As You Sow

AS YOU SOW

*Three Studies
in the Social Consequences
of Agribusiness*

by WALTER GOLDSCHMIDT

foreword by Senator Gaylord Nelson

 ALLANHELD, OSMUN & CO. PUBLISHERS
MONTCLAIR

ABIGAIL E. WEEKS MEMORIAL LIBRARY
UNION COLLEGE
BARBOURVILLE, KENTUCKY

ALLANHELD, OSMUN AND CO. PUBLISHERS, INC.
Published in the United States of America in 1978
by Allanheld, Osmun and Co. Publishers, Inc.
19 Brunswick Road, Montclair, N.J. 07042

Copyright, 1947 by Walter Goldschmidt
Copyright © 1978 by Walter Goldschmidt

As You Sow was originally published in 1947
by The Free Press, Glencoe, Illinois.

All rights reserved. No part of this publication
may be reproduced, stored in a retrieval system, or
transmitted in any form or by any means, electronic,
mechanical, photocopying, recording, or otherwise,
without prior permission of the publisher.

Library of Congress Cataloging in Publication Data

Goldschmidt, Walter Rochs, 1913-
  As you sow: Three studies in the social
consequences of agribusiness.

  CONTENTS: As you sow.—Small business and the community.—
  1. Agriculture—Social aspects—California—Case
studies. 2. Agricultural industries—California—Case
studies. 3. California—Rural conditions—Case studies.
4. Cities and towns—California—Case studies.
I. Title.
HD1775.C2G62   338.1'09794   77-84435
ISBN 0-916672-10-7
ISBN 0-916672-11-5 pbk.

Printed in the United States of America

To Paul S. Taylor

WHO HAS DEVOTED HIS LIFE TO
THE USES OF SCHOLARSHIP IN
THE INTEREST OF SOCIETY.

FOREWORD

Corporate control of our farm production is growing throughout the nation. What once was viewed as a peculiar aberration of California and a few other places, is now a factor in every area and aspect of American agriculture. The studies made by Walter Goldschmidt over thirty years ago and republished in this volume are the only detailed examination ever made of what corporate agriculture means for the character of life in American rural communities. For these reasons they are more important today than they were when they were first published.

This country has given inadequate attention to many of its precious resources. One of these resources is its pool of independent farmers. The family farm provides a social environment in which the central virtues of American life are fostered. It is at once a business, a job and a set of family relationships. At best, it does not provide an easy life and in bad times there are often harsh difficulties. But it provides a good life, and one in which independence, industry, hard work, foresight, cooperation and other qualities central to America's needs are fostered. For most of our history, the family farm has been the seedbed of our culture.

This relationship was well understood by the founders of our nation, and support for it was written into our constitution and reaffirmed in legislation, particularly the homestead laws and the Reclamation Act of 1902. The independent family farm is therefore an institution created by the foresight and planning of the makers of America. But throughout our history there have been those who, in the pursuit of selfish interests, in their desire for wealth and power, have threatened this traditional American institution. It is currently being threatened by the corporate control of agriculture.

The Reclamation Act, for instance, was specifically designed to foster family farming, but the law has been seriously distorted by successive administrations. For millions of acres, with billions of dollars in federal tax dollar subsidies, federal reclamation law has failed to encourage family farming. Instead, it has all too often merely lined the pockets of wealthy investors. Where there should have been flourishing communities there are, instead, the desolate corporate farm towns this book describes. New federal regulations and legislation that has been introduced in Congress would help to turn this Act to its original intentions. This is but one aspect, however, of an ever-increasing erosion—largely sponsored by the government—of the position of the family farm.

My predecessor as Chairman of the Senate Small Business Committee, the late Senator James Murray of Montana, was fully aware of this danger. When he learned about Goldschmidt's research on the social effects of industrialized agriculture, he published it as a committee print in 1946. It had an immediate impact and was widely quoted throughout the nation, for it gave irrefutable evidence of what we all intuitively know—that corporate control of agriculture undermines these traditional rural values.

Walter Goldschmidt's studies of three California towns have become classics. The comparison of Arvin and Dinuba remains so important that it has been twice reprinted in the records of the Senate Committee on Small Business, and references to it abound in the literature dealing with American agriculture.

When Professor Goldschmidt testified before our committee in 1972, he revealed aspects of the study that shed further light on what agribusiness does to American traditions: the efforts to sabotage and suppress his investigation. That shocking story he has now presented in detail for the first time in this book. Goldschmidt is well aware that this was not a personal attack; it was not an attack on the quality of his work but was made because those business interests well knew the social consequences of their modes of production.

This story shows that what is happening to our farming is not merely a rural problem, but a national one. For those who cherish the American tradition, for those who worry about the erosion of our way of life, this book is essential reading.

GAYLORD NELSON

CONTENTS

FOREWORD BY SENATOR GAYLORD NELSON vii
PREFACE xvii
ACKNOWLEDGEMENTS xxi
INTRODUCTION: AGRICULTURE AND THE SOCIAL ORDER xxiii

PART I: AS YOU SOW

I.	The Place of California Agriculture in American Farm Life	3
II.	Industrialized Farming and the Rural Community	22
III.	Basic Structure	55
IV.	Social Status and Social Experience	80
V.	Social Status and Religious Life	124
VI.	Cohesion, Conflict and Control	148
VII.	Variations in the Social Pattern: Small Farms	186
VIII.	Variations in the Social Pattern: Large Farms	203
IX.	Industrial Agriculture and Urbanized Farm People	221
X.	Social Directions	239

PART II: AGRIBUSINESS AND THE RURAL COMMUNITY

	Introduction	279
XI.	Nature of Investigation	286
XII.	Historical Background of Arvin and Dinuba	292
XIII.	Agriculture in Arvin and Dinuba	304
XIV.	The People of Arvin and Dinuba	321
XV.	Social Aspects of Community Life	344
XVI.	Retail Business in Arvin and Dinuba	381
XVII.	The Causes for the Social Differentiation	392

Appendix
- A. Sources of Data, Methodology, and Sampling Technique — 425
- B. Agricultural Data, Sources, and Methods — 428
- C. Analysis of Monthly Labor Requirements — 439
- D. Method of Obtaining Population Figures — 444
- E. Method of Determining Level-of-Living Index — 445
- F. Association Between Social Phenomena — 447
- G. Business Enterprise Data: Sources and Methods — 449

PART III: AGRIBUSINESS AND POLITICAL POWER

INDEX

LIST OF TABLES, CHARTS, AND FIGURES

PART I

Tables
1. Number of Persons of Various Ethnic Groups in California, 1890–1940 — 17
2. Gainfully Employed Workers in California Agriculture by Ethnic Group, 1930 — 18
3. Crop Acreages in Northern Kern County 1931 and 1936 — 30
4. Consumption of Home-Produced Foods in California Compared to Other Areas — 31
5. Acreage, Yield, and Production of Potatoes — 31
6. Farm Size and Value, Wasco Township — 32
7. Average Size of Farms and Average Value of Farms and Farm Equipment, Kern County, 1870–1940 — 33
8. Allocation of Costs: Potato Production — 35
9. Allocation of Costs: Sugar Beets — 35
10. Summary of Allocation of Costs and Income: Cotton — 36
11. Total Labor Requirements in Man-Days of Selected Crops, Kern County — 38
12. Estimated Minimum Requirements for Seasonal Workers, Kern County, 1939 — 39

13.	Estimates of Population Growth, Wasco, 1930-41	51
14.	Proportionate Distribution of Occupational Groups	58
15.	Monthly Variation in State Relief Administration Case Load in Wasco Area and the Labor Demand for Kern County	82
16.	Workers, Wages, and Labor Cost of Potato Harvest Operations, 1940	87
17.	Economic Activities According to Status and Sex	91
18.	Occupational Characteristics of the Wasco Voting Precincts	93
19.	Expressed Occupational Ambitions of High School Students	99
20.	Occupational Characteristics of Twelve Selected Organizations in Wasco	103
21.	Proportions of Occupation Classes Belonging to any Club or Church	103
22.	Recreational Activities of Resettled Migrants in Kern County (8 Communities)	119
23.	Occupational Characteristics of Library Subscribers	121
24.	Occupational Characteristics of Churches	136
25.	Changes in Church Habits of Recent Arrivals	144
26.	Reasons for Coming to California and for Choice of Community of 45 Resettled Migrant Families	151
27.	Occupational Shifts of Recent Arrivals into Wasco	154
28.	Summary of Occupational Shifts	154
29.	Land Use and Value of Commodities in Dinuba	189
30.	Classification of Dinuba Population According to Occupation	191
31.	Participation in Social and Recreational Activities in Dinuba	195
32.	Class Character of Dinuba Churches	199
33.	Land Use and Value of Commodities in Arvin	204
34.	Classification of Arvin Population According to Occupation	206
35.	Participation in Social and Recreational Activities in Arvin	210
36.	Class Character of Arvin Churches	213
37.	Proportion of Farms and Farm Lands in Different Size Classes in Arvin, Wasco and Dinuba (1940)	218

Charts

1.	Allocation of Costs and Profits in Cotton Cultivation, Kern County, California, 1940	37
2.	Estimates of Population Growth, Wasco, 1930-1941	52
3.	Reciprocal Relationship of Relief Cases to Farm Labor Requirements	83
4.	Growth of the Wasco Schools as Indicated by Annual Average Daily Attendance—1908-1939	96
5.	Occupational Characteristics of Clubs with Differing Status	104

xii   CONTENTS

6.	Number of Club Memberships Per 100 Persons Registered in Occupational Class	105
7.	Occupational Characteristics of Churches with Differing Status	137
8.	Size of Farm and Occupation Distribution	219

PART II

Tables

1.	Comparison of Population and Farming in the Small Communities in Madera, Tulare, and Kern Counties	290
2.	Shipment of Fruits and Vegetables from Arvin, 1921–43	295
3.	Quality of Soil in Arvin and Dinuba	302
4.	Comparative Irrigation Costs: Arvin and Dinuba	302
5.	Comparison of Number of Farm Operators as Reported in Agricultural Adjustment Agency Records and as Indicated by Schedules	305
6.	Major Crop Classes in Arvin and Dinuba, 1940	308
7.	Estimated Gross Farm Income by Principal Sources: Arvin and Dinuba	308
8.	Number of Farms and Acreages, Classified by Type: Arvin and Dinuba, 1940	309
9.	Distribution of Farms and Productive Land by Size of Farms: Arvin and Dinuba	309
10.	Number of Ownership Units and Acreage by Size of Holdings: Arvin and Dinuba, 1940	314
11.	Tenure of Farm Operators: Arvin and Dinuba, 1940	315
12.	Variation in Tenancy by Size of Farms: Arvin and Dinuba, 1940	315
13.	Residence of Landowners: Arvin and Dinuba, 1940	316
14.	Monthly Labor Requirements: Arvin and Dinuba	316
15.	Number of Workers Required for Farm Operations During Month of Peak Labor Demand: Arvin and Dinuba	318
16.	Population of Arvin and Dinuba, 1944	322
17.	Average Size of Household by Major Occupation Groups: Arvin and Dinuba	323
18.	Distribution of Families by Size of Households: Arvin and Dinuba	323
19.	Birthplace of Family Heads: Arvin and Dinuba	326
20.	Year of Arrival in Community of Family Heads: Arvin and Dinuba	326
21.	Levels of Education of Family Heads: Arvin and Dinuba	328

CONTENTS xiii

22. Distribution of Families by Employment of Chief Breadwinner, Arvin and Dinuba — 329
23. Income Distribution in Arvin and Dinuba — 330
24. Estimated Median Income of Major Occupational Groups: Arvin and Dinuba — 332
25. Incidence of Selected Individual Items on the Level-of-Living Scale: Arvin and Dinuba — 333
26. Occupation of Members in Selected Arvin and Dinuba Clubs — 356
27. Families Reporting Participation in Various Classes of Social Organizations: Arvin and Dinuba — 358
28. Families Reporting Participation in Social Organizations, Classified by Occupation of Family Head: Arvin and Dinuba — 358
29. Club Memberships of Persons 12 Years Old and Over, Classified by Occupation of Family Head: Arvin and Dinuba — 359
30. Families Participating in Social Activities Other Than Clubs and Churches: Arvin and Dinuba — 360
31. Individuals Participating in Social Activities Other Than Clubs and Churches: Arvin and Dinuba — 361
32. Families Reporting Participation in Social Events Other Than Clubs or Churches, Classified by Occupation of Head: Arvin and Dinuba — 361
33. Motion Pictures as a Source of Recreation for Different Occupation Groups: Arvin and Dinuba — 362
34. Individual Church Participation Among Persons 12 Years Old and Over, Classified by Occupation Groups: Arvin and Dinuba — 368
35. Proportion of Persons from Independently Employed Families and from Labor Families Participating in Churches of Different Social Status: Arvin and Dinuba — 370
36. Occupation of Members of Selected Churches in Arvin and Dinuba — 371
37. Persons Who Consider the Local Community as "Home Town" in Arvin and Dinuba — 375
38. Summary of Important Social Differentiations: Arvin and Dinuba — 376
39. Comparison of Business Enterprises and Volume of Business: Arvin and Dinuba — 382
40. Number of Businesses and Volume of Business by Major Category: Arvin and Dinuba, 1943 — 386
41. Size of Business Enterprises by Volume of Retail Sales: Arvin and Dinuba — 390
42. Size of Business Enterprises by Estimated Pecuniary Strength: Arvin and Dinuba — 390
43. Date of Civic Developments in Arvin and Dinuba — 404

xiv CONTENTS

44. Intensive Land Use in Arvin (1931, 1932, and 1940) Compared with Land Use in Neighboring Communities 409
45. Diagrammatic Presentation of Causative Forces Responsible for the Character of Arvin as Contrasted with Dinuba 418
46. Gross Income Per Acre and Total Gross Income for Crops: Arvin and Dinuba 432
47. Estimated Head of Livestock and Gross Income from Stock: Arvin and Dinuba 432
48. Feed Requirements for Livestock 434
49. Dollar Value of Commodities Produced in Arvin and Dinuba 434
50. Itemized Comparative Costs of Irrigation in Arvin and Dinuba by Size of Farm 438
51. Calculations of Labor Requirements, by Months and by Crop Classes: Arvin 441
52. Calculations of Labor Requirements, by Months and by Crop Classes: Dinuba 442
53. Estimated Monthly Labor Requirements and Theoretical Source of Labor Supply: Arvin 442
54. Estimated Monthly Labor Requirements and Theoretical Source of Labor Supply: Dinuba 443
55. Calculations in the Computation of Arvin and Dinuba Population from Schedule Data 444
56. Frequency Distributions of Items on the Material Level-of-Living Scale and Value of Items 446
57. Association of Social Phenomena with Occupation and Income: Arvin and Dinuba 448

Figures

1. Upper San Joaquin Valley California 288
2. Gross Farm Income by Principal Sources 307
3. Comparisons in Size of Farming Operations 311
4. Size Distribution of Farms and of Cropland Acreage in Farms 312
5. Distribution of Farms by Size in Acre-Equivalent Units 313
6. Monthly Labor Requirements and Source of Supply 319
7. Age Distribution of Arvin & Dinuba Population Compared to San Joaquin Valley 327
8. Occupational Structure 331
9. Distribution of Families According to Level of Living 334
10. Scattergram Showing Relationship Between Level of Living and Income 336
11. Distribution of Index of Home Conditions 337
12. City of Arvin, Kern County, California 338
13. City of Dinuba, Tulare County, California 340

14.	Participation in Social Activities by Occupation Groups	363
15.	Occupational Structure of Selected Arvin and Dinuba Congregations	372
16.	Number of Business Enterprises and Gross Volume of Retail Sales	383
17.	Dollar Volume of Sales Reported in Major Classes of Business Enterprise	384
18.	Distribution of Retail Sales among Various Classes of Enterprise	385
19.	Divergence in the Distribution of Capital Investment and Gross Volume of Business in Arvin Compared to Dinuba	389
20.	Growth of Annual Average Daily Attendance	403
21.	Growth of Average Daily Attendance in Arvin Compared to Wasco, California	406
22.	Comparison of Carlot Shipments of Fruits and Vegetables (1921–1942) Between Arvin and Selected Kern County Communities	408

PREFACE

From industrialized sowing of the soil is reaped an urbanized rural society. This is the lesson which the present study teaches us. Many changes in social relationships and in the functioning of social institutions—sometimes subtle, sometimes blatant—are the component parts of this urbanization, and an intelligent planning for the future of rural society must recognize the import and content of this transformation.

Both in popular thought and in sociological doctrine, rural life has been set apart from that of the city. Rural ties are said to be closer; face-to-face contacts are said to dominate social relationships. The individual is said to be evaluated in terms of his own true worth. Rural institutions are said to derive from common needs and not only serve them but serve also to integrate the society and unite its members. Sometimes less laudatory features are pointed out. Rural people are said to be backward, naturally cautious, and individualistic, less educated and less concerned with progress. A livelihood is said to satisfy their wants.

The present volume shows that these generalizations do not hold for California rural society. In the California community, which is the subject of this study, social ties are not close, invidious social distinctions are maintained without reference to personal qualities. Most institutions serve to maintain these distinctions rather than to destroy them for the sake of common interest. On the other hand, the people are neither backward nor uneducated, but are interested in progress in the way that concept is usually understood in American society. They are a part of that society, and not a separate entity.

This is a community study, but whether it is the study of communities depends upon our definition of that concept. For our data show, as intimated above, that the town and its surrounding rural population form a community only in the political sense. The ties which bind the individuals living in this area are subservient to the ties of social classes and cliques which are at all times dominant. It is this fact more than any other which compels us to consider the rural community as urbanized, and which makes us loath to consider it a community in that sense of the term which implies social unity and homogeneity. Remnants of community life remain, to be sure, but when they are brought under closer scrutiny it is clear that they serve but a segment of the population which dwells in the area.

A few general statements will serve to orient the reader. At the time the study was made, the community of Wasco was an unincorporated town of over 5,000 persons, while perhaps another 5,000 lived in the immediate vicinity. Wasco lies on the floor of the Great Central Valley of California, near its southern end. The land which is now so rich and fruitful was once desert, reclaimed to man's more urgent uses by the gasoline, electric, and Diesel pumps which lift the water from the underground table. Save for an unimpressive oil field nearby, it is dependent entirely for its resources on the products of its soil.

This study is a case history. It is the result of eight months' study as participant observers in Wasco and a month each in the other two towns. We—my wife and I—made every effort to participate in Wasco society on that level which might be considered normal for persons of our background. We joined in community meetings, school functions, and club affairs; we attended churches and fraternized with as many groups as we could. Furthermore, interviews were held with persons of all walks of life, with emphasis either upon the historical or developmental aspects of the town, or upon that person's relationships to the community. All available and pertinent statistical material was examined, membership lists were analyzed, and many chance observations and unsolicited remarks were recorded. Similar techniques were used in Arvin and Dinuba in addition to specific statistical information collected.

The detailed information on Wasco is given a broader meaning through the analysis of two similar neighboring towns, Dinuba and Arvin. The study of these latter communities was made after the analysis of Wasco was completed, and it was therefore possible to check the conclusions reached there.

Arvin, which lies some 40 miles southeast of Wasco, had a somewhat smaller population and a similar pattern of industrialized production. The land there was for the most part, however, operated in large units, much of it under corporate control. Dinuba is some 80 miles north of Wasco in the raisin grape area south of Fresno. It had a somewhat larger population, and though production was similarly industrialized, it was surrounded by small family farms. The general character of these two communities conforms to the pattern uncovered in Wasco, but the difference in the scale of operation allows us to see the effects of size on the character, and especially on the quality, of rural community life.

The visit in Wasco started in the fall of 1940 and lasted into the following summer; the visits to Arvin and Dinuba were made during the spring of 1944. Data collected in the field refer, therefore, to those periods unless otherwise specified.

The urbanization thesis developed in this study suggests that the local elite in these communities maintains direct ties to the centers of power and influence in our national society. Part Three, which is an historical account of the attack made on the comparative investigation of Arvin and Dinuba, and of the broader implications of that attack, is a demonstration of this characteristic of industrialized agriculture.

The implications of this thesis do not, therefore, end at California's borders. Nor do they extend only as far as industrialization has already been found. Mechanization and industrialized production will inevitably come to dominate the rural scene in all America. Neither wishful thinking nor nostalgic legislation will prevent this course of events. To those who look backward, this trend presents a doleful picture. But such a view is not justified. Though the traditional has its endearing charms, it is not without its costs, while urban society has much to commend it. The importance lies, however, in the recognition both of the possible dangers and the inherent values of an urbanized rural society. It is not impossible to salvage the good from tradition and still capture the best that technological efficiency has to offer. But if we are to accomplish this a realistic view must be taken; reality must replace stereotype. The traditional bases for farm policy must be reviewed in terms of the future social picture in rural America.

ACKNOWLEDGEMENTS

In preparing this second edition of *As You Sow* I have incurred further indebtednesses. In addition to those who are acknowledged in the preface to the first edition and in the footnote on page 304, I want to thank the following for help in preparation of new material: Varden Fuller, Isao Fujimoto, Paul Lasky, Phillip LeVeen, Angus McDonald, Jerry Moles, and David Weiman. I want also to thank the officers of Free Press for releasing to me the rights to *As You Sow*.

My indebtedness to Paul Taylor is of an entirely different order; his influence upon me and this work runs deep. The same is true for my wife, Gale, to whom the first edition was dedicated, and who joins me in the rededication of the work to Paul.

INTRODUCTION
Agriculture and the Social Order

THE ISSUES

Controversy over the control of land is as old as America. National policy from the outset formed the development of a land of free-holding husbandmen, owning the soil they tilled. Private interests have constantly challenged this policy, seeking to establish large holdings in which the sweat of the hard work would be shed by others—slaves, indentured servants or wage workers. This conflict between independent small holders and concentrated ownership has taken on a new, twentieth century character: giant corporations are increasingly invading agricultural production.

The three studies in this volume examine the consequences of corporate farming for the character of American life. The first demonstrates, through a detailed examination of one community, the social consequences of industrialized production. Its central theme is that the fruits of this mode of production are the urbanization of the rural community: as you sow, so shall you reap.

The next study takes this analysis a second step. The comparison of two closely comparable towns, one surrounded by family farms and the other by giant agricultural enterprises, shows that the quality of rural life is seriously eroded by corporate operation.

The third study is an examination of the influence of this kind of agricultural production on our national institutions. By examining the controversy engendered by the comparative study, it shows how big business operators utilize the media to suppress free inquiry, influence legislation to further their self-interests, and punish those who hold other views.

The three studies relate to events in the 1940's, though for reasons soon to be addressed, they are more relevant to events of today than they were to that earlier time. *As You Sow* was based upon research done in 1940-41 and published just 30 years ago. Significantly, at that time, Joseph Henry Jackson, then the most influential reviewer on the West Coast, wrote: "If the author's words are heeded, *As You Sow* may well be spoken of 30 years from now, as the most important volume on our social and agricultural structure written in this decade."[1]

The second study was made in the spring of 1944. It was designed specifically to investigate the social consequences of corporate farming; that is, to test the validity of the agrarian assumptions by the use of sociological research techniques. These assumptions had long been expressed in law, most particularly in the Reclamation Act of 1902 (and its subsequent amendments). This law provided that irrigation water developed through federal subsidy must be allocated to lands held in family-size units. The question at issue was whether this law should be applied to the Central Valley Project of California which was then nearing completion of its first construction phase. It was thus a study addressing itself to public policy. *Agribusiness and the Rural Community* was published in 1946 as a Committee Print of the Senate Small Business Committee under the title *Small Business and the Community*.

of Agriculture on funds provided by the Department of Interior published by a Senate committee? The third study, which is newly written, is directed to that question. Most of the land in the area targeted for benefit by the Central Valley Project was in large holdings owned by a few giant corporations. From the moment they learned of the investigation, the representatives of these corporate interests initiated an attack on the research which did not abate even after the study was published. The attack reached the highest offices in Washington and the Department of Agriculture feared to publish it. So a senator forced it from the Secretary of Agriculture. The details of this attack and of the consequences it has had for American rural life and institutions is therefore an example of the social effects of corporate agriculture that extend far beyond the confines of the towns and villages where farming takes place.

The issue remains alive today. The Central Valley Project has been delivering water for nearly 30 years; the laws supporting the agrarian position remain on the books and have been found applicable to California in court tests.[2] They are not, however, being enforced.[3] Such "compliance" as takes place, is usually mere subterfuge.[4] Vast expanses of land that was arid in 1944, particularly on the west side of the San Joaquin Valley, are green and luxurious as a result of the Central Valley Project waters—and virtually barren of farmsteads and rural communities. The former commissioner of the Bureau of Reclamation is seeking ways to prevent the lands from becoming available to working farmers with modest holdings.[5] The present secretary has stated firmly that the reclamation laws will be administered in accordance with the intent of Congress, while Senators Nelson, Haskell, Abourezk and Metcalf have introduced a bill, The Reclamation Lands Family Farm Act, which would require going back to the intentions of the original law.[6] We may confidently anticipate a major confrontation.

THE SPREAD OF AGRIBUSINESS

The issues raised in this book are not, however, local ones. When the studies were made, corporate farming was rare outside of California, Arizona, and Florida—and of course Hawaii. As in so many other ways, California has also offered a vision of the future of agriculture, and now agribusiness is threatening to engulf those areas of traditional agrarian enterprise. The number of farms in America declined from 6.5 million in 1920 to 2.8 million in 1975. Over the past two decades at least 100,000 independent farmers went out of business each year, 2,000 per week. Self-employment in agriculture declined from 7.9 million in 1949 to 3.5 million in 1973. It is estimated that one independent businessman goes out of business for each six farmers—another 300 each week.

It is not possible to measure precisely the degree to which farm production is in the hands of corporate interests. It is a subject on which little research has been done and mass statistics can be confusing. Some corporate farmers are really family farms while only 8 percent of all farming corporations (*i.e.*, about 1,000) hold 71 percent of the corporation-operated farm land.[7] These large-scale operations account for about 5 percent of the total acreage in agricultural production in the United States. But this is not the whole story.

First, some specialty crops are heavily controlled by a few large operations. Second, corporations that are primarily engaged in other enterprises and where agricultural operations account for less than 10 percent of their gross income do not have to report their farm operations separately. Thus Tenneco, the conglomerate with many enterprises is not included in such surveys because it is not *primarily* agricultural, though it controls nearly two million acres of farm land. The same applies to Boeing, Goodyear, Purex, Penn Central, Standard Oil of California, Prudential Insurance, and Bank of America.[8]

The third, more insidious, form of corporate control is by the large processors through contracts with the growers, an organizational form known as vertical integration. Vertical integration means bringing together two or more successive steps of production or distribution under the ownership or control of a single company. Vertical integration can be accomplished by direct ownership in the hands of a conglomerate. "An example [of such vertical integration] is Tenneco, Inc., a conglomeration with $3.4 billion in assets, that has told its stockholders it is developing a food system based on 'integration from seedling to supermarket.'"[9]

Vertical integration can also be achieved through "contract farming," the more important element in corporate control. Contract farming involves a contract between farmers and companies that specify the conditions of production or marketing of the commodity produced. Vertical integrators are most important in animal products (meat, poultry, milk and eggs) and in specialty crops. The vertical integrators are usually feed supply houses, processors or marketing operators.

A detailed analysis of vertical integration in various commodities has been made by Roy.[10]

A speech by Don Paarlberg, former Director of Agricultural Economics quotes a 1963 study that indicates 10 percent of American agricultural production was controlled in this way at that time.[11] However, certain crops are dominated by this system (fresh market milk and broilers, 95%; vegetable seeds, 90%; hybrid seed corn and sugar, 75%; citrus fruit, 65%; vegetable, 60% and turkeys, 50%). A closer breakdown of fruits, nuts and vegetables would increase the percentage for many specific crops. A 1970 study shows increases and gives the following figures: sugar beets and sugar cane, 100%; broilers, 97%; processing vegetables, 95%; citrus fruits, 85%; potatoes, 70%; turkeys, 54%; eggs, 40%.[12] Undoubtedly the trend continues.

This is how it affects the production process:

> In contract farming, the corporation contracts for use of the farmer's land and its production resources. In doing so, it gains many of the advantages of family farming (primarily cheap labor) without taking from the farmer the risks of ownership. The farmer sells his commodities directly to the packer or processor at a fixed price agreed on in advance. In ten years, from 1954 to 1964, the broiler industry went from 3- to 98-percent integrator-controlled. Mergers of processing and slaughtering firms increased at a rate of 41 percent during the four years 1960–64. As a result, the open market, the traditional cushion between the farmer and his corporate buyers, is gone. The chicken farmer is no longer protected by competitive bidding in the marketplace. If a farmer wants to sell chicken, he must sell to a corporation through a contract with a fixed formula price or not at all. There is still an open market for cattle and hogs but it, too, is succumbing to contract agriculture, as Swift and other companies increasingly buy fed cattle directly from the feedlot at a fixed price.[13]

Harrison Wilford has described the results of such integration in the poultry industry as it affects the farmers:

> The dirt-poor hill country of Northern Alabama was the scene of bizarre events in the spring of 1970. Its poor, white, chicken farmers,

rugged individualists to a man, had organized and were out on strike—the first time for farmers anywhere in the South. These family farmers with their rough blue overalls and Jeffersonian agrarian values, walked picket lines before the gates of Pillsbury, Ralston-Purina, and the other food conglomerates which bought their chickens for processing. Equally unprecedented was the decision of federal meat inspectors in the chicken plants to honor the pickets and refuse to enter the plants. Strangest of all, truckloads of black industrial unionists from Birmingham arrived at one plant to cheer the farmers on. The locals swore that the ghosts of Tom Watson and the Populists could be seen dancing in the shadows, their dream of a labor-farmer coalition against the trusts come true at last.

These events were stimulated by profound economic grievances which foreshadow problems for the consumer as well. A study by USDA economists recently reported that poultry growers in Northern Alabama work for an average of *minus* 36 cents an hour. Their economic plight reflects the outcomes of the farmers' man-to-man encounters with the $300,000,000 corporations which buy their chickens.

The problems of the poultry grower have a common cause with the problems of farm workers, environmentalists, and consumers when they confront this nation's agricultural establishment: organized bargaining power too heavily weighted on the side of agribusiness. The concentration of meat production and marketing power in relatively few food conglomerates over the last two decades has not been matched by compensatory restructuring of consumer and farmer power. In dealing with the farmer suppliers at one end and the consumer at the other, Swift, Pillsbury, Ralston Purina, Central Soya and the other agribusiness giants still maintain a man-to-man, eyeball-to-eyeball contact with unorganized individuals. The unequal relationship encourages an irresponsible marketing power which permits the corporation to pass the costs of its mistakes and excessive profit margins either forward to the consumer or backward to the supplier. This imbalance assumes classic proportions in the chicken country of the Deep South. . . .

The infiltration of the corporate state into agriculture is having a profound effect on the economic and social relationships of rural America. As large integrated companies move in, they force more and more family farmers to lose their independent status and become, in effect, organization men in overalls. Large corporations have recently moved into cattle ranching, cotton growing, orcharding and other kinds of farming. Dow Chemical now grows catfish in Texas; Purex is growing vegetables on thousands of acres in the Southwest; American Cyanamid and John Hancock Mutual Life Insurance Company have a joint venture to grow corn, wheat and soybeans on a 35,000 acre farm in North Carolina. Swift, Tenneco, Textron, Campbell Soups, Ralston-Purina, Pillsbury, and Central Soya dominate the beef and chicken industry. When corporations of this size go into farming, they pull the whole agricultural establishment in their wake. Congressional committees and the federal farm bureaucracy become more attuned to the interests of corporate agribusiness and less sensitive to the needs of small farmers, the rural poor and the consumer.

The corporatization of agriculture has been more rapid in the chicken industry than anywhere else. The chicken farmers of Mississippi, Georgia, Alabama and Arkansas provide a melancholy model of what the new industrial state may hold in store for rural people.[14]

The executive vice-president of the National Council of Agricultural Employers has stated that its 800 members hire 80 percent of the agricultural laborers in the United States.[15] These are not all individual corporation or farm operators, but processors, "cooperatives," and other integrated groups. Eight hundred such units have effective determination of the circumstances of some two million agricultural laborers — the largest block of underprivileged workers in the United States.

In Nebraska, the introduction of pivot irrigation is having a similar influence. In this heart of traditional farming has come a new type of operator; the custom farm manager:

The custom manager is significantly different from the traditional farm manager who makes arrangements with a tenant farmer and otherwise manages a farm for widows, retired farmers, and non-farm heirs. The custom manager actually operates the farm with hired employees, providing an entire package of farm services on a fee basis. The custom farm manager is frequently in the business of recruiting absentee investors and brokering land purchases for them.[16]

One well-known custom farm manager . . . is the proprietor of Williams Management Company which actively recruits investors to develop pivot systems. Most of his investors have been Norfolk-area persons or Nebraska residents who are not primarily engaged in farming. His 1974 customers included a fertilizer dealer, irrigation equipment dealers, several bankers, a bank-owned subsidiary corporation, a life insurance salesman and a gasoline retailer. He also serves several non-local clients, including a New Jersey investor whom he claims to have made a millionaire. Williams Management Company hires 14 employees year-round, has grossed $3.5 million for its clients, currently custom operates 63 pivot systems and owns $400,000 worth of farm equipment.[17]

The corporate control over American agricultural production can be seen to take many forms. First, there are the giant agricultural landholding producers, such as those that developed early in California, Hawaii, Arizona, and Florida. Second, there has been the entry directly into production by large corporations. Third, there has been the use of contract farming to control the production of formerly independent farmers, sometimes reducing them to little more than laborers and occasionally to something less. Fourth, new technologies, such as Nebraska irrigation, is developing a new breed of manager-operated enterprise. While the precise degree of corporate control cannot be ascertained, it quite clearly is no longer a limited problem, but reaches into every state in the nation.

THE MYTH OF THE ECONOMY OF SCALE

There is a theme in American culture that is sometimes called "Social Darwinism"; a belief in the survival of the fittest. This theory is a justification of wealth and power on the basis that those who have it deserve it because they are more efficient, more capable, more energetic. This thesis justifies the growth of large corporations in the belief that they are more effective, and that in the end everybody benefits through production efficiency.

This is a myth. Economists have made repeated studies on the returns in agriculture as a function of scale of operations. The classic summary study on the economics of scale was prepared by J. Patrick Madden and published by the USDA.[18]

INTRODUCTION xxxi

In a foreword to this report, Warren R. Bailey, Deputy Director of the Farm Production Economics Division of the Economics Research Service wrote:

> In the report, Dr. Madden had pulled together and summarized the research results of many independent studies that directly or indirectly had dealt with the economies of size in farming. . . . His central conclusion was that full-scale, fully mechanized one-man farms achieve most of the economies due to size of operation. Their costs per unit of output are equal to or lower than those of much larger farming operations.[19]

This report examines such diverse production units as: cling peaches in Yuba City, California; Iowa cash grain and crop-livestock farms; irrigated cotton farms in Texas and California; cash crop farms in Kern, Yolo, and Imperial counties, California; wheat farms in the Columbia basin of Oregon; beef feedlots in California and Colorado; and dairy farms in New England, Iowa, Minnesota and Arizona. The cost efficiency curves in each instance flatten out at the level of operations that one or two persons can handle and sometimes actually rise with larger operations. Just what the optimum size is varies with crop and other circumstances, but in very few instances do substantial economies appear beyond modest-sized operations, despite their intensive use of mechanization. This is true on a cost-accounting, profit producing basis of calculation.

There are, though, socially more important measurements of efficiency. Thus Karl Lee found in California that while larger farms had greater returns in capital, medium sized farms maximized work opportunity, total production, trade, and income, as cited in *As You Sow*.[20]

It is characteristic of the American culture that we economize on labor and consume vast amounts of power — sometimes using 100 calories of fossil fuel to produce one calorie for human consumption. Yet this economy of labor is also illusory. When a tractor draws a combine to harvest wheat, the farmer is employing hundreds of hours of urban manpower expended in the steel mills and the oil refineries. All who work in the tractor and farm equipment plants, in the fertilizer and pest-control chemicals plants, and a fair portion of those producing oil, steel and other ingredients for our mechanized farms, are in fact part of the agricultural production team.[21] The farming sector of our economy appears to have dwindled remarkably, when in fact a large portion are agriculturalists working in the urban industrial environment. But of course the true irony of our agricultural economy is that we promulgate labor saving devices through capital-intensive land-extensive production and create thereby an army of low paid farm workers and a large pool of unemployed.

Our use of land is profligate. It stands in direct contrast to the pattern that has developed in Japan where the productivity per acre is approximately 10 times that of the United States.[22]

America's agricultural productivity has been prodigious. The capacity of the American farms to support a large non-farm population is a remarkable feat. But it is not the economies of large-scale operations that have brought about this capacity. Indeed, this productivity is not achieved by any kind of economy, but by the profligate use of resources and by the rich lands that lie within our boundaries.

SOURCES OF CORPORATE ADVANTAGE

If the corporation is not more efficient, the argument goes, then why is it pushing out the independent farm operator? The answer is clear: Governmental and other institutional policies have favored the large grower and given impetus to the constant process of industrialization and corporate control. The most important of these special advantages are (1) the agricultural support programs, (2) tax policies, (3) agricultural labor policies, and (4) the research-orientation of the USDA and of the land grant colleges.

In the development of these advantages, corporate interests have repeatedly and effectively hidden behind the image of the farmer, the mythical downtrodden hayseed who is at once benighted and exploited and yet the "backbone" of our country. Especially since the dark days of American agriculture in the interwar years, when both the prosperity of the twenties and the depression of the thirties seemed to force farm prices down, this image has been used for the promulgation of farm policies. Since these policies have benefited the large operators far more than the family farmer—and occasionally were actually against the interests of the latter—the results are often ironical.

In the depth of the depression, when farm foreclosures were threatening millions of farmers, the Franklin Roosevelt administration initiated a program of agricultural relief. In contrast to most New Deal welfare programs, agricultural relief did not require a "means test." Instead, the amount of subsidy payments were directly proportional to the total productivity of the farm enterprise, so that the more a person (or corporation) owned, the more relief he (or it) received. The concept was based upon the assumption that the family farm was universal and that the farm population therefore shared equally in the general depression. In this situation, the corporate operators, with tax lawyers, economic consultants, etc., could take massive advantage of the program in ways not open to the small operator. A ceiling of $55,000 per farm was recently imposed, but it can easily be circumvented. Thus, in one year, 1970, 10 corporate operations received $18.3 million in cash subsidies from agricultural relief programs; the largest two, J. G. Boswell Co. and Giffen, Inc. received $4.4 and $4 million respectively.[23] Payments of comparable size are made to such big operators each year, and have been for 40 years. While the $1.1 million received by Tenneco is a small fraction of its $158 million total net earnings, it is not a trivial amount. We must remember that the flexibility of the large international operations makes it possible to take advantage of such regulations. Thus, according to the same source, "Boswell is an old hand at the subsidy game. Two years ago he took advantage of a bounty offered by Australia to grow cotton, and received $500,000. At the same time, he received $3 million from the U.S. for not growing cotton on his farms." In short, American agricultural relief policy has subsized the corporate interest in agricultural production.

The influence of tax laws is more insidious and even more pervasive. I know of no general study of the influence of the IRS on the American culture, but I suspect that it has been profound. Every business and professional man must shape his behavior in some degree to the effects of tax policy. A whole industry of lawyers and accountants has arisen as a result of these regulations, like camp followers in old military campaigns. Even our morality has been adapted to the income tax: It is right and proper to take advantage of every tax feature possible, without regard to any general principle of fairness or obligation to share one's burden. And the tax laws offer many opportunities for the astute and those who are diligent in the pursuit of their self-interest. Among those elements particularly relevant to agriculture are the differential payment for capital gains as against "ordinary" income, accounting on a cash versus accrual basis, investment credit, and depreciation allowances. The progressive nature of the tax structure makes these more important to the rich than to others, and of course the rich have also the ability to purchase the use of that cadre of experts. The influence on agriculture has been profound. Many of the laws that treat agriculture favorably are purportedly designed as an aid to the family farmer who cannot afford high priced accountants and is felt to deserve these tax "breaks." Philip Raup has said:

Because we make extensive use of a graduated and progressive income tax, it follows that any concessions or favored tax treatment extended to farmers inevitably results in more favored treatment for those with higher incomes. The option to report on a cash basis or an accrual basis is an example of favored treatment, as is the opportunity to charge off a part of the costs of soil conservation practices as current expense.[24]

As I see it, there are two basic avenues by which tax regulation contributes to corporate control of agriculture. One of these is the "tax shelter" for high-income urban people, the other is accounting advantages to vertically integrated corporations that can use accounting devices to shift their income and losses so as to minimize their taxable income.

We are all familiar with publicized instances of the use of

agricultural enterprises as tax shelters by public figures like John Wayne, but we are less aware that hundreds of thousands of doctors, lawyers, and other professional and businesspeople have tax consultants and accountants who redirect their cash income into "tax shelters." This is the basis for the development of the pivot irrigation schemes in Nebraska, already discussed. A similar set of activities has affected the meat industry through corporate control of feedlots. Tax policies have also had adverse effects through the increased use of land as an investment. In Minnesota between 1950–1967, the proportion of land sales to investors, as distinct from farmers, ranged from 11 percent to 17 percent, according to a detailed study by Philip Raup.[25]

The use of agricultural tax advantage by integrated industries is also described by Raup:

> Consider an integrated firm involving a ranch, a cow herd, a feedlot complex, and a slaughtering plant. It will pay to operate the slaughtering plant as a producer's corporation, with only enough profit to provide incentive bonuses for management, and do the same with feedlots. All profits can be pushed down the integrated chain and converted into capital by heavy investment in breeding stock, land-improving practices, water supply, irrigation, and other improvements. When the cattle are sold, any gain will be taxed at capital gains rates.[26]

Beef production is rapidly moving down the road that poultry production has traveled. Meisner and Rhodes report:

> In 1962 the commercial feeders fed about one-third of the fed cattle; in 1973, they fed two-thirds. . . . The nation's supply of beef is now more concentrated than data on feedlot plant sizes suggest. USDA data show approximately 2,000 feedlots produce over two-thirds of the nation's beef. However, a few multi-lot firms control a surprisingly large fraction of national output. Two multi-lot firms supply three percent of the nation's fed beef. One of these firms has announced plans to supply five percent of the nation's fed beef in the future. Seventeen firms supply one-eighth of the nation's beef.
> In addition to this concentrated level of horizontal integration, some vertical integration continues. Physical and financial inputs are controlled by these vertically integrated firms. A few major cattle

feeding firms control fed beef production from the intermediate growth stage of the animal on through slaughter. Feedlot firms even provide direct loans to investors in custom feeding in some cases through financial subsidiaries.[27]

This situation is in large measure a product of tax policy, as Matthews and Rhodes show:

The limited partnership has contributed to the formation and growth of larger firms in the cattle feeding industry. Firms utilizing funds have been able to utilize more fully their existing feedlot capacity, to expand existing lots, and to acquire more lots until now the multi-lot cattle feeding firm is becoming common. Capacities of these "super firms" now reach and exceed 100,000 head. Much of this growth activity has occurred simultaneously with the adoption of the limited partnership by these firms. The limited partnership has been seized upon by these entrepreneurs as an opportunity to achieve rapid growth; the results have accentuated the shift in the location of the fed cattle industry from the farmer feedlots of the Midwest to the domain of the super firms with funds in the High Plains and Southwest. As the structure in the cattle feeding industry shifts from one made up of numerous small- to medium-sized feedlots to one made up of fewer firms with much larger feedlot capacities, previously existing market relations begin to break down. Such related industries as slaughter and processing plants, grain suppliers, and trucking services are attracted towards the location of the larger firms.

The presence of large firms operating with fund money presents a different slant to profit motivation. Under a fund arrangement, most feedlot firms derive their returns from charging management fees for their services, together with feed markups, feedlot charges, and perhaps a share of the profits upon termination of the fund. All these avenues for compensation minimize greatly the risk capital of the feedlot and its subsidiary: the fund management. . . . Fund capital, sometimes referred to as "funny money," is contributed by high tax bracket investors. Their capital, if successfully applied to create operating losses, represents an "IRS loan." . . . The investor has simply taken money he ordinarily would have paid to the government as federal income taxes and delayed his tax liability until the fund terminates. . . . The fund management receives contributions from investors who in effect receive an interest-free loan from the government. Such investors are not so demanding that they receive a minimum return on "their" investment, as the investment is really being sponsored by the government. Capital obtained from such investors presents a significant advantage to fund management over other firms, corporate or otherwise, whose capital suppliers are more demanding that an economic pre-tax return be forthcoming. In the cattle feeding industry both the family feeder and the corporate feedlot operating without tax-benefit capital are disadvantaged relative to the fund feedlots.[28]

A similar process is now under way in hog production, the traditional "mortage lifter" for the young farmer.[29]
 The bigger the income, the more "valuable" these losses are. Consider the following inversion noted in a National Planning Association pamphlet:

Taxpayers with *under $50,000* adjusted gross income showed farm profits of $5.1 billion and losses of $1.7 billion, a ratio of 5:2.
 Taxpayers with adjusted gross income *over $500,000* show profits of $2 million and losses of $14 million, a ratio of 1:7.[30]

According to Jim Hightower, Research Director of the Agribusiness Accountability Project, Tenneco received a tax credit of $13.2 million in 1969.[31]
 The exclusion of agricultural labor from the legislation governing unionization is the third major element in the advantages to corporate agriculture. The relevant legislation, known as the National Labor Relations Act, includes the Wagner Act of 1935, and the Taft-Hartley and Landrum-Griffin amendments of 1947 and 1959. These are the instruments that protected union organization and are generally credited with the increased income and power of the labor sector of the economy. Along with domestic servants and family members, agricultural laborers are simply excluded from the protection provided by the NLRA. The exclusion was not debated, according to Varden Fuller, but "reflected some degree of implict and potential agrarian hostility." The argument was that agriculture was in some way different and that the farmer needed the protection from the power of labor.[32]
 The traditional farm laborer in the agricultural heartland is the "hired hand," a man of comparable background to his boss, working alongside him and often sharing his table. But

the mass of agricultural laborers are not of that variety; they are low paid, often ethnically differentiated and usually migratory workers. There are an estimated 2½ million of them in America, and about half of this number are employed by 2 percent of the producers. The concentration is even greater when we consider the degree to which employment is controlled through various organizations. As noted earlier, 800 organizations control the employment of 80 percent of the laborers. These workers constitute the largest block of disadvantaged workers in America.

In order to understand how the low wages paid farm labor is disadvantageous to the family farmer, we must recognize the operation of the market. The family farmer's income derives in part from his capital investment, in part from managerial skill, but in large part from the value of his labor input. Commodity prices will be affected by prevailing wages; the farmer competing with poorly paid workers thus receives less compensation for his work. The matter was neatly presented by R. L. Adams in his *Handbook on Managing Western Farms and Ranches:*

> The attitude of large-farm operators, who hire all their work done, is to seek a profit from the service of those whom they employ. Their interest is for an ample supply of labor obtainable for wages as low as is consistent with the maintenance of prices for farm products, because the larger the group of workers can be drawn, the easier can they be procured when wanted, and with less demand for high wages and accommodations.
>
> The working farmer who does his own work and whose product is placed in competition with products of other farmers, prefer high wage scales so that the cost of labor entering into the goods of his competitors will force up the selling price of goods, and hence give him a higher return.[33]

The fourth element in furthering the interests of corporate farming has been the government-sponsored research agencies. When American agrarian policy took root during the Civil War, it was recognized that something we now call "R and D" (research and development) must be provided for the farmers, and the Department of Agriculture and the land grant college systems were born. The importance of these programs for the commercialization of the traditional American farm and the emergence of an educated rural population (and also the concept of universal education) cannot be overestimated.

But the agrarian orientation of this research and training program has disappeared. Not that the programs have been eliminated (an estimated half billion dollars in research alone is spent each year), but that they have been directed to the interests of agribusiness. A detailed examination of this phenomenon was made by Jim Hightower. He writes:

> *It is agribusiness that is helped.* In particular, farm machinery and chemical in-put companies are the primary beneficiaries. Big business interests are called upon by land grant staff to participate directly in the planning, research and development stages of mechanization projects. The interests of agribusiness literally are designed with the product. No one else is consulted.[34]

We need not here go over the details of Hightower's impressive demonstration of this thesis. It is sufficient merely to add that, in addition to serving the corporate interests in the character of research and neglecting the needs of the traditional farmer, the agricultural research activities have set the tone and the character of rural American culture. It has helped to develop that overly mechanized, capital-intensive, city-oriented pattern of production that has contributed to the flight from rural America and the decline of traditional virtues.

This brings us back to the third study in this volume, which is a detailed examination of how corporate interests intervene in research and reshape governmental agencies to their purpose. The demise of the Bureau of Agricultural Economics eliminated virtually all sociologically oriented research activities from the Department of Agriculture.

AGRIBUSINESS AND THE AMERICAN CULTURE

Every nation and every region has a distinct character. Crossing the Channel from England to France, the Rhine from

France to Germany, or the Alps into Italy, takes a traveller from one culture to another. Each is unique in its basic outlook to life and the character of its interpersonal relationships, however much bluejeans and Volkswagens or the latest fad in popular music have been universalized. Each society has its own culture, its national character. These are not unchanging; Victorian England was certainly different from Elizabethan. It is the eternal quest of anthropology to understand the forces that shape these different cultures as they occur in time and space, and everything from climate to genetics to toilet-training practices has been evoked to account for them.

It is my opinion that the most important single factor in the formulation of the character of nations is its basic mode of production and the way that production is organized. The American character was forged in its rural hinterland: the frontiersman melding into the freeholding farmer created a pattern consisting of egalitarianism, personal independence, the demand for hard work and ingenuity, self-discipline, with its ultimate reward in a personal success. This syndrome of values and attitudes has become known as the "Protestant ethic," for these were the qualities promulgated by early puritanism.

The relationship between the Protestant ethic, social egalitarianism and industriousness has been a major theme in the sociology of history by such scholars as Tawney and Weber, and was first observed on the ground by that remarkable traveller de Tocqueville when he visited us in 1831. It was also recognized by those who sponsored Jeffersonian agrarianism. If this thesis is correct, then the alteration of the basic organization of production implicit in the growth of corporate farming can be expected to have far-reaching effects on the quality of the American culture. Indeed, that is the central thesis of *As You Sow*. I want now to review the evidence available that the implications of the studies reported here do in fact have such an effect. Though there are no investigations as comprehensive as those of Wasco, Arvin and Dinuba, there is a growing corpus of data which is indicative.

INTRODUCTION   xli

Let us begin this review with evidence for the continuing influence in California. The appropriate place to begin is with a reexamination of the Arvin-Dinuba contrast. As a summer project, Bruce La Rose made a series of comparisons in 1970 based on data from published sources.[35] He found the earlier contrasts substantiated a quarter century later in such matters as level of education, number of social and religious institutions, local newspapers, and paved roads. According to the census, median family income was 37 percent greater in Dinuba than in Arvin, retail establishments were nearly twice as numerous and, on a per capita basis, there was 40 percent more local trade. These contrasts continue despite the fact that in the intervening years, the agricultural base for Arvin grew enormously—thanks to the irrigation waters made available by the Central Valley Project.

I have also reexamined some of the data relating to the communities of the upper San Joaquin Valley, using the data from Table 1 of the *Agribusiness and the Rural Community*.[36] That table shows the population and average farm size for 25 towns lying on the floor of the three-county upper San Joaquin Valley area, excluding the county seats and other cities. The data demonstrate that where the towns are surrounded by large farms, the population per acre declines. A regression curve (Pearson's r) was calculated between two variables: average farm size and number of acres required to support the local residents. The correlation coefficient is .54 with a probability that this relationship would occur by chance being less than one in a thousand. Put another way, the 13 towns with the larger farm size support a population of 9.6 persons per 100 "acre-equivalent" acres, whereas the 12 towns with the smaller farms support a population of 15.1 persons per 100 acres.

Now it is of particular importance to remember that, though the number of people supported is greater, nonetheless, the average income in the small farm town of Dinuba is appreciably greater than in the larger farm community of Arvin, and they have a higher standard of living. When we examine the total household income (as determined from the schedules) in relation to the basic agricultural resource income (based on farm record analyses), we find there are $30 in extra circulation for every $100 of income in Arvin. The circulation in Dinuba is $101 for each $100 of resource income. This 3:1 ratio is an expression of the degree to which small farm operations are supportive of local business enterprise.[37]

Isao Fujimoto has recently examined the social and economic facilities in 130 towns of the eight-county San Joaquin Valley area.[38] He has scaled these towns in terms of the number of classes of facilities they possess, using a total of 41 categories. He has shown that there is a relationship between the number of such facilities and the size of farms (as determined by examining aerial photographs): findings that are consistent with those in the Arvin-Dinuba investigation. The towns surrounded by small-scale cropping patterns show a higher value for 9 out of 13 selected essential services.

Fujimoto included in his analysis 21 of the 25 towns in the upper San Joaquin Valley listed in Table 1 of *Agribusiness and the Rural Community* (p. 290). I found that there was a negative correlation between average farm size in 1940 and the number of facilities in the community some thirty years later ($r = -.42$). This figure is significant at the .1 level of probability, suggesting the continuing effects of scale of operation.

Phillip LeVeen has made a comparative analysis of 1970 an area of large-scale farming, and the other an area of small family operations.[39] He isolated two sets of census tracts to establish areas of farmer-intensive and labor-intensive agriculture. (In this area of specialty crop production, all farmers must hire labor at times of seasonal peak demand.) The former were those tracts in which 50 percent or more of the labor force was identified as "farm worker," the latter where 20 percent or more persons reported self-employment.

The labor-intensive area included a labor force of 5,156 persons of which 2,784 (54%) were agricultural workers and only 356 (6.9%) were self-employed in farming enterprises. The farmer-intensive area included a labor force of 12,454 persons of which 4,421 (35.5%) were farm workers and 3,363 (27%) were self-employed in agriculture. The median income of the latter group was 23 percent greater than the former and home ownership was 137 percent greater. On the other hand, there were 80 percent as many households living below the poverty level and crowding in the household (ratio of people to rooms exceeds 1.51) was less than half (43%) as frequent.

LeVeen made a separate analysis of Spanish surname persons, a population that provides much of the farm labor. There were 2,346 in the labor force in the labor-intensive area of which 1,572 were agricultural workers. In the farmer-intensive area there were 2,181 Spanish surname persons in the labor force, of which 1,117 were agricultural laborers. The Spanish surname population in the farmer-intensive area had median incomes 12 percent greater than those in the labor-intensive area and were home owners just twice as often. Crowding in their homes was only 76 percent as frequent. There were, however, 21 percent more of them below the poverty level.

A recent analysis of water districts in California made by Merrill Goodall and his associates leads us into a different area of concern.[40] California laws enable the formation of local districts to provide for social services under diverse kinds of regulations. According to the Goodall study, there are some 4,235 such special civil districts (not including school districts) in California, of which 886 are concerned with water. Though there are some 20 classes of districts, the significant distinction for our purposes is in the manner in which governing boards are selected. There are three forms: boards are elected by constituency consisting of certified voters on a one-man/one-vote basis; boards elected on a property valuation basis (one-dollar/one-vote) and those where boards are appointed by elected officials. The first of these may be called democratic, the second elitist. While only 11 percent of the districts established before 1950 were of the elitist variety, 25 percent of those established between 1950 and 1969 were.

It should be recognized that these districts are governmental entities.

A few of the classes of districts responsible for water utility functions are virtually indistinguishable from general governments.

Thus, in 1971, 16 of the community services districts provided fire protection, 28 were active in waste disposal, 8 maintained recreation and park programs, 21 were responsible for lighting and lighting maintenance, 2 supplied library services, 1 had local and regional planning responsibilities, 2 provided police protection, 8 constructed and maintained streets and roads, and 1 supplied ambulance service.[41]

Despite this fact, the management of such districts is subject to little electoral control. Even in those where the franchise is based upon residence, voter turnout rarely reaches a third of the electorate. It is not possible to determine how many voters turn out in the elitist districts. This is how the authors describe the situation with respect to the 72 California water districts formed between 1960 and 1969.

California Water Districts are formed by petition of property owners and can perform many significant services. . . . They can, for example, construct and maintain project works for irrigation, domestic, industrial and municipal purposes. They may acquire and construct necessary facilities to provide sewer service. They also can issue both general obligation and revenue bonds and bring eminent domain proceedings to purchase and condemn property for district purposes. Finally, this type of a district may form any number of special inprovement districts within its boundaries and issue bonds to finance improvements within these "mini-districts." These special improvement districts, incidentally, are governed by the same board that governs the parent district. With this vast array of powers and the resulting impact these districts can have on the residents of the districts, it is interesting to note that participation in elections is restricted to property owners who may cast one vote for each dollar's worth of land to which they hold title as shown on the district's assessment roll. Voters may vote in person or by proxy. Members of the governing board need not be residents. Districts may be divided into separate wards or divisions for the purpose of electing directors. Owners of property constitute the electorate not only on questions of district formation and representation on the board of directors but also on the incurring of bonded indebtedness. It is not surprising that this type of district is popular with landowners, especially landowners with large holdings. . . . In the Westlands Water District, for example, a district which comprises 597,778 acres and has more than 3,000 landowners, ten landowners account for 43 percent of all the land in the district. This situation, coupled with assessed valuation voting, means that a handful or so of corporations and individuals effectively controls district elections. Nominating petitions for the 1971 board elections in Westlands indicate how trusts and corporations relate to political influence. In that year, according to the information on nominating petitions on file in the Fresno County Elections Department, a current board of directors member signed a nominating petition in the following manner: in his own name; as vice-president of one corporation; as president of another; and as trustee of a children's trust.

In some property-test districts a clear majority of the votes cast is at the disposal of no more than four or five landowners; Westlands is such a district. In others, a single owner can cast the majority of all votes; Tulare Lake Water Storage District in the large-scale farming areas of the southern San Joaquin Valley, and the Irvine Ranch Water District in once-agricultural but now rapidly urbanizing Orange County, are examples. In many other districts, our data show a strong trend toward a more consolidated ownership of land. Berrenda Mesa Water District, a California Water District in the southern San Joaquin, exemplifies that trend. Districts which set property tests for voting tend to be incorporated in areas where relatively large-scale farming is the norm. The recent expansion of property qualification districts and of increasingly extensive corporate agriculture cluster in the southern and western San Joaquin.[42]

Thus far I have brought together evidence of the continued pattern of corporate farming and its sociological implications for California. I want now to show that the social results of this form of economy are similar wherever corporate farming is found. I shall begin by citing the study of social class structure in rural America made by T. Lynn Smith.[43] Smith divides rural society into five classes based upon diverse criteria for which the 1959 census provides evidence: an upper class of independent farm operators, a lower class of wage laborers and poorer tenant farmers, and three levels of middle class. In a detailed examination of selected counties, he shows how in some areas one class tends to be dominant, a different one, depending upon local conditions and economy. In highly industrialized agricultural areas such as Imperial Valley in California, or Palm Beach in Florida, there is a heavy concentration of lower-class people, relatively small representation of the middle groups, and an upper class slightly larger than usual, but still less than five percent of the total population. Smith sees this as a two-class system. Smith also shows the prevalence of each class for the 50 states of the Union.

A detailed analysis has been made of large-scale agriculture in the United States by Radoje Nikolitch, based on the 1964 census of agriculture.[44] His Figure 1 shows the proportion of total agricultural production for each of 49 states (Alaska is omitted) that is accounted for by the 31,000 largest farms — i.e., agricultural enterprises that had a total value of products sold of $100,000 or more.

I have made an analysis of the relationship between the prevalence of corporate farms, based on Nikolitch's 1964 data, and the prevalence of lower-class persons as shown by Smith.[45] The two sets of data have a correlation coefficient of .76 (Pearson's r). Such a close relationship demonstrates that the formation of a class-oriented society of the kind I have described for California is a direct consequence of the incidence of large-scale agriculture; that is, it will appear wherever such organization prevails.

A few studies in America's agricultural heartland have been made showing how this process affects the rural communities of traditional agriculture. The study already cited on the development of pivot agriculture in Nebraska has shown how a new form of management has invaded the area.

The social and political consequences of absentee investor financing are . . . worrisome. Traditionally, rural Midwestern communities have placed a high value on equality and independence and self-reliance. These values have shaped a social structure which is relatively free of class division.

This will change under the emerging pattern of ownership which we have described here. The classic urban-industrial division between ownership, management, and labor is already apparent in many of the larger farms in Holt and Dundy County. Interestingly, the growing importance of the custom farm manager reflects the situation in major manufacturing corporations where management has emerged as the controlling group . . .[46]

A more detailed and intimate investigation of the sociological consequences of this new externally financed, management controlled farming has been made in rural Missouri by William D. Heffernan.[47] Heffernan studied the social attitudes and participation of rural people engaged in poultry production—an industry that we have already seen has become dominated by outside corporations through vertical integration. He found that the owner-manager of the corporate structured poultry enterprise was differentiated from the family farmers (whether still independent or integrated through a corporate contract) and the laborers in income, social status, and a number of other important variables. This labor group was significantly higher in two measures of an index of social alienation (the source of powerlessness and normlessness), and in the degree of informal social interaction. A pattern of social involvement with voluntary organizations showed the same kind of differential that appears in California communities: workers average membership of .37 and a participation score of .88 in contrast to the owner-manager group with 3.61 membership per person and a participation score of 18.72. A similar pattern was demonstrated for political involvement. Most significantly, Heffernan says "this type of agricultural structure suggests the development of two rather distinct classes for rural America which undermines the traditional American ideal of Equality."[48]

Studies made by Heffernan and Lasley of the grape production area in Missouri show similar tendencies.[49] They are here distinguishing between agricultural operation on the basis of financial resources—an appropriate recognition of the increased importance of capital in the modern farming enterprise. Lasley and Heffernan found that there is a gradual encroachment of externally financed, management oriented operations in this specialty crop area. These managerial persons are less involved with the local community—especially its social interaction.

A more personal view of this situation was expressed by an Iowa minister:

I live in a community of 2,000 persons and a county with a population of 8,000. Imagine, if you will, the impact this trend toward commercialization is having upon our economy. First, we are all losing our population to urban areas as they leave the farms. This has reduced the economic growth factor throughout the county. As the service area is reduced, so the need for servicing units has declined and we lose more population to the urban centers. At the same time, the commercial investors are gaining a stronger hold in the farm economy. It takes no imagination to see that absentee investors have no concern for what happens to community economic pattern or community organization where they have their investment. Educational facilities may deteriorate, religious institutions may disintegrate, and social organization may evaporate, but it will not affect the investor nor his investment.[50]

FARM POLICY AND AMERICAN CULTURE

The studies of Wasco and of Arvin and Dinuba show in detail the character of the rural community that develops under industrialized and corporate agricultural production. In this introduction I have shown that such farming is growing rapidly in the United States, and have given evidence that the social consequences of such production are similar wherever they occur. This growth of corporate agriculture is not inevitable nor simply a product of efficiency, but it is rather a result of the emergence of national policies favorable to large-scale enterprises. Some of these policies were promulgated by corporate interests. Others, ostensibly at least, were formulated in the desire to protect the family farmer, but have had the opposite effect.

The sociological consequences of agricultural organization are not difficult to understand. When farms are of a generally uniform size, there can be little concentration of powers, and social interaction operates on the premise of equality. Where large-scale and corporate agriculture develops, it follows not only that there are great differences in the level of control among the managerial group, but that a cadre of economically dependent laborers will emerge. From this there follows a system of social distinctions, with a powerful group

INTRODUCTION   xlix

and a relatively alienated and disaffected working class. The economically and socially advantaged groups look outside the community for both their economic and social needs, so that both local business and local social organization wither. Increased power in the hands of a small sector tends also to be self-reinforcing, so that once the process is initiated, it will continue to grow, unless measures are taken to counteract it.

Rhodes and Kyle, impressed with the juggernaut of corporate growth, warn us of the corporation's peculiar power for survival in dramatic terms:

> Many farmers still do not take the possibility of a corporate agriculture seriously because they don't believe that it can happen. Twenty years ago, almost no one believed it could happen; *today the corporations themselves, and growing numbers of integrated or displaced farmers know that corporations can succeed in various parts of both field crop and livestock production.*
>
> Those farmers miss the point who laugh at certain operating errors made by corporate farmers. For example, while the errors made by Penn Central appear to have been tremendous, that huge railroad system *still exists.* As another example, I.T.& T. grew so fast and so large, not because of any exceptional operating efficiency, but rather, because it had a deliberate and successful strategy of growth via acquistion and merger.
>
> *The capacity of the giant corporation to grow and grow, despite the lack of any real competitive edge over individual farmers in a traditional accounting sense, is the crucial difference between the corporate and the individual competitor.*[51]

The rural sector of our society was once the predominant element, and the degree to which the frontier in America and the establishment of agrarian policies has influenced our national society is not always fully appreciated. It is now a relatively small fraction of the American populace, yet it has served as a continuing wellspring for that national culture. The passing of the traditional farm population from the American scene will have profound effects on our national character. Senator Wayne Morse put the matter explicitly:

> We talk about political democracy, but we cannot have it without economic democracy. We cannot have political freedom of choice

for the individual without economic freedom of choice for the individual. Therefore, I say again today on the floor of the Senate, if I were to be asked to name one thing—if I were limited to the naming of one thing only—which I think is the greatest guarantee of the perpetuity of our democratic form of government, what I would name would be private home ownership in the city and family-farm ownership in the country. On that type of ownership, I think, is dependent, more than we sometimes fully realize, our whole system of political and economic freedom of choice for the individual.[52]

The social picture described in the three studies in this volume, therefore, have relevance to the emerging character of the American culture as well as to the nature of our rural landscape. Whether that scene will continue to change toward industrialized production and corporate control will depend upon the policies that are formulated; will depend upon whether reclamation projects will create many small farms or subsidize giant corporations; whether labor and tax policies will continue to favor giant corporations and investment interest or will serve the needs of the farmer; whether government in general will turn back to its historic concern with individual welfare. These policies are not only relevant to the rural communities, but to the very continuance of the American heritage.

NOTES

1. Joseph Henry Jackson, "A Bookman's Notebook," *San Francisco Chronicle* (July 22, 1947).
2. The landmark decision with respect to agriculture was handed down in the case of Ben Yellen, *et al.* versus Walter J. Hickel by Judge William Murray of the U.S. District Court in 1971.
3. Angus McDonald, "Reclamation Law Violations of the Department of Interior," (1977). Personal files, courtesy of Angus McDonald.
4. David M. Weiman, "The Effect of Federal Law and Policy in Family Farming, with Special Reference to the Westlands Water District as an Example of the Law and Policy," in *Will the Family Farm Survive in America?* Joint Hearings before the Select Committee on Small Business and the Committee on Interior and Insular Affairs; 94th Congress, First Session (July 17, 1975), pp. 13-44. David M. Weiman, statement before the Subcommittee on Water and Power Resources, Committee on Interior and Insular Affairs, House of Representatives (April 20, 1977). Mimeographed.
5. An editorial in *The Fresno Bee* (May 16, 1977) says, in part: "According to a story by George Baker of the Bee's Washington bureau, [Gilbert] Stamm [recently retired commissioner of the Bureau of Reclamation] has called on Fresno's two representatives in Congress and talked to them about the problems of landowners in the Kings River services area who are under court order to break up their holdings.

"Stamm says he wasn't working for the landowners when he dropped in on Rep. John Krebs. He was just curious to know what Krebs was thinking about the matter, Stamm says.

"Krebs, however, tells it differently. He says Stamm explored the possibility of Krebs' introducing legislation to nullify the court order and permit the landowners to retain their holdings. Krebs says he isn't interested. . . .

"The court opinion that so interests Stamm holds that the landowners who use Kings River water stored in Pine Flat Dam near Fresno are subject to the 160-acre limitation. . . ."

6. "Interior Secretary Cecil B. Andrus has stopped all excess land sales in reclamation areas pending the formulation of regulations governing the sales, and his order goes far beyond a federal court order [by Judge Barrington D. Parlor in August, 1976] to include prohibition on approval of recordable contracts." George L. Baker, "Andrus Orders Halt to Excess Land Sales in All Areas," *The Fresno Bee* (July 7, 1977). Preliminary regulations were announced in mid-August, 1977, and as of this writing are being subjected to public review. The Reclamation Lands Family Farm Act is reported in the *Congressional Record*, Vol. 123, No. 114.
7. *Corporations with Farm Operations.* Economics Research Service, USDA, Report 209 (June 1971).
8. Statement of Jim Hightower, *Role of Giant Corporations.* Hearings before the Subcommittee on Monopoly of the Select Committee on Small Business, U.S. Senate, 92nd Congress (Nov. 30 and Dec. 1, 1971; March 1 and 2, 1972), Part 3, p.3725. (Hereinafter *Giant Corporations.*)

9. Oren Lee Stanley testimony in *Giant Corporations*, Part 3, p. 3864.

10. Ewell Paul Roy, *Contract Farming*, U.S.A. (Danville, Ill.: The Interstate Printers and Publishers Inc., 1963).

11. Don Paarlberg, "Future of the Family Farm." Speech before the annual convention of the American Milk Producers Federation (November 30, 1971). *Giant Corporations*, Part 3B, pp. 5072-5087.

12. Ronald L. Mighell and William S. Hoofnagel, *Contract Production and Vertical Integration in Farming, 1960 and 1970*. Economic Research Service, USDA, Economic Report 479 (Washington, April 1972).

13. Harrison Welford, testimony in *Giant Corporations*, Part 3, p. 3693.

14. Harrison Welford, "Sowing the Wind: The Politics of Food Safety and Agribusiness" in *Giant Corporations*, Part 3, pp. 3705-6.

15. Richard V. Thornton, testimony in *Giant Corporations*, Part 3, pp. 4088-4092.

16. *Wheels of Fortune: A Report on the Impact of Center Pivot Irrigation on the Ownership of Land in Nebraska* (Walthill, Nebr.: Center for Rural Affairs, 1976) p. 51. Mimeographed.

17. *Ibid.*, p. 50.

18. J. Patrick Madden, *Economics of Size in Farming: Theory, Analytic Procedures, and a Review of Selected Studies*. Economic Research Service, USDA. Agricultural Economic Report No. 107 (February 1967).

19. Warren R. Bailey, Foreword to reissue edition of Madden, *op. cit.* Reproduced in *Farmworkers in Rural America 1971-1972*. Hearings before the Subcommittee on Migratory Labor of the Committee on Labor and Public Welfare, U.S. Senate, 92nd Congress, Part 5A, p. 3468.

20. See page 24.

21. Michael Perelman makes the same point in "Efficiency and Agriculture" (typescript, Economics Department, Chico State College). *Giant Corporations*, Part 3B, pp. 5165-5177.

22. Y. Hayami and V. Ruttan, *Agricultural Development* (Baltimore: The Johns Hopkins Press, 1971), pp. 72-73.

23. "The Agri-Welfare Roll," *Ramparts* (October 1971). Reprinted in the *Congressional Record* (Nov. 2, 1971), as extension of remarks by Rep. Charles B. Rangel.

24. Philip M. Raup, "Some Issues Raised by the Expansion of Corporation Farming." Statement in *Corporate Farming: The Effects of Corporation Farming on Small Business*. Hearings before the Subcommittee on Monopoly of the Select Committee on Small Business, U.S. Senate, 90th Congress, 2nd Session (May 20 and 21, July 22, 1968), p. 245.

25. *Ibid.*, p. 243.

26. P. M. Raup, *Corporate Farming in the United States*. Scientific Journal Series Paper No. 8187, Minnesota Agricultural Experimental Station (December 1972), p. 11. Mimeographed.

27. Joseph C. Meisner and V. James Rhodes, *The Changing Structure of U.S. Cattle Feeding*. U. of Missouri, Columbia, Agricultural Economics, Special Report 167 (August 1975).

28. Stephan F. Matthews and V. James Rhodes, *The Use of Public Limited Partnership Financing in Agriculture for Income Tax Shelter.* Studies of the organization and control of the U. S. Food System, North Central Regional Research Project 117, Monograph 1. (Madison: University of Wisconsin, College of Agriculture and Life Sciences, July 1975), p. 26.

29. Faculty of the Department of Agricultural Economics, University of Missouri-Columbia, *Policy Issues in Missouri Agriculture 1976,* p. 9. Mimeographed.

30. National Planning Association, *The Effects of Federal Income Taxes on the Structure of Agriculture.* Pamphlet No. 131 (1972), p. 140.

31. Jim Hightower, *Giant Corporations,* Part 3, p. 3725.

32. Varden Fuller, *The Struggle for Public Policy on Farm Labor-Management Relations.* MS. (Davis: Department of Agricultural Economics, University of California, n.d.), p. 11. Fuller notes an ironic twist to the problems of unionization in agriculture. With the introduction of conglomerates into agribusiness, there is a new vulnerability to labor demands. Meanwhile, Cesar Chavez, the United Farm Workers president, has used effectively the secondary boycott on table grapes and lettuce, which is forbidden under the NLRA, so that some employers now want to bring agriculture under its provision whereas UFW does not. The situation in California, with its highly controversial Agriculture Labor Board, is now in a state of dynamic flux.

33. Quoted by P. S. Taylor. Hearings before a Subcommittee of the Committee on Education and Labor, U.S. Senate, 76th Congress, 3rd Session (1939), Part 47, p. 17218.

34. Jim Hightower, *Hard Tomatoes, Hard Times: A Report of the Agribusiness Accountability Project on the Failure of America's Land Grant College Complex.* (Cambridge, Mass.: Schenkman Publ. Co. 1973), p. 31. (Emphasis in original.)

35. Bruce L. La Rose, "Arvin and Dinuba Revisited: A New Look at Community Structure and the Effects of Scale of Operation," *Giant Corporations,* Part 3, pp. 4076-83.

36. See page 290.

37. As the source of data on farm income was derived from agricultural production records while the family income was calculated from responses to the questionnaires, the *absolute* values are not useful. However, the *relative* values between Arvin and Dinuba are significant. It might also be noted that Arvin probably represents a relatively high ratio for large farm communities, inasmuch as it is unusual in the size of population supported under these conditions.

38. Isao Fujimoto, *The Communities of the San Joaquin Valley: The Relation between Scale of Farming, Water Use, and the Quality of Life.* MS. Testimony before the Federal Task Force on Westlands, California, Sacramento (Aug. 4, 1977). The use of this preliminary analysis is with the kind permission of Dr. Fujimoto.

39. Phillip LeVeen, *Agricultural Development and Rural Poverty,* Department of Agricultural and Resource Economics, University of California, Berkeley. MS. Chapter 1. Cited by kind permission of Dr. LeVeen.

40. Merrill R. Goodall, John D. Sullivan and Tim De Young, *California Water: A New Political Economy* (Montclair, N.J.: Allanheld, Osmun & Co., 1978).

41. Goodall, Sullivan and De Young, *ibid.,* pp. 15, 18.

42. Goodall, Sullivan and De Young, *ibid.*, pp. 24-25, 29-30.

43. T. Lynn Smith, "A Study of Social Stratification in the Agricultural Sections of the U.S.: Nature, Data, Procedures, and Preliminary Results," *Rural Sociology*, Vol. 34, No. 4 (1969), pp. 496-509.

44. Radoje Nikolitch, *Our 31,000 Largest Farms.* Agricultural Economics Report No. 175, Economic Research Service (March, 1970).

45. Walter Goldschmidt, "Large Scale Agriculture and the Rural Social Structure," *Rural Sociology* (In press).

46. Wheels of Fortune, *op. cit.*, pp. 61-62.

47. William D. Heffernan, "Sociological Dimensions of Agricultural Structures in the United States," *Sociologia Ruralis*, XII, No. 31 (1972), pp. 481-499.

48. *Ibid.*, p. 497.

49. William D. Heffernan and Paul Lasley, *Structural Changes in Agriculture and the Rural Community* (n.d.), Mimeographed, Paul Lasley and William D. Heffernan, "Structural Changes in Central Missouri's Grape Industry," paper presented to the annual meeting of the Rural Sociological Society (1976).

50. Lester L. Moore, pastor of the United Methodist Church, Corning, Iowa, in testimony before the Senate Committee on Small Business, U.S. Senate, 90th Congress; 2nd Session (May 21, 1968). *Corporate Farming*, pp. 173-4.

51. V. James Rhodes and Leonard R. Kyle, "A Corporate Agriculture," in *Who Will Control U.S. Agriculture?* No. 3 (of a series of 6), North Central Regional Extension Publication 32, (Urbana-Champagne University of Illinois Extension Publication, College of Agriculture, Cooperative Extension Service, Special Publication 28. No date. (Emphasis in original.)

52. *Congressional Record* (May 7, 1959), p. 7677.

PART I

As You Sow

ACKNOWLEDGMENTS

The contributions of innumerable citizens and colleagues have made the present volume possible, and to all of them I would like to express my deep appreciation. Particularly do I wish to express my appreciation to Paul S. Taylor of the Department of Economics of the University of California, whose help began with the inception of the study as an idea and has continued through to its completion. Dorothy S. Thomas and Robert H. Lowie have also served to stimulate me and to improve the quality of the work, as have many former members of the Bureau of Agricultural Economics, especially John Provinse, Lloyd Fisher, Davis McEntire, Varden Fuller, Marion Clawson, and Carl C. Taylor. Our visit to Wasco was made under a collaboratorship with the Bureau of Agricultural Economics, but neither that agency nor any other branch of the government is to be held responsible either for the factual content or the sociological analyses. Many others performed special tasks in the preparation of the manuscript: Mary Montgomery in editing, Patricia Mathews, Bethel Webb and Helen Rosenberg in typing, and the personnel of WPA Project No. 165-2-08-374 in tabulating statistical data.

In the course of our visits many close bonds were developed. Some persons knew rather precisely the nature of the investigation, others vaguely that it was an historical study or, falsely, one of many romantic notions, and most—such is the urbanity of these towns—knew nothing whatsoever of the study. To these friends and strangers we are permanently indebted, and from them we have quoted liberally in the hope that thus we may better interpret their, and our, society.

Finally, and most particularly, I thank my wife, who participated in the development of this work from the first exploratory discussion to the final proof. Her assistance in the field was indispensable, and her influence is to be found on every page.

CHAPTER I

THE PLACE OF CALIFORNIA AGRICULTURE IN AMERICAN FARM LIFE

TENURE PATTERNS IN AMERICA

THREE FUNDAMENTAL and divergent traditions of farming may be isolated in America: the small landholding pattern introduced in New England and the North Atlantic by early colonization; the plantation system of the South; and the industrial farming and large-scale ranching of the Southwest. There are small farms in the South and West and large ones in the East and Middle West, but the farm economy and rural life in each area can only be understood in terms of these basic traditions, and a knowledge of the differences between them and the essential characteristics of each will help to clarify present-day farm problems and future farm policy.

The farm pattern of the North was the pattern of the self-sufficient small farm, owned and operated on a modest scale. On it were produced the basic crops in the American diet—grains, potatoes, and livestock products. The farmer was a husbandman, close to his soil, producing much of his own needs, and maintaining maximum independence from the city. The tradition of the small independent farmer has spread throughout most of the nation. The slow movement westward during the first half century of our national life was in very large part a spread of this pattern. Settlers moved into the frontier country and hewed for themselves a farm out of the wilderness. The development and spread of this major trend was given official recognition in the Pre-emption laws which assured the settlers title to their land. It was developed into the dominant pattern by passage of the Homestead Law which made it possible for individuals of initiative to make a livelihood at a minimal cost by merely building a homestead and working the land. So firmly rooted in American tradition is this pattern that it is hardly necessary to elaborate upon it. Novelists have filled our shelves with tales of this sturdy element in our economy. Orators refer to it when they speak of the glories of farm life, administrators inevitably formulate national farm policy in terms of it, and many of us have tended to accept this tradition not only as real, but as universal throughout America.

The South developed a very different pattern. The early and successful—from the point of view of the landed gentry—introduction of slaves into the area created a different type of production and a different social system. Instead of small farms producing largely for home consumption, there were great estates producing single crops of goods—usually cotton—for the export market. The landowner remained distant from the soil, and even further from the actual work of tilling that soil. He did not produce his own needs, but bought them from the urban centers with money obtained from the sale of his cotton. This pattern also spread westward, but its course was checked by the Civil War. Though the Civil War abolished the legal institution of slavery, it did not wipe out the social order which slavery had engendered. Under the sharecropper system, which has come to replace slavery as the fundamental economic pattern, the dependence of the Negro and the poor white worker upon the land owner is virtually complete. Strong caste barriers combine with this economic dependence to preserve the social system of the antebellum South. Here lies a great exception to the traditional democracy of American rural life. The character of Southern economy and the structure of Southern society have been recorded in detail by the economists and sociologists, and have reached the people through the medium of literature. But this recognition has not altered the popular concept of rural America. The South has been recognized as a great economic problem, but only as an exceptional and localized aberration on the small-farm tradition. It has had little effect upon American agricultural policy.

Agriculture in the Southwest conforms to neither of these patterns. And unlike farming in other sections of the country, it is relatively poorly understood, relatively little has been written about it, and its peculiar problems are frequently overlooked in the formation of national agricultural policy.[1] In part this is because it is not easily characterized, and in part because it is remote—or has been—from the major currents of American life.

The industrialized agricultural pattern has its origin in an amalgamation of several historic traditions. It received its early impetus from the Spanish *hacienda,* and it was further developed by the giant land grants and land grabs of the early period of California statehood. Its origin in part goes to an amalgamation of Northern and Southern traditions, for both groups came to California, and California farming contains elements of each. And while the small farm exists in California as well as the large holding, the tenure relationship, the organization of the farm enterprise, and the attitudes of the people are neither those of the North nor of the South.

The pattern of the North created a social system in which local democracy could flourish and the farmer had a large measure of autonomy. To be sure, the farmer was usually looked down upon by the townspeople, and he has been described as heavily subject to the pressures in the market place.[2] But in the long run, the yokel or rube from the countryside had a measure of economic and social independence rarely achieved among the tillers of the soil anywhere else in the world. In contrast, the social system of the South has been one of extremes—the very rich juxtaposed to the poor. The landowners, the aristocracy of the South, look up to no one, but the sharecropper and tenant farmer have no social standing.

The social status system, the relation of farmer to townsman and of the worker to the land, these are the subject of detailed analysis in the chapters which follow. It is an urban pattern, for

[1] It is not without interest that the great novels based upon California rural life are proletarian rather than agrarian in tone.
[2] Thorstein Veblen has discussed this with bitter sarcasm in his essay "The Case of America," in the section entitled "The Independent Farmers." Reprinted in *What Veblen Taught* (Wesley C. Mitchell, editor), The Viking Press, New York, 1936.

just as agricultural production is handled like business and manufacturing, so, too, the social relationships follow the pattern of those in the city.

LAND TENURE IN CALIFORNIA

California's heritage from Spain, under whose flag she once stood, was a heritage of large landholdings. The *hacienda* was a small principality, in which the landlord lived supreme, and the labor was done by impressed Indians whose major compensations were admittance into the realm of Christendom. Spanish land grants, the spurious often along with the real, were recognized by the American government as valid claims, upon the acquisition of California. The importance of these grants may be seen from the fact that by 1934, 8.5 millions of the 55 million acres which had been transferred from the public domain to private title had entered such private ownership as Spanish grants. Their importance is, however, even greater than these figures indicate, first, because the lands under such grants included much of the State's finest, and second, because through the recognition of the Spanish tenure system the tradition of large landholdings was continued into the American period.[3]

Large-scale landholdings were further augmented by grants of land to railroads amounting to 11.5 million acres. Both these lands and the Spanish grants included much of the best acreage in the state. Such grants gave further impetus to the tradition of large-scale ownership and curtailed to that degree the opportunity for land settlement in the small farm tradition.

This tradition of large holdings and the attitudes of officials during the sixties and seventies, created a favorable climate for the acquisition of large holdings by land grabs. Much of the 8.5 million acres of land to which the state had title was sold to speculators, without limitation on acreage, at $1.25 per acre. For

[3] Leon Key, *The History of the Policies in Disposing of the Public Lands in California, 1769-1900.* Ms., University of California, Berkeley, 1937 (M. A. Thesis). Data obtained from A. E. Douhan, Acting Assistant Commissioner, General Land Office, by letter dated October 4, 1934.

PLACE OF CALIFORNIA AGRICULTURE IN AMERICAN FARM LIFE 7

a summary description of land acquisition we can rely upon the historian, Paul Wallace Gates.

Land monopolization in California dates back to the Spanish and Mexican periods when large grants were made to favored individuals. . . . Following 1848 there came a rapid influx of settlers which, together with the large profits realized from the grazing industry in the interior valleys, created a land boom and led to extensive purchases. With great areas of land in the San Joaquin and Sacramento Valleys open to cash purchase the opportunity for speculative profits was unparalleled elsewhere; nor was the opportunity neglected. From 1862 to 1880 land sales and warrant and scrip entries in California were on an enormous scale, surpassing all other states for the period and in some years comprising well over half of the sales for the entire country. In the single year, ending June 30, 1869, 1,726,794 acres were sold in this state by the Federal government and for the entire period from 1862 to 1880 well over 7,000,000 acres were entered with cash, warrants, or scrip. It should also be remembered that the State of California which received 8,426,380 acres from the Federal government was disposing of its most valuable holdings at this time.

Greatest of all the speculators operating in California was William S. Chapman, whose political influence stretched from Sacramento to St. Paul, Minnesota, and Washington, D. C. Of him it was said, with apparent justice, that land officers, judges, local legislators, officials in the Department of the Interior, and even higher dignitaries were ready and anxious to do him favors, frequently of no mean significance. Between 1868 and 1871 Chapman entered at the Federal land offices approximately 650,000 acres of land in California and Nevada with cash, scrip, and warrants. At the same time he entered additional land through dummy entrymen, purchased many thousands of acres of "swamp" lands from the State of California, and otherwise added to his possessions till they totaled over 1,000,000 acres. Fraud, bribery, false swearing, forgery, and other crimes were charged against him but he passed them off with little trouble. The most remarkable feature about his vast acquisitions is that when plotted on a land-use map today they appear to be among the choicest of the lands. Chapman was not able to retain this vast empire for long. He became deeply involved in a grand canal project and eventually lost his lands, many of them going to a more constructive but equally spectacular land plunger, Henry Miller.

Miller, unlike Chapman, bought lands for his cattle business which was his main interest. As the activities of his firm—Miller and Lux, of which he was the chief promoter—expanded, he pushed its land acquisitions until they mounted to over a million acres. One hundred and eighty-one thousand acres of this amount were acquired directly from the Federal government, with cash, Agricultural College scrip, and military warrants; large amounts were purchased from Chapman and other big land speculators and from the State of California. Miller's lands were slowly irrigated, parts were disposed of to small farmers, and upon them today exists a veritable agricultural empire.

Other large purchasers of land in California were Isaac Friedlander, E. H. Miller, and John W. Mitchell, who acquired 214,000, 105,000, 78,000 acres respectively. The total amount purchased from the Federal government by Chapman, Miller and Lux, Friedlander, E. H. Miller, and Mitchell was one and a quarter million acres. Forty-three other large purchasers acquired 905,000 acres of land in the sixties in California. Buying in advance of settlement, these men were virtually thwarting the Homestead Law in California, where, because of the enormous monopolization above outlined, homesteaders later were able to find little good land.[4]

While lands sold under acts devised to create small holdings after the pattern of northern development included 15 million acres, such lands were frequently sold in large tracts by means of various fraudulent devices.

The massive holdings acquired during the last century are not, of course, still operated as single farms. But their former existence had certain direct and specific effects. The first of these was to create a pattern or tradition of large landholdings and tenure relationships which has dominated California's agricultural scene. The second was to create a demand for cheap labor which, once supplied, came to be capitalized into the value of the land itself. The third was to make the lands subject to speculation and speculative prices, and such prices have regularly constituted a burden upon the working farmer who attempted to wrest a livelihood from the soil.

Great acreages of California's fertile valley lands have been subdivided by speculators and colonized by hopeful "pioneers." Sometimes these settlements resulted only in blasted hopes and shattered bank accounts. Frequently, however, some present thriving community—and Wasco is one such community—has grown out of these very settlements. Such thriving communities are no guarantee that everything was always easy. The tradition is widespread in the West that it takes three failures to make a

[4] Paul Wallace Gates, "The Homestead Law in an Incongruous Land System," *American Historical Review,* July, 1936, pp. 668-69.

is a specialist in one or two heavily soil-depleting annual crops. He therefore does not want to own large acreages of land on which he would have to plant soil-replenishment crops, and which at best would take too much of his operating capital. Therefore he leases land for that period of time during which it can produce his special crop, and when it is exhausted he moves his operations to new lands. He frequently owns one piece of land, on which such permanent investments as packing sheds, labor camps, and the like are placed. In addition, he will lease a number of pieces for two or three-year periods, after which the owner will plant alfalfa to rebuild the soil. This pattern developed first in the Salinas and Imperial Valleys during the early twenties, and is particularly associated with lettuce, melons, and carrots. In recent years it has invaded the San Joaquin Valley, and is found associated with potatoes in the neighborhood of Wasco. The mobile farmer is a speculator, investing heavily on a short-term basis. His money is a gamble on the crop, while there is little investment in land or capital equipment. Permanent investments are largely in farm machinery. In Imperial County, where the pattern is most prominent, the total investment in farm machinery exceeds the total investment in farm buildings. It is specialized farm equipment, usually expensive and of limited usefulness, that forms the key to this type of farming. The operator must have a large amount of it and wants to use it as fully as possible. The geographical scatter of his operations means that he must be able to move his equipment from place to place. For this purpose a tractor rig has been developed, on which tractors and other heavy equipment can be hoisted off the ground and pulled from one piece of land to the next. The "farmer" engaged in this kind of production is much more concerned with matters pertaining to the market than he is with matters pertaining to the soil. His judgments as to the amount of planting, the proper time of maturation, and the particular place to which to ship his products are the most important he must make. Prices fluctuate seasonally and spatially, and his entire operation is a gamble on price. The economics of this type of production do not motivate the operator to maintain soil fertility; to consider the welfare of the local community in which his leased lands lie; nor to have any concern over the long-term welfare of his labor.

The third type of large farm unit that has grown up in California is that created by the consolidation of numerous farms. A continuous process of breaking and joining of tracts takes place in any dynamic farm community. In many communities of California, of which Wasco is one, the original farm size was too small for the character of farm operations, the dominant standards of the area, and the increasing efficiency of farm machinery. There is a natural tendency for such units to adjust in size. In Wasco the original settlement was mostly in 20-acre tracts, and many were smaller. Now the average farm is over 100 acres and hardly a single full-time unit is based on as few as 20 acres. This consolidation is a healthy adjustment to a form of disequilibrium. Some such consolidation, however, results in very large production units. Usually this is the case when an operator has invested in a processing plant. Thus, the ownership of a potato shed in Wasco or a raisin packing plant in Dinuba usually motivates the operator to increase his holdings. What happens is this: a successful operator decides he can function better if he has his own packing shed. He invests in a packing shed, but finds it difficult to maintain an orderly flow of produce into the shed, and he also wants to maintain the quality of his produce in order that his merchandise will be considered premium by the buyers and will move more rapidly and command a higher price. He may solve his problem by purchasing the fruit on the tree or vine, hiring his own crew and managing the later stages of farm production. Such purchasing is frequent in the citrus area of Southern California, and quite general in grape and deciduous fruit production. But the producer may find it difficult to assure an even flow of prime quality fruits, even if he contracts in advance. He may also feel that he stands to profit more if he owns the fruit from the outset. So he is motivated to own and operate enough land to utilize his packing plant. As his operations grow, they approach in size and organization the operation of the factory farms. Such a process of accretion lies in the history of the Wasco Creamery, and a similar pattern is involved in the development of grape production by the Schenley Corporation, distillers.

Attempts have been made to determine the degree to which large-scale operations and industrialized farming dominate the agricultural scene in California. The census, for instance, reports that 4 per cent of all farms in California have 1,000 acres or more, and that these farms own 66 per cent of the total farm acreage and 35 per cent of the land under actual cultivation in the state. A study recently made of irrigable lands in three counties in the San Joaquin Valley shows that the 2.5 per cent of the owners holding 640 or more acres of irrigable land own 52 per cent of all land in the area. If we direct our attention to the farm as an operating unit, less than 4 per cent of the farmers operate over 640 acres, but they utilize 58 per cent of all land in the area.[5] No statistics can give a full appreciation of the importance of industrialized operations because even the modest grower uses methods, organizes his operations, and maintains attitudes established by the large grower. The family farmer in Wasco, Dinuba, and elsewhere in California must compete with these large enterprises and frequently is dependent upon one of them for financing, processing, or marketing his goods. He finds himself a part of a system of social attitudes, ethics, and social values which he can rarely escape. In that way the whole agricultural production is industrialized.

FARM PRODUCTION IN CALIFORNIA

California produces commercially every major commodity grown anywhere in the United States, except tobacco, soy beans, and peanuts, and in addition produces numerous items which are found nowhere else. This marked diversity of production lends special interest to the farming in the state, and makes California farming a matter of particular interest to the nation. California produces all the domestic almonds, artichokes, raisins, olives, and dried apricots, peaches, pears, and figs in the

[5] Edwin E. Wilson and Marion Clawson, *Agricultural Land Ownership and Operation in the Southern San Joaquin Valley* (Mimeographed), Bureau of Agricultural Economics, Berkeley, June, 1945, Tables 3 and 15.

United States. It produces 22 per cent of all commercial vegetables and 46 per cent of all fruits and nuts.[6] Fruits, nuts, and vegetables make up 41 per cent of all production by volume shipped out of the state, compared with but 7 per cent of the volume in the nation as a whole.

At the same time that California farms are producing commodities for nation- and world-wide shipment, they fail to furnish the staple food products for local consumption. About 226 million dollars' worth of fruits, nuts, and vegetables were produced annually between 1930 and 1939 in California, of which 177 million (about 80 per cent) was shipped out. But the 189 million dollar livestock production had to be augmented by 81 million dollars' worth of net inshipment, and the 36 million dollars' worth of grains by 7 million dollars net inshipment.[7] California farms produce a great variety of commodities and export a large portion of them, yet many staple needs in the local diet are not met by production. There are many interesting economic problems associated with this situation, but one aspect of it particularly attracts our attention. This is that those commodities which constitute a disproportionately large share of the agricultural enterprise in California are those which are subject to the greater fluctuations in market value, while the "deficit" crops in California are those characterized by relative stability in prices and production. It seems probable that the specialty crops which dominate California actually return more income per acre and therefore afford a "higher" use of the land resources. Whether or not this is the case, it is clearly true that these commodities offer greater speculative possibilities, afford the farmers an opportunity to get rich quick, and also carry a greater threat to the operators' economic security. This speculative character of farming in California is an important psychological as well as economic attribute, and some of its direct influences will become clear in the subsequent story of Wasco and her neighboring communities.

[6] Wendell T. Calhoun, "State Balance of Trade in California's Farm Products," Western Farm Economics Association, California Meeting, Berkeley, Calif., March 14, 1946, Table 6. Data based upon 10 year average, 1930-1939.
[7] *Ibid.*, Table 4.

PLACE OF CALIFORNIA AGRICULTURE IN AMERICAN FARM LIFE 15

FARM LABOR IN CALIFORNIA

Approximately 350,000 persons were employed in the production of agricultural goods in the State of California in September, 1939.[8] One-third of these are farm operators and their families and two-thirds are laborers. The number of "unpaid family workers," as the Census calls those who help on the farm without compensation, is small. In addition to these there are many who engage in agricultural processing, while during years of low industrial employment there are great numbers of persons who seek employment in agriculture.

Three fundamental facts must be recognized with respect to farm labor in California. First, the origin of large-scale farming and the continuance of industrialized agriculture are dependent upon an abundant supply of cheap (relative to price) wage labor. Second, no group as such has remained as farm labor in California for more than a single generation. Third, it has been necessary for large-scale farm operators to maintain a flow of workers into California in order that they can continue their operations under normal price conditions.

Since the Indians were impressed into service on Spanish missions and ranches, a colorful and diverse array of workers have labored in California's fields. During the first two decades of American statehood, California's agriculture was largely devoted to stock and grain production. While these commodities were produced on giant land holdings, the amount of labor required was not great, and the industrialized pattern of production was not established. In 1869 the transcontinental railroad was completed, and by 1870 the Chinese were available as an abundant supply of agricultural labor. Their continued immigration for over a decade maintained this supply of exceedingly cheap workers. It was during this decade that the production of fruits on an intensive basis came to be an important part of California's agriculture, and the entire organization of the farm

[8] According to the Sixteenth Census of Agriculture (Vol. III, *General Report*, Chapter VI, Table 10). The total employment in agriculture is greater, because of the seasonality of farm employment.

enterprise and land values were based upon the continued existence of such labor. Wages of $1 per day or $25 per month, and with extremely low costs for board, coupled with the employers' complete lack of responsibility toward the workers when not needed, made for a labor supply which was often considered cheaper than slave labor. The use of Chinese labor did not require capital investment, as did slaves, nor very much in the way of housing and equipment. The Chinese worker was generally recognized as performing his duties well and rapidly.

When further immigration of Chinese was excluded and the resident Chinese began to move away from farm work, the growers, whose expectation of profit was based upon such a labor supply, began to seek elsewhere for the necessary labor. For nearly twenty years the labor demand was met by the remaining Chinese, the first immigrant Japanese, and above all the industrial workers who could not find employment in the cities because of the depression of the nineties. By the turn of the century, when industrial employment drained the Caucasian workers back to the cities, the Japanese were sufficiently numerous to assure abundant field workers. They continued to come to California through the first decade of the century, and were supplemented by Hindus. Before World War I, industrial unemployment again assured growers a full supply of workers. Meanwhile immigration from Mexico was beginning. During the war there was an acute shortage of workers in agriculture, from the growers' point of view. A number of emergency measures were taken, including use of juveniles and urban workers (based on patriotic appeal), and the importation of Mexicans.

During the twenties the farm labor supply was constantly augmented by a great immigration of Mexican workers and the lesser immigration of Filipinos. These groups replaced the Chinese and Japanese in that they worked for low wages and demanded a minimum of responsibility from the employers.

It should be mentioned that from time to time, from 1850 to World War II, efforts were made to bring Negro workers into California's fields. While some Negro labor has served California farmers, they have always been few in number. Probably the greatest influx was during and just after the First World

enterprise and land values were based upon the continued existence of such labor. Wages of $1 per day or $25 per month, and with extremely low costs for board, coupled with the employers' complete lack of responsibility toward the workers when not needed, made for a labor supply which was often considered cheaper than slave labor. The use of Chinese labor did not require capital investment, as did slaves, nor very much in the way of housing and equipment. The Chinese worker was generally recognized as performing his duties well and rapidly.

When further immigration of Chinese was excluded and the resident Chinese began to move away from farm work, the growers, whose expectation of profit was based upon such a labor supply, began to seek elsewhere for the necessary labor. For nearly twenty years the labor demand was met by the remaining Chinese, the first immigrant Japanese, and above all the industrial workers who could not find employment in the cities because of the depression of the nineties. By the turn of the century, when industrial employment drained the Caucasian workers back to the cities, the Japanese were sufficiently numerous to assure abundant field workers. They continued to come to California through the first decade of the century, and were supplemented by Hindus. Before World War I, industrial unemployment again assured growers a full supply of workers. Meanwhile immigration from Mexico was beginning. During the war there was an acute shortage of workers in agriculture, from the growers' point of view. A number of emergency measures were taken, including use of juveniles and urban workers (based on patriotic appeal), and the importation of Mexicans.

During the twenties the farm labor supply was constantly augmented by a great immigration of Mexican workers and the lesser immigration of Filipinos. These groups replaced the Chinese and Japanese in that they worked for low wages and demanded a minimum of responsibility from the employers.

It should be mentioned that from time to time, from 1850 to World War II, efforts were made to bring Negro workers into California's fields. While some Negro labor has served California farmers, they have always been few in number. Probably the greatest influx was during and just after the First World

PLACE OF CALIFORNIA AGRICULTURE IN AMERICAN FARM LIFE 17

War, when large acreages were planted to cotton. While Negroes now constitute one of the largest minority groups in the state, they are heavily urban, with 70 per cent of the 1940 total living in Los Angeles and Alameda Counties.

The accompanying tabulation shows the growth and decline of different minor racial and ethnic groups in California. The data on Mexicans are available for only three decades and two

TABLE I.—NUMBER OF PERSONS OF VARIOUS ETHNIC GROUPS IN CALIFORNIA, 1890-1940

Year	Mexican [1]	Negro	Japanese	Chinese	Filipino	Indian
1890	....	11,322	1,147	72,472	0	16,624
1900	....	11,045	10,151	45,743	0	15,377
1910	48,391	21,645	41,356	36,248	5	16,371
1920	121,176	38,763	71,952	28,812	2,674	17,360
1930	368,013	81,048	97,456	37,361	30,470	19,212
1940	....	124,306	93,717	39,556	31,408	18,675

[1] Separate classification of Mexicans was made only in 1930. The 1910 and 1920 figures are estimated.
SOURCE: Charles N. Reynolds, *Basic Information on Race and Nativity*, Statistical Memorandum No. 3 (Race and Nativity Series), Population Committee for the Central Valley Project Studies, Dec. 3, 1943, p. 1.

of these are estimates, but their importance in California is clearly demonstrated. There has been a steady growth of the Negro population during the fifty years since 1890. During that half century the Japanese increased to a peak of nearly 100,000 while the Chinese declined. As a result of wartime relocation policy, the Japanese will probably be insignificant in number in California. The Filipino immigration is recent and the number is small. However, most of these are employed men, since families did not enter.

A careful analysis of the agricultural labor force made in 1930 enables us to see the situation as of that year.[9] By 1930

[9] George M. Peterson, *Composition and Characteristics of the Agricultural Population in California*, Agricultural Experiment Station Bulletin 630, June, 1939, Berkeley, California.

native whites made up over half the labor force (including operators) in the agriculture of the state, and together with foreign-born whites, nearly 62 per cent of the laborers. However, Mexicans, Filipinos, and Japanese, though each did not make up a great proportion of the labor force, were predominantly engaged in farm work. The Negro and Chinese were, on the other hand, more frequently engaged in urban pursuits. Table 2 shows that

TABLE 2.—GAINFULLY EMPLOYED WORKERS IN CALIFORNIA AGRICULTURE BY ETHNIC GROUP, 1930

Ethnic group	Total in farm pursuits			Wage workers as per cent of total in farm pursuits	Proportion in ethnic group in farm pursuits
	Owners, tenants, managers and foremen	Wage workers	Total [1]		
	No.	*No.*	*No.*	*Pct.*	*Pct.*
Native white	85,980	84,069	170,049	49.5	12.3
Foreign born white	40,854	33,035	73,889	44.7	18.6
Mexican	1,417	41,191	42,608	96.7	37.0
Japanese	4,784	14,569	19,353	75.3	54.8
Filipino	231	16,100	16,331	98.6	60.2
Indian	797	2,306	3,103	74.3	55.4
Chinese	450	2,191	2,641	83.0	13.5
Negro	488	1,907	2,395	79.6	8.3
Other	211	1,444	1,655	87.2	70.8
Total	135,212	196,812	332,024	58.6	16.5

[1] Excludes 3,581 special workers unclassified by race, including bookkeepers, clerks, engineers, tractor and truck drivers.
SOURCE: George M. Peterson, *Composition and Character of the Agricultural Population in California*, University of California Agricultural Experiment Station, Bulletin 630, June, 1939, Tables 5 and 6.

most of the whites (both native and foreign born) were operators, while most individuals in the other groups were employed as wage hands.

By 1930 the native white farm laborers comprised nearly half of the wage workers, while Mexicans, foreign born whites, Japanese and Filipinos made up most of the remainder, in the order mentioned. By that year Chinese and Indians were insignificant, while the Negroes and Hindus had never been important. The decade of the thirties, however, brought further changes in the composition of the agricultural population. For it was during that decade that the great migration of destitute citizens from the Southwest, particularly from Oklahoma, Texas, and Arkansas, took place.

The migration of the thirties and the conditions of the migrants have been brought forcefully to the attention of the nation by Steinbeck's novel, *The Grapes of Wrath,* by Carey McWilliams' *Factories in the Field,* by many public notices of the problem and finally, at the end of the decade by the detailed examinations of the Committee on Violation of Free Speech and Rights of Labor (the La Follette Committee) and of the Committee on Interstate Migration of Destitute Citizens (Tolan Committee). This migration for the first time brought into California native white American families who settled in great numbers in the rural areas and furnished the army of cheap labor that is requisite for the continued functioning of the industrialized agriculture of California.

Though the migration into California during the thirties received a great deal of public attention, it was not of unusual magnitude in California's history. California's phenomenal population growth in the last century has been almost entirely from migration and hardly at all from natural increase. The migration of the twenties was nearly twice as great as that of the thirties; the decade before that it was just as great, and in the first five years since 1940 there had already been as much migration as there was during the thirties. Nor was the migration limited to the rural areas. One-third of the migrants settled in the larger cities (over 100,000 population) while only one-fourth of them moved to communities of less than 2,500 population. Nor were the immigrants during the thirties all of one class. A survey made in 1939 showed that they were distributed among the major occupation categories in almost identical proportions as the total California population at the time of the 1930 census.[10]

What, then, set the migration of the thirties apart from previous decades? First, a large proportion of those seeking new homes in the West were destitute. Second, the depressed condition of agriculture and the low wages created an unfavorable environment in which these immigrants could seek their fortune. Finally, the large army of immigrants—especially those from the depressed agricultural states of the Southwest and the region of the "dust bowl"—formed the first native white American families who endeavored to make their livelihood as wage workers on the California farms. These Okies, as they have been called, moved westward in their broken-down cars, with bag and baggage, children and pets, to fill the role that the Coolie Chinese originally created. They have been the ultimate successors to that long and unbroken line of farm laborers—Chinese, Japanese, fruit tramp, Filipino, and Mexican.

Low-paid insecure labor devoid of any real participation in community life was rationalized by farm operators in California on the basis of race. The poor economic position and the social segregation were taken as evidence that those groups were inferior to the American farmer, and the farmer rationalized his demands for labor importation on the basis that the difficult work in his fields could be performed only by these "inferior races." The presence of these foreign elements had not been suffered without considerable resistance on the part of many of California's citizens, for it was generally recognized that traditional American institutions could not be built on the basis of a segregated and destitute citizenry. It was this realization, together with the organized efforts of labor, which feared the competition of these foreign elements, that secured successively the restrictions on immigration of Asiatic peoples. Meanwhile, however, California's industrialized farming was predicated on the basis of such a labor supply, and the operator had to work to insure the continuance of these needed hands.

The destitute migrants from Oklahoma, Texas, Arkansas, and

[10] Seymour J. Janow and Davis McEntire, "Migration to California," *Land Policy Review*, July-August, 1940, United States Government Printing Office, Washington.

PLACE OF CALIFORNIA AGRICULTURE IN AMERICAN FARM LIFE 21

other drought and depression-ridden states stepped into the picture as the Mexicans were beginning to move out; they stepped into the status of these Mexican and Asiatic workers, and inherited the attitudes and prejudices of the resident citizenry of California. The nature of the adjustment that has been made and the type of rural community which has evolved is presented in the detailed picture of Wasco, Dinuba, and Arvin.

CHAPTER II

INDUSTRIALIZED FARMING AND THE RURAL COMMUNITY

THE NATURE OF INDUSTRIALIZED FARMING

WASCO HAS, in the past thirty years, been transformed from a pioneer community into a center for industrialized farming enterprises. It was an urbanized farmer who said: "There is one thing I want you to put down in your book. Farming in this country *is a business, it is not a way of life.*" This was no big landed gentryman, but the operator of a 200-acre farm, a man who himself can qualify as a pioneer and who built up his holdings by the sweat of family labor. From its very outset, Wasco lay in an area of highly industrialized agriculture; for this industrialized farming has its roots in early California land policy and has continued unbroken to the very present. The history of the industrialization of the California rural scene has been documented especially by Taylor and Vasey, McWilliams and Fuller.[1] Taylor and Vasey present the components of this form of agriculture:

Together with crop intensification and large-scale production organization have come commercialization of California agriculture, higher capitalization, increased production for a cash market, and a high cash

[1] The history of California's agricultural labor has been described, first by Paul S. Taylor and Tom Vasey in two articles, "Historical Background of California Farm Labor," and "Contemporary Background of California Farm Labor," *Rural Sociology*, Vol. I, Numbers 3 and 4, 1936; second by Carey McWilliams, *Factories in the Field;* and third by Varden Fuller, "The Supply of Agricultural Labor as a Factor in the Evolution of Farm Organization in California," Exhibit 8762A, Part 54, *Hearings Before a Subcommittee of the Committee on Education and Labor*, United States Senate, 76th Congress, 3rd Session, pursuant to S. Res. 266 (74th Congress), Washington, 1940 (hereafter referred to as *La Follette Hearings*).

expenditure for wage labor. Each of these developments contributes to the industrialization of labor relations. . . .

The family farm, which still expresses the national ideal, is subordinate in California to the influence of agriculture on an industrialized pattern.[2]

The farm operators have recognized this industrialization, as Taylor pointed out in a quotation from the *Western Grower and Shipper,* which says:

> California is not unfriendly to husbandry and farming as a mode of life, but costly experience has shown that a large percentage of its acres, no matter how attractive to the inexperienced eye, are not suited to such purposes. The history of attempted development of many sections now successful under industrialized agriculture to small farming is a history of blasted hopes and broken hearts. And nature, not man, has been responsible.[3]

Though the nature of California's climate and terrain make industrialized farming profitable, we must beware of the simplistic explanation in this statement. The early establishment of great land holdings acquired through genuine and spurious Spanish grants presented the background for the present agricultural pattern.[4] The introduction of cheap labor which heightened land values has been a heavy contributing factor, as Fuller has shown.[5] And the development of urban values in the rural society has created strong pressures toward the perfection and continuation of the industrialized farming pattern which itself

---

[2] Taylor and Vasey, *op. cit.,* pp. 403-4, 419.

[3] From "Census Truths," *Western Grower and Shipper,* October, 1939, p. 7, and quoted in the testimony of Paul S. Taylor, *La Follette Hearings,* Dec. 6, 1939, Pt. 47, p. 17224.

[4] Carey McWilliams states that "Migratory labor . . . is a result of the character of California agriculture, but (this) . . . is, in turn, a consequence of the type of land ownership in California." *Op. cit.,* p. 25.

[5] "Wherever intensive cultivation had already begun or was in prospect, land values were capitalized on the basis of actual or anticipated returns from the employment of the cheap and convenient Chinese labor supply. To the prospective small operator, this meant paying so high a price for land as to permit him a labor return approximately equal to the wages of Chinese. . . . Such a prospect did not encourage either European immigrants or people from the East to come to California. . . . Thus, in order to subdivide and sell the large holdings to prospective small operators, a considerable depreciation in valuation would have to be suffered. . . ." Fuller, *op. cit.,* p. 19878.

is responsible for the existence of these urban values in the rural society.

While industrial farming has largely developed in areas where the scale of operations are great, large-scale operations are not synonymous with industrial farming. It is possible to have large units measured by acreage or by production, where many of the essential elements of industrialization are not present. It is not only possible, but in California irrigated farming areas frequently the case, that small units show every other feature of industrial enterprise—intensive production, large investment, impersonal hiring, and complete commercialization. Similarly, production efficiency does not rest upon scale of operations. A detailed analysis made by the Bureau of Agricultural Economics shows the relation of size of farm to efficiency in production and concludes as follows:

> The large and medium-large farms [averaging 1,894 and 179 acres, respectively] have a slight advantage over the medium size farms [averaging 52 acres] in output per unit capital employed. But judging from past performance the medium-size summer-field-crop and dairy farms and the medium-large fruit farms have the advantage over other size groups studied in maximizing work opportunity, agricultural production, and the potential trade, or in maximizing income for the maximum number of people directly dependent upon agriculture for their livelihood.[6]

It is significant that only from a personal pecuniary calculus do large-scale operations appear advantageous over more modest farming enterprises. Smaller units are more productive of total commodities, total income, and people supported.

DEVELOPMENT OF INDUSTRIALIZED FARMING IN WASCO

Wasco itself has grown rapidly out of the fertile desert soil. Save for a few early homesteads, the land was all held by the Kern County Land Company, that great landowning corporation developed by Haggin and Carr in the early days of California's

---

[6] J. Karl Lee, *Economics of the Scale of Farm Operations in the Southern San Joaquin Valley, California,* Bureau of Agricultural Economics, Berkeley, 1946 (Mimeographed).

statehood. Prior to 1907 the town was peopled by cowhands, section hands, and the few independent farmers. It was a negligible aggregate of a few buildings housing saloons, a hotel, and a store. Its lands were considered adequate only as pasturage for sheep. Its sudden growth in 1907 was the result of a colonization scheme which opened to farming nine sections of desert land. This land, like miles lying in either direction, had not previously been opened for sale, according to the man who promoted the settlement at Wasco, because the Land Company did not consider the income from such a transaction sufficient to compensate for the increased costs of fencing and protecting the vast herds of stock. The promoter, aided by business sentiment against this restriction on population growth, induced the Company to part with the small parcel, which he then subdivided and sold to members of his organization in tracts of from two and a half to twenty acres. These lands were opened in the late winter of 1907 and the colonists prepared to farm this arid land the coming season. The hardships these people suffered in coming to so hostile an environment are still poignant in memory and have won for the colonists the name of pioneer.

The settlers' organization which opened up this land was made up of persons who, for various reasons, wished to change their economic conditions. One was a middle-aged Eastern business man who had lost his job and was considered too old to be employed. Another, a lawyer, a third, a doctor, and a fourth, a professor, were motivated partly by reasons of health, believing that the desert atmosphere and the farm life would improve their condition. Some were clerks, who in classic resentment of the control of the boss desired to be on their own. Others were young men who had a small stake in a world of limited opportunities, some were given their start by farmer parents in neighboring regions. Before they met at the organization office in Los Angeles they were all completely unknown to one another, but they each bought, one might say, an interest in the new community. The organizer of this colony has himself given expression to this aspect of the enterprise, for the basis of the philosophy by which he sold his scheme was that in bringing together an aggregate of people he created new values.[7] Whether his advertisements actually reflected his own philosophy or influenced his customers, the fact remains that these individuals had a real financial, as well as social, interest in the new community that came into being at that time.

Like pioneers, during this early period, the colonists had a common enemy. The enemy was the desert, and it had two aspects: the drought on one hand, and the infestation of rabbits on the other. Both were the subject of concerted action of that group which had put its stake in Wasco. The colonists still like to tell of the rabbit fence that was built around the nine sections with community money, and the rabbit drives, in which all the young men participated, to kill out the rabbits which had converged upon the greenery of the newly created oasis. The water problem had been anticipated, and a water company had been formed by the organizer. A clause had been inserted into the contract requiring the land owners to take shares on a per acre basis. But the co-operative distribution of water pumped by gasoline engine and carried in open canals proved unsuccessful. It is little wonder, therefore, that the major business of the first civic organization in Wasco, the Improvement Club, was directed toward a solution of the water problem. It is characteristic of our American culture that this solution was derived not from a higher concentration on co-operative effort, but on an individual basis. It is the first of the technological developments that altered the economy of the region and therefore it is worthwhile to examine the nature of the solution.

The water corporation was a stock company. The plan was to pump water to the surface with gasoline engines and distribute it in open canals. The inefficiency of the early internal combustion engine and the high degree of loss due to seepage and evaporation made it virtually impossible to get water to the far corners of the colony. The importance to the farmers of having irrigation water at the exact time they needed it added to the problem. After the colonists had dislodged one or two of the

[7] In a brochure, he proclaims: "You are worth $1,500 just because you sit in that chair . . . your family has great value to you in a new community group for acre gardens. Alone, you lose it."

original men in charge, a movement started which led to the dissolution of the company, for at about that time the power lines of one of the major utilities companies were brought to the community, and it became possible for the individual farmers to install electric pumps. Thus, the water problem was defeated by individual effort of the farmers, with the technological aid of an outside corporation of major size, and this solution destroyed one of the focal points of community effort.

So the course of Wasco's star was set by the nature of her physical and social environment. Long before the community existed, the agricultural enterprises were established against which her farmers had to compete, and the pattern was set. The very plan of establishing a colony on irrigated lands inevitably called for the production of cash crops at a high cost with abundant cheap labor. Though the hardships were to be great and many farms were to be lost in the struggle to bring Wasco into the pattern, it was inevitable from the outset that she should be set up on an industrialized basis. That is, inevitable in an economic sense. For the cash outlay for expensive equipment necessary to pump water meant producing high-value cash crops. And in order to realize the necessary return to cover these costs the new farmers had to compete with established enterprises. Thus they were immediately caught in the established pattern of farming.

CHARACTERISTICS OF WASCO'S AGRICULTURAL INDUSTRY

What, then, are the characteristics of this industrialization? Its first characteristic is its intensity of production as indicated by crop specialization, thorough cash cropping, high per acre yield, the utilization of irrigation, and a high dependence upon farm machinery.

The farm operators in the Wasco area tend to specialize in two crops. The most usual combination is potatoes and cotton. Others grow sugar beets, melons, grapes (but rarely are new vineyards now put in). The dairy farms are completely specialized to that one product. Furthermore, farmers who specialize in two or three crops always consider one of these as their major interest.

A farmer will grow cotton and a few potatoes, or potatoes and a little cotton. The farmers who gave figures on the cost of production of cotton, potatoes, and beets felt competent only to present figures on one crop. The other crop is a result of compliance with the Federal AAA program, or the feeling of safety a second crop affords. The farmer is not only specialized, but also is proud of his specialization. He maintains firmly that you have to know how to raise potatoes or cotton in this country, that "the old dumb-bells just can't farm any more." Crop specialization is indicated statistically in the census by the appearance of only 100 "general" farms out of the 2,397 farms in the county, the others being specialized in one or, at most, two crops.[8]

This tendency to specialize in one or two cash crops has very clear effects upon the social and physical landscape. Basically, it expresses the competition between the old traditional rural values and the urban value system. One of the first evidences of this meets the eye immediately—the virtual disappearance of the barnyard. Practically no farmers milk cows; almost as few have chickens; a garden is considered a luxury, not because it is work to plant one, but because it is considered cheaper to buy the products at the market and turn the land into cash crops. Flower gardens around a home are also a luxury. One farm wife expressed herself clearly when she said, "My husband would plow up that rose garden if I'd let him. He'd plow right up to the bedroom window." The disappearance of the barnyard has also meant the "emancipation" of the farm wife. With barnyard chores eliminated and with electrical labor-saving devices and smaller families, the line, "but a woman's work is never done," is no longer applicable and she is freed for social activities, just as the housewife of the towns. These changes have tended to break down the traditional barrier between the country and town people.

There are other psychological effects. The farmer is planting with one eye on his furrows and the other cocked at the market.

[8] *15th Census of the United States: 1930*, Agriculture, Vol. III, Pt. 3, p. 387. "General" farms are those "where the value of the products from any one source did *not* represent as much as 40 per cent of the total value of all the products on the farm." (P. 3.)

INDUSTRIALIZED FARMING AND THE RURAL COMMUNITY 29

When the total investment is in cash crop, it becomes a basic matter with the small farmer to hit the right market. Farmers consider that during the harvest season they should be at the marketing center rather than in the fields. The entrepreneur's insight into market conditions is more important than his managerial ability in supervising the harvest.

Certain events can indicate the effect of this aspect of farming as it appears to the local people. In 1936 the yield in potatoes was at its prime, and the price of potatoes skyrocketed. Potatoes that make a neat farming profit at $1 a sack sold for as high as $4.50. Costs were low in that year, especially labor, so that the net farming profits were astronomical; one farmer reputedly made a million and a quarter on his crop that season. The picture has been preserved in such exaggerated stories as the one claiming that "three people were killed in the scramble when a sack of potatoes fell from a truck." Many a completely mortgaged farm was paid for with a little patch of potatoes. "The year 1936 is what ruined this country," the merchants say. "Ever since then everybody has been figuring he'd make a killing in potatoes and he invests everything he has." [9] But the 1936 crop did not change the basic trend of events in Wasco; it merely brought them to the fore and won over to urban monetary standards the remainder who were still thinking of farming "as a way of life."

Specialized farming means production of cash crops. We have already pointed out that specialization spelt the doom of the barnyard. It has meant likewise that all the products of the farm are sold for cash. Table 3 shows the major crops grown in the Wasco area—products with low on-farm utility and high cash value.

It is, of course, necessary for all farms to sell some of their goods for money under our economic system, yet traditionally the farm produces most of the food for the farm household. Though the trend away from production for home use is general, it has gone especially far in Wasco. This appears clearly

[9] The Kern County and local potato shipments doubled the following year.

from the census data. The opposite pole from cash cropping is the self-sufficient farm. In Kern County only 35 of the 2,397 farms were of this type.[10] It is doubtful if any of these are in the Wasco area. Even more significant is the fact that the farmer and his family consumed only $371,000 worth of the $14,900,000 he produced in that year.[11] This means that about 2.5 per cent of the farm products were used by the farmer and his

TABLE 3.—CROP ACREAGES IN NORTHERN KERN COUNTY 1931 AND 1936 [1]

Crop	1931 acreage	1936 acreage
Fruits and olives	2,405	1,946
Grapes (table, wine, and raisin)	10,932	9,808
Potatoes	5,000	9,000
Sweet potatoes and onions	910	1,500
Cantaloupes and watermelons	2,097	700
Alfalfa	6,254	2,398
Cotton	19,157	20,000

[1] Northern Kern County . . . "all land north of Seventh Standard Road that is irrigable" and comprises lands that are in vicinity of neighboring towns of equal size.
SOURCE: *Soil Survey*, by A. C. Anderson and J. L. Retzer, United States Department of Agriculture, and Bruce C. Owen, Leighton F. Koehler, and Ralph C. Cole, University of California, Ms. Project #1006, USDA, June, 1936, pp. 38-40.

family, the rest was sold for money with which to buy food, clothes, and other necessities and luxuries.

While no data are available specifically for Wasco, the difference between the California pattern and other portions of the United States is shown in the accompanying table (Table 4) developed by the Consumer Purchases Study and based upon three California agricultural counties (San Joaquin, Orange, and Riverside).

[10] *15th Census of the United States: 1930*, Agriculture, Vol. III, Pt. 3, p. 387. Self-sufficient farms are those on which over half of the total products is consumed on the farm.
[11] *Ibid.*, p. 398.

High farm yields further characterize this intensive land cultivation. In the Wasco area, the average yield per acre of early

TABLE 4.—CONSUMPTION OF HOME-PRODUCED FOODS IN CALIFORNIA COMPARED TO OTHER AREAS

Area	Number of families using home-produced food			Average value of food per person per meal	
	Milk	Pork	Garden	Home production	Purchased
	Pct.	Pct.	Pct.	Cents	Cents
California	53	0	29	2.6	6.6
North Dakota–Kansas	100	76	72	5.1	3.8
Pennsylvania–Ohio	84	72	100	5.7	3.5
Georgia–Mississippi	96	96	96	7.7	2.5

SOURCE: Hazel K. Stiebeling, et al., *Family Food Consumption and Dietary Levels*, Farm Series, p. 51.

potatoes was from 240 sacks in 1937 to 198 sacks in 1940 (Table 5). Furthermore, acres of land with as much as 600 sacks

TABLE 5.—ACREAGE, YIELD, AND PRODUCTION OF POTATOES

Year	Acres	Production (sacks)	Yield	County yield
1937	16,277	3,916,500	240	205.6
1938	15,817	3,447,900	218	185.4
1939	16,906	3,366,600	199	187.1
1940	17,406	3,456,000	198	183.3

SOURCE: *Marketing Kern County Early Irish Potatoes*, by John B. Schneider, M. A. Lindsay, G. B. Alcorn, and H. W. Longfellow, Agricultural Extension Service, University of California, Bakersfield, 1940-41.

(30 tons) have been reported and good farmers expect 250 sacks to the acre. The average cotton production in the county was

631 pounds of lint per acre, though farmers in Wasco considered two bales (1,000 pounds) a normally good yield.

Practically all farms around Wasco are irrigated and irrigation is another feature of intensive farming. It is not mere contour irrigation with surface water, but the careful distribution of water raised about 100 feet from an underground table over land that has been perfectly leveled. Of the 566 farms in the Wasco area in 1935, 539 were irrigated, and virtually all the crops are produced on irrigated soil (Table 6).

TABLE 6.—FARM SIZE AND VALUE, WASCO TOWNSHIP

Item	Total	Average per farm	Irrigated	Average per farm
Number of farms	566	..	539	....
Number of acres	49,165	87	...	....
Crop land harvested, in acres	29,644	52	29,233	54.2
Total value of land	$8,058,870	$14,238 [1]	......	....

[1] Or a value of $164 per acre.

SOURCE: United States Census of Agriculture, photostated sheet on 9th Township, Kern County, 1935.

Another aspect of the intensive character of farming is the use of modern machinery, especially power equipment. Though a few farmers maintain a team to help with cultivation, virtually none of them attempts to work without at least one tractor. The land is leveled, prepared, planted, and cultivated with tractors, and the potatoes are dug by a tractor-drawn machine. We have already indicated that the individual farm irrigation systems with costly wells and pumps were the harbinger of farm mechanization. These power pumps, operated by gasoline, electricity, gas, or butane, are an important item in the farm operations and in the farm costs.

The tractor is both a necessity and a luxury. Under the competitive system, no man can make much money following a team. The tractor is a source of pride, and many a farmer referred almost affectionately to the tractor, as a young man might to his car. The long straight furrow takes on new connotations after a farmer has said with pride: "With this tractor, you can cultivate right up to the roots; you can put that dirt right where you want it." A tractor salesman said that the farmers in the area over-buy on farm equipment and tend to follow styles in the nature of machinery they use. Table 7 shows the steady

TABLE 7.—AVERAGE SIZE OF FARMS AND AVERAGE VALUE OF FARMS AND FARM EQUIPMENT, KERN COUNTRY, 1870-1940

Year	Total farms	Average size of farm		Average farm values	
		All land	Crop land	Land and buildings	Farm equipment
	Number	Acres	Acres	Dollars	Dollars
1870	86	2,900	105	3,960	163
1880	282	1,880	284	6,830	220
1890	730	975	191	13,600	305
1900	1,098	1,431	295	17,900	316
1910	1,167	1,202	270	21,606	526
1920	2,020	741	197	32,257	1,035
1925	2,793	462	97	23,841	1,048
1930	2,397	712	79	31,076	1,294
1935	2,584	626	91	18,822	.....
1940	2,188	705	138	30,854	2,153

SOURCE: United States Decennial Census and Census of Agriculture for years specified.

growth of farm equipment in Kern County, from a value of $526 per farm in 1910 to $2,153 per farm in 1940.

The intensive use of land has been discussed as one characteristic of industrialization. A second is the high capital requirements. In a sense this latter is merely the obverse of the former, for each of the factors which are part of intensive land use are likewise items of cost which lead to difficult capital requirements.

A major factor in the cost of production is the high evaluation upon the land—values which create a heavy interest burden upon the crops to be produced, which limit the uses to which it is put, and which require the further intensification of efforts if a going enterprise is to be maintained.

The cost of improved land around Wasco was $200-300 per acre during the low-price period of the late thirties. At the lower rate, a farm of the size recommended by the local Agricultural Planning Committee, namely, 80 acres, would cost $16,000.[12] An 80-acre farm requires at least one tractor and one pump, plus other equipment which would add from three to five thousand dollars. The psychological effect of such investments is far-reaching, and there is no wonder that the farmer in California feels himself and comports himself like a business man.

Farm values can best be understood in terms of production costs, for as such they appear in the operations of owner, tenant, or manager. Leading growers of several commodities presented cost of production figures, two of which are presented below. These show the heavy expenditure required in the production of crops. While these figures are not averages, they nevertheless represent estimates based upon successful individual farm operations.

At the average yield of 198 sacks per acre achieved in 1940, the cost of bringing potatoes to maturity is $94.75 and the costs of putting them in cars is $70.49, or a total production cost of $165.24 (Table 8).

The costs of bringing sugar beets to market is considerably less, yet it is not small. The production costs are almost $50, while the sliding scale of harvest pay established by law and the trucking charges to shipping point bring the costs up another $22 (Table 9).

Data were collected on cotton production costs from 7 farms in Kern County. These units ranged in size from 13 to 60 acres. Though they are not considered "typical," the range and aver-

---

[12] County and Community Committee of Farmers, *Brief of Land Use Survey of Kern County: Description, Problems, Recommendations.* Bakersfield, 1940, pp. 40-41.

INDUSTRIALIZED FARMING AND THE RURAL COMMUNITY 35

TABLE 8.—ALLOCATION OF COSTS: POTATO PRODUCTION

Production of crop on a per acre basis		*Harvesting on a per sack basis*	
1. Rent	$25.00	1. Hauling	$ 0.05
2. Preparing soil, plowing and discing	2.75	2. Digger and picking crew	.11
3. Planting	3.25	3. Washing	.09
4. Seed (ca. 15 sacks at $2.36)	35.00	4. Sacks	.10
5. Fertilizer (5-6 sacks per acre at $2.50)	13.75	5. Inspection	.006
6. Power (for water)	6.50	Total	$ 0.356
7. Irrigation labor	6.00	Average yield	× 198
8. Cultivation	2.50	Harvest cost per acre	$ 70.49
Total production	$94.75	Production cost per acre	94.75
		Total cost per acre	$165.24

SOURCE: Local potato farmer (based upon 1940 costs and wages).

TABLE 9.—ALLOCATION OF COSTS: SUGAR BEETS

Production (per acre)		*Harvesting*		
		Yield	Per ton	Per acre
Rent	$20.00	Trucking:		
Chopping	6.50[1]	18	$0.50	$ 9.00
Hoeing (twice)	2.50[1]	19	.50	9.50
Irrigation (water)	6.00	Labor:[1]		
Irrigation (labor)	3.00	15	.82	12.32
Plowing, discing and making beds	4.50	16	.78	12.48
Planting	1.00	17	.75	12.75
Seed	2.25	*18*	*.72*	*12.96*
Cultivation	2.00	*19*	*.70*	*13.30*
Labor overseer	1.00	20	.69	13.80
		21	.68	14.28
Total	$48.75	22	.67	14.74
		Average harvest cost		21.96
		Production cost		48.75
		Total cost		$70.71

[1] Costs set by established government wage rates. The sliding scale for labor of topping is based upon the variation in speed as the yield varies, since low yield is largely a function of size of tubers.

Italicized figures are local average yields as given by farmer reporting.

SOURCE: Operator of sugar beet enterprise (based upon 1940 costs and wages).

age costs are illustrative of the factors in cotton production (Table 10). The accounting was set up in such a way that the residual net profit after the farmer's labor and the interest on his investment were paid was allocated to the operator's managerial skill. Chart 1 displays graphically the major average

TABLE 10.—SUMMARY OF ALLOCATION OF COSTS AND INCOME: COTTON

Item	Range		Average costs	
	High	Low	Amount	Proportion of total
Costs				
Total costs	$119.76	$70.79	$90.25	100.0%
Labor (wage)	61.16	35.38	48.80	54.1
Labor (farmer's)	9.53	.58	2.47	2.7
Capital investment	35.48 [1]	6.77	17.55 [1]	19.4
Materials, overhead, depreciation	27.44	16.52	21.43	23.8
Income				
Total net income	67.20	13.43	37.12	100.0
Managerial profit	49.57	1.86	28.92	78.0
Interest on investment	13.19 [1]	.17	5.73 [1]	15.4
Farmer's labor	9.53	.58	2.47	6.6

[1] Rental included in interest costs but not in interest income.
SOURCE: *Third Annual Report, Kern County Cotton Enterprise Efficiency Study for the 1940 Crop Year.*

allocations of costs and the several sources of income in the operation of the farming enterprise.

Translating these figures into the quantity of operating capital required to bring a crop to market—this is not the capital value of the farm but the capital value of the annual crop—we find that the sum varies from over $2,000 to nearly $5,000 for the minimum size of unit acceptable to the Agricultural Planning Committee (40 acres, but letting 10 acres lie fallow). Despite these costs, the sentiment prevails that size of units should increase, and that farms of less than 80 acres should not exist,

ALLOCATION OF COSTS AND PROFITS IN COTTON CULTIVATION
KERN COUNTY, CALIFORNIA, 1940

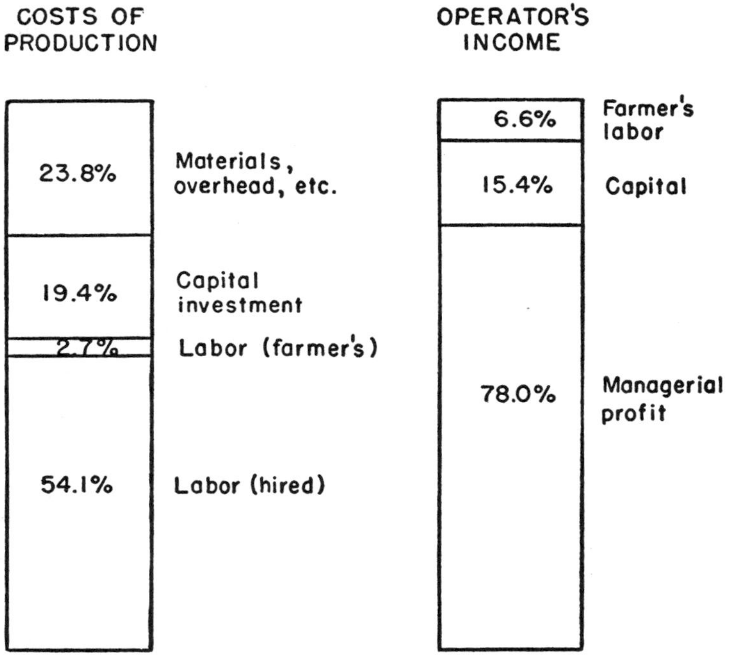

COSTS OF PRODUCTION

%	Category
23.8%	Materials, overhead, etc.
19.4%	Capital investment
2.7%	Labor (farmer's)
54.1%	Labor (hired)

OPERATOR'S INCOME

%	Category
6.6%	Farmer's labor
15.4%	Capital
78.0%	Managerial profit

SOURCE: Third Annual Report, Kern County Cotton Enterprise Efficiency Study for the 1940 Crop Year, (see Table 10).

CHART I

while units of 160 acres should be maintained. The farmer who is content with 40 acres is generally considered unprogressive. The 20-acre plats which were originally established are all either held or operated in connection with other land. This pressure toward expansion was expressed in many different ways. One farmer was discovered who had just bought a tractor. "You

TABLE II.—TOTAL LABOR REQUIREMENTS IN MAN-DAYS OF SELECTED CROPS, KERN COUNTY

Crop	Total	Permanent	Seasonal	Percentage of workers seasonally employed
Alfalfa	194,942	194,942	0	0
Cotton	480,611	182,726	297,885	62
Grapes	441,753	181,010	260,743	59
Onions	18,302	3,452	14,850	81
Potatoes	268,588	169,016	99,572	33
Sugar beets	19,788	3,135	16,653	86
Totals	1,423,984	734,281	689,703	48
All crops	1,643,783	834,091	808,692	49.2

SOURCE: *Agriculture Labor Requirements and Supply, Kern County*, by R. L. Adams, June, 1940, Mimeo. Rep. No. 70, Giannini Foundation of Agr. Econ., Table 4, p. 8.

watch him," his neighbor said, "next year he will be wanting to farm eighty." Another said that he had made enough money the previous year to buy 20 acres, but that he was going to try renting one more year. He hoped to get ahead sufficiently to have 40, for 20 acres was not enough for a living.

This need for capital is not necessarily met out of the operator's pocket. Estimates of the proportion of operators dependent upon crop financing varied between 75 and 90 per cent. It is generally considered good practice to borrow at least a portion of the production cost, since it does not tie up for the whole year capital that is needed only during the peak cost period.

INDUSTRIALIZED FARMING AND THE RURAL COMMUNITY 39

But the effects upon the pattern of farming are essentially the same whether the operator has or borrows this capital. In either case he must emphasize cash returns and the reduction of costs; in either case he is entrepreneur for a highly capitalized business unit.

The third major aspect of industrialized agriculture is its heavy labor requirement. According to the Census, three-fourths

TABLE 12.—ESTIMATED MINIMUM REQUIREMENTS FOR SEASONAL WORKERS, KERN COUNTY, 1939

Month	Resident	Number transient	Total
January	1,300	500	1,800
February	650	200	850
March	750	600	1,350
April	800	750	1,550
May	2,100	700	2,800
June	2,400	850	3,250
July	1,250	550	1,800
August	1,750	700	2,450
September	1,700	750	2,450
October	4,000	2,250	6,250
November	3,000	1,700	4,700
December	2,750	1,400	4,100

SOURCE: *Agricultural Labor Requirements and Supply, Kern County*, by R. L. Adams, June, 1940, Mimeo. Rep. No. 70, Giannini Foundation of Agr. Econ., Table 8, p. 15.

of all farms hired labor for cash wages during 1939 (as against a national average of about one-third). The crop requirements in Kern County have been worked out by R. L. Adams and show not only the heavy requirements for labor but the importance of seasonal workers (Table 11).

On the basis of the data in Table 11, an estimate of the minimum monthly labor requirements for Kern County has been made. These are presented in Table 12. Before the war drained off farm workers, the available supply of hands in Kern County to do this work was estimated at from three times this demand in peak season to twenty times the demand in slack season. The working force in agriculture in Kern County is predominantly hired labor; the farm operator and his family contributing only a small part of the work. In September of 1939, according to the Sixteenth U. S. Census (Agriculture, 1940), there were approximately 13,000 persons employed in agriculture in Kern County. Over four out of every five of these were hired workers, and less than one either a farm operator or a member of his family. In the United States as a whole, the category of unpaid family labor comprised about one-third of all workers at that time. In Kern County about 5 per cent fell in this category. Of the 10,724 hired workers, only 1,084, or about 10 per cent were hired by the month, 2,731 or 20 per cent by the day or week, while the remainder were hired on a piece rate, hourly or contractual basis.

From the farm operator's point of view, labor needs can best be understood in terms of labor costs. The allocation of production costs for three of the leading crops in the area has been shown. In one, cotton, these costs represent over half of the total production costs (see Chart 1) and in the other two they represent well over a third. That these labor costs are paid out as cash wages is indicated by the fact that only 2.7 per cent were allocated to the farmer's own services, and this demonstrates the small proportion of the total farm work which he performs. The right hand column on this chart demonstrates that his own labor does not account for a significant proportion of his income, but that this income is allocated to his entrepreneurial efforts.

If these industrial features of farming around Wasco are to be considered the causative force in creating an urbanized type of society, then it must be expected that they have immediate psychological effects upon the farm operators. The social identity of the farmer has changed with the development of the United States, as Paul Johnstone has pointed out.[13] The Wasco farmer is more and more identifying himself with the business entrepreneur, as the quotation at the beginning of this chapter

[13] Paul Johnstone, "On the Identification of the Farmer," *Rural Sociology*, Vol. 5, No. 1, March, 1940.

suggests. His income derives largely from returns upon entrepreneurial efficiency and secondarily from interest on investments, while only in small measure from his own toil. Furthermore, his entrepreneurial efficiency depends upon wise buying and selling, and above all, on maximizing the returns from expenditures for hired labor. In this last lies the most insistent psychological factor which influences the farmer's thinking. Therefore, though the farmer and the laborers on his farm are virtually interdependent and together bring the product to market, there is nevertheless a source of conflict in their economic relationships. The impersonal character of most of the hiring does not serve to ameliorate this situation. The farmer's increased business contacts with equipment merchants, gasoline salesmen, power representatives and the like as well as with the marketing agents further develop the urban outlook. The large sums of money handled by the farmer also has an effect on his way of thinking regarding his own personal expenditures, which in turn influences his whole scheme of values.

EFFECTS OF INDUSTRIALIZED AGRICULTURE ON THE TOWN

The industrialization of agriculture has not only altered the psychological and social attitudes of the people on the land, it has also affected the people of the town who serve the farm population. Though Wasco falls within the Census definition of a city, being an aggregate of over 4,000 people, it is the smallest place the farmer can go for his needs. There are no smaller satellite neighborhoods or shopping centers which enable him to avoid coming to Wasco, except for one or two nearby road crossings with bars or filling stations. There is, at a greater distance, an oil town which is in many ways socially and economically dependent on Wasco. It is the only town now represented by a separate column of social notes in the local newspaper, although in 1921 there were three others, which have since either grown to independent status or dwindled to nothing.

While Wasco is the smallest town to which the local farmer can go, it is capable of serving all his needs. There he can buy his groceries, clothes, lumber, furniture, or car; his farm equipment or seed; and there he can market his potatoes or beets, gin his cotton, or process his milk. Likewise it contains his church, schools, and many governmental agencies. When the local resident searches elsewhere for his goods or services it is almost invariably because of personal preference. In this sense, Wasco is a self-sufficient economic unit. Its complete dependence upon the outside world, not only as the source of goods, but also as the impetus of the economic and social forces, stands in marked contrast to this apparent independence, and in marked contrast to the pioneer type of community.

The first change in the rural community, as has already been suggested, is the influence of large outside corporations. Big business is involved in the farm enterprise to an extent much greater than is frequently realized, and the representatives of big business are the leaders in the local community. When electrical power was first brought to Wasco by one of the great utilities companies, it was a boon to the farmer who was fighting for his share of the insufficient water supply; it was also the introduction of large corporation interest in the town. Even gas is piped in by the major distributor of this utility in Southern California though capped natural gas wells lie a few miles away.

The bank is a branch of one of the largest banking institutions in America. Its representative is a community leader, yet his position is quite different from that of the small-town banker as traditionally conceived—the locally successful financier firmly rooted to his community. The patrons of the bank may argue at length over the relative merits of chain banking, with its unlimited resources, and the local bank, which does not have to get outside approval of loans. Whatever the farmer's choice, the fact remains that the local banker is a representative of an outside large corporation, with which his natural economic interests lie. The fact that he enters fully into community affairs does not alter the case, for the corporations are fully cognizant of the value of good will and the need for an effective representative not only of their economic interest but of their social point of view. Gasoline distributors have played an important role in local business and social life. Petroleum products are vital to mechanized agriculture and the sales in

Wasco are large. Four oil companies maintain distribution plants; their managers are community leaders and their salesmen are persons of social prominence in the town.[14] Smaller business enterprises are also affected by the growing tendency toward chain operation. There are several small grocery stores, but also two large supermarkets which are members of chain enterprises centered outside Wasco. The smaller grocers tend to sell exclusively to one or another of the social or ethnic groups, but the chain stores serve all segments of the society. Of the three automobile dealers only one is limited in its operation to Wasco, another is a branch of the nearest city dealer, and the third is the central office for a small syndicate. One of the two drugstores and both the variety stores are syndicate members. Even two of the bars and pool halls are said to be chain operated. Hardware and farm implement sales are completely dominated by outside corporations, and only the much smaller of two lumber companies is locally owned. Some types of stores are completely free of outside domination; notable among them are the clothing, furniture, and restaurant businesses. Except for one hotel, bar, and restaurant combination, all purely local enterprises are on a very modest scale.

There is one local corporation of major size, and its paramount interests and activities lie outside the local community. In this corporation is embodied all the tradition of the local entrepreneur as a community and business leader, yet the very continuation of the enterprise was dependent upon the development of outside interests. Its major battles for growth and survival have been with outside large corporations, unions, gov-

[14] The implications of the trend toward increased mechanization upon rural society has been pointed out by C. Horace Hamilton. He says, "The invention of the machine and . . . their exploitation by monopolistic corporations may be considered as one very effective means by which a nonagricultural economic group cuts out for itself a juicy slice of agricultural income. In this sense farm machinery manufacturers and the large oil companies are engaged in the process of agricultural production, without having to take nearly so many of the risks as does the farmer." "Social Effects of Mechanization of Agriculture," *Rural Sociology*, Vol. 4, p. 15. He goes on to quote the Federal Trade Commission which points out that the International Harvester Company made its record-breaking profits in 1937, when farm income was 18 per cent below the 1929 level.

ernmental control, and the need for an established external market. This corporation grew out of a farmers' co-operative creamery established to improve marketing facilities for a number of local dairymen in 1915. Like most co-operative effort in Wasco, it proved unsuccessful, and was reorganized upon a corporate basis. During the twenties, its growth, in connection with a construction company, was phenomenal, and its president and chief stockholder became a local leader in community affairs. During that decade the major enterprise of the corporation was the subdivision of a tract of land, and the development and construction of an elite residential section. Though an outside market was developed for the creamery products, the major interests of the corporation were local, and, in turn, the local people looked up to the corporation as their leading business and a source of community well-being. With the onset of the thirties, the situation began to change. The construction phase of the enterprise was dropped, and in its stead a second creamery plant was established in a nearby city, and most of the operations were centered there. As a result, the local interests not only dwindled, but also the local payroll was lessened. With increased economic depression, the need for controlling sales outlets was recognized, so that a chain of "malt shops" was established in Los Angeles to insure a market. This meant that now there was only one of the two plants and only one of the eight malt shops in Wasco, and though the central offices remain there the outside interests are dominant. On the other hand, the creamery established dairies of its own, so that a large proportion of its milk supply was directly controlled. Several factors were responsible for this integration. The competition from larger milk distributing corporations forced the creamery to maintain a certain supply of products. The increased dairy regulations in the Los Angeles milkshed made it difficult for the small operator to supply milk. Finally, the value of land in the Wasco region increased with the development of potatoes, making it difficult to maintain a dairy with the resulting high fixed overhead except under highly efficient business practices. The necessity under AAA regulations of maintaining some land under cover crop insured a supply of hay to the dairymen that

INDUSTRIALIZED FARMING AND THE RURAL COMMUNITY 45

remained. But now dairying, like the other Wasco farming enterprises discussed above, is a completely integrated industry—there are no small farmers supplying a few cans of milk. The economic interest of major corporations and chain enterprises has thus wrought changes in the town itself. These corporations have sent in representatives who have, by and large, taken the dominant social role in the community. In this way the whole social structure has been affected, and the natural external loyalties of this group further the disintegration of the unified community. Though these changes are not in themselves entirely dependent upon industrialized agriculture, this form of economy has been favorable to corporate interests. The great demand for capital quickens the interest of lending agencies; the growing universality of power equipment has supported several implement houses; this equipment plus pumped water has brought in electric, gas, and gasoline enterprises, and the large labor population has made cut-rate stores profitable.

The increase of the influence of outside governmental agencies, county, state, and national, is another aspect of this externalizing of the local community. Its application to the local scene is, of course, merely a manifestation of the trend toward governmental centralization, yet its effects are potent.

It is a matter of local choice that the community is not incorporated. (It has, in fact, since become incorporated.) In the middle twenties, it actually became a civic entity, but this was short-lived as a number of farmers succeeded in forcing disincorporation through legal action. Instead of incorporating, a public utilities district was established to maintain the water and sewage systems. This is the only completely local public service operated in Wasco.

Considerable local autonomy prevails in the public schools. The local school board is elected by the people; it determines (within the framework of state law) wages and salaries, can hire and fire, and decides on the disbursement of funds unless a vote of the people is required. While the curriculum and nature of teaching are established by the school officials in conjunction with the county offices, the trustees can and do exert considerable influence over the actual class work. In this way, the community exercises some control over the knowledge and development of its young.

Another elective local officer (who works through the county) is the constable. He is the chief law-enforcing agent in the community. The Justice of the Peace and a county deputy sheriff work in conjunction with him. Similarly, a local voluntary fire department co-operates with the county department. Other county organized administrative agencies include public welfare and health.

During the thirties the major state institution in the community was the State Relief Administration. This was administered entirely from without, employing virtually no local people, and under no local control. A great deal of criticism and abuse was directed against this agency and those others established for the purpose of assisting indigent and unemployed persons. Such reaction stems from several sources. The resentment of an outside power entering into community affairs is supported by the tradition of local autonomy, and is fostered by the dominant element of the community itself. The fact that the philosophy of unemployment relief runs counter to the complex of pioneer traditions, such as rugged individualism, personal sacrifice, and individual fitness in the struggle for existence, offers a climate of opinion that makes the program particularly vulnerable to criticism. Many farmers have recognized that, since the presence of cheap labor is necessary to their agricultural economy, some form of unemployment aid is necessary during times of economic depression. Even these, however, objected to the administration policies. They would have the relief administered entirely for their own needs with all aid terminated as soon as work is available and reinstituted when work is over. Since off-season support of farm labor has never been considered the responsibility of the farmer, there is little recognition of the function the welfare agencies perform in maintaining sufficient workers on a low wage-scale basis.

Hostility has also been expressed towards the Agricultural Adjustment Agency, though it gives assistance to the growers themselves.[15] Here external control is the center of attack, and the committee members themselves have not only asked for more local committee autonomy, but have actually taken it upon themselves. Most of the Wasco committeemen operate moderately large farms; they are successful men fully imbued with the concept of farming as a business enterprise. Their attitude toward "parity payments" does not stem from resentment of the big payments received by the very large operators; they have fought valiantly for the rights of both large and small. Their objection is with the effect upon their operating costs and taxes, and also with the curtailment of their freedom of action. Since they are not in need of subsistence, they do not look upon the payments as a means of assisting distressed farmers. These attitudes substantiate their major claim that the AAA program is not suited to their mode of farming. It is interesting that the very farmers who object to unemployment assistance for labor insist that "parity payments" are different in kind from such aid. No one has ever made the claim that the relief check is a means of maintaining the purchasing parity of the workingman's dollar, while only those few local farmers who are on marginal or submarginal farms recognize the relief aspect of "parity payments." The fact that most of the farmers are business men with large capital investments and a considerable margin of profit makes it difficult for them to view these payments in the light of relief. But unless they can see greater profit through failure to comply with the AAA plan, they have no hesitancy in taking payments, and this without any loss of self-esteem or any hostility on the part of the citizenry. On the other hand, there is no feeling of shame in failure to comply with the rulings of this agency if such a failure proves to be profitable to themselves.

The trends toward industrial and governmental concentration that have just been described have slowly and inexorably invaded the local autonomy and independence of the small com-

[15] The older name Agricultural Adjustment Agency has been used because it was used during the period to which this study applies, and because it is the better known term. Its functions are currently under the Production and Marketing Administration.

munity throughout America, but most particularly where farming itself is caught in the vortex of industrialization. The change of local social attitudes by the introduction of personal representatives of big business and government in the rural community is only part of the story. The urban newspapers with their syndicated columns tend more and more to replace the local newspaper as a source of information and opinion formation. The radio has brought into the homes of nearly every rural resident the values and attitude systems of the outside world. Both these media, through their advertising, have had the effect of creating standard urban wants among the rural people. The motion pictures have not only had an effect upon local attitudes, but tend to establish patterns of behavior by precept. The automobile has been of very great influence. The mobility it affords emancipates the individual from the fortuitous ties of propinquity and enables him to seek social outlets where they are most congenial. This inevitably tends to destroy the neighborhood as a unit of social action and dissipates local loyalties.

These technological developments for living, together and in combination with growing direct economic influences from urban centers, have deprived the local community of much of its function and even more of its social solidarity.

BACKGROUND OF THE FARM LABORERS

We have discussed the agricultural economy and its effects upon town and country alike. Throughout, the importance of the existence of a large farm labor population has been stressed. A brief résumé of the background of this laboring group is necessary to our understanding of the community.

Farm laborers may be divided into two groups: Those who are permanently employed by a single farmer, and those who work by the day or hour, or on a contract or piecework basis. The steady hand may be, but is not usually, of the "hired man" type of employee. Only very occasionally does he eat or live with the farm family; he much more frequently has a separate cabin. He is employed on a permanent basis only in the sense that he is paid by the month; when the work stops, his employment likewise terminates. Frequently he continues to live on the farm, but it is only the rare farmer who feels it necessary to keep him employed the year round. Prior to 1930 field labor was performed mostly by minority races, Chinese, Japanese, Hindu, Filipino, Mexican, and Negro. The white agricultural worker was the unmarried fruit tramp or "bindle stiff," whose contact with the rural community was nil. In the last decade there was an influx of a new type of laborer: whites from the Southern Plains region who came with their families in search of employment. Immigration into California has been a steady phenomenon for nearly a century, but the social consequences of the immigration in the decade of the thirties has had a special effect.[16] Both the absolute and proportional in-migration of the twenties exceeded the in-migration of the past decade. During the earlier period two and a quarter million persons came into California, while the most reliable evidence indicates that the thirties brought in but one million, one hundred thousand. The immigrants were drawn from all occupations and "generally are a cross section of the occupational structure of the States from which they came," [17] and furthermore the "distribution of occupations pursued by migrant family heads in California in 1939 was strikingly similar to the occupational structure of the California population of 1930." [18]

The important difference between the migration of the thirties and that of earlier decades was in the economic circumstance

[16] Persons born outside the state have constituted from 55 to 80 per cent of the population during various census years in California. In 1930 67 per cent were born outside the state. Native births have always constituted but a small portion of the growth of the state's population. See Charles N. Reynolds and Sara Miles, *Migration*, Statistical Memorandum No. 6 (Growth of Population Series), Population Committee for the Central Valley Project Studies, July 5, 1944, Table 1.

[17] Seymour Janow and Davis McEntire, "The Migrants VI: Migration to California," *Land Policy Review*, Vol. III, No. 4, 1940, p. 32. In the studies of migrants into California, statistics were obtained through a census of school children throughout the state. "Migrants" were defined as all persons entering California since January 1, 1930. The coverage of California schools was virtually complete, but, of course, the sample was of those individuals having children in schools, therefore excluding single persons.

[18] Janow and McEntire, *op. cit.*, p. 32.

which surrounded them. For the movement of people in those earlier years was in response to an attractive force of economic opportunity in the Far West, while in the thirties this pull was not so much responsible as a push from areas of distress. This means that the migrants left because their situation became untenable in view of economic circumstances in their native state, and they had to go elsewhere. It also means that there were no ready opportunities in California for economic betterment, so that the already impoverished migrants remained destitute and had to scramble over the countryside to seek a livelihood as best they could during an era of economic depression.

Kern County received the greatest proportionate increase of population of any county in the state, and the rural areas in many cases show increases in school enrollments of over 50 per cent.[19] Wasco is a community with such a large influx. Approximately 2,500 persons came into Wasco from outside of California between 1930 and 1939, according to the school survey.[20] Over two-thirds of these came from Oklahoma, Texas, and Arkansas. The growth of population which this increase implies may be inferred from the increase in water users over this period, and from the school survey (Table 13).

This population came largely from the area of depressed agricultural conditions as a result partly of the drought and partly of increased farm mechanization.[21] In their own parlance these people had been "blown out" and "tractored out." The people who came into the rural areas were virtually destitute and were in search of any type of employment they could find.[22] The major labor market which was open was provided by agri-

[19] Davis McEntire and N. L. Whetten, "The Migrants I: Recent Migration to the Pacific Coast," *Land Policy Review*, Vol. II, No. 5, 1939. See especially the map, p. 11.
[20] Data collected through California public schools.
[21] Paul S. Taylor says, "Heavy displacement of farmers and laborers, as a result of increasing mechanization, is already in progress in several important cotton areas." "Power Farming and Labor Displacement in the Cotton Belt, 1937," *Monthly Labor Review*, March and April, 1938, p. 1.
[22] "The average financial inventory (of resettled migrant families in California) at the time of arrival consisted of the following items: Approximately $100 in cash on hand, $20 in household goods, automobile valued at about $100, and other assets including clothing valued at about $60. The average total value of assets was therefore less than $300." Varden Fuller, "Resettlement of Migrants in Rural California Communities," Ms., p. 54.

culture, especially harvesting work, and this market they flooded. They more than replaced the repatriated Mexican workers and the workers immobilized by the residence laws governing eligibility for public relief. As destitute agricultural laborers

TABLE 13.—ESTIMATES OF POPULATION GROWTH, WASCO, 1930-41

Year	Estimate from water users			Immigration increment estimate	
	Number of water users	Persons per outlet [1]	Population estimate	Families enumerated [2]	Population estimate
1930	572	2.7	1,548	..	1,548
1931	583	2.8	1,632	19	1,738
1932	612	2.9	1,775	14	1,878
1933	586	2.9	1,699	7	1,948
1934	608	3.0	1,824	12	2,068
1935	650	3.1	2,015	38	2,448
1936	700	3.2	2,240	40	2,848
1937	907	3.3	2,993	49	3,338
1938	962	3.3	3,175	41	3,746
1939	1,075	3.4	3,655	30	4,048
1940	1,131	3.5	4,000	12	4,168
1941	1,134	3.6	4,082	..	.....

[1] Established by the 1930 and 1940 Census data, with a sliding scale for intervening years; 1930 and 1940 figures are from the U. S. Decennial Census.

[2] Studies have indicated a net increment of 10 persons for each family enumerated in this school census.

SOURCE: Water Users, from records of the Wasco Public Utilities District. Immigration Increment, from California Location Census.

dependent upon intermittent employment and public welfare they became known to the rural and small town population; their poverty, their peculiarity of dress and speech, and the fact that they came from outside marked them as a class apart, and they came to be referred to by such derogatory epithets as "Okie" and "Arkie." [23]

[23] The literature on these migrants is by now fairly voluminous. John Steinbeck's *The Grapes of Wrath* is the outstanding fictional account; Dorothea

ESTIMATES OF POPULATION GROWTH, WASCO, 1930–1941

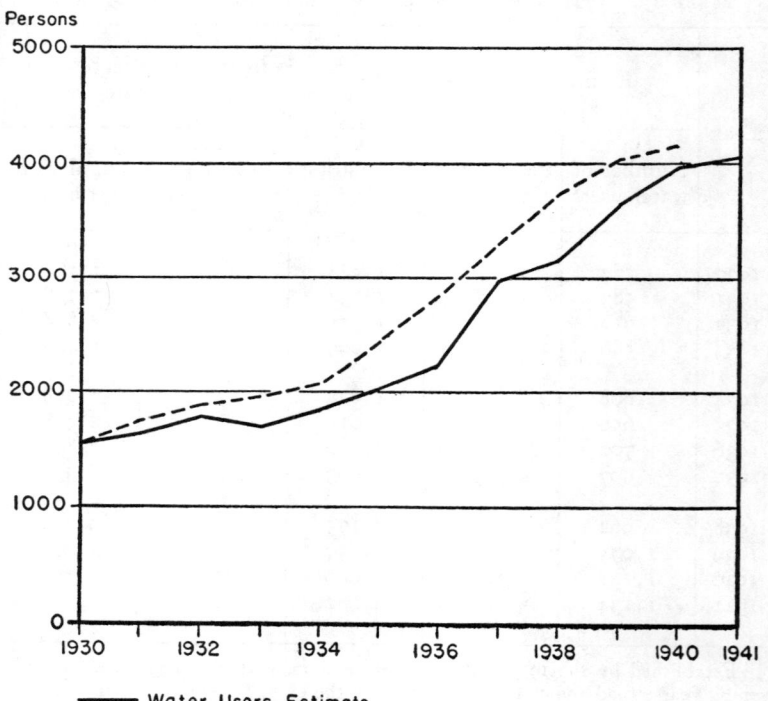

——— Water Users Estimate
——— Immigration Increment Estimate

SOURCES:
    Wasco Public Utilities District Records
    California Location Census
    See Table 13.

CHART 2

This new laboring element in California differed from its numerous predecessors in the combination of two characteristics: They were of the white race, and they came as families. Earlier white migrants had quickly gained a higher status and were absorbed in the population. These two items made it both possible and necessary for them to differ in another and more important way; they tended to settle down in the communities and become permanent laboring citizens. Despite local opinion, the "Okie" did not come to California out of wanderlust, and neither does he want to move about in California now. From a survey of resettled migrants made in 1939, it was learned that most of these laboring families came directly to California from their home, that half of them came directly to the community in which they had permanently established themselves,[24] that most of them intended to remain in the community in which they were at the time of the interview, that almost half of them have bought homes, and that over 70 per cent are registered voters. These facts clearly indicate what every Wasco resident knows, that the "Okie" is a permanent part of his community.

This large sessile labor population, like the growing influence of outside business and governmental interests and the technological developments as the radio, moving pictures, and automobile, has been a contributing factor in the shift away from community homogeneity toward a more urban rural environment. First, the fact of a large labor population increases the size of the local community so that personal face-to-face relationships are no longer universally possible. Second, the great diversity of economic conditions and social backgrounds make closer interpersonal relationships undesirable to the people

Lange and Paul S. Taylor's *American Exodus* describes the movement both in words and photographs. A case study made by the Farm Security Administration (*A Study of 6,655 Migrant Households in California*, 1938, processed report directed by Jonathan Garst, San Francisco, 1939) has been supplemented by other official bulletins. The La Follette and Tolan Hearings include data on the situation and the causes of migration.

[24] Varden Fuller, "Resettlement of Migrants in Rural Communities of California," Ms., pp. 51, 73.

themselves. These factors have tended more and more to render inoperative those normal modes of social sanctions based upon personal approbation and censure. In its stead there has developed a system of social values based upon pecuniary and occupational standards, paralleling that found in the city.

CHAPTER III

BASIC STRUCTURE

THE ECONOMIC BASIS OF SOCIAL DISTINCTIONS

THE COMMUNITY of Wasco—the town and the surrounding countryside together—includes between seven and eight thousand individuals. The diversity of cultural background and the division of economic interests are more evident in this aggregate than is their unity, and in this respect it duplicates the city. Negroes and Mexicans, whites from the sharecropper South, German Mennonites, Catholics, representatives of big business, small shopkeepers, all make a diversified list with variations of great importance, yet the patterns of behavior are not so chaotic as this record would imply. They vary from individual to individual, but they also approach norms within certain basic classifications, norms which differ significantly according to social class. And the most significant variations in behavior correlate in general with the groups which have divergent economic interests. It is for this reason that the important social groupings in the community must be established, and this chapter will attempt to classify the population into such groups. Certain basic cultural desires on the part of all members of the society, however, affect the life of all classes and groups, and the significant variation in behavior is very largely an expression of the degree of attainment of these values. In order to classify the society it becomes necessary to define the nature of the social goals.

Social worth is determined in this rural community, as in most of our society, by an interdependent triad: occupation, money worth or income, and material possessions. The very interdependence of these things makes it difficult to select one as the most important, while the high degree of correlation between occupation, income, and possessions makes it unnecessary. The core of these three items is money: occupation represents its means of acquisition, income is the amount available, and possessions are the public assertion of that income. And, in general, income as such is determined by the public through knowledge of occupation and evidences of conspicuous consumption. It is impossible for an investigator not armed with the legal instrument of subpoena to obtain information on income and only with difficulty and uncertainty on expenditures, and for that reason occupation must be used as the instrument for establishing social position. Occupation is, after all, the major orientation of the newcomer into the society, for just as in the simpler societies the stranger is oriented by real or fictitious consanguinity, so the stranger in Wasco is oriented in terms of his occupation through the inclusive question, "What do you do?" It is generally accepted that the source of a person's income be public knowledge but the amount is a matter of speculation and gossip, established by the process of reckoning from occupation on one side and from expenditures on the other. And for this reason the purchase of consumers goods is *de facto* a social gesture as well as an economic act. Especially is this true of homes and house furnishings, of cars, and of luxury items. Modern devices which increase leisure and mobility and serve creature comforts are popular, while silver, linens, and other more conspicuously luxury goods are limited to the more affluent. The compulsion to spending can best be viewed when farm profits have been abnormally great, as in 1936, when potato prices were high. Then farmers bought houses, hired interior decorators, acquired two and three new cars, and the like.

The major criterion for establishing social differences will, therefore, be occupation which implies income and wealth as well, and involves not only the economic activities devoted to the acquisition of money, but also by implication and less perfectly the nature of expenditures for the gratification of physical and social wants. This fiscal-occupational classification is an adequate device for determining social position because it is used by the members of the society themselves.

A series of five occupational distinctions have been utilized to indicate the variations in social status in the community, and while these only imperfectly reflect the social classes and status levels to be defined they can be used to indicate the existence of social distinctions. These occupational groupings have been adapted from the work of Alba M. Edwards.[1] They are as follows:

A. Professionals, Managers and Proprietors. Professionals, including physicians, nurses, teachers, ministers, and a few other highly trained occupations; managers and proprietors of commercial establishments, including trained managers of large farms.

B. Farm Operators. Either tenant or owners of farms.

C. Clerical Workers. All white collar workers not included in A above, such as clerks, salesmen, secretaries, and the like.

D. Skilled Labor. Skilled and semi-skilled workers including mechanics, truck and bus drivers, public services, construction and mechanical workers, school janitors, and the like, as well as carpenters, painters, plumbers.

E. Unskilled Labor. Unskilled laborers, whether farm labor or not.

F. Non-employed. Housewives, unemployed, unknown occupations.

We may fairly consider classes A, C, D, and E a descending scale of social worth, though with exceptions established on the basis of various factors as indicated in the text. Farmers show variation in social status from A to D, but for the most part fall between A and C.

In the absence of census data on these occupational classes, we must use two available indices for the distribution of occupations; namely, the results of a survey made of school children,[2] and the voting registration of the several precincts of the Wasco township for the November, 1940, elections. The following Table shows roughly the distribution of the occupation groups in

[1] Alba M. Edwards, *A Social-Economic Grouping of the Gainful Workers of the United States: 1930*, U. S. Dept. of Commerce, Bureau of the Census, Washington, 1938, and coded according to the *Alphabetical Index of Occupations by Industries and Economic Groups*.

[2] California Location Census, a survey of families who have entered California in the period 1930-39 taken through the public schools of the State.

Wasco and among the migrants (Table 14). Since voting registration is somewhat selective, we cannot interpret these figures too literally.

TABLE 14.—PROPORTIONATE DISTRIBUTION OF OCCUPATIONAL GROUPS

Occupational class	Voting registration		School survey families	
	No.	Per cent	No.	Per cent
A. Professionals, managers, and proprietors	231	15.1	14	7.6
B. Farm operators	197	12.9	17	9.2
C. Clerical workers	130	8.5	3	1.6
D. Skilled laborers	491	32.1	64	34.6
E. Unskilled laborers	482	31.4	87	47.0
Total	1,531	100.0	185	100.0

SOURCE: California Location Census and Voting Registration for 1940 elections, Wasco Township.

THE TWO SOCIAL CLASSES

On this basis two all-pervasive social groups may be established.[3] One of them is made up of business men, farm operators, professionals, and the regular employees of business houses, both white collar and skilled, and some semi-skilled labor. (Groups A to D in the above list.) The other is made up of the agricultural laborers, both regularly employed and seasonal, and the other forms of common labor in the community. (Group E in the above list.) It also includes persons of other occupations whose work is directed toward this group, such as storekeepers

[3] The remainder of this chapter will be devoted to presenting the nature of the social cleavages in the society. The following sections will describe the nature of the social behavior in terms of the groupings established in this. Statistical documentation of the validity of the social differences has been relegated to the later chapters.

who sell only to members of this class. These two classes may be called upper and lower, and in a loose way those terms will be used below, but because these terms have a variety of meanings, it will be better to establish a set of terms that are more descriptive of the actual relationship. The former of the two will therefore be called the *nuclear* group, or the functioning members of the Wasco community, and the latter will be called *outsiders,* or non-members.

This terminology expresses both the historical and the immediate aspects of the social situation. The nuclear group is that body which grew up with Wasco and inherited the institutions of the community—that body to which Wasco belongs. The outsiders are those who have arrived somewhat later to serve as agricultural laborers. They remain outside the social walls of the community, against which they are constantly impinging. They are not accepted into community life, and they are not considered in community affairs. Though more recent, this outsider class is not new—it has existed as long as, and to the extent that, industrialized agriculture has prevailed. It is a necessary concomitant of agriculture which requires a large amount of unskilled labor. It has, as indicated in the preceding chapter, changed its ethnic composition. And with this change has come a new set of social problems.

The established psychological attitudes and the sanctioned social behavior easily separated the minority ethnic groups from the dominant or nuclear element in the society. Any social advancement of a Negro or Mexican was within his own group; he did not enter the social sphere of the white community. He had fewer social possibilities, and his externality remained complete. As a result of common physical characteristics, common social backgrounds, in the case of the Mexican a distinct language, and because the dominant group insisted upon their geographical segregation, the two minority groups developed an internal unity which resulted in their having communities of their own. The "Mexican colony" and the "nigger town" still exist as separate entities. The white laborers, unlike the colored groups, do not have the identity of physical and social characteristics to set them off from the nuclear population, nor do they have any mechanisms by which they could organize into a community with internal status differentiations. Though economic pressure tends to force them into delimited subdivisions with poorer housing facilities, actually they are scattered throughout the town wherever poorer houses exist, or wherever property deeds do not contain building restriction clauses. As a result of all these factors, they consistently impinge upon the nuclear group and some attain membership in it. But because of the social barriers that have been created, and because of the limitations upon economic advancement, the group as a whole remains separate.

Members of both classes generally give overt expression to this class distinction. It may be the minister of the most elegant church in town saying, "The migrants don't come here because they don't feel comfortable," or it might be almost any of the outsiders saying, "To tell you the truth, I don't like the Baptist church here because they are a different class of people, and I'd rather stay around my own class."

While Wasco is in a region of industrialized agriculture with dominantly urban values, the poorest of the white agricultural workers have come from an area where different conditions prevail; where population is sparse, great wealth is rare, and differentiations in social position either are not dependent upon the possession of luxury goods, or the people are themselves in such poor and backward country that few could afford them. Many of them did not have modern plumbing, houses with several rooms, special clothes for Sunday, trade unions or other secular organizations, nor rural slum areas. Their religious observances were largely of the "old time religion" type; their occupational experience mostly as farm tenants, or farm or other unskilled labor. This is not, however, true of all of them. Data have been collected which show the variety of occupations of the new arrivals into California and of the resettled agricultural workers. Whatever the previous circumstances, most of them have, since coming to California or before, adopted the standards of value of the dominant group in the area. A few have maintained their old behavior patterns, yet it is difficult, if not impossible, to ascertain to what extent their living conditions are determined by their values and to what extent they are forced upon them by economic circumstances.

In short, it is impossible to generalize that part of the behavior of these agricultural laborers which is not directly determined by the economic forces to which they are subject. Their backgrounds and histories are too complex and varied to make such generalizations valid. And, since they remain a disorganized aggregate, they have not developed any internal sanctions which would tend to unify their social behavior. The only generally accepted sanctions for attitudes and actions among this group are those imposed upon them by the nuclear group in their desire to achieve acceptance in that society. Nevertheless, members of the nuclear group do tend to make generalizations regarding the behavior and character of the laborers, and usually base their own actions upon these preconceived attitudes.

The popular picture of the "Okie" with straight blond hair, lean face and body, dressed in bib overall or apron and sunbonnet is filled out with imputed character designations. That imputed character is a bad one, with a ready rationalization for the many exceptions that have come to the individual's attention. Members of the nuclear group usually describe the "Okie" as ignorant and uneducated, dirty of habit if not of mind, slothful, unambitious, and dependent. He may be viewed now as emotional, again as phlegmatic; sometimes as sullen and unfriendly; again as arrogant and over-bearing. Not rarely is he accused of being dishonest. These characteristics are sometimes considered innate (a local physician spoke of them as a separate breed); sometimes lack of education is held responsible. As a matter of fact, the farm workers display as great a variety of characteristics as are found in any group of equally divergent backgrounds. Cases are often cited from personal experience illustrating each characteristic, for as in any group individuals may be found to conform to them. It is true that the level of educational attainment and the apparent capacity to learn is generally lower among the workers than among the nuclear group. The opportunities and facilities for learning have not been so readily available to many of them, and migration from town to town and the necessity for the children to work are instrumentalities enough to bring this about. Many dirty homes can be pointed out among them, as well as exceptionally clean ones. Yet the circumstances of their living are not readily conducive to the maintenance of middle-class standards of cleanliness. Many have spent days and weeks in idleness, yet a local leader remarked with astonishment that laborers generally preferred working for wages to getting relief. A long history of malnutrition and lack of dietary knowledge, coupled with poor living conditions generally, have not been conducive to vigorous bodies capable of sustained physical exertion, yet the work these laborers perform is long and hard. Emotional religious practices are generally cited as examples of emotionalism in their nature, yet the function of such religion for those who participate can be understood in terms of their social and economic situation. Court records do not uphold the imputation of dishonesty since local arrests and convictions did not rise proportionally with population. In summation, the bad and good is mixed among the "Okie" as it is among any population; and while the condemnation made by the nuclear group can be applied to individuals, they are not justified generalizations for the group as a whole. The valid generalizations regarding their behavior are those which derive from common economic and social circumstances, and will be discussed in greater detail below.

While the two social classes in Wasco are interdependent parts of a functioning economic system, and together bring farm products to the market, they are also in direct economic competition. For the wages that the one receives come directly out of the profits of members of the other—"managerial profits" derived from the use of hired labor. Resulting conflicts have been expressed in strikes which have involved violence, but for the most part it is latent, rarely rising to the surface. The farmer needs the worker and the worker needs the job, and an agreement is usually maintained. But the farmer is interested in having a large number of laborers unused to achieving the social values of the dominant group, and satisfied with few of the luxuries of modern society, so that his desires conflict with the social desires of the laborer. One of the leaders of the nuclear group expressed this all too clearly. "The trouble," he said, "is that we have educated them too much. They are dissatisfied with their work and who will then scrub our floors. Don't think that I disapprove of education. . . ."

Wasco, then, is an aggregate of people divided into two groups, social classes with the same basic values but with different social experiences and differing interest in the economic system. The one has inherited the traditional life of the community in the pioneer sense; the other remains an outsider. These two classes are not only distinguished by differences in social status; they are also in competition. They are in turn divisible into less clearly differentiated subgroups, according to their prestige in the value system of the society. Three separate levels of social status may be segregated in the nuclear class: an elite, a middle group, and a marginal group. This is a conceptual device for dividing a continuum of variation into broad categories, but it is of real value in helping to understand the social relationships, and in describing the nature of social life in the community. Furthermore, since the citizen tends to accord like status to groups who associate together (that is, to classify their associates unconsciously on a status basis), this conceptualization has validity. The levels of status are not the same kind of social entity as the social classes just defined, however. The individual manifests at every hand his realization of the class to which he belongs, and it is possible to awaken in him loyalties to these groups, while the conceptual levels of prestige are not overtly recognized.

THE NUCLEAR GROUP

The highest level in Wasco society is made up of the representatives of the large corporations which have branch offices in the community, the persons who are in administrative positions in the single large local corporation, the members of the medical profession, and a few local business people of long residence (group A in the occupation list), and the most successful large growers (part of group B). Economically, they are all well off, not only in that they possess most of the goods which have prestige, but also in that they have more than reasonable certainty that they will continue in this economic position for the remainder of their lifetime. They are not an aristocracy in the sense of the upper classes of the South, and they are not extreme wealthy. In neighboring communities where the land is subdivided in larger units, there are usually a number of families with great holdings, but in Wasco there are but one or two. This class is comfortably housed in dwellings usually having a spare bedroom or two. They are never highly elaborate or ostentatious. They do not indulge in such wealth displays as yachts, summer homes, chauffeurs, or even regular maids, probably because few or none can afford even the least of these. None of them is a capitalist in the sense that his living comes solely from invested moneys; therefore, even the elite in Wasco habitually work a normal set of hours each day. They are, however, capitalists in the sense that either they have administrative positions in large capital interests, or their work is directed toward the end of seeing that their capital investments pay proper dividends. As pointed out in the preceding chapter, this is true of even the farmer whose holdings are moderate.

Because Wasco is not a unit separate from the remainder of the county, state, and nation, these individuals are not a complacent elite, sure of their own standing. Those whose position is highest have entered a wider social arena in which their ambitions are directed upward. Thus, a farmer of the elite group entertains an exclusive county organization rather than participates in a community social event. Others achieve outside recognition through developing political interests or spreading their economic activities over a wider area. There is no tradition of an upper class with certain prerogatives; membership is attained through the economic struggle and it is maintained by continual social and economic effort. And there is always a higher social rung to egg on the individual. As the Negroes in the South would say, they are all "strainers," straining to achieve ever higher social standing.

The middle group in Wasco is made up of local entrepreneurs and the operators of eighty to two hundred-acre farms (groups A and B of the occupation list); school teachers; lesser representatives of the big corporations, such as gasoline and power sales-

that they will continue in this economic position for the remainder of their lifetime. They are not an aristocracy in the sense of the upper classes of the South, and they are not extreme wealthy. In neighboring communities where the land is subdivided in larger units, there are usually a number of families with great holdings, but in Wasco there are but one or two. This class is comfortably housed in dwellings usually having a spare bedroom or two. They are never highly elaborate or ostentatious. They do not indulge in such wealth displays as yachts, summer homes, chauffeurs, or even regular maids, probably because few or none can afford even the least of these. None of them is a capitalist in the sense that his living comes solely from invested moneys; therefore, even the elite in Wasco habitually work a normal set of hours each day. They are, however, capitalists in the sense that either they have administrative positions in large capital interests, or their work is directed toward the end of seeing that their capital investments pay proper dividends. As pointed out in the preceding chapter, this is true of even the farmer whose holdings are moderate.

Because Wasco is not a unit separate from the remainder of the county, state, and nation, these individuals are not a complacent elite, sure of their own standing. Those whose position is highest have entered a wider social arena in which their ambitions are directed upward. Thus, a farmer of the elite group entertains an exclusive county organization rather than participates in a community social event. Others achieve outside recognition through developing political interests or spreading their economic activities over a wider area. There is no tradition of an upper class with certain prerogatives; membership is attained through the economic struggle and it is maintained by continual social and economic effort. And there is always a higher social rung to egg on the individual. As the Negroes in the South would say, they are all "strainers," straining to achieve ever higher social standing.

The middle group in Wasco is made up of local entrepreneurs and the operators of eighty to two hundred-acre farms (groups A and B of the occupation list); school teachers; lesser representatives of the big corporations, such as gasoline and power salesmen (group C); most skilled laborers; and some semi-skilled laborers who have had long residence in the community (group D). They are the substantial citizenry who, for the most part, are living well. They usually have all the "modern conveniences," such as new gas ranges, shining kitchen sinks, and frigidaires; like all other classes in Wasco, they usually have a car and it is frequently new. Installment buying makes it possible for these people of modest means to acquire this assortment before they have the requisite capital, and it is generally recognized that possession does not connote full ownership. This has reduced the prestige value of these material possessions. Their houses can be classified into two types. The older persons in this class who have lived there a long time are in the older section of town in rather large bungalows built in the early twenties. The younger group and those who have come into Wasco during its recent growth have for the most part built or rented new bungalows with one or two bedrooms. When built by the present inhabitant, they are generally financed through FHA loans, usually in the newer subdivisions in the better but not the best section of town. The social life of the middle group is more closely bound up with the town than any other group in Wasco's social structure. Those special occupational groups, like oil workers and school teachers, form a partial exception to this statement. The pattern of social behavior is virtually the same as with the elite, but on a less ambitious scale. It tends, also, to be more intimately connected with the church, usually either the Methodist, Baptist, Catholic, or Seventh-Day Adventist.

The marginal group consists largely of regularly employed workers, such as mechanics, clerks at small stores, assistants at filling stations, and the like (C and D). The smallest farmer, renting less than eighty acres of land can also be classed in this category. They are the least clearly defined unit in the nucleus. They live in the older houses of the town, many in the section called Little Oklahoma City, and many of them are former outsiders who have attained membership in the community by length of residence and permanent employment. They are likely to have some of the modern conveniences, but not all. Their floors are typically covered with linoleum rugs, their houses are old and require repair. They are insecure economically as well as socially, and their wants remain great. They are part of the nuclear group because they are known to that group, as the poor in the pioneer type of community are known to it. Their church affiliation may be with the established churches, but is frequently in one of the two older revivalistic sects. If so, they form the pillars of those churches, in which they associate with the outsider group.

THE OUTSIDER GROUP

The outsiders consist of three separate categories distinguished by ethnic origins: the white, Negro, and Mexican laborers.[4] They are economically insecure and most of them have at one time or another received some form of unemployment assistance. It is possible to consider the three as a single class, because they are accorded similar treatment by the nuclear group and have the same economic circumstances. But since they each remain to themselves and, in fact, have some manifestations of hostility, they cannot be considered a functioning unit. Allusion has already been made to some of the distinctions between the minority races and the "Okie." The primary distinction lies in the fact that the white can potentially attain the higher status, which the Negro can never, and the Mexican can only with difficulty. The second distinction is that the two minority races have an internal cohesion which the white group lacks. This is derived from their geographical and social segregation, and results in quite different social behavior.

The Negroes and Mexicans each concentrate in certain sections of the town, though some of each live in the neighborhood dominated by the other, and some whites are interspersed in the

[4] The distinction between Mexican, Negro and white among the outsider group are largely an expression of social avoidance between persons of separate ethnic origins. The fact that the Mexican and Negro have physical characteristics by which they may be identified is a social fact of considerable significance to the structure of Wasco society. In the following we shall occasionally refer to these ethnic groups as races, without any imputation of a biologic basis for differentials in behavior, except as biology is raised to an important consideration by the society itself.

Mexican neighborhood. Between Negro and Mexican there appears to be no friction or ill-feeling; their relations seem amicable. Despite these friendly relationships and their close physical proximity, there is no evidence of close social ties. The fact of being a Negro or Mexican is a potent fact in establishing social intercourse; and most social action takes place within each of these groups. No Negro-Mexican marriages were noted, but because this aspect of the Wasco social structure was not subjected to detailed examination, the absence of evidence is not conclusive.

The Mexican, being Catholic, has a point of contact with the whites that the Negro does not have, even though the church does not bring the Mexican and the white into very close social contact. Catholic leaders have expressed differential attitudes toward the two groups, considering the Mexicans like children. The church sponsors separate social affairs for each group. In light of this it is interesting that one completely assimilated person of Mexican descent who has become a member of the nuclear group has renounced the Catholic faith and joined a Protestant church.

The dominant attitude of the nuclear group toward the Negro is one of complete superiority. Its members have no social relationships with him, except under patronizing circumstances. The Negro will perform in a white church or the whites will be invited to come to money-raising functions at the Negro church; the whites will be condescending and the Negro not so much subservient as deferent. The Negroes have escaped so many violations of their privacies and legal rights by leaving the South that they feel well treated. They also manifest fewer of the obsequious qualities which are important to their well-being in the South. Nevertheless, they must maintain a respectful attitude and their occasional failure to do so is the subject of ill-feeling among the whites. The Negro child in school is frequently aggressive in over-compensation and is condemned for not "keeping his place." The complete segregation and the formally recognized and socially sanctioned forms of behavior in their relationship make social behavior between them more "natural" than it is between the nuclear group and the other two outsider races.

Not only does the white outsider come from the region where the more virulent forms of race prejudice are found, but he is also in direct economic competition with the minority races. As a result, the segregation is fully as complete, and the relationship more antagonistic than is manifested between nuclear group and Negro, though there are no evidences of open hostility. On the other hand, the enforced closer association between the two groups has had some effect in breaking down the prejudiced attitudes of the whites. As one Negro storekeeper said, "It seems like the white folks don't feel so bitey as they do down South. Down there they won't come into your place because they are afraid that someone down the street won't like it. When they see that other people won't talk about them they don't mind coming in. They are a little standoffish here at first. I've seen them come in at first like they were afraid of us, but pretty soon they find out we are civilized. One woman wouldn't come in for a long time, but finally she sent her children in." Though there is a tendency for the workers to be hired by race, the three races often work in the same field together, and one of the most active labor contractors is a Negro preacher. One white outsider woman expressed the effect of this interrelationship by saying that when her husband first came out here he didn't like to work in the same field with a Negro, and that it "nearly killed him" to work for one, but now he has extreme respect for the honesty and reliability of this contractor. That the traditional prejudices have not broken down sufficiently for co-operative action was manifested by the wife of a former union officer who refused to join a union with Negroes in it because "you can't equalize me with no nigger."

The white outsiders form an aggregate which is a part of this economic class, but which manifests little evidence of social unity. We have already indicated that they represent a variety of economic backgrounds, and possess no effective institutional mechanisms for organization and unity. They form an economic class that has by and large accepted the values of the nuclear community.

Several factors lead us to the conclusion that the status drives of the outsider group are directed toward membership in the community of Wasco rather than toward status desires within their own group. The first of these is their own statements, especially the often repeated ones that they want "a steady job." Desire for permanent work is an economic one, but permanent employment is not the only possible adjustment. It is possible to make a highly successful adjustment on a permanently migratory basis, and the laborers themselves recognize that year-round farm employment means less income during the season of high labor demand, when hourly or piece rates net more per day. Secondly, they want a "place of their own." To the newcomer this usually means a small farm—"just two acres." This ambition tends to become moderated to merely a small house on a little plot of land in town. This desire gets frequent expression among those who have not acquired one, while half of a group of resettled migrants recently studied had purchased real property.[5] A third factor indicating the direction of social desires is for education for their children, and a general appreciation of the facilities provided for this purpose by the community.

It is equally clear that the migratory workers have tended to settle down and remain in one place. The study mentioned above indicates that 84 per cent of the families intended to stay in the community in which they settled, while almost half of the families moved directly to their community of settlement from their state of origin.[6] Furthermore, the laboring group has tended less and less to be entirely migratory, and has remained more and more in one place. This is indicated by the disappearance of squatters' shacks and tents in the last prewar years. It can be demonstrated statistically by the reduction in the fluctuation of the average attendance in the schools. Migrant workers take their children in and out of schools as they move from town to town. In the early part of the 1930's this created a great fluctuation in the monthly averages of average daily attendance in the elementary school, but this fluctuation declined steadily

[5] Fuller, "Resettlement of Migrants in Rural Communities of California," Ms., p. 67.
[6] *Ibid.*, p. 51, 67.

after 1935. Such a decline means that there is an increasing number of laborers who remain in one community during the school semester, or at least maintain a home there for their children.

We have, then, evidence that the families of agricultural workers are becoming a physical part of the total community, and that their ambitions lie in that direction. But in the community only the nuclear group can confer either status or membership, for, as we have already said, the outsiders have no mechanisms at the present time for establishing and maintaining their group entity. Though there is a large neighborhood made up of agricultural workers only, there are no evidences of neighborhood activities or neighborhood solidarity. That smaller cliques exist, independent of any formal organization, there can hardly be any doubt, but there is no evidence that such groups play a large part in the social life of the outsider, and the outsider consistently denies any regular social contacts of this sort. There are, of course, two institutions which can serve to bring together members of the outsider class: the union and the church. The union has at different times been an effective weapon in obtaining economic advantages for the laborer (see Chapter VI). In Wasco at the time the study was made it was subject to a leadership more interested in public relief than increased wages, and was shaken by the racial prejudices of these leaders. The situation in Wasco was less favorable than in neighboring towns, as the district organizer said in the following:

> Wasco is different from other towns. There is a higher percentage of workers there who become home owners. It might be because the relief office is there or because rents are cheaper.
> It is the hardest town to organize, and there is more hostility to organized labor there than anywhere else. At Arvin the Chamber of Commerce supported the [Government sponsored low-cost] housing plan, and so did the merchants, but not in Wasco.
> The Mexican population is different too. At the union meetings the majority of the union members were drunk, and they are hard to organize. The Mexicans in a neighboring town were easiest to organize. The Wasco Mexicans don't get along with them at all.
> The Wasco Negroes believe in nationalism, that is, they believe that the Negro must solve his own problem, and that their problems are

BASIC STRUCTURE 71

not the problems of the working class. Under the domination of the church and the police, these people were taught that the Negro must believe in the Negroes helping themselves. A former deputy sheriff, a preacher in a big frame building, and a grocery store owner who has a bunch of labor contractors are responsible for this set of ideas among the Wasco Negroes.

These people from Oklahoma aren't very class-conscious. It isn't in their background.

Union organization fails to unify the farm labor group, particularly in Wasco, because the workers are not willing to identify themselves as laborers. This is partly because such identification, and the whole philosophy of unionism is foreign to their background, and partly because such identification, constitutes a denial of community values. Instead, the individual worker strives for status as an individual.

The church has failed to serve the purpose of bringing the laborer into a unified social class for other reasons. First, many persons do not care for church membership, and so belong to none. Second, the churches are many in number and split the outsider group into small factions. Even for those who are brought together by the church, their religious ideology precludes the development of class-consciousness. For the outsider religions are non-class-conscious, if not actually anti-class-conscious. Though church membership reflects class distinctions of which both member and minister are aware, the philosophy their religions espouse negates the importance of mundane social considerations in view of the greater truths of eternity. This, as will be shown below, is particularly true of those denominations serving entirely the outsider group. For other of the outsider churches, there appears to be a kind of institutional social mobility, whereby the whole congregation moves toward social acceptance in the community. This condition again leads to a denial of labor-class identification, which would be a check against such social acceptance.

If the outsider's social ambitions are directed toward membership in the community, it must be equally clear that these desires are frustrated by the circumstances in which he is thrust. For the acquisition by the outsider of status, or even recognition of a minimal kind, is rare and the possibilities of satisfaction limited. Such frustrations find their sublimations in different ways. The church serves this end admirably, for in denying the reality of the social and economic system in which its members have an unenviable position, it sets up a putative society with transcendental values and criteria for membership. Liquor, of course, serves as escape from this social situation as well as from more personal difficulties. Finally, a form of sublimation, or partial fulfillment through symbolism, is obtained through the purchase of items in the inventory of middle-class well-being. It is not infrequent that a new and expensive electric refrigerator is found in a small shack, and one of the most expensive kind shone through the flap of a tent. Cabinet radios are similarly found, and the outsider is frequently criticized by nuclear persons for the money he spends on automobiles. These items have their practical functions; they serve some segment of creature comfort. But they are purchased at the sacrifice of other items which might serve more basic needs, or at the sacrifice of savings, which might serve the original purpose more satisfactorily but only after a long period of time and over many hazards.

Considering, then, that the white outsider himself conceives of social status with reference to the values of the nuclear group, it is permissible to use them for purposes of social segmentation, and therefore the outsider may be divided into groups according to the permanence of his employment. The laborers who are permanently employed gain permanent residence thereby, and those social advantages which result from permanent residence. Their relationship to the community is set in terms of their employment, so that they become known to at least a segment of the nuclear group as the worker on a particular ranch. The seasonal worker has no such ties with the community, and may be known to none of the nuclear residents, frequently not even those for whom he works under contract, even though he spends the greater part of the year in the community.

Members of the nuclear group are in the habit of making a distinction between agricultural laborers which, in a general way, follows this dichotomy; namely between "dust-bowlers" and "Okies." The Okie is, as we have already indicated, characterized as a congenital ne'er-do-well without ambition or desire, while the "dust-bowler" is a person of ability and good character who is temporarily in bad circumstances. In the words of one farmer, "The dust-bowl people who came out here have settled down and become real citizens. There isn't one of them that hasn't gotten a steady job and settled down. But these Okies who come out here, who weren't anything before they left, don't amount to anything. They are filthy dirty—you give them a decent house and in a couple of weeks they are spitting through the cracks. Why, yes, I've seen it myself." Another says, "They are Okies back home, just as much as they are here, and never would amount to a damn."

This distinction between agricultural laborers who have and those who have not achieved the standards of the dominant group is certainly valid, though we cannot accept the imputed attributes. The agricultural laborers make the same sort of distinction. One of them spoke in shocked tones of the deplorable condition of the people in a certain region in Oklahoma; another laughingly said that the Oklahoman has just as much prejudice against the Arkansas people, as the Californians do against the Oklahomans. But these statements came from persons who would, from their economic circumstances and general living conditions, have been branded "Okies," not dust-bowlers.

The important thing is that, while the distinction exists, the nuclear member makes the assumption that the agricultural laborer is an Okie, with the social connotations already described, until he proves himself otherwise. As one outsider woman said, with keen insight into the tendency of persons to generalize regarding people unknown to them, "You know, one person can cause a lot of trouble for others. You can't blame these people for feeling that you can't trust those Okies. There are some that make them feel that way." The outsider can only establish the fact that he is not an Okie by advancing his economic position, and the first advancement possible is to permanent employment status. The most frequent opportunities are in dairies or as permanent hired hands on middle-size farms. A few opportunities are found in the town as service station attendants or bus drivers, and these jobs most frequently lead to recognition by the community.

The permanently employed group of outsiders either live in a small house in Little Oklahoma City or on the land of the farmer for whom he works. The farmers frequently furnish their regular laborers a house comparable to that which they would have in town, namely a three-room bungalow with linoleum-covered or bare floors, and electricity. For this he usually does not have to pay any rental, for the house is considered a regular perquisite. Socially, he tends to remain separate, knowing only a few intimates, his nearest neighbors or his working companions. If he goes to church, it is almost always to one of the newer sects in the community, while most frequently he merely sends his children to Sunday School. For those who do attend church it becomes the center of all their social and recreational activities.

The temporarily employed may have the same living conditions, but more frequently they are less favorable. Many avail themselves of the cabins that have been built in congested courts like the one-room tourist cabins of an earlier period, usually furnished with electricity, running water in the yard, and a common toilet which may or may not be of the flush type. Others live "on the desert," where they have their tents and accumulate shacks by gradual accretion. This practice is frowned upon by the health authorities of the county, and has virtually disappeared, except that during the season when much labor is needed tents are found in uninhabited groves. Such migrants (or families who have their homes in some other community) may also come in homemade trailers and settle either in places where accommodations are available or on empty lots near a filling station or the home of a friend. Like all the preceding groups, they have cars which are essential to their occupation. Occasionally they are quite new, but cars six or eight years old are more usual. Some also have acquired such things as washing machines, refrigerators, and furniture.

The Negroes live in a 20-acre tract that was subdivided by

BASIC STRUCTURE

one of the older citizens and sold to them on a small payment plan. It lies outside the area served by the public utilities district, but water has been furnished them. There are, however, no sewers. The housing in this Negro community is the poorest in Wasco, few of the dwellings are painted, and none is of substantial size. Some of the Negroes and Mexicans in the district have stores and others have rent-houses for Negroes, but none is well off. Very few of the Negroes escape permanently the relief rolls. The Negro has his own churches, of which there are three, his own stores for immediate necessities, and even a civic organization. These represent some of the elements of internal unity lacking among the white outsider. There are also status differentials but the nature of these was not determined in view of the fact that the major problems here are concerned with the white group. A few leaders are well known to many white business men.

The Mexican lives in similar circumstances, with less clear social segregation and with more variation in living conditions. Many of them live in the Negro district, but there is an area in Wasco known as the Mexican colony. There are a number of stores operated by Mexican entrepreneurs, and one restaurant that is occasionally visited by whites. Though they do not have a church of their own, they remain fairly segregated under the Catholic roof. The unpainted barn-like building of a Mexican Pentecostal group still stands, but has not been in use for a year. The Mexicans, too, have enough civic unity to be able, for instance, to have a float representing them in the local parade, and there are status differentials among them.

LESSER SOCIAL GROUPINGS

In each of the social groups described there exist smaller units which are, however, of a different order. One is the family; the other is the clique. Of the family—the biological family consisting of a married couple and its dependents, usually children—little need be said. It is economically communal, sharing the profits of labor and the costs of living. With the highly developed tendency in the society to segregate social activities on both sex and age lines the family plays a relatively small part in the community social life, except for some families of German descent. The status of one member of a family affects that of the others: the school child may be an agricultural laborer's son and therefore is an Okie; the business man derives prestige from his wife's social activities; and the success of their children redound to the parents' credit.

The cliques are made up of persons of similar social background and tastes; they are, as one person put it, people who are "our kind." One clique may be clearly defined, another but vaguely, and always it is a highly fluid unit. An individual may have full membership or he may remain on the peripheries. Usually the members of a clique are in about the same economic circumstances and have about the same amount of prestige in the community. The primary function of the clique is to delimit the group in which the individual has social experience, where he derives the pleasure of belonging and associating with other beings. It supplements and often supplants the function of the family. Secondly, it is the group which determines the minor sanctions of social behavior, for the member will tend to behave according to the norm of his group on penalty of ostracism, while the person hoping to attain membership will conduct himself acceptably. The third function of the clique is to serve as a means of recognizing the social position and tastes of the individual members, because as their behavior tends to approach a norm, so the expectancy of that behavior can be predicted by the person less intimately acquainted. This is important in making proper adjustments upon social contact, and is necessary in a society where the norms of conduct vary as greatly as in Wasco.

Several factors operative in Wasco tend to segregate the individuals of each class into smaller units. One of the most important of these is his attitude toward drinking. One of the first things that the newcomer hears about Wasco is that it is divided between the drinkers and the non-drinkers. Such statements refer, of course, only to the nuclear group. Since the

BASIC STRUCTURE

clique is a unit for social participation, attitudes toward drinking are naturally important considerations in establishing membership, for drinking is a determinative of social behavior. Religion also tends to separate the population into smaller groups. There are many churches in Wasco, yet many attend no church. Since a congeries of taboos regarding social behavior are associated with religion, it is natural for the religious and the non-religious persons (or rather church-goers and persons who do not go to church) to find their social interests divergent. The religious group is re-divided by the different sects. This is in part because of the difference in status-level of the different denominations, and in part because the church organization itself presents the machinery for cohesion. Occupation is another factor in segregation. Farmers have in the past tended to remain separate from the townspeople, but this distinction is breaking down. The teachers and the oil workers tend to consort with their own occupational group. Clubs and orders in the community bring together individuals who have like social interests, and thus set up cliques. The tendency to age-grading is manifest in many aspects of the social pattern, and cliques are inclined to be unified by age categories. A set of young high school graduates can be distinguished from a group of pre-married and just married people; a group of mothers of young children can be separated from those whose children are well along in school. This age-grading is formalized not only in the schools, which separate classes by age, but also by many organizations which have special units for younger people. Where the family has remained strong, as with some of the Germans, it has the same functions as the clique, while family dissolution and age-grading are correlated social phenomena.

SUMMARY

Fundamental to the understanding of Wasco society is its division into two separate social classes: an upper one which has continued from pioneer days and has inherited the ties, institutions, and attitudes of the old community, and therefore forms the social nucleus; and a lower one which is made up of persons who have come to the town later, who do not have access to most of the older social institutions, and who therefore remain outside the normal spheres of community activity. This distinction transcends all others in importance with respect to social and economic behavior of the people themselves, and therefore is basic to an understanding of the social structure of Wasco. Each of these classes is, in turn, subdivided into more or less well-defined status levels with varying amounts of prestige. The nuclear group includes an elite, a middle group, and a marginal group which are generally differentiated by occupation and economic circumstances, and whose daily social and economic activities tend each to vary from the other. The outsiders are segregated first on a racial basis, with little or no social contact between the Mexicans, Negroes, and whites. The Mexicans and Negroes each have their own community with special institutions serving the group as a whole and some evidence of social solidarity. The whites, however, do not have any homogeneity, except insofar as it derives from the common effort to attain acceptance in the nuclear community. On this basis two levels of status may be seen, one with relative permanence and stability and another with no established ties whatsoever.

The rural community everywhere in America, as in human society without exception, recognizes levels of prestige and creates and maintains social distinctions on the basis of some calculus of personal worth. In Wasco, however, there is a very real difference in the character of the social structure from that more generally found in the rural communities where farming is not industrialized. This difference lies in two things. First, that social evaluations are made at such a social distance that symbols are used in the determination of social worth, rather than a true evaluation of the individual on the basis of personally known qualities. Thus occupation and the pecuniary calculus generally establish the individual's social standing, with a general tendency to class people accordingly. Second, the society is divided into two fundamental groups who, though they are mutually dependent, are in direct economic competition.

Between such groups there are not merely differences in social standing, but a lack of social contact, quite different modes of behavior, and most particularly great differences in natural economic interests. In these matters, social relationships are like those to be found in the cities rather than those of the farm community as generally known.

CHAPTER IV

SOCIAL STATUS AND SOCIAL EXPERIENCE

THE VARIATION in the social activities of the Wasco citizenry makes clear the necessity for a classification such as the one established in the preceding chapter. It is only by discussing them with reference to the norms for social classes that description becomes feasible. Conversely, the existence of norms for social groups substantiates the established categories.

By social experience is meant the gamut of activities which fill the lives of the people, and which they engage in together with other persons; patterns of behavior, established by cultural tradition, that serve to determine the individual's place in the social aggregate.

MEANS OF LIVELIHOOD

Seasonal Rhythm. The most compelling of the individual's activities are those devoted to the business of getting a living; for not only do they occupy a major portion of the waking hours of each person, but they are also indicative of his social status and his level of living. As a background to the economic activities of all and sundry, there is an insistent rhythm established by the march of the seasons which determine crop maturity, employment, and business activity in turn. The two major crops, potatoes and cotton, create a double beat to the annual cycle—a rhythm which should be briefly described.

In the winter, as the last of the cotton is picked and the cotton "bollies" (the cotton that is picked from the dried bush with the pod adhering) are being pulled, the cold rains and the tulle fogs settle over the countryside. This is a relatively dormant period, when the farmer is preparing his soil and doing the tasks that have accumulated during busier seasons. At this time there is plenty of work for the farmer and his regularly hired hand, but none for the seasonal workers; the merchants' business is slow; the town is dead even on Saturday night. Toward the end of February more and more tractors are crawling up and down the land, first preparing the long potato field and then sowing the potatoes into the ground and leaving the soil behind wrinkled in deep furrows. A few added laborers drive tractors or work in the sheds cutting the potatoes for seed, and business begins to pick up. During the "hundred days" in which the potatoes mature the cotton beds are prepared and the seed dropped in the trough of shallow furrows. The town remains quiescent; work is still scarce. Purchases are limited to the necessities, while talk of potato prices grows in pace with the vines. By the end of April the first shipments of potatoes are announced, trailer houses appear in empty places, and campers occasionally along the highway. The sheds along the railroad tracks begin to hum as the washers are put to work; the laborers in the field and the graders in the shed have money in their pockets. Saturday night becomes the active time it classically is in agricultural communities. Preachers exhort the public on the street; a roller-skating rink blares out canned music under a tent. The merchants remain open until late and look to this period as the key to their year's earnings. If potato prices are rising the car salesmen begin to seek out the farmers to discuss the merits of the latest model, while the farmer's face reflects a downward curve of the market. By the middle of July the potato digger has eaten its way under all the deep furrows and left the ground flat and firmly packed behind it. Labor demand drops off, the trailers disappear, and the farmers have a short vacation after the cotton is once more irrigated.

In September the vacation is over, the schools are busy, the two gins begin to hum as the trailers and trucks filled with cotton drive up to the scales. The town is again active, this time with less excitement over price, with not quite so many outside workers, and with a longer and slower pull to the end. The pickers go over the fields once, then again, and by the third time the year is over. Work drops off as the farmers contract for a few laborers to pull the "bollies." Most of the workers are out of a job and drawing assistance from one of the relief agencies.

The rhythmic variation affects the tempo of life of the whole community (Table 15 and Chart 3). Employment rises and falls

TABLE 15.—MONTHLY VARIATION IN STATE RELIEF ADMINISTRATION CASE LOAD IN WASCO AREA AND THE LABOR DEMAND FOR KERN COUNTY

Month	Case load		Labor required		Money order receipts	
	No.	Index [1]	No.	Index [1]	Amt.	Index [1]
January	1,215.5	1.47	361	.54	13,471	.98
February	1,292.7	1.57	186	.28	11,666	.85
March	1,197.4	1.45	318	.47	11,826	.86
April	1,039.3	1.26	386	.57	12,452	.91
May	739.0	.90	734	1.09	13,186	.96
June	471.1	.57	851	1.26	16,823	1.23
July	614.7	.75	464	.69	14,304	1.04
August	736.3	.89	637	.95	12,222	.89
September	681.0	.83	631	.94	12,213	.89
October	531.8	.64	1,556	2.31	16,002	1.17
November	510.7	.62	1,082	1.61	15,343	1.12
December	866.5	1.05	876	1.30	14,864	1.09
Average annual	824.6	1.00	673.5	1.00	13,712	1.00

[1] Relation of monthly average to annual average.
SOURCES: Case load for Wasco district, taken from SRA weekly report on applications and case load statistics (form 213-K). Labor demand from R. L. Adams, Agricultural Labor Requirements and Supply, June, 1940, Mimeo. Report No. 70, Giannini Foundation of Agricultural Economics. Money order receipts from records of the Wasco Post Office.

with the advent of the harvest season and the population increases and decreases. Relief rolls rise and fall conversely with them. Business activity similarly rises and falls in the same rhythm. But this is a pattern of intensity, for the actual work varies with occupation, which in turn expresses sexual, age, and

RECIPROCAL RELATIONSHIP OF RELIEF CASES TO FARM LABOR REQUIREMENTS

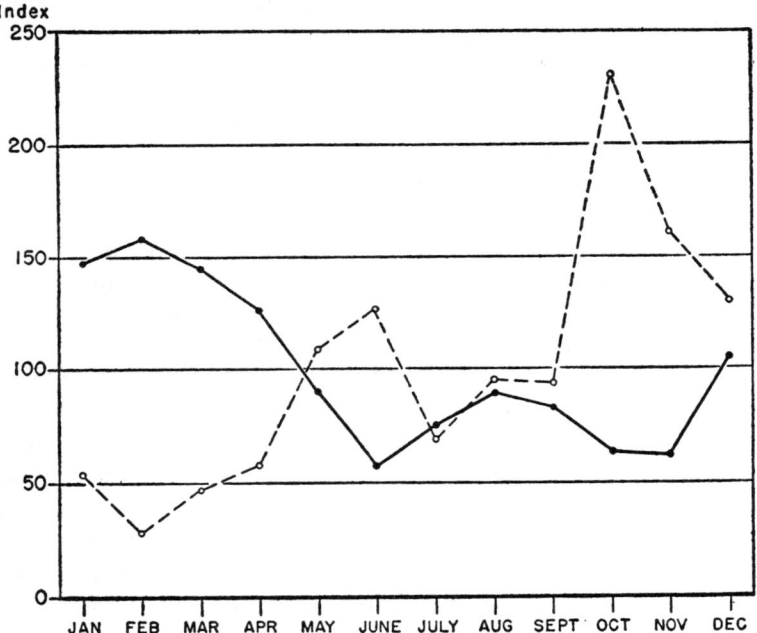

———— Average Monthly State Relief Administration Case Load Wasco Area, 1938–1940.

–o– –o– Average Monthly Farm Labor Requirement, Kern County (Index figures give relationship of monthly average to annual average).

SOURCE:
Case Load: Form 213K, SRA Weekly Report on Application and Case Load Statistics.

Labor Demand: R. L. Adams, Agricultural Labor Requirements and Supply, Kern County.

See Table 15.

CHART 3

social differentiation. The economic activities of the men can best be described in three categories: the farm operator, the business people of the town, and the farm laborers.

Farm Operators. The work of the growers in the above cycle is the most insistent and continuous of any. Every farmer declares that farming in California not only requires more ability than dry farming, but it also requires infinitely more work. Since most of them have at one time or another engaged in dry farming, and some quite recently, there seems no reason to doubt their statement. The farm operator is, after all, expecting a great deal in return for his work, and he conscientiously piles work upon work in an effort to increase these returns. Adages which suggest the insistence of farm work understate the reality; tractors driving through the night make working from "sun to sun" seem easy. Though field work is relatively slow in the middle of winter and for a few weeks in August, it never ceases. The pressure is relieved, and the hired hands are released, but there is always field work to be done and the operator remains to do it. A whole mass of socioeconomic forces make him want to increase his holdings, and with this increase the responsibility grows, the work grows, the tensions grow. Some producers have acquired farms which they feel are large enough, but most are still hoping and trying to expand. Farms of 160-200 acres are often considered the optimum size for it is large enough to require the full managerial ability of the owner, and also large enough to make the most of a full complement of power equipment.

The farmer of a forty-acre tract can do most of his own work other than the actual harvesting, except that he may require one hand to help him plant and irrigate. Any larger farm requires one man during much of the year, and farms over 120 acres require at least one and usually two hands hired all the year round. This means that the operator's time tends to be devoted more and more to managerial work, and the operator of two or three hundred acres, with perhaps a potato shed to manage as well spends almost all his time watching over the labors of others. The tradition of the dirt farmer remains, however, and the farm operator who is not in his field each day to direct activities is contemptuously referred to as "farming from the saloons." It is not without some satisfaction that operators are pointed out who delegate this managerial duty to others and are now losing their holdings. The large farms of a thousand or more acres are in a different category, because the managers are highly trained professionals, receiving good salaries. It is no hollow tradition, this insistence on the farmer remaining in contact with the soil, for the permanent labor hired at a hundred dollars a month on a straight salary basis can hardly be expected to be a first-class manager with requisite training and with his full interest in getting the most out of the soil. The tradition means, moreover, that when the managerial tasks do not consume the operator's time, he is actually on the tractor, looking to the pump, or doing other tasks which fill not only his day, but also his year.

The Townspeople. It is difficult, if not impossible, to find anything in the life of the business people of Wasco that is in any way unique. The mechanics and clerks go to work at eight and leave at five, a pattern measured by a raucous shop whistle. The salesmen wear pressed suits, the waitresses gingham dresses, the filling station attendants the company uniform. Many townspeople know their fellows by their first names and use them in ordinary business transactions—more than in the cities. But this in no way alters the nature of the business relationship; the car buyer and the salesman are as wary as they would be if entirely unknown to one another. And the first name acquaintance is not universal; the laborer remains outside this sphere of intimacy. There is probably a larger proportion of business proprietors in Wasco than in the city, but, as has already been pointed out, they are being crowded in many fields by chain operators and outside corporations.

The Farm Laborer. The economic activity of the agricultural worker is directly tied with the seasonal rhythm of the crops. The permanently hired hand receives from sixty to a hundred dollars per month, occasionally more, plus perquisites of an unfurnished house, space for a small garden, and sometimes gasoline.[1] For this he works at least ten hours a day, though the dairy farmers and some others require more. His work includes driving the tractor for preparing seed beds, planting and harvesting, irrigating, maintaining equipment, and sometimes acting as foreman. Some farmers feel that the returns for hiring a competent man, who can be relied upon in crises, are great enough to justify premium wages which may run as high as $135 (including perquisites), but most operators bargain more closely in the labor market, and $90 is generally considered good pay for all the services one man can perform in a month.

The seasonal employee is usually paid on a piece-work or hourly basis. In this way not only is the laborer's inefficiency accounted for in his wages, but also many of the labor costs of operation inefficiencies are passed on to him. Special skills or aptitudes earn a premium to the worker, and the person lacking them is at a disadvantage. It is for this reason that field operations requiring stooping are often segregated on a racial basis. The Filipino and Mexican, who after long years of practice have developed the requisite skill and stamina, are almost exclusively hired to thin beets and onions and to harvest lettuce. Other workers frequently state that they have had to abandon such employment as they could not keep up the pace set by the Filipino. The operator would be willing to give such employment to them, as the pay is on a per-acre basis.

The potato crop is harvested on an assembly chain pattern, and the industrialized nature of this operation warrants a full description. The potatoes are planted in broad ridges separated by deep furrows which serve for irrigation. The mechanical digger is drawn by a tractor, and consists essentially of a blade which cuts under the ridge, a belt which carries the potatoes up and separates them from the dirt, and drops them back on the earth, and a roller which tramps down the bed so that the potatoes lie on top of the soil. The potato picker wears about his waist a broad belt to which are attached hooks. On these he impales the number of sacks which he will need in order to

[1] These wage figures, and all subsequent ones, are based upon 1940-1941 data. Obviously great changes in income have occurred due to wartime labor shortage.

complete his "space." Each picker is allotted a certain space of from thirty to sixty paces along the row which he must harvest before the digger returns on its circuit. His work consists in filling the sacks and setting them in a row. The normal field employs about 24 such hands when a single-row mechanical digger is used. About every fourth or fifth circuit of the digger a truck comes to pick up the sacked potatoes. A crew of four swampers and a driver load the truck as it moves down the row and hauls the potatoes to the shed. The potatoes are then dumped into a bin feeding a chain which carries them through the washer. They are automatically graded by size, but eight or ten women "grade out" the potatoes which have been burnt by the sun or affected by blight or rot. The chain carries the potatoes to the sacks in which they are to be shipped. These are filled and weighed by the "jiggers," then sewed and hauled to the cars. Table 16 shows the workers required, the mode of

TABLE 16.—WORKERS, WAGES, AND LABOR COST OF POTATO HARVEST OPERATIONS, 1940

No.	Type of work	Wage scale	Wages per man-day	Cost per day
48	Field operations [1] Pickers	35¢ per hr.	$3.50	$168.00
4	Tractor and digger operators	40¢ per hr.	4.00	16.00
	Shed operations			
10	Swampers	9¢ per ton	5.40	54.00
9	Graders	50¢ per car	4.00	36.00
2	Dumpers	65¢ per car	5.20	10.40
2	Jiggers	65¢ per car	5.20	10.40
2	Sewers	65¢ per car	5.20	10.40
2	Loaders	65¢ per car	5.20	10.40
2	Side men	65¢ per car	5.20	10.40
				$326.00

[1] Two field crews operating for one shed crew.
SOURCE: Verbal statement of active potato producer.

payment and the labor costs of the operation given by a successful grower who has his own shed. Variations in yield, grade, and wages affect this setup.

This operation covers four acres on each of two separate fields with a normal yield of 300 sacks to the acre, working a ten-hour day. The labor cost of $326 per day for harvesting the crop suggests the importance of hired labor to the farm operator. Timing is a very important factor in the harvesting of Wasco potatoes as they may be spoiled by a short exposure to the sun, while delays add to the labor cost. In this operation the grower's full day is devoted to non-farm activities, largely managerial or administrative. The operator who furnished these particular figures also hired a "row boss" to supervise field activities and act as timekeeper, and had a special agent to handle sales.

The assembly-line aspect of potato harvesting is not duplicated in the cotton field. These pickers follow along the rows filling long canvas bags. These are then weighed and the weight recorded either on a ticket which is given the worker, or in the timekeeper's book. The cotton is hauled to the gin in trailers where it awaits being processed, and where it passes out of the farmer's hands.

The tasks these workers perform are hard, and working under pressure in a temperature normally around 100° F. requires real stamina. There is no wonder that many of the less hardy workers prefer to remain on the public welfare rolls as long as possible, thus bringing on the virulent censure of the nuclear population. Some of the work, like the sugar beet thinning, requires a kind of suppleness that is foreign to the muscular habits of the white worker. Perhaps the surprise expressed by one of the members of the elite is justified. "The marvel has been that they will work at all, getting only a little more than they did on relief," he said. "It is something that I didn't expect with this changing of the social order." The workers in the field feel that the forty cents an hour rate is good wages, and with two members of the family working, the eight dollars that they make each day suffices for their physical, if not their social, needs. The difficulty is not insufficient pay, but under-employment. In Wasco there are only two periods when labor is needed in large quantities, and even at these times there is an oversupply of workers. During part of the year the laborers move out of Wasco to work fields that mature at times when work is scarce in Wasco. But this moving is costly, often requiring double rent payments, large gasoline expenditures, and the added cost of living on the road. The worker frequently has a regular work connection in a distant town, but this does not prevent him from being without work much of the time, even during the season of general employment. Almost two months after the potato season had opened, a number of laborers with good work connections in Wasco had had only fifteen to twenty days of employment.

The worker employed on a monthly basis is better off in that he has a fixed income, but there are only a few such jobs, and since they pay less per day than seasonal work, and since it is often impossible for the wife to work, the difference is not very great. To this must be added the fact that most workers in Wasco employed on a so-called permanent basis do not have employment security, and the worker who has sacrificed the higher seasonal wage rate during the harvest period, still fears being laid off during the slack season (Table 11). This is not conducive to stability or the interest in workmanship that the farmer wants.

Women's Work. The work of the man, whatever his class, is theoretically that of providing the necessities and luxuries of the family; the woman's job is to care for provisions once they have been brought into the household. This fundamental sexual division of labor, though not sanctioned through any express tabus or elaborated beliefs, is maintained in the thinking of the people even to a greater degree than it is actually practiced. For although the woman has entered into the field of man's activities and the working wife is accepted without question in Wasco society, the man has been reluctant to take over any of the household duties. It is woman's work to prepare the food, keep the house clean, wash and repair clothes, and care for the children. Frequently she manages all the affairs of the household, making purchases and keeping accounts. We may divide the women into three groups: those who work only in the home (found in every class), those who work as clerks, teachers, or in some other business enterprise (predominantly in the middle nuclear group), and those who work as agricultural laborers (outsiders only).

The majority of the nuclear group women who are married do not engage in any remunerative occupation but devote all their energies to attending to the household, and their spare time to recreational activities which also serve to establish and maintain the social position and relationships of the family. The business of keeping house requires over half of the woman's time, sometimes virtually all. But the definite trend away from large families, the absence of any gardening or other outdoor chores, and the possession of mechanical devices which simplify household tasks, all serve to give the woman more and more freedom from her primary economic function (household duties), to devote to her secondary one (acquisition of status through social participation). These observations apply as much to the wives of farmers as they do to the women of the town, but not to the farm laborers.

There is no loss of status through the woman's working if the job itself is not "degrading." It is the norm for unmarried women who are no longer in school to work for a salary as office or sales help, and some women have become entrepreneurs. Though there is a tendency for them to stop working after marriage, many of them continue at their occupation, at least until they have children. This means that the new family will have more money at the expense of operational efficiency and ability to engage in the normal leisure-status activities of the women. The important point is that there are no direct pressures brought by the society on the women, the choice is made on the basis of personal predilection and the evaluation of the social and economic results. Very frequently the wife of a small entrepreneur will assist her husband in his business, sometimes to keep books and more frequently to help during rush hours or to relieve him for lunch. The farm wife rarely helps her husband in farm work, and rarely has a garden to tend, so that much of the traditional drudgery of the farm wife no longer exists.

The outsider wife either works in the fields or potato sheds with her husband, or she is busy maintaining a household. Very

TABLE 17.—ECONOMIC ACTIVITIES ACCORDING TO STATUS AND SEX

Social status		Men	Women
Nuclear group	Elite	Farmer devoting almost all time to managerial activities Corporation executives and a few successful entrepreneurs Professionals	Managing household usually with maid or part-time paid assistance Much club work, entertaining, and cultivation of leisure-time activities
	Middle	Farmers hiring labor most of year Professionals, especially teachers Salesmen, clerks, technical and other white collar workers Skilled laborers and some semi-skilled workers such as school custodians, mechanics, and oil workers	Housekeeping, rarely with help Often working for wages or to help husband in business Church and club work important
	Marginal	A few "worker-farmers" Most semi-skilled laborers like bus drivers, mechanics, etc., and some skilled laborers	Keeping house is major task Church work may be prominent but little formal club work or entertainment
Outsiders	Permanently employed	Agricultural laborers, dairymen, general hands, tractor drivers, irrigators, occasionally harvest-crew foremen	House work, with occasional gardening or chicken raising Sometimes work in fields during harvest
	Seasonally employed	Harvest hands and seasonal workers as required	All housework, rarely a garden Often works alongside of husband in field

rarely she works as a maid, for but few women in Wasco have assistance in their household, and when they do they usually prefer a Mexican or Negro woman. As an agricultural worker the woman has exactly the same duties as her husband, and is working at the same time that he is. This means temporary curtailment of all possible household activities. It means that children of about ten years are expected to care for the house or trailer and their younger brothers and sisters, while the older children often help in the fields. If they are too young to be allowed to work according to law, they may assist their parents in small ways. Very frequently pre-school age children are seen in the field, alternately playing and helping their parents.

The economic activities of the several social groups have been summarized in Table 17.

ECONOMIC NEIGHBORHOODS

The neighborhood has a special place in American society. Rural sociologists have shown that in many farm areas the people living within a small area tend to have such a degree of close association that the neighborhood forms the major social environment for the individual.[2] In the cities, however, the neighborhoods tend to have an economic basis. Rather than representing an arena for social action, the unity of the neighborhood in an urban environment generally develops in response to economic pressures. Even where they are unified by common racial and national backgrounds, the economic pressures have generally been responsible for the appearance of unity. Such economic neighborhoods are familiar in every American community, which has its "wrong side of the tracks."

The neighborhood in Wasco conforms more to the urban than the rural pattern. Those who dwell in the open country rarely show any special degree of association with their immediate neighbors, but seek their social ties on the basis of common interests. There are no rural schools or open country churches which might serve to bring people from a particular section together. The absence of barriers to communication—of breaks

[2] Charles H. Cooley in his *Social Organization* cites the neighborhood as a primary group—that first group beyond the immediate family in which the individual is socialized. Based upon his conceptualization, sociologists have been able to delimit areas of close social interrelationships (cf. J. H. Kolb, *Rural Primary Groups, A Study of Agricultural Neighborhoods*, Research Bulletin No. 51, Agr. Exp. Station of the Univ. of Wisconsin, Madison, 1921).

in the continuity of farms by hill, wood, or stream—deprives the area of a natural basis for delimiting such groupings. Some neighborhood action was found in one area, where the flow of a stream affected the water table and created a particular economic situation which gave a common interest to the neighbors. Some of the neighborhood activities went beyond this common interest. By and large, however, little evidence existed of specially close interrelationships among farmers based upon nearness.

In town, neighborhoods are clearly economic. A drive through the streets immediately reveals the dilapidated Negro quarters, the impoverished Mexican section, the area built up by migrants from the dust-bowl, the residential area of the elite, and areas of intermediate or mixed status. Table 18 shows the occu-

TABLE 18.—OCCUPATIONAL CHARACTERISTICS OF THE WASCO VOTING PRECINCTS

Occupation class	Proportion of voting precinct						
	I	II	III	IV	V	VI	VII
A. Professionals, managers, and proprietors	28	28	27	24	10	8	3
B. Farm operators	7	2	2	2	1	4	1
C. Clerical workers	18	12	13	12	8	8	1
D. Skilled laborers	37	39	43	49	46	36	11
E. Unskilled laborers	10	19	15	13	35	44	84
Total	100	100	100	100	100	100	100

SOURCE: Tabulated from voting registration sheets, 1939. Based upon 1,760 persons listed, of which 1,131 were classified by occupation. The remainder were chiefly housewives.

pation classification of voting registrants of the precincts. Such voting units do not conform to the boundaries of economic neighborhoods, but the table reflects their effect. Voting precinct I which includes the best residential district, shows fewest laborers and most in farming and white collar pursuits. Precincts II, III, and IV are in mixed areas. Precinct V includes the area of settlement of migratory workers, and this is shown by the proportion of laborers tabulated. Precinct VI includes the Mexican colony and VII the Negro colony. This last precinct conforms most closely to economic boundaries, and therefore the high proportion of laboring people is most accurately reflected.

The pressures forcing segregation are made on an economic basis, but that does not belie their essential social motivation. The Negro and Mexican are forced to live in their own neighborhoods, and while such direct pressure cannot be brought against white unskilled laborers, the economic pressures can. Land titles often contain restriction clauses which effectively maintain the quality of the districts, and these clauses are enforced by the neighbors, as was witnessed when a permanently employed laborer tried to build a modest house in one of the areas restricted by contract clauses. Land values express this social differentiation of the neighborhoods.

Such neighborhoods have little social cohesion. Social contacts are not set within such neighborhoods, and there are no formalizations of the neighborhood as a social unit. Primary group relationships in Wasco—that is, the social group in which attitudes and behavior are established—are not based upon such geographical units, but rather on common interests which derive from similarity in age, marital status, morals, and recreation habits.

THE EDUCATIONAL SYSTEM

The schools are the major public institution of the community. They serve not only to educate the young and to inculcate in them the mores of our society, but they form the major integrative force in the community. By mandate they are all-inclusive, bringing the young of every race, creed, and economic status together. It is the single institution which brings together people in Wasco irrespective of race or status. And if the schools fail completely to integrate the social classes into a true community, they serve this end far more than any other institution.

At the time Wasco was settled and for 20 years prior there were two or three single-teacher schools in the area. Since 1908 the school enrollment has increased steadily until in 1940 the average daily attendance reached about 1,400. This growth is presented graphically in Chart 4. The plateau on the Chart shows that Wasco had achieved its agricultural growth in the middle twenties, after which no more large tracts were broken into small farming units. The sudden upswing in the curve coincides with the influx of laborers who came to California in search for employment and settled in the community as shown on Chart 2. The last five years brought an increment of 70 per cent in school attendance.

The increase in enrollment was accompanied by an increase in plant, and as early as 1929 the half-million mark was reached in school property evaluation. Soon after the establishment of the colony in 1907 a grammar school was built. A high school was started in 1915 and by 1917 the first unit was built. Building after building has been added, the most recent acquisition being a junior high school, administratively a part of the elementary school. The high school has an elaborate auditorium, a well-equipped gymnasium, and a football field with lights for night games.

The school system has suffered some change in status during its history. An early high school principal was a community leader with a firm conviction of the value of "cultural" as opposed to "practical" education. He was responsible for the construction of the auditorium which is unusually lavish. He stressed the arts and classical languages at the expense of commercial and agricultural courses. He likewise insisted that the teachers become integral parts of the community. They were encouraged to join the best clubs and attend the elite church. Since his departure these activities are not emphasized, and some teachers report actual discouragement of such participation. Newer teachers do not join and older ones drop out. Fewer teachers are now church members, and they tend to develop fewer ties within the community and to maintain social interests outside the community. Men teachers are becoming more numerous. They generally participate in community affairs in

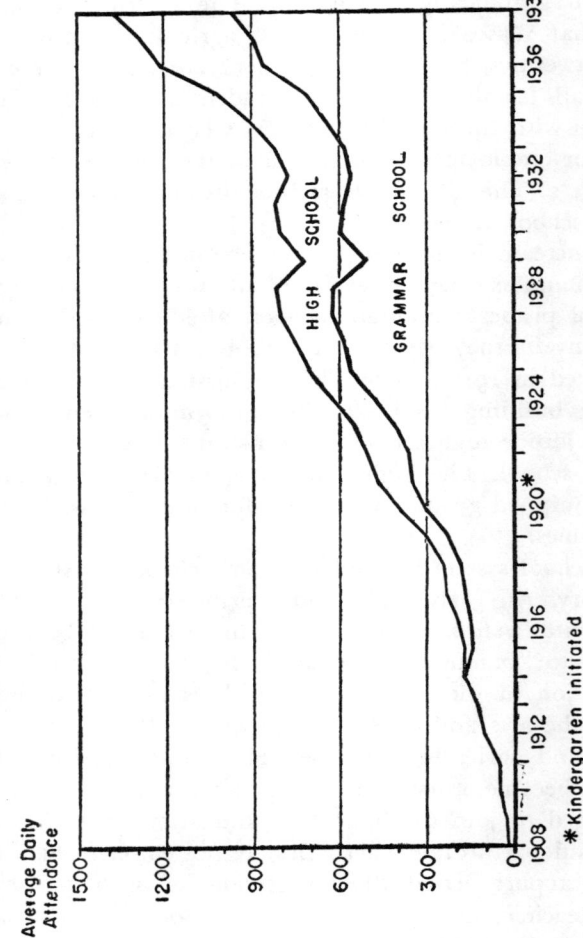

close association with the business men. Along with this shift in the status of teachers has come a new emphasis on education for livelihood, though the two facts are not necessarily associated. In part both reflect the interests and attitudes of the later school principals, yet both changes conform to dominant social opinion.

The schools, it must be recognized, are subject to two dominant direct influences. On the one hand, they must conform to the county and state patterns for schools, for they receive county and state funds and are integrated into the state-wide system. They must maintain certain records, conform to certain standards, and include certain prescribed courses. The community also has influence over the operation of the schools. School boards are elected for the elementary and high school, and these exert influence over the school chiefly in two ways: determination of expenditures and hiring of teaching staff. The democratic processes make it possible for the citizen to have an appropriate measure of influence over the schools and the education of the young. That this measure of influence resides largely in the nuclear group is shown by the fact that no laborers have ever been elected to a school board, and by the real fear shown over the threat that such a representative should be elected. This is discussed in a later section. There appears to be a reluctance to grant permanent tenure to teachers. Very few in the high school are granted a permanent right to their job. State law provides for automatic tenure after a period of teaching in elementary schools, but the school board at one time tried to insert a waiver of tenure in teacher contracts.[3] Such reluctance to grant permanent tenure appears to reflect a desire to maintain firmer control over the school.

Teachers in general bring their behavior into close conformity with the moral strictures established by the more conservative elements in the community. Public acknowledgment of smoking

[3] The following appeared in the minutes of the school board: "Board discussed matter of teachers who will become permanent. Stated tenure will not influence Board in the matter of discharge. Those who will become permanent will be asked to sign agreement to resign at the end of any term at the pleasure of the Board."

is avoided by women teachers and drinking by both men and women. Among a growing number of women teachers, social life is largely carried on outside the community.

While there is evidence in testimony that the teacher has lost status in the community, the school remains the most important single institution in the eyes of the citizens, whatever their walk of life. The quality of buildings and grounds and of the facilities made available at the schools appeared to be a point of personal pride among numerous people in the town. The quality of the schools is the most cogent argument for the existence of a strong community spirit, just as the school serves as a major integrating force in the community. The emphasis such references generally receive indicates that the quality of the building and the availability of equipment are more important to the citizenry than either quality of teaching or breadth of education. Since Wasco had swung away from a period of "cultural" education, the emphasis upon practical courses at the expense of language, history, and arts is understandable.

The student entering high school makes a choice between one of five programs of study: College preparatory, agriculture, industrial arts, home making, and commercial. College preparatory courses conform to the standards of the state institutions of higher learning and include four years of English (two each of grammar and literature), two years of mathematics (algebra and plane geometry), two years of history ("world" and United States), at least two in one foreign language, and a variety of courses ranging from mechanical drawing to "social problems." The other programs of study are far more specialized, requiring four years of English and one each of mathematics, social studies, and United States history. Other subjects, outside the special field, are elective. Four courses are given in agriculture, all of which the agriculture students take. There are nine commercial courses, six home economics courses, and five industrial arts classes.

In an effort to determine what schooling meant to the students who were enrolled, certain school forms were examined. Since the Wasco school did not utilize this form, those from a neighboring high school were used. Among other things this form inquired: What kind of work would you like to do after leaving school? What kind of work will you probably be doing? Name the three types of employment you are most interested in. The answers to these questions were not kept separate, since they are, in essence, the same question. The accompanying tabulation shows the answers, taking for each student each answer that fell in a separate category. The occupational background of this group of 94 students appears in the right-hand column which gives employment of that parent who had the socially highest classification of occupation. The answers were given in more specific terms and represent a wider array of answers than appear on Table 19. Most frequent among boys were "mechanic"

TABLE 19.—EXPRESSED OCCUPATIONAL AMBITIONS OF HIGH SCHOOL STUDENTS [1]

	Boys	Girls	Total	Occupation of parents [2]	
				Number	Per cent
A. Professionals, managers, and proprietors	22	13	35	3	3
B. Farm operators	10	0	10	19	20
C. Clerical, etc.	6	18	24	3	3
D. Skilled laborers	29	11	40	20	21
E. Unskilled laborers	3	0	3	41	44
F. Unemployed, unknown	5	15	20	8	9
G. Aviator or air stewardess	14	3	17	..	...
Total	89	60	149	94	100

[1] Obtained from farms at a neighboring high school. Responses to questions: "What kind of work do you want to do after leaving school? What kind of work will you probably be doing? Name the three types of employment you are most interested in." Personnel inventory taken from entering Freshmen; 94 questionnaires (58 boys and 36 girls) were analyzed and multiple responses counted separately.

[2] Where both parents work, or where one parent carries two jobs, highest ranking position was selected.

SOURCE: Personnel Inventory, neighboring high school.

(18 instances), "aviator" (15 instances), and "farmer" (10). Among girls (who more frequently refused to make a choice) was stenographer or secretary (13). Five wanted to be hair dressers and 6 wanted to be home makers. Only one boy and one girl wanted to be a "business" person. Authors, actors, veterinaries, baseball players, missionaries were all represented.

Table 19 shows clearly the desire to achieve higher status, yet the limited nature of these ambitions is also quite apparent. Children most frequently wanted to have occupations other than their parents whether the parents were high or low on this scale. For instance, only 4 of the 19 farm boys wanted to be farmers. Though the answers tabulated here show the undesirability of farm labor as an occupation, they show that freshman students are not heavily aware of the lesser social distinctions which mark the levels of local society. A similar set of statements from seniors might be revealing but unfortunately were not available.

Social democracy is not perfect in Wasco schools, but it is far greater than in any other area of life activities in the community. We have already stated that the schools are the major integrating force, and it is this measure of democracy that makes them so. There have been efforts to segregate the Negroes or the migrant workers, on the basis that they are poorer students, but such efforts have never succeeded, and all groups mingle together. Negro-white clashes have been reported, but they are not frequent. The different groups tend to maintain their own social interests, but segregations of this kind are not rigorous. Teachers report that the tendency for nuclear children to keep the outsider away from social activities has diminished. The successful migrant football player is a strong democratizing influence, and at least one such boy came after early rebuffs to be accepted at parties of the nuclear students as a result of his athletic prowess. For the general group in high school, segregation roughly along class lines as already defined was found, but there are more opportunities and successes in breaching these class lines than is found in the community as a whole, and class strictures are diminishing.

SOCIAL LIFE

It is in the leisure-time activities that the most significant variations occur with respect to the social divisions, for it is in these pursuits that social status, social membership, and invidious social distinctions can best be expressed. For, while the Wasco citizen is steeped in the philosophy of personal freedom of choice, he recognizes the compulsive force of the job he has to do, the control of the "boss" and the necessity of "making a living." On the other hand, he is rarely aware of the social pressures which mold his use of time not spent in the pursuit of a living. Occasional references to the oppression of social duties and compulsions to engage in certain types of recreational activity indicate the existence of social forces which are only dimly recognized as such by the citizenry.

The leisure activities of Wasco may be brought under two headings, social recreation and commercial entertainment. These are very different in character and in social implications. The one implies group activity and social participation, the other means individual activity without social ties. The one is local, indigenous not in the sense of originating historically on the spot, but having its source with the people of the community. The other is imported from outside. The one may be considered rural or small town, however much it is patterned after city behavior, the other is entirely urban. Above all, the social recreations are almost exclusively for the nuclear group and tend to solidify that group, whereas commercial recreations know no class lines.

ORGANIZED SOCIAL RECREATION

We may say, then, that the social recreations involve group participation, create a sense of belonging, delimit social groups, and give prestige to the participant. They are limited by class lines and status barriers, and, in fact, there is a dearth of such forms of recreation among the outsider class.

Associations in Wasco. The clearest exemplification of the status activities is expressed in those sponsored by the various formalized organizations such as the commercial clubs, the women's organizations, and the secret orders, to which we must first direct our attention. The associations or clubs of Wasco may be divided into three categories with respect to their major orientation. The first are those created to further common socioeconomic interests: the service clubs, occupational organizations, such as the P.T.A., Farm Bureau, Associated Farmers, and the moribund Agricultural Workers' Union. The Grange, though a secret order, fits this category better than any other. Likewise, the American Legion is a sufficient social force as an action group to be included here. The second are the organizations which are purely socializing in character. The women's clubs, the secret orders, and the social organizations in connection with the churches exist primarily to promote and institutionalize certain forms of social intercourse. The third category is the club oriented around some hobby or game, and includes the golf, camera, rifle, and card clubs.

Status Differential Among Associations. The first thing to note about the clubs, whether it be the most exclusive organization or the theoretically all-inclusive Parent-Teachers Association, is the practically complete absence of agricultural or other unskilled workers, as well as of members of the minority races. Data are presented in Tables 20 and 21 and in Charts 5 and 6. In short, the clubs serve as an instrument for organized social action and activity within the nuclear group, whereas they do not serve to bring the nuclear group and the outsider together. This thoroughgoing class limitation on club life means that the outsider group does not participate in any of the socioeconomic activities which are the province of club organizations, thereby depriving them not only of a sense of belonging, but also of any voice in social controls and pressures exerted by the clubs.

Not only do the clubs express the distinction between the nuclear and outsider social classes, but also each expresses its own level of status within the community. This status level is determined by its membership composition, and is maintained, on the one hand, by limitations on that membership and, on the other, by certain forms of prestigeful social activity. Thus, of the three service clubs (I, II, and III of the Service and Spe-

SOCIAL STATUS AND SOCIAL EXPERIENCE

TABLE 20.—OCCUPATIONAL CHARACTERISTICS OF TWELVE SELECTED ORGANIZATIONS IN WASCO

Occupation class	Men's orders		Service and special interest					Women's clubs				Recreation	Total
	I	II	I	II	III	IV	V	I	II	III	IV		
A. Professionals, managers, and proprietors	46	25	94	54	78	31	39	79	48	23	40	47	45.6
B. Farm operators	16	8	3	15	11	7	13	14	21	39	6	5	15.5
C. Clerical workers	14	12	0	31	2	21	5	7	7	2	33	16	8.9
D. Skilled laborers	23	25	3	0	9	38	35	0	21	32	21	32	25.2
E. Unskilled laborers	1	30	0	0	0	3	8	0	3	4	0	0	4.8
Total	100	100	100	100	100	100	100	100	100	100	100	100	100

SOURCE: Data obtained by interview and from membership rolls. The number of members of known occupation were, respectively: 70, 24, 37, 26, 66, 29, 283, 14, 118, 82, 52, and 19.

TABLE 21.—PROPORTIONS OF OCCUPATION CLASSES BELONGING TO ANY CLUB OR CHURCH [1]

Occupation class	Voting registrants	Club membership		Church membership	
		No.	Per 100 registrants	No.	Per 100 registrants
A. Professionals, managers, and proprietors	231	374	161.9	169	73.2
B. Farm operators	197	127	64.5	221	112.8
C. Clerical workers	130	73	56.2	84	64.6
D. Skilled laborers	491	207	42.2	285	58.0
E. Unskilled laborers	482	39	8.1	174	36.1
Total	1,531	820	53.6	933	60.9

[1] Each member of family is included in occupational class of its head, therefore it is possible to have more than one church membership per person among farm operators. These figures cannot be taken as literal representations of membership, but only for their distributional value.

SOURCE: Data on occupation and membership obtained from membership rolls and by interviews.

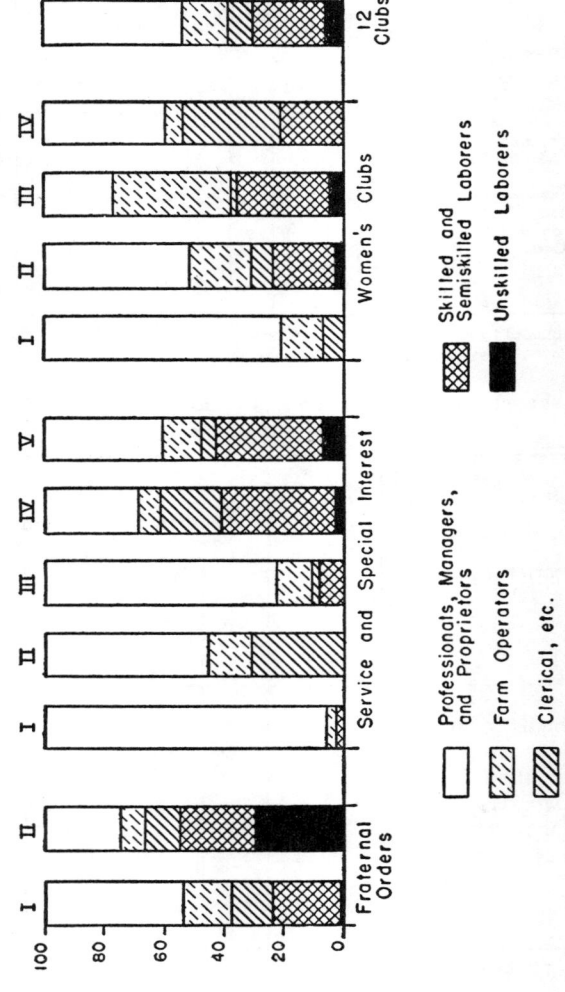

CHART 5

NUMBER OF CLUB MEMBERSHIPS PER 100 PERSONS REGISTERED IN OCCUPATIONAL CLASS

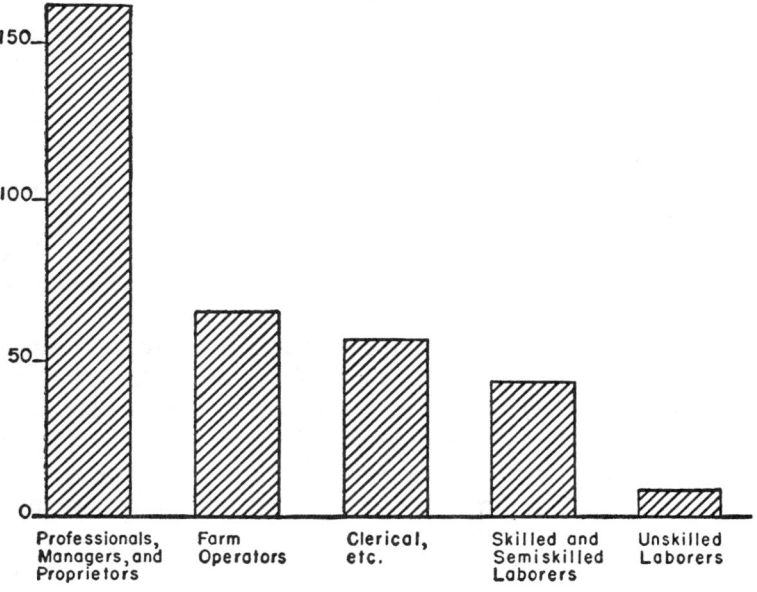

SOURCE· Table 21.

CHART 6

cial Interest Clubs in Chart 5), the first is the oldest; it meets at lunch time which requires freedom from economic pressure in the midst of the day, and it is made up almost entirely of the managerial-entrepreneur-professional group, including most of the managers of the big corporations. This is the most exclusive of the clubs, carrying more status than the other two. Number II is almost as old, has much of the same membership but many others as well, and serves especially the needs of the smaller merchant class. It maintains none of the trappings of prestige, meeting in the evening in a public building, and having a membership open to all business people, including farmers. Consequently belonging to this organization carries none of the subtler status connotations but denotes rather membership in the nuclear element of the community. The third service club is new and very active in sponsoring civic projects. It is made up almost exclusively of small merchants and assistants in larger organizations. Its evening meetings suggest less freedom of movement. The membership composition is thus more strikingly different than Chart 5 indicates, being made up of small shopkeepers, such as barbers and butchers who were "overlooked" by the older organization, yet anxious to participate in service club activities.

Recent changes in the existing women's clubs are suggestive of some of the social changes that have taken place. Since the early twenties, there have been two women's clubs (II and III in the Chart), one made up mostly of the women of the town (II), the other of the women of the open country (III). As the membership of each grew, the town-country division became less sharp. It was recently decided that two organizations were unnecessary, so they merged. While remnants of the old cleavage remain in the internal politics of the club, their unification shows the similarity in leisure activities and social values between town and country women. Meanwhile, a separate club has been established for the women under thirty (IV), splitting the group on an age basis. At about the same time a new club (I) of very small membership was formed, representing a select group of old Wasco residents, thus separating a group purely on a status basis. This club was organized after the clique had been established and it not only maintained a closed membership, but also included only persons who were "permanent" residents, thus giving specific expression to the status value of length of residence.

The secret orders likewise represent different status levels. Club I, for instance, has no members of the outsider class, while many belong to the other organization. Almost all the corporation officials belong to the former, while none is a member of the latter. The distinction was recognized by an officer of the latter group when he stated that his organization was "less exclusive." Another person made the statement that it would be impossible to become a high school principal without membership in the former order. Such a statement in itself suggests the social potency of the group, whether it is actually a true statement or not, and would never be asserted for the second organization.

The hobbies, games, etc., of the amusement clubs are forms of leisure activities and, therefore, in themselves express economic status. Except for the fundamental dichotomy of the social classes, they do not, however, give expression to the levels of prestige within the community.

Individual Status and Club Activities. If the clubs have varying status levels, and the individual gets prestige through membership, this is not to imply that all members of the club have identical social position. For the club frequently serves as a social matrix wherein the individual attains membership in the group and status in the eyes of the community. Conversely, persons of more or less standing in the organization have more or less control or influence over the club's activities.

It is only in the meetings and other activities of the various clubs that the citizens of Wasco regularly congregate in large groups as participants, and it is through these activities that the individual becomes generally known to the community. This function is recognized by the newcomer to the community, and several women expressed their indebtedness to the club to which they belong, as it enabled them to "get acquainted." Its importance to women whose economic activities are more confining and who, at the same time, have more free time for social activities is clear. Yet there is recognition of this need by the merchants "on the street." This necessity is, in itself, a departure from the pioneer community. There remains a tradition that the women of the community call on any newcomer, but in practice it is rare, and apparently has been for many years past. In short, the former small town technique for bringing the stranger into the social life of the community is almost defunct, and the club supplies its substitute.

Social participation for many residents, old as well as new, takes place in the club environment. Consider the account of one person who participated in the founding of the women's club. Her testimony to the importance of the institution runs as follows:

> I had been raised to believe that if a woman did nothing more than make a home, her life was a failure. And living out on the ranch I got terribly lonesome. So I took all the magazines I had and all the roses and drove our Cadillac around to the homes of different people. They never asked me in, but just asked how much I wanted for the roses and magazines. They never had anyone come to their doors except peddlers and salespeople. There were more neighbors then than there are now [that is, smaller farms and more closely settled farm homes]. One day there were several women together at my house, and I had organized entertainment and refreshments for them. We had such a good time that we decided to get together regularly, and we finally decided that we would form a club, and meet every two weeks, as that would be a relaxation from the daily drudgery of farm work. Club-work had been my life back East, so naturally I wanted to have a club out here. I never would be president.

Membership in associations may come to form a social environment in which a person can exercise his special talents. Playing bridge, reading and reviewing books, acting, handicrafts are all social assets which may operate through a club not necessarily given to that single activity. They therefore not only serve as recreation, but give the individual a personal sense of accomplishment and recognition among his fellows, and at the same time enrich the life of the community. Such special talents may substitute for financial status in establishing the individual within the nuclear group or some particular segment of it. One woman, speaking of her special talent, recognized it as a surrogate for wealth:

You might say that this group represents the cream of society. Most of the women are pretty well-to-do. I don't really belong with them, but then I felt that it would look funny for me to drop out. I can't keep up with them—clothes, and entertaining and all—but I suppose I give something else. I just have to look at it that way. They have promised not to make a great deal of the entertaining, but you know how those things are.

Her activities were not unique. At one time the rivalry between two women for social standing within the community was said to revolve about a certain special talent, and each set herself up as an expert in that field. Neither woman had an economic status that would assure social acceptance, but each had achieved a large measure of status in the community.

The formalization of social acceptance implied by club membership and participation can have a strong effect on the individual personality. It was said of one woman that her personal frustrations were resolved through active club participation: "She fussed with her husband all the time till she became a club member, but now everything seems to be all right in her home."

The social function performed by the formal organizations must be understood in reference to the social structure of the community and the social desires and ambitions of its people. It will be remembered that Wasco society is divided into two groups, one of which includes all those who participate in social organizations, while the other includes only persons who remain outside of such activities. The former is, in turn, divided into three separate levels of status, which must be recognized as rather fluid groupings between which social relationships are not barred. Among persons falling in the marginal level, participation in the clubs and organizations offers public evidence of acceptance in the nuclear group of the community. For persons of middle standing, active participation becomes a means of asserting and advancing in social status, while among the upper stratum, the social organization is a matrix for social leadership. Those persons whose top standing in local society is beyond cavil need not participate in clubs of the kind that are available to all of nuclear society, and when they do, they will frequently give it only perfunctory attention. The members of this elite in Wasco can be assured their status with respect to other members of the community, but they characteristically direct their social attentions to a wider community such as the elite of the county. In this environment their status is no longer to be taken for granted. One such person, for instance, had a party for city guests rather than participate in a general community festivity. Thus what is the desideratum of the lower group, and the framework for social expression of another, may be disdained by a third.

Clubs and Civic Action. The club, then, becomes at the same time a criterion for social status and a matrix in which status advances can be made. It will be well to describe some of the outward aspects of that club life. Most of the energies of most of the clubs of Wasco are directed toward maintaining the club's existence (elections, etc.), or its recreational activities. But the leading non-fraternal organizations maintain a tradition of public works which lends them prestige in the community, and causes them to serve as more or less powerful pressure groups.

The minutes of the meetings of one of the special interest clubs were examined for a period covering one year, and approximately three-fourths of the items recorded during that year had to do with the business necessary to the continuation of the organization and its recreational activities. The remaining fourth had to do with maintenance of a few civic activities; namely, bringing pressure to bear upon the construction of a highway underpass, arranging for the establishment of a Boy Scout troop, objecting to the existent cemetery district, furthering a volunteer fire department, participating in community charities, and aiding in the creation of a community baseball league.

In general, the business of the service clubs is conducted by the board of control or similar body vested with authority, while the meetings are devoted chiefly to entertainment. Yet a certain amount of business is transacted at each meeting. The several service clubs are asked to express their views on matters of general public concern, and it is not only interesting but also very significant that the assumption is made that their views express those of the community. In regard to the reorganization of the cemetery district, the district trustees serving the county asked the several clubs to vote on the matter, so that they could be "guided by the voice of the people." Wasco was not incorporated and therefore did not provide regular elections to serve this purpose. It has since been incorporated. The three clubs, representing only the business element, were considered a sufficiently accurate sample. And sufficiently accurate it is, within the accepted point of view of the social boundaries of the community. The same attitude was exemplified when one service organization sponsored a public discussion of city incorporation. There were neither Mexicans, Negroes, nor agricultural workers present. The vote of this group was considered sufficient to express the attitude of the people.

Insight into attitudes regarding the rights of various persons to participate in community affairs was gained from questions raised at the meeting and in conversations after it. One farmer felt that he should have a right to vote on the matter of incorporation because he owned town property, though he did not live in the area. Another questioned whether a person might vote if he did not own property in the proposed area of incorporation. That this was assumed to have reference to members of the outsider group was apparent from a conversation with a local merchant who was in favor of the issue. He said: "That is a foolish question. Of course, it doesn't seem right for these people who just come here for a little while and who don't have any real interest in the community to vote on questions pertaining to it—these Okies for example. But then, it's in the constitution, and has been a principle of our government for a long time." In discussing the failure to get a representative group of people out to decide on community problems, one of the leading corporation representatives expressed the dominant point of view. "Yes," he said, "what this town needs is a good active Chamber of Commerce." Thus firmly entrenched is the presupposition that the business people and the community are one and the same; that an interest in the community means a vested economic interest only.

Just as the club is used to determine public opinion, so it is a means of influencing public policy. Since the town is unincorporated and relatively few matters are determined by vote of the local populace, the clubs exert a not inconsiderable influence upon community activities. If a recreational project is undertaken, if a new civic enterprise is desired, if a change in existing public or private services is wanted, the service and civic clubs are utilized as the institutional mechanism through which these things are accomplished. And since membership in these clubs is highly selected not only on the basis of income but also of occupation, the direction of the public activities are highly selected on the basis of economic interest.

Similarly, the club is an instrument for the formulation of public opinion. The tradition of the regular speaker of the meeting lends itself naturally to a discussion of matters of public policy, and the use of the club as a means of influencing public opinion is readily recognized. For instance, attitudes regarding *The Grapes of Wrath* were crystallized in a speech at the leading service club, and the vituperation against the book was echoed by persons who heard the talk or read of it in the local paper, but who had not read the book itself. More subtle and probably more penetrating than the formal talks are the effects of crystallization of opinion regarding Federal controls, taxes, unions, foreign governments, and other matters external to Wasco itself, through the informal discussion at the dinner table. In a social environment selected for common economic interests the prejudices and points of view of the members receive the moral support of group sanction. And since, in the dominant club at least, the leadership is in the hands of the representatives of outside corporations, the direction of these prejudices are not determined solely by the problems of the local community.

Community of Interest and the Geographical Community. In Table 20, showing the occupational characteristics of the club memberships, it was made clear that the organizations represent largely the business and professional groups in the community, and that the laborer has virtually no voice in the club life. In short, the club does not represent the geographical community, but merely a segment of it, selected on an occupational basis. We have pointed out that the club is a vital influence in community activities. Because of these factors, it is of extreme importance that the club is rarely a purely local product, but represents a continuum of interest and has direct connections with the outside world. Every club and order of major importance in the community is either a chapter of or an affiliate with some general national or international organization. This means very simply that the institutional machinery of the non-governmental socioeconomic activities bring together not members of a geographical segment of the social universe, but a class segment determined on occupational-economic lines. The visiting banker has entree to the dominant clubs of the community to which the local agricultural worker does not have access.

Here the significance is apparent when we contrast the service clubs of today with the original organization established by the colonists just a single generation ago. The old Improvement Club was established to determine the policy of the settlers with regard to a community fund that had been created by the system of land allotments. This club, and the first women's club as well, were organized for the purpose of determining specific policies regarding local problems, more especially such problems relating to the development of agriculture as crop research, rabbit destruction, and, above all, water supply. Though there were differences of economic interests which were expressed in heated debate in meetings, there were no exclusions from participation. Furthermore, the club was a local growth, meeting local problems. Briefly, it was community in character, including all white residents (racial barriers have always existed) and excluding all outsiders.

This is simply a reflection of the situation of the time, for Wasco was then a small group of farmers fighting for subsistence, with no room for class differentiation, no large labor group, and, above all, a set of common enemies against which united action was possible and necessary. In the space of a third of a century a shift to the opposite pole is evident, with the virtual exclusion of labor from community participation, and differences between labor and management as the major source of the breach in the society.

The Club Meeting. We have discussed the socioeconomic

aspects of club life at length because they furnish the institutionalized mechanism for most social activity within the community. They establish class lines; they are determinative of social position within these class lines; they present the matrix for social action, prestigeful, economic, and political. Perhaps a simple description of the nature of club activities can present more concretely these social facts.

The members of a leading service club foregather in front of the dining hall and engage in small talk, shaking the hand of each newcomer and greeting him informally. As they file in, each selects the badge with his name, business, and nickname, and takes his place at the table. After the "Star-spangled Banner" is sung, they sit down. During the meal there is goodnatured banter and small talk about events of the day. It is tabu to address fellow members by their surnames. A breach of this tabu is punished by a ten-cent fine, and in the course of the dinner a dozen or so members have been fined on this pretext or some other. This money is raffled at the end of the meeting. By these trivial techniques, an atmosphere of comradery is created which is intended to induce a spirit of good feeling among these business rivals and associates. One cannot escape the observation that this performance acts as a form of ceremonial license to divest the members of their normal social attitudes of self-interest. Toward the end of dinner, business is introduced. "President John," says a corporation manager, "a member of the cemetery board of trustees asked me to get the voice of the club before deciding what action to take in regard to the re-formation of the cemetery district." There is confused discussion ending in a vote, which, as already stated, is taken along with that of a few other clubs as the public opinion regarding the matter. After the ice cream, a speaker is introduced, and perhaps a visiting member from another town says a few words.

The women's clubs have their own meeting house, and usually gather in the mid-afternoon. Their meetings, far from fostering an environment of informality, are conducted along rigorous parliamentarian lines, in itself a form of ceremonialism. After a pledge to the flag and recital of the motto, there follows a regular business meeting, according to the procedure set forth in Robert's *Rules of Order*. Rarely is there any business not connected with the club's own activities, though these clubs occasionally take part in community matters. After the business has been conducted, the meeting is turned over to the program chairman, who has arranged for a talk or some other form of entertainment.

This may be considered the general pattern for club life in the community, though the smaller clubs tend to hold less rigidly to the formalization imposed by Robert. Patriotism is a frequent keynote; sentimentalism often evidenced. Welfare work, such as the making of layettes, individual charity, such as the giving of Christmas candies, provide the semblance of meaning to the club's existence, but merely camouflage the major functions already defined.

Age-grading and Sex Division in Club Life. We may note also an incipient tendency toward age-grading and sexual dichotomy in the clubs; a tendency which correlates with the divergence of social interests along these lines, and with the failure of the family to provide the major outlet for social and recreational activities. Thus in Wasco there are a women's club and a men's service club for adults under thirty, while the children are, of course, separated on a rigorous age-grade system by the schools. The same applies to the religious organizations and other large clubs, which usually have their young people's groups. Similarly the fraternal orders have "women's auxiliaries," while all the major clubs are rigorously divided on a sex basis. Sex and age segregation not only serves to keep persons together who are of like tastes, but also eliminates intra-organizational rivalry between these groups. It effectively gives women and young people a means of expressing their status drives in a society where age and sex traditionally carry certain prerogatives.

THE CLIQUE

Though the club serves as the institutionalized framework for much of the non-economic activity in the community, it is too large a unit for the everyday forms of social recreation. For these there is a smaller and more natural unit, the clique. The clique may be defined as a small group of persons who, from personal choice, congregate for most non-economic and unformalized social activities. The club is, as a rule, too formalized, almost always too large, and frequently must include persons of divergent tastes and attitudes, to furnish the truly sympathetic and intimate group. Hobby clubs and special sections of the larger clubs could perform these functions, but essentially they are aggregates formed out of special interests, and not from the general interests which characterize cliques. Terming the cliques natural and saying that they are the result of personal choice does not deny their social implications, but asserts them. They are "natural" in the sense that they develop out of socially conditioned predilections and prejudices and not out of artificial or legalistic barriers. They are not merely fortuitous. The racial and class segregations are immediately apparent. The tendency to form within age levels is also obvious. The most elite group includes people of middle age with grown children; another clique consists of married couples, most of whom have young children; there is a "gang" of boys out of high school that congregate at one of the restaurants. Above all, the clear tendency to congregate into economic status levels prevails. The wives of the managers of two large corporations and of a leading farm operator form a small closed group. A group of seven couples—five corporation officials, an entrepreneur and a cattle rancher—forms another. The most elite women's clique in town has formalized its group by establishing an exclusive club (and becoming part of a national order). But even within this group of fourteen women there is at least one clique made up of the socially dominant few, women who shop in the city, who keep horses, and maintain other forms of leisure-class conspicuous consumption.

The groupings on a status and tabu basis are the closest social units beyond the family. They replace the neighborhood as a social entity, for the prevalence of the automobile has made space obsolete as a criterion for social relationship. They have taken over the function of socializing the individual to the minor overtones of community life, for in them are carried out the major portions of the non-economic forms of social intercourse. The community as such has largely lost its power to establish sanctioned forms of behavior, except through its legal machinery. The churches fought school dances and the use of liquor, but the outside world has been too much with them. The Protestant churches can still maintain a tabu on dances, the theater, and drinking, but they cannot make of these the basis for social acceptance, since other social groups exist which tolerate these forms of behavior. The religious neighbor who pries into the affairs of a drinking person can be told off without loss of social or economic position. This is not to deny the existence of a sense of belonging to the whole community—that is, among the nuclear group—but merely that the community has ceased to function as a selective agent for particular forms of morality. There is some evidence that a new morality is set by the community, but this does not emanate from the church.

Different cliques are generally recognized by members of the community, but no one knows all that exist, and since they are highly fluid groupings, it would be artificial to attempt an enumeration. The clique serves, however, to establish the social position of its members, not only with respect to status values, but also with respect to their moral predilections and social behavior. Though it is impossible to assert that no cliques exist within the outsider group, it is quite apparent that the outsider has relatively few such social units other than among the church members. All the agricultural laborers interviewed denied having any regular coterie of friends or pattern of visiting relationships, except one group of interrelated families, and the members of the strictly outsider churches.

COMMERCIAL ENTERTAINMENT

The commercial entertainments of the small town differ little from those of the city, from which, in fact, they are imported. Status, social membership, and prejudice appear only on the fringes of the activities associated with these forms of leisure-time pursuits.

The Motion Pictures. The motion picture may well be considered the most important commercialized entertainment on the Wasco scene. The single theater is operated by a small syndicate, showing three separate bills and usually five separate "feature" pictures each week. The pictures include the latest and best from Hollywood, as well as thriller serials and Westerns. These latter are shown on the week ends, presumably because they appeal to the children who should not be kept up late during the week, but also because they appeal to the laborers. The local manager made the statement that many of the outsider group would ask if the picture had any shooting in it, and would not see a show that had none. One of the syndicate officials stated that most of the patrons were of the laboring class, and if this is the case they are apparently as willing to see the most publicized pictures as they are the thrillers, for the most popular pictures of the year 1940-41 include only so-called "class A" shows.[4] The theater takes the general point of view that it is not responsible for the moral welfare of the people, and books its pictures insofar as possible on the expectancy of returns at the box office. The local women's organizations protested the showing of *Of Mice and Men,* but there is no organized means of restraining the theater owner. In this instance the operator refused to comply with the request because of the investment he had already made in booking the film. The show was censured on the basis of alleged immoral precept which would have a bad influence upon the children, and the operator took the point of view that the parents were responsible for their children's attendance. There was no community protest against the showing of *The Grapes of Wrath,* which deals more directly with the local problem of farm labor, and this picture was, along with *Gone with the Wind,* the best attended show of 1939-40. Many objections to the portrayal of farm life, however, were received from the people.

[4] The theater manager listed the following as best at the box office: *This Thing Called Love, Philadelphia Story,* the *Hardy* series, *Road to Zanzibar, Love Thy Neighbor, Return of Frank James, Western Union, The Westerner* (the last three are class A Westerners), *Foreign Correspondent, Buck Private, In the Navy, High Sierra* (gangster), and *Knute Rockne, All American.* These thirteen are selected out of a total of 312 shows in the year ending August 1, 1941. The theater owner did not divulge attendance figures.

Probably the most reliable source of information regarding the distribution of the use of the movies as a form of entertainment can be obtained from the Consumer Purchases Study, which shows from 84 to 90 per cent of the population attending, according to the various occupation groups, for village and country people in the Pacific area. There is more variation with income, yet in the lowest income bracket 70 per cent of the families indicate some attendance. Furthermore, approximately a third of all expenditures for recreation of families of all occupation and income classes are spent on the moving picture, more than on any other single item. Table 22 shows that this form

TABLE 22.—RECREATIONAL ACTIVITIES OF RESETTLED MIGRANTS IN KERN COUNTY (8 COMMUNITIES)

Nature of recreation	Number of responses	Proportion of families [1]
Moving pictures	73	40
Radio	53	29
Social functions (schools, churches, etc.)	54	30
Outings	47	26
Reading	50	27
Visiting	37	20
None or very little	28	15
Other	32	17

[1] Proportion of families in sample responding specific item of recreation; many gave more than one response.

of recreation was most frequently reported by migratory laborers in Kern County.

A questionnaire taken from a sample of the population in Arvin and Dinuba shows a similar dependence upon this type of recreation. Three-fourths of all families reported some movie attendance, with weekly or even more frequent attendance. One-fourth of all families reported that motion pictures formed the sole recognized form of social recreation. All occupation groups attended in great proportions, but the laborers generally are more dependent upon this recreation than are other occupation groups.[5]

The theater, like all the forms of commercial entertainment, does not serve to unify the participants in the way clubs do. Nevertheless, the proximity that results from group attendance violates the sense of social segregation sufficiently that the managers find it desirable to separate racial groups. Such segregation cannot apply to the white agricultural laborer, for obvious legal and social reasons, but the minority groups of outsider status—Negro and Mexican—are expected to sit in a special section.

The Radio. The social impact of the radio is similar to that of the motion picture. The radio is a completely external form of entertainment requiring no social participation, having no differential with respect to social class, and affording vicarious participation with the outside world. According to the advance releases of the Consumer Purchases Study, 93.7 per cent of the California farm families and 92.4 per cent of the Pacific village families had radios in 1936. In the survey made of resettled migrants, the radio was second only to the movie as a stated form of entertainment among this group, approximately a fourth mentioning it as a form of recreation.

Reading. According to these same schedules, reading is almost as important an item in the recreational activities of the resettled migrant group. Among the nuclear population, reading must be very much more widespread as is indicated by the magazine stalls and the library records. Magazines are more frequently found in homes than are books. According to one merchant dealing in magazines, the women's journals, especially the *Woman's Home Companion* and the *Ladies' Home Journal* are the most popular, but it must be remembered that the trade in pulp magazines is divided among innumerable different titles. This dealer handled forty-four detective and adventure titles,

[5] See chapters VII and VIII for a discussion of recreational activities in Arvin and Dinuba, the other two California communities studied. These aspects of social life are presented in detail in the final report on the study of those two towns (see footnote 1, chapter VII).

fourteen love-story magazines, and eleven movie magazines, practically all of the pulp class. Another form of reading has pervaded the school age population, the comic-book magazines, of which some eighty titles are handled. One merchant maintained he sold six hundred of these magazines per month, each of which is regularly traded among the children. According to teachers, these magazines satisfy the reading desires of many of the students, even in high school.

A major source of recreational reading is the local branch of the County Library, which had a circulation of about 30,000 books in the year ending June, 1940. The increase in circulation in the past decade has not kept pace with the population increase, and this may largely be accounted for by the fact that the outsider group does not utilize the library to the extent of other classes. Table 23 shows only one unskilled laborer using

TABLE 23.—OCCUPATIONAL CHARACTERISTICS OF LIBRARY SUBSCRIBERS

Occupation class	Number of borrowers	Proportion of users	Users per 100 registrants
A. Professionals, managers, and proprietors	181	25.7	78.4
B. Farm operators	50	7.1	25.4
C. Clerical workers	87	12.4	66.9
D. Skilled laborers	270	38.3	78.0
E. Unskilled laborers	116	16.5	24.1
Total employed	704	100.0	46.0

SOURCE: Kern County public library records.

the library for each four registered as a voter, compared to 3 in 4 of both the professional-entrepreneurial and the skilled labor classes. It is interesting, however, that farmers and farm laborers show about the same proportion of users. Furthermore, agricultural workers frequently mention reading books their children bring home (not included in this count of users). However, it must be remembered that a larger proportion of farmers vote, and that these figures show only readers per voting population. No investigation has been made of the selective factor of books used, except that fiction is by far more popular than nonfiction.

Within the nuclear group there is a clear prestige value in owning books, and some of the middle group and elite are subscribers to book clubs, buying books they frequently do not read. But, for the most part, books other than occasional gift copies and the Bible are rarely found in the parlors, whatever the social status. The prestige value of intellectual interests is even better exemplified by the existence of a reading group. A former teacher, an exceptionally widely read person, started a class made up entirely of women of elite status in the community. In her own words, "I had a class of women who wanted to learn things, and they let me do the reading for them. . . . I had to be pretty careful about politics. . . . Last year we studied world history from 5000 B.C. to the World War. Of course, we never got up to the war. This year we are studying absolute monarchs, people like Caesar, Jenghiz Khan, etc. We are making it a practice to do our own study work these last two years. I thought it best, for they had gotten in the habit of being dependent."

Other Commercial Entertainment. There are in Wasco several establishments where drinking, pool, cards, and dancing are made available to the general public. One bar, in conjunction with a hotel, offers dancing and occasional traveling road shows, and caters to the business people from nearby cities, as well as to the upper brackets in the local social hierarchy. Here the differentiation is on a purely status basis, that is, not merely racial. This was exemplified by a recommendation voiced by the patrons that the place charge more for drinks "in order to keep out the riff-raff." Two other bars are attended by local citizens of good standing. One of these offers cards, the other dancing. Neither has the prestige of the first, but both are regularly patronized by the business people. Two bars are run in connection with pool halls and operated by a local entrepreneur in conjunction with establishments in other towns, and card games are in progress much of the time. Much of their clientele is made up of laborers. There are also bars in outlying districts, which are frequented mostly by the farm operators. The Mexicans and Negroes have several separate bars or stores where liquor is available. Public drinking and gambling more than other commercial forms of entertainment follow the major social cleavages, though the nature of the business enterprise makes this an imperfect separation.

Other forms of commercial entertainment are the temporary shows, carnivals, etc., that pass through the community. A traveling skating rink is set up during the busy season; various clubs sponsor professional shows and carnivals, sometimes as methods of making money, sometimes for the prestige value of the production.

The processes of urbanization in the field of leisure-time pursuits are taking place in several ways. The commercial entertainments are the imported products from the city, and play the same role with the same impersonal atmosphere of similar establishments on the urban scene. The social recreations segregate the social classes, serving to develop internal bonds within the nuclear group and to establish the exclusion of the outsider. At the same time they establish formalized connections with persons of similar status outside the community, and in this way negate pure localism as a basis for social attitudes and actions.

CHAPTER V

SOCIAL STATUS AND RELIGIOUS LIFE

CHURCHES AND THEIR APPEAL

"The churches in Wasco tend," according to the minister in its leading church, "to represent the different elements in the San Joaquin Valley." Such a statement leads us naturally to a closer scrutiny of the position of the church in the social hierarchy. The church—at least the Protestant church—is as much a social institution as it is a religious one. When a resident decides to belong to a church, and when he selects the denomination to which he will adhere, he makes a fundamental social choice which will affect his associates and his social behavior for the duration of his residence. And his choice is as much influenced by social considerations as by religious ones. Because the church plays an important social role—one of the most important of any institution in community life—it must be subjected to careful analysis. The value judgments made with respect to these institutions are evaluations of their social position and do not reflect upon their religious tenets, which are outside the province of this study. Nor is there any implication that congregations elsewhere have the same relative social position that they display in Wasco.

There are ten Christian churches for whites alone in the community, not counting a small Mormon group and the one or two unorganized religious groups which meet in private homes. Besides these, there are three Negro organizations and there was at one time a Mexican Pentecostal group. Before examining the nature of social separation of these denominations, it will be well to acquaint ourselves with the variation in religious content of some of the more important Protestant sects serving the whites of the community.

The first church in the community has a moderately elaborate structure surrounded by shrubs and lawns, with a special recreation room, and an air of middle-class well-being. It is the congregation of the elite. Its leading patrons are select, even among this elite. Its services are quiet and orderly; its sermons innocuous admonitions to moral conduct, or intellectualized explanations of the workings of God with man. It is said that an earlier minister left at the behest of one of the leading contributors because he preached the doctrine of equal rights, co-operative activity, and sharing of wealth. The sermon is preceded by a fixed ritual, including music by a vested choir, organ accompaniment, and the funereal hush of the carpeted and insulated edifice. Lay participation is hardly more than in the Catholic ritual, two or three hymns and the reading of the responses constituting the whole. To this service the congregation takes its obligation lightly; rarely are there more than two or three dozen well-clad substantial citizens present. Communion with God may be had or left, as the spirit moves, so long as the appearances of membership are maintained.

Coming down but half a step, we may place two or three congregations on a social level, the differences between them not being those of social status. Comfortable, unelaborate structures, completely adequate in size to meet the requirements of the congregation, house the religious services. The sermons are more fervid, the spirit is less subdued, and the lay participation is more spontaneous. Correlatively the congregation is more active, the pews are more nearly filled each week, revivalistic meetings are undertaken, and the emotional appeal of Protestantism more manifest.

These congregations endeavor to bring together persons from widely different walks of life. Their success has not been great among the outsider group, yet they are not entirely without representation from farm laborers. The influence of social factors upon church affiliation is illustrated by the case of a person of Mexican ancestry who has succeeded in becoming identified with the nuclear group in the community. This shift not only involved acquiring a white-collar job and marriage outside the Mexican group but also the rejection of the Catholic church, to which most Mexicans in Wasco belong, in favor of a Protestant congregation. According to several statements, teachers formerly considered it incumbent upon them to affiliate with the social elite church in the community, but now readily join either congregation at the next level or none at all. While this is a form of emancipation from social pressure, it is also significant that this change is associated with the general lowering of the social status of the teachers as a whole, who are no longer exhorted to attend church and take part in club activities, but appear to be discouraged from the latter.

Stepping down once more in the social scale, we arrive at the level of the revivalistic churches. The buildings compare favorably with the preceding churches; they are newer, but not quite so nicely designed, so carefully finished, so well appointed, nor so centrally located, lying rather in the poorer sections of the community. The preachers are graduates of religious colleges but not graduates of general schools of higher learning. Informality may be considered the keynote of the services; for want of better clothes the congregation is modestly clad, the services are filled with colloquial expressions and homely illustrations, the participation of the congregation is easy and unselfconscious.

The emphasis on personal salvation and the intellectual-emotional appeal to the personal experience, following the pattern described in the Bible for the night of Pentecost, are not the annual or biennial expression of an itinerant evangelist, but the week-by-week fare of the Sunday services, heightened by the temporary elaboration of the revival meeting. The nature of the appeal of these sects and the spirit of their meetings can perhaps be caught in a sermon, and for that reason one is reproduced here very nearly as it was presented. For background, it may be added that this sermon was accompanied by the "Amens!" of the audience, as well as the presence of twisting and crying children and the informality of persons entering and leaving the congregation.

You know, folks, the other day, I was visiting some friends of mine on a farm back East. I took a couple of days off and had a visit with some people. The farmer asked me if I had ever seen a mechanical corn-picker, and I said I'd like very much to see one, for I never had. Well, he got out his tractor and rigged up the corn-picker. It had some boards to the side, set together about an inch or two apart, and the stalk went between these and they just lifted the corn off the stalk and a belt took it back and put it in a wagon that followed. That was fine, but I still wasn't convinced, and I asked my friend what they did about stalks that were blown down, and he laughed, and said that they had taken care of that. They have experimented and bred for years and they have gotten a pure bred corn that will stand up. It sends its roots way down in the soil, and the wind can blow and the rains can come, but that corn stalk stands right up. The farmer pays twice as much for that corn, because it is pure bred, and will stand up no matter how hard the wind blows.

What we need is more people that will stand up. We need to have people who are firmly rooted in their faith, and when the winds of adversity blow they stand right up to their God. We need real blue bloods. You know, a lot of people think that blue bloods all live in Kentucky, but the real blue bloods are those who are firm in their faith. You know there are plenty of blue bloods in the church, for in heaven everybody is a blue blood—no matter how poor you are.

Well, I just got off on this story. The collection is taken, and so you won't have to pay an extra dime for it.

[After a reading from the Bible] So no man can know when Judgment Day will come. There will be nothing different in the air, there will be no signs to show that Judgment is coming, one hour or one day or one week or one month before Judgment Day.

[The story of the flood was presented] Nobody paid any attention to the warning, for they were all living a life of sin. They ate, they drank, they married and gave in marriage, the night before Judgment. There was no difference between the night before Judgment and the night before, or the week before or the month before.

Abraham was willing to leave Egypt when God told him to. He didn't say he was too old to be moving. He didn't say, "You can't teach an old dog new tricks," and refuse to go. He went out to the promised land. Abraham later left, and went to Egypt. He said that the grass is greener over there. But he should have stayed and prayed the rain down from heaven, and made the grass green where he was. The same is true of the people in the church. They should go to their own church to pray, and not go to another one because it is doing better.

Abraham divided the land with Lot, saying there is enough for all of us in this wide world. And Lot went into the valley, and Abraham into the mountains. It is good to go into the mountains once in a while, and be alone, and pray, where the filth of man does not keep God away.

And three spirits came to Abraham, and he ran out to meet them, for he recognized them, and he welcomed them into his house. He didn't have to go to Sarah and tell her to put these cards away, and to hide that bottle, and to get rid of those *True Story* magazines. They may be true stories, but if they are, I'd pray to God that I could forget it and that He would forgive me. Amen, brother, amen.

The Lord decided to tell Abraham what He had planned, and He stayed behind after the others left. He decided to tell Abraham, because he managed well his household. Note that, he managed his household WELL. His daughter didn't manage his household, his son didn't, but Abraham managed his household. The son didn't come home at 2 A.M. and then when his father said, "Get up, go to Sunday school," he didn't answer, "No, I don't want to." He probably took them behind the woodshed. The woodshed is a fine place to learn things—more is learned there than at any college. Maybe the methods of impressing aren't the same, but you learn there. I remember the lessons that I learned behind the woodshed—and they didn't hurt me any, I don't seem so bad off.

About two years ago I visited in the home of a deacon, I won't say where, but it wasn't in California. The son came in and said, "Give me the keys. I want to use the car this afternoon." The deacon handed over the keys, and said, "Where are you going?" The son said, "I'm going to the movies with some friends. By the way, give me some money." "Well," said the father, handing over some money, "come back early for I want you to go to the young people's meeting." Why, that boy shouldn't pollute the church with his presence, after going to the movies on Sunday afternoon. Before I'd let that boy go to church, I'd scrub him good and clean with soap and a scalding bath, and I'd have him pray for about two hours, to get that filth off of him. And I'd take that deacon, that would let his children act that way, behind the woodshed. And I'd take his deaconship away from him.

Abraham tried to get the Lord not to bring destruction upon Sodom and Gomorrah. He asked the Lord if He would leave the city if he found fifty righteous men. Then he asked forty-five, then forty, and so on. He jewed the Lord down till He was willing to have ten good men in the city. He must have been counting—there's Lot and his family, and there are almost ten, right there.

The Lord went to Sodom and called on Lot. Lot wouldn't let the Lord sleep in the streets, for he knew the corruption of the people in the city. He made Him come into the house. The Lord told him what He planned, and Lot went to his sons-in-law, and to the people. They just laughed at him. They said, why Lot has been out to visit that crazy uncle Abraham out in the mountains, and he has been talking again. They ought to lock him up. And the people tried to get the angels, but the angels brought Lot out and with his wife and daughters.

They led them out of the city. And as they walked away from Sodom, Lot's wife said, "I have to look back. All my friends back there, that I will never see again." "The Lord said that we must never look back." "But our friends are back there. We used to play a few innocent hands of bridge, and have such good times together." And she looked back and was turned into a pillar of salt. But Lot did not look back.

You have it better than Lot's wife, for you have a chance to repent. She would have been happy to repent a million times over, but the Lord didn't give her a chance to repent, nor did He give the fallen angels a chance to repent. But, you, my friends, can repent now, before it is too late.

And the day before Judgment was no different from any other day. They were not able to notice any difference between the day before Judgment and the day before that, nor the week before that, nor any other time.

The son of Nebuchadnezzar was drinking wine, and he ordered that the great chalices of some temple be brought in, filled with wine, and they all drank from that. God saw this, and He sent a warning—just the handwriting on the wall, no arms, body, or anything else. They were all afraid, as all wicked people are of supernatural things. They called in the fortune-tellers, and all the people who thought they might be able to read the handwriting of God, but none of them could. Finally, the king's wife said that she knew a man of God who might be able to read, and they brought David out from the dungeon. God always has somebody in the gap, so that the people had a warning. David wasn't afraid to tell the king that his kingdom would perish and that it would be divided between the Meads and the Persians— he wasn't afraid to tell them, though he had been brought in from the dungeon. And the next day one in every two was taken away.

And the last night before Judgment was like all the rest. It was no different from the day before, nor the week before, but was like all the rest.

After the sermon was over and the prayer offered, while the choir sang "Almost Believing," the evangelist came through the audience, and spoke to each man separately. Meanwhile most of the congregation went forward to the altar and were kneeling and praying, each aloud and for himself. The evangelist put his hand on each man's back, drew each to him insinuatingly, and asked them in a lowered voice, "Have you been saved? Don't you want to be saved today? It would be terrible to have to face Judgment Day without being saved, wouldn't it? Why wait, why not come up now?"

This sermon may be taken as a typical, though somewhat highly organized, example of the appeal that the churches on this level make to their audience. The major theme presents clearly the familiar fear psychology appeal for adherents based upon the threat of eternal retribution, plus the salesmanship technique of "act quickly, limited offer." If we examine some of the asides we glean still more of the special aspects of the appeal the institution has for its followers. Note first the homely quality of the illustrations, the corn-picker, the references to bridge, to the woodshed, to those familiar items of family quarrels, car keys, and the movies. Above all, we have here just an aside, a reference to the dominance in the hierarchy of values in the putative society of the Kingdom of God: "The real blue bloods are those who are firm in their faith." "In heaven everybody is a blue blood—no matter how poor you are."

This revivalistic religion has direct emotional appeal for salvation; it is presented in the homely fashion of the layman, and individual participation is heightened not only by Amens and much singing but also by shouted prayers, each person to himself. Still, as we shall see shortly, it is far more subdued than the schismatic churches. Its appeals are not pure release; there is a direct call to the reason. The individual does not merely shout his woes publicly; he is exhorted to make a rational choice, within the frame of reference that has been set.

Here, then, is a homier atmosphere for the people who have been accustomed to attending church "where you're just raised up among folks" and "you could go [dressed] any old way," and, as will shortly be shown, it has drawn many from the established churches. The special appeals of the homier atmosphere and the lay participation draw heavily on that part of the population whose ties are with the churches which in Wasco are serving the nuclear class. In their social aspects, rather than in the special sectarian tenets, lies their particular attraction to this group. This has been forceful enough, not merely to catch a few strays, but to create a major shift in church participation.

As between one and another of the denominations which are on this same level, there is little to choose, and consequently no major shift has been observed. As between the belief in the ability to talk in tongues and the rejection of that belief, little in itself can affect the ordinary layman to whom the refinements of Biblical interpretations and theological philosophy are of minor concern. The ministers of these churches themselves treat lightly the existence of the different sects, comparing the situation to that found with commercial services, where personal whim leads to one or another grocer, and where space limitations require multiple gasoline stations. In part, this negation of sectarian differences is an attempt to create the illusion of unity with the churches on a higher social plane. The seminary ministers are quite conscious of the social distinctions between congregations; they minimize the agricultural labor adherents on the one hand, and the sectarian differences on the other.

The schismatic Pentecostal church represents a still lower level on the scale of formality, a higher one on the scale of emotional appeal. The small frame building housing this group stands in an outlying section of town. Inside there is ample evidence that "people living in tents would not feel uncomfortable." The pews are unfinished benches, embellished with the carved names of the bored unimpressed. Behind the altar the choir is seated on similar furniture and on the wall behind them are religious pictures, an electric sign advertising the young people's association and another proclaiming "Jesus Saves." A flag, a calendar, and other embellishments further relieve the dirty blue walls.

The services are conducted by a "brother" who "swamps" on a potato truck during the week. On one Sunday there were not over twenty persons, mostly women above forty, but some men and younger women. Several had children in their arms, while one young man sat in the rear, aloof to the whole proceedings. Young people sometimes go to these meetings, they say, merely for their entertainment value. They are more numerous in the evening services, when in the rear of the church flirtations and courtships are carried on, another aspect of the social appeal of the church. But these young people are not left unaffected by the services, even when their attention appears to be directed to other things. The description of part of a Sunday service from field notes will indicate the nature of this religious observance.

At the time I entered, a woman in the choir was giving testimonial and asking prayer for a young couple who had just come from Oklahoma. "And you just pray that those two children will get work. They came out here without a cent, and they have gone North now, but they will need work." This is to the accompaniment of "Hallelujahs" and "Amens" by the preacher and a few in the congregation. Immediately as she sat down another woman arose and asked prayer for her daughter and son-in-law, "I just asked that boy (and I know he's a good boy at heart) if he had ever been in church and had the Lord grip him, and he said that one time he did, and he had often wondered about that. I think he can be saved, and I just hope that you will pray for those two and help them." A third arose and asked that we pray for her neighbor. "Her husband was in the insane asylum and she came to church and almost got religion, but just then her husband got well and came back." Now he is sick again. She told me that if she hadn't backslid she believes her husband would never have suffered so. "I think we should pray for her, and get her back into the church."

After these testimonials, everyone kneeled, bowed his head upon the bench and prayed aloud. At first only the voice of one or two individuals could be heard in agonized prayer, then more and more voices were raised out of the indeterminate murmur, shouting indistinguishable words. As each person finished he sat on the bench and waited till the rest were through, finally, only one shrill voice remained.

A hymn was started, the last praying woman arose and composed herself. After the song, there was a standing prayer led by the preacher, who walked up and down the platform, frequently turning his back on the congregation and looking upward stretched his arms over his head and shouted, "Jesus, Jesus, Jesus." The sermon followed.

At the outset the preacher explained that the Lord gave him his sermon, and that he considered this better than the usual method of asking blessings of a sermon already rendered. The sermon itself quite lacked coherent structure, it also lacked modulation. It was alternately a passage from the Bible and a few shouted comments regarding the content such as "the Lord says that if you are dirty you should wash, but He isn't speaking of the dirt of the earth, but the dirt of sin." In closing, he struck the salesmanship note, "Satan is working hard in the world today, because he knows his time is short. I can see that Jesus is getting ready to make His appearance soon, that the earthly kingdoms are destroying themselves. It is good to know we have the thing in hand for Jesus."

At the close there was a second standing prayer, then a duet in the inimitable flat nasal voice so typical of the singing in these churches, and the service was closed. Each person shook the hand of the others and said, "God bless you."

Personal participation, emotional release, informality, equality are all fulfilled in these services, three times each week for the fervent. We can hear their own expression of social anxieties and tensions in excerpts from their testimonials and prayers. The feeling of belonging was expressed in the Sunday evening testimonials. One said, "We should all pray for one another, pray for young and old alike. . . . We should pray for brotherly love. . . . There is no wrong in our acting like one big family, for that's what we are." A release from the personal sufferings is expressed in the following: "I've got a son in Oklahoma who's in trouble. Sometimes it takes trouble to make us appreciate the Lord. . . . It's wonderful to have someone to count on, but it's best to be in the arms of the Lord." But the greatest suffering of all, the common suffering of the selected group, is the economic worry and the feeling of inferiority engendered by the social system. For this reason a putative society is created by their wishful-thinking philosophy, a society in which they claim equality but in which they really feel themselves superior, for they are the saved. This is the society of the Kingdom of the Lord, and they "are all as precious in the eyes of the Lord." One called out in testimonial, "I've been broke, but you feel good if you know the Lord is watching you." Another professed that "I believe the less a person has of the world, the more they appreciate the Lord because they have to call on Him more." Again, "Sometimes I think I am worth nothing to the Lord or to anybody else, but when I realize what I am in His eyes, it makes me want to pray all the more."

Thus publicly proclaimed before their fellows and their God is their status in the commonly held dream world and the public negation of the real world of sin and disorder. There is little wonder that the depressed are drawn to this church, and that the more satisfied are repelled by it.

STATUS SEGREGATION IN THE CHURCH

Some of the psychological appeals of the different denominations were presented in the preceding account. There is another aspect to the appeals of the several churches—that of belonging to a group of kindred spirits. This is a potent factor in the selection of members on a class basis. People like to "be with their own kind" when being with others means remaining always on the peripheries of participation. Yet people do not want to associate with people who are "beneath them." These social aspects have led to class segregation and such segregation is a specific denial of the basic tenets of the Christian philosophy. The church members deny any policy of exclusion, and can document their denial with examples. Yet the exclusion is of such an insidious nature that it is felt at both ends, and there is a tacit recognition that certain churches are for certain people, and this is sometimes given overt expression.

The first exclusion is on a racial basis. No Negro and white person attend the same church, even though their religious convictions coincide. This exclusion is specifically denied to be mandatory, yet it is without exception maintained. A leading minister toyed with the problem that would arise if a Negro would ask to join his congregation. His statement in this regard suggests, however, the reality of the unformalized type of exclusion.

I would take it up before the Board of Deacons and recommend highly that he be admitted. There would have to be some reason, for instance he might be a teacher who had gone through our schools. I believe they would pass it. I would then let the church vote on the matter, and if there were dissenters, I would try to make the action unanimous. After that it would be a closed matter. If anyone objected, I would point out that this is a democratic organization and that the rule of the majority must be accepted. I think he would be taken in. I think he would have to—it would be all over town one way or the other.

A member of one of the poorer churches maintained, on the other hand, that her group has encouraged the Negroes to join, "but they just don't join. I don't know why unless it is because back East they don't mix with whites, and they don't feel free to."

The leading Negro congregation is Baptist, but all the white religious organizations have helped it to build its church, and they take what can only be called a patronizing attitude. The young people's organization of a leading church invited the Negroes to a meeting. The question of refreshments (raising the problem of Negroes and whites eating together) was solved by passing around nuts. The Negroes invite the whites to come to services, and the white pastors make a special point of trying to get a good turnout and make up a good collection for them.

The Mexicans stand in an apparently different relationship, with regard to the church, for they are almost all members of the Catholic congregation. But the segregation is nearly as great, for though they attend Mass together, they remain apart socially. This distinction was pointed out by the priest, who said:

> There is a large Mexican colony but there are also many Germans. There used to be one service in Spanish for them, but we have discontinued that. We make no distinctions between the two groups. Once a year we have a Spanish Mission for the Mexicans, which lasts a week.
>
> The Mexicans are children of nature, and do not take their religion very seriously. They have a kind of inferiority complex and feel that they are looked down on. Many of the Mexicans have devotions in their own homes—they have little altars. They like the trimmings better than the essentials; it is better that way than if they had nothing.
>
> We have card parties and socials to raise money. The Mexicans do not come to these. They would rather be with their kind. Every once in a while, usually in the spring, they have a fiesta. They have a good time. Some of the others come—it is open to everyone.

Here we have the internal segregation of the Mexicans. Since they are traditionally Catholic, we would expect very few among the Protestant churches, and in actuality there is but the single case mentioned.

But the segregation of the religious institutions on an economic basis interests us more here, and the segregation is striking, if not so complete. Table 24 and Chart 7 present the occupations of the members of the ten Wasco churches and show the clear differentials with regard to the occupational characteristics of the several congregations. If we look at the first of these churches, we see the statistical substantiation of the pastor's statement that his congregation is made up of "the progressive business men, the creamery people, the solid farmers and

TABLE 24.—OCCUPATIONAL CHARACTERISTICS OF CHURCHES

Occupation class	I Congregational	II Methodist	III Baptist	IV Catholic	V Christian Science	VI Seventh-Day Adventist	VII Nazarene	VIII Assembly of God	IX Church of Christ	X Schismatic Pentecost	All
A. Professionals, managers, and proprietors	50	16	16	16	82	15	11	0	0	0	18
B. Farm operators	20	26	29	22	9	40	22	30	22	0	24
C. Clerical, workers	11	14	12	14	9	3	0	10	3	1	9
D. Skilled laborers	18	41	28	26	0	37	45	40	36	17	30
E. Unskilled laborers	1	3	15	22	0	5	22	20	39	82	19
Total	100	100	100	100	100	100	100	100	100	100	100

SOURCE: Data obtained from membership rolls and by interview. The number of members of each church for whom occupation was determined, were, in order named: 152, 154, 189, 93, 11, 59, 72, 60, 80, and 72.

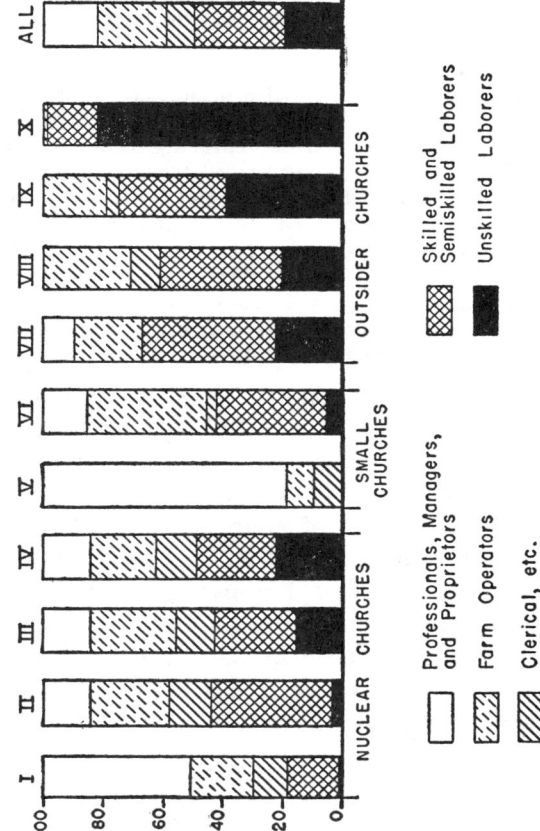

CHART 7

the school teachers." The agricultural laborers are completely unrepresented in this group. Of the relation with them the pastor said:

> The migrants don't come here. You can see why from the people who I said belong. We have a [missionary] camp of our own for the laborers on a large ranch. I didn't take the Government camp for those fellows are too well taken care of. Any minister will go there, for it's quite comfortable. But those workers are trying to do things for themselves. They have much to learn, and are trying. I think the situation is hopeful.
> The migrants don't come into our church because they don't feel comfortable. There isn't any feeling against them, but they aren't comfortable. They don't have the clothes, and we have a very pretty church here. They are more at home in the Church of Christ and the Nazarenes. Those churches are more like their homes. They can live in a tent and feel more comfortable there. I don't know whether my congregation would accept them. I haven't had any experience. The Methodists and Baptists might be able to give you information on that. These three churches represent the substance of the community.

Turning back to Chart 7 we see that these three Protestant churches of "substance" (I, II, and III) have fewest laborers and most of the entrepreneurial-professional group, leaving out the two small congregations. The Catholic church (IV) represents very nearly a cross-section of churchgoers in the community (compare the right-hand column). As we proceed down the line of outsider churches we find diminishing numbers of the top groups and increasing proportions of skilled and unskilled laborers, until we get to the schismatic Pentecostals (X) where virtual unanimity of workers is reached. This chart shows clearly the social divergence of the several sects in Wasco.

SOCIAL MOBILITY OF THE CHURCHES

Perhaps the most telling documentation of status differentiation among the religious bodies of Wasco may be gained from an understanding of the changes of status that the different churches as wholes have undergone. The leading churches—the four which make up the substance of Wasco—have not just recently attained their places, though their relative status may

SOCIAL STATUS AND RELIGIOUS LIFE 139

have undergone some modifications with the building of new edifices. But in the lower brackets, those called by the nuclear population the "Holy Roller" churches, the evidences of status change are manifest. One person recognized this change when he said, "I used to live across from one of those Holy Roller churches. My, but they were a noisy lot. They seem to have quieted down since then, though. They have built a new church and I suppose they have to live up to their new respectability." Such an observation might be written off to a development of understanding or acclimatization, but we have the following testimony from one of the ministers:

> The first two ministers here were just farmer-preachers who had had no education. They attracted most of the transient migratory workers. Many of the transient migratory type were attracted by his type of leadership, but my predecessor and I have kind of—now I don't want to put it so␣you misunderstand, but our special appeal is to the middle class. Poor people get a sensual or physical thrill and in that there is an attraction. I have had a frank Pentecostal preacher tell me that many of his congregation come to church for just that thrill. That is shallow thinking. Those poor folks get no other thrill out of life. But you can't build a church on that kind of element. My predecessor and I have appealed to a more sturdy and consistent type of people. We are appealing to the professional type of person. We are giving a sane intelligent presentation of the Gospel Truths.

This church, according to one of its own historians, grew out of the holiness movement of the latter half of the nineteenth century, which was the result of dissatisfactions in the Protestant churches and a desire for salvation through personal experience. It was established only in 1908. The church in Wasco is but a decade old, yet it has grown from meetings in a private home through a tent and two small buildings to its present plant, valued at $20,000. This new and elaborate plant has, itself, furthered the growth along the lines of conservatism, for "the work has taken on an impetus with the building of the modern church." Another cause for this growth "is the intensely sacrificial nature of our people. Our class is the middle to upper-lower class, and those are the most sacrificial. [There are] a half dozen field laborers, but the biggest part is middle class."

Another church of similar status is affiliated to the Assemblies of God. Like the preceding, it was organized in Wasco under a lay minister. Though the original congregation was largely made up of small farmers (this pastor also made a general disclaimer for any large labor membership), actually many agricultural laborers are included in the congregation. But the evidence for social advancement, at least in the relative scale, in the Wasco social hierarchy (for this church preceded the extensive growth of the white outsider group) can be seen in the nature of the schism that has taken place within the Pentecostal movement. The Pentecostal movement itself was away from "modernism" and "higher criticism" and toward a "return to the old truth," namely, "infillment of the spirit" and the "second personal crisis." The movement was also imbued with a spirit of democracy, and even an active participation, intellectual and emotional, by the laity.

But the processes of status advance by the church, with the acquisition of property and a history, and perhaps a vested interest in its own permanence as an established institution, have taken their toll from the original tenets, and in the past ten years there has been a schism on a nation-wide basis. The older church is the one discussed above, and the schismatic faction is represented by a Pentecostal group, a fully outsider religious body, poorest in equipment and with the poorest membership of all the churches of the community. (Column X in the preceding chart.) Of this split perhaps the statement of a former (lay) minister of the schismatic group is most telling:

> There is no difference between our church and the other Pentecostal church except that we believe that the spirit has the right of way. The Council has tightened down and become formalized. Back East they are free, but here (especially in Southern California) many of the churches have tightened down. Educated ministers and college students who are stiff shirts came in and some of the people fell for it.

This inhibition of the spirit which has resulted from the formalization was given expression by a classic statement of a person whose affiliation was with the older Pentecostal church back home. She did not like their congregation in Wasco because "they set you down," that is, "they won't let you get up and shout when you get the spirit, and that isn't right."

The church with lay participation, especially the emotional participation through the religious experience as exemplified by the shouting, talking in tongues, rolling, etc., of the revivalistic churches, is the special province of the underprivileged. They are manifested in the Negro churches, in the revivalistic cults of the Indians of North America, and other primitive groups in contact with western civilization, as well as in the white community that is our particular subject of study. But in this last, where the underprivileged persons succeed in advancing somewhat in the social scale, there are pressures upon the institution itself toward social advancement. An emotional church appealing to the "sensual" draws in a group, and a building is erected on a "faith basis." It grows under the impetus of lay participation, its coffers increase, and its building, outgrown or outmoded, is replaced with a more imposing structure. It becomes unseemly for the now relatively affluent church to have an uneducated minister, who, it is argued, cannot devote his full time to the congregation, so a preacher is hired from one of the seminaries of the parent church. Education, however, vests *de facto* authority in the minister's hands, inhibiting the congregation by precept, if not by direct effort on his part. "The sane intelligent presentation of the gospel" results in the "setting down" of the fervent adherents. The appeal goes out to the "stabler elements" who tend to take over the church. But this stabler element is made up of those who have made peace with their milieu, most frequently in terms of a fair amount of economic security; there still remain those distressed individuals whose emotional needs are not met by the intellectualized gospel of the seminary students. It is their turn for the new schism, the establishment of the new church where the "spirit has the right of way." And so the cycle is repeated.

Just as the poorer persons require the psychological reinforcement of the emotional religion and the negation of worldly goods, so do those better off find such a statement of the ethical situation at variance with their psychological needs. And as, first, the church exists in an environment in which prestige is expressed by evidences of economic worth, and, second, the congregation is exhorted to support the church to its fullest glory, there is a bourgeoisization of the church, to coin a phrase, that parallels the development of individual interest in worldly goods. The dilemma of the ethical system of the Protestant faith, which exhorts its followers on the one hand to reject the things of the world as unsuited to the servants of God, and on the other hand to the great virtues of industry, thrift and frugality, has not gone unheeded. Max Weber in his *Protestant Ethic* points out that "the whole history of monasticism is in a sense the history of a continual struggle with the problem of secularizing influence of wealth," and that "the same is true on a grand scale of the worldly asceticism of Puritanism." [1]

As a matter of fact, John Wesley himself recognized this very problem which he expressed in the following:

> I fear, wherever riches have increased, the essence of religion has decreased in the same proportion. Therefore I do not see how it is possible in the nature of things, for any revival of true religion to continue long. For religion must necessarily produce both industry and frugality, and these cannot but produce riches. But as riches increase, so will pride, anger, and love of the world in all its branches. How then is it possible that Methodism, that is, a religion of the heart, though it flourishes now as a green bay tree, should continue in this state? For the Methodists in every place grow diligent and frugal, consequently they increase in goods. Hence they proportionally increase in pride, in anger, in the desires of the flesh, the desire of the eyes, and the pride of life. So, although the form of the religion remains, the spirit is swiftly vanishing away.[2]

This frequently quoted passage from the Methodist leader implies what is clearly true, that the philosophy of emotional salvation for prestige in a putative society and of the negation of worldly systems of value appeals to the poor, and this for obvious reasons. That it applies to the church as a whole, as well as to the individual, is demonstrated in the data at Wasco, where the successive schisms of the Christian church, especially the Protestant, are demonstrated.

The Christian sects, from Catholicism through the Protestant factions of an earlier era, now serving stolidly a solid middle

[1] Max Weber, *The Protestant Ethic and the Spirit of Capitalism*, p. 174.
[2] Quoted in Southey, *Life of Wesley*, Chapter XXIX, 2nd American edition, II, p. 308, and again by Weber, *op. cit.*, p. 175.

SOCIAL STATUS AND RELIGIOUS LIFE 143

class, down to the Evangelical groups of modern origin, are represented in Wasco. Within the Evangelical sects the different stages are present. There are unorganized and unaffiliated groups meeting in homes representing the newest in point of time and the poorest in social status. Next are the schismatic Pentecostals, whose removal into an old building from a tent is less than two years old. Another church has but now obtained a full-time minister (completely dependent upon his services to the congregation for his livelihood), while two have attained plants rivaling the middle-class churches in value and elaboration, and these are completely dominated by the "stiff shirts" produced by the seminaries.

INDIVIDUAL STATUS AND RELIGIOUS PARTICIPATION

Thus far the discussion of religion in Wasco has centered about the church as an institution. We have pointed out that within the tenets of Christian doctrine the whole gamut of social classes can be accommodated, but that this can be done only with a variety of separate and very different institutional organizations. These different organizations, furthermore, appeal to persons of different social and economic status. It is therefore necessary to examine the nature of this differential appeal upon the individual.

Two major changes in church affiliation have been recorded for the outsider group in the tabulation of questions from 51 persons in Wasco. These are first, a shift away from church membership to nonparticipation, and second, a shift from churches of denominations which, in Wasco, serve the nuclear group toward those which serve largely outsiders.

Two-fifths of the sample at present attend no church. This figure cannot be compared with that for nonattendance formerly, because most individuals represented under that heading merely did not state their former church affiliations. It shows also that 28 of the 51 are members or attend churches of the outsider type, and that half the sample were formerly members of the nuclear type churches, but are no longer. This shift away from the nuclear churches is shown in the change in total allegiance of from 25 prior to migration to two at the present time, and neither of the two of this sample had membership in the churches they attended.

The pastor of one of the "substantial" churches expressed concern over such absences of the agricultural workers from the religious institutions. "It is true," he said, "that many of these people have left their religion behind them. I have frequently

TABLE 25.—CHANGES IN CHURCH HABITS OF RECENT ARRIVALS

Present church habits	Total	Before coming to Wasco attended		
		Revival-istic church	Nuclear church	No church (or no information)
Attend no church	21	4	12	5
Attend revivalistic churches	28	5	12	11
Attend nuclear churches	2	0	1	1
Total	51	9	25	17

SOURCE: Data obtained from interviews.

tried to get them into the church, but they don't seem interested. Many of them join the Pentecostal church. I have never thought of just why that might be, but many of them have pretty tough sledding, and also the emotional nature of the church appeals to them. The Baptist church in the region they come from is more emotional too. Most of the people I have talked to say they don't have the clothes to come to church and they don't feel well enough off. We just inducted a couple of agricultural laborers who have just come from Oklahoma. They have quite poor clothes but they don't seem to mind."

Even the churches that are considered by the nuclear population to be made up of agricultural laborers report this change in church participation. One of the pastors said, "Most of the recent immigrants go to the [Schismatic] Pentecostal church.

Our bus goes around and picks up about 35 of the migrant families' children. We haven't enough room in the bus to hold the adults. We have a ladies' missionary group, and they go around calling on the people. They can't get the adults. I have found that about 60 per cent of them were church people back home, and you'd be surprised at the number of former preachers who never darken the door of a church here in California. Their excuse is that 'people are so different out here.' "

The statements of the laborers themselves impress us with the direct social factors which they consider sufficient to account for these changes. One squatter said that a neighboring farmer had asked her to come to one of the leading churches. "They are good members," she said, "but we are poor people and everybody that goes there are up-to-date people." The wife of a permanently hired farm laborer had a similar invitation from his employer, but she went to the Pentecostal church. "We belonged to the Baptist back home. To tell the truth, I don't like the Baptist church here because they are a different class of people, and I'd rather stay around my own class. I don't like all the ways they believe in the Pentecostal church though." Here is not only an explanation on the basis of class differentiation, but the statement also that the change was made despite antithetical religious beliefs. Another laborer's wife made the following observation. "The children go to the Pentecostal Sunday School. We were Baptists back home, but we don't go to any church out here. We don't have the clothes. Back home there were little old meetings and you could go any old way. When you're just raised up among folks it's different from the way it is here."

Other shifts in church membership have already been mentioned; the Mexican with membership in the Protestant church and the teachers who no longer took up membership in the elite church at about the time their loss of social status in the community was being felt.

The recreational content of the church adds to the need for status unity. Aside from the relatively formalized church socials and the young people's and ladies' societies the church is an arena where friendships are created and courtships promulgated.

A young agricultural laborer who made the following statement could hardly expect to find his needs met if he went to the best church in town. He said, "I go to the Nazarene here. It's nicest and most up-to-date [his thinking does not even include the best] but I wouldn't say it's more friendly. That is how I get acquainted with the girls I know here. I wouldn't say that's the reason I go to church, for I like to hear a good preacher, but that's certainly one reason." As a matter of fact, the church is the only institutional mechanism available to the agricultural laborer which fulfills this need for expanding the social group beyond the family.

These several instances and statistics show that one feature of any Protestant church which particularly draws the individual is its social aspect, and more specifically its particular social status. The exceptional individual may demand a certain philosophy or religious content, but the vast majority seek to be with people of their own kind, avoiding situations where they feel inferior, yet not associating exclusively with people who are "beneath" them. The content of the services then adjusts, in the shifting process described in a preceding section, to the psychological requirements of the social and economic class of its adherents.

CIVIC INFLUENCE OF THE CHURCH

For all the hold the religious institutions of the community have over many persons of different stations of life in Wasco, each in his own way, the coverage of the church is far from complete, and its influence over the community as such is diminishing. Of six thousand or more whites and Mexicans served by the ten institutions here recorded, only about one thousand have direct affiliations. There are many more, of course, who are religious, that is, believe the major tenets of Christian ideology. Some of these frequently attend, others merely feel that if they "stay home and teach their children to do right, and don't bother anything, the Lord won't mind." The influence of the church is still great enough that nobody openly flaunts his disbelief in the major premises, but is no longer so great that it has the power of social ostracism.

The newcomer tells us, "This is one town where the church members don't come around and ask you to join." Probably the most significant indication of this can be seen in the small proportion of teachers who are members of the church, for teachers, as servants of the community, are expected to conform to all the dominant social dicta. Of the 66 teachers in the public schools of the community, only 18 have affiliation with a local church. The elite church still has most of the teachers and none belongs to the churches of the outsider group. This religious tolerance is an aspect of the urbanity manifested by the small community, yet it also reflects the loss of community status by the teachers.

The church was once the dominant social influence in Wasco. No person, public servant or not, could refuse participation without loss of status, and the non-believers and the indifferent felt obliged occasionally to put in their appearance at religious services. The church ban on drinking made Wasco a dry community during its early years. At a later date, about the close of World War I, one of the major conflicts was over the matter of school dances. In part the early victory in this matter over church conservatism was the result of a highly sophisticated school principal, but his very selection and the existence of potent forces of revolt are significant. The church now exerts great influence in the social affairs of only those who for one or another reason desire to be so influenced. In how far this diminution of the sphere of influence is a result of the development of industrialized agriculture it is difficult to say, but certainly the relationship is not purely fortuitous. The very fact of social exclusion and the tendency of each church to serve merely one class or status level are in themselves a voluntary restriction of the sphere of influence. Although their members have increased with the growth of population, the churches have suffered a net loss as a factor of control in the newer class society.

CHAPTER VI

COHESION, CONFLICT AND CONTROL

THE INDUSTRIALIZED character of the agriculture of California has resulted in the establishment of a social system comprised of two basic classes. These groups, with their differing modes of life, are the rural equivalent of the class structure generally associated with urban society; they are the primary mark of the urbanization of California rural life. The existence of these two antithetical groups gives rise to the following problems: Does the social class system create conflict situations; what is the nature of these conflicts; how does the dominant group control the submissive, and what are the checks against this control in the hands of the latter? It may be said from the outset that the social situation is conducive to conflict; that the controls by the nuclear group over the outsiders are substantial; that, above all, this situation is part and parcel of the greater social arena in which the conflict and controls are determined.

The terms cohesion, conflict, and control are used in their sociologic sense in this chapter. Since there are popular uses of these same words, a brief definition is apropos here. By social *cohesion* we mean those personal motivations (and by extension their outward manifestations) which strengthen the ties of any group of persons; in this instance with the community of Wasco. Social *conflict* is used to denote those situations where individuals or groups have interests directly contrary to other persons or groups, the fulfillment of which will act to the detriment of these others. Actual (physical) conflict can arise out of such situations, though it rarely does. Conflict may, but does not necessarily, involve hostility since it is not necessarily directly recognized as conflict of interests with another person or group. Social *control* denotes the influence or power of one individual or group over others, whether that power rests upon a use of force, upon legally established mechanisms, upon the powers of persuasion, upon established customs and attitudes of the people, or a combination of these. More generally it applies to extra-legal powers built upon custom and persuasion.

All societies carry these elements of cohesion, conflict, and control. The utopian societies without unfair social distinctions, without conflicting situations, and without controlling and submissive elements are formed only in the philosophers' studies. The anthropologists do not report them. Yet each society displays some means of welding the people into a functioning and interdependent whole, serving the social wants as well as the physical needs of its population. These cohesive forces vary greatly, both in kind and in degree. They are more apparent in the simpler societies with more fixed membership than they are in a modern community, particularly an urbanized community, where mobility is far greater. Yet at any one time, it is apparent that sufficient motivation exists to keep the people together. In earlier chapters the lack of cohesive ties between the nuclear population and the outsider group has been discussed in detail. Yet there are strong economic and social motivations which unify the population. Fundamentally, the worker, the farmer, and the townsmen co-operate in producing farm commodities, and each is necessary to the other. Any conflict situation is always mitigated by this economic interdependence.

COHESIVE FACTORS: THE OUTSIDER GROUP

The submissive element in the class structure has come into the rural area from the outside; it has come and it remains of its own free choice, so that the controls to which it is subject must be considered less odious than the economic oppressions of their places of former residence, for "if they don't like it here they can go back where they came from." That many of them do is well known, yet many more have remained in California. And, as has already been pointed out, not only do they remain in California, but also they select a specific community for resettlement and attempt to re-establish permanent homes in their new environment. Many make a single shift and come directly to their new homes; even those who follow crops often settle in one or another community which they then use as a base for their migratory activities. Before we examine the nature of the conflicts and controls to which they are subject in their new environment, it is necessary to examine the specific attractions which hold them in California and their new community. For, though it may be Hobson's choice, these agricultural workers have cast their lot with the California social situation.

The special attractions of resettlement may be understood under three heads: The immediate economic opportunities, the social emoluments of resettlement, and the expectancy of future social and economic gain. The basically economic motivation of their movement to California has been directly expressed by the migrants themselves. The drought and decreased farming opportunities resulting from mechanized farming (as expressed in the phrase "we are tractored out") have diminished the economic opportunity at the source of migration.[1] A survey of migration and resettlement enquired into the motivation of migrants moving into California (Table 26). From the nearest community included, a total of 45 of the 56 responses indicated the basic economic reason for this migration, while 40 out of 56 gave similar explanations for the choice of their community of settlement.

If the finding of work leads to resettlement in the community, other considerations are conducive to the maintenance of a home there, though it be only a boarded tent on the desert. Regular work contacts can best be established by means of permanent residence, and occasionally regular routes of migration are maintained because of permanent work contacts in different towns. Such work contacts can lead to permanent employment. A second economic factor is the establishment of credit which is an important consideration to the seasonally employed. Public welfare, especially medical aid, and those categories administered

[1] See Paul S. Taylor, "Power Farming and Labor Displacement in the Cotton Belt," *Monthly Labor Review*, Serial No. R 737, 1938.

by county agencies form a very real economic motive for permanent settlement. Finally, the desire to accumulate household goods and other evidences of middle-class well-being make it desirable to have a permanent establishment.

But the pressures toward resettlement in California not only have their economic aspect, but also their social. The Table just cited carries evidence of this. Thirty-five of those who came to

TABLE 26.—REASONS FOR COMING TO CALIFORNIA AND FOR CHOICE OF COMMUNITY OF 45 RESETTLED MIGRANT FAMILIES

	To secure work, reported by				Other reasons			
	Relatives	Friends	Ads	Unsp.[1]	Health	Climate	Visit	Other
Migration to California [2]	23	11	2	9	9	1	1	0
Choice of community [2]	7	7	1	25	3	1	9	3

[1] This category includes "followed crop," "better work opportunity," and like statements.
[2] More than one reason frequently given.
NOTE: Data from neighboring community and refers to spring, 1939.

California because of work opportunities learned of these from relatives or friends, and fourteen who settled in the community learned of work in this way. In addition to this, nine of those who settled there first came to visit. Similarly, of sixty immigrants of the outsider group interviewed in Wasco, thirty-two mentioned relatives as a reason for settling in the community, and forty stated that they had relatives in the town.

One of the major considerations in the resettlement of the laborers has been the schools. The attendance figures of the Wasco schools show that fewer withdrawals and delayed entrants occurred in the late than in the early part of the thirties. This indicates a progressive tendency toward maintaining permanent settlement. Some workers declare that they have come to California, and many that they remain in the community, because of the school facilities provided them by this State. The school is also a socializing agency, in that it is one of the few sources of social activity enjoyed by any of the outsider group. There is also the social aspect of the desire to accumulate household goods of prestige-bearing character, for these become tacit expressions of status within the outsider groups. In short, it is only through resettlement that the outsider can attain a measure of social belonging either to a smaller group or to the community itself, and this he is anxious to attain.

This desire to attain standing in the new community leads to the third basis for his choice of resettlement: the expectancy of future social and economic gain. The primary desires, as expressed by many workers, are a "steady job" and "a place of their own." The former is, of course, relatively rare, and when available often has specific drawbacks. The latter has in many cases been fulfilled, as is readily seen by driving through the "Little Oklahoma City" area of Wasco, or of any other small community in the California intensive farming area. In a study of resettled migrants, Fuller has pointed out that almost half of them have purchased real property.[2] Such homes represent not only economic advancement but also social gain, according to the standards of social worth set by the community and adopted by the outsider. Beyond these, and frequently in their stead, are the desires for consumer goods: cars, refrigerators, radios, and the like which are at the same time sources of physical satisfaction and emblems of the middle-class well-being for which they are striving. An often expressed, but rarely satisfied, desire is for a farm of their own. One worker says, "Above all, I would like to farm—I've done farming and I like it best of anything." A worker's wife says, "My husband is a cement worker for the WPA. We came out here on the desert [squatting on unimproved land] in the hopes of saving money so that we could buy some sort of place. We would like to buy a lot. We would like to buy a place and raise some chickens, and maybe later get a cow." This person is thinking in terms of the farm

[2] Varden Fuller, "Resettlement of Migrants in Rural Communities of California," Ms., p. 159.

enterprise of the East, rather than realistically of farming in this irrigation area. Such was also the case of the laborer who claimed he could make a living out of a farm here, even if he "just had a couple of acres." It is, nevertheless, the expression of a great majority of these resettled migrants, though occasionally one who has had the opportunity recognizes the limitations of marginal farming in the region saying, "It costs too much money to farm here in California." Finally, the expectation of future economic gains is in terms of ambition for children, who are to go to college, and here it may be that the realization can be fulfilled, for of the next generation this study cannot make any factual report.

SOCIAL MOBILITY

If these are the desires of the outsider group with respect to the community, it becomes essential to examine to what extent they are attained. For it is an essential characteristic of the open-class society that upward mobility is more than a theoretical possibility, and upon the ease or difficulty of such mobility rests the future of the social pattern.

Some evidence for social mobility can be obtained from the changes in occupation status of a sample of persons who entered California during the decade of the thirties. A survey of such families was made through the schools by the Bureau of Agricultural Economics in 1939. This survey elicited responses on questions as to the occupation of the parent of the child in school at the time of the survey and prior to coming to California. Table 27 presents the figures for the occupation at the present time according to occupation prior to removal. The subsequent tabulation (Table 28) summarizes some of the content, showing that four persons out of ten are working in the same occupation class, while of the remaining six, five are in an occupation bracket with less social status than prior to removal to California, or a net loss of 40 per cent in economic status. Referring back to Table 27, it is possible to note where the incidence of occupational shifts has occurred. A very large group has shifted into the relief brackets, and this shift has occurred in about the same proportion from every occupational bracket except the entrepreneurial-professional group. Many, but not all, of those persons in the relief bracket are seasonal farm laborers, for the survey was made at a low point in the annual labor

TABLE 27.—OCCUPATIONAL SHIFTS OF RECENT ARRIVALS INTO WASCO

Present occupation	Former occupation						Total
	A. Professionals, managers, and proprietors	B. Farm operators	C. Clerical workers	D. Skilled laborers	E. Unskilled laborers	R. Unemployed [1]	
A. Professionals, managers, and proprietors	7	3	2	1	1	0	14
B. Farm operators	2	10	0	4	1	0	17
C. Clerical workers	0	2	1	0	0	0	3
D. Skilled laborers	6	13	1	34	10	0	64
E. Unskilled laborers	3	32	1	12	37	2	87
F. Unemployed [1]	0	11	1	10	18	1	41
Total	18	71	6	61	67	3	226

[1] Unemployed or recipient of some form of public assistance.

TABLE 28.—SUMMARY OF OCCUPATIONAL SHIFTS

	Number	Per cent
No change in occupation class	90	40
Upward change in occupation class	24	10
Downward change in occupation class	112	50
Total	226	100

SOURCE: Table 27.

demand cycle. (See Chart 3.) A large amount of shifting takes place between skilled and unskilled workers, but the shift is approximately equal in both directions. The most significant shift is, however, from farmer to lower status. According to the data presented in the Table, 71 persons were farmers prior to coming to California. Only ten of these have remained farmers, while 56 have become laborers, or are on relief. If we simplify our classification to form a farmer-white-collar group and a laborer-relief group, there are only seven individuals who have raised their status as against 68 who have fallen into a lower bracket. These are indicated by the upper right and lower left boxes, respectively, on Table 27. Examining the seven more closely, we find only two who were agricultural laborers prior to coming to California. One of these has become a tenant farmer; the second operates a camp for migratory workers, and like all persons whose economic advancement derives from service to the outsider group, he does not have status within the nuclear group that is the normal concomitant of his occupation classification. Of the remaining five who have had this status advance, one is at present a real farm leader, one has had the help of local kinspeople of high status, and a third operates a service station. The other two might be called marginal farmers.

In order to arrive at an understanding of the nature of the adjustment of persons coming into the area in recent years, it will be well to examine a few cases in somewhat more detail. Ten synopses of individual histories, representing different types of adjustment to the local scene are therefore presented. The first five have become farm operators; the remainder are laborers. Of the latter, two have become integrated in the town, and one has obtained permanent employment on a farm. The other two have not become integrated into the community at all. Case A, that of a farmer now quite successful, indicates the ease with which economic advancement could be made under the expanding economy of the middle twenties—a degree of social mobility that he realizes as well as anyone else was not possible during the depression. To account for this change, he points to the labor displacement of mechanized farming practices on the one hand, and the increased size of farms on the other.

A. **Boom period immigrant.** Came to neighboring town from Oklahoma, where he had been farming, in 1925, after relative sent him newspaper clipping of farming opportunities. Both husband and wife had job arranged as agricultural laborers before coming West. Before year was over worked for gin, and gin manager persuaded him to take over a farm—"almost anyone could get a farm at that time." Farmed forty acres on a share basis. Now owns 100 acres and rents 360 more. Is well known in community but does not participate a great deal in activities. Is a member of Co-op gin and has refused to join Associated Farmers. Formerly belonged to church but has never belonged in California. One child prominent in school, two others in college, one doing graduate academic work.

The second case is of an individual who came to Wasco as a field hand and has become a successful farmer. Note, however, that he had had experience in large-scale cash farming, that he had no dependents, and that his wife could earn and save money and that he could borrow some cash from a relative. His aggressiveness and his ability to work very hard were, however, both essential qualities to his success. While his status in the community is not yet high, he stands a good chance of becoming a leading farmer. The third case likewise indicates the importance of a source of capital and of credit. Case D has utilized his resources as a skilled laborer to become a farmer, a situation which is not infrequent.

B. Agricultural laborer to farm operator. Came straight to Wasco from Arkansas in 1935, after having lost large farm due to illness. Wife remained in Arkansas and worked, only son was permanently employed elsewhere. Man worked as agricultural laborer as follows: hoed cotton, picked potatoes, followed grape harvest, returned for cotton picking, worked in dairy near Los Angeles. Wife arrived in December with $500 savings. He worked as farm laborer till September, and she in town, until September, when both picked cotton till Christmas. At that time there were two months of unemployment when he "pretty nearly went crazy." Obtained steady farm work till September, 1938, when he rented 20 acres of improved land, with savings plus sum borrowed from relative.

Farmed this land with team and borrowed equipment; aided by finance companies. Next year rented 40 acres and "made about $20,000." In 1940 operated, in conjunction with son, two tracts totaling 300 acres and claims a cash investment of over $10,000. Wife still working in town.

Man is well known in community, being subject both to praise and criticism for his aggressive economic advancement. Belongs to no clubs, though asked to join Grange which he declines because he has "never had time," and the Associated Farmers, which he declined because "the way I figure it, that organization is made up of a bunch of big fellows who run things, and I'm not one—yet." Wife a pillar of an outsider church.

C. Migration involving no change of status. After "eight drought years" sold farm in Western Oklahoma and came to Los Angeles in 1937. Spent three months at "a pretty good job," but became interested in farming in the San Joaquin Valley. Rented a farm from a man "who was hard to get along with" with $1,200 savings and financing made available because he had "friends working for cotton financing company." Now cash renting one place and share renting another, hires two regular hands at $65 and perquisites, keeps cows, chickens, and garden and plans diversified farming. Intends to make Wasco permanent home and wants to buy a farm.

Is known to farm circles, and belongs to Co-op gin. Has refused to join organizations and does not go to church.

D. Oil worker to farm operator. Raised on farms in Texas and Oklahoma, and spent some time in New Mexico and Arizona. Came to California in 1920 and worked as oil driller. Relatives in Wasco persuaded him to start farming. Farmed 40 acres as share tenant in 1930 and increased to 80 acres the following year. Leased land for three years, and bought land out of profits of high-priced 1936 potato crop. Has periodically throughout this time and is at present working in oil fields, maintaining that it is impossible to buy farm land in Wasco area without some other source of income, but wants to farm because of taste, and of greater security in old age. He now owns 100 acres of land and is referred to as a "wealthy man," but himself makes the observation that "you can't get out from under the finance company unless you work awfully hard and get the breaks." Belongs to Co-op gin, Grange and Masonic lodge, and formerly belonged to Farm Bureau. Refused to join Associated Farmers. Wife does not care for clubs.

The farmer in Case E is operating a small unit on share rental that furnished him a bare minimum income. Such units are rare in the area. This individual has no certainty of remaining a farm operator, and still has the social status of laborer, which is his more usual occupation. Advancement may follow, of course, if he is able to keep the farm and especially if he succeeds in expanding his operations. With farmers, size and tenure are important considerations for advancement, and the prevalent attitude is that a person cannot maintain a farm of less than 40 acres.

E. Marginal farm operator. Came to California in 1929, visiting relatives, worked on large corporation-ranch and then for two years on smaller farm where work was hardest he had ever done because "they put too much on you." "We worked regular except during the winter when work was slack and we were laid off. We moved here in 1934 and started buying this house in 1937. Since then have worked for different people. Rented 20 acres in 1935 for $1,000 with equipment and water furnished, but could not get the land the following year as owner did not want tenant. It was much better working by the day." This year renting 20 acres again, on share basis. Belongs to no organizations, and not known to community, lives in poor house and poor neighborhood. One daughter left school to be married secretly to truck driver by minister of outsider church, one son in high school who has no expressed ambition.

The remaining case histories present much more usual forms of adjustment. The first two (F and G) are persons who have achieved the upper status of the outsider groups, and are beginning to be known as "good workers" or "fine people" to members of the nuclear group. They would be pointed out as "dust-bowlers" rather than "Okies" by those who know them personally, though they have not attained membership in the nuclear group. These families have made a sincere effort at adjustment in terms of nuclear group values, and consider their social interests to be connected with the community. Any permanent semi-skilled or skilled job in the town would in time bring them into the nuclear group.

F. Agricultural laborer resettled in town: 1. Farmer all his life until "it got so you couldn't make a living in Oklahoma." Had a sale of stock and equipment to cover mortgages. Went to Arizona and back to Oklahoma "saying we wouldn't leave again, but in six months we were ready to go." Went back to Arizona and to California in spring of 1938, chopping onions and picking up potatoes. Husband now working for creamery for $3.50 per day. Have had help from local farmer, as well as from relief agency. Have purchased small home in "Little Oklahoma City." Do not go to church or "belong to any clubs or anything," though children go to outsider church. Not known to community, except one farm family who has befriended them, but say "we have done better than most people here . . . because we have worked hard."

G. Agricultural laborer resettled in town: 2. Came to Wasco in 1934 when times were bad in Arkansas and a cousin wrote of work. Worked for public utilities company during first summer, then worked as truck driver at dairy for four and a half years, at $110 per month, later did carpentry and miscellaneous agricultural labor and received public assistance for a short while. Meanwhile, had bought lot in "Little Oklahoma City," bought a house and moved it on lot. Also bought two shacks and moved them on lot and kept boarders during period of employment at creamery. Now working as cook in nearby city where defense work has created labor shortage.

Living in very neat and pleasantly furnished house. Woman claims to have been member of leading woman's club but dropped out because she "didn't care for it"; woman belongs to outsider church and hopes to send son to college to become minister. Son wants to go to Junior College and become civil servant—"something like a postmaster."

The wife in Case H expresses the values achieved by the two preceding ones in that she wants to "have a place of our own in town," even though it would probably be less adequate than her present exceptionally good accommodations. Her sphere of acquaintances is limited by farm living, but even more by her own reticence for she refuses to go to the established church with her employer because of a feeling of class inferiority, according to her own statement.

H. Regularly employed farm laborer living on farm. Was sharecropper in Arkansas till came to California in 1931. Returned in 1932 and came back to California in 1935, working in the potatoes in Wasco. Started working for present employer in November, 1939, but "wouldn't say it is better to work this way than just to work when you can get it. You don't make so much money when there is lots of work, but then it's steady." Hasn't tried to farm and on basis of relative's experience doesn't consider it feasible because "it just takes too much money." Woman wants to buy home of own in town for "we haven't ever had a place of our own since we have been married," but husband recently bought new car.

Live in new and very well built house belonging to farmer. Participates in no clubs or church, despite sincere effort on part of employer to get them to join the latter. Have adequate household furnishings including electric refrigerator. Plan to remain in California largely because children like the high school. They "can't say [they] are better off here; have more money to spend than back East, but back there you don't eat out of paper sacks."

The fourth of these laborers (I) represents the type of adjustment that involves the rejection of any settlement or integration into the community. His income as a migrating farm laborer is sufficient to maintain some aspects of middle-class standards and he prefers the wage advantages of migration to the social advantages of resettlement. Such workers frequently have work connections in several communities, but they have no vested interest in any particular one. Being less concerned with the prevalent attitudes of the elite, he has less reason to reject the union, and he is an active participant in that type of organization. Case J expresses a similar disregard for the community but is further characterized by not having broken her ties with the region of origin. Her migration back and forth between California and her home state is not an unusual occurrence and denotes complete failure to integrate into the California community.

I. Adjustment to seasonal migration. Came to California in 1933, obtained public assistance and agricultural work. At one time owned small tourist camp for agricultural workers, but sold this in 1939. Has relatives in Wasco working for oil company.

Now owns new car and home-built trailer house, and has regular migration route, working in grapes near Fresno, the cannery at Monterey, and picking cotton in Wasco during slack season. Wants steady job in oil fields but unable to find, and considers it better to move around than to remain in Wasco which he has tried. Belongs to AFL union though he resents the fact that the "big boys have kind of a racket." Wife formerly belonged to outsider church.

J. Not adjusted to new environment. Single woman who came to Wasco in 1938 for first time and had been back to Oklahoma three times by 1941. On last trip back to California was in accident and is temporarily unable to work in fields so is anxious to go back to Oklahoma. Works in harvesting crops, and has been on public welfare, whence she is now getting support. When in California lives with relatives in tent behind farm house, where the chief items of furniture are an electric washing machine and refrigerator, and a number of beds crowded together. Belongs to no clubs or church, finds entertainment in shows and dances.

As these cases indicate, social and economic advancement is a possibility, yet it is of rare occurrence. In order to advance to farmer status some private source of capital is necessary, and also, as one person stated, a few "breaks." Another condition is previous entrepreneurial experience. For the most part the adjustment is made on the outsider level, with economic and social desires oriented according to the standards of the local community, which means, among other things, adopting the prejudices of that group. Even workers following the crops become adjusted in this way through the use of one community as a base for operations, though some, as illustrated by cases I and J, have not acquired roots in any community.

Another form of advancement may be said to occur over generations; that is, through the advancement of the children. Here, of course, we cannot study the *fait accompli,* but certain observations may well be made. It has already been pointed out that the school is the chief integrating element in the community. Though there is some evidence of social segregation of migrant children, the school enforces a high degree of democracy. Competitive sports help give status to migrant and minority race children whose athletic prowess has been notable, and thus, tend to lessen the prejudice against these groups. Teachers state that social distinctions between the local people and the migrant are tending to disappear, and one agricultural laborer's child recently achieved the highest scholastic standing of his class. The frequent expressions of a desire on the part of parents for their children to attend college are also an indication of the recognition of this form of social advancement, though its achievement will be much rarer.

COHESIVE FACTORS: THE NUCLEAR GROUP

It is not only the laborer, but also the community which has had to make adjustments to the influx of migrants. Though its members complain of the changes wrought in the community by the immigration of destitute workers, they have derived many benefits from it. Above all, the farmer is completely dependent upon the seasonal worker under the established pattern of agriculture, and the large army of workers has made it possible for him to harvest his crops when and as he wants to, and at a cheap rate. This cheap harvest labor has been written into the value of the California farm lands.[3] Prior to the immi-

---

[3] *Vide* Varden Fuller, "The Supply of Agricultural Labor as a Factor in the Evolution of Farm Organization in California," *La Follette Hearings,* S. Res. 266, Part 54, p. 19878.

gration of white workers this labor had been done by a series of minority races who survived on a low standard of living. That they have been wanted, at least by some groups in the valley, is demonstrated by their specific efforts to obtain them.[4]

The nuclear group profits from the large laboring class by the shopkeeper's sales and enhanced real estate values. The growth of Wasco during the decade of the thirties, from a town of less than 1,600 to one well over twice that figure, means a necessary correlative increase in total business turnover. For instance, the total money orders of the Wasco Post Office increased from $83,000 in 1934 to almost $178,000 in 1940, and similarly the gross receipts for stamps more than doubled from about $8,000 in 1933 to nearly $17,000 in 1940.[5] The credit extended to these workers, not only for groceries, but also for household goods and cars, suggests that this asset is recognized by the local merchants.

Similarly, the local realtors have recognized this business asset, and Wasco, like most agricultural communities in the region, has its areas of cheap housing. One large tract, subdivided by several different property owners as early as 1925, sold at that time for $125 for a 45-foot lot and these were worth in 1940, according to subdividers, from $300 to $350 a lot. One real-estate broker subdivided 5 acres in this area in 1937 into 22 50-foot lots which have all been sold at $300. These he sold on a long-time payment plan, sometimes as little as $5 per month, and he claims that there have been no delinquencies.

[4] Recruiting of labor from the East has been practiced by farmers in both California and Arizona. Tetrau reproduces handbills and newspaper advertisements distributed and printed in Oklahoma and sponsored by the Farm Labor Service (*Migratory Cotton Pickers in Arizona*, WPA, Div. of Research, ch. VI, p. 61 ff.). California city newspapers carried articles quoting Frank Palomares, manager of the San Joaquin Valley Agricultural Labor Bureau, stating the need for farm hands in 1935, 1936, and 1937 (*La Follette Hearings*, S. Res. 266, Pt. 51, pp. 18843-18848). Payments for advertisements and labor scouts were made during these years and others (*idem*, pp. 18848, 18849). Workers state that advertisements in Oklahoma for California employment have been seen since 1938, but none so identifiable has been reproduced.

[5] These data were obtained from the local records of the United States Post Office of Wasco.

SOCIAL CONFLICT

Though the new social situation had clear advantages to both social groups, it is rife with latent conflict which gets expression in the more degrading phases of social exclusions, occasionally appears in open conflict, and has at certain times resulted in actual battle and bloodshed. Though the preceding chapters have indicated the nature of the social divergence between the two groups, the actual conflict situations remain to be discussed.

Economic Conflicts. It must be remembered that the outsider group in Wasco is a laboring group, made up of persons who, when working at all, are working for wages, and that those wages are always close to the margin of subsistence—would often have been below it if it were not for the public assistance received. The nuclear group may be considered an employer group, even though most of its members are actually working for salaries or wages. They are to be considered as employers because they have accepted the standards and leadership of the employer as the "natural system," and accept the ideology of this group, understanding social advancement in terms of degree of approximation to the employer's status. This does not necessarily mean that each person within the group approves the specific actions of the dominant element, but it indicates the basic dichotomy of the community regarding conflict situations.[6]

The economic conflict between these two groups in agriculture is a latent one, rising to the surface occasionally either as

---

[6] An advertisement which appeared during the cotton strike in the Tulare *Advance-Register,* demonstrates the assumption of certain dominant attitudes and at the same time implies their lack of universality. It reads: "Notice! To the Citizens of Tulare. We, the farmers of your community, whom you depend upon for support, feel you have nursed too long the Viper that is at your door. These communist agitators MUST be driven from town by you, and your harboring them further will prove to us your noncooperation with us, and make it necessary for us to give our support and trade to another town, that will support and cooperate with us. Farmers' Protective Association." Quoted by Paul S. Taylor and Clark Kerr, "Documentary History of the Strike of the Cotton Pickers in California, 1933," *La Follette Hearings,* Pt. 54, p. 19974.

individual and personal grudges or as mass action in the form of strikes. Twice during the depression the hostility developing out of the conflict situation rose to the point of physical violence. Such hostility is most apt to appear during times of stress, so that the decade of the thirties saw more open conflict than would appear during periods of economic stability or a boom period. Yet the essential conflict situation remains at such times too.

During the period, January, 1933, to June, 1939, inclusive, a total of 180 strikes were recorded in California agricultural industries, of which 150 were in field operations.[7] These 150 strikes in California varied by year from a third to all the agricultural strikes in the United States (43.5 per cent of total) and involved even larger aggregate proportions of workers (70 per cent of all agricultural workers).[8]

Of the strikes in California during this period, thirteen occurred within Kern County, of which five involved civil and criminal disturbances. Several of them are indicated as occurring in the vicinity of Wasco.[9]

The cause of over two-thirds of the strikes, according to this report, was wages and hours, while most of the remainder were for union recognition and discrimination.[10] Another tabulation with different definitions was compiled by J. C. Folsom.[11] It shows that of 96 agricultural strikes in California between 1933 and 1938, 63 were for "wages, hours and working conditions"; 14 more for "wages, hours and recognition"; 7 for "recognition"; 4 for "organization"; and 8 for other reasons.

These data demonstrate that Wasco lies well within the regions of strife in the most strife-ridden state so far as agricultural labor is concerned. Furthermore, this conflict is often accompanied by violence. Finally, the conflict is clearly rooted in the nature of the economic relations between the groups. Of these strikes, two were particularly virulent in the Wasco

[7] Henry R. Fowler, "Strikes in Agricultural Industry," *La Follette Hearings*, Appendix, p. 18380.
[8] *Ibid.*, Exhibit 7925, p. 17381.
[9] *Ibid.*, Exhibits 7922 and 7928, pp. 17379 and 17385, respectively.
[10] *Ibid.*, Exhibit 7926, p. 17383.
[11] *Ibid.*, Exhibit 7927, p. 17384. Quoted from J. C. Folsom, *Labor Disputes in Agriculture in the United States, 1927-1938*.

area, and the most important of these has been well documented.[12] The strike of 1933 started in Wasco, spread throughout the cotton area of the San Joaquin Valley, and resulted in several fatal shootings, innumerable arrests, and widespread ill-feeling. It involved not only the growers and processors on one hand and the workers on the other, but it also engulfed the whole of the community. Some of the social forces which lie behind strikes are shown by the following statements. "The Kern County Committee to resist the strikes, which was formed with the approval and support of a large meeting of growers held at Wasco, was composed of the directors of the Kern County Farm Bureau, the Executive Committee of the Kern County Chamber of Commerce, and representatives of other organizations." [13]

Again, "a number of school children were attracted to the cotton fields, and it was suggested that the schools be closed. . . ." [14] As a matter of fact, the growers made direct appeals to the citizenry by advertisements, such as one that appeared in the *Advance-Register* of Tulare, California, and quoted above,[15] and strenuously objected to what they considered the merchants' unfair siding with the laborers. Taylor and Kerr say:

> It greatly incensed the growers that the merchants should aid the strikers by extensions of credit and gifts. As one grower said, the merchants gave the farmers more trouble during the strike than any other element in the community. Or, as an official sympathetic to the workers put it, "The small local merchants are among the best friends of the laborers." The growers, regarding themselves as patrons of the merchants, believed they were entitled to full support in resisting a wage advance; they ignored the fact that the pickers are also patrons.[16]

If individual merchants considered their profits to lie with the laboring group, that is not to assert that the community as a whole, or even in large part, felt itself so aligned. For instance, in a neighboring community, "committees representing the Women's Club, P.T.A., Legion Auxiliary and American Legion . . . unanimously [agreed to] pass a resolution to declare the

---

[12] *Ibid.*, Exhibit 8764, Pt. 54, p. 19945, "Documentary History of the Strikes of the Cotton Pickers in California, 1933," by Paul S. Taylor and Clark Kerr.
[13] *Ibid.*, p. 19963.
[14] *Ibid.*, p. 19970.
[15] *V. supra*, p. 163, footnote 6.
[16] *Ibid.*, p. 19974.

[strikers' emergency] camp a health menace, and thus gave sanction to the health authority's closing them.[17] Shortly after the strike, the American Legion Post passed a "resolution expressing the Legion's disapproval of the appearance in Wasco of any speakers of avowed Communistic tendencies and asking that the churches, schools, etc., ban the presentation of any such speakers in any public or semi-public building. . . ."[18]

This 1933 strike involved shootings at which Wasco farmers were said to be present with guns. This strike, which raised wages from 60¢ to 75¢ for picking 100 pounds of cotton, is most vivid in the memory of the people of the community. A later strike in October, 1938, was much less effective and resulted in no violence. Nevertheless under the letterhead of the Associated Farmers the license numbers of cars connected with the strike were sent to farmers in nearby counties, with the notation that ". . . several caravans of strikers and agitators have gone from field to field in an endeavor to influence other pickers to leave their jobs."[19] This strike order led to at least one riot with a number of arrests, though these did not take place in Wasco.

Conflict over Unionization. If social and economic conflict exists over the matter of wage scales, as illustrated above, the conflict over unionization is much more real in the minds of most persons of the community, and the union has no status whatsoever in community life. It would, for instance, be impossible to propose that the sentiment of the union be canvassed on public issues in the way that other organizations in the town are unofficially polled. One young farmer said, "They ought to take a machine gun and shoot these [union] fellows down," and expanded his opinion of the union as an institution, and especially the vicious designs of their leadership. One of the major objections to the existence of the government farm labor camps was the fear they were the seed bed for radical activities, some going so far as to claim that the governmental agencies

[17] Quoted from the San Francisco *News,* Oct. 18, 1933, by Taylor and Kerr, *ibid.,* p. 19976.
[18] Minutes for November 15, 1933. Strike leaders were generally called communists in the daily papers.
[19] *La Follette Hearings,* S. Res. 266, Pt. 51, p. 18623.

sponsor communism. This double standard toward organization was derided by a liberal-minded small farmer speaking of one of his neighbors, "He used to be a construction laborer and you know they are all unionized. Now he says we must stop the workers in agriculture from joining unions."

The president of the local creamery is reported to be opposed to unionization. He is quoted as having planned the curtailment of trucking operations rather than reaching an agreement with the teamsters' union, which had been endeavoring to organize that aspect of the industry. One laborer stated, "I worked for them until they had this strike. The Old Man wouldn't have anything to do with unions, and he said he would go out of business before he would hire union labor. He cut off a bunch of workers, preparing to go out of business, and I was one of those let off. I didn't strike; it was the truck drivers who were striking. I didn't belong to any union—I was just laid off. The Old Man was a darn nice fellow—a good man to work for."

Later in this chapter we shall present some of the pressures against unionization. Here it is only necessary to point out that the union has neither any place in the organized social life of the community nor in the minds of its members as an acceptable means of achieving social and economic ends. Objections to the union may be vituperative as indicated by the person who simply wanted to shoot the leaders, or they may be rationalized by pointing out some of the evils attendant upon unionization, such as racketeering. The frequent acceptance of these attitudes by the persons who stand to gain by united economic pressure is manifested in the statement that "I haven't had to join a union yet," or more simply and directly "my husband doesn't belong because his boss doesn't believe in unions."

Political Conflict. One incident in Wasco showed more clearly than anything else the ramifications and intensity of the social antagonism and direct conflict between the nuclear and the outsider group beyond the economic sphere. On the day before an election for school board trustee, the phones of the nuclear members were busy carrying information that there was a campaign afoot to elect a "State Relief Administration candidate" —that is, a person currently receiving direct relief from the State

—as a member of the board of trustees, and advising all to be certain to vote the following day. The relief recipients had requested that school lunches made from surplus commodities be given their children without cost, and had been refused this request, and the "scare" developed that they were attempting to place their own member on the board. The assumption was that there would be a late hour attempt to rush the ballot box and write in the name of the two recipients of state aid who were leaders in the Workers' Alliance, a union of relief clients. The next day, though there was not a single ballot cast for these two persons, the vote was much heavier than in former years [20] and a long line of nuclear members awaited their turn at the booth during the closing hours of balloting. One nuclear member, who felt that the original request for free lunches was justifiable, said that she felt that it would not be bad to have a person on the board who represented those people, yet that if they got one member on this year, they would realize their power and eventually get control of the schools. Most of the persons felt that the original request was preposterous—"these people have gotten so they want everything for nothing"—and were fearful of the prospect of farm labor controlled schools.

It was impossible to determine the origin of this "scare." One of the "candidates" hotly denied the implication that he had entertained such an idea, and there certainly existed no mechanism by which a sufficiently large group could be organized to vote in that way, for neither the agricultural workers' nor the relief recipients' union was active enough. The validity of the "scare," however, has nothing to do with the implications of the situation; the important thing is that the sentiment of the nuclear group was so well organized against the outsider that the "scare" could have brought out such overwhelming reaction.

Other Sources of Conflict. Another manifestation of the social prejudices against the outsider group is the feeling toward the

[20] The newspaper showed votes of 415 and 422 for each of the two unopposed incumbents, who were re-elected to the school board (June 13, 1941), as against a total vote of 191 for the two opposing candidates in the election of the previous year (June 14, 1940). In short, the number of ballots increased from 191 to 422.

labor camps established by the Farm Security Administration. Hostility toward these camps was frequently expressed. One preacher felt that those who were not living in such camps (who were, in fact, living in growers' camps) were "trying to do something for themselves." Farm operators frequently expressed their dislike of the Farm Security Administration's camp near Wasco, and often refused to obtain labor from it. When pressed for reasons, they usually mentioned inefficiencies in administration or lack of satisfaction with previous experiences, or the unfortunate experience of a neighbor. These camps were referred to as hot-beds of radicalism, and as already stated the agency was accused of being communist controlled. The objection to these camps received official statement in the recommendation that they be discontinued.[21]

Such overt reactions to the latent hostility and mistrust, which have developed as a result of the general social exclusion described in the previous chapter, are rare. Yet enough instances of social antipathy have been adduced to indicate the existence of hostility toward the outsider group. It gets its clearest expression in feelings toward such institutions that serve the outsider class: unions, relief administrations, migrant camps, and even the revivalistic churches.

EXTERNAL LEADERSHIP IN CONFLICT SITUATIONS

These evidences of conflict in the social and economic spheres make more poignant the social dichotomy already described and lend more credence to our characterization of the social life as urbanized. What is more outstanding is the fact that the social conflicts which exist in Wasco are not only part and parcel of the conflict over a wider area, but are also very largely inspired from the outside. For the most part, the local small farmer, the local laborer, and the townsman are not interested in the generalized social conflict. Each is, of course, interested in his own economic gain and his own social position, with the result that

[21] *Brief of Land Use Survey of Kern County; Description, Problems, Recommendations, by County and Community Committees of Farmers*, 1940, and quoted *infra*, p. 174.

the psychological and social background for conflict exists, but he prefers to deal with his needs and desires in his own way. The 1933 strike, so well documented by Taylor and Kerr, had its very inception from outside the strike area. On September 21 the Bakersfield *Californian* reported, ". . . schedule for cotton picking is set at 60 cents for each 100 pounds at Fresno conference," while on the 25th the San Francisco *Western Worker* made rejoinder "Cotton pickers prepare to strike." [22] Thus, the opening shot for both sides was fired quite outside the region of conflict.

While the basic economic conflict existed in the agricultural area, the leadership of both factions came not only from outside Wasco but also, to a large extent, from outside agriculture. Wages to farm labor are set by a meeting of farmers before the San Joaquin Valley Agricultural Labor Bureau.[23]

This Bureau, according to its own by-laws, is made up of 17 members. It includes a high proportion of large business representatives, namely, a member from each of the seven San Joaquin Valley Counties (Stanislaus, Merced, Madera, Fresno, Kings, Tulare, and Kern), of the County Farm Bureau, and of the County Chamber of Commerce ("or in lieu of each organization accredited civic commercial organization") and one member each

[22] Quoted by Taylor and Kerr from newspapers cited, *La Follette Hearings*, S. Res. 266, Pt. 54, p. 19948.

[23] The *La Follette Hearings* give testimony to the method of setting wages, as follows:

SENATOR LA FOLLETTE: Now when it comes to the time of harvesting, what is your policy so far as the amount advanced to pay labor for picking is concerned, for example?

MR. JENSEN (Credit department of the Western Production Co., The Interstate Cotton Oil Co., the San Joaquin Cotton & Oil Co.): The policy is, within reasonable limits to advance those sums which the growers request with which to pay their harvest labor.

SENATOR LA FOLLETTE: And what standard, if any, did you set up to determine whether the growers' requests are reasonable and proper . . .

MR. JENSEN: Well, there is a custom in this state and in Arizona for the farmers to gather together prior to harvest and discuss a uniform picking rate of wage. The custom is also included, after that scale, so to speak, has been arrived at and agreed to, to request not only of us, but the other financing agencies, of which there are quite a number, that we assist them to conform to that. In effect, it amounts to a request that we advance a

COHESION, CONFLICT AND CONTROL 171

from the fresh fruit, the dried fruit, and the cotton industries, including all processors, marketers, shippers, and the like.[24]

According to the manager, the Bureau does not set the wages in the industry, but merely calls together farmers for the purpose of setting the wages. They are fixed in these meetings and the recommendation taken by the financing agencies as the basis for computing advances on harvesting the crops. There is no sliding scale nor any account taken of perquisites furnished. One farm operator has the following to say regarding this practice: "I never went to the meetings in Fresno where the farmers decided on the price scale. The gins are run by fellows who are [farm] operators, and they all go to those meetings. I can't get away. They should have meetings in each county. I usually pay above the set price. Most people around here pay more than the set prices. I figure those prices are for fellows who furnish houses to their people."

On the other side of the ledger, the laboring group was dominated by union and communist leadership. The 1933 strike was called by the Cannery and Agricultural Workers' Industrial Union, an affiliate of the Trade Union Unity League, and was considered to have been led by persons from outside with well-known communist affiliations. There were but a handful

certain scale, a certain amount per pound of lint cotton, and we, with some variations, largely conform to that. . . .
SENATOR LA FOLLETTE: Now, as I understand you, you say that the farmers get together in the various districts and fix or determine on what wage they are going to pay. How do you do that, do you know?
MR. JENSEN: In a general way. In both California and Arizona, there is an organization that serves as a labor bureau, so to speak, and it has a board of directors. Prior to the harvest time it sends out notices to the farmers that there has been called by the board of directors a meeting to be held at a certain date and requesting their attendance. Large numbers of farmers attend and after some debate they arrived at a scale of wage to be paid. . . .
SENATOR LA FOLLETTE: Do you know the name of the bureau in California?
MR. JENSEN: Yes. It is called the San Joaquin Valley Agricultural Labor Bureau (*La Follette Hearings*, S. Res. 266, Pt. 51, pp. 18582-3).

[24] By-Laws, Agricultural Labor Bureau of the San Joaquin Valley, reprinted in *La Follette Hearings*, S. Res. 266, Pt. 51, p. 18809 ff. The needs for a quorum (of ten) are met when "two agricultural members" are present. These may, by the statement of the by-laws, be corporation executives. (*Idem*, p. 18816, Exhibit 8427.)

of workers in Wasco affiliated with the United Cannery, Agricultural Packers, and Allied Workers of America (UCAPAWA), and a few more with the Workers' Alliance (union for the recipients of public assistance).

It has already been shown that many of the outsider group have accepted the nuclear group attitude toward the union. This was recognized by the district organizer for the UCAPAWA himself, when he stated that "these people from Oklahoma aren't very class-conscious. It isn't in their background." By this he meant not that they fail to recognize their social position, but that they are unwilling to act in terms of class unity, preferring to establish themselves as individuals and thus to avoid public actions which will identify them to the community as laborers.

The predominantly external origin of the conflict situation that develops hostility and open strife does not mean that there is no local conflict. The behavior of the nuclear group with respect to the school board election demonstrates the hostility, and the general social segregation has been documented in earlier chapters. The social and economic background for this class conflict exists and is a major characteristic of present day rural life in California, but the conflict in Wasco is but a part of a larger outside one.

SOCIAL CONTROLS

The externality of the economic conflict between outsider and nuclear groups brings to the fore the whole matter of social controls, to which our attention must be turned. By social controls is meant the exertion of influence or coercion by one person over other persons or groups, beyond any legally established powers. This is not to be construed as meaning that such controls are illegal, but merely extralegal. Neither does it mean that controls necessarily meet with opposition, or are even resented by the controlled group, for the most effective controls, those exerted over the employee by the employer, rarely meet with opposition. These are the "natural" controls of our social and economic system. Controls may vary in potency, according to the degree of effective resistance, and according to the number of persons so controlled. Social potency may be considered as pyramided.

Domination of Outsider Group by Nuclear Group. It will be best to begin with the lowest level of control, that which the nuclear group as a whole exerts over the outsider. We have already characterized the nuclear group as the one that has inherited the community, its institutions and its prerogatives as well as most of its assets. There has been sufficient demonstration of the fact that the civic organizations are made up almost completely of the nuclear group, and the example of the school board election shows clearly the popular horror of losing any of the political authority to the outsider class. As a matter of fact, no agricultural laborer is represented on any public board —school trustees, cemetery and water district trustees, or state or federal agricultural committees. The legal controls of these groups remain in the hands of the nuclear element of the community.

These are, of course, legally constituted authorities, and it may be assumed that in the course of time representatives of the outsider groups will appear in these capacities, and that the failure of the outsider to gain representation is merely an indication of its numerical minority situation. However, when civic problems are raised for which no vote is required, the "consensus of opinion" and the "cross-section of the community" are obtained through reference to the civic organizations made up entirely of nuclear members. Thus the whole matter of revamping the public cemetery, useful almost exclusively to the impoverished elements of the community, was debated within the service clubs, and the only spokesman for the poor was the Catholic priest, who had a few words to say on the matter. Similarly the water supply of the community is controlled by the nuclear group. When a WPA project was obtained for the purpose of installing a sewage system, a petition signed by 59 Negroes requested that the "honorable body . . . extend the sewer now in process of being constructed by the Wasco Public Utilities District into [the Negro district]." [25] This district lies

[25] Minutes of the Public Utilities District for October 7, 1936.

outside the limits of the utilities district but is furnished water at the regular charge made to subscribers within the district. The request was refused on a technicality and the matter dropped.[26]

At the meeting over incorporation, the question was raised as to whether the agricultural laborers had a legal or a moral right to vote on the issue. Again, a petition requesting free school lunches, presented by public assistance clients, was denied by the school board.

The laborer was not represented on the Land Use Planning Committee (a government-sponsored local body which recommends policy), or the Agricultural Adjustment Administration local committee, and this becomes significant when they deal directly with labor problems. In the summary of land-use problems of the 1940 report there are several references to the labor situation including the following problems under the heading "Relief."

1. Influx of homeless people create heavy relief cost, as well as serious housing, school, social and public health problems.
2. Relief payments too high to encourage work on farms, creating shortage of temporary help in some areas in spite of the presence of more workers than are needed, even in peak periods.[27]

The recommendations to meet these problems are as follows:

1. It would be better to eliminate the Government Camp and have housing provided by the farmers.
2. Relief payments and rules should be organized to encourage acceptance of farm work.[28]

The Wasco community recommendations were virtually the same, adding the specific recommendation that "wages on relief

[26] "The petition was read by the clerk and ordered filed, as the territory . . . lies outside the district and could not be considered at this time." (*Idem*.) It may well be noted here that fire hydrants and mains were installed after fire ravaged a part of this subdivision.

[27] *Brief of Land Use Survey of Kern County; Description, Problem, Recommendation, by County and Community Committees of Farmers,* 1940, compiled by Agricultural Extension Service of University of California, and the U. S. Department of Agriculture, Bakersfield, p. 3.

[28] *Ibid.*, p. 5.

should be less than farm labor rates to encourage relief clients to accept farm jobs."

Setting aside the extraordinary quality of the *non sequitur* in problem and recommendation number 1 that the housing shortage should be met by eliminating Federal housing facilities, there remains evidence that these recommendations have in mind only the welfare of the farmer group, and assume a position of antipathy to the interests of the laboring population.

There remains one quasi-political control exerted by the governmental agencies; namely, the activities of the health department in eliminating squatting on idle land. During the middle thirties, dwellings were placed along the roadside and in fields wherever this was possible, but these have largely been done away with. This elimination is the work of the health officials who desire to reduce the unsanitary housing conditions. Almost the last squatters in the Wasco area were removed in the arrest reported in the local newspaper as follows:

Charged with squatting on property without permission of the owners, six men and one woman were given sentences of 30 days in jail or the county road camp, which sentence was suspended on condition they move off the property within 5 days.

They were brought before [the] judge . . . on a complaint signed by [a member] of the County Health Department.

This treatment meant that the families would have to pay rent out of their small incomes, in many cases for houses inferior to those they had themselves built. One person had just spent, according to his own statement, thirty-five dollars, and "it came pretty hard after that outlay of capital."

Despite the general attitude of the evicted squatters, who considered the reasons of sanitation as merely a ruse, there can be no doubt that the health officers were motivated by the best interests of the public in bringing these charges. The fact remains, however, that the sanitation in camps operated by large growers is frequently inferior to that of the better squatter camps and the crowded conditions are much more dangerous to the public health.

A control of a somewhat different character is exerted by the landholders who have established neighborhood restrictions on building, which effectively prevent the construction of homes below certain arbitrary standards. These restrictions have never been established on an administrative basis, but have been written into contracts by those who have subdivided their acreage holdings. In effect this means that the agricultural laborer cannot live in certain sections of the town as he does not have the capital or the credit to build within the restriction limits. Since social worth is in part a function of neighborhood, the worker is prevented from attaining that form of prestige until after he has achieved economic status. In view of the fact that it has become the custom for the resettling laborer to build by slow accretions—his technique for circumventing his limited credit facilities—the disadvantages of geographical restrictions become more poignant as his dwelling improves.

One major controlling technique of our society is the control of the employer over the employee; a control which has become so thoroughly accepted that only under extreme provocation is it met with sanctioned counteraction. Since employee status is tantamount to outsider status, this means that a large part of the daily life of one segment of Wasco society is subject to the will of members of the remaining segment. The farm laborer, like any other, has the privilege of refusing or quitting his job, but if he accepts it he accepts also the conditions of working that are presented with it. Characteristically, the hours of work, the speed of work, lay-offs for whatever reason are determined by the employer. In order to prevent effective quitting by the working force, it has been of interest to the employer of large bodies of farm workers to maintain an oversupply of wage labor. The history of California farming is replete with examples of employer groups sponsoring movements into California from various parts of the world, from the introduction of the Japanese to the importation of Mexican nationals during World War II. California production depends upon an adequate number of wage workers, yet there is general recognition of the fact that employers overestimate the number of such workers needed. During the period of relative shortage of labor one of the chief complaints heard from farmer groups has been that it was impossible to maintain adequate control over labor to assure that the work could be performed under conditions demanded by the operators. It is in protection of these prerogatives that the employer group often opposes unionization, and this is explicit in the frequent complaint that "the unions are trying to run things." Indeed, the union is a mechanism not only for obtaining counter-control, in this case for the outsider group, but it is also trying to overthrow the mores of social control. For it is a part of the cultural tradition that social control is the prerogative of capital and the employer, a tradition that is accepted not only by the employer, but also by the outsider group.

Social Controls in the Nuclear Group. Within the nuclear group controls are of a somewhat different and more subtle nature. This group has already been characterized as maintaining many aspects of the primary group, capable of direct social pressures without economic weapons, that is, capable of ostracism and assigning status, on bases other than (but in conjunction with) economic position. The subtlest and probably the most effective is the establishment of patterns of behavior and the presumption of conformity. The influence by precept may be a strong one on the outsiders, whose desire to attain social recognition often results in a high degree of conformity, but since he does not belong to the social group, the major pressure, that of ostracism, cannot be brought to bear. This desire for conformity among the outsiders is at present one of the chief barriers toward unionization.

Within the nuclear group the pressures of this nature are stronger and more varied in character. It has already been shown that they are not so strong as they had once been; that the pressure to church attendance, the pressures against drinking, and the like, are not maintained. The "normality" of these controls makes it difficult to secure evidence of their existence, though occasionally the conflict appears on the surface. The pressure toward conformity of the young liberal thinker in the community was manifested repeatedly. The fear of "being caught" with books of liberal or radical social thought, or of expressing any politically unacceptable ideas, were indicated by several persons. The complete ostracism of the social worker attached to the State Relief Administration is a case in point here, the quite general assumption being that "all those relief workers are radicals."

It is highly significant of the urbanization of Wasco that these social pressures have changed their sphere of influence from the field of "morality," as exemplified by the earlier religion-drink-dance conflict, to the field of politico-economics, wherein the conflict between the social classes lies.

There are also less subtle pressures influencing the behavior of members of the nuclear group, economic pressures of the market place. The issue over incorporation expresses most clearly the nature of coercion which may manifest itself. As previously stated, the question was raised in a service-club-sponsored open meeting at which no person of the outsider group was present. It was raised by small shopkeepers, because of the economic benefits to them through the lowering of utilities rates, the elimination of private watchman fees, and the decreased competition from itinerant merchants. Attached to their banner was also the "intangible value" that organized community action might create. There were two groups bitterly opposed to incorporation: the farmers who were absentee owners of town site lands, and the large corporations, both for the reason that the benefits, which the small merchants would get for the increased taxation, would be burdens upon them. Incorporation had previously been dissipated by a legal suit brought by the absentee owners. The relative merits of the case are of no consequence here (it is clear that some would benefit while others would suffer loss), but it is of extreme importance that most of the small merchants would not take part in the discussion for fear of alienating customers. The lawyer who presented the issue in public meeting carefully avoided showing any prejudice in its favor, and was relieved when he received the approbation of known opponents to it. Reportedly the newspaper did not commit itself openly to a policy favoring the issue, for fear of reprisals by the advertisers, though the editors were so well known to the community that there could be no doubt of their attitude in the matter. One merchant wanted to print a series of articles in the paper but would not sign them. Another person said, "I can't take a stand because if I did the people would just take their business elsewhere." These restrictions are felt in other expressions of sentiment in public. A similar reticence was manifest in the discussion of national and international issues in public forums.

Social Controls of the Elite. These controls within the nuclear group are not distributed in a random fashion, but rather certain groups and individuals have higher degrees of potency. The social influence of the social organizations in the community has been demonstrated, and these organizations are the province of the nuclear group. But if we select those individuals who each belong to several organizations, we find a clear selection for certain occupations.[29] The overwhelming preponderance of the professional, manager, and proprietor class is not fortuitous. Of the fourteen persons of this category who belonged to five or more organizations, eight were the representatives of large corporations. Their repeated appearance and their status within these clubs are evidence of their important position in the society as local policy-makers. It contrasts clearly with the fact that only three small local entrepreneurs were represented.

Just as club membership and social leadership are sponsored by the corporations as a major source of public good-will, the skilled workers in the corporation offices are encouraged to participate in the lesser social affairs. The control that the corporation has over its representatives and employees may involve requiring them to join certain organizations, to move to a new community, to leave their families, or to inculcate manners, if not actual social attitudes, and may even influence their living arrangements. Usually, to be sure, any inconveniences are compensated for by added pay or covering expenses. For the most part they are accepted as "part of the job."

External Controls. This influence of the corporation, of course, leads us directly outside the community, for the local managers

[29] Families with memberships in three or more of the ten organizations analyzed consist of the following proportions: (A) Professional, managerial and proprietary, 53 cases; (B) farmers, 10 cases; (C) clerical, 3 cases; (D) skilled and semi-skilled, 23 cases. Of the 15 who belong to five or more, only one belonged to any class other than the first, and he was the local constable. Many farmers belong to farm organizations which were specifically excluded from this analysis.

are themselves the employees of others. This is quite clearly not an unimportant point, for when the major conflicts of the society are examined, the influence of the external social matrix is seen to be dominant. We have shown the influence of the large corporations in establishing a wage rate for hired labor, which is in turn enforced by the simple procedure of advancing that specified sum to the farmer for payment. The *La Follette Hearings* carry the testimony of the farm operator who paid higher wages because he financed himself.[30] The same situation occurred in Wasco. One farmer, financed through the local branch of a chain ginning corporation, said, "They never told me what to pay. They won't advance more than the wage scale for picking, and one year my wife and I got out and picked cotton ourselves so we could make up the difference between what we got and what we paid." The gin advanced money for wages on the basis of pounds picked, and this farmer was able to use that money financed for his family labor in order to pay what he considered a fair wage. During the violent strike of 1933 he gave the following account: "I didn't attempt to get pickers. They were striking for $1.00; the price was set at 60¢ and I was paying 75¢. There were several who said they would pick for me, but I told them not to. To tell the truth, I was pretty well caught up, and my wife and I went out and picked what there was. Lots of people objected to my attitude about the strike because I wouldn't go out and help. They don't seem to hold it against me now. One of the gin owners said he knew about my attitude, but for me to just forget about it, that I was a good customer, and he would continue to give me credit."

These statements, carrying no hint of persecution, show at once the controls and the acceptance of these controls by a person known for his liberal attitudes. He was not told what to

[30] SENATOR LA FOLLETTE: How did it happen you set your wages above the scale? [*i.e.,* at $1.00 and $1.15 for first and second pickings].
MRS. NICHOLS: Because we finance ourselves.
SENATOR LA FOLLETTE: What do you mean by that?
MRS. NICHOLS: We don't have to take finance money from the gin.
SENATOR LA FOLLETTE: And how does that make any difference?
MRS. NICHOLS: We are not told what to do. We can be our own boss. (*La Follette Hearings,* S. Res. 266, Pt. 51, p. 18635.)

COHESION, CONFLICT AND CONTROL 181

pay, yet he avoided the determination only at extreme physical sacrifice. Again, the gin operator forgave the farmer a transgression of what he must have conceived as the farmer's simplest moral debt; namely, to aid in breaking the strike.

It is not only in the overt threat and conflict that the controls appear. The criticisms of *The Grapes of Wrath* by persons who had not read the book reflect the phrases of speakers at the service clubs. The popular disrespect of the Federal agricultural workers' camps is but the reiteration of a set of attitudes handed down from outside of the community itself. They are the continuation of attitudes promulgated by the Chamber of Commerce [31] and by the California Farm Bureau Federation [32] before the camp near Wasco was created.

This policy with regard to the Federal camps is exactly the one that formed the basis of the illogical recommendation of the County Land Use Planning Committee, that housing conditions be improved by the abolition of the Federal camp.[33] We find it likewise expressed by farmers of Wasco, who refuse to hire labor from these camps.

The same situation obtains with respect to union attitudes and, while the developmnt of prejudicial feeling far antedates

[31] Excerpt from report of the Tenth Annual State-wide Meeting of California State Chamber of Commerce, November, 1935 (Los Angeles), which recommends that housing facilities be created and furthermore that "camp supervisor be under control of individual grower or committee or group of growers" and that "camp should be strictly limited to migratory labor for needed workers during harvest season, and that strict regulation be enacted against establishment of permanent residence of any group or groups in relation to relief conditions." (*La Follette Hearings*, S. Res. 266, Pt. 68, p. 24927.)

[32] *Vide* letter signed by Ray Pike and obtained from their files, dated December 11, 1935. It says in part:

"The subject of Migratory Laborer Camps has been much discussed throughout the State during the last several months. This has been largely brought about because of the fear that one of the Federal Departments may proceed with its plan for establishing 15 or more very large camps throughout the State, and that they will be operated by Federal appointees, favoring the communistic viewpoint.

"It is our belief that no Federal aid should be accepted for the building of such camps unless the camps may be locally operated and controlled by the farmers operating in the district. . . ." (*Ibid.*, Pt. 68, pp. 25169, 25170.)

[33] *Vide supra*, p. 174.

the existence of the present local anti-labor farmer organizations, this propaganda has been continuous and effectual.[34] It is, as a matter of fact, the very core of the interests of the Associated Farmers. The arguments against unionization are as old as the conflict itself, and are reiterated in speech after speech by the organizations dominated by the large growers.[35]

Walter Garrison spoke to the California Fruit Growers and Farmers in 1936, saying that "for many years the farmers of California have been the victims of vicious assaults. . . . The records of [the Associated Farmers] office . . . show that of the last thirty-six agricultural strikes in California, twenty-four were controlled and dominated by a few known Communists." [36] A press release from the Associated Farmers states, "Farmers will not submit to the organization of their workers . . . ," [37] while Philip Bancroft sums up the whole attitude of this group in a speech before the California Fruit Growers and Farmers in 1937. He says: "We [farmers] believe that unionization of farm labor, under existing conditions, would be absolutely ruinous to us as well as to the laborers themselves, [because] . . . first, . . .

[34] The development of the philosophy of rural life which identifies the farmer with the business man, and opposed to the laborer, is given trenchant examination by Paul H. Johnstone in his essay, "On the Identification of the Farmer," *Rural Sociology*, Vol. 5, No. 1, 1940.

[35] *Vide La Follette Hearings*, S. Res. 266, Pt. 68, pp. 25184-25270, giving speeches, press releases, and correspondence on this subject.

While the present discussion is developed out of data presented to that committee in 1939-40, preoccupation of the Associated Farmers with the labor situation continues. In the annual meeting of the Board of Directors in December, 1945, six resolutions were passed, including (1) a recommendation to transfer the Federal Farm Placement Service to the Department of Agriculture, that governmental employment agencies be returned to the State, and that farm labor be handled separately from industrial labor, (2) opposition to extension of unemployment insurance to agricultural labor, (3) opposition to so-called liberalization of the California Unemployment Insurance Act, and (4) the continued (and increased) appropriation for farm labor activities of the War Food Administration and Agricultural Extension Service (labor importation). Of twenty-four other items, all of paragraph-length, discussed in the December 20 issue of the *Associated Farmer,* ten were reports on unions and union activities, eight referred to other matters pertaining to wages, five referred to Communist or Socialist activities and one had reference to farm prices.

[36] *Idem*, p. 25184.

[37] *Idem*, p. 25185.

the perishable nature of his crops, . . . second, the typical farmer is much closer to his workers and on a much friendlier basis with them . . . third . . . most of the farm work is seasonal . . . [and] finally, the farmers are not able to pass on their increased costs to the consumers. . . ." [38] Rather than quote more examples of anti-union attitude in the higher brackets of this farmer organization, we can show not only this attitude, but also the very purpose of the Associated Farmers, the most active of the state-wide employer groups, in the following statement made by its executive secretary: "The Associated Farmer . . . was not organized for any purpose except to defeat the unionization of farms and to stop the agitation of radical organizers. . . ." [39]

It must be understood that every community or group in America is subjected to the efforts of many persons and organizations to crystallize and direct public opinion. The success achieved by the various sources of opinion formation are dependent only partly on either the inherent correctness of such opinions or the skill in presenting them, but rests in very large measure upon the climate of opinion and the social relationships and attitudes that exist in the community. For this reason, of the many forms of propaganda to which the people of Wasco are subjected, those which have real appeal to the community are the ones which both emanate from the elite in the community, and conform to traditional attitudes carried over from an earlier period. It is therefore not surprising that attitudes toward governmental innovations, to union activities among workers, to the Farm Security Administration camps, and public welfare activities tend to reflect those of dominant business interests and the large farmer. They also are made to appeal to traditional behavior in American rural society. The adoption of such attitudes by persons whose economic status is indifferently involved or adversely affected is a public assertion that the individual has identified himself with the group that expounds those ideas. Such attitude formation expresses itself within the

---

[38] *La Follette Hearings*, S. Res. 266, Pt. 68, pp. 25187-8.
[39] *Idem*, p. 25194. Letter to the editor of the *Saturday Evening Post* in reference to an article by George Creel, dated February 6, 1934.

nuclear group, but is effective beyond that group to the outsiders. Farm operators and community members generally indicate a strong disapproval of relief, particularly emphasizing the external control. The economic basis for their attitudes becomes explicit when they assert that relief should be discontinued for all persons whenever farmers need labor and should at all times be below prevailing wages. As a matter of fact most public assistance followed such policy but the rapidity and universality of termination and the level of wages was still unsuitable. Such attitudes among the nuclear group act as a strong incentive for outsiders to get off welfare rolls. Similar attitudes with respect to union activity prevail. At no time was a member of the nuclear group heard to express publicly his approval of unionization, while many condemned them mildly or violently. Sympathetic attitudes toward such organization, particularly among agricultural workers, was kept quiet. In such an environment it is not surprising that workers indicate reluctance to participate in union affairs if they desire to acquire social acceptance in the community.

Governmental Agencies and Social Controls. It is true that federal and state agencies organized to meet depression and war conditions, and backed with governmental sanction and large blocks of money, have taken powers which were historically in the hands of private citizens. They have influenced the rate of wages through relief standards, determined amounts and the nature of crops through AAA regulations, effectively competed in the credit market, both for farm operations and personal services, and they have affected the building trade through Federal assistance for private housing. And to most of those activities a vociferous leadership finds exception, for there has been a real invasion of local autonomy. But these forms of social control were not taken away from the local merchant and the small farmer. Rather they were taken from an elite which largely represents another outside influence, that of the corporation. We have shown how they have influenced wages through wage-setting hearings, influenced farming practices through financing, taken leadership over community affairs, and have been influential in directing public sentiment on subjects of national and local policy. Resentment of large corporations has often been expressed and occasionally still is, but these expressions are rare compared with those toward governmental and union controls.

SUMMARY

Controls over the behavior of Wasco residents are circumscribed by American law and custom and by the potential mobility of the population. Within the framework, the degree of influence exerted by persons of higher social status over those of lesser standing is considerable. These controls rest largely upon the direct control of the employer over his employee, the controls of the market place, and the influence exerted by the force of prestige itself. The areas of behavior in which conformity has come to be expected appear to have shifted from the sphere of morality to politico-economic attitudes and actions.

But the most insistent implications of the data on both social controls and social conflict are the strong influences exerted from outside the community. While the essential conflict situations are inherent in the economic and social structure of the community, they are in reality but the reflections of similar conflicts found in the industrial society of the nation as a whole. Examination of the sources of action in conflict situations and of controls exerted immediately carry one outside the community itself into the fountainheads of divergent ideas and desires.

CHAPTER VII

VARIATIONS IN THE SOCIAL PATTERN: SMALL FARMS

INTRODUCTION

IF THE characteristics of the farming community are indeed a function of the industrial pattern of farming operations, then they should appear throughout the area of industrialized agriculture. Furthermore the degree of urbanization should vary with differences in the degree to which the agricultural operations take on the character of the factory. Such a test has been made possible by the subsequent detailed analysis of two communities lying near Wasco, in the area of intensive irrigated farming, which are the subject of this and the succeeding chapter.

Dinuba and Arvin, the two communities subjected to this later analysis, lie north and south of Wasco, within about fifty miles. They enjoy the same general characteristics in soil and climate, have been subjected to the same major influences of the agricultural economy and are part of a single culture area. Their chief divergence lies in the fact that one of them, Dinuba, is surrounded by farms of modest proportions while the other is to a great extent farmed in large tracts. It was indeed this difference which motivated the investigation, for the analysis of these two towns was originally made in order to determine the nature and extent of the effects of large-scale farming operations upon the local community.[1]

[1] The study of Arvin and Dinuba was designed to furnish specific information with respect to the acreage limitation provision of Reclamation Law as applied to conditions in the area to be served by the Central Valley Project of California. A series of studies (Central Valley Project Studies) were instigated by the Bureau of Reclamation, with one problem raising the question of applicability of the law to California, and another assessing the

Since scale of operations is an important element in the industrial character of farming, it would be expected in terms of the fundamental hypothesis of the present volume, that certain important social differences appear between Arvin and Dinuba. Yet, because industrialization is not entirely dependent upon large acreages in common ownership, certain essential urban characteristics so vital to the proper understanding of Wasco society appear in both Arvin and Dinuba.

DINUBA AGRICULTURE

Industrialized farming has the following primary characteristics: intensive cultivation, high per-acre and per-farm capital investment, high specialization in single crops on individual farms, highly mechanized operations, large requirements of wage labor hired on an impersonal basis, and large-scale operations. On each of these counts, with the single exception of large farms, Dinuba farming fits the industrialized pattern. When the farming is examined in greater detail, we can see the extent to which these characteristics appear and dominate the farming scene. Dinuba agriculture is specialized to the production of

social effects of the project upon the State. The assumption of value in small farms to the welfare of the nation rests upon the existence of a causal relationship between size of holdings and the nature of society. A detailed comparative study using the insights gained from the investigation at Wasco was designed to test the validity of such an assumption.

The investigations utilized many of the same techniques applied in Wasco, but without the same intimate knowledge because of time limitations. On the other hand, three sources of statistical information are available for these two communities which did not exist for the earlier study: (1) a schedule of population, social participation and level of living taken from a 10 per cent random sample, (2) analysis of Agricultural Adjustment Agency records for size and type of farming, and (3) analysis of sales tax data for volume and characteristics of the business enterprises of the community.

A detailed description of the social and economic aspects of Arvin and Dinuba, and an analysis of the effects of large-scale operation upon community life in areas of industrial farming has been published elsewhere. Walter R. Goldschmidt, *Small Business and the Community, A Study in the Central Valley of California on Effects of Scale of Farm Operations,* Report of the Special Committee to Study Problems of American Small Business, United States Senate (79th Congress, 2nd Session). Government Printing Office, Washington, December 23, 1946.

raisin grapes. Of the 34,000 acres within the area of Dinuba, over 16,000 acres are devoted to orchard and vineyard, and by far the greater portion of this to the latter. Of the remainder, nearly 5,000 acres are devoted to forage crops—alfalfa and sorghums, and nearly 3,000 acres to cotton and vegetables.[2]

Orchard, vineyard, forage crops, cotton and vegetables are all irrigated crops. Together they comprise about three-fourths of all the land in the area. They produce a gross income of from $32 per acre for forage crops to $108 per acre for orchard and vineyard. These figures are based upon average yields and 1935-1939 prices. The forage income is low because the figures do not include value added by feeding livestock and selling meat and milk. The total annual value of fruit and grapes is one and three-quarters million dollars, while total production of all commodities has an annual value of two and one-half millions. These figures are indicative of the intensity of crop production.

The degree of farm specialization is extremely high. Three-fourths of all farms depend chiefly upon fruits as a source of income and over two-thirds of these have 80 per cent or more of their total acreage in fruits. About two-thirds of the remaining farms are devoted chiefly to summer field crops. Diversity in operations is the exception rather than the rule.

Labor requirements on farms in Dinuba are very great. An estimated 3½ million man-hours of labor are demanded by the crops in the community, or 133 man-hours per acre of used land each year. Such a demand on human energies—especially when the degree of mechanization of field work is considered—is a further sign of the intensity of land use.

These data indicate the amount of hired labor required. Because farms are small the relatively large number of farm operators can perform, if they work full time, 60 per cent of all farm labor in the community. In addition approximately 550 family heads work at farm labor as their chief or only means of support and another 600 persons work part-time in the fields. They

---

[2] These figures apply to the year 1940, and are based upon the records of the Agricultural Adjustment Agency. The area surrounding Dinuba within which the people go to that town for normal shopping and service needs was determined by interview, and that area included in statistical analyses.

VARIATIONS IN THE SOCIAL PATTERN: SMALL FARMS 189

cannot work the full year—indeed can expect full employment only three or four months of the time. Despite this fact, about 1,600 additional workers are required for farm operations during the month of September, when harvesting activities are at their peak. Thus, while nearly two-thirds of the work can be performed by the 722 farm operators, an additional require-

TABLE 29.—LAND USE AND VALUE OF COMMODITIES IN DINUBA

Commodity	Acreage		Value	
	Acres	Per cent	Dollars	Per cent
Orchard and vineyard	16,295	50	1,752,000	69
Row crops	2,646	8	212,000	8
Forage crops	4,749	15	152,000	6
Grain	1,020	3	24,000	1
Other land uses [1]	7,818	24	....	...
Livestock [2]	......	...	400,000	16
Total	32,528	100	2,540,000	100

[1] Not including lanes and buildings. Includes range, pasture and fallow and idle lands and a few acres of unclassified cropland.
[2] Value of livestock deducting cost of feed, except pasture. Locally grown feeds accredited to value of land in specified crops, though produced for feed locally.
SOURCE: Records of the Agricultural Adjustment Administration.

ment of 2,700 workers must be met out of the ranks of labor. Such workers are characteristically employed in large crews, frequently through contractors, and the personal relationship to the worker implied in the phrase "hired man" is a rare exception, even when farms are small.

The small scale of operations in Dinuba affects the social picture. It has the direct effect of cutting down the proportion of the dependent laborer population and of increasing that of the independent, stable and secure farmer group. The average farm in Dinuba contains 57 acres of land, including idle land and land devoted to homes and buildings. Nearly 90 per cent of all units are less than 80 acres in extent, and they contain nearly 60 per cent of the total acreage. Only about one per cent of the farms have over 320 acres and these contain but 8 per cent of all cropland. While farms are small in Dinuba compared to Wasco or Arvin or to the general size of operations under the industrialized pattern of farming, it must be recognized that these farms are not small in the more general sense of the term; that they still require great investments of capital and labor and bring adequate incomes even with the unfavorable prices of the late thirties.

DINUBA POPULATION

There are about 7,000 persons living in and around Dinuba who look to that community for their basic needs, supported directly or indirectly by the 2.5 million dollar annual agricultural production. Some of these must, of course, seek employment elsewhere part of the year, while outsiders must supplement this group during harvest season. Approximately one-third of the employed family heads are farm operators, another third are agricultural wage workers, while the remainder are divided among the different working groups in the town (Table 30). Exact comparison with the Wasco data (Table 14) is not possible, but they indicate broadly that the independently employed and salaried groups (the first three categories in the tabulation) are more important numerically in Dinuba. Over half of the gainfully employed fall in these brackets in Dinuba, against between a fifth and a third in Wasco. The Wasco farm population is less than half as great as that of Dinuba according to these estimates.

Dinuba is an older community than Wasco. Its start came from the development of irrigation in 1882 when the "76 Land and Water Company" was formed to convert the wheat lands to intensive irrigation uses. In 1888 the present irrigation district was created as a public organization under state law, and the town of Dinuba began. Schools had already been in operation in the area, and by 1900 a high school was created. The town was incorporated in 1906. The steady growth of the community,

VARIATIONS IN THE SOCIAL PATTERN: SMALL FARMS 191

both in its physical aspects and its population continued through World War I but when the demand and the price for raisins dropped in the early twenties the town suffered economic distress and lost somewhat in population.

The greater age of the community not only means a more firmly established set of institutions, but also affects the charac-

TABLE 30.—CLASSIFICATION OF DINUBA POPULATION ACCORDING TO OCCUPATION

Occupation class	Family heads		Average size family	Total population	
	No.	Per cent		No.	Per cent
A. Professionals, managers, and proprietors	264	13.8	3.31	874	12.7
B. Farm operators	661	34.5	3.27	2,161	31.4
C. Clerical workers	61	3.2	3.31	202	2.9
D. Skilled laborers	313	16.3	3.45	1,080	15.7
E. Unskilled laborers (farm)	557	29.0	4.22	2,351	34.2
Unskilled laborers (non-farm)	61	3.2	3.45	210	3.1
Total	1,917	100.0	3.43	6,878	100.0
Non-employed	244		2.17	529	

SOURCE: Schedule data.

ter of the population. An analysis of the age distribution shows a larger proportion of the population above seventy years of age than for the San Joaquin Valley as a whole, and considerably more than in Arvin. One result of this older population is a relatively small average-size family and a relatively larger number of small families. Thus 9 per cent have but a single member and an additional 30 per cent include only 2 persons. The occupational differences in size of family are also revealing. Farm operators have smaller families than the traditional occupation groups of the towns—merchants, professional, and white collar workers. The really large families are found among the farm workers.

Though Dinuba is old enough to have a fairly stable population, and though there has been no increase in its population for the past 20 years, nevertheless, only half the family heads have had 20 years' residence in Dinuba, and nearly one-fourth have come in 1940 or later. This instability is found predominantly among the laboring group, for three-fourths have less than 20 years' tenure and over a third have arrived in the town in 1940 or later.

Eighty-one per cent of the family heads are American born and the remainder represent a wide array of origins, including Asiatic, Armenian, Mexican, Russian, and Canadian. A small Japanese colony had been evacuated at the time the studies were made, but a Korean colony remained. Nineteen per cent of the family heads were California born, while the remainder have come from various parts of the United States with a slight preponderance from the states of Oklahoma, Texas, and Missouri—the source area for the migration of farm labor in the thirties. The largest ethnic groups in the area are the colony of Armenians, the Koreans, and before evacuation, the Japanese. A group of Mennonites made up of persons of various nationality backgrounds, chiefly Russian, German, and Canadian, form a separate community based upon common attitudes differing from those prevalent in Dinuba.

The population of Dinuba may be characterized as an aggregation of persons from a wide variety of backgrounds but predominantly American whites, with a relatively large proportion in the older age brackets, and with a large number displaying a high degree of mobility. About one-third are farmers, one-third are farm laborers, and the remainder engaged in the various service occupations of the town.

SOCIAL STRUCTURE

The significant segregations of the population of Dinuba, like those of Wasco, are occupational and ethnic. While the general pattern is the same, and similar relationships between the several classes exist, the lines of cleavage are less sharp and the social distance not so great in Dinuba as they are in Wasco. There is a greater wealth of institutions, a larger and more diversified stable population, and particularly more persons whose social affiliations are determined not by the dominant pecuniary values of urban society but rather by the specific attitudes and ethos of one or another cultural subgroup. It is significant that while in Wasco the major ethnic groups were considered simply as outsiders and had a status commensurate with laborers of the white race, in Dinuba these groups generally had greater economic independence and a higher social position. In Dinuba the Armenians, the Mennonites, and to a lesser extent the Japanese (before Pearl Harbor) and the Koreans are occasionally accepted in community institutions in a manner that does not take place with respect to either the Mexicans or Negroes of Wasco.

Evidence of economic well-being, as reflected by material possessions and reported income, was obtained from the Dinuba sample interviewed. About one-eighth of the population fell in the upper quarter of each of the three indices developed from this data, and this group must be viewed as an elite. Only one out of the 26 families included in this elite obtained his livelihood as a laborer. A large group of persons have free social access to this elite by belonging to the same clubs and churches so that, though gradations in prestige exist, this larger group must be viewed as a single social class, comprising about a third of the total population.

Of the remaining two-thirds there are many whose activities center about some focus of interest, usually a church, and who have a common bond with others, thus forming a sub-community or strong in-group. Here would be placed all the Armenians and Koreans, and the Mennonites, and other minor religious colonies. These groups breach occupation barriers, including among their numbers both farm operators—usually small landowners—and farm laborers, plus a few in the service and industries of the town. They are by-passed by the dominant community pattern of pecuniary values and are far less urbanized. Within each sphere the individual is known to all and a more rural and homogeneous atmosphere prevails, while the relationships between members of these groups and the dominant elements of the community are fairly remote. This latter relationship is, however, vitally different from that which characterizes the relationship between outside and nuclear groups in Wasco. For these strong in-groups maintain a solidarity on their own volition, rejecting the value system of the community for their own, usually religiously inspired one and eschewing any close social ties with the community. Furthermore, they have stable tenure, permanence in the community and are not an impoverished class. A third or more of the population must be included in this category.

There remains, however, a third class whose relationships are those of the outsider to the community, and whose status and social conditions correspond exactly to that group in Wasco. It is comprised almost entirely of farm laborers living in poor economic circumstances and having only the most tenuous ties with the dominant elements of the community. Eight per cent of the total population sampled participated in none of the affairs of the community whatsoever and many others in very little more. Thirteen per cent of the residents stated that they did not consider Dinuba their home town. These social relationships can be visualized in terms of the following diagrammatic sketch:

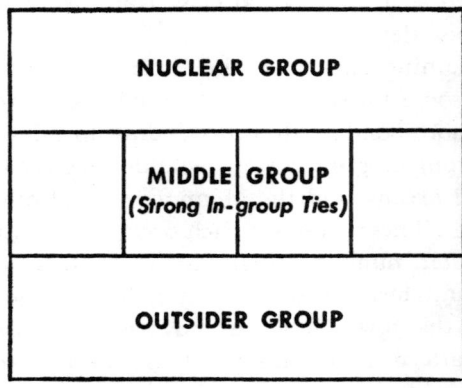

SOCIAL PARTICIPATION

Of the categories of social activity and recreation subjected to investigation, church attendance exceeds all other forms in Dinuba, while motion pictures are second. Over 80 per cent of the families have members in churches and over 70 per cent report moving picture attendance. This is a greater degree of church attendance reported than for Wasco (Table 21), while it is a smaller movie attendance than reported in the Consumer Purchases study for village and country people in the Pacific. No other category of social activity or recreation involves over half the population. Table 31 shows the relative importance of the different categories of social activity.

TABLE 31.—PARTICIPATION IN SOCIAL AND RECREATIONAL ACTIVITIES IN DINUBA

Type of activity	Families reporting [1]		Individuals reporting [2]	
	No.	Per cent	No.	Per cent
Clubs [3]	103	47	...	..
Churches	175	82	370	72
School events	70	33	203	28
Other community events	86	40	231	32
Dances	49	23	98	13
Card parties	29	14	55	8
Picnics	91	43	288	39
Motion pictures	145	71	456	62

[1] Based upon a sample of 206 families.
[2] Based upon total population of sample, or 731 persons, except in the case of churches, which is based upon total population aged 12 years old and over, or 515 individuals.
[3] Data for individual participation not available.
SOURCE: Schedule data.

Though membership in the various non-religious associations is not as frequent as are other activities, the importance of such organizations should not be underestimated. In Wasco memberships in the dominant social clubs not only assured upper-class status in the community, but were necessary in order to have the opportunity to participate in many of the decisions affecting community welfare. Since Dinuba has elective officials the civic importance of the social organizations is somewhat diminished, yet there is little doubt that the clubs set the tone and character of the community.

A meeting sponsored by the Chamber of Commerce is in point. This public dinner meeting was called by a group of community leaders to discuss the problems and prospects for planning community improvements. Not only was the meeting called jointly by two associations, but almost every speaker called upon represented some such group. The individual comes to be represented in important community decisions by the elected representative of his social group.

A complete catalogue of Dinuba associations is difficult, but a list of the better known organizations is indicative. There are two merchants' associations, three service clubs, a local business men's club for social purposes, and the volunteer firemen who form a closed social group. There is an active Legion with its auxiliary, a chapter of the Masonic order (with its women's, girls', and boys' auxiliaries), a local chapter of the Modern Woodmen of America, and the I.O.O.F. For women there are four recognized associations and one P.T.A. The Red Cross is not without its social aspects. Farmers have, aside from commodity associations and an organization which aids in obtaining labor, a local Farm Bureau Center and a chapter of the Grange. The Legion, the Women's Club, the Red Cross, and two fraternal orders each have their own meeting halls. In addition one service club has sponsored a recreation hall for youth and two others have each furnished meeting places for Boy Scout troops. Most of these buildings are generally available to the public—or to segments of the public—for recreational and meeting purposes.

As in Wasco, most of these organizations are the province of the upper group in the community, and particularly of the merchants and professional people. Labor is sparsely represented among them. In Dinuba nearly half of all memberships re-

VARIATIONS IN THE SOCIAL PATTERN: SMALL FARMS 197

ported were held by persons gaining their livelihood from white-collar activities while 89 memberships were held by the farmer group and only 40 by all laborers combined. There were 158 memberships for each 100 persons in the white-collar category, 57 for each 100 persons in the farmer category and only 16 for each 100 labor persons. This pattern follows closely that of Wasco.[3]

The service clubs and the American Legion have the widest representation of memberships, while fraternal orders are represented among only 15 per cent of the families, and farm organizations among only 12 per cent. Less than one family in ten has a member of a woman's organization. Ninety-eight per cent of all Rotary Club members whose occupations could be determined were of the farmer-white-collar group; 96 per cent of the Dinuba women's club and 79 per cent of the Legionnaires fell in this category. Here again the pattern established in Wasco in which laborers rarely have the intimate contacts of club association, is found in Dinuba. Comparable data were not obtained for other organizations.

It is also significant that, though the community consists in very large part of people who work as wage labor, unionization has not proceeded very far. Only five per cent of the families interviewed held membership in any union, and no local chapters were reported. Here again the Wasco pattern is reflected.

DINUBA CHURCHES

Religion affects the lives of a large proportion of the Dinuba population, judged by the proportions who belong to or regularly attend one of the fourteen or more local congregations. Seventy-two per cent of the population 12 years old and over reported religious participation, with very little difference between the separate occupation classes except that farmers appear

[3] It should be noted that in Wasco, information was obtained from club records while here it was obtained from persons. Since farmer organizations were not included in the Wasco data, but were for Dinuba, one would expect Wasco farmer memberships to appear more rarely. Since the figure is actually somewhat greater, there is clear evidence that Wasco farmers participate much more in social organizations.

to be more devout. Differences in sources of data make direct comparison with Wasco impossible, but the number and kind of churches and the heavier participation among the laboring group suggest that a similar pattern exists. The fact that there are more churches with a smaller total population and that the churches appear to be much more fully attended suggests that the degree of religious affiliation and participation is greater in Dinuba than in Wasco.

The Dinuba churches include the Presbyterian, Christian, Methodist, Baptist, two Seventh-Day Adventist congregations, a Zion Mennonite and a Mennonite Brethren, Church of the Nazarene, Assembly of God, Church of God, Church of Christ, Four-Square Church, Korean Presbyterian, and Armenian church. Prior to evacuation of the Japanese there was a Japanese Buddhist group; there was a Mexican Pentecostal for a while, and Mormons, Catholics, and Lutherans periodically meet in Dinuba. These congregations, like those in Wasco, tend to "represent the different elements" in the community. These may be divided into four categories: churches of high, intermediate, and low social standing, and churches which serve some particular segment of the community which has strong in-group ties and which cannot readily be assigned social status in terms of the dominant pecuniary values. The first four churches have high status in Dinuba, the Nazarene and Assembly of God have intermediate status, while the Church of God, Church of Christ, and Four-Square Church have little or no social standing. The Seventh-Day Adventists (with their own school) and the Mennonite churches and the churches serving persons of common racial or ethnic origin must be considered as part of the fourth category. Judgments with respect to social standing are based upon general observation of type of service, age of the institution and character of the building, and upon expressed attitudes of the people. They are corroborated by the data on participation (Table 32). Only one-third of the four congregations with high status are laborers, while in the churches of intermediate and low status two-thirds are laborers. The proportion of laborers in the in-group congregations correspond closely to the proportion of the laborers in the whole community. Though

TABLE 32.—CLASS CHARACTER OF DINUBA CHURCHES

	Per cent of membership among:	
	Independently employed	Wage laborers
High status churches	67	33
Intermediate status churches	36	64
Low status churches	37	63
In-group churches	45	55
All churches	55	45

SOURCE: Schedule data.

the pattern of social segregation is similar to that found in Wasco, Dinuba churches afford more opportunity for social contacts between different occupations.

SOCIAL ORGANIZATION AND COMMUNITY ACTION

The city of Dinuba is incorporated and therefore represents a body which can act in response to the expression of public sentiment. Herein lies the greatest civic difference from Wasco. Incorporation is nearly 40 years old, and expressions of pride in the city's achievements are frequently heard.

A council of five is elected for a four-year term, three at one time, two at another. Each councilman has charge of one particular phase of the city's activities—police and fire, finance, city properties, parks, and waste disposal, or streets, sewers, and water. The operations of particular aspects of city government are therefore subject to the direct review and approval of the electorate. A heated election had taken place immediately prior to the period of field investigations, resulting in the deposition of one of the councilmen whose policies were objectionable to a segment of the population. Feeling in the matter was still in evidence on both sides.

Physical improvements—paving and a sewage system—were inaugurated before World War I. Early in the twenties the community, in expectation of continued growth commensurate with that which resulted from the highly favorable raisin prices, inaugurated a civic development which included paving and lighting virtually every street, laying sidewalks throughout town, completing the sewage system and establishing a water system and parks. As a result the physical appearance of the community was and remains one of the best of any town its size in the area. The slump in grapes during the early twenties left an indebtedness that destroyed property values and burdened the community for fifteen years.

This development came at the time when speculative farming in the area was at its peak. It was the result of the adoption of pecuniary standards by the rank and file of the population, and of a money prosperity which distorted both values and judgment. It is Dinuba's counterpart of the 1936 potato prices in Wasco, on a bigger scale over a longer period and with more far-reaching effects. At the same time it was the civic counterpart of the "silk shirt" era.

Many individuals lost heavily as a result of individual and community spending, based upon the capitalized value of wartime raisin prices. But the community has managed to straighten its affairs by a system of refinancing and the sale of tax-deeded lands. As a community, therefore, it is now in excellent condition, with a great many public improvements and a low bonded debt. Improvements continue to be made. The current mayor (at the time of field research) prided himself upon his contribution to community welfare—a municipal garbage disposal system and cleaned up alleyways.

The city furnishes a number of services. In addition to street paving, street lighting, and sewage and garbage disposal, the city has a municipal water system and has established two parks and has the property for a third one which is currently being improved. The city maintains a four-man police force and a fire department which is largely manned by volunteers and works co-operatively with the county fire department.

Civic leadership in Dinuba, like that in Wasco, rests largely with a small group of merchants, teachers, and other professional persons. The influence of the Chamber of Commerce meeting, the action of organizations in setting the patterns of behavior and the discussions with local citizens all offer testimonial to that effect. In the recent election, for instance, the candidates were associated in people's minds with certain organizations, even though no official sponsorship was announced. Yet there is a real difference in the fact that the mechanism exists in which the people may express a preference, irrespective of creed, color, or social affiliations.

The broader base for democratic action shows itself by the continued existence of the larger of the two newspapers, a semiweekly. It has long maintained an outspoken attitude, both with respect to internal politics in the community and with respect to the encroachment of outside interests upon the community. The editor claims to have publicly fought the acquisition of the two local banks by the chain banking system, the development of large-scale farming enterprises and similar economic interests, and to have maintained his paper by subscriptions in the face of a boycott by advertisers. All these statements were not checked, but some editorials were examined which expressed opinions undoubtedly free of any coercive pressures by economic interests. This local paper continues to take a positive stand with respect to major local issues, along with furnishing a vehicle for the expression of social solidarity in the community. The wartime phase of this latter service has been to print all pictures of local servicemen submitted, by printing a special sheet of hometown news for them, distributed by the local Rotary, and by publishing an annual volume containing pictures and records of local people in the armed forces.

Social activity takes place outside the political sphere, and important civic enterprises are sponsored by various groups in the community. The Legion and Rotary have each sponsored Scout troops and furnished them with a meeting place. The Y's Men's Club has initiated a downtown recreation center, and weekly dances are held in the clubhouse of the Women's Club. It will be seen that the influence of formal organizations upon the welfare of the community is very great, and that this influence is made to reach beyond class lines, though leadership rests with those of upper class status.

SUMMARY

The community of Dinuba presents a significant variation on the pattern of industrialized farming. With a large number of small units and very few acres held in large tracts, there is a large body of stable farm population with community-centered interest, while the proportion of the population with negligible interests remains small. This appears to be the result on the one hand of the absence of a wealthy class with social ties in great urban centers and on the other hand, of the relatively small population having poor circumstances and few roots in the local community.

CHAPTER VIII

VARIATIONS IN THE SOCIAL PATTERN: LARGE FARMS

ARVIN AGRICULTURE

ARVIN IS the community center for an area devoted predominantly to large-scale industrialized agricultural enterprise. About ten thousand acres of the exceptionally fertile land in the area is held and operated by the DiGiorgio Fruit Corporation. This organization, with its subsidiaries and affiliates extends the length and breadth of the United States, and is a potent influence on the marketing of fresh fruits and vegetables. This, at least, was the opinion of a federal grand jury which indicted the owner and a number of corporations in its control for their monopolistic practices, an indictment to which the accused plead *nolo contendere,* on the basis of which the corporations involved were subjected to fines.[1]

The average Arvin farm is large—497 acres. While 40 per cent of all units are less than 80 acres in extent, these comprise but 4 per cent of all the acreage. The 22 units containing a section or more of land each, on the other hand, hold over two-thirds of all the acreage in farms within the community. Arvin, therefore, is not without its small farmers, yet these are few in contrast with Wasco and especially with Dinuba. Farming is dominated by a handful of larger growers who hold most of the acreage.

[1] United States *vs.* California Fruit Growers Exchange, *et al.,* No. 15167 (criminal) District Court of the United States for the Southern District of California, Central Division, September Term, 1941. The accusation read in part that the indicted were ". . . engaged in a wrongful and unlawful combination and conspiracy to fix, control, regulate and stabilize prices at which citrus and deciduous fruits are marketed and sold in interstate commerce . . . by controlling and restricting the channels and methods of distribution, which combination and conspiracy has been in restraint of trade and commerce."

Not only are Arvin farms large in scale, but they have all the other attributes of industrialization. The proportion of land devoted to intensive uses within the boundary of the community is somewhat less than in Dinuba, but the absolute acreage was equally great in 1940, and has since increased, as the area of intensive crop use has been expanding greatly in response to wartime prices. Nearly half of all farm land was devoted to irrigated agriculture, and this area accounted for over four-fifths of the two and a half million dollar value of crops produced (Table 33). The value of the crops from these irrigated

TABLE 33.—LAND USE AND VALUE OF COMMODITIES IN ARVIN

Commodity	Acreage		Value	
	Acres	Per cent	Dollars	Per cent
Orchard and vineyard	7,875	18	847,000	35
Row crops	8,980	21	1,009,000	41
Forage crops	3,774	9	163,000	7
Grain	15,994	38	222,000	9
Other land uses [1]	6,037	14	....	...
Livestock [2]	......	...	197,000	8
Total	42,660	100	2,438,000	100

[1] Not including lanes and buildings Includes range, pasture and fallow and idle land, and a few acres of unclassified cropland.
[2] Value of livestock deducting cost of feed, except pasture. Locally grown feeds accredited to value of land in specified crops, though produced for feeding locally.
SOURCE: Records of the Agricultural Adjustment Administration.

lands is $100 per year, based upon prices of the late thirties and upon average yields.

Arvin's production is more evenly spread over a variety of commodities than either Dinuba or Wasco, though the individual farms tend to be highly specialized. Two-thirds of all farms having fruit as their major crop devote over 80 acres to that one category, while a third of all farms are devoted chiefly to row crops. There is a growing tendency among the very large operators to diversify their land use in order to maximize the use of their buildings, equipment, and managerial labor, and incidentally to improve their bargaining position for labor. The DiGiorgio interests in Arvin have endeavored to grow a variety of fruits and vegetables in order that the flow of commodities through their packing sheds is continued for as long a season as possible. Yet this diversification is different in character from the old-fashioned "general" farm, for each product is a highly specialized operation, each is produced for cash sale to Eastern markets, and none is utilized simply for rotation to soil building crops.

The intensive character of farming means great requirements for labor. Cotton and potatoes each require well over 100 man-hours of work per year for each acre of land, while deciduous fruits require over 500 hours of labor for each acre. A total of 2.9 million hours of work are required for the commodities produced, of which only a fraction (about one-seventh) can be done by the farm operators, assuming each works full time. Most of the work (73 per cent) can be done by resident hired labor, while during three months of peak requirement it is necessary to import workers to fill out the necessary force. It is not surprising, therefore, that two-thirds of the family heads (940) in the community obtain their living as farm laborers, while nearly 700 additional workers perform such labor on a part-time basis. With this large labor supply, it is still necessary to import nearly 1,200 workers during the peak month of employment (July).

ARVIN POPULATION

Approximately 6,400 persons are residents in Arvin. This is 20 per cent fewer than in Dinuba despite the fact that the value of farm production is the same. Nearly three-fourths of this population is dependent upon agricultural wages for its support, while the proportion who have independent employment represent but a small fraction of the people (Table 34). These population statistics, when viewed in terms of the social and economic position of wage labor in California agriculture, present the most telling story of the effect upon the rural community of large-scale farm enterprise under industrialized production. For in Arvin more than eight persons out of ten are directly dependent upon a small fraction of the population for their means of livelihood.

In Wasco we have seen that, though mobile, farm labor is motivated toward settling in one community. Arvin has not gone

TABLE 34.—CLASSIFICATION OF ARVIN POPULATION ACCORDING TO OCCUPATION

Occupation class	Family heads		Average size	Total population	
	Number	Per cent		Number	Per cent
A. Professionals, managers, and proprietors	82	5.9	3.50	287	4.6
B. Farm operators	141	10.1	3.57	403	8.1
C. Clerical workers	20	1.4	3.50	70	1.1
D. Skilled laborers	200	14.3	3.90	780	12.7
E. Unskilled laborers	955	68.3	4.75	4,536	73.5
Total	1,398	100.0	4.23	6,076	100.0
Non-employed	81		2.63	212	

SOURCE: Schedule data.

very far in this process. Over half the residents in Arvin have lived in the community four years or less, irrespective of occupation, and three-fourths came in 1935 or later. The proportion of laborers of recent tenure in the community is greater than for the remainder of the population. It must be remembered that Arvin is a younger town than Dinuba or Wasco. It was first subjected to irrigation in 1910, and a school was established at the townsite in 1913. The growth of schools in Arvin and Wasco shows a very similar pattern, with the Wasco school population about four years ahead of the Arvin population until the middle thirties.

Very few Arvin residents are native Californians (4 per cent of the heads of families) while nearly two-thirds of the family heads were born in either Oklahoma, Texas, or Arkansas. Twelve per cent of the family heads were born outside of the United States, half of these in Mexico. Thus the population of Arvin is made up in very large part of depression and post-depression migrants from the "dustbowl" states, who have settled temporarily where work opportunities exist. The fact that so large a portion of the Arvin residents came to the community since 1940 does not reflect a sudden growth—on the contrary, the student population was less at the time of field investigation (spring, 1944) than it was in 1940.

The age composition of the Arvin population reflects a pattern of family migration, and the effect of the draft and war opportunities upon the community. Forty per cent of the people are under 15 years of age, nearly 20 per cent are in their thirties, and only about 10 per cent are in their twenties. Only a small fraction of persons are 60 and over. Families tend to be much larger in Arvin than in Dinuba, with nearly a fourth composed of six or more persons and less than a fourth composed of only one or two individuals. The average family is 4.23 persons, or nearly a fourth greater than in Dinuba. This difference in part reflects the larger proportion of labor whose families are far the largest of any occupation group. The younger composition of the population with families relatively intact, is also a factor contributing to this difference. As in Dinuba, Arvin farm families are about the same size as those of professional and business people, whereas the truly large families are found among farm laborers (3.57 for farmers as against 4.75 for farm laborers).

While a heterogeneity of origins can be recognized among the people of Arvin, by far the greatest bulk of the population are farm laborers recently come to the community from the Southwest—and serving as wage labor in the fields. The most striking characteristic of the population is its great proportion of such labor and the small fraction of persons with relative independence, security, or long tenure.

SOCIAL STRUCTURE

If occupation is the diagnostic criterion of social status, it follows that in Arvin the proportion of persons of outside position is far greater than those whose position can be described as nuclear. This is clearly the case. Whereas social distinctions in Dinuba are less finely drawn than in Wasco, they are far sharper in Arvin than in either of the other communities. As a matter of fact, a great social hiatus between the farm laborer on one hand and the farmer and white-collar worker must be recognized. These two groups represent two separate worlds with but the most tenuous ties between them.

Ten of the 132 families interviewed in Arvin were in the top quarter of the brackets of each of the three indices of economic well-being: income, material possessions, and condition of home. Nine of these were from among the farmer and merchant class, and all these nine belonged to the single leading church, or to no church at all. Among this group there were 23 persons twelve years old and over. They had a total of 53 club memberships including all but one of those reported for the two major civic associations. Another 8 families in the same occupation categories had above-average living conditions and income, and held 15 club memberships among them. Some of them belonged to the poorer churches. A third group of the farmer-white-collar category had poor economic circumstances, rarely participated in any associations and never in the leading church. Only eleven families of the laboring group fell in the upper half of the three indices of economic well-being. One of these belonged to the high status church, and among them they had nine club memberships. Possibly a single skilled laborer in the sample was in a position to associate freely among the social group made up of the dominant farmers and merchants.

These facts show that while being in the farmer or in the business and professional categories is virtually a necessity for participation in the leading affairs of the community, such occupation does not insure top social position. In the upper bracket of the Arvin social structure, we can certainly include all the first group of 9 families, probably the second group of 8 families, and one labor family. These 18 families in our sample of 132 represent 14 per cent of the resident population. They are not a homogeneous unit, though they have easy and fairly close social relationships. A small portion, mostly operators of larger farm units, participate chiefly in the social affairs of the nearby city of Bakersfield and, like similar elements in Wasco, find their true social status in this larger environment.

Of the remaining 114 families only 21 hold any membership in associations of the local community and only 71 hold membership in some local church. In all, about 75 families (two-thirds) participate in some local activity, though these ties are frequently tenuous and with but a handful of persons of similar status and with equally tenuous ties. Thus if we eliminate those whose only membership is in the churches of lowest social standing, the number of families drops to 50. Twenty-seven of the 75 families denied participating in any community-located recreation and nearly half did not consider Arvin their home town.

From an examination of the behavior of these families it is apparent that the degree to which they have ties varies considerably, and that about half of them have absolutely none with Arvin while the remainder have established social contacts within their status group and have begun to look upon Arvin as their home. In summary, the status system in Arvin can be illustrated with the following diagrammatic sketch:

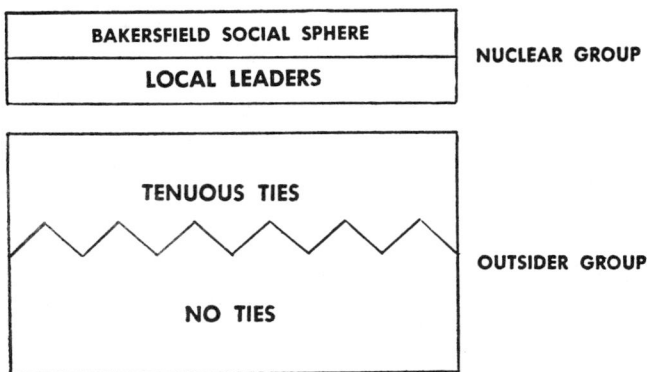

Perhaps the segregation of the two worlds can best be illustrated by two statements of a single member of the top echelon group. In one context she referred to the nuclear group as "All Arvin" while in another context she considered Arvin an "Okie Town."

SOCIAL PARTICIPATION

Participation in the social affairs of Arvin is largely limited to the nuclear group. As in Dinuba, the degree of such activities is limited or widespread according to the degree of social contact the activities imply. Thus two-thirds of the population go to movies, which does not imply any social intercourse, one-third go on picnics, which are generally limited to a family or a very small group of families, while only very small groups participate in the more social forms of recreation—dancing, school, and other community events (Table 35).

TABLE 35.—PARTICIPATION IN SOCIAL AND RECREATIONAL ACTIVITIES IN ARVIN

Type of activity	Families reporting [1]		Individuals reporting [2]	
	No.	Per cent	No.	Per cent
Clubs [3]	41	31	...	..
Churches	91	69	221	59
School events	34	26	88	16
Other community events	12	9	51	9
Dances	19	14	38	7
Card parties	10	8	18	3
Picnics	52	39	209	38
Motion pictures	110	84	387	67

[1] Based upon a sample of 132 families.
[2] Based upon total population in sample, or 558 persons, except in the case of churches, which is based upon total population 12 years old and over, or 372 persons.
[3] Data for individual participation not available.
SOURCE: Schedule data.

There are not many organizations centered in Arvin—a complete list includes two civic groups, the local Boosters and the international Lions, the Parent-Teachers Association, a local group of the State Guard, the Farm Bureau Federation, a Boy Scout and Campfire Girl group. There are no local chapters of lodges, veterans' associations, or women's clubs, nor any active local union organization. The absence of such organizations at once deprives the community of media for social contact and reflects the lack of community action. As one merchant stated, in discussing the beginning of the Lions Club, "The merchants didn't even know one another. At the first meeting we had a contest to see who could call each other by his first name, and found that none of us knew many of them. . . . I am rarely on the other side of the street and know only one merchant over there."

With so little social contact within the nuclear group, it is not surprising that contact with the labor groups is rare. While 70 per cent of the farmer and white-collar families report club activities, only 17 per cent of the farm labor families have such memberships. Stated otherwise, for every 100 persons in the farm-labor category 7 memberships in some form of social organization were reported. In contrast to this, white-collar workers reported 92 memberships and farmers 124 per 100 persons. Here we see the farmers, where farm operations are large, taking the lead in the degree of social participation. The relative proportions between farmer and towns were reversed from those found in Dinuba and Wasco. This corresponds to other observations regarding the relative social position of the farmer in Arvin, as contrasted with the other two communities. In Arvin the elite is predominantly of the farm-operator group, while the merchants and professional people are secondary. In Wasco the elite rather evenly represented the two groups, while the farmer in Dinuba was rarely a civic and social leader in the community. Income and other social data support this view of the relative status of the two groups. In Arvin, for instance, the median reported farm income was approximately $3,750 per year, the white-collar workers about $3,000. In Dinuba these figures were reversed with $2,800 and $3,650 respectively.

Examination of club memberships shows the degree to which social activities are the province of the nuclear group. The two major civic organizations have a combined membership of 124.

Seven of these memberships are held by persons in the labor category, 119 of them by farmers and white-collar workers. The only adult organization to which workers belong to any great extent is the Parent-Teachers Association. About three-fifths of its 40 members come from the laboring group.

The exclusion of outsiders must be understood in terms of the behavior of both groups. Social distinctions which exist operate both upon the included and the excluded. A Parent-Teachers' president claims to have endeavored to bring the laboring people into the association, but found it difficult to develop interest among them and to get the other parents to accept these outsiders on terms of equality.

The records of one other club were examined, the Farm Center. This organization is devoted to farmer interests and has only a few sustaining memberships from other occupations. Operators of farms in all size categories are members of this organization; in fact the distribution by size of farms owned by members is the same as the size distribution of all Arvin farms. Yet it is of interest that an officer of this club remarked that "the small farmers attend Center meetings more regularly . . . but the larger farmers seem to take a more active part in the working of the organization."

To a far greater extent than either in Dinuba or Wasco, social activities within the community are limited to a small segment of the population, while there exist few media for social intercourse between persons independently employed and those who work for wages.

ARVIN CHURCHES

The pattern of church participation follows that found in Wasco with a sharp segregation of a single church which serves almost exclusively the nuclear group and a number of other congregations serving the outsiders. The absence of a stable middle group in the society is reflected in the fact that there is only one congregation serving the stabler element and adhering to the older established Protestant faiths. According to the schedules taken in Arvin, half the members of the single congregation serving chiefly the upper class consisted of farmers and white-collar workers. Forty per cent of that occupation category reporting church participation, referred to that congregation. In this count, persons attending church regularly were included, whether actual members or not. When membership rolls were analyzed, the congregation proved to have three-quarters of its membership from farmers and white-collar workers, and only a tenth from the farm-labor category. Intermediate status churches showed a fair representation of persons from the farmer and white-collar occupations, but congregations with low social standing included very few participants other than laborers. The proportions, as indicated by the schedules, are shown in Table 36.

TABLE 36.—CLASS CHARACTER OF ARVIN CHURCHES

	Per cent of membership among:	
	Independently employed	Wage laborers
High status churches	50	50
Intermediate status churches	19	81
Low status churches	7	93
In-group churches	18	82
All churches	19	81

SOURCE: Schedule data.

The Nazarene and Assembly of God, like the comparable congregations both in Wasco and Dinuba, have built fairly elaborate churches, have developed a philosophy and a service more like the older sects and have sent out their appeal to the stabler elements in the community. Their history parallels exactly that found among the same denominations of Wasco, with shifts not only in the quality of their housing, but in the character of their service and the type of membership. As a result, a third of the congregation of one of these two churches is from the farmer-white-collar class, whereas, in the nuclear group church three-fourths of the congregation is so constituted. The Assembly of God and Nazarene congregations are the main source of contact between the outside and the nuclear groups. The ministers have moved away from their working-class heritage in the nature of their appeal.

The third group of churches in the hierarchical order have much poorer facilities, usually unpainted shacks and sometimes no regular place of worship. They are served by lay ministers whose livelihood comes from employment as labor. These religious bodies rarely participate in community events or engage in co-operative endeavors. Membership in these congregations therefore establishes practically no ties between the individual and the community of Arvin; it certainly establishes no social contact with any of the elite.

In this discussion of the hierarchy of religious bodies the Catholic congregation has been omitted. Here, as in Wasco, the activities are so largely devoted to religious service and the social contact so limited, that participation is hardly an act having any status connotations. In some ways its standing is like those churches in Dinuba which show strong in-group affiliations, but unlike those, the church does not serve as an active social center and the members do not find in it a common source of social action within the community.

CIVIC ACTION IN ARVIN

The fact that the civic organizations are virtually the exclusive province of the nuclear group takes on added significance when the nature of civic action in Arvin is examined. Arvin, like Wasco and in contrast to Dinuba, has never been incorporated. Therefore no machinery exists for making civic decisions, and the actions of the clubs in the town take on a double importance. The manner in which such decisions were arrived at in Wasco has already been illustrated. That a similar procedure characterizes such action in Arvin was attested to by the statement of a county official before one of these clubs. "You will have to let me know about your community problems," he said, "for you know more about your needs than I do. You have to let me know how you want the law administered, because I don't want to run your labor off to some other town." Not only do the county officials respond to the will of this segment, but action is occasionally initiated by them for community improvements and changes.

The key to civic action in Arvin lies in this situation. That such a process, whatever its merits, does not utilize the democratic processes, and fails to recognize the inherent right of every resident to a part in the decisions affecting his home town, goes without saying. That the process has not provided a complement of community facilities comparable to Dinuba and many other towns of equal resources, offers further criticism of this method of decision-making.

The reason for the failure of many communities in California, after they have reached and passed a population of 2,500, to incorporate into a body politic is not easy to assess. Undoubtedly there are many contributing causes. We may rule out relative age as a primary cause. For instance, Dinuba incorporated in 1906. A comparable date for both Arvin and Wasco (in terms of years of existence and size of population) would place the incorporation date in the middle or early twenties. A primary reason for the failure must be placed with the transient nature of the population. It has already been shown that a great proportion of the Arvin population has no recognizable or self-recognized allegiance to the community. Such persons will have little interest in incorporation. On the other hand, the nuclear element in the population fears the voting powers of the outsider element. That, at least, is the opinion of some of the local people. In Wasco certain propertied farmers and some outside corporations, who feel they have little to gain by incorporation yet have to pay a large share of the cost, are said to be inhibiting factors to such development. In Kern County, furthermore, a strong county organization, performing many services, has discouraged the incorporation of small towns, furnishing them with certain services at a lower cost to the local taxpayer than they would have if they furnished it themselves.

Failure to incorporate usually is costly to the small shopkeeper, who gets the most benefit from the local police and fire departments and other improvements initiated. But the community as an entity suffers, both from lack of facilities to maintain a proper physical environment and from the lack of community solidarity and spirit. Arvin, for instance, has practically no paving, street lights, or sidewalks. It has been slow in getting adequate water and sewage facilities, and has not had sufficient control over those which do exist. It has no park and has inadequate schools. The town is poorly laid out, the houses are crowded together and there appear to be no restrictions on the nature or location of buildings. The result of such a situation is that Arvin is less a community than an agglomeration of houses.

It has already been shown that the social picture is similar, with at least a third of the population having no ties whatsoever to Arvin as a social entity, with the remainder of the labor population having only the weakest local roots while the elite of the community find their social interests lie in the larger cities of Bakersfield and Los Angeles. There remain very few with the interest of Arvin at heart, and these do not readily recognize the interest of the whole community, but merely that small segment which makes up the nucleus.

The effects of such disunity are far-reaching. Marshaling the support of citizens for civic enterprises, getting them to devote time and energy to social ends rather than to their own personal interests, is, at best, difficult. In Arvin there are very few persons to draw upon. For such leadership cannot come from a group whose tenure is unstable and who have security neither of economic nor of social position. One group from which leadership is usually obtained, the school teachers, find the Arvin environment so uninviting that they most generally live in Bakersfield and commute the 22 miles daily. As a group they offer little to community life beyond the call of their duties as teachers, and this forms a great loss to the local population. In contrast to Dinuba, where teachers not only are leaders of student affairs, but where they have been partly responsible for the creation of civic enterprises, the absence of teacher leadership in Arvin can well be seen. The situation is aggravated by

VARIATIONS IN THE SOCIAL PATTERN: LARGE FARMS 217

the lack of a local high school and by the high rate of teacher turnover in the Arvin schools. The very absence of a high school must in part be laid to the fact that there was not a sufficiently vocal and organized leadership to demand the creation of a high school in the community, until many years after a reasonable high school age population existed.

AGRICULTURAL COMPARISONS

The brief presentation of the social organization of Arvin and Dinuba serves to deepen our perspective of the Wasco scene. In the following chapter the implications of similarities and divergences among the three communities are developed. Before entering into such an analysis it will be helpful to review some of the similarities and differences in the economy of the three communities.

The primary characteristics of industrialized farm operations have been stated already. Briefly, they are: production exclusively for cash sale, intense specialization of farm operations, intensive land use, high capital requirements for production, demand for large amounts of labor, and large-scale farm enterprises. In all three communities farmers specialize in single crops, produce practically nothing for home consumption, engage in an intensive form of cultivation on irrigated land with high values, utilizing large amounts of production capital and many man-hours of labor on each acre. In Dinuba fruits, especially raisin grapes, predominate, with little cotton and vegetable crops, while in the other two towns the proportion of the acreage in row crops is much greater.

The major variation in farming, however, is in the size of farms. The older Dinuba was established on a small-farm basis, and in 1940 the average size was 57 acres. In Wasco, farm units averaged 140 acres and in Arvin had an average of nearly 500 acres. Intensity of land use varied somewhat, and if such is calculated into size of unit, the differences become less in extent, though the relationship remains the same. If acreage is standardized according to its capacity to produce income, a fairer measure of farm size is had. It has become customary to standardize acreage for such purposes in terms of that amount of land devoted to a specific crop which will produce an income equivalent to that of an acre of irrigated alfalfa. Under such calculations half an acre of orchard, seven-tenths of an acre of cotton or seven acres of grain land would be called a "standard acre." The average farm size in terms of standard acres is 84 in Dinuba, 101 in Wasco and 247 in Arvin. Another measure of farm size as it affects a community is the proportion of farms and of farm land held in various size units. Table 37 shows these distributions for Dinuba, Wasco and Arvin.

TABLE 37.—PROPORTION OF FARMS AND FARM LANDS IN DIFFERENT SIZE CLASSES IN ARVIN, WASCO AND DINUBA (1940)

Size categories	Distribution of farms			Distribution of farm land		
	Arvin	Wasco	Dinuba	Arvin	Wasco	Dinuba
Under 160 acres	56.4	72.9	94.1	8.9	31.0	74.8
160-639 acres	27.0	23.5	5.3	23.8	44.9	21.8
640 and over	16.0	3.6	.6	66.3	24.1	3.4
	100.0	100.0	100.0	100.0	100.0	100.0

SOURCE: Based upon records of the Agricultural Adjustment Administration.

Scale of farming is an important element in industrialization. It is not in itself a necessary element, for the production may show every other characteristic of industrialization even though farms are of modest proportions. This is true in the three communities discussed here. However, within a common economy, variation in size of farms do produce differences in the degree of industrialization.

The most important concomitant of large-scale operations is the composition of the population it produces. With a given amount of available land, the larger the farming units are, the fewer will be the number of farm operators. And, if farming is equally intensive, the proportion of farm laborers will increase

SIZE OF FARM AND OCCUPATION DISTRIBUTION

DISTRIBUTION OF FARMLAND ACCORDING TO SIZE OF FARM:

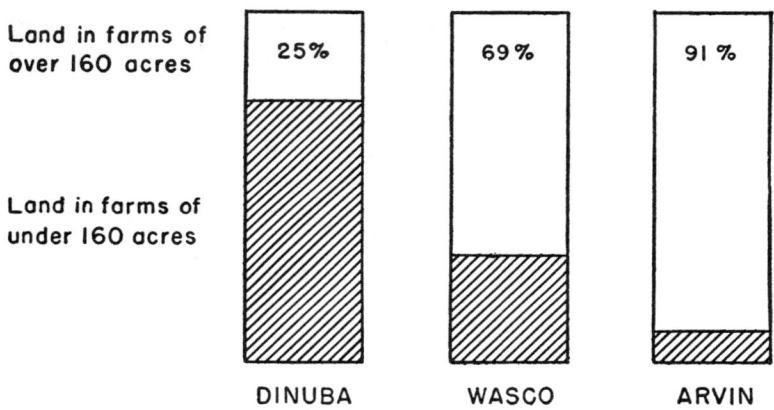

DISTRIBUTION OF EMPLOYED PERSONS ACCORDING TO OCCUPATION STATUS:

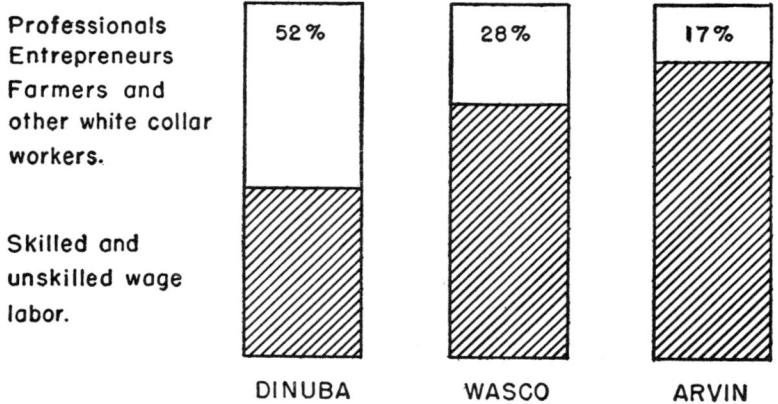

SOURCE: Tables 14, 30, 35 and 37.

CHART 8

as size of farm units are increased. It is therefore a characteristic of large-scale operations that the community is composed overwhelmingly of laborers and the number of persons independently employed is decreased. This relationship is shown in Chart 8, where the upper bars indicate the proportion of land held in units of 160 acres or more and the lower bars show the proportion of wage workers.

In view of the economic and social position of agricultural workers in the industrial farming areas, this differential in the composition of the population has a decisive effect upon the degree of urbanization of the communities involved.

CHAPTER IX

INDUSTRIAL AGRICULTURE AND URBANIZED FARM PEOPLE

URBAN AND RURAL LIFE

THE DICHOTOMY between town and country has held the imagination of America. At this point it is necessary to define these modes of life more thoroughly. It is not merely the province of the sociologists who recognize a rural and an urban field within the discipline, nor of the census taker, who for decades has made that segregation a primary one in his enumeration. Far more, it has been a source of divergent political attitudes since the foundation of our nation and repeatedly is made the basis for various kinds of public action. One of its earliest manifestations has been the establishment of political capitals in the smaller cities rather than in the urban centers. Another has been the maintenance of the system of county governments which largely serve the rural people. The establishment of Land Grant Colleges throughout the West, with their emphasis upon rural society, physically and psychologically separated from the universities with their more urban influences, is not entirely unrelated to this dichotomy.

The separation and antagonism between city and country can be found in popular literature and more abundantly perhaps in popular thought. The terms hick, rube, and yokel express contempt for the unsophisticated country-bumpkin. He is a man of narrow horizons perhaps, unaware of the value of money. He is an easy prey to the city slicker, whose sophistication is great, whose evaluation of money is such that he will hazard his soul in order to obtain it from the hayseed newly come to town. Behind such characterizations lies an element of truth which it is necessary to explore before proceeding to an analysis of the urban quality of California's rural scene.

The German sociologist Tönnies [1] has set up the differentiation in a polar scale, recognizing that no society is purely urban and none purely rural. He suggests the term *Gemeinschaft* as that which characterizes rural life, emphasizing both the commonality of origin and of spirit. The opposite pole is the *Gesellschaft* where the organization is based upon special interests and associations of convenience. Louis Wirth has defined urban civilization in its contrast to the primitive and rural, and his discussion furnishes us the basis for the present one.[2]

It should be remembered that urban civilization is a product of the massing of people together in the cities, and that this in turn can take place only when the technology and resources are sufficient to emancipate great numbers from responsibility of wresting a livelihood from the soil. Thus, while urban culture is found sporadically in the ancient world, it has been with the advent of the technological development of the industrial revolution that urban society really began to flourish. It is not surprising, therefore, to find urbanism follow technology into rural areas. While urban civilization must be viewed as a product of the cities, it must also be recognized that it is not confined to cities. Indeed, it is the essence of this volume to show that it is not so confined.

Let us first define urban culture as it applies to city life. The best sociological definition of the city is that it is a heterogeneous agglomeration of persons in a large and densely settled area. The heterogeneity furnishes us with the most important element in the growth of urban civilization. Cities have rarely if ever reproduced themselves; they are built up by immigration from

---

[1] Ferdinand Tönnies, *Gemeinschaft und Gesellschaft*, Leipzig, 1887, translated and edited by Charles P. Loomis as *Fundamental Concepts of Sociology*, American Book Co., New York, 1940.

[2] An excellent discussion of this dichotomy is found in the talks by Robert Redfield and Louis Wirth entitled respectively, "The Folk Society and Culture" and "The Urban Society and Civilization," *Eleven Twenty-Six, A Decade of Social Service Research*, edited by Louis Wirth. Wirth's article entitled "Urbanism as a Way of Life," *American Journal of Sociology*, Vol. XLII, 1938, was used as a basis for the present discussion.

outside. The origins of these people are diverse; they do not have a set of common customs and common social values. Standards are not uniform. Heterogeneity of origins is matched by heterogeneity of occupations. The economy of city life is, and must be, an economy of specialized functions and high economic interdependence of the individuals composing the society. This means that the individual specializes in some phase of the total economy, and we are only now learning the degree to which such specialization may be carried. This specialization at once reinforces the heterogeneity of origins and creates a situation wherein the individual loses contact with the total society and sees only the fragment which his life activities reach.

Without common background and common activities, the values men live by must seek common expression. In the economic activities of man the money calculus brings diverse wares and activities into a single system. It is therefore not surprising that in the social affairs pecuniary values replace the more personal value system of rural or folk society. If money is good, the possession of money is *prima facie* evidence that the individual is good, and social calculus in urban society rests on this assumption. On such a basis rests a system of social distinctions that differentiates the elite from the masses and presents rungs in the social scheme. This system of pecuniary values is reinforced by the development of common interests within segments of the society resting on the base of similar economic activities. Therefore occupation, or mode of livelihood, comes to play a strong part in the social structure of city life.

Perhaps it will be well to digress here. In primitive societies such as, for instance, those of the Pueblo Indians of the Southwest, the population has a common set of traditions and customs. The norms of behavior are established; they set not only the life activities of each person according to age, sex, and other individual qualities, but they define closely his behavior and his personality. Evaluations are made on such a basis, so that social standing rests largely upon the individual's adjustment to these norms. If ownership of goods—material items, ceremonial apparatus, or magical formulae—bear prestige it is not because they may be translated into other goods or the services of others, but because such ownership reaffirms the position of the owner *vis-à-vis* the norms of his own society. Even in those primitive societies where a money economy exists, such as among the natives of the Northwest Coast of America, the function that money plays is socially and psychologically very different from that in urban society. It is not, for one thing, used as a common calculator of all values—not at least till the American trader and museum collector makes a money offer. On the other hand, the values these people live by—and each has its set of values—not only are firmly established, but they are continually reinforced by the art, the literature, the superstitions, the religion, and the social relationships of the community. All the activities of the life of a Zuñi or a Kwakiutl reinforce the primary social values; the essential correctness of social judgments are daily proved to be right within the frame of reference the society establishes.

In urban society there is no common set of values and no common ethical system of behavior reinforcing these values. In common parlance, "things don't add up." Or rather, the only way you can add the behavior of the bootblack and the banker, the priest and the panderer are by means of a pecuniary calculus. If perhaps it has not gone that far, it has yet not lacked much. Lincoln Steffens or any of the muckrakers furnish us a ready reference.

Perhaps nowhere does this pecuniary calculus so readily meet the eye as in the housing of the people of the separate social classes. While food differentials are probably more important to the individual's physical well-being, and while clothing makes a ready reference to social status, the house a man lives in is a lasting monument to his social position. The great gulf between the dwellings of the elite set in the midst of vast personal parks and those of the crowded slums is perhaps the most characteristic scene of urban society. And such monuments afford the outsider a judgment neither of the heart nor of the brain of the inhabitant, but merely of his purse.

A fiscal elite, a divergence of social standing, and a tendency toward associations through common special interests together have the effect of creating a system of social controls in which money is the key to power. For in a society of interdependent economic activities there also grows an internal conflict between the several segments. Such conflict in urban society has repeatedly led to open warfare, both on the grand scale implied by social revolution and on the smaller scale of industrial disputes. For, though money is an important element in social potency, it is not the only source, and the banding together of special groups, motivated by common interests and desirous of a greater share of the values created by co-operative action, can present a formidable counterbalance to the power amassed by the fiscal elite. In urban society the individual generally expresses his social potency through association with fellows who have a common set of interests, and these interests are usually oriented in strictly pecuniary terms. The growing importance of the organizations serving the special interests of some segments of the population is a major trend in modern social behavior. The influence of professional organizations, commercial associations, and labor groups upon national policy is generally recognized, but they are equally influential over social behavior in every community, as we have seen in Wasco.

Simpler forms of society have their own social structure, and the elite of such social groupings maintain their position by recourse to a variety of techniques, of which established custom and superstitious awe are probably the most important. In many ways, the very homogeneity of such a population makes the elite more secure in its social position. It cannot, therefore, be said that invidious social distinctions are the province of urban society. The difference lies in the basis upon which they rest.

If this characterization of urbanism seems a harsh one, the implication is not entirely justified. One must not lose sight of the fact that the technological development in the past several centuries was a product of the urban rather than the rural element in life. Not only is this true of the material aspects of living, but the development of arts, letters, and science, ever since the astronomers of the Nile and the writings of Homer, have predominantly been urban products. The very freedom from tradition that results in a pecuniary social calculus, carries with it the promise of new forms of thought. If on one hand folk songs and handicrafts are lost in the process of urbanization, the creation of artistic masterpieces is made possible only when the restraints of tradition are lifted.

THE DIFFUSION OF URBANISM IN AMERICA

The polar extremes of rural and urban culture appear overstated, whether we refer to the popular notions of rube and city slicker or whether we have reference to the sociological analysis. It is a contrast, perhaps, between the city life of a New York or a Paris against the largely self-sufficient farming of a backwoods America or a European peasant community. Yet the overstatement is more apparent than real. In the first place, the cities are composed so largely of persons recently from the country, and in many American instances have themselves so recently been rural areas, that there remains a strong ameliorating rural influence. Secondly and more importantly, urban civilization has constantly and persistently diffused into the rural areas of America and in a more attenuated form has reached every primitive outpost in the world. The hill-billy myth is not made up out of the whole cloth, yet nobody seriously considers such characteristics are applicable to a great portion of our agricultural population. The mail-order houses have reached the remote corners of our society, and the mail-order houses are but two or three years behind the finest urban shops in cut of clothes and home decor, and right with them in modern mechanical contrivances.

In its encroachment upon the countryside, urban civilization has left islands of folk culture in the mountain fastnesses and distant valleys. Parts of the Old South, Appalachian and Ozark mountaineers, the Spanish Americans of New Mexico, the poor dwellers in bottom lands and cut-over areas in various parts of the Middle West, and an occasional community with strong religious ties maintain social values almost uninfluenced by the pecuniary calculus of the cities and keep customs foreign to the norm of American urban life. But the great areas of American farm production have been caught in the major current of urban economy. Commercial farming and the first stages of industrialization are found throughout the great productive areas in the Middle Western states and the Plains area. Consequently, money has come to be a predominant element in social relationships as well as in economic activities. Yet there remains in such environments a great deal of the rural culture. Its continuance rests, above all, upon the relative homogeneity of social backgrounds and economic activity, and the absence of specialization of functions, especially the specialization of the managerial functions from those of labor. The commercial farming of Iowa or Pennsylvania differs from the industrialized operations in the production of agricultural commodities in California. So, too, the urbanization of communities in those regions, though far removed from conditions in similar regions a century or two ago, is a far cry from the urbanization in California. The growth of industrial farming throughout the nation is reserved for later discussion, but clearly California is in the vanguard of this trend. And differences of degree can be found in California.

URBAN CULTURE IN CALIFORNIA RURAL AREAS

In terms of these ideas and on the basis of data presented in the preceding chapters, we can attempt to assess the nature of urbanization in California rural life. The first urban characteristic is heterogeneity. The diverse origins of a pioneer community are to be expected, but the degree to which the population of each of the communities analyzed here is made up by recent immigration does not rest upon their newness. Certainly the growth in each area is dependent upon immigration, but the continual influx and turnover of a relatively old community like Dinuba goes beyond the necessities of pioneer areas. Even in Arvin recency of growth cannot account for the volume of immigration, since half of all the families arrived after its present size was achieved. In all three towns the broad scatter of birthplaces covers most of the United States and includes many from foreign lands. The history of labor in California assures us that each community represents such a wide array of origins.

Diversity of backgrounds is matched by diversity of social

action. In Wasco the nature of the living conditions and of the daily activities of the separate social classes was described. Yet this description involves a degree of generalization and simplification greater than the ethnologist employs in describing the totality of a primitive or folk culture. The lifeways of a potato grower is divergent from those of a grape producer, and increasingly the economic activities of the laborer are becoming more specialized and hence more divergent from one another. The workers on an individual farm do not all perform the same tasks. We have examined the labor composition of a potato-digging crew, a good example of the degree to which special skills and aptitudes are utilized through a fine division of labor, and the degree to which the individual producer of commodities addresses himself to but a small segment of the total production. Such activity does not have to be contrasted against a primitive community, but is sharply divergent from the activities of the traditional hired man on the commercial farms elsewhere in modern America. The essential criterion of heterogeneity, both in origin and in present circumstances, is therefore fully met. It is a characteristic of the production of commodities in Dinuba as well as in Arvin, though in Dinuba there remains a larger segment which can and does diversify its activities.

Pecuniary standards dominate the system of social values throughout the area under discussion. Each community has a social structure which rests upon the possession of wealth and the characteristic occupations which reflect that wealth. The class structure of each community can best be understood in terms of occupation. The association of people in clubs, interest groups, cliques, and even churches follows the essentially occupation cleavage and demonstrate the degree to which occupation determines such associations.

Pecuniary standards show themselves vividly in church behavior where they stand in contrast to the equalitarian ethics of Christian ideology. Not only is this shown by the segregation of social classes in different denominations, but further evidence of the significance of money values derives from the behavior of the newer sects. These religious groups show a pattern of vertical mobility, rising in wealth, in the well-being of members and ultimately taking on the airs of the "higher" elements in society.

Nowhere, however, is the pecuniary character of social relationships more clearly shown than on the farm enterprise itself. It is not merely that crops are grown for cash and sold in the market, but it is that cash returns dominate the behavior of the farmers in every facet of their activity. The value of production for household use, when weighed in the scales of cash returns, is found wanting. Sharing of implements and trading labor are so rare as to appear unique in California's fields. A cash settlement is the solution, and practically all share arrangements on equipment are handled on a rental basis. The growth of the independent equipment operator working on a contract basis is a case in point. The calculations of land value carry such exactitude that the farm wife must fight to maintain a screen of garden between the planting and the home until such affluence is attained that conspicuous display is in order. But pecuniary values are displayed most blatantly when money is freed by exceptionally favorable prices in relation to costs. The early twenties in Dinuba and the fortunate break in potato prices and yields in Wasco in 1936 both developed a spirit of conspicuous consumption that accentuated the essentially pecuniary social motivation.

The producer has two fundamental market transactions to make. The first is his bargaining for the services of labor and the second is the sale of his commodities in the market place. Except for such large enterprises as the DiGiorgio holdings, the farmer's potency as a seller is limited. Yet fairly modest growers hire the services of brokers, utilize modern technology and direct most of their personal energies toward a favorable place in the marketing picture. In the market for labor, the farmer generally is in a better position to bargain. His interest in his laborer rarely extends beyond the assurance that he gets labor at the cheapest possible cost. The almost universal application of piece-rate wages serves completely to destroy any vestige of personal relationship between the buyer and seller in the labor market. The rare exception noted, of the cotton grower paying above market price—which he rationalized in terms of good investment—not only appears unique to the outside observer but marked him locally as a person apart.

The emphasis upon money values and the other aspects of urbanization are not limited to large farms. They are found throughout the area where operations are carried on in the intensive, expensive techniques of irrigated specialty crop production. But large operations have been influential in the establishment of the pattern. Historically, they set the pattern of production-for-market and established the pool of low-cost labor. Currently, they are a dominating factor in the functioning economy, so that even where whole communities consist of modest operations their influence is inescapable. Where groups exist which form an exception to the pattern they are always found to be small growers. Thus in Dinuba the existence of special "in-group" churches were recognized, and the membership of these had a degree of social cohesion based upon common origins and common ethical values resting upon a non-pecuniary base. These represent islands engulfed by the dominant stream of social forces in the larger community. That they should be found in the community of small farms is to be expected, since such groups invariably are made up of small farmers. Yet a similar group with a high degree of social cohesion is found just outside the boundaries of the Arvin community. These, too, are small operators whose commonality rests upon their common Danish origin and the strong sense of co-operation engendered by their forebears. Such exceptions should not blind us to the more overpowering cultural tendency in rural areas any more than would the similar social groups found within the confines of the city. Yet their effect, where their number is as great as it is in Dinuba, has a strong ameliorating influence. That religious bodies can sometimes prevent the schools from giving dances is a measure of their force in preserving older rural Protestant mores.

It is essential to realize that a money-oriented society is in turn based upon the controls of the market place and the hierarchy of elites that exist in the greater society. The extent to which this dependency is developed, determines in large measure the extent to which this outside influence pervades the social relationships within the community. The nature of these controls has been indicated in a preceding chapter. They rest upon the need for urban goods, the demand for capital, the dependency on nation-wide markets and above all upon the recognition of common interests along occupational and class lines rather than within the local community. In Wasco we have shown the influence of the great corporations upon the activities of mundane civic affairs—corporations which are caught up in the major structure of American economy.[3]

With a society segmented along economic class lines, of which occupation is a fundamental criterion, it is to be expected that civic action and social force operates through associations of persons with common interests. The common economic interests of farmers as a group have long been recognized. Organizations such as the Farm Bureau and Grange have a long history of speaking for the farmer, and as such represent the first step in this direction. Their organizations are community oriented— that is, endeavor to bring together farmers from a single community as a unit. There is still sufficient common interest to maintain active local groups, but a newer basis for organization along even more highly specialized lines is rapidly gaining in popularity. This is best exemplified by the commodity associations, formed in order to settle problems common to the producers of single crops. The associations of various fruit producers have long been active, while new groups are continually coming into being. Characteristically such commodity associations bring together the growers over a larger region—a hundred or more miles if the crops are grown over so large an area. Such associations have not been analyzed in this study because they do not form a part of community life. They go outside of it. It is not surprising that such associations appeal particularly to the large growers rather than to the small. It is not only that the large growers have greater mobility or that they have the

[3] Pacific Gas and Electric Company, Southern California Edison Company and Bank of America, whose local representatives take an active part in Wasco's civic affairs, are listed among the 200 largest non-financial corporations and the 50 largest financial corporations in the report of the National Resources Board, *The Structure of the American Economy* (Part I, Chart I, p. 158), Government Printing Office, Washington, D. C., 1939.

freedom to engage in these "managerial" capacities, but these growers generally find their social associations over a wider area and have less interest in the purely local milieu.

If the farm operator is thus influenced in his social action, it is not surprising that the townspeople themselves are so associated. Unlike the producers of agricultural commodities, the merchants can rarely be associated in smaller interest groups specialized to one or another type of activity. However, they do have several such organizations in the two communities which can possibly support them. In Wasco, at least, such groups represent status differentials. Their effectiveness in civic affairs and their bland assumption of representativeness have already been demonstrated.

In such a milieu of special organizations, their absence among the farm-labor population represents a real exception. The failure of laboring groups to band together in order to promote their own interests rests upon several factors. In the first place, the origin of the laboring population must not be overlooked. The typical farm worker of today is a recent migrant from Oklahoma, Arkansas, or Texas. These are regions which have preserved more of the rural qualities than almost any other states in America. This background does not include a society organized along special interest lines, and they are slow to acquire such behavior. Again, their occupation history shows that a large proportion of them have been farmers in the past. They do not identify themselves with a laboring class because they are only temporarily non-farmers, and certainly only temporarily farm laborers. At least that is the way most of them feel. And it is certainly the way in which they want to be identified to the community in which they live, where they readily recognize that labor status means no social status.

Yet these elements in their cultural background and their social position do nòt form the full explanation. They are sufficient to keep them from organizing of their own accord. But urban labor organizations, as we have already seen, have made repeated and conscientious efforts to form permanent and lasting unions among the farm workers, yet only the shed workers are organized in any numbers. But we have also seen the concerted efforts made to prevent and inhibit such organization. The very need for such effort on the part of the farmers in order to maintain unorganized labor is evidence of the great pull—perhaps one should say push—toward organizations along special interest lines. And though labor organizations are still unimportant in California's fields, they do exist.

In this discussion of the urban character of the rural community stress has been placed on those elements which are basic and fundamental rather than those which are superficial. Yet it would hardly be proper to overlook those characteristics which are generally recognized as indices of urbanization. Such characteristics as crowded slums areas, small families, and high insanity rates are generally found among urban societies. Information on the first two of these is available.

The rural slums in California have received their fair share of attention, and it is not the purpose to elaborate on them here. They were described for Wasco. In that community three separate neighborhoods within the town were distinguished: one almost exclusively Negro, which did not have the advantage of all the public utilities available to the other areas; a second predominantly Mexican but including others as well; and a third known as "Little Oklahoma City," made up mostly of migrant workers. In addition a number of outlying areas were devoted to makeshift housing, the most dramatic of which was the open land "on the desert," on which homes were built from scraps of lumber and tin. Particularly inadequate were the houses in this last and in the Negro area. In Arvin the degree of crowding was far greater. Only for two blocks along a single street were lots universally 50 or more feet wide and 100 or more feet deep. Elsewhere, where such lots existed, a pattern of placing two or more units on each lot was established, so that half the houses front on the alleys. Crowdedness within such units is also marked. Nearly three-fourths of the Arvin population had one person or more per room in the house, and 44 per cent had 1.5 or more persons per room. Crowdedness of dwelling units form only one measurement of poor living conditions, but the quality of the board shacks which house great proportions of the Arvin residents is in keeping with this index. When farmers furnish labor homes, these are generally close together, frequently utilize common plumbing facilities or outdoor toilets, and rarely have two or more rooms. A fourth of the Arvin families had no water in their homes.

One of the features which marks Dinuba off from her two sister communities is the relatively few quarters which may be designated as slums. A housing map shows only a few areas where separate units are close together. One of these is the area inhabited by Asiatics. Other areas showed some crowding. Only one-fourth of the homes had more than one person per room, less than a fifth had 1.5 persons per room, only one-tenth failed to have water piped into the house.

Small families are an index of urban centers. Family size has steadily declined in America as her earlier rural heritage has given way before encroaching urbanization. The place of the industrialized farm community in this trend is of interest. The average family unit in America in 1940 was 3.78 persons, but the farm population had an average family of 4.25. In the South, where both industrialization and urban production is at a minimum, the family averages 4.50 persons. But the farm population in California shows only 3.61 persons per family—less than the total national average. The data from schedules taken in Arvin and Dinuba show average families of 4.23 and 3.78 respectively. It would seem, therefore, that family size in Arvin indicates less urbanization than Dinuba, and that both communities are less urban than the average for California farm population.

However, if the data for the two communities are broken down by occupation, it is shown that the farmers themselves tend to have small families: 3.57 in Arvin and 3.27 in Dinuba. These are very nearly the same as those found among the merchant and white-collar classes. The large average family is the result of the large proportion of agricultural workers who characteristically have large families (4.75 in Arvin and 4.22 in Dinuba). Because there are so many of this class in Arvin the total effect upon the average is greater. Those very families who bring up the average size are the ones who have migrated from the Southwestern states in recent years, an area which has been least affected by urban characteristics. The index of urbanism presented by family size suggests that the farmers and small-town merchants have accepted urban standards, though the laborers have not. This is in accord with other evidence that it is only the farm laborer who maintains traditional rural attitudes. The index does not show any significant difference between Arvin and Dinuba.

DIFFERENTIALS IN URBANISM

It has been a corollary of our major thesis that the degree of urbanization varies with the degree to which farm operations have become industrialized. Thus while the three communities represent a high development of urban culture, it should be greatest in Arvin and least in Dinuba, with Wasco in the intermediate position. Certain statistical evidence is at hand which is an indication of the differentials, especially between Arvin and Dinuba where data are fully comparable. There is the evidence of slum conditions, the evidence of associational activity, and finally the evidence of family size. Other data of a descriptive nature further develops the relationship of the three communities.

The housing conditions in Arvin were shown to be consistently worse by measurements of crowding and by other measures. Level of living indices of material possession showed the failure of many families to have items generally accorded to be desirable in modern life. Observations on the condition in which the home was found showed marked divergence. General observation, however, is sufficient to show the differential with respect to inadequate housing. Such observation may be summed up simply as follows: in Arvin inadequate homes were the rule, in Wasco there were large areas of inadequate housing but other areas of good and superior homes, while in Dinuba the areas of poor housing were few and small, while substantial dwellings were the rule.

With respect to size of family, the data suggest a greater degree of urban development in Dinuba than Arvin, though the non-labor population in both communities follows closely the urban pattern. This difference, however, reflects the newness and greater population turnover in Arvin, but does present an exception to the other data available.

The heterogeneous quality of the population is not easy to assess. It is clear that the number of persons born in California was greater in Dinuba than in Arvin, while the number of persons coming into the community from outside in recent years was far greater in Arvin. Data from the school survey made in 1939 suggests that Wasco has a central position with respect to this index of heterogeneous origins. At the same time, there are more groups in Dinuba which maintain within themselves a separate set of cultural attitudes. Similar groups do not exist in Arvin and are relatively unimportant in Wasco. Yet these groups have, in themselves, folk culture. The very fact of their group activity based upon common non-pecuniary values stands in contrast to the extreme individuation among the farmlabor class in all three communities. This labor class is clearly largest in Arvin and smallest in Dinuba.

Social expression through association of like-minded individuals appears upon first blush to have the highest development in Dinuba. Here again, the occupational differential must be examined. If this is done it will be seen that the farmer in Arvin participates in such activities more frequently than in Dinuba, while Arvin merchants participate less frequently. The two groups combined in Arvin participate more than the two combined in Dinuba. It is the large proportion of laborers, who in both communities rarely engage in associational activities that reduces the over-all social participation in Arvin to below the figures for Dinuba.

Little positive can be asserted on the basis of these indices of urbanism, though they are suggestive. Closer scrutiny of the social scene clarifies some of the differences. The orientation of social action along interest-group lines typifies urban conditions while action encompassing the community and directed toward common welfare typifies rural life. In Arvin, Wasco, and Dinuba, such community-oriented action as exists consistently excludes the laboring class, and therefore contains an element of urbanism at the outset. The broader the base of activity is, and the more directly it is concerned with community-wide problems, the less it denotes urban behavior. A review of some of the kinds of group activities for community welfare in the three towns is therefore in point.

In Dinuba community civic affairs are resolved by popular vote. The fact of incorporation assures the community of a degree of action based upon residence that is not available to the other towns. Wasco has a vestige of such action in the formation of a public utilities district, through which a few decisions are made by popular vote. Arvin has no such group, other than those provided by state law. Here, then, a clear distinction in degree and direction is manifested.

Civic action, however, involves affairs outside the legal framework, even where a corporate community exists. The character of social action can best be judged by the analysis of an example. The community dinner called by the commercial organizations to discuss postwar development is illustrative for Dinuba. Though no special interests and economic conflict were involved, the dining hall was crowded with the hundred and fifty participants. It is significant to our discussion of the urban character of community action that each speaker represented some organized group, with the exception of one who represented an outlying neighborhood. Yet the representation covered very nearly the whole range of interests, always with the exception of labor.

In contrast to this meeting stands that held in Wasco to discuss the issue of incorporation. Here the attendance was not half as great, though an issue was involved. More significant, however, was the fact that the dominant spirit was hostile to an idea which, whatever its alternative defects and merits, was designed to increase community solidarity. The difference between these two meetings is difficult to catch in an objective description without going into great detail, yet it was a very wide one. In Arvin there were no opportunities to observe a community meeting, and it is doubtful that one has ever been held. The failure to continue community social affairs because of lack of interest and leadership, and the development of social action through the two dominant associations is indicative of the manner in which civic decisions are made—when they rest upon local choice.

One more illustration will suffice. In Dinuba there are two newspapers. They have a long history of community action and one is particularly oriented to local interests. Its practice during the war of publishing an average of a half dozen or more pictures of local service people—regardless of race or occupation—in each issue and its other community-interest activities have already been described. Its news is almost all local, and it reports on as many as five separate local neighborhoods or nearby communities. The editor claims to have weathered an advertisers' boycott, brought on by a fight for local enterprise, by getting subscriber support. The Wasco paper is overwhelmingly supported by advertisements from outside corporations and it is doubtful if a stand could be taken against the interest of that group. The paper is devoted chiefly to local news, but it has less such information. The Arvin paper is very much smaller in volume, and has very little local news. These newspapers reflect the differential in local interest of the population of each community.

On the basis of civic action it seems apparent that the degree of urbanization varies among the three communities generally with the degree to which their basic resources have been organized along industrial lines. Their differences, though they make for considerable variation within the general pattern, do not obscure the more fundamental similarities which differentiate California rural life from truly rural folk society or even from areas where commercial farming predominates.

CHAPTER X

SOCIAL DIRECTIONS

STEREOTYPE AND SOCIAL REALITY

FARM POLICY must be formulated in full recognition of the growing urbanization of rural society. For the past quarter century farm programs have been developed in terms of a stereotype of rural life which no longer reflects social reality. It is this failure to adjust agricultural planning to the world of today that has, more than anything else, spelled out the failure of our vast farm program to accomplish its stated ends. The picture of Wasco and the urbanity of its people serves as an important background for the re-evaluation of American rural policy.

Farm policy has been written for a rural world that is backward, homogeneous, and submissive. The backwardness of the farm population is implied by the elaborate structure designed to bring adult education to our rural people. No other element in our population has a government-sponsored program such as the Extension Service which is designed to teach farmers how to increase their productiveness and their wives how to make their hats. The value of this program of education cannot be questioned and its original formulation grew out of an era of rural backwardness. However, the assumption that the farm population, or more specifically the farm operators, are the group most in need of such information is of doubtful validity. The assumption of backwardness this program implies is unsubstantiated.

The homogeneity of the farm population is implied by the programs created for the relief of distress among them during and since the depression. It is not the place here to go into the historic development of, the rationalization for, nor the calculations of the parity principle and the creation of the Agricultural

Adjustment Agency. It is sufficient to point out that the need for some form of farm relief was clear even before the general depression of the thirties, and that low prices for farm commodities was a contributory cause to rural economic distress. But no other relief measure created during the depression was based upon an occupation or industry group in our society. Furthermore, every other relief measure made requisite a verification that the individual needed such relief. The parity price program, however, was the relief of an industry which not only assumed that the industry as such needed aid—the only comparable situation in American life is the subsidies to the merchant marine—but that help should be given in direct rather than in inverse proportion to individual well-being. The only assumption under which such a program makes sense is that the farm population is a homogeneous one—that differences in wealth among them are insignificant.

The inability of the farmers to protect themselves against the depredations of a more militant urban population—which for want of a better term has been called submissiveness—is implicit in the multitude of laws which exempt farmers from labor-union action. During the twelve years of the Roosevelt administration laws were created to protect the process of collective bargaining, to set minimum standards for employment conditions, and to insure workers against the hazards of illness, old age, and unemployment. Virtually every legal restriction upon industry for the protection of the worker and of his right to organize exempt the farm operator. Such exemptions not only imply a homogeneity in which restrictions are unnecessary, but that farmers have a peculiar quality of meekness which requires that they must themselves be protected.

As we have seen, rural society is not characterized by such terms as backward, homogeneous, and submissive. Certainly not that half of the farm population which produces 90 per cent of the commodities which enter into commercial channels, and least of all those operators whose farms are organized along the industrialized pattern existing in California. It is indeed for a stereotype rural society that farm policy has been written, and it is this unrealistic quality which must be overcome if our rural climate is going to fulfill the expectations that the people of America have for it.

What, then, has protected the myth of the country yokel in our national life? It is supported at once by sentimental tradition and the profit motive. The farm home, with sons helping father, with mother in the kitchen and the hired man a part of the family; with Sunday night suppers and social decisions reached around the cracker barrel—this picture is "as American as apple pie." It is hallowed in our poetry, our art, our novels, and our soap opera. It grew out of homesteading and free land, and has in the past been a real and living tradition for a segment of our farm population. To be sure, it was not applicable to much of our rural society, and the area of applicability has long been dwindling. Yet it has its basis in an historic reality; reality which appeals most particularly to that segment of the urban population which somewhat wistfully remembers an earlier farm life somewhat, if not exactly, like that tradition.

With such a sentimental basis the rural stereotype is a natural means of appealing to the public and its legislative representatives. Whenever the appeal serves the interest of some special pleader it is readily called forth. It has been under this appeal that the price support legislation has been developed on one hand and farm-labor exemptions maintained on the other. The advantage of both sets of laws to those very farm operators who least fit the characterization needs hardly any discussion; employers generally like support for their prices and dislike legal responsibility for the welfare of their labor.

The stereotype has one other advantage over reality. Reality is far more complex than a putative social order and such complexity makes legislative decisions far more difficult. The California industrial farm, the Iowa homestead, and the Southern plantation are different kinds of economic organizations with inherently different problems and surrounded by different social worlds; the problem of creating farm policy which meets the needs of each yet does not do harm to the other is not simple. The lawmakers' task, especially for our world in transition, cannot be an easy one.

THE NATIONAL TREND TOWARD INDUSTRIALIZED FARMING

If the story of Wasco were the story of some small cultural island within the body economic of United States agriculture, the need for special recognition in the laws of the land would be negligible. There are many small areas in the American scene which for some reason or another have not been caught up in the main current of American life.[1] But Wasco is characteristic of rural society in most of California, while more and more evidence arises to indicate that California stands merely at the vanguard of what is the major trend in American agriculture. Indeed the inexorable progress of the industrial revolution has touched all phases of modern life; and where it has once touched the old form appears ever supplanted by the new. It would be difficult to conceive that there could be any turning away from mechanization of farming; and it is equally difficult to visualize such mechanization without growing industrialization and the urbanizing influences that follow.

Census data are indicative of the trend. Average farm size has increased fairly regularly since 1900, and between 1930 and 1940 increased 11 per cent. This average obscures real events, for many new part-time farms (less than 20 acres in extent) also came into being during this decade. Each size group between 20 and 260 acres has decreased in importance during the decade of the thirties, whereas the number of farm units over 1,000 acres in size increased by a fourth and the acreage of such units by a third. It is those very units which most nearly fit the stereotype of farming in America which have shown the greatest mortality.

Farm mechanization has grown with farm size, but at a more rapid pace. The number of tractors increased by two-thirds during the decade of the thirties, despite the industrial depression that prevented many a grower from buying what he wanted. Farm electrification more than doubled during the same period.

[1] The difficulty encountered by James West in finding a subject community that would fit this stereotype without also involving foreign groups is significant. See the introduction in *Plainville, U. S. A.*, Columbia University Press, New York, 1945.

Since the 1940 census the amount of machinery has increased greatly. Not only have the number of tractors and combines increased, but a great development of new forms of farm machinery has taken place—the Rust cotton-picker, corn-pickers, cane cutters, the development of "sheared" sugar-beet seed that eliminates hand chopping, and dozens of minor developments. These war-borne inventions have not come into their full use; much less have their full effects been felt by the farming population. They cannot fail of furthering the processes of industrialization.

That industrialization is engulfing broader acres of American farming is a matter that has received official recognition before now. In the opening remarks to the *Supplementary Hearings* held by the Committee on Free Speech and the Rights of Labor in Washington, Senator La Follette pointed to the growing area of influence of the industrial farm.

The peculiar problems raised by the so-called migratory farm family which follows a nomadic way of life precluding any normal home or community advantages is not confined to California. The irrigated areas of Idaho and Arizona; the Yakima Valley of Washington; the Willamette and Hood River Valleys of Oregon; the beet-sugar areas of Colorado; the Rio Grande and Winter Garden areas of southern Texas; the Mississippi Delta and Texan cotton area; the berry regions of Louisiana, Mississippi, Arkansas and Michigan; the Florida vegetable and citrus area; and the truck and vegetable farms of eastern Virginia, Maryland and New Jersey—all receive an annual influx of migratory farm workers. . . .

Nor is California the only locale in which industrialized agriculture has developed to a degree worthy of observation. . . . Although California leads all of the other states in the number of its large-scale farms, they have developed or are beginning to appear in substantial numbers in such widely scattered states as Arizona, Texas, Washington, Louisiana, Arkansas, Oregon, Missouri, Ohio, Pennsylvania, New York, Virginia, North Carolina, Florida, Georgia, and South Carolina. As yet this problem . . . is restricted to less than 1 per cent of the Nation's farms. . . . But there is great significance in this 1 per cent of the Nation's large-scale or corporate farms, when one considers the large number of their employees, their increasing share of agricultural income, and their impact upon the future welfare of the "family farmer" in a competitive commercial agriculture. . . .[2]

[2] *Supplementary Hearings*, S. Res. 266, Pt. 1, pp. 2, 3.

Paul Taylor made a trip through the Corn Belt in 1940, and found that the mechanization in that area had proceeded far. He says:

> To most Americans the "migrant problem" seems a long way off. The trek to the Pacific Coast is not just the product of a great drought on the Plains. That stream of distress is the end result of a long process going on from New Jersey to California and from North Dakota to Florida. . . .
> Still fewer Americans know that in the Corn Belt, citadel of conservative, stable farming, the same forces are at work—excepting drought—which produced the Joads. . . . Today opportunity for the common man is narrowing over the lands of the Corn Belt. Only last August a regional official of the United States Department of Agriculture told the House Committee on Interstate Migration that twenty-five thousand Middle Western farmers are not able to find farms to rent. . . .
> One result of mechanization is bigger farms and fewer men. Another is transformation of the occupation itself. Steadily, and in recent years rapidly, it is doing to farming what machines have done to domestic handicraft production over the past century. The results of the process to both industry and agriculture are decidedly upsetting, if not revolutionary. Where industrialization of agriculture runs its full course the term "farmer" no more suggests a man with hand on the plow than "manufacturer" now means what it once did—a maker of things by hand.
> The march of mechanization is not limited to corn. It has been sweeping at an accelerated rate over one section or another of the Wheat Belt for fifteen years. In 1932 Edwin Bates described the spread over the Inland Empire of what a leading wheat farmer called "virtually a factory system of production". . .
> Power farming in important sections of the Cotton Belt is producing effects comparable to those in corn and wheat. . . . Within the past generation fruit and vegetable production has run far on the course of mechanization. It is characterized by large-scale operation, in competition with which small family farmers find survival difficult. . . . On the muck lands of the Florida Everglades the large-scale pattern of commercial truck farming is being repeated. . . . Even in the cattle industry similar forces are at work, with mechanization.[3]

Industrial farming is therefore not merely something to be dealt with in California; it is not simply a function of an his-

[3] Paul Schuster Taylor, "Good-by to the Homestead Farm, The Machine Advances in the Corn Belt," *Harper's Magazine*, May, 1941, pp. 596 ff.

toric tradition and a favorable physical environment—it is a new mode of production that will transform the American landscape and make ever rarer those scenes of rural well-being and simplicity that fit the stereotype of art and politics. Senator La Follette continues in his statement:

> There are ominous signs that the Nation is confronted with a transition from the traditional "family farm" toward industrialized or corporate agriculture. Farming as a way of life is threatened. This transition challenges long-accepted national ideals of the farmer on his own land. If our national agriculture faces the same cycle that changed the form of industry from 1870 to 1930, the problem should be fully recognized.

Industrial farming does indeed carry a threat to tradition; it carries a promise as well.

FARM POLICY SINCE 1933: PRICE SUPPORT

In this chapter we shall endeavor to suggest certain characteristics that farm policy should have in the light of social conditions in the California community. In order to do this, it is necessary briefly to examine farm policy in somewhat greater detail. Two aspects of that policy have been crucial from the point of view of rural society—price support and labor legislation. Other programs, conservation (as distinct from price support), credit, farm purchase programs, debt moratoria, and educational activities, have all had their effect upon rural conditions and the support of farmers, but none has been so important to the American agricultural plant as price support and labor legislation.

The watchword of the price support program is "parity." Parity is a concept of a "proper" ratio between farm commodities and other goods on the market. A parity price is that price which meets this standard of equity between farm and nonfarm goods. It may be, and has been, calculated according to a variety of formulae, but fundamentally it is a price for cotton or wheat or some other "basic" crop, which would give to the farmer the equivalent in purchasing power of the same amount of goods produced in the "base period," usually the average between 1910 and 1914, and taking into consideration the cost of production and increased technical proficiency. This price-guarantee program has been attached to a crop curtailment one, on the principle that low prices have resulted from surplus commodities and that decreased production would thereby tend to raise prices. Such curtailment would, of course, only represent an advantage for the individual farmer if all farmers reduced their productivity. Since it was always better for the individual to stay out of the program it was necessary to induce farmers to enter. Thus parity prices were not guaranteed an individual unless he reduced his own production. Actually, he did not reduce production, but merely reduced the acreage of the land devoted to that crop and planted a soil-building one instead. He could, however, intensify production on the remainder and he could rent or purchase additional lands, and cultivate them in the same manner, without foregoing "parity payments."

A great deal of discussion has been centered about the proper calculations of parity; about the relative merits of various base periods, and about other factors in the calculated formula. Such discussions can mean many dollars to this or that group of producer and are therefore subject to rigid examination. By nature, however, they overlook the more fundamental issues that are involved. One of the few really to see beyond the arithmetic and into the morality of the parity principle is T. W. Schultz.[4] Schultz points out that the purpose of the parity price system was twofold: to re-allocate agricultural resources and to redistribute wealth among farm people. Schultz claims it met neither end. We need not concern ourselves here with the former, but the latter is of extreme importance to our interest in farm policy.

The parity program, like federal relief, bank holidays, and other measures undertaken during the dark days of 1933, was essentially one of relief. But unlike other measures taken for the welfare of people, this one was for the welfare of an industry. Its philosophy is based upon the principle that agricultural commodities deserve a "just" share of total national income, irrespective of efficiency in production or the willingness of people to buy the commodities. Not only does it assert that there is a

[4] Theodore W. Schultz, *Redirecting Farm Policy*, Macmillan Co., New York, 1943.

just share of the national income which should go to agriculture, but it completely fails of apportioning that share equitably within the industry. For whatever changes have been made in the amount and nature of the payments and qualifications for payments, one principle has always held. Stated negatively, that principle is that individual need shall never be a criterion for receiving payment under the Agricultural Adjustment Act. In positive terms, payments to farmers have been made in proportion to his pre-existing well-being, for the bigger the operations the more money he is "entitled" to. In later years an upper limit of $10,000 has been placed on the amount of payment to any single farm, but even this limitation is not upon an individual, who may have a number of separate units. Such a policy has, of course, had the effect of eliminating the stigma of relief from the program, and as we have seen in Wasco, such a conception of the program is completely absent in its operations. It of course can be a very major source of income on big operations while it can be of very limited assistance to the small farmer whose production, because of little or poor land, is already low. Such a program cannot possibly have a beneficial—that is, equalizing—effect upon the distribution of income among farm operators because of the very basis upon which parity payments rest. When tenants, sharecroppers, and laborers are considered, the effect upon income distribution appears to further the economic differences between the wealthy and the underprivileged.

Certain facts lead us to believe that the agricultural adjustment program has increased the gulf between the advantaged and the disadvantaged classes in farm production. Schultz points out that "White operators in Mississippi with incomes of $1,000 or less received about $55 from AAA, whereas those with incomes of $3,000 or better averaged well over $1,000 in cash payments from AAA. The effect of the commodity loans upon the distribution has been similar. When the loan rates have been above market prices, farmers with the most land and crops have gained much more from the loans than have farmers with low or inadequate incomes." [5]

[5] Schultz, *op. cit.*, pp. 20-21.

But inequality and disproportionality in payment is not the only means of creating a differential. In general owners are better off than tenants, tenants than sharecroppers, and sharecroppers better off than farm laborers. Yet the effect of the AAA has been to help the land owner to displace tenants, to reduce sharecroppers to wage workers, and to curtail the opportunity for farm employment for the workers. Professor Gillette pointed out that in certain areas of the Wheat Belt, farms were being operated in increasing numbers by managers rather than by tenants.[6] Thus, the working farmers were being displaced in order that the owner could get the full benefit of governmental subsidy. Others have pointed out that the tendency toward farm mechanization was hastened by the AAA payments, which afforded the landowner both the means and the incentive to replace the sharecropper system with a system of hired labor. Under the provisions of the Act, the government payment was to be shared, in proportion to the general crop-sharing arrangement, between the farmer and the cropper. But there was no provision which effectively prevented the farm owner from doing away with the sharecropping system and instituting a hired labor operation which gave the former tenant an even smaller share of the total production as laborer and none of the government check. Finally, the farm program carried no guarantees for the laborer. On the contrary, since the payments to farmers were tied in with crop reduction programs, the net effect of the parity policy was to reduce the total employment opportunities, and insofar as it was an effective instrument in crop curtailment, and insofar as it was an incentive to further mechanization, the program inevitably had the effect of worsening labor conditions.

It is clear that the inequalities in the farm enterprise cannot all be laid at the door of the farm program of the past dozen years, and indeed it cannot positively be asserted that the rela-

[6] "Two or three men in Bottineau County [North Dakota] are operating forty-five quarter sections of land, with a very few men as hired laborers. Incidentally, the undertaking is to garner in the federal allotment rather than for bona fide production. This alone has caused the displacement of many small farmers and scores of laborers." J. M. Gillette, "Social-Economic Submergence in a Plains State," *Rural Sociology*, Vol. 5, No. 1, March, 1940, pp. 64-5.

tive position of the disadvantaged agricultural classes was worse under the program than it would have been if the depression conditions of the early thirties had been allowed to continue without aid. Still it can readily be seen that the program itself failed to relieve distress where that relief was most urgent and failed to equalize conditions in agriculture. Furthermore, whatever ameliorating effect the parity program had was partially or totally off-set by their influences toward the further reduction in economic status of the more disadvantaged groups in agriculture. The reason for this failure lies in the fundamental misconception that is at the philosophical root of the program; the misconception that results from directing a farm program in terms of a fallacious stereotype rather than social reality.

FARM POLICY SINCE 1933: LABOR

The second major aspect of farm policy during the New Deal era in America is the relationship between the farmer and his labor. It has been an extremely negative policy. It is an ironic fact that during the dozen years when industrial labor gained a series of rights and privileges, those workers with the worst conditions of any large group in America were rigorously kept outside the scope of such legislation. The policy is therefore negative with respect to farm labor, but it is positive with respect to the farmer himself.

One of the earliest developments in social legislation was the attempt to curtail the use of children in industrial occupations. Very little of the body of law created to protect children against exploitation and to assure their opportunity for education and advancement has been made to apply to farm labor. Yet, according to Beatrice McConnell of the U. S. Children's Bureau, in testimony before the La Follette Committee in 1940, more children were employed in agriculture than in all nonagricultural occupations combined.[7] She quotes from a series of studies made of agricultural activities under industrial conditions throughout the United States which point to the prevalent use of children under sixteen. The purposes of child labor laws are three-

[7] La Follette Committee, *Supplementary Hearing.*, Part 3, p 790 ff.

fold: to protect growing youngsters from unhealthy physical environments, to insure their continued education, and to protect them from human relations in which they are at a disadvantage because of immaturity. Agricultural exemption from such laws is predicated on the assumption that farm children work for their parents under healthy conditions: physical and social. The fact is that the majority of hired child laborers in agriculture are seasonally employed, work in groups for persons other than relatives, and often do work far too difficult for frail bodies. Parental employment is usually exempted from these provisions irrespective of the character of work, so that special agricultural exemptions are unnecessary.

The Fair Labor Standards Act of 1938 exempts farm labor from its provisions. Under this exemption, it has been ruled that all field employees and all those engaged in the first processing of fruits and other perishable goods are agricultural labor. Packing industries are exempted from 14 weeks of their seasonal operations, except that they may not employ a person more than 12 hours per day or 56 hours per week. Thus, except insofar as state school laws effectively prohibit young people from working, or where state welfare codes rule on the conditions for the employment of children in agriculture, there is no control over working conditions for young people on farms, either family or industrial.

Workers engaged in purely agricultural pursuits were excluded from both the old-age and the unemployment insurance programs under the Social Security Act of 1935. According to A. J. Altmeyer, this exemption was made despite the general recognition of their need for protection, because of the administrative difficulties involved.[8] Yet by the time the Social Security Act of 1939 was passed, when half a million or more people, previously covered, were excluded by the adoption of a broad definition of farm labor, techniques for covering all industrial farm employment had long been known. Broadening of the definition of farm labor to include all possible cases offered a direct rejection of the policies advocated by the administrators

[8] A. J. Altmeyer, "Social Security for 'Industrialized' Agriculture," *Social Security Bulletin*, Vol. 8, No. 3, March, 1945.

of the Social Security program. Altmeyer gives the following explanation as to the logic behind such a policy:

> This broadening of the definition of agricultural labor was largely motivated, according to a report of the House Ways and Means Committee, by a desire to relieve a tax inequity, said to exist under the definition used in the regulations, between large and small farm operators. It was argued at hearings on the amendments that the small farmer ordinarily did not process his product on his farm but turned it over to commercial processors or co-operatives. These establishments, being off the farm, were not exempt from the payment of social security contributions, and the costs of their contributions, it was contended, were passed back to the small farmer. On the other hand, it was pointed out, large farm operators, having sufficient production to justify the maintenance of a processing or packing plant on their farms, were not required to pay social security contributions. Exempting the activities of the commercial processors and co-operatives would, it was believed, remove the competitive advantage enjoyed by the large farmers.[9]

The fact is, of course, that inclusion of farm labor would serve to protect the small farmer, who must compete against the large operator hiring cheap labor without guarantees, and who thus devaluates the worth of a day's work.

Farm labor is also excluded from the unemployment insurance feature of the Social Security Act. Because this portion of the program is administered by the state, individual states may define this as they see fit. But field hands remain without coverage at any time. The Wagner Act, which protects the bargaining and unionization rights of workers likewise excludes farm workers. During the war farm labor was subjected to special laws administered by separate agencies from those which covered urban workers. Thus wage ceilings were set by an agency attached to the Department of Agriculture, which had always devoted itself to the interest of the farm operators. Special employment offices were created, and these were attached to the Extension Service, and were closely aligned with the farmer group. Finally special draft exemptions and labor importation both served to maintain artificially a large supply of farm workers—a protection that no other industry, however basic to the war effort, received.

[9] Altmeyer, *op. cit.*, pp. 2, 3.

Harry Schwartz discusses these sanctions as follows:

> ... After the passage of the Farm Labor Act of 1943 in the spring of that year, the determination of "prevailing wages" to be paid foreign and domestic workers transported under this act came largely under the control of growers in each community. In this way grower wage-fixing action received government sanction and aid in making it effective.
>
> Similarly, the government war program for regulating farm wages has in part become identified with farmer wage fixing. Thus, the government order setting ceiling wages for picking raisin grapes in 1943 specified exactly the same rates as those set by the growers acting through the San Joaquin Valley Labor Bureau. This sort of government intervention strengthens growers' hands in fixing wage rates since it lends these rates legal sanction, and threatens severe fines or imprisonment for farmers willing to raise rates. Such one-sided government action—in which workers have had almost no representation to date—seems of questionable wisdom from a social viewpoint.[10]

Special legislation of this kind can best be understood in terms of Congressional attitudes. The following is the statement of a Congressman regarding labor relations in agriculture:

> The habits and customs of agriculture of necessity have been different than those of industry. The farmers and workers are thrown in close daily contact with one another. They, in many cases, eat at a common table. Their children attend the same school. Their families bow together in religious worship. They discuss together the common problems of our economic and political life. The farmer, his family, and the laborers work together as one unit. In the times of stress, in the handling of livestock or perishable agricultural commodities, of impending epidemics and at many other times the farmer and laborer must stand shoulder to shoulder against the common enemy. This develops a unity of interest which is not found in industry. This unity is more effective to remove labor disturbances than any law can be.[11]

Such an idyllic picture does not hold for Wasco or Arvin, nor even for Dinuba where small-scale industrial farming is the rule. Indeed it does not hold for any of the over three million seasonal workers in agriculture, nor for very many of the seven hundred thousand "hired hands," whose position most closely

---

[10] Harry Schwartz, *Seasonal Farm Labor in the United States*, Columbia University Studies in the History of American Agriculture, New York, 1945, p. 72.

[11] *Congressional Record*, Washington, Feb. 23, 1939.

resembles the Congressman's portraiture. Indeed, farm-labor policy is predicated on the same fallacy that parity payments are; that rural society is homogeneous and unified, where cupidity is unknown, and tranquillity the keynote. The nature of farm wages, the conditions of work, the character of social controls, and the economic and social status of labor, as these appear in Wasco, suggest that those very laws from which farmers are exempt are most clearly needed if rural society is to meet even those standards of life that are offered by the cities.

Indeed, the essential paradox in farm policy since 1933 has been that policies which were created to serve a fallacious stereotype have tended inexorably to destroy the elements of truth behind that stereotype.

PRINCIPLES FOR A FARM POLICY

Legislation for agriculture in terms of a stereotype out of keeping with reality can serve neither the interests of the land nor of the nation. The course of American land policy was set with the Preëmption and Homestead laws of nearly a century ago. The Far West and the South were outside of the main current of that tradition. The South because of its devotion to cotton, and the West because of its remoteness and relative undevelopment, seemed mere aberrations hardly to be taken seriously by policy makers. Now the Far West has not only become of major importance (and less remote), but evidence is at hand that its pattern has influenced agricultural production throughout the nation.

Before World War I farm policy rested largely upon the principle of homesteading and the family farm. The existence of plentiful good land strongly influenced all of the American economy. It meant that, indeed, the industrious and willing had no need to suffer a secondary role in society, for independence was theirs for the work and the asking. It meant that free men could not be exploited; that an underprivileged class could not be maintained. Only in the South where elaborate legal machinery was established and a strong cultural tradition enforced, and in California, where an army of legally restricted foreigners ignorant of law and discriminated against by it, could such undemocratic forms continue. But free land is gone, and the single base for American farm policy—both legal and economic—has thereby gone, too. The tradition remains; the social stereotype brought from an earlier era resounds in the halls of Congress, even as the very laws created by it are hastening the processes of industrialized farming and an urbanized farm society.

Formulation of a farm policy is imperative. The present transitionary stage presents the opportunity still for preserving the good in the American tradition and at the same time capturing the inherent values of efficient production on an industrialized basis. The absence of formulated policy and recognized goals leads only to chaos, and under chaotic conditions strong-willed men can serve their own interests at the expense of the public good.

Three fundamental principles must underlie any constructive farm policy consistent with American democratic traditions:

> The full utilization of American productive capacity to insure the welfare of all the people and the strength of our nation;
>
> The preservation of our natural resources to insure that maximum production can continue without loss from earlier exploitation of the land;
>
> The promotion of equity and opportunity for those whose life work is devoted to the production of agricultural commodities.

The tradition of scarcity economics—so firmly rooted in a past of insufficiency for life—is out of keeping with the needs and capabilities of the modern world. The efforts made artificially to maintain scarcities in the interest of the producing group served inevitably to further the impoverishment of the nation. The social cost of scarcity—artificial or actual—and of the failure to promote full consumption was writ large during the recent national emergency when millions were found unfit or inadequate for the duties that had to be performed. Little further need be said concerning the first principle in sound agricultural policy; its formulation does not emerge from the present study but its overwhelming importance requires that it be mentioned.

Conservation of natural resources is again so fundamental and obvious an element in sound policy formulation that it need hardly be belabored here. Conservation of resources is actually a part of full production. It is the assurance that full production can be continued indefinitely through time. The two principles are not in conflict, for full production can only mean maximum production without depleting the resource base from which it is derived. In the past we as a nation have lived largely on our capital. The depletion of minerals and forests has left us poorer than we should presently find ourselves, and the mining of soil and misuse of land has been a grave error. Foresighted men of affairs have seen this and deplored it for at least half a century, and more recently concerted efforts have been made to stem the tide of destruction. It yet remains, however, to make conservation a fundamental basis for determination of agricultural policy, transcending all other considerations. If this principle appears self-evident, consider only our many failures to act upon its obvious wisdom.

To understand the principle of equity for the producers in agriculture, it is only necessary to review existing inequities in both the legal and social structure of the agricultural community. Of the nearly fifteen million producers of farm commodities, the major economic sanctions developed during the past 12 years serves only about three million commercial farmers. Programs designed to help them, often in direct violation of consumer interests and the principle of full consumption, have been supported by money counted in billions. And this money has gone in disproportionate amounts to that portion of this group which has the highest economic status.[12] At the same time, farm labor received nothing except relief, economically the

[12] Mr. Rudolph M. Evans, administrator, Agricultural Adjustment Administration, in testimony before the Tolan Committee pointed out that 90 per cent of the payments were under $150. In response to a request from Congressman Osmers of the Committee, a tabulation showing portion of payments in various size categories shows that the remaining operators received over half the total payments by dollar value. *Hearings*, Part 8, pp. 3232 and 3244.

most inefficient and socially the most derogatory of all public welfare expenditures. And it has been tellingly argued that relief is a direct subsidy to the hiring farmer, for it holds his worker during the season he is not needed without expense to the farmer himself. Not only did the legislation of the thirties fail to assure equity to the farm worker, but it also denied him those guarantees against poverty and distress which protected the industrial worker.

Stated in positive terms, equity as our underlying principle of farm policy means that all public policy must be designed to support the working farmer against the aggressive economic policies of growing rural industrialists, and the rights of labor against oppressive actions of small groups seeking personal aggrandizements. This in no way implies the necessity of breaking up corporate holdings or collectivizing farm production, but merely that those legal apparatuses which now serve the interests of a minority be jettisoned and new legal forms supporting the farm worker and the working farmer placed in their stead.

THE PRINCIPLE OF EQUITY IN POLICY

Thus far our discussion of farm policy has remained detached from the situation in the California rural community. Its burden has been that farm policy was not tied to social reality and that therefore it could not possibly serve its own stated ends. It has been shown that in actual fact it has not fulfilled its purposes in the past, despite great and commendable organization and, in terms of peacetime expenditures, vast sums of money. In order to understand specific policy, three principles upon which it should rest were enumerated, of which the one that interests us here is the principle of equity.

The present discussion assumes the continuation of the parity principle—that is, the principle that the total agricultural enterprise in America will continue to get a "just" proportion of total income, most likely based upon a price calculus. But whereas policy in the past stopped here, we shall use this as our point of departure, and consider the question of equity among the different groups engaged in agricultural production. Our discussion of equity resolves into two fundamental questions: (1) equity for whom and (2) equity in what. For it is necessary to see who fails of getting his share in the values of rural life and what these values are which are not fairly apportioned. Equity for whom means equity for all those engaged in the production of farm commodities—whether industrialized operator, family farmer, hired hand, or migratory worker. We have seen that in Wasco there were between 6 and 8 in the labor category for every 10 persons engaged in farming. In Arvin, this proportion rose to about 9 out of 10. In the United States as a whole the proportion is not so great, yet it is highly significant—far more so than generally recognized. A statistical analysis recently made attempts to determine the importance of various groups helping to produce farm goods.[13] According to the estimates presented, the total working force in agriculture is about 14.5 million persons, and is divided into the following employment categories:

Commercial farmers	
employing more labor than they perform themselves	1,000,000
employing only supplemental labor	1,200,000
employing no labor	1,100,000
Total commercial farmers	3,300,000
Wage laborers	
sharecroppers	600,000
"hired hands"	700,000
seasonal workers receiving 8 months or more of farm work	500,000
seasonal workers receiving less than 8 months of farm work, but constantly in labor market	1,500,000
workers only seasonally in farm labor market	1,500,000
Total wage workers	4,800,000
Others in farm-working force	
unpaid family labor	4,200,000
non-commercial farmers (part-time, residential and subsistence farmers)	2,200,000
Total others in farm-working force	6,400,000

[13] Walter R. Goldschmidt, "Employment Categories in American Agriculture," *Journal of Farm Economics*, in press (August, 1947).

This tabulation demonstrates what raw census data obscure. The hired labor category is nearly half again as great as the commercial farm category, and is more than double the number of operators who hire labor. Only one million of the agricultural working force are more concerned with the problem of hiring than they are with the productivity of their own labor. While farmers hiring labor produce the major portion of the farm products which enter into the commercial market, they constitute but a small segment of the population engaged in the production. Such a tabulation further shows that a farm policy of protecting the hiring farmers against the farm worker is not protecting the interests of the "agricultural" population. It shows, too, that the farmer hired by the month—the traditional "hired hand"—makes up a very small portion of all wage workers in agriculture.

The question of equity for whom means equity for these different employment groups—it means legislative protection for the noncommercial farmer, the sharecropper, and the farm worker equivalent to the protection for the commercial and labor-hiring farm operators.

Wherein does equity fail? What form must equity take in order to assure us that these groups in agriculture will get their fair share of the economic and social rewards of which agriculture has claimed its full deserts?

First, there are the basic amenities of life which are the expected heritage of Americans. We have seen that these were available to the worker in Wasco to but a limited extent and that as a result not only was his mode of life below acceptable standards, but his opportunities for higher expectations, either for himself or for his children, were also impaired. These low standards rested first of all upon low wages. A recent study of farm wage rates shows that in terms of purchasing power, farm wages have remained the same as they were in 1910.[14] California wages have been slightly, but not materially, above national levels, but when adjusted for higher living costs even this difference appears to be absorbed. At the same time industrial

[14] Louis J. Ducoff, *Wages in Agricultural Labor in the United States*, Tech. Bul. No. 895, USDA, Washington, 1945.

wages and industrial labor's purchasing power has nearly doubled. Also, concurrently, the productivity per worker in agriculture has nearly doubled, as it did in industry.[15] In California, during the thirties, the proportion of crop value that went into wages dropped from 25 to 15 per cent, and remained there as late as 1939.[16] Comparisons between farm-labor earnings and industrial earnings from 1940 to 1944 show that the latter are consistently double the former.[17] Agricultural wages are lower than that of any category of worker except hotel employees, whose income is largely derived from tips. Such measurements give statistical precision to the generally recognized fact that farm labor is poorly paid labor.

But the low economic level of wage workers is not wholly dependent upon low wages. We have seen that in Wasco, there was a sharp variation in demand for labor at different seasons of the year. Such a demand curve is forced by the seasons of the year and the fact that farmers do not organize their operations to maximize the employment opportunity for their labor. In California as a whole it is possible for only 60 per cent of the workers required during the peak season of employment to get as much as 6 months work during a year, assuming that all labor is used to its fullest capacity.[18] This seasonally enforced underemployment is a grave source of economic distress.

During times of economic depression this underemployment is far graver than that resulting from seasonality of demand. For as wages go down more members of the family enter the labor market and the employment opportunities are spread ever thinner. During times of industrial depression the entry of urban workers into the market depresses agricultural wages and further

[15] *1946 Agricultural Outlook*, Bureau of Agricultural Economics, USDA, p. 15.
[16] "Supplemental Statement on the Trends of Farm Agricultural Income and the Industrial Wage Bill in California, 1924-1939," prepared by James E. Ward, La Follette Committee, *Hearings*, Exhibit 9574, p. 22518.
[17] William H. Metzler, *Two Years of Wage Stabilization*, Bureau of Agricultural Economics, Berkeley, 1946.
[18] California Emergency Farm Labor Project, *Labor Requirements for California Crops*, Agricultural Extension Service, University of California and U. S. Dept. Agriculture, March, 1945.

spreads work opportunity, thus doubly affecting the economic position of the farm laborer.

The principle of equity in agriculture therefore means the assurance that a fair share of the returns to agriculture be distributed to those who have in the past been a highly underprivileged group. Agriculture as a whole has asked for income "parity" with the urban industries. If the principle is good, then it is proper to ask for a parity for the laboring element of the farm population. Statistics are available to show that they have not, in the past, had such parity. But because parity calculations based on group income are not conducive to equity, another mode of calculation must be applied. This would be a guaranteed minimum wage for work, and a recognition of the opportunity hazards of the job in the form of unemployment insurance.

But a host of other aspects of farm conditions separate from, though not unrelated to, economic circumstances also require the ministrations of an agricultural program. The social instability is as real as the economic insecurity. For the social position of the farm laborer is much like that of the farmers themselves fifty years ago, before rural education programs had been instituted. The Extension Service developed the social potentialities of the rustic farmer by offering him a meeting place, inducing him to participate, and furnishing him with educational materials. This service has been an important agency in overcoming the less good aspects of rural society by the very process of making the farmer a more social being. Today it is the farm wage worker who needs these services: a meeting place, an inducement to participate socially with his fellows, and a source of information and education. Such a program would create among the presently out-caste workers that same sense of belonging and personal security that the Extension Service developed among the farmers.

We saw in Wasco that aside from a few churches the farm worker had no social institutions. The degree of social isolation of the average farm worker is very high. The absence of community feeling, the failure to participate in social decisions, the lack of representations in the machinery of government and of quasi-official agencies, all converge to create a sense of personal frustration and above all of inferiority. Coupled with these isolations is the effect of a migratory life, the impermanence of residence that results from a constant search for work opportunities, and the resulting failures to form strong social attachments of an informal nature. There exist, too, the constant under-current of social hostility, the social isolation of the students in school, the absence of greetings from employers, and the latent hostilities which arise with an issue or an imagined issue such as the school election. Finally, and most devastating, are the memories of open clashes, of past strikes, of hostility to the agencies who endeavored to help them during their worst times, and the very remoteness of the source of decisions affecting their every-day lives.

It is a truism that one cannot legislate social equality and social acceptance. No law, constitutional or otherwise, can make one man look upon another as an equal. But laws can and have made it possible for one group to gain its self-respect and thus, inevitably, a measure of respect from others of their community. Equity in agriculture means, therefore, a program which will aid in bringing the farm laborer into community life, not as an equal, but as a full citizen. Several steps are required. First, efforts must be made to reduce the demand for migration, and aid the individual worker in settling in one community. The strong drive in this direction among the regular farm workers is evident, but the economic deterrents are great. Second, a program of education and assistance, for which the Extension Service, with its use of local organization and its social aspects, offers us an excellent pattern. Finally, a protection of the right of farm workers to organize their own groups based upon common economic and social interests is requisite. Such protection, as we have seen, is required because the climate of hostility and the active preventative measures have effectively hindered the successful development of organizations of laborers.

A farm policy designed to produce equity among the working force in agriculture must recognize the right of all groups to a fair share of the products of their work. It must not only offer economic satisfactions adequate to the needs and deserts of the workers, but must recognize those social values subsumed under the phrase *full citizenship*. It must afford to the farm workers and minor producers those values which have been developed among the commercial farmers in the past half century.

TOWARD THE IMPLEMENTATION OF EQUITY IN RURAL SOCIETY

Urban life has invaded the countryside. Its characteristics will in time pervade every aspect of the rural scene while the bucolic life which is now a tradition will become a memory. Already it is no more than that in the vanguard of our production areas in irrigated California—and in New Jersey, Florida, Texas, and elsewhere where intensive efficient farming is the watchword. It carries with it the promise of more food for the consumer, cheaper production, more income for agriculture and therefore a better life. Wherever the industrial revolution has touched, it has carried this promise of greater wealth and leisure for humanity. Wherever it has touched it has, ironically, carried with it the threat of estrangement, depersonalization, and impoverishment. It carries now to agriculture and rural society both this promise and this threat. Yet the enrichment can be assured only if the impoverishment is prevented. It is for that reason that the principle of equity takes on particular significance in the formulation of rural policy.

Let us review a few fundamental facts:

1. The industrialization of farm production is well under way and follows the general pattern of industrialization that has taken place in other branches of production.

2. The increased and ever-increasing machinery and equipment will make it possible to produce food in plenty with an ever-decreasing working force on the production end.

3. With industrialization has come a class system and a social pattern in agriculture that is essentially similar to those found in urban areas.

4. With only the rarest exceptions do any of the legal protections for wage workers in agriculture exist, though the agricultural industry has been and without doubt will continue to be allocated its share of total national income.

5. The conditions of farm workers, both social and economic, are substandard and not conducive to a healthy social order.

6. The number of wage workers is greater than the number of agricultural employers, while the farm operators who do not hire labor, and many who hire some supplemental work done, derive their income from the value of the work they perform rather than from their entrepreneurial profits.

7. Farm policy has not been successful in halting the trend toward industrialized farming, and there is evidence to show that both price and labor policies have actually hastened the process.

8. Efficiency of operations, when measured by productive use of land or income returns to the farm-working force is not greater on large-scale farm operations than it is on farms of moderate size capable of utilizing modern small-size power equipment.

9. The rural values are generally translated into pecuniary terms and therefore social status and personal self-respect are in a very large measure determined by the financial condition of the individual.

10. Rural society under industrial conditions has not only excluded from social participation the wage-working group, but has effectively and in many instances advertently prevented the development of associations within the laboring group itself, thereby preventing it from developing a sense of, and capacity for, social belonging as well as from participating in community decisions.

11. The exclusion of labor from participation in the community is also the result of their poverty, poor living conditions, low educational opportunities, and the instability which results from the necessity of constant migration.

The implementation of the equity principle in agriculture cannot be accomplished by a single legislative panacea. But it can be done within the framework of laws already existing, or laws patterned after similar ones applicable in other parts of our economy. In developing the legal framework it is first assumed that all three principles of sound policy enumerated in an earlier section of this chapter will be adopted: that production at full capacity will be maintained and land resources conserved. Presumably the former, in times of economic stress, will mean the continuation and further development of consumer subsidies while the latter will involve direct aid to farm operators in soil building and protection activities. It is presumed also that price support, which according to law now continues at least through the year 1948, will be continued indefinitely under some reasonable formula. It is, however, assumed that the implementation of these policies will mean, on the one hand, that crop curtailment for the purpose of reducing production will be discontinued. On the other hand, soil conservation and building programs, in the interest of national welfare and with proper compensation for the service, will become compulsory. The former assumption takes away the odiousness of compliance while the latter takes away the choice.

The first legal device necessary is the establishment of minimum wages. The extension of minimum wages and of conditions of working, regulation of hours and provision of compensation for over-time to farm workers has long been advocated. We have already seen that it is administratively feasible, and Senator La Follette introduced a bill providing for such extension into the Senate as early as 1941. Such an absolute minimum, based upon minimum standards of decency for living, should represent a floor under which wages cannot go. The assurance of farm prices and consumption will carry the guarantee that the farm operators can pay such prices as will meet those minimum standards.

But minimum wages do not guarantee reasonable equity. As the value of a man's work rises, either because technological development renders him a more efficient producer or because price rises make his products worth more on the market, the worker has a right to share in such increases. If farmers' parity prices rise because of increased cost of living, the worker's income should most clearly rise proportionately, since he will suffer similar increases in expenditure. Such a share arrangement can be attached to the parity payment principle. Indeed, it is the only way the parity principle can overcome disparity. Thus guaranteed parity prices will carry with them a guarantee that as prices rise, minimum wages will also be increased. Since parity prices are calculated on the basis of costs of other commodities, fixed minimum wages can be set with respect to an assumed set of parity rates. As parity prices increase above this figure, a proportional increase in farm wages will not act as a hardship upon farmers but will assure parity wages for the workers.

A word must be inserted here on the position of the small farmer—the traditional American farmer—with relation to wages and prices. While the stereotype painted in an earlier section has been shown as false, this does not deny the existence of small-scale farmers with high personal independence, nor does it deny that farm policy should not be directed toward maintaining such operators and integrating them into the picture of industrialized farming. It is frequently asserted that high wages place a hardship upon these small farmers. There are three reasons why this is not true of those farmers who do more of their own farm work than they hire done. First, since as a nation we are committed to a policy of supporting all people at some level of decency, unemployment and low wages, which go together, create burdens on the taxpayer and a subsidy for the hiring farmer. Second, farm income is derived from commodity prices and these in turn rest upon high consumer income, so that the farmer gains from high wages. Third, the farm operator who does his own work gets compensated for it in the sale of his products in direct proportion to the value of his labor; if farm wage workers are getting paid a small wage, then his work is worth only that wage. Obviously these factors apply only to the general wage level—not to the wages that he himself pays (though we have seen in Wasco the payment of wages by small growers above those set by the large). There are an estimated 80,000 farm operators in America whose operations are highly dependent upon farm labor and only a million whose production is dependent upon as much or more hired work than the farm operator performs. In contrast, there are well over two million commercial farmers who hire no labor or who do more work than such labor as they do hire. If there is any truth left behind the family-farm tradition, it resides in this group rather than in the employer group.

The attachment of wages to the parity principle has another important effect. In our discussion of the operations of parity it was shown that it had a tendency to reduce sharecroppers and farm tenants to laborers, while landowners took over the operation of farms themselves. Such an effect results from the failure of parity to provide for equity. If the assurance to farmers carried with it the assurance to laborers in fair measure, then the profit would not accrue to farm operators from creaming off the additional worth of a day's work performed by others, but would go, as it should, to the workers in just proportion. In this way the parity principle could be maintained without continuing to disrupt the established economic order. The displacement of labor and the amalgamation of farms would rest upon economic principles of efficiency and not upon governmental subsidy.

Thus it appears that minimum wages—particularly parity wages—not only offer economic assurance to the wage workers themselves, but carry with them the promise of continuing that very element of farm life which has the highest value from the standpoint of American tradition—the independent farmer.

The second legal device is the establishment of agricultural workers' right to organize, the establishment of machinery for collective bargaining, and for the arbitration and determination of wages and conditions of work. The development of a minimum wage law, like the concept of a parity price, does not displace bargaining. It merely places a floor under the prices for a commodity and a day's labor.

The extension of the principles set forth in the Wagner Labor Relations Act to cover farm workers is necessary for several reasons. The most important of these reasons is that in the past there has been concerted and organized effort to prevent farm workers from organizing and a complete absence of the fundamental principles of collective bargaining. In the absence of machinery for the fair establishment of the value of work in agriculture, both farmer and laborer have lost. Labor because it has, in the nature of things, suffered wages and working conditions and living conditions that would not be tolerated by urban workers. Farmers because in the development of wage policies set in the high councils of industrial farmers, they have had to suffer insecure labor supplies, disorganized labor market, and strikes in which they had little to gain and much to lose. But the economic necessity for the establishment and recognition of labor organization is not the only one. We have seen in the communities presented here the complete absence of secular organization among that third or half or two-thirds of the total community whose income is dependent upon farm wages. We have seen community decisions reached—decisions affecting the laborer as much or more than they did the other elements in the community—without a voice raised by or for the working group. Even when local citizens realize the failure of representation from the working group in civic affairs, there is in fact no means of reaching them. The urban character of social relationships means, as we saw in the preceding chapter, that the individual must participate in the total community as a member of a group whose interests are held in common and must be presented through spokesmen for such a group. If a labor union, or some other organization whose membership represented the farm wage worker, had existed in Wasco when the cemetery question arose or when the incorporation decisions were raised, or if it had existed in Dinuba at the time the Chamber of Commerce held its post-war planning session, then labor would have at least had the opportunity to be heard. To be sure, if labor were represented by organized groups, the threatened attempt to elect a representative to civic bodies would become a reality, and the promises of county officials to run the government according to the needs of the employer segment would not be so readily made. We have seen that the absence of such organization has not been fortuitous, and that its failure has been detrimental to democratic action in the rural community.

A third major device is necessary to the establishment of equity among the agricultural working force. For wage rates and economic well-being, organized activity and social participation all require a measure of security in tenure as farm workers and as community residents. It is for this reason that the extension of the principles of social security, and most particularly the payment of unemployment insurance, is requisite for the development of equitable economic and social conditions. We have seen that the economic conditions of farm labor rest heavily upon seasonality of employment and over-crowding of the labor market. Such seasonal fluctuations in the labor market as are unavoidable inevitably create hardships and costs to someone. That these hardships and costs should be borne, as they were in early years of California agriculture, by the laborers themselves is hardly in keeping with the principle of equity. That they should be borne by the public at large in support of the few to whom labor availability is a direct advantage, is likewise of doubtful equity. So long as this is the case the operator who hires labor has no personal incentive to utilize the worker in such a way as to maximize his employment opportunity. Without a system of employment security the guarantee of minimum wages is meaningless, for no reasonable wage can, of itself, carry the family needs on the basis of six months' employment. Without employment security union protection of employees' rights is also meaningless, for the fluctuations of the labor force will make impossible the necessary continuity of the farm-working force. But with a measure of employment security, it will be possible to induce employers of large amounts of labor to organize their farm work along lines which will spread the season of employment. Some large operators have found such a system advantageous for economic reasons, but where specific pressure is absent few have adopted such a policy.

These three fundamental extensions of legal protection for the economic and social welfare of the farm worker make possible and in a large measure require certain laws of lesser but nevertheless significant proportions. Here again, nothing new in legal devices nor in administrative problems arise. These lesser problems are (1) the development of an adult education system patterned after the Extension Service, (2) the creation of an employment service operated from the standpoint of getting the worker jobs, (3) the development of community labor pools among farmers, and (4) the establishment of a housing program to fit the workers' needs.

The Federal and State Extension Service, designed primarily to bring new techniques in production and living into farms and farm homes is, theoretically, open to the use of all comers. The very nature of its administration and the natural direction of its energies has made it, in fact, almost exclusively a farmer welfare and educational program. Certainly the farm laborer never joins the Farm Bureau meetings and rarely gets service from the extension agent, at least under industrial farming conditions. Yet the need of educational service is far greater among farm laborers than it is among farm operators.

Such a program should have two facets: the education of the worker to enable him better to serve agricultural production and enhance his personal value, and the education of the householder to the full potential usefulness of a limited income. Farm work, like industrial work, is improved by the possession of skills. As industrialization progresses, new and more skills will be required of the worker. The need for information to new workers in agriculture of even such simple operations as the picking of fruit, was recognized during the war emergency. But education of workers in the care and treatment of farm machinery, and in the execution of simple repairs, will become increasingly important as more farms become mechanized. The value of such a program will be great to the farm operators who have complained loud and bitterly, and not without cause, of the damage done to equipment, stock, trees, and soil by careless handling. Yet even more important than this aspect of an education program is the homemaking aspect. For a knowledge of purchasing, of saving, of full utilization and of those arts which will make life esthetically more satisfying are of the greatest importance to the redevelopment of the personal self-respect of the farm worker.

The simplest expedient for the development of such a program would be to attach it to the existing agricultural extension program. A common program might be developed in time, or in areas not yet industrialized. But it is doubtful if such a program could function in Wasco or Arvin, for instance, if it were attached to the county agent's office. The mutual antagonisms and the distrust between farmer and laborer would repel the worker. They would not participate for, like the worker who was invited by her farmer employer to accompany her to church, they would want to be with people of their own class. Until such a program has developed the group self-respect of the working class, any educational program must remain separate from the Extension Service and from farmer participation. It must also be administered by those whose primary consideration is the welfare of the worker. But if such a program is to succeed, it can best pattern itself after the Extension Service, which has so raised the standards and capabilities of the farming population. Most particularly can it emulate this group in the development of social relationships among its constituency and of leadership and spokesmen for the group as a whole.

An agricultural employment service is requisite, if rationalization of the farm-labor market is to be achieved. The great oversupply of workers, the long, expensive, and useless migrations, and the lack of adjustment of employee capabilities to employer needs can all be ameliorated by an information and placement service. The need for such service has been recognized by farm operators during the period of wartime labor shortage. If full employment is achieved, the continued need of such a service will be demanded by farmers, who cannot recruit their workers individually and in mutual competition and maintain an effective production force. If unemployment should again create the distress that existed during the last economic depression, then the need to help the worker get employment with the least cost to him in time and money will be equally important.

Such an employment service should be equipped with information on the character of employment and the volume of workers at hand in various parts of the state. It should have a knowledge of the work requirements of various tasks, in order to direct employees to the kinds of work for which they are capable. In this way both employer and employee will have a central meeting place for workers not only within the community, but over the entire area of potential migration. Operation of social security and fair labor programs will require the existence of an employment service for the certification of agricultural employees to eligibility for its benefits. The effective operation of such a program like that of education, requires that the agency be an impartial one. The development of an employment service under an agency which is aligned with either group would immediately nullify its effectiveness because the other would avoid its use.

In order to increase the efficiency of the working force and to maximize the season of farm employment, the continuation of a wartime expedient is recommended. During the war, organizations of farmers have been established for the sole purpose of creating a labor-demand pool. Such co-operative effort among farm operators was made necessary by the program of labor importation, for it was necessary to guarantee such workers a minimum period of employment. What was done as a wartime expedient for foreign labor can certainly be made a peacetime policy for citizen workers.

The creation—or continuance—of such organizations can serve the farm operators in many ways. It will effectively eliminate labor pirating and the bidding up of wages during periods when workers are scarce. It can develop the local labor market, so that a large part of the labor force has permanent local residence, thereby enriching the community in many ways. It can also serve as a bargaining agency for farmers in the establishment of agricultural wages. In this way the local farmer who cannot attend wage hearings in distant places can make his own attitudes and desires known in the processes of reaching group decisions.

Because of lack of residence and other disadvantages of farm-labor work, much welfare legislation has been unavailable to the laboring class. Among these are aids to aged and sick. The stabilization of farm work will go far to alleviate this situation, because it will make the worker a full-fledged local citizen. One further aid, made available to low-income workers in other categories of employment, is the extension of assistance in housing for farm workers.

The physical need for housing among farm workers is a well-known reality. Housing as a psychological need among farm workers has been demonstrated in an earlier chapter. The need is not merely for better temporary housing in operators' camps or other emergency facilities in areas which need large harvest crews. Such housing has in the past been furnished workers, though much more, and much improved units, could be provided. But the housing need is for homes, separate and personally owned.

The farm worker now serving agriculture is a man who has always been close to the soil. Many came from non-industrial farms. Most of them, and more particularly their wives, have a strong desire to own a house and some land. Industrial farming does not make the very small farm—under 10 acres—feasible, but it should not deny the half-acre plot or the city lot to its workers. But in the absence of security of tenure as a farm worker and the resulting handicap to credit, the farm worker has been able only to buy land at high prices in poorer sections. These he could buy on credit furnished by the seller, but his house had to be pieced together out of scraps.

The result of this has been the continuation of poor housing and the creation of economic neighborhoods which are virtually slums. Residence in such houses and in such areas carries with it a social stigma and supports class feelings in the community. Any program of housing for the workers should recognize that most of them want and should have permanent residence in some one community, that they want to own houses personally rather than rent them, that they should be separate and placed where the individual wants them, that they should have adequate land to allow for home gardens and poultry, when these are desired, and that they should be modest but in keeping with the social values recognized by the community.

RURAL SOCIETY IN THE WORLD OF THE FUTURE

Industrial agriculture brings an urbanized society, and industrialization is taking over the rural scene. But the kind of urban society that exists in the future depends upon the agricultural policy that develops in the next few years. If we continue to promulgate laws based upon an outmoded and unrealistic stereotype, our rural communities will be peopled with unstable and insecure workers, spotted with rural slums, broken by class schisms, and devoid of those democratic qualities that have served rural America in the past.

But what will rural life be like if we plan for it in terms of actual rural values and social relationships, in the manner of the program just outlined? It will not be made to fit the stereotype, to be sure, but it can be made to fit American ideals.

The legal structure outlined would first of all professionalize our farm labor. A professionalized farm-labor group will be a stabilized one; capable, self-conscious, and self-respecting. The farmers in such a community will not be able to profit from inadequate wages and lack of responsibility to labor but will be able to operate more efficiently because of stable supply of workers who have the requisite skills. The economic status of the farmer will rest more heavily upon his own efficiency and skill than upon his opportunity to take advantage of low-cost labor and government expenditures. The rural community will therefore become more stable, more democratic, and economically more sound.

Not only will programs which insure maximum employment, unemployment compensation, educational and informational services, and housing stabilize the life of the individual farm workers. It will also stabilize the wage worker as a group. For three-quarters of a century a series of workers have been imported or have come into California to do the field work, and as each came it as rapidly went. It is a significant fact that no single group has dominated the agricultural working force for more than a generation. Each has sought escape from the work and the working conditions as soon as the opportunity presented itself. Not only does this suggest condemnation of the conditions of work, but it also creates a hardship upon the farmer who must always have an untrained working force. A stable group, recognizing farm work as their life work and capable of making it a satisfactory one will therefore tend to become more competent and responsible.

Such a labor force will be self-conscious. The workers will engage in more and more mutual activities, and the union or other farm-labor organization will take an increasingly prominent place in farm life. As group action makes for a sense of belonging and the mutual reinforcement of attitudes and ideals, the personal humility now found among the group will be replaced by the normal dignity that man should have. This replacement of personal attitude will be a primary factor in the development and the fulfillment of standards of behavior of the community as a whole among the working element. More than any single factor, it will do away with the need for those escapes from reality provided by drink and emotional religion. It will make possible joint action in affairs with other elements in the community, because the embarrassment of insecurity will be lifted.

A professionalized working force will have other effects. It will, of necessity, remove farm work as a category of employment which anyone can have. The recognition of a group having a prior claim to the work opportunities on farms will mean that the unemployed industrial workers, the housewives, and school children can only get farm employment when the supply of recognized farm workers is exhausted. An efficiently operated rural economy would have enough professional workers to fill all the long-term jobs in the industry but would require a seasonal emergency force. Such a force can be, as it has been, recruited from persons not normally in the labor market.

The farmers in a rural society in which the principle of equity was maintained by protection of the workers, would prosper in proportion to their own proficiency as farmers. The creation of large-scale enterprises would rest upon the inherent efficiency they may have, rather than upon inadequate compensation to the workers and their dependence upon public money for their off-season support. The working farmer, dependent upon his own labor, would find his work worth more in terms of production if large-scale farming cannot undersell him by producing with low-paid labor. These policies would therefore act as fully to protect the small farm as it would serve to improve the conditions of labor.

We may confidently expect that one result of such a rural social order would hasten mechanization on farms. Mechanization is frequently viewed with considerable alarm, though its opponents are never willing to carry their position to its logical reduction to absurdity. Mechanization, however, can bring agricultural products to market and to the consumer at a lower cost. It is therefore generally beneficial. It will also increase the total national production and reduce the amount of farm employment required. If, however, these tendencies take place in a world of full employment, they need not cause distress. If unemployment exists and we cannot afford to purchase the commodities produced, then it will be our failure to utilize efficient production rather than efficiency itself which is to blame.

The community serving rural people will become a more stable and democratic one if equity is achieved among the farmworking force. It will become more stable because it will have a constant population. The merchants will find that a group of stable and solvent farm workers will increase their business and thus further prosperity. Social institutions, churches, and schools will be able to plan for a future of relative certainty because the constant shifting both in numbers and in degree of well-being will be replaced by relative stability. Above all, the community bound together by common geographical location can become a community bound by common ties. The creation of a professionalized labor force will not do away with the natural conflicts between employer and employee, it will not result in social equality that makes all men have the same amount of prestige, it will not create a utopia; but it will create a social body in which the individuals all participate, and in which they have, in accordance with American tradition and law, an equal voice in the decisions facing the community. We discovered the paradox that agricultural planning in terms of a fallacious stereotype of rural society tended inevitably to destroy those vestiges of reality behind the stereotype. It is equally true and equally paradoxical that planning in terms of social reality can create those very values which were characterized in that social stereotype.

PART II
Agribusiness and the Rural Community

INTRODUCTION

The family farm is the classic example of the American small business enterprise. For generations this institution and the community it supports have held the esteem of all who have known and understood the American heritage. Statesmen, historians, economists, and sociologists have generally agreed that the spread of the family farm over the land has laid the economic base for the liberties and the democratic institutions which this Nation counts as its greatest asset.

The great declaration by Daniel Webster still stands as perhaps the clearest and most authentic expression of America's deeprooted belief in the intimate and causal relation between the family farm and the distinctively popular character of our Government.

Our New England ancestors—

he said—

brought thither no great capitals from Europe; and if they had, there was nothing productive in which they could have been invested. They left behind them the whole feudal policy of the other continent. * * * They came to a new country. There were as yet no lands yielding rent, and no tenants rendering service. The whole soil was unreclaimed from barbarism. They were themselves either from their original condition, or from the necessity of their common interest, nearly on a level in respect to property. Their situation demanded a parceling out and division of the land, and it may fairly be said that this necessary act *fixed the future frame and form of their government.* [Webster's italics.] The character of their political institutions was determined by the fundamental laws respecting property. * * * The consequence of all these causes has been a great subdivision of the soil and a great equality of condition; the true basis, most certainly, of popular government. * * *

The advances in technology during the past century have greatly benefited farmers who, with their families, work the land. The industrial revolution has eased the burden of the farmer and rendered his labors more productive. Yet these technological advances have, at the same time, brought a threat to the very institution to whose personnel they have brought so much aid. The threat is this: That with increased mechanization will come increased industrialization of the farm enterprise; that with industrialization will come an increasing concentration of economic power in the hands of fewer and fewer men at the head of great organizations, and an end to that broad diffusion of social and economic benefits that has long been characteristic of American rural communities.

There is foundation for the belief that industrialization is on the increase. The United States Census of Agriculture has been recording the gradual increase in average farm size in America. This is not a result of the disappearance of undersized farms; family farmers on the better lands appear to be particularly vulnerable. Census statistics are supported by other information. In those areas particularly suitable to high-value specialty crops, the concentration of land and production into large units has been reported by various agencies and students of American agriculture. A committee of the United States Senate has pointed out that within the decade of the thirties the percentage of all farms in California which produce just over one-half the total agricultural production of that State fell from 10 to 6.8 percent, marking a growth in concentration of nearly one-third. It is not without significance as evidence of this trend that at least one group of specialty crop producers has so far changed its character away from that of family farmers and in the direction of becoming industrialists that it has found itself indicted for violation of the antitrust laws of the Nation.

The development of large-scale farming has been foremost in California. The influence of Spanish land policy, the monopolization of large areas by early comers after American statehood, the soil and climate favorable to the production of specialty crops, and congeries of other historic and economic circumstances have made California particularly amenable to industrialized agricultural production. But development of this pattern of agriculture, often operated like industry from urban centers and worked by wage labor, is not peculiar to any one part of the nation. It has been reported in some degree from all sections.

Whether industrialization of farming is a threat not only to the family farm, but also to the rural society founded upon the family farm, is the specific subject of the present report. The purpose of this study is to test by contemporary field research the historic hypothesis that the institution of small independent farmers is indeed the agent which creates the homogenous community, both socially and economically democratic.

The present inquiry consists of a detailed analysis and comparison of two communities, one where agricultural operations are on a modest scale, the other where large factory-like techniques are practiced. Both communities lie in the fertile southern San Joaquin Valley in the Great Central Valley of California, where highly developed and richly productive agriculture is characteristic. Limitations of time and resources dictated that no more than two communities be studied. Numerous other pairs might have been chosen which doubtless would have yielded comparable results.

The two communities studied here naturally vary in some degree with respect to proportions of surrounding lands devoted to this or that crop, with respect to age, to depth of water lift for irrigation, etc., as well as with respect to the scale of the farm enterprises which surround them. Controls as perfect as are possible in the chemist's laboratory are not found in social organizations. Yet the approximation to complete control achieved by selection of the communities of Arvin and Dinuba is surprisingly high. Other factors, besides the difference in scale of farming, which might have produced or contributed to the striking contrasts of Arvin and Dinuba have been carefully examined. On this basis the conclusion has been reached that the primary, and by all odds the factor of greatest weight in producing the essential differences in these two communities, was the characteristic difference in the scale of farming—large or small—upon which each was founded. There is every reason to believe that the results obtained by this study are generally applicable wherever like economic conditions prevail.

A variety of techniques were used to gather the data upon which this study is based. Fundamental were the schedules which afford data on population composition, social participation, and level of living. They were obtained by two field enumerations over a period of 4 weeks in each community (spring, 1944) based upon a 10 percent sample of the houses in the town and surround country. The information from this source was enriched by interviews with community leaders taken by the author. The area surrounding each community was determined by a well-established technique of community delineation long used by rural sociologists and executed by a person trained in its application.

Statistical data were obtained from several sources other than the schedule. Certain data were available from county and community files. Special mention should be made of two sources. Data on size of farms, acreage devoted to various crops, and yields were obtained from the records of the Agricultural Adjustment Administration, analyzed by competent agricultural economists. The data on number and volume of business enterprises were extracted from the records of the Sales Tax Division of the California State Board of Equalization. These data were made applicable to the community as delineated, including the agricultural areas.

The author makes grateful acknowledgment to those numerous persons who by their counsel and as participants in the study have made its execution possible. Members of the communities of Arvin and Dinuba were generous in their cooperation.

SUMMARY OF FINDINGS

Certain conclusions are particularly significant to the small businessman, and to an understanding of the importance of his place in a community. Not only does the small farm itself constitute small business, but it supports flourishing small commercial business.

Analysis of the business conditions in the communities of Arvin and Dinuba shows that—

(1) The small farm community supported 62 separate business establishments, to but 35 in the large-farm community; a ratio in favor of the small-farm community of nearly 2:1.

(2) The volume of retail trade in the small-farm community during the 12-month period analyzed was $4,383,000 as against only $2,535,000 in the large-farm community. Retail trade in the

small-farm community was greater by 61 percent. (See figure and table, pp. 83 and 84.)

(3) The expenditure for household supplies and building equipment was over three times as great in the small-farm community as it was in the large-farm community.

The investigation disclosed other vast differences in the economic and social life of the two communities, and affords strong support for the belief that small farms provide the basis for a richer community life and a greater sum of those values for which America stands, than do industrialized farms of the usual type.

It was found that—

(4) The small farm supports in the local community a larger number of people per dollar volume of agricultural production than an area devoted to larger-scale enterprises, a difference in its favor of about 20 percent.

(5) Notwithstanding their greater numbers, people in the small-farm community have a better average standard of living than those living in the community of large-scale farms.

(6) Over one-half the breadwinners in the small-farm community are independently employed businessmen, persons in white-collar employment, or farmers; in the large-farm community the proportion is less than one-fifth.

(7) Less than one-third of the breadwinners in the small-farm community are agricultural wage laborers (characteristically landless, and with low and insecure income) while the proportion of persons in this position reaches the astonishing figure of nearly two-thirds of all persons gainfully employed in the large-farm community.

(8) Physical facilities for community living—paved streets, sidewalks, garbage disposal, sewage disposal, and other public services—are far greater in the small-farm community; indeed, in the industrial-farm community some of these facilities are entirely wanting.

(9) Schools are more plentiful and offer broader services in the small-farm community, which is provided with four elementary schools and one high school; the large-farm community has but a single elementary school.

(10) The small-farm community is provided with three parks for recreation; the large-farm community has a single playground, loaned by a corporation.

(11) The small-farm town has more than twice the number of organizations for civic improvement and social recreation than its large-farm counterpart.

(12) Provision for public recreation centers, Boy Scout troops, and similar facilities for enriching the lives of the inhabitants is proportioned in the two communities in the same general way, favoring the small-farm community.

(13) The small-farm community supports two newspapers, each with many times the news space carried in the single paper of the industrialized-farm community.

(14) Churches bear the ratio 2:1 between the communities, with the greater number of churches and churchgoers in the small-farm community.

(15) Facilities for making decisions on community welfare through local popular elections are available to people in the small-farm community; in the large-farm community such decisions are in the hands of officials of the county.

These differences are sufficiently great in number and degree to affirm the thesis that small farms bear a very important relation to the character of American rural society. It must be realized that the two communities of Arvin and Dinuba were carefully selected to reflect the difference in size of enterprise, and not extraneous factors. The agricultural production in the two communities was virtually the same in volume—2½ million dollars per annum in each—so that the resource base was strictly comparable. Both communities produce specialized crops of high value and high cost of production, utilizing irrigation and large bodies of special harvest labor. The two communities are in the same climate zone, about equidistant from small cities and major urban centers, similarly served by highways and railroads, and without any significant advantages from nonagricultural resources or from manufacturing or processing. The reported differences in the communities may properly be assigned confidently and overwhelmingly to the scale-of-farming factor.

The reasons seem clear. The small-farm community is a population of middle-class persons with a high degree of stability in income and tenure, and a strong economic and social interest in their community. Differences in wealth among them are not great, and the people generally associate together in those organizations which serve the community. Where farms are large, on the other hand, the population consists of relatively few persons with economic stability, and of large numbers whose only tie to the community is their uncertain and relatively low-income job. Differences in wealth are great among members of this community, and social contacts between them are rare. Indeed, even the operators of large-scale farms frequently are absentees; and if they do live in Arvin, they as often seek their recreation in the nearby city. Their interest in the social life of the community is hardly greater than that of the laborer whose tenure is transitory. Even the businessmen of the large-farm community frequently express their feelings of impermanence; and the financial investment in the community, kept usually at a minimum, reflects the same view. Attitudes such as these are not conducive to stability and the rich kind of rural community life which is properly associated with the traditional family farm.

CHAPTER XI
NATURE OF INVESTIGATION
PURPOSE

This study of two rural communities is an endeavor to analyze social causation. In it an attempt has been made to demonstrate the kind of society that results when large-scale farm operations dominate the economy of a community as contrasted with society under moderate-size farm operations. To this end a detailed analysis of two towns lying in the industrialized specialty-crop farming area of California's Central Valley, one surrounded by large farms and the other by enterprises of moderate size, was made. The present report sets forth in detail the social and pertinent agricultural and other economic facts about each community, and concludes with an analysis of these differences which indicates the extent to which they may properly be attributable to the scale of farm operations.

It should be made clear at the outset that this report is a study of the social and business effects of large-scale farming operations as they apply to the local agricultural community. Investigation of the effects upon major urban centers or the character of social and economic conditions of the Central Valley or of the State as a whole are not a subject of the present analysis, except insofar as they are affected by the welfare of the local community.

Arvin and Dinuba, the communities studied, are not a sample of all communities of California or of the Central Valley. They are cases, a method which has gained acceptance in the social sciences generally and particularly in the study of the community.

It has been the method used by Lynd for Middletown, by Warner for Yankee City, and by every student of the rural community. The case study depends not upon adequacy of sample but upon the soundness of the selection of the cases as representative of the phenomena subjected to analysis.

CHOICE OF COMMUNITIES

The importance of proper selection was recognized at the outset, and extreme care was used to get a fair and representative selection. The fundamental criteria were that the two communities (1) be sufficiently similar in size so that they could be expected to support similar institutions; (2) have similar and, if possible, reasonably diverse agriculture; (3) have existed for enough years to allow time for the development of social institutions; (4) not be confused with extraneous advantages, such as large mineral deposits; and, of course, (5) that the farm size be significantly divergent.

The two communities chosen for this investigation were Arvin (Kern County), as a large-scale farming community, and Dinuba (Tulare County), for the community surrounded by farms of moderate size.[1]

Certain vital statistical information was being collected for other purposes for the agricultural areas of Madera, Kern, and Tulare Counties, and therefore it was desirable to select a community from within that area. Furthermore, this includes most of the "project area" of the Central Valley project, and it seemed desirable to remain within the geographic region in which this development was to take place. It was important to have communities of sufficient size to support social and economic institutions yet not so large that the totality of these could not be grasped in the limited time available for field study. In practice this meant a community of not under 2,500 and not over 10,000 population. It was also desirable to have communities which farmer and laborer both utilized; where institutions served both these segments of the population, since both groups are an essential part of farm production in the area. Finally, the towns should be of sufficient age so that they have had the opportunity for the development of social and economic institutions.

Table 1 shows the communities of Madera, Kern, and Tulare

[1]It is more economic to use the expression "large farm community" and "small farm community," and these will be used in the discussions that follow. A clear picture of the actual situation with regard to size is presented in a subsequent section terms will thus be recognized as having comparative rather than absolute value. The term "small farm" as used here may better be considered a family-sized commercial farm, and must not be confused either with part-time or subsistence farms.

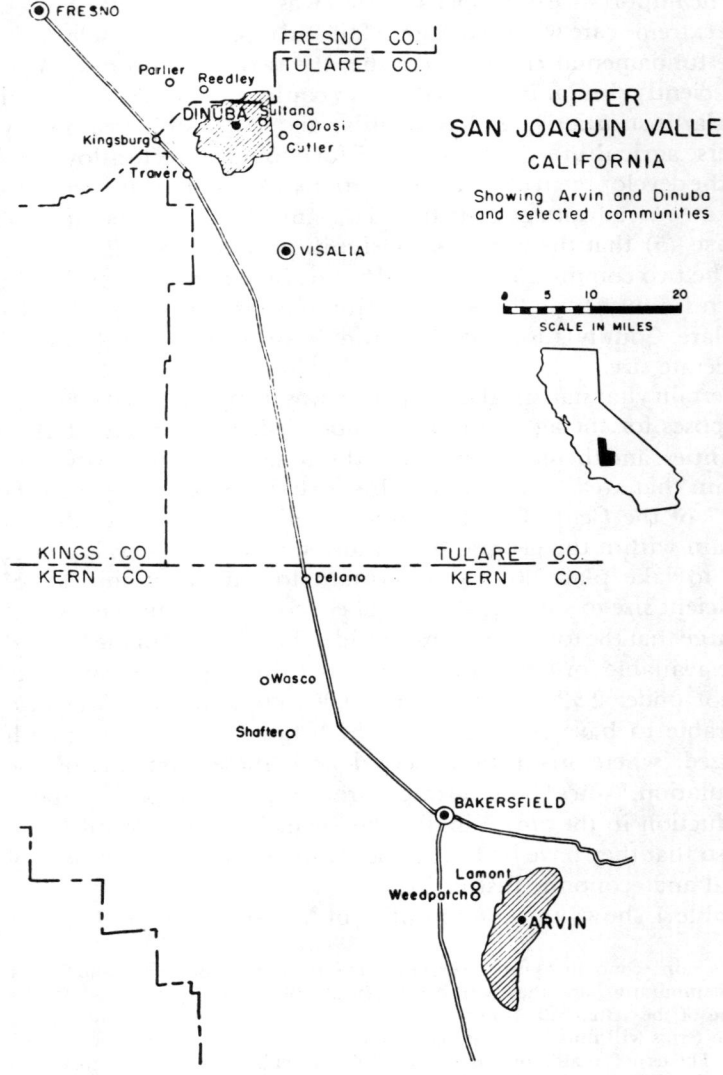

FIGURE No. 1

Counties from which a choice was made. The figures are based upon estimated boundaries around each community, but indicate the relationship in population, land use, and size of farms. (Boundaries were more accurately drawn for the two communities studies, and agricultural and population figures do not conform exactly to these rougher approximations which were used at the time of selection.) The towns are in order of average acre-equivalent farm size.[2] Communities near the opposite poles were selected though extremes were not sought.

In practice, the strictures were not easy to apply, especially the stricture that the communities be similar. In the first place, as everyone acquainted with California agriculture knows, there is a wide diversity of crops, soils, and water conditions, and it is impossible to find communities identical in these respects. Yet it was possible to get general similarity with respect to quality of soil, major agriculture production, and the influence of nonagricultural resources.

Details of the agriculture are presented in a later section, where a thorough analysis of the characteristics of farming and types of production is made. A few significant comparisons will show the validity and limitations of the selection. In both communities a variety of crops, and very similar crops, were grown. The Dinuba area, however, is far more highly specialized than the Arvin one, with over two-thirds of the total value of production in fruit and grapes, chiefly the latter. Cotton and vegetables are more plentiful in Arvin than in Dinuba though they are grown in both communities. Forage crops and livestock were very nearly the same in the two areas. The total estimated value of production in the two communities was nearly identical. In summary, the agricultural production in the two communities has about the same dollar value and includes most of the same products, but Dinuba is more specialized to fruit and has relatively small amounts of cotton and vegetables, while Arvin has greater diversity, with emphasis on cotton and vegetables.

In selecting the communities it was desirable that they be located similarly with respect to highways, railroads, and cities. This was achieved with a considerable degree of success. Both communities

[2]This adaptation of the standard acre has been worked out on the basis of data available. (See Methodology in appendix B.)

TABLE 1.—*Comparison of population and farming in the small communities in Madera, Tulare, and Kern Counties*

Community [1]	Population			Number of farms [4]	Size of farms	
	Town [2]	Open country [3]	Total		Acres	A-E acres [5]
Richgrove (T)			325	18	642	304
Buttonwillow (K)	685	1,755	2,440	98	432	291
Arvin (K)	4,042	631	4,673	137	297	247
Earlimart (T)	1,174	1,936	3,110	150	247	234
Lemoucove (T)			930	44	104	223
Pixley (T)	1,625	1,530	3,155	180	232	192
Tipton (T)			1,807	166	222	182
Alpaugh (T)	638	1,086	1,724	133	490	167
Lamont (K)			1,220	85	156	165
Delano (K)	4,573	1,535	6,108	341	177	159
Woodville (T)			1,130	112	156	155
Woodlake (T)	1,146	2,934	4,080	215	110	152
Goshen (T)			1,436	104	160	148
Chowchilla (M)	1,957	2,190	4,147	430	215	139
McFarland (K)	2,120	1,894	4,014	115	188	138
Exeter (T)	3,883	2,554	6,437	364	68	124
Shafter (K)	1,258	5,067	6,325	300	102	108
Wasco (K)	4,916	5,338	10,254	190	128	101
Lindsay (T)	4,397	3,521	7,918	577	77	101
Berenda-Fairmead (M)	353	1,763	2,116	238	216	94
Dinuba (T)	3,790	3,877	7,667	635	45	84
Strathmore (T)			1,680	214	43	81
Terra Bella (T)			1,580	141	131	76
Orosi-Cutler (T)	917	2,778	3,695	451	69	76
Ivanhoe (T)	814	780	1,594	159	41	73

[1] In order of average A-E size of farm (right-hand column). Letter in parentheses indicates county in which community falls.
[2] Based upon 1940 census of population.
[3] Based upon population of 1935 as indicated on dot map prepared by the Bureau of Agricultural Economics (Berkeley), increased proportionally to increases in rural areas for each minor civil division according to 1940 census. Community boundaries are approximate.
[4] Based upon AAA data. Since community boundaries were approximated, too literal reading of this figure is not appropriate.
[5] An acre-equivalent (A-E) acre is that area of land in any crop which has the normal income potential of an acre of alfalfa. For fuller explanation see appendix B.

N. B.—The data referring to Arvin and Dinuba do not exactly correspond to data presented elsewhere since the area included with the community boundary is a less accurate approximation. These data are less exact, but appropriate for the comparative purposes of this table.

lie off major motor highways, though both are served by paved roads. Both communities are served by the railroads for freight only, though at one time Dinuba also had passenger service. Both communities lie sufficiently distant from major cities so that they can reasonably be expected to provide more than emergency services to the local population. Arvin is 22 miles from Bakersfield, Dinuba is 20 miles from Visalia and 30 from Fresno. Neither community serves a tourist population, though Arvin has in the past taken advantage of its location for holding glider meets and thereby gained publicity if not actual economic advantage.

Arvin lies just south of fairly extensive oil fields, and there is sufficient likelihood of finding underlying strata of oil to induce oil companies to maintain leases on mineral rights of Arvin lands. Most landowners in the community have lease contracts which pay $5 per acre per year. Dinuba has no comparable source of revenue.

Oil production does not materially affect the character of the community, however, since very few persons secure their livelihood from this resource, either as laborers in the oil fields or as a result of oil pumping. There are but two or three small productive wells within the community boundary.

The greatest differential between the two communities, other than the size of farming operations, is their history. Dinuba is 20 to 25 years older than Arvin. This difference was not avoidable, however, because of the history of land settlement within the State. During the early period of irrigation development there was a general tendency to break up holdings and sell them to settlers. After the turn of the century, and especially since World War I, larger landowners have tended to keep their holdings after acquiring irrigation water. Therefore the large farm communities tend to be younger than the small farm communities. In a later section the influence of the age of the community will be dealt with at greater length.

Finally, the ethnic composition was a matter of importance. For obvious reasons it was preferable to have a community made up of native white Americans. While there are foreign groups in each community, foreigners are not an important element in either town. There are a few Mexican families in each, a number of Negroes in Arvin, and some Koreans in Dinuba. There were formerly Japanese in Dinuba and Filipinos in Arvin, but the Japanese have all been evacuated and the Filipinos have left. A contingent of German Mennonites in Dinuba has had some influence upon the community but not an extensive one. The effect of alien cultures on the character of the two communities is negligible.

METHODOLOGY

A variety of methods, procedures, and techniques were used in developing the information in this study. Included are community delineation, interviews, schedules, analysis of club and church membership lists, and compilation of statistical data from a variety of sources. A group of three spent a month in each community to take the interviews and schedules. In addition, one person spent a few days to delineate the community boundaries. Details of procedure, together with a copy of the schedule used, are given in appendix A.

CHAPTER XII

HISTORICAL BACKGROUND OF ARVIN AND DINUBA

Before the analysis and comparison of the social picture of the two communities can be meaningful, it is necessary to have a clear picture of their resources, physical setting, and historical development.

ARVIN

SETTING

Arvin lies south and east of Bakersfield, about 10 miles from the highway running eastward to Arizona and about the same distance from the highway south to Los Angeles. The climate is that of a desert, with less than 10 inches average annual rainfall. The soil has been built into alluvial fans by streams out of the mountains to the east and is of excellent quality. The farming area is quite flat, with a very gentle slope to the north and west. A few miles east of Arvin are the foothills of the Tehachapi Range, bare of trees but covered with good range grass. Most of the land in these foothills belongs to the great El Tejon ranch. To the south of Arvin lies undeveloped land, though more and more of this is now being cultivated by the use of deep wells and heavy-duty pumps. There is still considerable land available for development in this area, but unless the water supply is augmented it is doubtful if sufficient water is available for the continued irrigation of lands now using ground waters. The land to the north and west has for a long while been held in very large holdings, and most of it is now owned and operated by the DiGiorgio Fruit Corp. The community is bounded on the north by a small draw which is often rendered impassable by floods. Westward from the town there is a large area of moderately large farms, and this extends unbroken into the neighboring communities of Weedpatch and Lamont. Weedpatch derives its name from the fact that after the spring floods weeds in this area grow over the head of a man on horseback. It was the earliest community in the area, but at present is merely a crossroads center. Lamont, north of Weedpatch, has come to be a large center for laborers. Neither of these communities is as active commercially as Arvin, however, and neither of them presents a great threat with respect to trade potentials. For instance, the county has decided to place the proposed high school at Arvin rather than near the other two communities.

HISTORY

Arvin lies in the shadow of one of the oldest large ranches in the State—the El Tejon. But this ranch apparently has had little or no direct effect upon the community. Much of the flat land around Arvin was homesteaded at about the turn of the century. In 1910 a colony was started in Arvin dependent upon community irrigation wells. At this time many of the homesteaders sold their holdings to these settlers for about $10 an acre. This was the beginning of the development of intensive farming in the community, and many of the small farms today have come down from this early period. During these early days the settlers suffered the hardships of the pioneer. The route to the nearest railroad was the dust-covered buggy tracks running across the desert. In 1912, according to one woman who is still in the community, she was the only farm wife in the area, and while there was electricity for pumping irrigation water, there was none for household use. During the second decade of the century more land was developed. It was during this period that the largest single holding was developed, as well as many other units now in operation. Land values rose from the $10 per acre which the original homesteaders received from their sales to about $100 an acre, which is said to have been the average price during the First World War.

Cattle were the first agricultural commodity produced in the area, but diversified farming came in with the development of small ranches in the period 1910-15. Walnuts and hops were produced quite early. It is generally claimed that it took three "generations" of farmers to make a farm; that is, that the investment of two failures were required before a man could make money by farming. Two classes of crops have in the course of time proved themselves profitable under the relatively high water cost—field crops and fruit produced to meet the early-season market. The land and climate is ideally suited to the cultivation of cotton under irrigation, and the early growing season makes it possible for fruits to mature for the earliest market and thereby bring premium prices. Grapes are harvested as early as July and plums frequently in May. According to one pioneer farmer it was cotton that saved the Arvin area. Cotton was first cultivated in the 1920's and is still an important crop. The earliest data available on cotton in the community indicate that there were 7,756 acres in the Arvin-Weedpatch-Lamont area in 1931 and 9,306 in 1932.[3] The Agricultural Adjustment Agency data for 1940 indicate 6,533 acres in cotton in the Arvin community alone (15 percent of all cropland reported). While the total acreage in cotton has remained fairly constant since the early 1930's, it is now far less important proportionately than formerly.

The average farm in Arvin is quite large, though, as already indicated, not the largest in the San Joaquin Valley. The reasons for this lie both in history and environment and are compounded of the following factors: Nature and cost of water development, the historical timing of the development around Arvin, the fact of DiGiorgio developing land within that community, and the type of crops grown in the area.

As stated above, Arvin lies in a desert which, though occasionally flooded by melting snows and spring rains, has no stable surface-water supply. The underground water table was such that it could not be developed until a certain level of pump efficiency was reached. Thus it was that though the area had been homesteaded, and one of California's oldest and largest cattle ranches was developed in the neighborhood, the region was unsettled at the beginning of the twentieth century. In 1910 the first concerted effort at land settlement was made. This colony formed the basis of the present community and has left its mark on the present land pattern.

The tenure pattern just after 1910 included a number of small units in a colony, a number of homesteaded tracts, a considerable acreage in large holdings, and, apparently, some moderately large

[3] Data compiled by Kern County Agricultural Commissioner obtained from the files of the farm advisor, Kern County. See also later discussions.

holdings. Intensive farming was rare, with permanent planting first being attempted.

Arvin's development during the 1920's and early 1930's was not rapid, but from about 1935 to the present time there has been a great increase in the acreage of land under cultivation. This development has mostly been in field crops and alfalfa, with cotton and potatoes the principal crops grown. There has been a continuous development of vines and tree fruits also. Table 2 shows the shipments of fruit and vegetables from 1921 to 1943. While tree fruit increased by about 50 percent and grapes doubled during the last 10 years, the shipment of vegetables (mostly potatoes) increased tenfold.

TABLE 2.—*Shipment of fruits and vegetables from Arvin, 1921–43*

Year	Cars shipped				
	Tree fruit	Grapes	Vegetables	Unspecified	Total
	Cars	*Cars*	*Cars*	*Cars*	*Cars*
1921		4	31		35
1922	47	25	205		277
1923	78	134	194		406
1924		705	191		896
1925	17½	1,505	47		1,569½
1926	24	1,222½	160		1,406½
1927	42½	1,174	213	128½	1,558
1928	95	1,213	42	122½	1,172½
1929		1,653½		143½	1,797
1930	128½	1,500	275		1,904
1931	156½	1,269½	112	156	1,694
1932	219	1,595	210	162	2,186
1933	191	1,492½	17	113	1,812½
1934	251	1,619½	123	191½	2,185
1935	160	1,904	37	44	2,145
1936	292½	2,520½		149	2,962
1937	338½	3,675½	45½	90½	4,150
1938	361	3,035½	410	131	3,937
1939	393	2,491½	592	245	4,313
1940	389½	3,240½	564		4,194
1941	325	2,365½	1,171		3,861½
1942	326½	2,569	1,577	368	4,840½
1943	328	2,898½	2,872	719	8,617½

NOTE.—Carlot shipments are a measure of volume the value of which varies with the class of commodity. They furnish only an approximation of the value or acreage. Neither cotton nor alfalfa is reported. These classes of commodity accounted for 47.5 percent of the irrigated acreage in 1940 and 61 to 63 percent in 1931–32.

Source: Based upon the records in the office of the Kern County Agricultural Commissioner. Truck shipments converted to carlot basis.

The most recent developments have almost universally been in large tracts and on a highly speculative basis, with large investments in pumps and land leveling. The need for deep wells and powerful pumps has inhibited the growth of small operators. To utilize these deep wells fully, joint use must be made of them either by incorporation, partnerships, or cooperative arrangements. There are several such arrangements; some of 20 years' standing are now operating successfully. Such practices are readily feasible, but the need for group action and large capital outlay inhibits their development.

The growth of speculative development of farming operations, the tendency to concentrate on annual crops, and the development of large tracts are all part of the dominant pattern of Arvin's agriculture, and set it off from the Dinuba pattern and from family farming in general. It is a development which appears elsewhere in the State; the Imperial Valley, the Salinas Valley, the Sacramento-San Joaquin Delta, the west side of Fresno County, and in parts of Kern County, especially lands along Highway 99 which have recently been released from stock raising uses for intensive agriculture. In Arvin it overlies older patterns of large operations as well as a pattern of small operations as exemplified by the present descendents of the 1910 colonization.

DINUBA

SETTING

Dinuba lies about 10 miles east of Highway 99, about 32 miles southeast of Fresno and about 20 miles north of Visalia, in the northwestern corner of Tulare County. It is in the southern end of the grape-producing area which centers in Fresno County, and is supplied with water by the Kings River, supplemented with water pumped from a shallow underground basin. Unlike Arvin, Dinuba is surrounded by neighboring communities which rival it in importance and size. The nearest of these, about 7 miles away, is Reedley, a grape-producing community. Next is Kingsbury, a thriving community of comparable size, lying on Highway 99. Smaller in size, though fairly independent of Dinuba, is the town of Orosi, directly to the east. Selma, Parlier, and Sanger are towns of comparable size within a radius of 12 miles. There are numerous subcommunities or neighborhoods near Dinuba, some within the Dinuba boundaries and some outside them. Sultana and North Dinuba are in the former category, while Cutler, Yettem, and Orange Cove are important small centers just outside the boundaries of Dinuba, as delineated.

The soils around Dinuba are generally of good quality. About 6 miles south of Dinuba are some poor salt grasslands which are used almost exclusively for grazing stock. In this area there are few houses. In all other directions from Dinuba, intensive agriculture extends unbroken until the orbit of a neighboring community is reached.

Dinuba, like Arvin, lies on the flat plain of the San Joaquin Valley. It, too, is close to the foothills, being but 3 miles from the nearest promontory. The soils are especially suited for the development of grapes, but appear to be excellent as well for numerous field crops including cotton. The growing season is long and the same general climate as in Arvin prevails except that there is a slightly greater rainfall and shorter growing season. Since crops are irrigated, precipitation is not a direct advantage, while the later spring means that Dinuba growers cannot bring their produce to market as early as Arvin growers can. Early markets are not important to raisin production, and Dinuba is in an area favorable to field-drying grapes because of the dry and warm (but not too hot) season after the grapes are ripe.

HISTORY

The Dinuba area produced grain during the seventies and eighties. At that time the dominant community was Traver, which served as the shipping point for the grain and the residence for laborers. Dinuba did not exist at that time. Early descriptions of Traver indicate that it was typically "wild west," and that it was apparently destined to be one of the major cities of the San Joaquin Valley. The irrigation development which was to be the basis of Traver's further development proved its undoing and created Dinuba.

During the seventies there was a large cattle and grain ranch in southern Fresno County which used the brand "76." In 1882 a group of men, including the owners of the "76" ranch, started an irrigation development called the 76 Ranch & Water Co. According to Frank Adams, this company was successful from the start.[4] It sold both land and water rights, the latter being made appurtenant to the land, each 40-acre right calling for 40 inches of water. An initial charge of $200 was made for each 40-acre right and an annual assessment of $20 covered operation and maintenance. The

[4]Frank Adams, Irrigation Districts in California, Bull. 21, 1929, State of California, Department of Public Works, Sacramento, 1930, p. 214.

individual owner had to build adequate laterals when these were necessary to bring the water to his land.

The Alta Irrigation District was formed in 1888, and is one of three original Wright Act irrigation districts that have been continuously active since their formation. In 1890 the district purchased the system built by the "76" company for $410,000.

The district has been involved in much litigation, and disputes over water rights have in the past resulted in violence. Adams describes some of its problems:

> From the early days Alta Irrigation District was involved in litigation respecting its water rights. There was also litigation regarding the legality of certain acts of the board of directors, the first bond issue, out of which the system was purchased, being declared void by the superior court on August 18, 1898, when bonds of this issue in the amount of $543,000 were outstanding. These were the dark days of the district. For several years most of the district assessments remained unpaid and development was halted, although the canal system was continued in operation and the district organization remained more or less active. In 1901 a compromise with the bondholders was reached. Under this compromise 5-percent refunding bonds in the amount of $500,000 were issued on February 4, 1902, $492,000 of these being used to redeem all of the outstanding bonds and the defaulted interest coupons for the years 1898, 1899, and 1900. The basis for exchange was $0.75 on the dollar. Since this refunding, the district has been in sound financial condition, meeting all interest and principal payments as due, and even retiring bonds in the amount of $53,500 in advance of maturity out of accumulated surplus.[5]

In 1888 the towns of Reedley and Dinuba were formed. Irrigation of the higher lands around Dinuba flushed alkali to the surface of the soil around Traver, and this, in conjunction with a number of fires, caused the earlier town to be abandoned. Several houses and buildings were moved from Traver to Dinuba, and quite a few of the people of Traver established residence in the new community. With this start, the town grew steadily.

There had been rural schools within the community boundary (as delineated) as early as 1879, but the first Dinuba school was started in 1889. This school grew steadily through the nineties. In 1899 a high school was established. During these early years additional land was constantly being brought under irrigation,

[5] Frank Adams, ibid.

and the creation of small farming units continued. By 1900 there were three general stores, a furniture store and funeral parlor, a newspaper, one or two doctors, a hotel, two smithies, two livery stables, and a packing shed. A basis for social participation was also established, with at least three churches, a community hall in which groups could meet and amateur theatricals were performed, and a public park in which regular band concerts were given. The reverse of this bright coin of the gay nineties was a "Chinatown," with its saloon and redlight district.

Dinuba was incorporated in 1906, and since that time has had its own local government. A second newspaper was started in 1903, a water system was developed the same year; the year before that a bank was set up by local capital, and in 1910 a second bank was organized. In 1915 the first general large public-works development was undertaken.

During the First World War prices were good and prosperity was general, and after the war there was a great boom. The population grew to an all-time peak in 1922. The average daily attendance in the several elementary schools shot from 700 to 1,250 during the 4 years 1918-22. It was during this postwar period, when the price of raisins was good, that the townspeople thought that their community would develop into a major urban center. The farmers overexpanded on the basis of these prices, the city made elaborate improvements which eventually created burdensome assessments on real estate but which had the immediate effect during the construction period of furthering the inflationary economy.

At this time the town had a professional baseball team and a well-paid full-time chamber of commerce secretary. The community had enjoyed high prices and exuberant prosperity, and the people acted as if it were a permanent expectation.

In 1922 the situation changed; many small fortunes and many small savings were lost. The farmers who had mortgaged their home farms for an extra piece of land often lost both; people who had built homes in town had to pay high construction costs and higher tax assessments for paving, lighting, and the civic improvements. The population declined rapidly, so that the average daily attendance at the schools was reduced from the 1922 peak of 1,250 back to 1,000 in 1926, and it remained under 1,100 for the next 10 years. During this period both banks closed and were taken over by chain systems, and the financial position of the community was very low. Dinuba was then "the best-lighted cemetery ever seen," according to drummers.

In 1937 the town reorganized its finances, and economic conditions are much improved. At present, the high prices have brought on another boom period, but the chastened community, like the chastened farmer, has carefully avoided overexpansion, but is preparing for postwar improvements on a modest scale. Though it was not without individual heartaches and losses, the community has come through the war and depression in good order and now has many civic advantages and practically no debt.

The land of Dinuba was owned in large tracts prior to irrigation development, but the owners, over a period of years, sold off their holdings in small units. In this way the community was built upon small farm operations, though a few big operators have always existed in the area. Though it is impossible to determine all the reasons for the development of small holdings, some of the important ones can be indicated. The Alta irrigation system was developed in the early period of California fruit production and, though large-scale field operations were prevalent in California, large-scale fruit operations were not then frequently attempted. It seems that the landowners considered their best opportunity to be in the profits from direct sales at the enhanced land values, rather than the more speculative operation in the new industry. Land costs were high at the very beginning of the development. A significant item in the predominance of small-scale operations is the fact that the land was developed by irrigation under the Wright Act, an act which was purposely drawn to assist the development of small farming. Some large growers have always farmed in the area, though none on the scale of the largest Arvin operations.

No adequate picture of the size of farms throughout Dinuba history is available, but in recent years some large-scale operations have developed. These have been created by the consolidation of holdings by packers and shippers, motivated by a desire to integrate their activities sufficiently to enable them to be assured of an adequate pack.

During the last 15 years successful packers have gradually increased their holdings. One of these operators was quoted as saying that by having holdings and a packing shed in combination he could make money when the small farmers could not. This could be accomplished by means of three advantages: (1) Growing a premium quality which brought 10 cents more per pack, (2) saving 5 cents per pack on commission, and (3) avoiding the direct packing charges. He considered he made $250 per car more than the farmers did, and is assured of 200 cars per season through his own production.

The development of these integrated operations is viewed with some alarm by the small growers, who recognize that in times of unfavorable prices the packers can refuse to handle the independent operator's produce. Large-scale operations may become important in Dinuba but are not now, nor have they been a dominant factor in the community since the development of irrigation.

COMPARATIVE NOTES

The geographic bases of Arvin and Dinuba are quite similar. Both are surrounded by flat lands with good to moderately good soils capable of growing fruits and vegetables with good yields and quality, when supplied with adequate irrigation water (table 3). Arvin, however, has more good soil within the area, and is much less hemmed in by rival communities. Neither town has any great advantage with respect to climate. Arvin's is slightly favorable in that it can produce for an earlier market while Dinuba has a climate peculiarly advantageous to raisin production. Neither has any great advantage with respect to location. Dinuba is somewhat more central to the traffic within the State, and is slightly better supplied with railroad facilities; but Arvin is better located with respect to urban and eastern markets. Potential and actual oil deposits give an economic advantage to Arvin over Dinuba, but this is not of sufficient importance to account for any great divergence between the two towns.

The greatest differences between the two communities, other than the differential in size of farm operations, are the nature and cost of water supply and the history and age of the communities. Arvin is completely dependent upon ground waters for irrigation, while Dinuba secures the major portion of its supply as surface irrigation by a diversion from the Kings River, and uses ground water only as a supplement. A careful analysis of cost of water under average conditions in the two communities shows that water costs more in Arvin than Dinuba (table 4). The cost analysis, made

TABLE 3.—*Quality of soil in Arvin and Dinuba*

Soil class	Arvin		Dinuba	
	Acres	Percent	Acres	Percent
1 and 2	33,348	52.5	23,186	54.8
3	25,408	40.0	7,827	18.5
4	4,764	7.5	5,950	11.7
5 and 6	0	0	6,347	15.0
Total	63,520	100.0	43,310	100.0

Source: Data obtained by planimeter readings from soil map of each community as delineated. Soil map prepared by Bureau of Agricultural Economics, based upon soil-classification map by Walter W. Weir and R. Earl Storie, Division of Soil Technology, University of California.

for farms of the average size in each community, shows that the average per acre cost of water in Arvin is $6.92 (2 feet 11 inches duty) and Dinuba is $4 (2 feet 6 inches duty). While this difference is not great, compared with the total annual cost of land, the difference would be very great between Arvin and Dinuba for farms of similar size. Arvin units of 57 acres would pay over $14 per acre for water. Such excessive water costs can be and regularly are avoided by cooperative use of wells and pumps, either between two or three neighbors or among a large group.

There is a general attitude in Arvin that water cannot be developed by the small operator because of the very large capital outlay. However, three items should be borne in mind. First, the water table was around 50 feet when the land was first brought into production, a lift that is not out of line with water lifts in other areas. Second, there are small units in the area which have been

TABLE 4.—*Comparative irrigation costs: Arvin and Dinuba*

Item of cost	Arvin		Dinuba, 57-acre farm basis
	497-acre farm basis [1]	57-acre farm basis [2]	
Total investment	$13,500.00	$3,700.00	$1,200.00
Annual costs:			
Fixed costs [3]	1,404.00	385.00	159.00
Repair and emergency	120.00	40.00	8.00
Electric energy	1,915.00	384.00	61.00
Total annual costs	3,439.00	809.00	228.00
Investment per acre	27.00	65.00	21.60
Annual cost per acre	6.92	14.19	4.00
Annual cost per acre-foot	2.37	4.87	1.59

[1] Average farm size in Arvin.
[2] 57 acres is the Dinuba average farm size.
[3] Includes interest and depreciation at 5 percent each, tax of 4 mills, and for Dinuba a charge for gravity water delivered at 60 cents per acre.

For more detailed analysis of water costs, and for sources and necessary assumptions, see appendix B.

farmed continuously for a quarter of a century. These usually obtain water under some form of cooperative arrangement that enables several units to share the investment and pumping charges. Finally, the cost of water is an item which is reflected in the value of land, since land values are based upon the capitalized potential net income. High water costs do not render small farming impossible, yet it must be recognized that the great expense and the resulting high risk in the development of Arvin lands, together with the cultural inertia in forming cooperative arrangements, serve to inhibit the growth of small farming. Therefore, while small farming is feasible and profitable, with proper price relationships, the economics of the Arvin situation under present conditions militate against the development of the family farm and in favor of corporation agriculture.

The historical differences between the two communities may be examined under two phases: the age of the communities, and the era of the communities. Dinuba is approximately 20 years older than Arvin, and reached its population maturity during the early 1920's. Arvin cannot yet be called a mature community, since there is a great deal of land being developed. The relative age of the two towns is shown by the growth of the annual average daily attendance of the elementary schools in the area. The first Dinuba area school started in 1879, while the first school in the Arvin area began in 1902. The growth curve in the two areas shows a remarkable parallel development, with slow growth during the first 15 years, rapid growth for the next 20, followed by a cessation of growth in later years. The growth period in Arvin shows a somewhat sharper ascent (fig. 21). The period in which a community comes into being affects its character. Arvin grew up after World War I and Dinuba before it. This has had certain direct effects; for instance, a small town which came into being during the 1920's would rarely have two banks, because chain banking became prominent in California during that period and these are in a position to avoid such a situation. On the other hand, the increased use of automobile traffic, and the assistance furnished by the Federal Government through WPA would suggest that streets would be paved and sidewalks laid relatively earlier in the newer town than the older. A detailed analysis of the effect of the historical differences between Arvin and Dinuba will be presented in a later section.

CHAPTER XIII

AGRICULTURE IN ARVIN AND DINUBA

INTRODUCTION

California agricultural production is industrialized. Its major characteristics are high degree of specialization on the farm; general use of power equipment; high value and intensive use of land; large capital requirements; and heavy dependence upon hired labor. Both Arvin and Dinuba fit this pattern. Furthermore, most of the same commodities are produced, but they are produced in different proportions. Finally, the scale of operations differs, for while both communities have a wide range of farm size, the farms at Arvin are generally larger while those in Dinuba are mostly of very moderate size. In order to understand the nature of the economic and social conditions, it will be necessary to examine the agriculture of each community in detail.

From the standpoint of community comparisons, the most significant fact is that the same total dollar volume of agricultural production—2½ million dollars—was brought to the market in Arvin and in Dinuba.

Special data have been available on the agriculture of the two communities. Statistical data on size and type of farm, on tenure, and on acreage in various major crops have been obtained from the worksheet records of the Agricultural Adjustment Agency. These data have been developed by the Bureau of Agricultural Economics for use in other studies relative to the economic effects of scale of farm operation, and the data cover three counties in the upper San Joaquin Valley.[6] While only worksheet farms of the Agricultural

[6]For the detailed analysis and a discussion of the methods of collecting this information, see Edwin E. Wilson and Marion Clawson, Agricultural Land Ownership and Operation in the Southern San Joaquin Valley. Bureau of Agricultural Economics, Berkeley, 1945 (mimeographed). These data also entered into the analysis of the scale of farm operations. (See J. Karl Lee, Relative Efficiency of Farms of Varying Size in the Southern San Joaquin Valley, California, Bureau of Agricultural Economics, 1945.)

Adjustment Agency were included, this is very nearly all farms in the area. Actually more units were included than were included by the United States Census of Agriculture. Furthermore, some indication of the accuracy of these sources is shown by the agreement between the Agricultural Adjustment Agency data and the schedule data from each community (table 5). The Arvin agreement is nearly perfect, while in Dinuba the questionnaire included 90 percent of the number enumerated by the Agricultural Adjustment Agency records.

TABLE 5.—*Comparison of number of farm operators as reported in Agricultural Adjustment Agency records and as indicated by schedules*

Community	Number of Agricultural Adjustment Agency operating units	Number of farm operators on basis of questionnaire
Arvin	133	140
Dinuba	722	650

The Agricultural Adjustment Agency crop and type of farm data relate to 1940. The use of 1940 rather than a later year was dictated by considerations outside the scope of this study, but its effects must be recognized. The differences between 1940 and 1944 agriculture are not significant in Dinuba, where most land has been in intensive production for a long time and much of it is in permanent plantings. A slight shift from grapes into commercial vegetables has occurred. Expansion is no longer possible, since all good lands have long been intensively farmed. In Arvin the agriculture has changed measurably. In about 1937 a development started which brought about 11,000 acres into production by 1940 and which has continued at approximately the same rate since then. Much of this new land was shifted from dry-farmed grain to irrigated potato and other row-crop production, while some shifted directly from desert to intensive uses. Probably about 6,000 acres of land were brought into intensive use for the first time during the 3 years 1941-43 inclusive. It must be noted that population and other social data refer to 1944, business data to 1943, while agricultural production data refer to 1940. This means that the production base supporting Arvin's population and business at the time for which data in these categories apply are underestimated. The 3- to 4-year offset is more than enough to account for any expected lag in volume of business or in population growth. Arvin's population, as indicated by school enrollment, shows no gain since 1940.

VOLUME OF PRODUCTION AND MAJOR CROPS

The acreage distribution in the two communities and the proportion of total acreage by major crop classes are given in table 6. There were 46,126 acres in farms in Arvin as against 34,202 in Dinuba (1940). If grain and idle or unused lands are excluded, there are 22,000 acres in Arvin compared to 24,000 acres in Dinuba. The following are the major intensive land uses in Arvin and Dinuba:

Intensive land uses	Arvin	Dinuba
	Percent	*Percent*
Orchard and vineyard	36	65
Row crops	41	11
Forage crops	17	19
Other intensive uses	6	5
Total	100	100

This emphasizes the major difference between the two communities; namely, the heavy dependence of Dinuba upon one category (and in fact, upon grapes alone), in contrast to the balance in Arvin between fruit and row crops.

An estimate has been made of the gross farm income, based upon local yields and acreage. The total income in 1940 was approximately 2½ million dollars in each of the two communities. Table 7 shows the distributions of this income by major commodity classes, and the same information is presented graphically in figure 2. This demonstrates again the great value of fruit in Dinuba while the row crops make up but a small total value. These latter have become more important in both communities during the last 3 years, but they are still but a small proportion of the total value of the Dinuba production.

TYPES AND SIZE OF FARMS

The analysis of the Agricultural Adjustment Agency data segregated all farms into 10 major classes. Table 8 shows the

GROSS FARM INCOME BY PRINCIPAL SOURCES

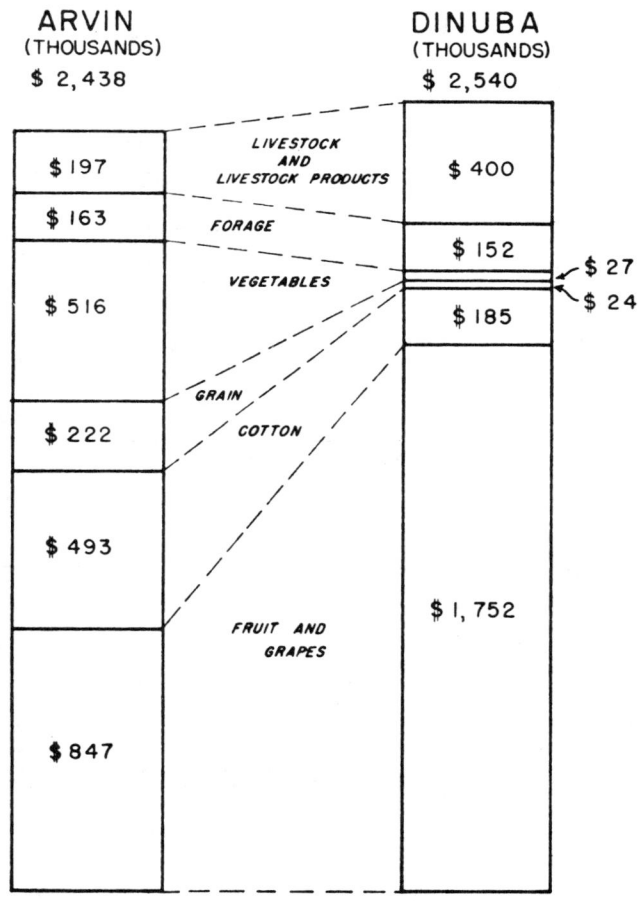

SOURCE: AGRICULTURAL ADJUSTMENT AGENCY RECORDS AS ANALYZED BY BUREAU OF AGRICULTURAL ECONOMICS. DATA REFERS TO 1940 CROP YEAR FOR ARVIN AND DINUBA AS DELINEATED FOR COMPARATIVE COMMUNITY STUDY. DOLLAR VOLUME OF PRODUCTS ESTABLISHED BY USING 1940 PRICE LEVELS AND AVERAGE YIELDS

FIGURE No. 2

TABLE 6.—*Major crop classes in Arvin and Dinuba, 1940*

Crop class	Arvin		Dinuba	
	Acres	Percent	Acres	Percent
Orchard and vineyard	7,875	17.0	16,295	47.7
Cotton	6,274		2,358	
Sugar beets	32		0	
Potatoes	2,047		10	
Commercial vegetables	627		278	
Total row	8,980	19.4	2,646	7.7
Wheat	12,004		76	
Barley	3,990		944	
Total grain	15,994	34.6	1,020	3.0
Alfalfa	3,284		3,060	
Ladino	377		737	
Hay and sorghum	113		952	
Total forage	3,774	8.4	4,749	13.9
Other crops	1,317	2.9	1,268	3.7
Range land	170		8	
Noncrop pasture	1,078		4,234	
Summer fallow and idle	3,472		2,308	
Total noncrop	4,720	10.2	6,550	19.1
Lanes and buildings	3,464	7.5	1,674	4.9
Total land in farm	46,124	100.0	34,202	100.0

Source: Agricultural Adjustment Agency data for communities as delineated.

TABLE 7.—*Estimated gross farm income by principal sources: Arvin and Dinuba* [1]

Crop class	Arvin		Dinuba	
	$1,000	Percent	$1,000	Percent
Fruit	847	35	1,752	69
Cotton (lint and seed)	493	20	185	7
Grain	222	9	24	1
Potatoes, vegetables, and sugar beets	516	21	27	1
Forage crops	163	7	152	6
Livestock and livestock products [1]	197	8	400	16
Total gross income	2,438	100	2,540	100

[1] Gross value of each commodity. Value of commodities fed to livestock, both that grown locally and the necessary purchase from outside ($51,000 worth in Dinuba, none in Arvin), deducted from gross income from livestock and livestock products.
For method of calculation see appendix B.

Source: Agricultural Adjustment Agency data for communities as delineated.

number of farms and the acreage in each class. Detailed description of these classes appears in appendix B. The summer-field-crop farms, and to a lesser extent the summer-and-winter-field-crop farms, produce most of the cotton, potatoes, and vegetables. Fruit ranches are broken into two categories on the basis of degree of specialization.

AGRIBUSINESS AND THE RURAL COMMUNITY

TABLE 8.—*Number of farms and acreages, classified by type: Arvin and Dinuba, 1940*

Farm class [1]	Arvin				Dinuba			
	Number	Percent	Acres	Percent	Number	Percent	Acres	Percent
Forage livestock	0	0	0	0	8	1.1	611	1.8
Specialized fruit	30	22.6	1,229	2.7	397	55.0	14,916	43.6
Major fruit	17	12.8	9,055	19.6	152	21.1	8,012	23.4
Winter field crops	25	18.8	16,763	36.3	5	.7	329	1.0
Winter and summer field	13	9.8	6,118	13.3	16	2.2	1,995	5.8
Summer field crops	41	30.7	11,871	25.7	104	14.4	6,473	18.9
Small ranches, idle and part-time farms	7	5.3	1,090	2.4	40	5.5	1,866	5.5
Total	133	100.0	46,126	100.0	722	100.0	34,202	100.0

[1] Definitions of farm classes are given in appendix B.
Source: Agricultural Adjustment Agency data for communities as delineated.

Average farm size in the two communities varies significantly, though both communities have very small and very large units. Three measures of farm size are indicated in figure 3. The upper squares represent the average area of farms in each community. Arvin farms average 497 acres as compared with 57 acres in Dinuba, or about 9 times as large.

The distribution of farms and of productive land according to size is shown in table 9. From this tabulation, it can readily be seen that there are numerous operations of modest size in Arvin, but that 7 farms operate 42 percent of the cropland and orchard and 22 farms operate two-thirds of all such land in the community. The heavy preponderance of small farms in Dinuba is equally evident, with 94 percent of the farms under 160 acres and very few units in

TABLE 9.—*Distribution of farms and productive land by size of farms: Arvin and Dinuba*

Size category [1]	Arvin			Dinuba		
	Number of farms	Acres	Percent of acreage	Number of farms	Acres	Percent of acreage
Under 80	53	1,600	3.8	624	16,261	57.7
80 to 160	22	2,142	5.1	55	4,789	17.1
160 to 320	18	3,898	9.3	33	4,794	17.1
320 to 640	18	6,067	14.5	5	1,337	4.7
640 to 1,280	15	10,081	24.1	4	963	3.4
Over 1,280	7	17,983	43.2	1	²8	²0.0
Total	133	41,771	100.0	722	28,152	100.0

[1] Size category based upon acreage of cropland and orchard only.
² Acreage in large unit which only partially lies in community. Amounts to less than 0.5 percent.
Source: Agricultural Adjustment Agency records.

the upper brackets. Figure 4 shows both the distribution of farms by size and the acreage of all cropland, orchard, and vineyard by size. While number of units decreases as size increases in both areas, the total crop acreage in farms in Arvin increases as the size increases.

Summer-field-crop farms tend to be larger than the average of all farms in the community, but the difference is not very great. In Dinuba about 70 percent are under 80 acres in size, as against 87 percent for all farms. In Arvin about 20 percent are in this small category and 35 percent are under 160 acres while 40 percent of all farms are under 80 and 55 percent under 160. Summer field crops are a somewhat less intensive operation than fruit, so that somewhat larger units would be expected.

Acreage in farms, and even cropland acreage as used above, is not an entirely satisfactory measure of farm size. An acre of wheat and an acre of grapes differ extremely in the amount of labor required, amount of capital invested, and potential income. In order to discuss farm size on a more comparable basis, a unit of measurement has been devised which expresses the potential income from an area of land. This unit has here been called an acre-equivalent (abbreviated A-E), and may be defined as that area of any cropland which under normal conditions has the potential capacity to return income equivalent to that of an acre of irrigated alfalfa. (See appendix B for method of calculation and factors used.) In terms of this measurement, the average farm unit in Arvin is 285 acre-equivalent units against 89 in Dinuba (fig. 3). Figure 5 shows the distribution of farms by size categories measured in acreage-equivalents. The heavy concentration of Dinuba units in the brackets between 50 and 200 units is clearly evident. In Arvin nearly half the farms are under 100 such units in size, though most of the acreage is controlled under farms of the larger categories.

The accompanying figures Nos. 3, 4, and 5 apply to farms as operating units. Since tenancy is prevalent, the same picture need not apply to farm ownership. Analysis has been made of ownership units, which may or may not be operated as one farm but which include all the lands within the community owned by one individual. There are 214 such units in Arvin with an average size of 176 acres, and 753 units in Dinuba with an average size of 45 acres.

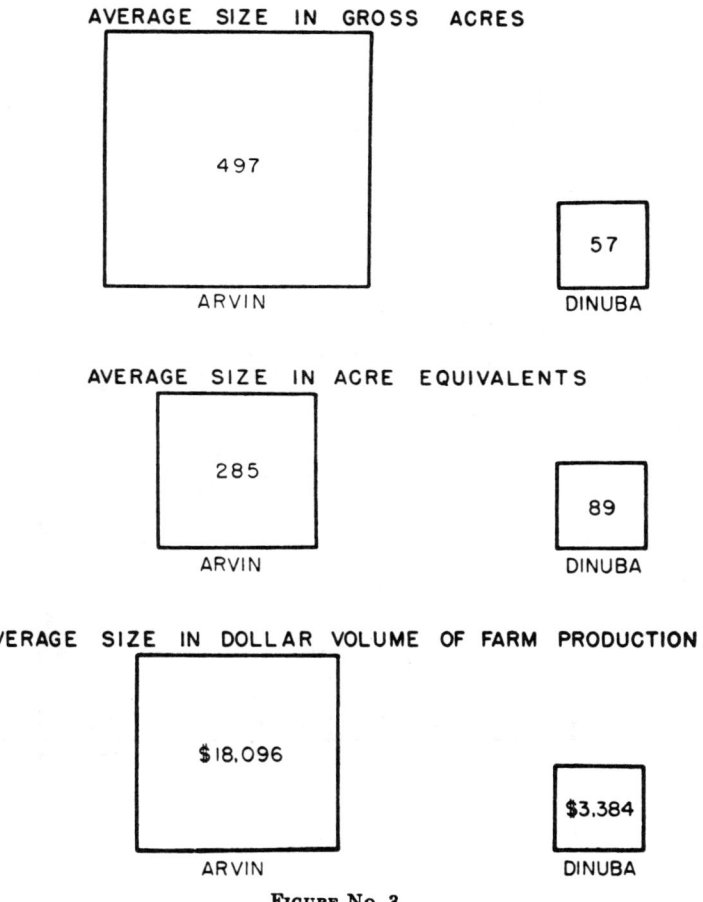

Figure No. 3

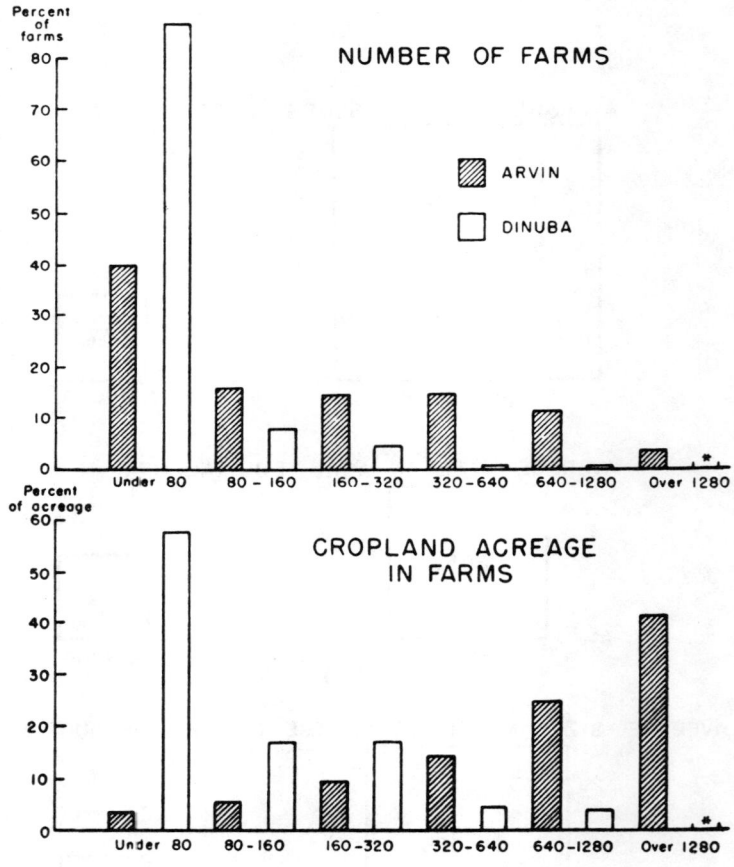

* Less than .05 %

Source: Agricultural Adjustment Agency data

FIGURE No. 4

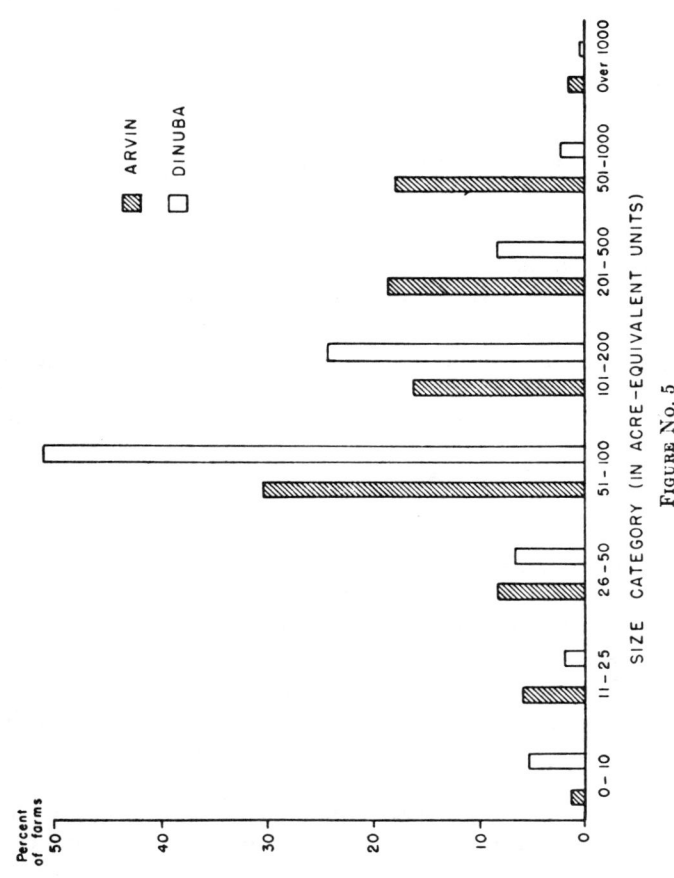

Figure No. 5

TABLE 10.—*Number of ownership units and acreage by size of holdings: Arvin and Dinuba, 1940*

Size class	Arvin				Dinuba			
	Number	Percent	Acres	Percent	Number	Percent	Acres	Percent
0 to 80	100	46.8	3,483	9.2	668	88.7	19,088	56.3
80.1 to 160	49	22.8	7,466	19.8	42	5.6	4,678	13.8
160.1 to 640	52	24.3	11,696	31.0	38	5.0	7,063	20.9
640.1 and up	13	6.1	15,083	40.0	5	.7	3,049	9.0
Total	214	100.0	37,728	100.0	753	100.0	33,878	100.0

NOTE.—Where part of unit is held within community boundaries and part outside, acreage within boundaries only was included, but placed in size category based upon total holdings. Such situation reported for Arvin only.

Source: Agricultural Adjustment Agency data for communities as delineated.

Table 10 shows that nearly half the holdings in Arvin are under 80 acres but have only 9 percent of the land, whereas 30 percent of the farm holdings over 160 acres have 71 percent of the land. In Dinuba nearly 90 percent of all ownership units are less than 80 acres, and operate 56 percent of the land, while the small percent of the owners who have over 160 acres (5.7 percent) operate 30 percent of the land.

FARM TENURE

More than three-fourths of Dinuba farmers own all the land they operate, while only 35 percent of the Arvin farmers are full owners. The proportion of full owners, part owners, and tenants is shown in table 11. In Dinuba, tenancy is not directly associated with size, but in Arvin the smaller farms are rarely tenant-operated while the larger categories are tenant-operated slightly over half the time. The relationship between size of operating units and tenure is shown in table 12.

The place of residence of landowners in the two areas presents the same contrast (table 13). Less than a third of the owners give Arvin as their residence, and only two-thirds live in Kern County. Seventy percent of Dinuba owners reside in the community, and 84 percent live in Tulare County. Arvin landowners are often distant from the town, with 31 percent residing outside the San Joaquin Valley as compared with only 5 percent of the Dinuba owners.

Arvin and Dinuba are in fairly strong contrast with respect to tenure characteristics. Arvin has a high proportion of tenancy,

TABLE 11.—*Tenure of farm operators: Arvin and Dinuba, 1940*

	Arvin		Dinuba	
	Number	Percent	Number	Percent
Full owners	43	35.0	562	77.8
Part owners	28	22.7	59	8.2
Tenants	52	42.3	101	14.0
Total	123	100.0	722	100.0

Source: Agricultural Adjustment Agency data for communities as delineated.

TABLE 12.—*Variation in tenancy by size of farms: Arvin and Dinuba, 1940*

Size, class	Arvin			Dinuba		
	Owners and part owners	Tenants		Owners and part owners	Tenants	
	Number	Number	Percent	Number	Number	Percent
0 to 80	36	14	28	540	84	13
80.1 to 160	7	10	59	44	11	20
160.1 to 640	18	16	47	33	5	13
Over 640	10	12	55	4	1	20
Total	71	52	42	621	101	14

Source: Agricultural Adjustment Agency for communities as delineated.

especially among the larger units, and the owners frequently live not only away from Arvin but at a considerable distance. Dinuba has a very high proportion of owner-operated farms and most of the landowners live in the community or in the San Joaquin Valley.

FARM LABOR REQUIREMENTS

In a farming system where at least half of the total labor performed in the production of goods is paid for in the form of direct wages, the situation and condition of labor requires a great deal of attention. There are interesting similarities and differences between the labor pattern in Arvin and Dinuba.

An estimate has been made of the total requirement for manual labor on Arvin and Dinuba farms in terms of man-hours of work. These estimates are based largely on the records of farmers in the area, combined with the 1940 crop data from the Agricultural Adjustment Agency cards, but complemented with information on some crops from other sources (see Appendix C for details). On the

TABLE 13.—*Residence of landowners: Arvin and Dinuba, 1940*

Residence of owner	Arvin		Dinuba	
	Number	Percent	Number	Percent
With community address	60	32.1	529	70.7
Elsewhere in county	59	31.6	101	13.5
Elsewhere in San Joaquin Valley	10	5.3	81	10.8
Elsewhere in California	53	28.3	34	4.5
Outside California	5	2.7	4	0.5
Total [1]	187	100.0	749	100.0

[1] Owner's residence not recorded: Arvin 27; Dinuba 4.
Source: Agricultural Adjustment Agency data for community as delineated.

basis of this information, the total labor requirements and the monthly distribution were calculated for the two communities (table 14). Arvin has a total requirement of 2.9 million man-hours of work per year and Dinuba 3.5 million man-hours. The 20 percent additional labor requirement on Dinuba farms means that a greater portion of the total value of production must go to labor (including farmers' own labor), assuming equal wages.[7]

The seasonal fluctuation in labor requirement is great in both communities. Arvin demand varies from 132,000 hours in March to

TABLE 14.—*Monthly labor requirements: Arvin and Dinuba*

Month	Arvin		Dinuba	
	Man-hours	Percentage of average	Man-hours	Percentage of average
	Thousands	Percent	Thousands	Percent
January	149	62	189	65
February	138	58	243	84
March	132	55	227	79
April	218	91	265	92
May	248	102	234	81
June	333	138	250	87
July	525	218	393	136
August	151	63	299	104
September	372	155	669	231
October	294	122	392	135
November	137	57	124	43
December	189	78	175	61
Total	2,886		3,460	
Average	241	100	289	100

For methods of computation, source of data, and detailed analysis see appendix C.

[7] The analysis of farm efficiency made by Karl Lee (op. cit.) shows that a greater amount of labor is required per acre and per unit of production on small farms than on large. Smaller units, according to this same study, are more intensively operated.

525,000 hours in July (or four times the minimum). Dinuba demand for labor varies from 124,000 hours in November to 669,000 in September (over five times the minimum). Seasonality of employment opportunity is a serious problem in both towns, but is worse in Dinuba than Arvin.

These figures represent labor requirements on all farms, or the demand for labor. On the supply side, several classes of labor may be segregated: The farm operator, the resident full-time farm laborer, the resident part-time worker, and the outside transient worker. It may be assumed that, in general, the labor is performed by the operator when he can do it, by resident labor when there is too much for the operator, and by part-time and migratory workers only after the resident labor is fully employed. In actual practice, there will be many exceptions, but as a general rule this relationship will apply. In this way, the itinerant worker will receive the residual employment. It must be remembered that the resident laborer of Arvin and Dinuba may also be an itinerant laborer in any other community, while the itinerant laborer is the resident of some other town.

Figure 6 shows graphically the monthly fluctuation in labor demand for the two towns, and the proportion of this demand which must be filled by hired labor and by migrant workers living outside the community. Hatchures show the source of such labor. The lower portion represents the labor performed by the farm operators, on the assumption that each operator works full time (250 hours per month) when there is work to be done. Since many operators, especially on larger units, are occupied with management, this may overstate somewhat the actual hours of labor they can accomplish. It is assumed that this managerial function results in at least equivalent labor savings. Unpaid family labor has not been included as it does not play an important role in the economy of industrialized farming. The next section of the bar shows the work done by full-time hired labor resident in the community. The supply is predicated upon the data from schedules. The third section shows other family members who perform farm labor for wages on a part-time basis, the supply of which was determined by the schedules. Full-time labor is assumed to work 200 hours per month when work is available and part-time labor 100 hours per month when work is available. In Dinuba, no hired labor is required in November or December, but in Arvin there is always work for some hired hands. The resident labor in each community is sufficient to cover most of the demand. In both communities outside workers are necessary during the three peak months.

No doubt outside workers are normally in each community at other times, competing with local labor, but they are not absolutely needed. The upper portion of the bar represents that portion of the available work which must be done by these itinerant workers. Table 15 shows the break-down of workers for the two communities for the month of peak employment, based upon the assumption given. During other months, the number of itinerant workers is fewer, and during most months, even the resident labor is not fully employed. In Dinuba there are seasons when the operators are themselves not fully employed. Arvin requires approximately 1,200 workers, Dinuba 1,400 in the peak months. Dinuba can furnish this class of workers about 20 percent more total employment.

TABLE 15.—*Number of workers required for farm operations during month of peak labor demand: Arvin and Dinuba*

Class of labor	Arvin (July)		Dinuba (September)	
	Man-hours	Persons	Man-hours	Persons
	Thousands	*Number*	*Thousands*	*Number*
Farm operator (250 hours each)	33	133	180	722
Resident labor (200 hours each)	188	940	110	550
Part-time resident labor (100 hours each)	69	690	60	600
Itinerant labor (200 hours each)	235	1,175	319	1,595
Total	525	2,938	669	3,467

Source: Total labor requirements based upon data developed by the staff of the Bureau of Agricultural Economics (Berkeley); number of operators based upon Agricultural Adjustment Agency records; and amount of resident labor based upon schedule data. For more details, see appendix C, tables 53 and 54.

The significant facts which emerge from this analysis are:

(1) Both the small-farm and large-farm communities have high labor demands, which fluctuate seasonally.

(2) More labor is required on Dinuba than on Arvin farms.

(3) A far larger proportion of labor on Dinuba farms is performed by the operators, while resident hired labor makes up a smaller proportion than in Arvin. Nearly the same absolute amount of resident hired labor is available in both communities.

(4) Dinuba requires more outside labor at the peak month than

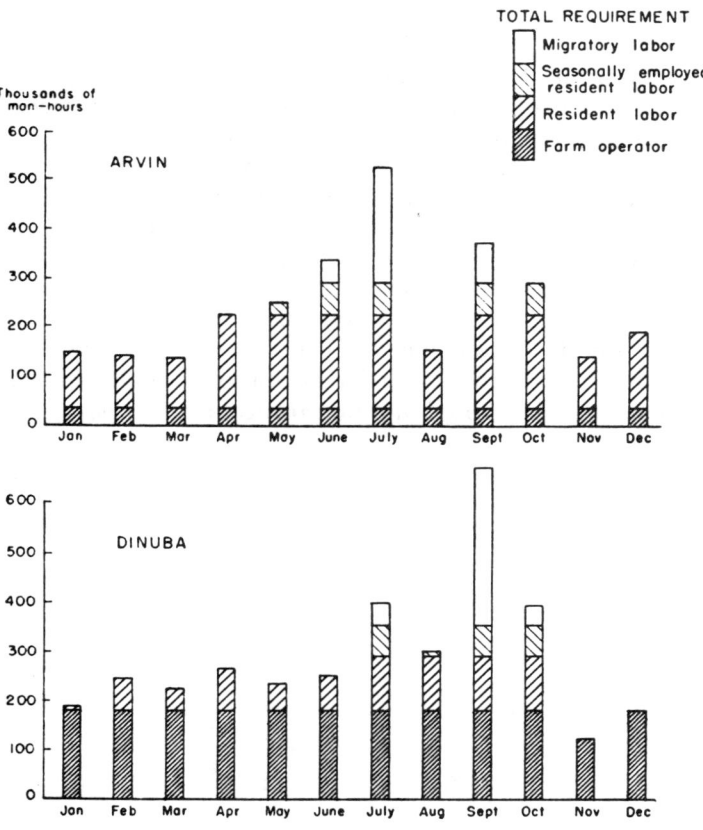

FIGURE No. 6

Arvin, but the itinerant worker gets less total employment than in Arvin.

Most of these facts relate to the degree of specialization rather than the size of operations. In Arvin the relative diversity makes for a longer working season.

SUMMARY

Agriculture in Arvin and Dinuba is intensive and specialized; the basic products are of the highly speculative type which are marketed outside the State. High capital requirements, high production costs, and intensive seasonal use of labor are characteristic of each. In these conditions the two communities reflect the pattern throughout the Central Valley of California, and may be considered generally representative of the California type of agricultural production. They differ in the crops grown; Arvin having more field crops and Dinuba more fruit, but each having acreages of both. Dinuba farming is far more specialized, as one crop heavily predominates, and this results in higher seasonal labor requirements, though not in significantly different requirements for outside labor.

CHAPTER XIV

THE PEOPLE OF ARVIN AND DINUBA

The population of the Arvin community is 6,200; of the Dinuba community, 7,400. The people in each community are directly or indirectly dependent upon agriculture for their livelihood. In this chapter an effort will be made to show who these people are, their background, their education, their social and economic conditions. Not only does this involve comparisons between the two towns but an understanding of the internal variation of each.

NUMBER OF PERSONS

The population of Arvin and Dinuba was determined by the questionnaires, and may be accepted as reasonably accurate. The houses in each community were numbered in sequence and questionnaires were taken at each tenth house, on the basis of which the total population was estimated. The method of estimating the population is discussed in appendix D.

The fact that small farms support more population than large farms is in itself significant. There are 3.01 persons supported for each $1,000 of agricultural production in Dinuba as against 2.45 persons in Arvin. Both communities require a seasonal labor supply and conversely furnish inadequate employment to resident labor, both in about the same degree.

Both communities have approximately half their total population within the congested area and half living in the open country (table 16). In Dinuba the congested area was defined by the city limits. In Arvin an arbitrary line of demarcation was established so as to include all more or less contiguous congested areas. (See figure 12).

Both communities consist predominantly of caucasians. The schedules show 85 percent of the family heads are native-born whites in Arvin, 6 percent are Mexicans, 3 percent Negroes, and 2 percent European-born. In Dinuba, 81 percent were native-born

TABLE 16.—*Population of Arvin and Dinuba, 1944*

	Arvin		Dinuba	
	Number	Percent	Number	Percent
Town residents	3,139	50.3	3,750	50.6
Open country residents	3,097	49.7	3,654	49.4
Total population	6,236	100.0	7,404	100.0

Source: Schedule data.

white, 7 percent Mexican, and the remainder were persons from different parts of Europe, including Italy, Portugal, Poland, Germany, Yugoslavia, and Russia. The largest single group of foreign-born whites were Armenians with eight families recorded (4 percent of the schedules). One Negro, one Korean, and one Chinese were found in the sample. A group belonging to the Mennonite Church, while not a separate racial or nationality group, have such cultural homogeneity that they should be segregated from the rest. The 17 families classified in this category, mostly American-born, represent 8 percent of the total Dinuba population.

The racial characteristics of the two communities are similar, with very nearly identical proportion of native whites, Mexicans as the major group of nonwhites, and a variety of individual representatives of Europeans. A group of Filipino workers formerly lived in Arvin but are now gone; a number of Japanese families have been evacuated from Dinuba. Most of the Mexicans in both communities, and all of the Arvin Negroes are agricultural laborers.

SIZE OF FAMILIES

A striking difference between Arvin and Dinuba is the large difference in the size of families. In Arvin the average household contains 4.2 persons while in Dinuba it has only 3.4 persons.[8] Two

---

[8] The family for purposes of this study includes all members of the household at the time of interview, whether related or not. There were very few roomers, boarders, or hired men. Separate establishments (such as labor homes or multiple apartments) were counted individually. It is interesting to note that in the town of Dinuba the average family was 3.33, which corresponds closely to the figure 3.27 given for Dinuba in the 1940 census. This is the only category for which such comparable data are available.

important facts are responsible for this: in Dinuba there are many more elderly and retired couples and families from which grown children have separated, and in Arvin there are more farm laborers from the southwest with characteristically large families. Table 17 shows the size of families by major occupational groupings. Each category in Arvin is larger than the comparable occupation category in Dinuba, but in no case is the difference so great as the difference in the total. Farm laborers in both communities have the largest families, and the preponderance of this category in Arvin, to a very large extent, accounts for the difference between the family size in the two towns.

The distributions of families by size categories shows the high proportion of one- and two-person families in Dinuba and the proportionately fewer large families (table 18).

TABLE 17.—*Average size of household by major occupation groups: Arvin and Dinuba*

Occupation category	Number of persons in household	
	Arvin	Dinuba
Farm operator	3.57	3.27
Business, professional and white collar worker	3.50	3.31
Farm labor	4.75	4.22
Other labor	3.90	3.45
Nonemployed	2.62	2.17
All groups	4.23	3.43

Source: Schedule data.

TABLE 18.—*Distribution of families by size of households: Arvin and Dinuba*

Size category	Arvin	Dinuba
	Percent	Percent
1 person	4	9
2 persons	15	30
3 to 5 persons	58	48
6 persons or over	23	13
Total	100	100

Source: Schedule data.

Population statistics in wartime are subject to error because of the numbers in the armed forces. Twenty percent of the Dinuba families had sons, daughters, or husbands in the services against but 10 percent in Arvin. Dinuba families have contributed about

590 persons to the armed services as compared with but 280 persons from Arvin, or about 1 person per 5 families in Arvin against nearly 1 in 3 in Dinuba. Farmers in both communities have contributed heavily to the services, 29 percent of them in Arvin having members in the service against 25 percent in Dinuba. Only 9 percent of Arvin labor families have boys or girls in the services, and only 10 percent of the Arvin white-collar families are represented there. In Dinuba 15 percent of the laborers have family members in the Army or Navy, while all other groups run between 20 and 25 percent.

Any immediate family member (son, daughter, or spouse) regardless of age or marital status, who was outside the household was enumerated, but not included in the population estimates. In Arvin 16 percent of the families (about 25 percent of all labor families) had persons living away from home. In Dinuba this proportion is greater, with 36 percent of the families reporting members outside the household. Dinuba families had sons, daughters, or husbands away from home, either in the services or living outside the home in 41 percent of the cases. In Arvin these were only reported in 24 percent of all families. These absent family members somewhat correct the impression made by the small size of Dinuba families and account for much of the difference in family size between the two.

The data on family size in these two communities have some interesting general connotations. It is generally the case nationally that the farm families are large and town families small. This is not the case in either of these two communities, where the farm families are smaller than the community average and comparable to the business, professional, and white-collar workers. It is the farm laborers who have the large families. This close similarity in size of family between the farm operators and the business groups and the divergence in size of family between these groups and the laboring class offers a pattern which is displayed repeatedly and presents an index to the urbanization of the farm population.

AGE DISTRIBUTION

The median age of Arvin residents is 20 years; of Dinuba is 27 years. Figure 7 shows an age-distribution pyramid of all members in the household interviewed, undifferentiated by sex for Arvin and Dinuba, and for the total population of the eight counties of the San Joaquin Valley in 1940. The greater number of old people in the Dinuba population and the relatively few in their early productive years show clearly in this chart. In both the communities the draft and urban-work opportunities have reduced the number of people between ages of 15 and 30. Both pyramids show the effects of increased birth rate of the past few years. Arvin has a strikingly large number of adults in the thirties, and thus has many more children under 15 than Dinuba. Dinuba's population in all respects shows closer similarity to the total San Joaquin age distribution. It may be described as normal, mature, or stable in comparison with Arvin's. Each community has just half of its total population in the productive ages 20 to 64.

These differences are largely attributable to the age of the two communities, for Arvin displays the age distribution of a new town with a large number of young adults and their children and very few persons in the old-age categories.

SOCIAL BACKGROUND

Only a small proportion of the people are native Californians. In Arvin about 4 percent of family heads and in Dinuba about 19 percent were born in California. The Arvin population originated predominantly in the States of Oklahoma, Texas, and Arkansas, for 63 percent of the family heads were born in these States. Twelve percent of the family heads were foreign born, most of these in Mexico. Though the California-born family heads were far more numerous in Dinuba, they are still a minority. Oklahoma, Texas, Missouri, and Kansas were the birthplaces of just one-third of the total, while another 19 percent were born outside the United States. These data, based upon the schedules, are presented in table 19.

Both communities have a relatively large number of newcomers, but this group is far more numerous in Arvin than in Dinuba. Over half the Arvin residents came there in 1940 or later, while only about a fourth came to Dinuba during the same period. The longest residents in the Arvin sample came to the community in 1919, while a few Dinubans had been resident since before the turn of the century. The year of arrival of family heads, by 5-year intervals, is shown in table 20. Data are presented for the total population and for the laboring group alone.

TABLE 19.—*Birthplace of family heads: Arvin and Dinuba*

Place of birth	Family heads			
	Arvin		Dinuba	
	Number reported	Percent	Number reported	Percent
All American-born	117	88	166	81
California	5	4	39	19
Oklahoma	41	32	23	11
Texas	22	16	16	8
Arkansas	21	15	6	3
Missouri	4	3	16	8
Kansas	4	3	14	7
Kentucky	2	2	7	3
All others	18	13	45	22
All foreign-born	15	12	40	19
Mexico	9	6	7	3
Canada	3	3	8	4
Armenia	0	0	7	3
Russia	0	0	6	3
All others	3	3	12	6
Total	132	100	206	100

Source: Schedule data.

TABLE 20.—*Year of arrival in community of family heads: Arvin and Dinuba*

Date of arrival	Arvin				Dinuba			
	All family heads reporting		Labor family heads reporting		All family heads reporting		Labor family heads reporting	
	Number	Percent	Number	Percent	Number	Percent	Number	Percent
Before 1910	0	0	0	0	31	15	3	3
1910–14	0	0	0	0	21	10	6	7
1915–19	3	2	1	1	22	11	4	4
1920–24	9	7	7	7	27	13	13	14
1925–29	8	6	4	4	10	5	5	6
1930–34	11	8	7	7	14	7	8	9
1935–39	32	24	24	24	33	16	18	20
1940–44 [1]	69	53	57	57	48	23	33	37
Total	132	100	100	100	206	100	90	100

[1] Includes first quarter of 1944.

Source: Schedule data.

The differences in length of residence between Arvin and Dinuba have three basic causes—(1) the relative age of the two communities; (2) the proportion of the population made up of the low-security; low-stability laboring group; and (3) the relative social integration of the two communities. Obviously, since Dinuba is the older community it has older residents. This does not account for all the difference. School data show that Arvin's

AGE DISTRIBUTION OF ARVIN & DINUBA POPULATION COMPARED TO SAN JOAQUIN VALLEY

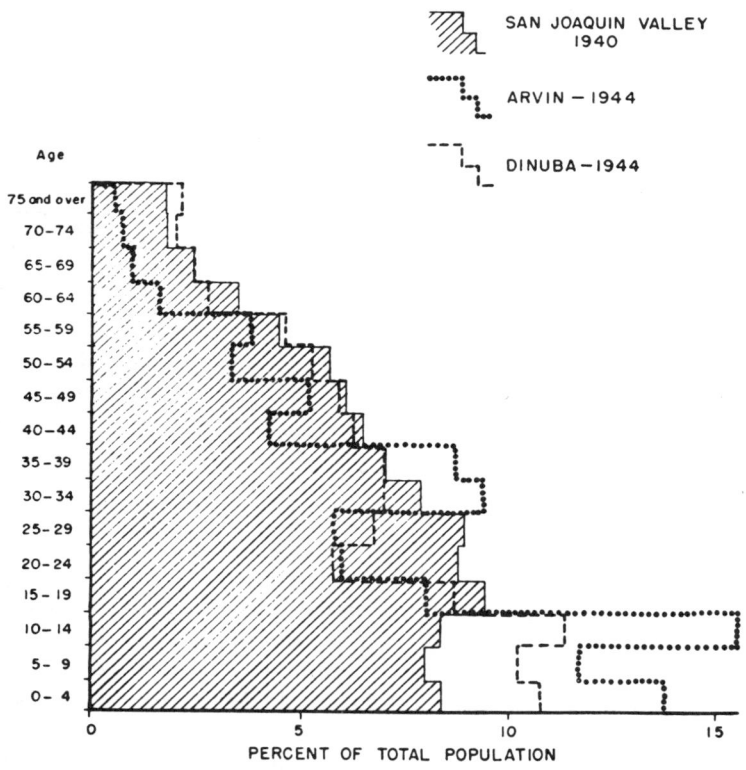

Source: Schedule data, U.S. Census, 1940

FIGURE NO. 7

population has not grown since 1940, yet over half the present population arrived in 1940 or later. This indicates a large rate of population turn-over. Labor shows shorter residence than the population as a whole (the differences is especially great in Dinuba), and the proportion of farm labor which arrived in 1940 or later is 61 percent in Arvin and 45 percent in Dinuba.

Most of the people in each community have grammar-school education. Eight years is both modal and median for educational attainment of family heads. Though the proportion of persons with high-school diplomas and college training is twice as great in Dinuba as in Arvin, Dinuba family heads have only 0.8 year additional education on the average. The educational attainment of family heads is presented in table 21.

TABLE 21.—*Levels of education of family heads: Arvin and Dinuba*

Educational attainment	Arvin		Dinuba	
	Family heads reporting		Family heads reporting	
	Number	Percent	Number	Percent
No education	3	2	8	4
1 to 4 years	15	12	19	10
5 to 7 years	38	31	40	20
8 years	40	32	53	26
9 to 11 years	14	11	30	15
12 years	8	6	31	15
13 or more years	8	6	19	10
Total	126	100	200	100
Average number of years	7.6		8.4	

Source: Schedule data.

OCCUPATIONAL STRUCTURE

From the standpoint of understanding the inherent social structure of the two communities and their fundamental social and economic problems, the occupation structure is the most significant fact about their population. In Arvin 80 percent of the families secure their livelihood from wage labor, while only 20 percent are independent farm operators, entrepreneurs, or whitecollar employees. In Dinuba each of these categories accounts for half of the gainfully employed. This difference heavily affects the character of the community under the prevailing system of hired labor in California agriculture. The most significant difference in the population of the two towns is in the proportion of hired farm laborers in each. Occupation is the basis of social class in rural California, as will be shown later.[9]

[9] See also Social Structure of a California Rural Community, by Walter R. Goldschmidt, Ph. D. thesis. University of California, Berkeley, 1942.

TABLE 22.—*Distribution of families by employment of chief breadwinner, Arvin and Dinuba* [1]

Occupation category	Arvin		Dinuba	
	Number	Percent	Number	Percent
Farm operator	14	10.6	65	30.6
Farm foreman	4	3.0	3	1.4
Other farm labor	76	57.6	52	24.4
Merchants, professionals	8	6.1	26	12.2
Other white collar	2	1.5	6	2.8
Skilled labor	7	5.3	15	7.0
Semiskilled labor	8	6.1	10	4.7
Service labor	5	3.7	6	2.8
Unskilled labor	0	0.0	6	2.8
Not gainfully employed [2]	8	6.01	24	11.3
Total	132	100.0	213	100.0

[1] Head of family, if fully employed; or if he has greatest amount of employment; otherwise, most important breadwinner in family.
[2] Not gainfully employed, includes all persons unemployed except seasonally unemployed persons, all retired persons, and families whose chief support comes from a person in the armed services.
Source: Schedule data.

The occupation according to 10 major groups are shown in table 22. While this gives a clear picture of the major occupational categories, the individual cells are too small to permit of further statistical analysis. For that reason the following groupings have been made:

```
                              Farm operator:       Percent
 1. Farm operator               Arvin............ 11.3    Farmer and white collar:  Percent
                                Dinuba........... 34.4     Arvin................ 19.4
 2. Merchant and professional  White collar worker:         Dinuba............... 51.3
 3. Other white collar          Arvin............  8.1
                                Dinuba........... 16.9
 4. Skilled labor              Nonfarm labor:
 5. Semiskilled labor           Arvin............ 16.1
 6. Service labor               Dinuba........... 19.6   Laborers:
 7. Unskilled labor            Farm labor:                 Arvin................ 80.6
 8. Farm foremen                Arvin............ 64.5     Dinuba............... 48.7
 9. Farm labor                  Dinuba........... 29.1
10. Nonemployed.
```

Despite the great difference shown in these figures between the occupational structure of Arvin and Dinuba, these figures actually understate the proportion of farm laborers. Neither residents in the Government camp just outside the Arvin community boundary nor the residents on the DiGiorgio holdings were included. All of the former (about 200 families) and nearly all of the latter (about 150 families) are farm laborers. Though the Government camp is outside the community, many of the residents work within the Arvin area. The DiGiorgio camps are within the community boundaries. Nevertheless, accepting these figures at face value, we find a striking difference between the two communities.

INCOME

Estimates of the distribution of income in the two communities can be had by means of data obtained from the schedule. Each person interviewed indicated the income bracket in which he fell during the calendar year of 1943. The information was probably fairly accurate since it was obtained shortly after respondents had filed income tax returns. Because the upper bracket was open, it is impossible to determine average income, so median figures must suffice. Wartime farm prices and farm wage rates have undoubtedly had a great effect both on the absolute values and on the distribution of incomes so that they cannot be considered normal. This is an error which must be recognized, though there is no adequate means of correcting it. Table 23 shows the income distribution by brackets for both communities. Groupings are made which divide the sample into four approximately equal parts. It will be seen that Dinuba has a larger group in the lowest quartile, but that Arvin has more incomes falling below the median.

TABLE 23.—*Income distribution in Arvin and Dinuba*

Income bracket	Arvin		Dinuba		Total	
	Number	Percent	Number	Percent	Number	Percent
Under $750	10	8	28	14	38	12
$751 to $1,250	22	17	27	13	49	15
$1,251 to $1,750	15	12	18	9	33	10
$1,751 to $2,250	28	22	33	16	61	18
$2,251 to $2,750	25	20	27	13	52	16
$2,751 to $3,250	6	5	19	10	25	8
$3,251 to $4,250	9	7	19	10	28	9
$4,251 to $5,250	1	1	7	4	8	2
$5,251 to $11,000	5	4	13	6	18	6
Over $11,000	5	4	9	5	14	4
Total	126	100	200	100	326	100
Not recorded	5		13		18	
Total	131		213		344	

Source: Schedule data.

The estimated median income of the four major occupational groupings in Arvin and Dinuba is shown in table 24. Dinuba has a slightly higher median income than Arvin, a difference that results from the large size of the low-income labor group in Arvin as compared to Dinuba. The figures on the income of farm labor are

AGRIBUSINESS AND THE RURAL COMMUNITY

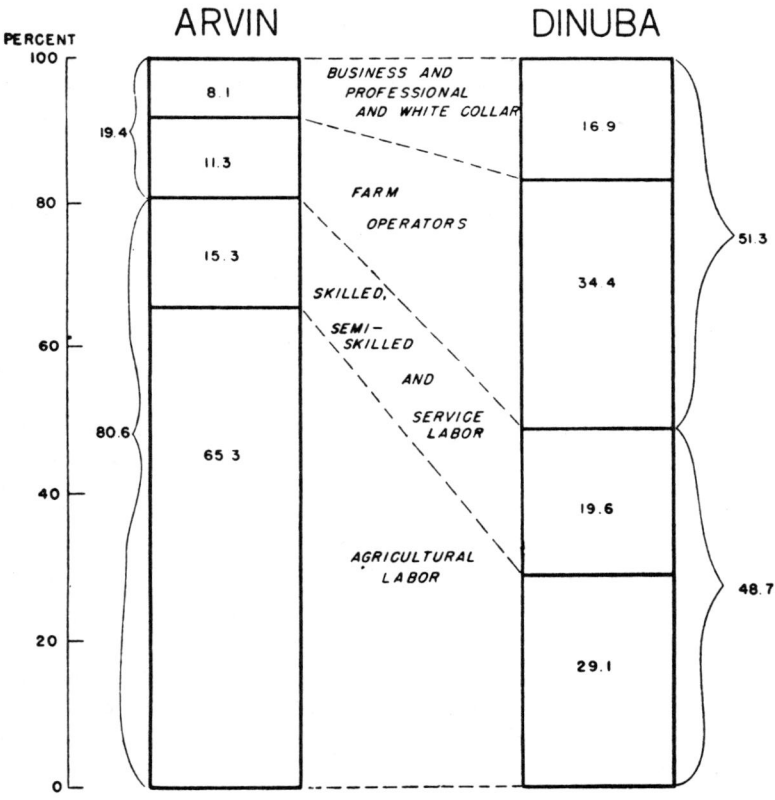

Figure No. 8

the same for both communities but the proportion of farm laborers is so much larger in Arvin that the average is reduced. A comparison of income per person, rather than per family, would show a greater divergence between the two communities, since Arvin, with smaller median incomes, has larger families.

TABLE 24.—*Estimated median income of major occupational groups: Arvin and Dinuba*

Occupational group	Arvin	Dinuba
White-collar worker	$3,000	$3,650
Farm operator	3,750	2,850
Farm labor	2,000	2,000
Other labor	1,600	2,000
All gainfully employed	2,100	2,350

Source: Schedule data.

Some occupational differences in income are particularly of interest. In Arvin 70 percent of the farmers and white-collar workers and 36 percent of the laborers were above the median income. In Dinuba the proportions are 65 and 40 respectively.[10] The difference in the position of the farm operator in the two communities is also significant. In Arvin the farmer has a higher median income than the white-collar worker while in Dinuba the reverse is true. This difference is clearly reflected in the social position of these two groups, as will be shown later.

LIVING CONDITIONS

Two measurements were obtained which indicate that the people of Dinuba live under material conditions that are measureably better than those enjoyed by the Arvin residents. The first of these is a level-of-living index based upon the possession of a series of items, while the second was an evaluation of the condition of the home based upon the observations of the enumerators.

[10] The association between social phenomena analyzed and the differences between the two communities were computed by a variety of techniques. Computations and chi square and T were considered most accurate and a table of results is presented in Appendix F. Chi square shows the probability of any difference being the result of chance, and T is a measure of degree of association roughly corresponding to the correlation coefficient. The variation in income was determined to be significant and the degree of relationship between occupation and income in the two communities is about the same magnitude.

The frequency of occurrence of seven of the eight items which make up the level-of-living scale is shown in table 25. Several items, which for purposes of making the level-of-living index were broken into series, have been simplified for purposes of this tabulation. Thus the degree of crowding is here indicated by a break between those with less than one person per room and those with more, while three categories were used for purposes of calculating the index.

TABLE 25.—*Incidence of selected individual items on the level-of-living scale: Arvin and Dinuba*

Item	Arvin		Dinuba	
	Number reporting	Percent	Number reporting	Percent
1. Less than 1 person per room	36	28	149	72
2. Water in home	99	75	185	90
3. Electric lighting in home	128	97	203	98
4. Mechanical refrigeration	75	57	154	75
5. Radio	113	86	190	92
6. Telephone	17	13	80	39
7. Automobile	109	83	170	82

Source: Schedule data.

With a single exception (possession of automobiles) Dinuba people are better off than people in Arvin. The possession of electricity in the home is very nearly universal in both communities, but the difference in the possession of the other five items between Arvin and Dinuba is quite great. It should be pointed out that the lack of crowding in Dinuba is in part a reflection of the fact that more people are away from their homes, either in the armed service, or making homes of their own. The difference in this item is therefore somewhat exaggerated.

On the basis of these seven items and one other (type of home construction) a level of living scale was constructed with a range from 0 to 44.[11] Figure 9 shows the frequency distribution of level-of-living scores in Arvin and Dinuba, and the median and mean scores of each. It will be seen that Dinubans have an appreciably higher level.

Level of living as measured by this index is clearly associated with occupation. Only 21 percent of Arvin laborers have an index

[11] The method of calculating this index is presented in appendix E.

DISTRIBUTION OF FAMILIES ACCORDING TO LEVEL OF LIVING

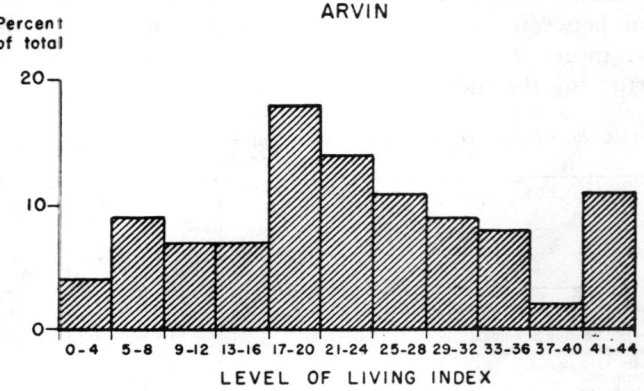

FIGURE No. 9

above the median point of the combined sample, while 70 percent of the independently employed farmers and white-collar workers are in this category. In Dinuba 43 percent of the laborers are above the median, and nearly 90 percent of the independently employed fall in the upper brackets. (The median point was calculated for the combined sample.) That a statistically significant association between occupation and living conditions exists was indicated by the Chi Square Test.[12]

There is a similar association between level of living and income. The relation between these two factors is shown in the accompanying scattergram (fig. 10). It is readily seen that the upper income brackets regularly have a high level of living, but the lower brackets frequently have a high level of living, too. This is the result of two things; first, the fact that the income in any single year is not the determining factor for the attainment of a relatively high level of living, and second, that the items in the index were too basic and too nearly universal, and were too few in number to form a sufficiently sensitive reflection of living conditions or social position.

A second measure of living conditions was a more subjective evaluation of the premises and of the interior and exterior of the home made by the enumerator. This is a rough measure of the personal standards of cleanliness and orderliness within the financial ability of the individual family. No doubt the standards were affected by cash outlay, but a family placing a high premium on these values, and who correspondingly maintained a neat and orderly home and garden would be rated good even though the income was quite limited. A scoring system from 0 to 9 was developed, by giving the best and poorest values for each of the three enumerated items the value of 3 and 0, respectively, and intermediate items values between. Figure 11 shows the cumulative percents at each score for Arvin and Dinuba, first for each community and second for the fundamental occupational dichotomy within each. Dinuba's score is superior, and the condition of laborers' homes is somewhat better there than in Arvin, yet basically the difference lies between the laborer on one hand and the farmer and white-collar worker on the other.

The occupational differences in the condition of the home which were found are statistically significant, according to the Chi Square Test.[13] In Arvin, 32 percent of the laborers and 67 percent of the farmers and white-collar workers fall above the median point with respect to this evaluation of the home. Corresponding proportions in Dinuba were 40 percent and 65 percent. The table in

[12]See appendix F.
[13]See appendix F.

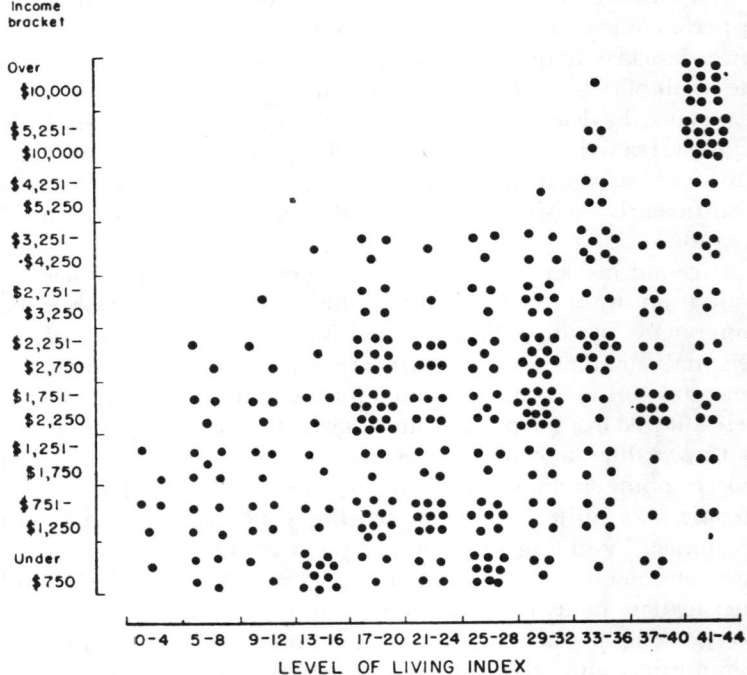

SCATTERGRAM SHOWING RELATIONSHIP BETWEEN LEVEL OF LIVING AND INCOME

Source: Schedule data

FIGURE No. 10

appendix F indicates that the association appears to be somewhat less close in Dinuba than in Arvin. Furthermore, home conditions being less dependent on economic status, they show a lower degree of association with occupation than does the index of level of living as measured by material possessions. The association between living conditions and income is slightly closer than between living conditions and occupation in Arvin; is somewhat less close in Dinuba.

These calculations show several things: (1) that Arvin condi-

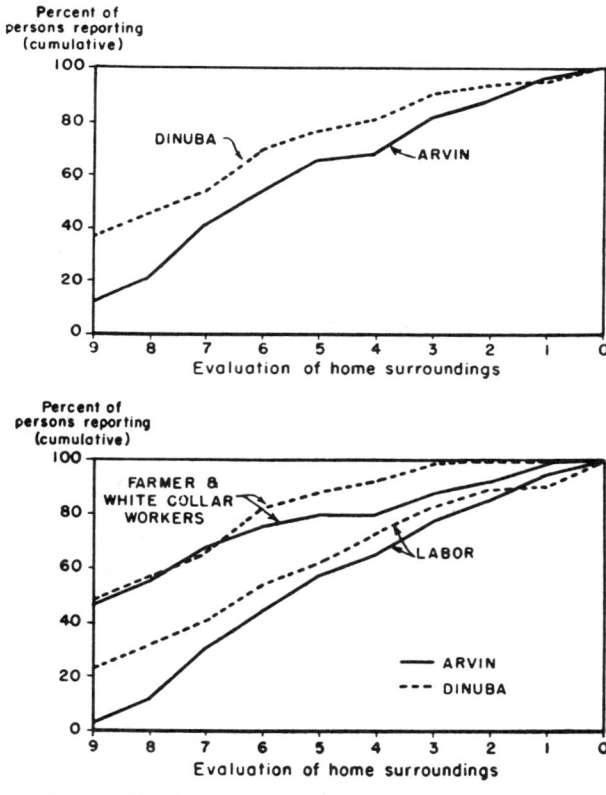

FIGURE No. 11

tions are consistently poorer than Dinuba ones, (2) that there is a significant association between occupation and conditions of living, (3) that these conditions as measured by income, level of living, and conditions of the home are all closely interrelated, and (4) that the poorer conditions in Arvin are therefore a direct function of the great preponderance of the farm labor group in that community.

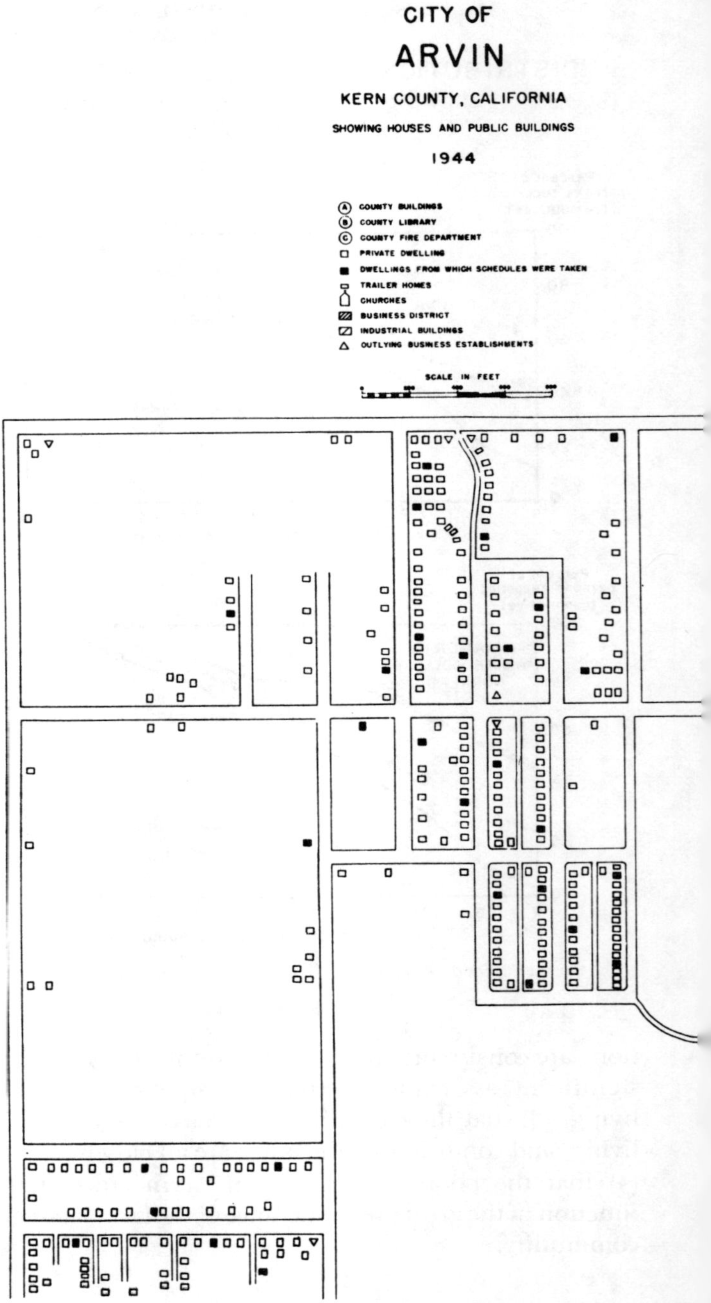

CITY OF
ARVIN

KERN COUNTY, CALIFORNIA
SHOWING HOUSES AND PUBLIC BUILDINGS

1944

- Ⓐ COUNTY BUILDINGS
- Ⓑ COUNTY LIBRARY
- Ⓒ COUNTY FIRE DEPARTMENT
- ☐ PRIVATE DWELLING
- ■ DWELLINGS FROM WHICH SCHEDULES WERE TAKEN
- ▯ TRAILER HOMES
- ⌂ CHURCHES
- ▨ BUSINESS DISTRICT
- ▨ INDUSTRIAL BUILDINGS
- △ OUTLYING BUSINESS ESTABLISHMENTS

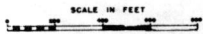
SCALE IN FEET

FIGURE NO. 12

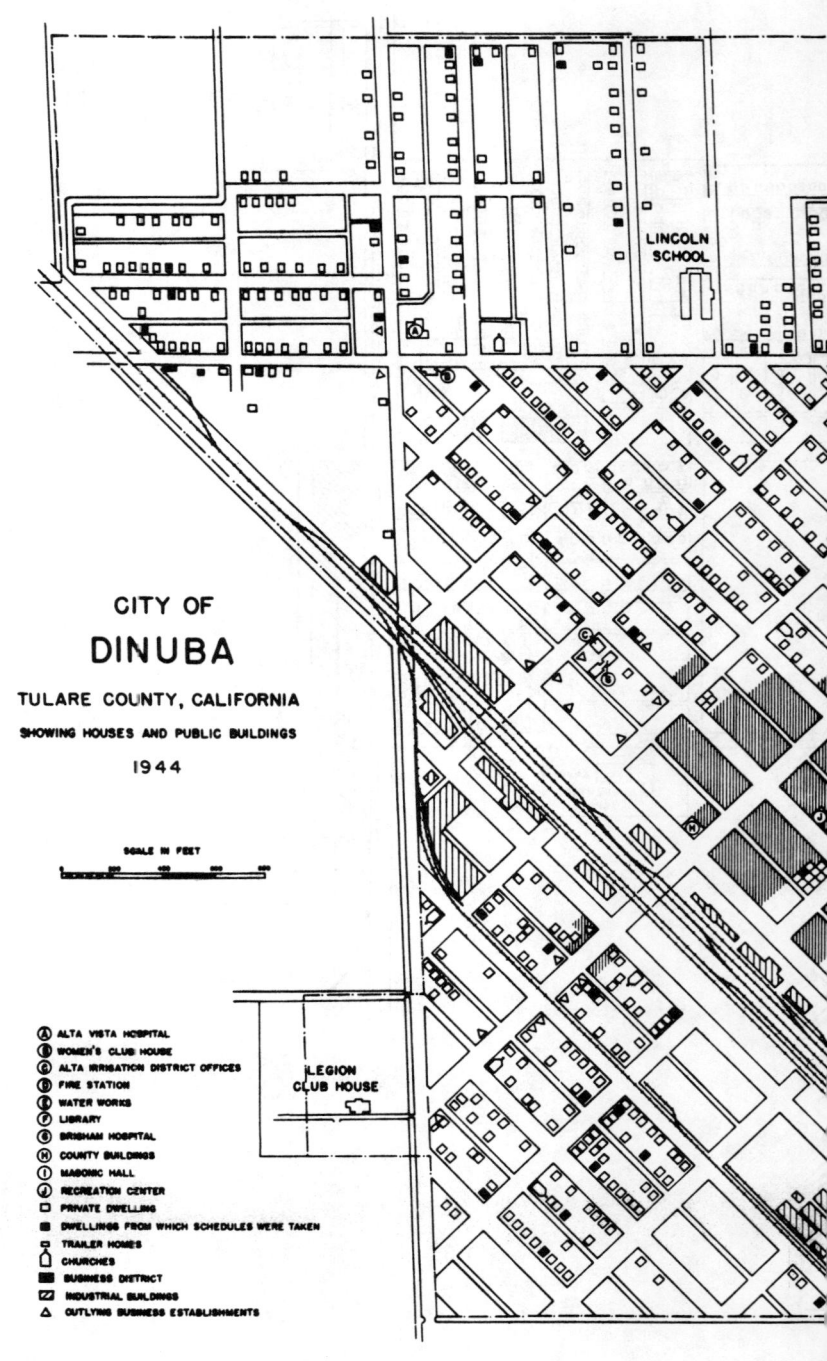

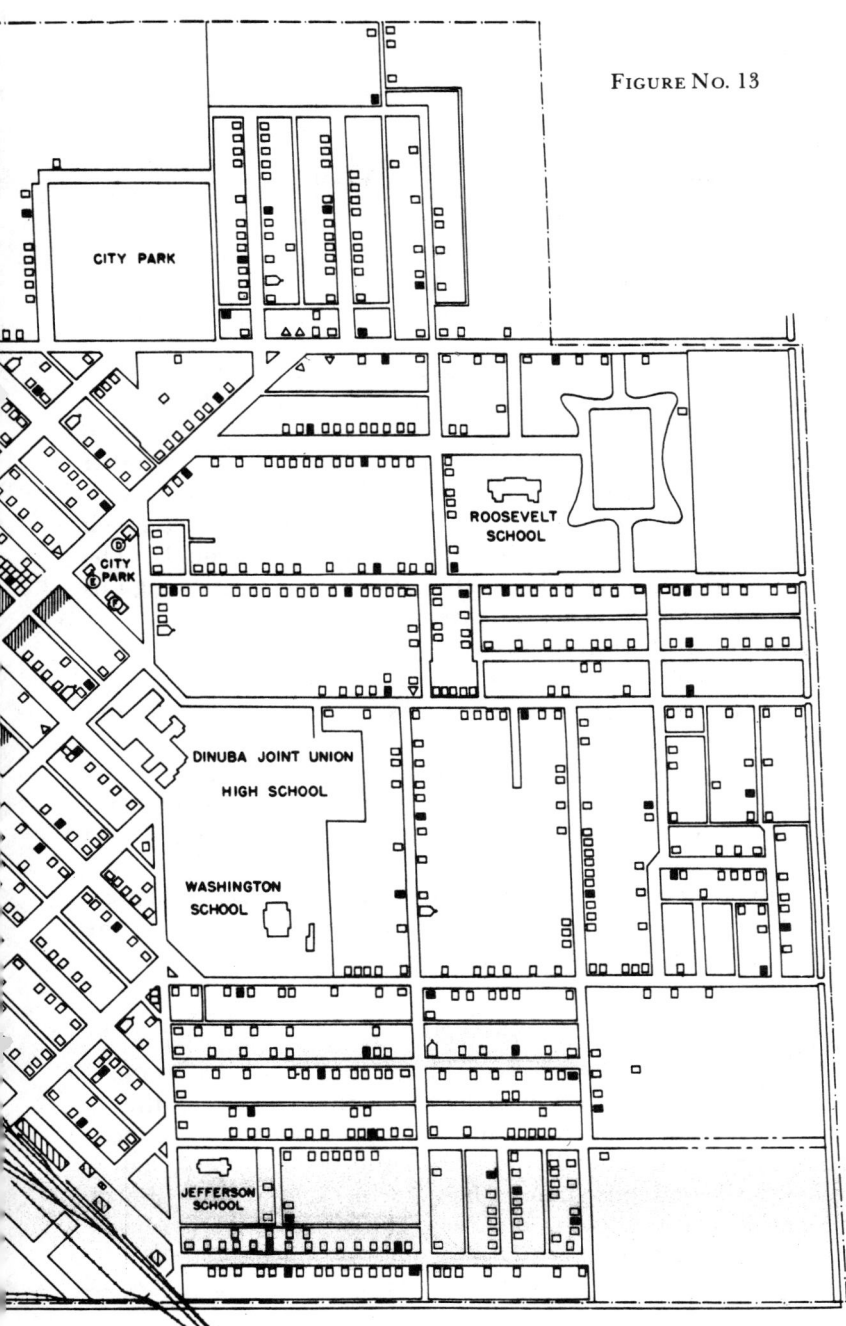

Figure No. 13

PATTERN OF SETTLEMENT

Some appreciation of the nature of the two communities can be had by the examination of maps showing the location of business districts, residences, churches, and public buildings. Such maps reproduced on figures 12 and 13, which are on the same scale to allow for ready comparison. The rectangles representing individual residences are of such a size that they represent the minimum adequate floor space considered necessary for a family of four or five persons.

The relative crowding of the houses is immediately apparent. Few areas in Arvin have 50-foot lots and most of them do not have full depth. Throughout certain districts it has been the practice to place two units on a single lot, one facing the alley and the other the street. Dinuba has some relatively poor areas with a fair degree of crowding, but these are far less crowded and involve a much smaller proportion of the total number of households. The characteristic lot in Dinuba is 50 or more feet wide, running full way to the alley, with but a single family unit.

Not only are there differences in the houses, but we find a much larger business district. Both communities have an "industrial" district, which contains packing sheds, storage for gasoline and similar types of enterprises.

Maps of the rural area would show a great difference in the pattern of settlement. In Arvin there is usually a large distance between each farm house, but near the farm house there is generally also a labor camp with 4 to 20 or more separate dwelling units. In Dinuba the homes are scattered fairly evenly over the area, with few units at any great distance from any neighbor, while the crowded aspect of the labor camp is rarely found.

SUMMARY

This section has been devoted to the presentation of a statistical analysis of the population of the two communities, based upon the 10 percent sample of households enumerated. These statistics show that the community of Dinuba has a somewhat larger population than Arvin. The average size of household is much larger in Arvin, partly because Arvin has a younger age composition, partly because it has a smaller contingent in the armed forces, and very largely because of the greater proportion of wage-worker families in Arvin, families which are consistently larger than families in the other occupation groups.

The racial composition and ethnic backgrounds of the two groups are quite similar. The only important exception is that Arvin residents have a much shorter tenure in the community, and they come largely from the States of Oklahoma, Texas, and Arkansas. Family heads in Dinuba are more frequently native Californians, more of them are foreign-born, while those from elsewhere in the United States represent a wider array of origins. More important than origin appears to be the length of residence, for over half the population came to Arvin in 1940 or later as against but 23 percent in Dinuba with such brief tenure.

Almost every family head in each community had some education, and most had completed elementary school. Dinubans more frequently had college training, but there was less than a year's difference in average number of years of school completed between the family heads in Arvin and those of Dinuba.

The most significant population differential between the two communities is the occupation of the family heads. Eighty percent of the Arvin population works for wages, while in Dinuba this group represents just half of all the families. There are far more farmers, more business people, and more skilled workers in Dinuba than in Arvin. This is important because of the high association between occupation and social status.

The median income in Arvin is somewhat smaller than in Dinuba. The differential here is undoubtedly affected by both the high wage rates and high farm prices at the time the study was made. In Arvin the farm operators are better off than the merchants, while in Dinuba the reverse situation exists. Average level of living and the evaluation of living conditions both indicate that the Arvin families live in less desirable surroundings than those of Dinuba. These items, income, level of living, and conditions of the house are all clearly associated with occupation.

CHAPTER XV

SOCIAL ASPECTS OF COMMUNITY LIFE

The differences between Arvin and Dinuba strike the casual observer immediately, for their appearance is demonstrative of divergent social characteristics. Driving into Dinuba from any direction one approaches the business section of the town by going through tree-lined streets flanked by rows of substantial dwellings. The business section of town is made up of brick buildings, many two stories high, and gives the appearance of stability and prosperity. The streets are wide and well paved, both in the business and residential sections. Approaching Arvin from either direction, one moves from the open country immediately into the small business section. The main street is lined with low stucco buildings and service stations for a distance of about two blocks. The side streets are entirely unpaved; there are no sidewalks, and the houses are crowded so close together that in some sections of town half of them front on the alleys. One single street for a distance of about two blocks is lined with houses where lawns have been planted.

GOVERNMENT

Dinuba is an incorporated community and has a local government; Arvin is governed by the county. Incorporation is a matter of local action, and affects the life of the community in many ways. Incorporation and the quality of community government are important to this analysis not only because they affect the lives of the citizens, but because they are indicative of the spirit and motivation of the community.

The fact that Arvin has never constituted itself a civic body undoubtedly finds its root cause in the lack of any real civic unity. This lack of unity, which in essence makes two communities out of Arvin (one of farmers and one of laborers) will be analyzed later. Some Arvin residents find the reason for failure to incorporate in this fact alone, such as a minister who said that property owners do not want incorporation because they fear that the laborers would then "run the town." This is certainly not the only cause.

It should be pointed out that many California towns remain unincorporated, and this is particularly true of the towns in Kern County. Kern is a wealthy county and it has a strong and effective county government capable of furnishing services to the local communities. Each town has a fire department with adequate and modern equipment; each of the townships has a deputy sheriff, who is also adequately equipped. The county has a planning board which is at the service of local groups in unincorporated communities. For instance, Arvin has been furnished with modern stucco buildings (an attractive type of architecture admirably adapted to the desert climate) for its fire department, for local offices of the sheriff, the welfare department, the health department, and the agricultural representative, and a community hall and kitchen. Such county-furnished facilities are as elaborate as the local electorate could furnish for itself, and reduce the incentive to incorporate.

Incorporation has advantages and disadvantages. It is argued that the large corporations and absentee landholders do not favor it because their taxes are increased while they receive little or not direct benefit, that local merchants and professional people usually are in favor of having city government because they get needed services—such as a local police force—which save them money. It also is said to "promote" the community, thereby increasing the value of their business. Other citizens probably weigh these benefits against the cost with varying results. Social considerations favor incorporation, provided the city government does not become corrupt. This is because an incorporated city can perform needed services to local people over which they have direct control, and because it encourages a spirit of community solidarity which will otherwise have no means of developing. These generalizations are substantiated by the situation in Arvin and Dinuba.

Though the county has furnished some things to Arvin, it has not provided it with others. Not until 1940 was there a sewage-disposal plant. Water and garbage service is provided by private enterprisers, with no direct popular control over their activities.

Certain congested areas in Arvin are only now getting an adequate water supply from a central system. Street paving, the building of sidewalks, street lighting, parks, and such matters are supplied by the county.

Decisions as to the expenditure of money for such civic improvements and the general welfare are remote from the people who are to be affected by them. One important county official addressed the Booster Club of Arvin somewhat as follows: "You will have to let me know about your community problems, for you know more about the needs of your town than I do. I don't know what you need. You have to let me know how you want the law administered, because I don't want to run your labor off to some other town." This club is composed largely of farm operators. This is not an isolated case. When the community wants a park, a school, or lights, it must form a committee to wait on the county officials, or the county commissioners ask the leading clubs what their pleasure is with respect to certain decisions. In thus arriving at decisions, only a small segment of the community is formally consulted. However just and equitable the decisions are, they are participated in by only a small section of the community.

Without a civic entity, and with limited participation in community decisions, there is a serious lack of spirit and solidarity. Lack of unity even among the merchants along the main street was so great that one of them described it as follows:

> Prior to 2 years ago, when some Bakersfield men organized a chapter of the Lions Club, the merchants didn't even know each other. At the first meeting we had a sort of contest to see who could call each other by their first name, and found that none of us knew many of them. We worked here during the day and went home at night and never gave a thought about the other man on the street.
>
> I am rarely on the other side of the street, and still know only one of the merchants over there.

Dinuba's incorporation dates from 1906, and city government is a very real part of Dinuba life. A council of five is elected for a 4-year term, three at one time and two at another. A heated biennial election had been held just prior to the time of field investigations for the present study, and the issues were still fresh in the minds of civic leaders, issues involving local problems which the local electorate decided at the polls.

In the course of its history, the city has paved many miles of streets and laid many miles of sidewalks. It has established a water system, a sewerage system, and a garbage-disposal system; it has placed electric lights along its streets throughout town, has created two parks and is creating a third one, and maintains police and fire departments. The council selects a chairman who is the mayor, and each councilman is in charge of one of five departments. These are (1) police and fire, (2) streets, sewers, and water, (3) parks and waste disposal, (4) city properties, and (5) finance. The operation of the city government is therefore close to the people.

In final analysis, the worth of this must be measured in accomplishment. The police force of four maintains order in the community. Court actions are confined largely to "driving while intoxicated" charges. Houses of prostitution in the community were readily eliminated at the specific request of the War Department.

The fire department is efficient. Its rapid response to a fire and its consideration of property owners, as well as its interest in fire prevention, was observed. The department is jointly operated with the county. There are four paid firemen who operate the county engines outside the city limit and both county and city engines within the city. In addition, there is a volunteer group which serves both town and county. These men serve at nominal pay, and have, after a pattern frequently found in rural California, made a social organization out of the department.

The present mayor claims responsibility for establishing the city garbage system. Four years ago garbage collection was a private franchise. It was expensive and few people availed themselves of the service. It is now a city service, paid for out of an addition of 50 cents to the monthly water charge. After many years of inadequate service, the alleys had become very dirty and the mayor hired a crew to clean them up. Adequate garbage service has made it possible to keep the alleys clean. The mayor was particularly proud that no WPA help was required on this project, and that the service is done at so small a charge without resorting to feeding garbage to hogs. He avoided this because of the nuisance to householders of segregating garbage, and because he anticipates that this practice will eventually be outlawed.

Most of the streets are paved and lighted with electroliers. They are kept unusually clean, and together with the planting of trees

for the community. The dinner followed close upon the heated city elections, and the traces of ill-feeling remained, though officially denied.

This privately sponsored meeting was not attended by representatives of farm laborers or other laboring groups. Since it was an open meeting, they could have participated if they were sufficiently motivated, though with the same psychological and social barriers that would keep them out of such a meeting in Arvin. The absence of laborers is not felt so keenly since they form a smaller portion of the population than in Arvin. However, the principle remains.

SCHOOLS

The first school in the Dinuba area started in 1879 with 13 pupils, the second in 1884 with 20. In 1889 an elementary school was opened in Dinuba proper with an average daily attendance of 43. In 1944, the Dinuba Elementary School, housed in four separate units scattered through town, has an average daily attendance of 605, but at one time had as many as 940. In the rural area there are four schools, and a portion of another from which the children come to the Dinuba High School. These rural schools have an average daily attendance of 350, but at one time had 450. The highest combined average daily attendance was in 1922-23, when the figure was 1,251. The boundaries of these school districts fit very closely the boundary of the community as delineated.

In the Arvin area two schools were opened in 1902-3, with a total average daily attendance of 29. A school was opened at Arvin in 1914-15. These three schools reached a combined average daily attendance of 1,242, and the Arvin school reached a peak of 683 in 1940-41 and is still close to that level. District boundaries conform poorly to the community boundary as delineated, with one of the three schools serving neighboring Weedpatch as well as many homes in the Arvin area. Strictly speaking, therefore, the school attendance never reached as high a figure in Arvin as it did in Dinuba. This is to be expected, for Arvin is presently smaller than Dinuba, and the Dinbua population is considerably less than its post-World War I peak. The close parallel in the growth of the two communities is shown in figure 20, which gives the growth curve of the elementary-school attendance for both towns on the same scale, but with Arvin dates set back 20 years. The similarity in growth pattern is striking.

If attention is given to the elementary school in the towns, rather than to all schools in the area, the same similarity in growth pattern is found. Again the growth curves are closely parallel but Arvin is about 24 years later than Dinuba, rather than 20. Since this does not represent town residence, but merely the pupils from that geographic area which the town school serves, the comparison is of less value than the more inclusive one, and is indicated merely further to substantiate the general similarity in growth and the relative age of each community.

Both Arvin and Dinuba have modern school plants. The Arvin buildings are newer than the Dinuba ones, but are somewhat more crowded. Both conditions would be expected in view of the history of the two communities. Arvin has somewhat greater average daily attendance per teacher—30 as compared with 26. A very significant difference, however lies in the nature of the planning. Dinuba has adopted an unusual plan of separating its school into four parts. Two units each serve the first four grades and the other two units serve grades 5 and 6 and grades 7 and 8. There are several advantages to this system. First, by placing the lowest grades at the opposite corners of town, the small children have relatively short distances to walk, second, the school playgrounds are scattered through town, and third, the age groups are separated. Undoubtedly the original cost as well as the upkeep is somewhat greater, with some disadvantages in the administration. For many reasons, this plan would not have the same advantageous effect in Arvin, where the district is large and the students are more widely scattered. Arvin has a system of bus transportation to bring the children the long distances to school.

The turn-over in teachers is an index to the school situation. In Dinuba 3 out of 22 teachers did not return for the 1943-44 session. In Arvin 14 of the 22 did not return. These figures apply only to the schools in the towns, but the other schools in the Arvin area had high turn-over rates—5 out of 8 and 4 out of 13. In the three schools combined, fewer than half the teachers had been there the preceding year. Such a high rate of turn-over indicates that the schools are viewed by teachers as a poor alternative and they tend to move away at their earliest opportunity. It means that the school cannot hold the best grade of teachers, and has fewer experienced ones. Rapid turn-over also means that the teacher does not become acquainted with the peculiar problems of the community and that the staff cannot develop the teamwork that is necessary.

From the community viewpoint, long teacher tenure means that the teacher plays an important role in the affairs of the community outside of the classroom. He serves not only as the vital leader of youth but in civic affairs in general. Dinuba has been particularly fortunate. The superintendent is recognized in all social gatherings as a leader; his advice is sought and his counsel followed. But he is not the only teacher who serves this vital function. For instance, one of the younger men on his staff—less than 10 years' tenure—already can boast of having been instrumental in starting a civic organization, and the youth service it performs, and has instigated other community improvements. The lack of this type of leadership is constantly made evident in Arvin. School and community functions suffer from an inadequate number of public-minded and trained citizens to supervise such affairs. The problem is aggravated by the fact that many of the teachers do not live in the community but commute from Bakersfield. These teachers naturally have less interest in the community, and most of them give no service to the community as a whole. This is particularly serious in a town which has few other sources of leadership.

The absence of a high school in Arvin is one of its most fundamental problems. It is recognized as such by Arvin people who have long sought a high school. In 1940-41 a study of the need was made,[14] and in October of 1941 a site was purchased just west of Arvin. Construction is planned for the postwar period. Whether it will be a full 4-year high school still remains in doubt. Arvin businessmen and resident farm operators are anxious to have the school built and presented a detailed statement of the advantages of an Arvin location over one in the Lamont-Weedpatch area. The report on site selection shows the average daily attendance for the four school districts which would be served by the proposed new high school and the high-school pupils resident in each. There

[14] School Site Report, Arvin Lamont Area, manuscript report prepared by the site selection committee of the Kern County High School. By Norman Pollasby, T. L. McCain, and Thomas L. Nelson.

were in January of 1941, when the data were assembled, 155 pupils in the Arvin school district and 271 in the 3 school districts which most nearly conform to Arvin boundaries. The plan includes a fourth district, which brings the high-school age population up to 390. These figures indicate a ratio of high-school pupils to elementary average daily attendance of 24 to 100. Using this ratio, the area would have had over 100 potential high-school pupils as early as 1925. This area centers at a distance of over 20 miles from the high school to which the pupils must ride.

The location of a high school is generally a matter of decision which goes beyond the local community, yet very properly the local population can influence a decision. The fact that Arvin does not have its own high-school facilities, though for nearly 20 years it has had an estimated high-school population of over 100, is evidence that insufficient influence and motivation could be mustered in the Arvin area.

The lack of high-school facilities is, in turn, a heavy detriment to the youth of the community. They must be on the bus as much as 2 hours a day, which gives them a very long school day and deprives them of hours when they could play, do chores, or earn spending money after school. According to local mothers, the rush, noise, and bustle of the bus ride is enervating. In the city school, the children find themselves among a large group of strangers. The requirement of catching the bus deprives them of time for extracurricular activities which would break down the barriers and otherwise give them satisfaction. These facts were set forth by an Arvin mother, who went on to say:

> The worst hardships of all are the discrimination that is made against local students (bus students) and their inability to participate fully in extracurricular activities because they have to go home by bus immediately after school is over. The school authorities try to put all the rural students into agriculture because they fell that they are all going to be farmers or laborers. They tried to put my sons into agriculture, and I went down not once, but twice, to have the schedule changed, because I want them to have a college preparatory course. The labor parents are not in a position to protest; if they do have the interest, they are licked by the fine surroundings and their own shyness.

The absence of a high school is a deprivation not only to the students but the entire community. The high school in Dinuba is a rallying place for community action, a center of cultural activities such as lectures and musicals, and a source of leadership. In addition, it furnishes the town a playground, gymnasium, and auditorium. Arvin, lacking a high school, is also lacking in these.

SOCIAL INSTITUTIONS

Both communities have institutions which have grown up in response to local needs and the natural desire of persons to have social contacts. In Arvin there is relative poverty of such institutions, their functions are more limited, and fewer people have access to them. In Dinuba the more numerous organizations are active, and many people participate.

In Arvin there are the following formal organizations: The Booster Club, the Lions Club, the Farm Bureau center and Farm Home center, a chapter of the State Guard, and the Parent Teacher's Association. In nearby Weedpatch, but with only a few Arvin participants, there is a Grange. This is a complete list of the formalized organizations by means of which Arvin residents get together for social functions or for any other kind of secular associated activities.

The Boosters is a local civic service club for men which meets once a month in the evenings. It was organized in 1921 as a civic improvement group and since that time has performed many useful community functions, largely as a group which induced the county to provide services. Among its first projects were obtaining a county road to the community and getting the area resurveyed. Its activities were largely responsible for getting a community hall, those street lights that are in Arvin, and the WPA-built sewage system. It has helped in two regular community events: The flower festival and the glider meet. The flower festival is a chamber of commerce activity which has publicized the famous Kern County wild flowers. In the spring the unplowed semidesert fields are transformed into a purple and gold carpet by the lupin and California poppies, and they attract thousands from Los Angeles and elsewhere. Some of the best fields are around Arvin, and the Boosters sponsored concessions and aided in the countywide festival. The slopes east of Arvin have air currents favorable to gliding, and the Boosters aid a glider society in Los Angeles in staging a meeting once a year. These events have been curtailed by the war. Recently the group has directed its attention to alleviating local problems, such as petitioning Federal agencies for more wholesale gasoline. Aside from regular monthly dinner meetings, the club has occasional social functions.

Forty of the eight-four members are farmers and thirty-nine are business, professional, or white-collar workers.[15] There are two farm foremen and one mechanic who belong. Other farm labor and the unskilled and semiskilled laboring groups are unrepresented in the organization. Many of the members live outside Arvin and belong because they have Arvin property or other interests in the community. These are included in the above tabulation.

The Lions Club has been organized but a few years. Prior to its organization there was no association of merchants in the community. With a much shorter history than the Booster Club, it cannot point to as many successful projects, though it performs very much the same kind of function. Its major service to date has been the bringing together of the merchants. According to several members of the Lions Club, the Boosters are predominantly interested in matters pertaining to farmer welfare, and for that reason the need for a separate civic organization was acute. Some anxiety over farmer control of the Lions Club was expressed. Of the 42 members of the Lions, 29 are merchants or professional people and 11 are farm operators (table 26). The remaining two are in the service trades. There are 27 persons (nearly two-thirds of total Lions membership) who have membership in both organizations.

The Arvin Farm Center has 70 members, of which 7 are nonfarmer "sustaining" members. The remaining 63 are farmers, and 34 of these operate less than 80 acres and 38 under 160 acres. The chairman of the center made the observation that "the small farmers attend center meetings more regularly than do the large farmers but the larger farmers seem to take more active part in the working of the organization." The Farm Center is a local organization of the county farm bureau and carries out the excellent educational work of that organization. There is a purely social aspect to the Farm Center meeting, for the men and women frequently have suppers and other social events.

The Parent-Teacher Association is the only social group which

---

[15] Occupational break-downs of all club members analyzed are given in table 26.

only nonreligious organization in which this group participates. Of the 56 members classified, 8 are farm laborers and 9 are other classes of workers. About 30 percent of the members are from the laboring group (table 26, p. 67). White-collar people account for half of the membership and farmers for a fifth.

TABLE 26.—*Occupation of members in selected Arvin and Dinuba clubs*

Occupation group [1]	Arvin clubs						Dinuba clubs					
	Booster		Lions		PTA		Rotary		Women's Club		American Legion	
	Number	Percent	Number	Percent	Number	Percent	Number	Percent	Number	Percent	Number	Percent
White-collar workers	39	46	29	69	27	48	36	84	57	57	58	53
Farmers	40	48	11	26	11	20	6	14	34	34	28	25
Farm labor	2	2	0	0	8	14	0	0	0	0	9	8
Other labor	3	4	2	5	9	16	1	2	3	3	14	13
Nonemployed	0	0	0	0	1	2	0	0	6	6	1	1
Total	84	100	42	100	56	100	43	100	100	100	110	100
Employment unknown	2		0		12		0		1		57	

[1] Occupation classification according to family head.
Source: Club records.

These organizations (and the State guard, which probably performs some recreational and social purposes in addition to its protective function) are all the organized social groups in the community. The Weedpatch Grange is an active group of small farmers, but practically none of the members live within the Arvin boundary, and the meeting place is outside it, too. There are no veterans' organizations, no lodges, no women's clubs, no sport clubs, or any other social group. Those who can afford it participate in Bakersfield "society."

A complete cataloging of the Dinuba social activities is more difficult because of the greater amount and variety of social life. An appreciation of the complexity can be obtained by a list of the major organizations. Dinuba merchants have two associations, the chamber of commerce and the business men's association, to serve their interest. In addition to this, there are two "service clubs," the Rotary, the Y's Men's Club, and the semisocial and purely local Young Business Men's Club. The volunteer firemen form a club which has a social function as well as its service to the community. The American Legion has a strong post, with a large and active membership, and a Legion auxiliary. There is a Masonic order with chapters of the Eastern Star, the Rainbow Girls, and the DeMolay. Women may belong to any of several clubs, the Dinuba Women's Club, the Garden Club, the Dinuba Women's Music Club, or to the Palace Club, a study group made up of old residents. Dinuba has an active chapter of the American Red Cross, which has its own meeting hall. There is one Parent-Teacher Association for the elementary school. Two farmer organizations, the Farm Center (with a home center) and the Grange, are active.

The PTA in Dinuba appears to be quite weak, with but few members and little activity. They formerly sponsored a "penny carnival" each year, but this was discontinued during the war. They had previously sponsored a Cub Scout pack, and this has been resumed though was not active at the time the field work was being done. There is no association for the high school, and the elementary schools are consolidated into one Parent-Teacher Association.

Elsewhere in this report are presented some of the outstanding activities of different clubs and their contribution to the community. A few general remarks will suffice here. These groups bring the following facilities for social gatherings to Dinuba: A hall for the meeting of the lodges, a large hall and park belonging to the American Legion, the clubhouse of the Women's Club, the recreation center and meeting place of the Y's Mens Club, and the Red Cross clubhouse. (See fig. 13.) These facilities do not merely serve the members but are available to the whole community. The Legion park has been used for picnics and carnivals, the Women's Club clubhouse is used for weekly dances of the high-school set, and the Y's Men's Club room is a recreation hall 6 nights a week.

Like Arvin clubs, the Dinuba associations tend to serve only certain elements in the population. While farm labor constitutes a third of the Dinuba population, it rarely belongs to social organizations in the community. Membership lists for the rotary women's clubs show no representatives of this group and only 8 percent of the American Legion membership are laborers.

Dinuba citizens have a complement of organizations which serve the community, and the number of persons who participate in them is greater. In Dinuba 45 percent of the families have a member who participates in some social activity, as against 32 percent in

TABLE 27.—*Families reporting participation in various classes of social organizations: Arvin and Dinuba*

Type of organization	Arvin		Dinuba	
	Number of families reporting	Percentage of all families	Number of families reporting	Percentage of all families
Service clubs [1]	13	10	42	20
Women's clubs [2]			19	9
Fraternal orders [3]	9	7	32	15
Parent-Teacher Association	14	11	14	7
Farm organizations [4]	9	7	24	12
Youth organizations	6	5	10	5
Church organizations	4	3	10	5
Unions	2	2	10	5
Others inside community	4	3	11	5
Others outside community	4	3	10	5
No participation	91	69	113	53

[1] This category includes in Arvin: Lions, Boosters, State guard; in Dinuba: Rotary, Y's Men's Club, merchants association, chamber of commerce, and American Legion.
[2] No women's club in Arvin.
[3] None meet in Arvin, though Arvin people belong; in Dinuba includes: Masons, Eastern Star, Rainbow Girls, De Molay, Independent Order of Odd Fellows, Modern Woodmen of America.
[4] Farm Center, Home Department, Associated Farmers, and (in Dinuba only) Grange.

Source: Schedule data.

Arvin. Table 27 shows that each major category of club, except the PTA and youth organization, has a larger participation in Arvin than in Dinuba.

Both the analysis of memberships and the schedule data show that in both communities the laborer rarely participates in any social organization. Table 28 shows the number and percent of the families in each occupation group having membership in any organization. This tabulation shows that the white-collar worker participates most fully, the farmer nearly as much, the town

TABLE 28.—*Families reporting participation in social organizations, classified by occupation of family head: Arvin and Dinuba*

Occupation group	Arvin			Dinuba		
	Total	Number reporting participation	Percentage	Total	Number reporting participation	Percentage
White-collar workers	10	7	70	32	27	84
Farmers	14	10	71	65	43	66
Farm labor	80	14	17	55	11	20
Other labor	20	8	40	37	16	43
Nonemployed	8	2	25	24	3	13
Total	132	41	31	[1] 213	100	47

[1] Information on 7 families lacking.

Source: Schedule data.

TABLE 29.—*Club memberships of persons 12 years old and over, classified by occupation of family head: Arvin and Dinuba*

Occupation groups	Arvin			Dinuba		
	Persons 12 and over	Memberships reported		Persons 12 and over	Memberships reported	
		Total	Per 100 persons		Total	Per 100 persons
White-collar worker	26	24	92	79	125	158
Farmer	37	46	124	156	89	57
Farm labor	240	17	7	156	20	13
Other labor	54	19	35	92	20	22
Nonemployed	15	3	20	32	5	16
Total	372	109	29	615	259	42

Source: Schedule data. Numbers refer to behavior of individuals in sample, not whole community.

laborer much less, and the farm laborer hardly at all. In Arvin the farmer and the white-collar worker participate equally, and the Arvin grower participates more frequently than the Dinuba farmer. There is somewhat more social participation among the Dinuba townspeople and farm laborers than among those groups in Arvin, but these differences are not great. A test of the statistical significance of these data shows that participation in clubs is highly associated with occupation status (appendix F).

The individual participation in organizations, as shown by the schedule data, is summarized in table 29. The number of memberships held by all members of the family 12 years old or over were recorded. No distinction is made between types of organization, membership in or outside of the community, or frequency of meetings. Basing these memberships on the number of persons 12 or over within the occupational groups and eliminating those who failed to answer this question, the number of memberships per 100 persons was calculated. This analysis further demonstrates the social segregation between farmer and white-collar worker on one hand and laborer on the other. This wide gulf exists in both communities, though there is somewhat more labor participation in Dinuba. It should be noted that in Arvin the farmers participate far more heavily in clubs than in Dinuba, where farmer memberships are but a third as great as memberships of whitecollar workers. Total participation is less in Arvin than in Dinuba, a difference which again is accounted for by the preponderance of laborers, who rarely participate in club activities because of the strong social barrier in both communities. These relationships are shown graphically in figure 14, along with other forms of participation.

OTHER SOCIAL PARTICIPATION

Organized club life is only one means of social participation. In order to obtain some appreciation of the nature of social life in the two communities, questions were included on the schedules designed to determine how many persons participated in other types of social activities. Six categories were included and an indication of the family member participating and the frequency of such participation. The six categories are: School events, other community events, dances, card parties or games, picnics, and movies. The last of these cannot be strictly considered a social event, since it does not require any active group participation and will be discussed separately.

Table 30 shows the number and percent of the families having members who participate in each of the five types of social activities (movies excluded) and the number reporting participation in some one of the five. Of these forms of recreation, picnics are the most frequent in both communities and about equally popular in each. The difference between Arvin and Dinuba is shown immediately in that only 58 percent of all families participate in social events in Arvin, while 71 percent do so in Dinuba. If those persons whose only form of recreation was picnics

TABLE 30.—*Families participating in social activities other than clubs and churches: Arvin and Dinuba*

Class of social activity	Arvin		Dinuba	
	Number reporting participation [1]	Percentage	Number reporting participation [1]	Percentage
School events	34	26	70	33
Other community events	12	9	86	40
Dances	19	14	49	23
Card parties	10	8	29	14
Picnics	52	39	91	43
All social events [2]	76	58	145	71

[1] Each family reported only once, no matter how many members participate, or how frequently or in how many types of events.
[2] Not the sum of column; represents all families participating in any one or more of above categories of social activity.

Source: Schedule data.

TABLE 31.—*Individuals participating in social activities other than clubs and churches: Arvin and Dinuba*

Class of social activity	Arvin		Dinuba	
	Number reporting participation	Percentage	Number reporting participation	Percentage
School events	88	16	203	28
Other community events	51	9	231	32
Dances	38	7	98	13
Card parties	18	3	55	8
Picnics	209	38	288	39

Source: Schedule data.

(which are usually family affairs) are eliminated, the Arvin participants would be reduced to 45 percent of the families, while the Dinuba participating families would not be reduced at all. Participation in community events and school affairs is relatively more popular in Dinuba than in Arvin. The failure of the community to provide opportunity must be considered a major cause of this lack of participation. Table 31 shows similar data, based upon individual participation rather than families. It represents more accurately the participation of individuals, demonstrates the degree to which total families participate in picnics and in general community events, but only a few members participate in the other activities.

Participants in general community events more nearly represent a Table 32 shows the participants by major occupational groupings, and relatively little difference is found. The Chi Square Test indicates that the probability of these occupational dif-

TABLE 32.—*Families reporting participation in social events other than clubs or churches, classified by occupation of head: Arvin and Dinuba*

Occupation group	Arvin		Dinuba	
	Number reporting participation	Percentage	Number reporting participation	Percentage
White-collar workers	8	80	28	93
Farm operator	9	70	44	72
Farm labor	43	54	37	74
Other labor	12	60	23	66
Nonemployed	4	50	13	56
Total	76	58	145	71

Source: Schedule data.

ferences being significant is relatively small, and the value of T for these communities is very close to zero (appendix F). That laborers participate in open social events very nearly as much as other groups shows that social participation is not foreign to the laborers' mode of life and that their failure to belong to clubs in both Arvin and Dinuba reflects the social barrier rather than any inherent reluctance to participate in social events. Striking, too, is the difference in the degree of social participation among farm labor families in Dinuba as compared with Arvin. It is clear that the greater opportunity for social activity coupled with a somewhat lessened social barrier has enabled the worker to find a richer social life. Social participation of the farm-operator group in the two communities is about the same.

Motion pictures have become the most important form of recreation to nearly all groups. Table 33 shows many more families attend movies in Arvin than all other forms of recreation combined, while in Dinuba as many attend movies as all other forms of recreation. This applies to families in practically all occupation groups to a like degree, though the nonemployed and the farmers find somewhat less use for this form of recreation. Movies are the sole reported form of recreation for over 30 percent of the Arvin families and for nearly 20 percent of the Dinuba families. The farm labor families are particularly dependent upon movies for their recreation, as this tabulation demonstrates.

TABLE 33.—*Motion pictures as a source of recreation for different occupation groups: Arvin and Dinuba*

Occupation group	Arvin				Dinuba			
	Families reporting movie attendance [1]		Families reporting movies as only recreation [2]		Families reporting movie attendance [1]		Families reporting movies as only recreation [2]	
	Number	Percent	Number	Percent	Number	Percent	Number	Percent
White-collar workers	9	90	1	10	28	93	2	7
Farm operator	10	77	3	13	39	64	8	13
Farm labor	69	86	29	36	45	82	16	29
Other labor	17	85	6	30	26	74	9	26
Nonemployed	5	63	2	25	7	30	3	13
Total	110	84	41	31	145	71	38	19

[1] All families reporting some member who attends motion pictures.
[2] All families who attend motion pictures in which no member participates in any other social activity.
SOURCE: Schedule data.

The social participation in Arvin and Dinuba has been summarized in graphic form in figure 14. This figure shows the difference in participation among farmers, white-collar workers, and laborers, and makes comparisons between the two communities and between five types of activities. School events and other community affairs are more frequently enjoyed in Dinuba than in

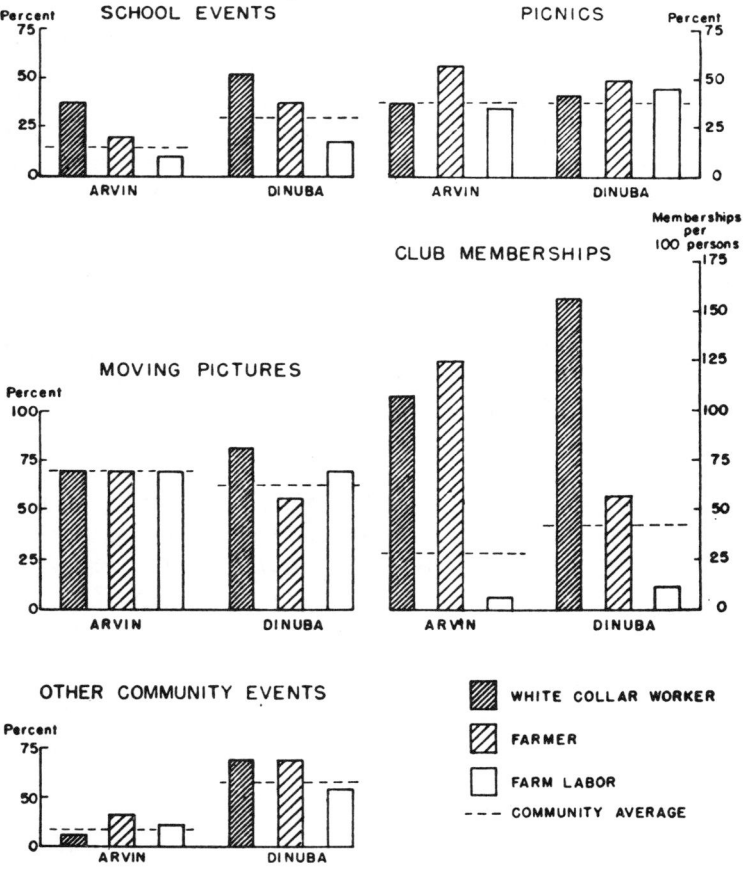

FIGURE No. 14

Arvin, and in general are more fully the province of the farmer and white-collar worker. Picnics and movies are more frequently family or individual affairs, and the occupational difference in participation is far less. There is less difference between the two communities in these categories of activity. Movies form the only category where Arvin participation is greater than Dinuba, and this is the least social of all forms of recreation.

Club participation remains the most striking differential between social classes. Among the white-collar workers in Arvin and Dinuba and the farmers in Arvin there is more than one membership for every person of 12 or over. Participation was not recorded among the younger group, and they were eliminated from all calculations. The ratio among laborers is only 1 membership for every 10 persons. The differential between Arvin and Dinuba is slight. Dinuba farmers participate far less than Arvin farmers do; Dinuba white-collar workers more.

These data show: (1) that Dinuba has a richer social life and more nearly full participation, (2) that laborers do not participate in the interpersonal types of social activity as frequently as other categories, but participate equally in the more individual forms of recreation, (3) laborers have hardly any participation in club activities where closed groups are involved and where social barriers are effective, and (4) this social differentiation is nearly equal in both communities.

THE PROBLEMS OF YOUTH

The conditions under which the young people are brought to adulthood is one criterion of the quality of a community. Since it is a sphere of activity in which the local population has a great deal of influence, the youth programs reflect community spirit.

Juvenile delinquency is a universal problem varying only in degree; it has been a particularly great problem during war years, and people in both Arvin and Dinuba were concerned with it. No statistical data were available on delinquency rates, but verbal testimony is indicative. This testimony was obtained from various school officials, county officers, and local leaders, and represents informal local opinion.

Such testimony brought out that the problem exists in both

make the Dinuba residential areas attractive. The paving and lighting, along with the sewage system, was established in the postwar boom period at excessive costs. At that time Dinuba was confidently expected to expand into a community of much larger size, and this expectation and high raisin prices conspired to create a spirit of overoptimism. The result was overexpansion, with the inevitable collapse that caused heartaches in the community. Assessments ran high, the town was overbuilt, houses and other property were lost, and the community came to the verge of bankruptcy. Prevalent local opinion does not blame this on corruption within the community, but rather on a combination of overoptimism and sharp sales practices during the inflation period after the last war.

A process of refinancing has been carried on during the past 7 years. The result is that the town is virtually debt-free. The largest block of bondholders agreed to accept 60 cents on the dollar for outstanding debts, which are now fully paid. Other bonds are still outstanding, but the city is trying to buy them up as fast as possible. The city took over property for taxes, and has sold most of it, so that it has money to buy bonds, but the holders are now unwilling to part with them, as there is a good rate of interest on these investments.

The two parks are exceptionally well kept. One is near the center of town, the other larger one at the outskirts. It has playground and picnic facilities. The schools furnish additional playgrounds and playing fields. The city has planted trees in a third park, but will not plant shrubs and lawn until the trees are sufficiently mature.

A chamber of commerce sponsored dinner on postwar planning, which took place the first evening of field study in the community, demonstrated the type of civic cooperation, the quality of leadership, the nature of local friction and rivalry, and the spirit of loyalty among community leaders. It was held at one of the churches; the ladies' aid prepared and served the dinner as a means of increasing their funds. The dinner was sponsored by two business organizations cooperatively, and about 150 persons participated in the event. More than a dozen civic leaders spoke on topics ranging from industrial activities and city finances to the development of a youth center and the planting of victory gardens. The ultimate purpose was to develop interest in postwar planning

communities, but is far more severe in Arvin than Dinuba. In both communities cases involving sexual promiscuity had recently been reported, and were mentioned by the citizens of the two towns. The Dinuba incident was a single affair and was played up in local papers, while the Arvin case involved a number of students over a period of time. Theft and pilfering were reported from both communities, but gambling apparently was a severe problem in Arvin only. In Dinuba, the justice of the peace considered the problem noteworthy, while the school principals, the mayor, and the PTA president stated that a few cases came up from time to time but the problem was not severe. The justice pointed out that it was associated with broken homes and poor economic conditions, and all agreed that the incidence of misbehavior was highest among the labor families. In Arvin the school principal, one merchant, and two of the ministers found the problem great and emphasized sexual promiscuity and gambling. The justice of the peace, one county sheriff, and one minister admitted to a real problem but did not emphasize it, while another sheriff and the PTA president did not consider it severe. While these accounts were at variance, they suggest that if the Dinuba situation is described as normal, the social conditions of Arvin youth must be considered bad. The association of juvenile delinquency with the laboring class, particularly children of white field hands, was generally agreed upon.

For purposes of the present study, community efforts to prevent juvenile delinquency are far more significant measures than the incidence of delinquency itself. For the latter may have many causes, while the efforts to prevent delinquency by means of social programs are direct testimonial to the degree of community solidarity and its social quality.

In Arvin, at the time of field study, the only active program was a series of baseball games for the older boys. This had been in progress for several weeks, and had the support of the sheriff's office and unofficial aid from the Lions Club. In addition there was a small Boy Scout troop and a Camp Fire Girl organization.

One Arvin merchant who took an active interest in community welfare became alarmed by the juvenile problem and determined to find why no county funds had been spent on playground facilities in Arvin. He discovered that no request had been made, and as a result of his action, Arvin secured lighting and equipment for the empty lot that had been loaned for use as a playing field by a private company. The lack of leadership was constantly cited as the cause for the dearth of facilities. The school superintendent contended that the Boy Scouts should be led by persons other than teachers but that nobody else would take the job and that it was often difficult to get the board of review out for a review meeting. The school itself sponsors a program of athletics for the children, and the school has a safety club and a youth council. These activities do not extend beyond school hours, and do not reach any of the young people beyond elementary-school age.

In Dinuba there are two Boy Scout troops, each with its own clubhouse. These are sponsored by the Rotary and the American Legion. A third troop is being planned and a Cub Scout pack has recently been organized. There is also a Girl Scout group sponsored by two teachers. The Masonic Lodge has a Rainbow Girls and a DeMolay group; there are weekly dances held by the high-school students at the women's club, and the Y's Men's club maintains a recreation hall.

This hall was created out of an old store building. A paid supervisor is on duty each night, and facilities for billiards, table tennis, shuffleboard and for reading and the cultivation of hobbies are all available there. The place accommodates from 30 to 80 boys each night in the week without any cost to them. As a public service, the establishment of this recreation hall deserves special merit because it was made available to the Dinuba youth at a real sacrifice in time and money by a group of citizens. It contrasts with the endeavor of a few public-spirited personalities who attempted to create a weekly "fun night" at the Arvin school and failed because of the lack of interest among community leaders and their unwillingness to make the necessary sacrifices.

These activities in Dinuba are over and above those made possible by the schools and the general park facilities available to the boys and girls. The difference between the two communities can be summarized as follows: An Arvin high-school youth can participate in ball games once or twice a week and can go to Scout meetings. Otherwise his only recreation is at the movies, a commercial skating rink open during the summer, or the pool halls. A Dinuba youth can go to a dance, play either on the school grounds under supervision or at a park, participate in high-school activities, can go to Scout meeting or to the DeMolay (or Rainbow) meeting, can spend his evenings in the recreation center, or can participate with others under supervision in one or more hobbies. There are three moving-picture theaters and a commercial dance hall, if he wishes to pay for his recreation. County libraries are available in both communities. Obviously the opportunities for social contacts and personal development are greater for the Dinuba youth than for those of Arvin.

It should be added that the Dinuba facilities are not locally considered adequate. Neither community has a swimming pool, and this lack is very keenly felt. There is insufficient playground equipment in the park, and there is no counterpart to the recreation center for the use of girls. At one time there was a WPA-sponsored recreation program which, according to the justice of the peace, lessened juvenile misbehavior. High-school students presented a symposium to the Dinuba Rotarians on juvenile delinquency and concluded that more facilities were needed.

THE SOCIAL ROLE OF THE CHURCH

Arvin has the following churches: Catholic, Union Congregational, Church of the Nazarene, Assembly of God Church, Missionary Baptist, Church of Christ, and Pentecostal. At some times there is a second Pentecostal church serving the Mexicans, and there is a group of adherents to Jehovah's Witnesses.

In Dinuba there are: Presbyterian, Christian Church, Methodist, Baptist, Seventh-Day Adventist (two groups), Zion Mennonite, Mennonite Brethren, Church of the Nazarene, Church of God, Assembly of God, Church of Christ, Four Square Church, Korean Presbyterian, and an Armenian Church. Prior to evacuation there was a Japanese Buddhist group and there has also been a Mexican Methodist congregation, while Mormons, Catholics, and Lutherans have meetings periodically in Dinuba, though no regular church. Both in the number of congregations and in the total amount of church facilities available, the Dinuba community is richer.

Despite the large number of churches in both communities, only about two-thirds of the population are either members or attend church regularly.[16] Table 34 shows that only 59 percent of Arvin persons 12 or over are church participants, against 72 percent in Dinuba. Each occupational group in Dinuba shows this greater participation. In both communities farmers have the highest record of memberships (leaving out nonemployed), farm labor next, while white-collar workers and other labor participate least.

TABLE 34.—*Individual church participation among persons 12 years old and over, classified by occupation groups: Arvin and Dinuba*

Occupation group	Arvin			Dinuba		
	Number in group	Participants	Percent	Number in group	Participants	Percent
White-collar worker	26	12	46	79	48	61
Farm operator	37	25	68	156	123	79
Farm labor	240	152	64	156	109	70
Other labor	54	25	46	92	56	61
Nonemployed	15	7	47	34	34	100
Total	372	221	59	517	370	72

N. B.—Church participants are all persons over 12 who either are members of a church in good standing, or who attend church at least 12 times per year. Number in group includes only persons 12 years old or over.

Source: Schedule data.

While club membership is a function of income and occupation, and nonorganized social activities show slight differentials between occupation groups, no such generalization can be made for participation in religious institutions. The percent variation between occupational categories in Arvin ran from 46 to 68 of the several major occupational groups; for Dinuba from 61 to 100 percent. The differential did not meet the Chi Square test of significance in either community. (See appendix F).

Interestingly, there is a tendency for low-income groups in Arvin to belong to churches more frequently than high-income groups, the direct opposite to the tendency in other forms of social participation. This is shown by a negative association between high occupation status and church membership—an association which fully meets the Chi Square test of significance. This partly explains why only one church is supported by the Arvin elite.

Since social criteria have been reflected in church participation

[16] All persons who belong to a church, whether or not they attend, and all persons who attend 12 or more times per year, even though not a member, are included in this count. Only persons 12 years old or older were included in this analysis.

elsewhere in California,[17] it is appropriate to examine the manner in which different elements of the population are segregated in existing religious institutions. In order to make such an analysis it is necessary to evaluate the social position of the different congregations in each community.[18] Eliminating memberships in groups without a formal organization in either town, a fourfold classification is suggested. Most congregations can be rated, on a pecuniary standard of values, into degrees of social standing, but some cannot. In the latter category, are the Catholid churches and those congregations which have a fairly recent history of persecution and wandering or for other reasons maintain strong in-group loyalties. Mennonite and Seventh-Day Adventist churches are included here. Congregations such as the Korean Presbyterian and Armenian churches, which serve only special racial or ethnic groups, are also placed in this category. These examples make up the Dinuban category of strong in-group churches, while in Arvin only the Catholic church was so classed.

The remaining three categories represent the social standing of the church in terms of dominant pecuniary standards. The upper group includes the earlier deonominations of Protestantism; in Arvin the Union Congregational and in Dinuba the Presbyterian, Christian, Methodist, and Baptist. They universally have substantial buildings and are the first recognized by the elite in the population. The second group is comprised of those newer denominations of Protestantism which have firmly established themselves in the local community. In both towns the Nazarene and Assembly of God churches are so classed. These congregations have good structures, professional pastors, and are recognized by the community as good substantial congregations. The third category consists of those churches which have poor facilities— usually unpainted frame structures without any elegance. Generally they are served by lay ministers. The elite hardly

[17]The role of the church in the California town has been described in Walter R. Goldschmidt's Class Denominationalism in the California Rural Churches, Journal of American Sociology, vol. XLIX, January 1944.
[18]It must be made clear that this analysis of church standing does not in any way reflect an evaluation either of the religious doctrines or of the quality of the membership of the separate congregations, but has reference only to the social status of the group within the community, with reference to community values, as the sociologists use that concept.

recognize their existence. In Arvin this group includes the Missionary Baptist, Pentecostal Church, Church of Christ, and Jehovah's Witnesses; in Dinuba the Church of God, the Four Square Church, and the Church of Christ.

Using this classification, we find that there are four churches of high and more or less equal status in Dinuba, but only one in Arvin, and that they account for 37 percent of the membership in Dinuba and 14 percent of Arvin churchgoers (table 35). Churches of lesser social standing are predominant in Arvin but unimportant in Dinuba. A large number of Dinubans go to other

TABLE 35.—*Proportion of persons from independently employed families and from labor families participating in churches of different social status: Arvin and Dinuba*

Church category	Arvin						Dinuba					
	Farmers and white-collar workers		All labor		Total [1]		Farmers and white-collar workers		All labor		Total [1]	
	Number	Percent	Number	Percent	Number	Percent	Number	Percent	Number	Percent	Number	Percent
I. High status	15	40	15	8	31	14	87	51	42	25	136	37
II. Intermediate status	8	22	38	21	46	21	4	2	7	4	12	3
III. Low status	5	14	69	39	80	36	14	8	24	15	51	14
IV. In-group churches	9	24	40	23	49	22	33	20	41	25	82	22
V. Other	0	0	10	6	10	5	9	5	12	7	25	7
VI. Outside community	0	0	5	3	5	2	24	14	39	24	64	17
Total	37	100	177	100	221	100	171	100	165	100	370	100

[1] Includes 7 nonemployed in Arvin, 34 in Dinuba.
Source: Schedule data.

communities because of their desire to participate in particular denominations, and because there are a number of other churches within a few miles of the community. Sixty percent of Arvin laborers go to churches of the newer sects with less social status in the community, against but 36 percent of the independently employed. A similar differential between the two occupation groups is found in Dinuba. While all groups go to church to very nearly the same extent, they do not go to the same churches but are segregated along occupational lines. The degree of association is shown in the table of appendix F.

Approaching the data from a different source, the pattern of membership in certain churches can be shown. Table 36 shows the occupational break-down of the three leading Protestant churches in Arvin, and five of the churches in Dinuba. Figure 15 summarizes this tabulation and shows the marked divergence between these congregations with respect to the means of livelihood of their members. Verbal testimony indicated that laborers only belonged to the remaining Arvin Protestant Congregations. The churches of high social status in Dinuba as in Arvin, have few farm workers among their members, but there are more churches which serve a mixed congregation and more persons who participate in church affairs together with persons from other walks of life.

TABLE 36.—*Occupation of members of selected churches in Arvin and Dinuba*

ARVIN

Occupation group	Congregational		Nazarene		Assembly of God	
	Number	Percent	Number	Percent	Number	Percent
White-collar	23	19	16	29	10	10
Farm operator	72	58	5	10	0	0
Farm labor	10	8	16	29	81	77
Other labor	19	15	17	32	14	13
Total	124	100	54	100	105	100
Nonemployed	6		4		7	

DINUBA

Occupation group	First Presbyterian		Christian		Zion Mennonites		Church of Nazarene		Assembly of God	
	Number	Percent	Number	Percent	Number	Percent	Number	Percent	Number	Percent
White-collar	102	47	54	38	16	8	17	18	20	22
Farm operator	94	43	68	48	141	72	35	37	33	37
Farm labor	6	3	4	3	¹ 22	12	22	24	23	25
Other labor	15	7	16	11	16	8	20	21	14	16
Total	217	100	142	100	195	100	94	100	90	100
Nonemployed	34		38		28		17		23	

¹ Includes some unspecified labor.
Source: Schedule data.

In Arvin there were clear expressions of opinion as to the social standing of the churches. Local citizens can and regularly did rate them. There is a similar social hierarchy in Dinuba, but it is not so clearly marked, and there are far more churches serving small social groups isolated because of a common background rather than because of their social or economic status in the community.

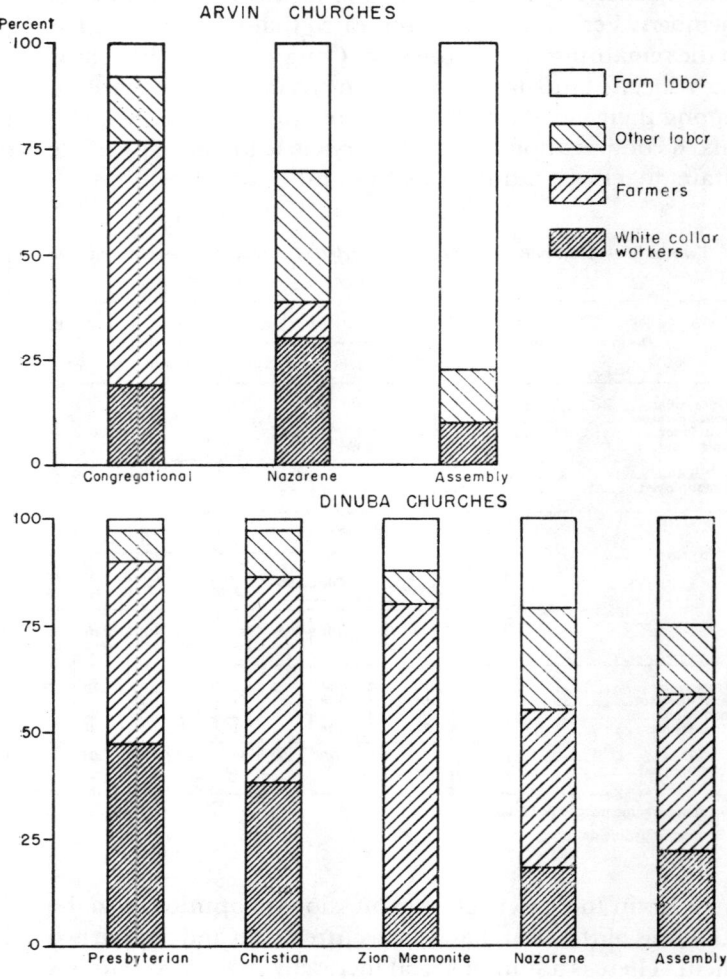

FIGURE No. 15

SOCIAL EVALUATIONS

Thus far the description of the social life in Arvin and Dinuba has largely rested upon factual data, with a minimum of descriptive material and subjective evaluation. In order to develop a rounded picture, the evaluation of community life made by the residents themselves must be recorded and the evidence of the spirit of the communities presented.

Arvin residents generally recognize the limitations of their community; some do not care, others are concerned but do not take action, while a few make an effort to improve the community. It is this last group which participates in Booster Club and Lions Club activities, and which endeavors to get a park, high school, and other facilities for Arvin. But there are too few who can and will devote their time and energy to the endless, and often thankless, task of community improvement.

At a Booster Club meeting, when this study was being discussed, one community leader said:

> We think we have a pretty good town and that we have done a lot for Arvin but we have to admit that we don't stack up very well against Dinuba. They have a high school, paved streets, good buildings, and so forth.

A small farmer blamed the poor quality of the Arvin community on the fact of absentee farm ownership and farm operation, and the fact that nobody made Arvin his permanent home. "I venture to say that 80 percent of the people here have no roots in the community," he said. He admitted many were buying their homes, but said that this was only because it was necessary to buy in order to have a place to live. Concerning this impermanence one woman who had come to Arvin as an agricultural worker said, "The trouble is mostly that people don't feel permanent here. Now we came here 9 years ago and we never expected to be permanent here. People feel transient." This woman felt Arvin was a poor place to raise children because there were no facilities for them and all they had to do was "lounge around the pool halls." The impermanence of the situation affects business people as well as laborers. One merchant said that "the trouble is that no one here plans for the future. People who start stores do not build them for permanent investments but build them cheaply with the idea of making as much money as quickly as possible while times are good. This does not lead to the kind of community where a man can plan for the future and set up a business that will go to his children."

A minister said of Arvin:

> The big farmers are not interested in the town; they go to Bakersfield or Los Angeles for all their wants and don't care whether the town is here or not. There is practically no one who is interested in the welfare of the community. The church should take care of that, but it can't because its congregation is made up of transient people who do not have a stake in the community.

Another minister said:

> Frankly, this is the worst town I have ever seen. I don't think there is another like it.

He pointed to the absence of sidewalks, and blamed the lack on the fact that there were not enough citizens interested in working for the community welfare. He went on to enumerate other failings, such as the failure to incorporate and the lack of parks.

This harsh judgment of the community is coupled with a feeling that the community has the potentialities of growth and improvement. For 25 years a nucleus of small farmers and merchants has existed upon which the town could build. The Booster Club has been in existence for nearly this length of time, and it and the Lions Club are filled with people who consider Arvin their home and want and expect it to become a better place. Yet they are evidently too small a group to make a thriving community comparable to Dinuba.

Criticisms in Dinuba were made of the operation of one or another civic function or of the activities of some club; they never reached the level of community condemnation. There was antagonism between parents who want their children to have an opportunity to dance and those who consider dancing morally reprehensible. Conflict of such kind, stemming from differing moral values, is to be found in every community. On the other hand, one merchant picked Dinuba as a place to start his business after he had spent several years traveling through the area, because he felt that it was the best town in which to raise a family.

One measure of community solidarity is the degree to which people feel an allegiance to the community. As a measure of such sentiment, the schedule included the question: "What do you consider your home town?" This question was always asked in this naive form and the primary response recorded. Table 37 shows the responses, first by occupation and second by years residence. Sixty-two percent of the Arvin residents considered Arvin their home town; 87 percent of the Dinubans considered that community their home town. The remainder indicated a former residence as their home town. In Dinuba four persons referred to a neighboring community as their home town as a result of the imperfect community boundaries that are inevitable. These are excluded from the analysis, along with those who did not respond to the question. The results of this question can be considered a rough measure of the degree of community solidarity and feeling of permanence.

TABLE 37.—*Persons who consider the local community as "home town" in Arvin and Dinuba* [1]

	Arvin			Dinuba		
	Total responses [2]	Arvin as home town	Percent	Total responses [2]	Dinuba as home town	Percent
By occupation:						
Farmer and white collar worker	24	20	83	89	81	91
Farm labor	77	42	55	55	43	78
All other	28	18	64	58	51	88
Total	129	80	62	202	175	87
By year of arrival:						
Before 1910	0	0	0	29	29	100
1911–29	25	21	84	80	80	100
1930–39	40	34	85	45	38	84
1940–42	36	19	53	23	15	65
1943–44	28	6	21	25	13	52
Total	129	80	62	202	175	87

[1] Analysis of responses to the question: "What is your home town?" See schedule, appendix A.
[2] Persons indicating neighboring town or failing to respond were eliminated from the analysis.
Source: Schedule data.

Laborers in both communities display the least interest in the community, as would be expected. Similarly, the length of residence plays an important part in the expression of this attitude. In every occupation category and in every length-of-residence category except one, a smaller proportion considers Arvin its home town than considers Dinuba its home town. Even among residents of 15 or more years in Arvin there is an appreciable group which does not consider that community as its home.

THE SOCIAL STRUCTURE IN ARVIN AND DINUBA

The analysis of the association between occupation, income, and the many aspects of social participation and social conditions demonstrates that these characteristics are closely interrelated. Social cleavages separate different segments of the population, and these groups or social classes form a status hierarchy. In some significant respects the social structure of Arvin and Dinuba is alike; in other respects it is different.

While the analysis in the preceding sections has not differentiated social status beyond occupational status, such a differentiation can be made. Table 38 summarizes the more important data on social participation for Arvin and Dinuba. It includes only information on occupation, income, level of living, condition of the home, club participation, and class of church, since these are the items which most clearly reflect social status.

TABLE 38.—*Summary of important social differentiations: Arvin and Dinuba*

Item	Arvin	Dinuba
	Percent	Percent
Farmers, merchants, and professionals as percent of total population [1]	17	43
Percent of population receiving over $3,250 annual income [2]	16	21
Percent of population in upper fourth in level of living index [3]	18	38
Percent of population in upper fourth in condition of home index [4]	12	36
Percent of top ranking club memberships in farmer and white-collar group [5]	95	94
Percent of top ranking church memberships in farmer and white-collar group [6]	76	88

[1] From table 22.
[2] From table 23.
[3] From figure 9. Includes all with index of 37 and over, or 24 percent of combined sample.
[4] From figure 11. Includes all with index of 9 (perfect score) or 27 percent of combined sample.
[5] From table 26. Includes Booster and Lions in Arvin and Rotary and Women's Club in Dinuba.
[6] From table 35. Includes Congregational Church in Arvin and First Presbyterian and Christian in Dinuba.

It will be seen that the upper bracket in Arvin represents from 12 to 18 percent of the families for each of the first four items indicated, while similar break-downs include from 21 to 43 percent in Dinuba. This leads immediately to the general conclusion that the upper class in Dinuba includes not only a greater number of people, but actually a much larger proportion. The next two items on the table give us an indication of the degree to which this small group dominates social activities in the two communities. It is readily seen that the small group generally includes a dominant proportion of those social activities which bear status in the community.

If we examine more closely the individual cases, we can obtain more evidence of social differentiation. In Arvin there are 10 families in the sample of 132 who were in the top fourth of income, of level-of-living index, and of the condition of the home index. Niine of these were either merchants or farm operators. These nine families either belonged to the top-ranking church or to none at all. The 23 persons 12 years old or over in this group held a total of 53 memberships, including all reported memberships in the Lions Club and all but one in the Boosters. Another group of eight farmer and white-collar families having good incomes and living conditions (i.e., above median in both categories) can be separated. This group has some members in churches other than that with the highest social standing, 1 of its group is a Booster, and among them hold 15 club memberships. The remaining seven families in the farmer-white-collar group do not participate in the older congregation, and among them hold only two club memberships. On the basis of what we know about social status in the community, we may therefore say that this last group has a status commensurate with the laborers.

These facts indicate that the upper class in Arvin comprises between 10 and 15 percent of the total resident population. Their ranks are not significantly augmented from among the labor group. Selecting those among the laborers who are in the upper half (not quartile) of income, level-of-living index, and index of home conditions, we find a group of 11 families. Only one of these belongs to the upper-class church while there are only nine club memberships among them. One skilled laborer in the group might qualify, since he participates in social activities rather frequently.

After eliminating the occupational group which meets the general criteria of upper class, there remain 115 families in the sample, representing 87 percent of the population. Of this group, only 21 hold memberships in local organizations, while 71 families belong to some local church. In all, about 75 families participate in some local activity, though these ties are frequently tenuous and often only with a handful of other persons with equally tenuous ties. If we eliminated those who only participated in the newer religious sects with but slight ties to the whole community, the number would be reduced from 75 to 50, or from two-thirds to less than half of the total population in this status group. Those who participate in organized social events also more frequently participate in group recreation than those who belong only to the church or to no organization at all. Twenty-seven families reported no membership in any community organization and no form of social participation other than movies or picnics (which are usually individual family affairs). This is a fifth of the total population and a fourth of the lower group.

The independent class of Arvin includes between 10 and 15 percent of the families, and is made up of farm operators and merchants, though such occupation status does not insure membership. They are split evenly between two groups—an elite whose status is established and a middle group whose status is less clear. A few families (about 4 in the sample) participate more fully in the society of Bakersfield than they do in local events.

The elite are universally in the highest income brackets and have material possessions and housing conditions which place them at the top of these categories as well. It is comprised mostly of farmers with a few from the merchant-professional category. As a group they hold nearly as many club memberships as all the remainder of the population combined. They frequently participate in the social events in Bakersfield and occasionally in Los Angeles, and are highly mobile, both in the geographic and social sense of that term. If they belong to any church, it is the upper status church.

The middle group has a lower income, poorer living conditions, and generally displays less evidence of social status in the community than the elite. It is made up of the remaining merchants and farmers, with perhaps a few skilled workers among them. They more rarely participate in city activities. This group has some members in churches of intermediate status.

The largely dependent class is made up almost entirely of farm laborers, though a small group of merchants and farm operators, on the basis of evidence of their social participation and living conditions, must be included. On the whole, this group participates very little in any activity other than the church, and rarely in the older church. They never enter the leading clubs. As a group they comprise about 85 percent of the total population, yet they remain outside the sphere of most community activities. A few of the skilled laborers with permanent jobs occasionally breach the line between this group and the upper class, but this is rare.

The church is the most frequent sphere for social contact among members of this class. Nearly two-thirds participate in this form of activity, while less than 20 percent are club members. In this group there are 34 persons (30 percent) whose only social activity is the church, 23 who only participate in community events and other nonorganized activity, and 27 who do not participate at all. Most of these latter groups have no ties whatsoever to Arvin, and the dependent class may be differentiated between those with local ties and those without any social ties whatsoever. Nearly half of the laborers did not consider Arvin their home town. Those who display little or no social participation rarely have an income or level of living index above the median point.

The social structure of Dinuba cannot be reduced to a linear scale with the same degree of accuracy. The greater wealth of institutions and the larger and more diversified stable population combine to create a far more complex situation. The dominant community pattern must be viewed as similar to Arvin, with a group of well-off persons in the upper ranges of level of living on one end of the scale and a group of impecunious laborers with poor living conditions and little or no social participation on the other.

There are 25 farmers and merchant families in the sample who fall in the upper-income brackets and in each of the measurement of living conditions (one laborer family also fell into this group). This 12 percent of the population forms an upper class, but its members must be augmented by another 20 to 25 percent who fall lower in the scale on these measurements, but who participate freely in the same churches and clubs. While there are gradations of prestige within this group, it would be difficult to make a segregation of the sort that was possible in Arvin.

Of the remaining two-thirds, there are quite a few whose social life revolves about their church. These groups are usually centered about the Mennonite, Lutheran, and Seventh-Day Adventist congregations, which develop a strong in-group loyalty and are capable of satisfying completely the social outlets of a large proportion of their congregations. Included among these are many of the stabler small farmers, most of whom own their own land. Such people are usually bypassed by the dominant community pattern of pecuniary values, having their own special interests and spheres of activity. They are not outsiders to community activity in the same sense that farm laborers are. The differences lie in that they have a stable tenure and a community of interests with a segment of the population, and that they can move into the social sphere of the larger community at will, but remain outside by choice. The laborer, on the other hand, does not have this stability, this participation in a small in-group, and can only with great difficulty become a part of the large community. Many of the more stable farm laborers—often farmers' sons—associate with these special groups, and mobility from laborer to farmer status is apparently more common while less social connotations are involved in this occupation differential.

Only a small segment of the population is without any ties whatsoever. Only 16 in our sample of 206 (8 percent) failed completely to participate in community affairs, compared to about 20 percent in Arvin. Only 13 percent rejected Dinuba as their home town. Some others have only the most tenuous ties with the community, but this group is much smaller, proportionately and absolutely, than the comparable Arvin group.

The fundamental similarity between Arvin and Dinuba is that there are upper and lower classes with little or no common interest or social intercourse; the one made up of independently employed persons and the other made up of wage laborers. The fundamental differences are, first, that in Arvin the upper group is extremely small while the lower group is quite large, whereas in Dinuba the upper group comprises about a third of the population. Second, in Arvin there is a sharp break between the upper group and the remainder, while in Dinuba there are even gradations from one to the other. Furthermore, there appears to be more opportunity for social intercourse, if not between the top and bottom, at least between successive groups so that social contact and mobility are possible without a change of occupation status.

CHAPTER XVI

RETAIL BUSINESS IN ARVIN AND DINUBA

INTRODUCTION

Retail business data for enterprises in the two communities were secured from the records of the California State Board of Equalization.[19] The board, along with other duties, keeps the records and accounts of the California sales and use tax, which covers virtually all retail sales with the exception of retail foods. Records are kept, not only on taxable sales but on total retail sales of all enterprises selling taxable items. The Research and Statistics Department of the Board, in cooperation with the Bureau of Agricultural Economics, analyzed the retail sales data for all rural communities in Madera, Kern, and Tulare Counties. They were made in early 1944 and refer to the 12-month period beginning October 1942 and ending September 1943. The use of this time period was dictated by the nature of the data available. Additional material is available on business enterprises from the Dun & Bradstreet Reference Book (January 1942).

NUMBER OF ENTERPRISES AND GROSS VOLUME OF BUSINESS

There is a marked difference in the volume of business and the number of business enterprises between the community of small farms and that of large farms. On virtually identical resource bases, as measured by dollar volume of production of agricultural commodities, the Dinuba merchants do approximately 4⅓ million dollars' worth of retail trade as against about 2½ million dollars' worth among Arvin merchants. On a population basis the dollar volume is somewhat less, but is nevertheless different to a significant degree. The number of business establishments in Dinuba is more than twice the number in Arvin, showing that the small farm population supports small business to a far greater extent.

[19]For a full discussion of the methods of developing these data, see appendix G.

According to the records of the board of equalization, there were 62 enterprises in Arvin holding a franchise to sell taxable items in the fall of 1943 and 141 in Dinuba, or a ratio of 4 to 9. Dun & Bradstreet listings for January 1942 show even greater divergence with 60 as against 155, or a ratio of less than 4 to 10. Retail trade reported to Arvin for the 12-month period studied was $2,535,000; for Dinuba during the same period it was $4,383,000 (fig. 16). This means that Arvin enjoyed $103 of retail trade for every $100 value of agricultural products, while Dinuba had $171 for every $100 value of agricultural product. Relating retail trade to resident population, we find $407 spent per person in Arvin and $592 per person in Dinuba.[20] These facts are summarized in table 39.

TABLE 39.—*Comparison of business enterprises and volume of business: Arvin and Dinuba*

	Arvin	Dinuba
Number of retail business enterprises	62	141
Volume of retail trade	$2,535,000	$4,383,000
Volume of trade per $100 agricultural production	$103	$171
Volume of trade per person	$407	$592

Source: Board of Equalization data.

The retail sales were reported by classes, and these have been brought together under nine headings in table 40. This summary was made in part to obscure data which might reveal the nature of any single enterprise and in part to simplify the materials. In each of these classes, with a single exception, the volume of retail trade is greater in Dinuba than in Arvin. The volume of trade per person is greater in 7 of the 9 categories (figs. 17 and 18).

Examination of table 40 shows that expenditure for food, for drugs and sundries, for liquor, and for gasoline and automotive supplies is not very different between the two communities. The last of them is the largest single item of expenditure, and on a per

[20] Analysis of the retail potentials in communities with differing size of farm units, based upon actual farm practices in California's Central Valley, is presented by J. Karl Lee in his study, Economics of Scale of Farming in the Southern San Joaquin Valley, Calif.. The relative intensity of operation, the greater use of labor on small farms, and most particularly the difference in distribution of farm income all make for greater economic prosperity among merchants and townspeople in the rural community serving small farms.

NUMBER OF BUSINESS ENTERPRISES AND GROSS VOLUME OF RETAIL SALES

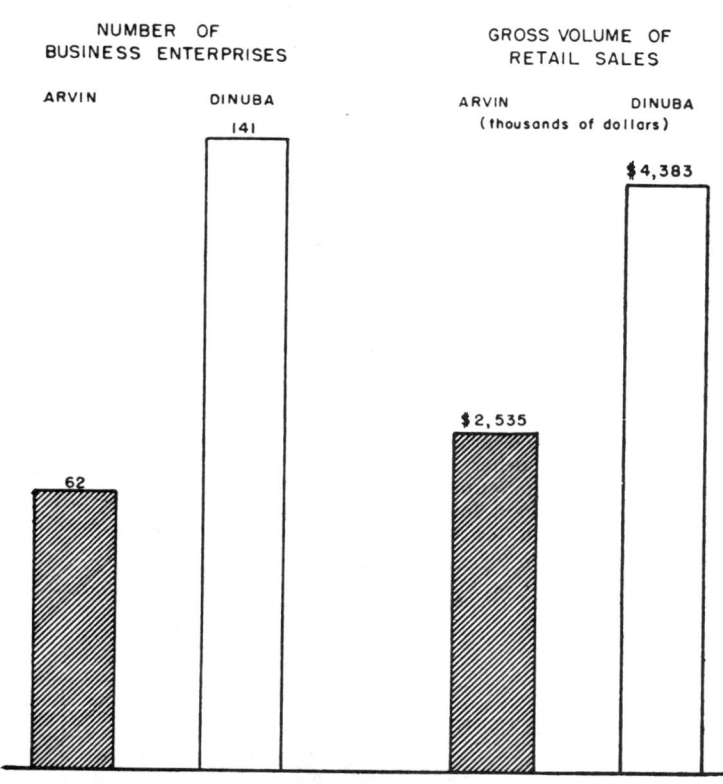

SOURCE: RECORDS OF THE STATE BOARD OF EQUALIZATION

FIGURE No. 16

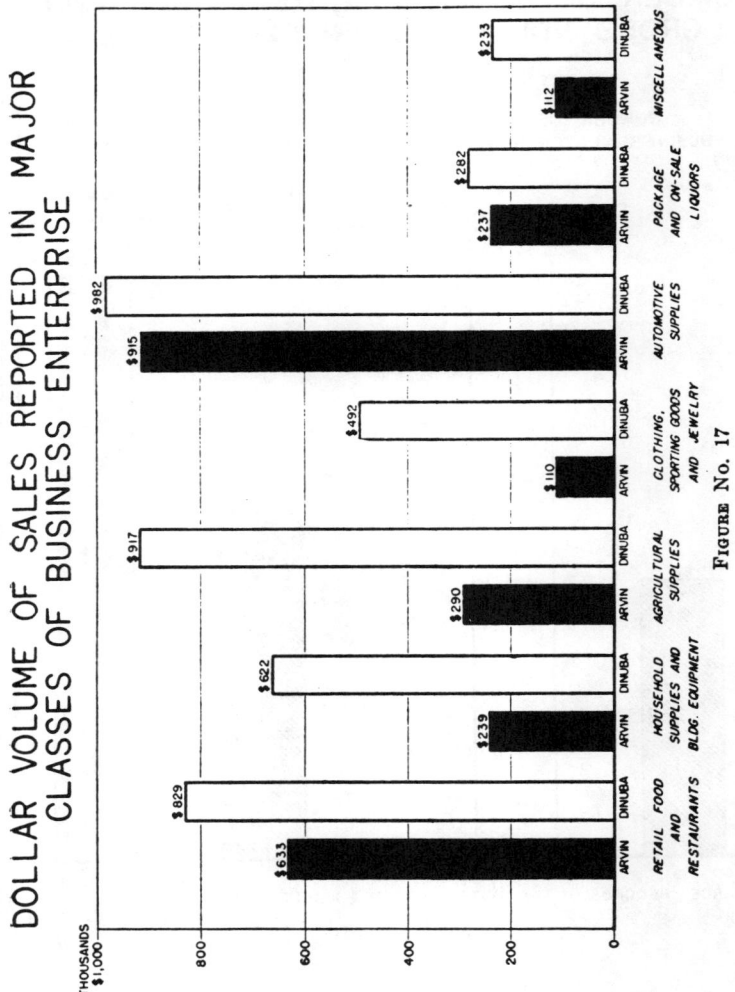

Figure No. 17

DISTRIBUTION OF RETAIL SALES AMONG VARIOUS CLASSES OF ENTERPRISE

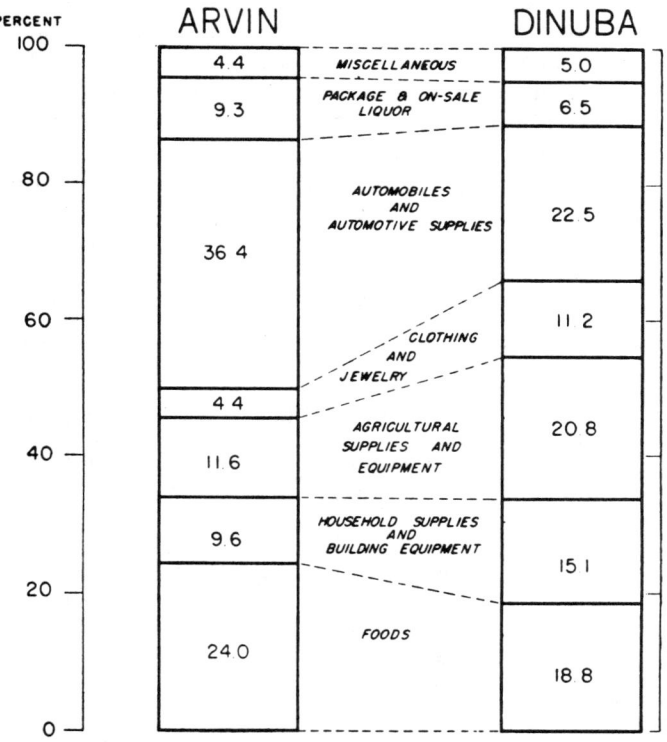

SOURCE: GROSS VOLUME OF SALES REPORTED TO CALIFORNIA STATE BOARD OF EQUALIZATION.

FIGURE No. 18

endeavors to bring together all classes in the community. Its service is to promote the welfare of the school and develop parent interest in school activities. The primary problem of the PTA is to maintain interest and develop adequate leadership. This problem is acute in Arvin, and it is difficult to get anyone to serve as chairman and to get many mothers to participate. The chairman at the time of the field studies was particularly anxious to develop the inherent value in the organization. She made two attempts to develop recreational facilities for the children. On Halloween the PTA put on a carnival, which was formerly a regular event but which had not been held for several years. The various organizations and groups had concessions, and in this way the PTA made quite a bit of money. It was a success from the recreational standpoint, as the children came in great numbers and talked of it for weeks later. However, there were some people who objected to it because the children trampled the grounds around the community hall and did other minor damage. The other activity was a "fun night." For 2 hours each Friday night schoolrooms were made available for children to play games. It was difficult to get sufficient chaperones; and, according to the chairman, the very persons who complained about the lack of facilities for their children consistently refused to help in these events. Some objected to the children dancing, others insisted that it close at 9 p.m., which didn't give the children a satisfactory and full evening. The chairman went on to say: "Some women felt this was for the riffraff and the poor people and they would not let their nice girls go to the fun night, and this was wrong and in direct opposition to the very purpose of the fun nights." After seven evenings the program was abandoned because of lack of interest and insufficient parent participation. Other persons had spoken of the rowdyism and vandalism at these community events, but neither the chairman nor the sheriff considered this a serious problem. "What," she said, "if they do a little damage? Why have these facilities unless you use them?"

The chairman felt that the participation of labor parents was very desirable and endeavored to get it, claiming that nobody tried to bring laborers into the meetings before. Her efforts have not been very successful. At one meeting it was possible for the principal to point out the single "Okie" present. The PTA is the

capita basis is greater in Arvin than in Dinuba. Those items with much higher retail volume in Dinuba are restaurant-bought food, clothing, and luxury goods, house furnishings and building supplies, and agricultural supplies. The single item in which Arvin has the greater volume of trade is public utilities, professional supplies, and industrial equipment. This category in Arvin is made up almost entirely of the last of these, and a large proportion is expenditures for agricultural equipment and cement pipe. Since the data refer to a period of intensive increase in irrigated area, the volume of business is undoubtedly inflated. On the other hand, the great divergence in the sale of fertilizers and farm supplies indicates the local Arvin practice of purchasing in carload lots directly from the distributor. While it demonstrates the difference in local trade, it is not as revealing as some of the other items.

TABLE 40.—*Number of businesses and volume of business by major category: Arvin and Dinuba, 1943*

Category of business	Arvin			Dinuba		
	Enterprises	Volume	Amount per person	Enterprises	Volume	*Amount per person
	Number	One thousand dollars	Dollars	Number	One thousand dollars	Dollars
Food retailers	11	592	95	17	712	96
Eating places	4	41	7	8	117	16
Clothing and luxury goods	3	110	18	12	493	67
Home furnishing and household construction	3	239	38	25	662	89
Gasoline, autos, and auto supplies	19	915	147	34	982	132
Drug stores and sundries	5	113	18	8	139	19
Liquor license establishments	9	232	37	9	287	39
Agricultural supplies	2	7	1	19	887	120
Miscellaneous [1]	6	286	46	9	104	14
Total	62	2,535	407	141	4,383	592

[1] Includes public utilities, professional supplies, and industrial equipment.
Source: Board of Equalization data.

Arvin merchants sell fewer clothing and household goods than Dinuba merchants; a difference of nearly 1 to 4 in the former and over 1 to 2 in the latter category. These are the items that are purchased by stable people who are improving their personal condition and their surroundings: they are items in the standard of living, and are the economic or business reflection of the difference in the standard of living as previously shown.

There is little difference in the actual dollar-volume sale of liquor vendors. However, liquor sales make up a far greater proportion of total retail trade in Arvin than they do in Dinuba (over 9 percent against less than 6 percent). Fuller knowledge of the situation suggests even greater divergence. State law in California provides for two classes of liquor license, a permit for "off sale" only, and a permit for "on sale." The former category sells package liquor only, while the latter provides for sale of drinks for consumption on the premises. The law further provides that all stores with the second type permit be prepared to sell food, and therefore the sales at such places include some restaurant sales. Field observation strongly suggests that the proportion of food sales is far greater in Dinuba than in Arvin. There are no off-sale enterprises in Dinuba, but one in Arvin.

To be sure, this is not a budget of expenditures for the families, but of the local trade—a measure of the opportunity for local community enterprise. A rough measure of the degree to which purchases were made in the nearby city and in the local community was obtained by means of the field schedule. Respondents were asked to indicate where they made purchases for certain categories of goods and services. Groceries and gasoline were predominantly purchased in the local community. Ninety-five percent of the responses from Arvin people referred to local purchases of groceries and 91 percent to local purchases of gasoline. In Dinuba, comparable figures were 96 and 92 percent. Clothing (men's and women's combined) showed a greatly divergent pattern, with Arvin people indicating in 31 percent of their responses that they bought their clothes in Arvin, and Dinubans indicating that they bought their clothes in Dinuba 68 percent of the time. If we can use the proportion of responses as a rough measure of the proportion of actual expenditures, the total Arvin expenditure for clothing and related goods would still be but half that in Dinuba. This suggests—although the data cannot prove it—that the actual volume of purchases by Arvin residents of those items which reflect standards and conditions of living are far less than in Dinuba. This is indicated despite the fact that a large number of families in Dinuba are in the older age groups where their needs are not so great and their wants more nearly fulfilled. This conclusion is in harmony with other facts about the level of living of the people in the two towns.

From the standpoint of opportunity created, and of the local community as a social environment, the difference is striking. The total volume of business, partly because of the difference in numbers supported and partly because of the difference in living conditions, is clearly greater in Dinuba than in Arvin. If we eliminate those items which are largely concerned with production itself, namely, agricultural supplies, industrial and transportation supplies, and automotive equipment (heavily influenced by sale of gasoline for power equipment), and leaving out liquor sales which are of a doubtful social value, we have a ratio of nearly 2 to 1 in the purchase of commodities.

SIZE AND TYPE OF BUSINESS ENTERPRISES

With far fewer stores, Arvin merchants have a larger average volume of business—$40,000 worth of business in Arvin against $31,000 business in Dinuba. Table 41 shows the distribution of retail enterprises by size categories of total sales. The distributions do not vary greatly, although the proportion of units under $10,000 total sales is greater in Dinuba, but above that figure is greater in Arvin. If, however, we analyze enterprises by estimated pecuniary strength, according to the Dun & Bradstreet ratings, we find a reversal of this situation. Seventy percent of the Arvin units have a rating of less than $2,000, against 45 percent in Dinuba (table 42). Though there are certain differences in the selection of enterprises in the two sources of data, over 90 percent of the cases refer to the same enterprises. This relationship is shown in figure 19. The bar charts show the high proportion of business enterprises in Arvin which have high gross cash sales and the low proportion which have high capital investments. In Dinuba, on the other hand, the correspondence between sales and capital investments is quite close. One inference from this chart is that the return to the entrepreneur on the basis of investment in the enterprise is higher in Arvin than in Dinuba. From the social point of view, however, an even more important fact emerges from this relationship. The Arvin merchant has a low financial investment in the community, which results in a generally low interest in the affairs and the welfare of the community. This is the statistical corroboration of the statement made by one Arvin merchant who said that the businessman in Arvin does not invest in his enterprise for

AGRIBUSINESS AND THE RURAL COMMUNITY

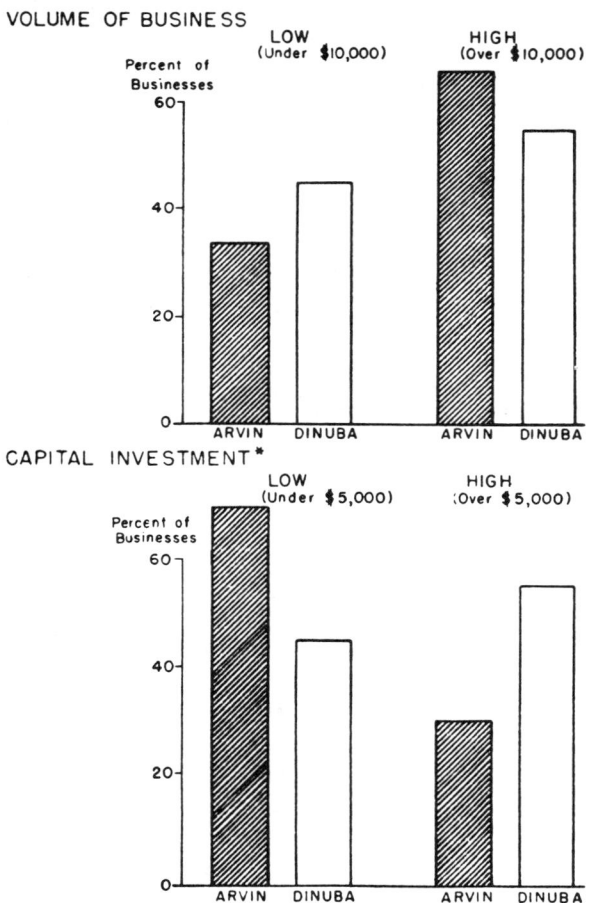

*The measure of capital investment is the Dun and Bradstreet (Reference Book, 1942) rating of "pecuniary strength", and is subject to the limitations of this data.

FIGURE No. 19

permanence, but endeavors to make a "killing" and get out. It is also reflected in the generally poorer quality of structures in the business district.

Another key to the nature of the business enterprise is derived from the kinds that are found, and their relative numbers. These data are presented in table 40, and can be summarized here. Enterprises selling food and automobile supplies are the two major kinds in Arvin and together comprise about half of all retail stores. These categories are important in Dinuba, but home-furnishing stores are second to automotive enterprises, and agricultural suppliers third.

Only five units are engaged in selling clothing, household goods, and building materials (9 percent) in Arvin, against 35 such units (25 percent) in Dinuba. On the other hand, the number of liquor sellers is the same in both communities, but percentwise

TABLE 41.—*Size of business enterprises by volume of retail sales: Arvin and Dinuba*

Size class by volume of annual retail sales	Arvin		Dinuba	
	Number	Percent	Number	Percent
Under $1,000 [1]	6	10	21	15
$1,000 to $10,000	15	24	43	30
$10,000 to $50,000	30	48	54	39
$50,000 to $100,000	5	8	11	8
$100,000 to $200,000	5	8	9	6
Over $200,000	1	2	3	2
Total	62	100	141	100

[1] Includes 2 Arvin and 6 Dinuba units without any sales but with records with the Board of Equalization.
Source: Board of Equalization data.

TABLE 42.—*Size of business enterprises by estimated pecuniary strength: Arvin and Dinuba*

Size class by estimated pecuniary strength	Arvin		Dinuba	
	Number	Percent	Number	Percent
Under $500	16	35	17	15
$500 to $2,000	16	35	35	30
$2,000 to $5,000	5	11	28	24
$5,000 to $20,000	6	12	20	17
$20,000 to $125,000	3	7	12	10
Over $125,000	0	0	5	4
Total [1]	46	100	117	100

[1] Ratings not made for 14 Arvin and 38 Dinuba enterprises.
Source: Dun & Bradstreet Reference Book, California, January 1942. Estimates of pecuniary strength are a form of credit evaluation which reflects total investment. The data bear the reservations and qualifications regularly made by the company issuing them.

make up a much greater proportion in Arvin than in Dinuba. As already indicated, the liquor sales places apparently do a larger total proportion of their business in the sale of liquor and alcoholic drinks, and less in the sale of food than these stores do in Dinuba.

SUMMARY

The business-enterprise data from the Board of Equalization show the difference in the kind of establishment locally supported and the volume and kind of expenditures made by the local people of each community. Dinuba has more enterprises, and they do a far greater total volume of business and a far greater per capita volume of business. They have a higher financial investment in the community (and a better credit-rating record) though on the average they do a smaller volume of business. Such a greater investment means a firmer interest on the part of the entrepreneur in the local community, and such interest is clearly evident in the analysis of other aspects of community life. The kinds of enterprises supported include many more of those which serve to improve family living.

The total volume of expenditure and the volume per person is appreciably smaller in Arvin than in Dinuba. The difference is partly made up by more purchases in the nearby urban centers, however. The evidence indicates that the Arvin purchases are to a far greater extent for such items of doubtful social value as liquor, and less for those items which make for better home living, such as household furnishings. The business enterprise data thus corroborate the evidence obtained from the schedule on level of living. It appears that Arvin purchasing power, buying habits, and tastes are not such as would support many business establishments serving the more basic needs for modern home living.

CHAPTER XVII

THE CAUSES FOR THE SOCIAL DIFFERENTIATION

THE HYPOTHESIS

The comparative analysis of Arvin and Dinuba, communities of large and small farms, was predicated under the following hypothesis: Within the framework of American tradition, what effect does scale of farm operations have upon the character of the rural community?

Essentially the technique has been to establish the area of similarity and difference between the two towns, assuming that the qualitative differences in social life rest upon fundamental causes in the economy of the communities. Had there been no other differences in the economy, history, or cultural origin of the people of the two towns, then we could simply assert that social differences were a function of scale of operations. Since, however, other possible explanatory causes for the social differentiation between Arvin and Dinuba exist, it is necessary to examine alternative possibilities with care to determine the area of influence that each exerts over the community. Recognition that other factors may be contributory causes does not relieve us from the need to evaluate importance of the various causative forces. This can be done first by determining the degree to which other factors are differentiated between Arvin and Dinuba, second by calling forth other relevant data from neighboring communities, and finally by setting up an explanatory hypothesis which will account for all known difference without either calling upon mystic and undefined causes or doing violence to accepted understanding of human social behavior.

ESSENTIAL CULTURAL SIMILARITIES

The differences between Arvin and Dinuba are differences within a broader framework of similarities. The necessary emphasis upon divergent social characteristics should not obscure this fundamental fact. Both communities belong to a common cultural heritage, so that, strictly speaking, the conclusions can have validity only in terms of that common tradition. They are, as a matter of fact, not so much differences in culture as they are differences in quality. The social conditions which have particularly attracted our attention are between good living conditions and bad, relative degrees of social equality, relative amounts of social homogeneity and participation, relative amounts of social services and of economic opportunity. These are differences on a scale of values, and acceptance of their significance implicitly recognizes that physical comfort, material possessions, social democracy, and economic opportunities are all desirable qualities in a community. Nobody imbued with American culture can cavil with such a scale of values.

The important thing here is that the two communities, therefore, do not have divergent value systems and social customs, but rather that they meet their own values with different degrees of success. If we may be allowed an analogy, the difference between Arvin and Dinuba are like those between two individuals with different degrees of health and vitality rather than like the differences between two individuals of divergent racial characteristics.

Essentially, Arvin and Dinuba are part of a common system of agricultural production, best understood as industrialized. Both also partake of a single culture pattern which, in turn, can best be described as urbanized.

By industrialized farming is meant the system of producing crops intensively, solely for the cash market, with a high degree of farm specialization, utilizing great quantities of capital and requiring a large input of labor hired on an impersonal basis. Large-scale operations tend to intensify these qualities, but the pattern is not dependent upon large units. It seems probable, however, that the existence of large-scale—particularly of corporate—operations within the broader area and with which the small farmer must compete is an essential element in developing the industrial pattern.

The urbanized culture pattern that results clearly reflects the social behavior of the cities and follows from the industrial nature of farm production. Its primary characteristic is the general acceptance of pecuniary standards of value and a social status system based upon money wealth. Such a set of values inevitably leads to a more or less closed class system based upon economic status, and expressed to the individual largely in terms of occupation. These features are common to Arvin and Dinuba, though the degree of social segregation and the social distance between occupational classes are markedly different. Urbanized culture has further effects. As a result of class stratification, and because of the complexity of society, there is a tendency toward developing social action in terms of special interests rather than on a community-wide basis. For that reason associations of like-minded persons tend to play a very important part in the functioning of the community. While specific differences have been noted, here again we get a common fundamental pattern. This aspect of urban culture is reflected in the specialization of the activities and interests of the individual—the tendency to be concerned with a single and very partial role in the total functioning of the economy. The farmer has traditionally held out against this aspect of the industrialization of the world. The farmer as jack-of-all-trades is the accepted American picture. Yet in the economy of agricultural production in the irrigated areas of California, the farm operator, like his city-dwelling cousin, has become specialized in his operations. The 40-acre farmer as well as the operator of 4,000 acres will show such specialization, though obviously there will remain considerable difference in degree.

It is against a background of such common cultural characteristics that the divergence between Arvin and Dinuba must be examined.

RECAPITULATION OF SOCIAL DIFFERENCES

Within the framework of cultural similarity, the differences between Arvin and Dinuba take a clearer meaning. The picture in Arvin may be contrasted with the Dinuba situation in the following way:

1. The greater number of persons dependent upon wages rather than upon entrepreneureal profit.

2. The lower general living conditions as measured by a level-of-living scale and the subjective evaluation of households.

3. The lower degree of stability of population.

4. The poorer physical appearance and condition of houses, streets, and public buildings.
5. The relative poverty of social services performed by the community.
6. The poorer schools, parks, and facilities offered youth.
7. The relative dearth of social organizations serving the individuals in the community and the community as a whole.
8. The fewer religious institutions.
9. The lesser degree of community loyalty expressed.
10. The apparently fewer decisions on community affairs made by the local community and the apparently smaller proportion of the population participating in such decisions.
11. The apparently greater degree of social segregation and greater social distance between the several groups in the community. (This and the preceding items have been labeled apparent because neither is amenable to statistical evaluation, though considerable evidence is at hand to indicate their existence.)
12. The lesser amount of retail trade, the fewer business establishments, and the low volume of trade in those classes of merchandise most generally accorded a high place in social values.

This constitutes a rather imposing list of social and economic factors, reflecting the quality of the society in the two communities, in which the one fulfills rather well our normal expectations of social life and the other consistently fulfills them less satisfactorily. The number of items and the consistency in their implications can hardly rest on purely fortuitous grounds.

POSSIBLE CAUSATIVE DIFFERENTIALS

However, as already indicated, other differences between Arvin and Dinuba than the scale of farm operations might be invoked as the cause for the qualitative differential between Arvin and Dinuba. While many of these differences are functionally interrelated, a listing of them under major headings will serve to clarify their importance. Obviously they are not all of like importance—some clearly are secondary reflections of more fundamental factors while others would appear to throw the advantage in the wrong direction. Differences in physical environment, cultural and demographic features, community history, agricultural production, and farm organization are listed.

	Arvin	Dinuba
I. Environmental factors:		
1. Land:		
(a) Area served	64,000 acres	43,000 acres
(b) Land in farms	46,000 acres	34,000 acres
(c) Intensive uses	22,000 acres	24,000 acres
(d) Land of soil classes 1 to 3	59,000 acres	31,000 acres
2. Water:		
(a) Source	Pumped	Surface supplemented with pumps
(b) Cost	$6.92 per acre	$4 per acre
3. Other resources:		
(a) Minerals	Oil leases, general	None
(b) Recreation	Little or none	Little or none
II. Cultural and demographic factors:		
1. Population of community	6,000	7,400
2. Cultural origins:		
(a) Native American	88 percent	81 percent
(b) Native Californian	4 percent	19 percent
(c) Dust Bowl migrants	63 percent	22 percent
(d) Median length of residence	Less than 5 years	15 to 20 years
3. Educational attainment (average for family heads)	7.6 years	8.4 years
4. Economic status:		
(a) Median income bracket	$1,751 to $2,250	$1,751 to $2,250
(b) Wage labor as proportion of family heads	81 percent	49 percent
III. Historic factors:		
1. Age of community (as of 1944)	31 years	56 years
2. Decade of major growth	1930–40	1910–20
IV. Agricultural production factors:		
1. Value of production (1940)	$2,438,000	$2,540,000
2. Type of farming:		
(a) Proportion irrigated land in orchard and vineyard	36 percent	65 percent
(b) Proportion in row crops	41 percent	11 percent
(c) Proportion in cotton	29 percent	7 percent
(d) Proportion of farms in fruit	35 percent	79 percent
(e) Proportion of farms in field crops	40 percent	17 percent
V. Farm organization factors:		
1. Tenure:		
(a) Tenancy	42 percent	14 percent
(b) Absentee ownership	36 percent	16 percent
2. Labor requirements:		
(a) Man-hours of labor required	2.9 million	3.5 million
(b) Requirement for hired labor	2.3 million	1.4 million
(c) Minimum labor requirement as percent of maximum	25 percent	20 percent
(d) Maximum outside seasonal workers required	1,175	1,595
3. Size of farm operations:		
(a) Number of farms over 160 acres	44 percent	6 percent
(b) Acreage in farms over 160 acres	91 percent	25 percent
(c) Average farm size	497 acres	57 acres
(d) Average value of production	$18,000	$3,400

Under these five headings are included 14 separate items, some with great differences, such as farm size and age of community; some with large differences, such as tenancy and major crops; some with practically no difference, such as intensive land use and value of production; and a few where the advantage would appear to lie with Arvin, such as available good land, other resources, and seasonality of employment. We shall discuss them seriatim.

ENVIRONMENTAL FACTORS

Factors in the environment are more impressive for their similarities than their divergences. The relationship of the community to neighboring towns and cities and to their markets, the availability of minerals, and the potential productivity of the land are all closely similar but somewhat favorable to Arvin. The only factor of the environment which is markedly divergent is the water resources. The question of environment, therefore, devolves upon the influence of this factor upon community life. This in turn must be separated into the influence of water resources on the size of farms on one hand and directly upon community organization on the other.

The discussion on relative cost of water showed that in Arvin the investment per farm was extremely high and because of depth of pumping, reasonably large acreages could be handled by single wells. In Dinuba, on the other hand, original cost was lower and during initial development no pump was required, though for full use of the land, investment had eventually to be made in pumps. On the other hand, given the size of farms as they exist in each community, the actual per-acre cost of water is not greatly different. As a matter of fact, the excess of cost of water in Arvin is less than the amount received by landowners for oil leases, so that any economic hardship directly resulting from water costs would be offset by gains from potential oil resources. Furthermore, both the costs and the gains are generally reflected in land values, and it is therefore doubtful if either has a long-run effect upon the returns to the farm operators.

The situation with respect to water has, however, had an effect upon size of farms in the Arvin area. The requirement for deep and expensive wells with large water flow has made it necessary to irrigate fairly large tracts with each pump—about 200 acres for efficient operation. Many farms in the Arvin area get water from wells owned either cooperatively or corporately, so that it is possible, even with this water situation, to operate small units efficiently; furthermore, most of the land is in units which are larger than the water requirements of single wells, and therefore farm size is not clearly dependent upon the need for deep wells. Nevertheless, this high initial investment has inhibited the development of small units and contrariwise been influential in the creation of larger ones. Furthermore, the depth to groundwater held up the intensive use of Arvin lands till efficient pumping plants were developed by engineers, so that the water situation was responsible for the late growth of Arvin. Summarizing, the water supply has had little or no effect upon the economic welfare of operating farmers that could create social poverty, but it has had some influence upon the size of farm units and upon the period of development of Arvin lands.

The availability of surface water in the Dinuba district and the relatively simple engineering and low investment in water resources made it possible to develop that area early. Establishment of an irrigation district under the original Wright Act made it advantageous to subdivide and sell the land. Thus the Dinuba water supply was a responsible agent in establishing farm size in that community.

CULTURAL AND DEMOGRAPHIC FACTORS

Several factors in the social background of the people who dwell in Arvin and Dinuba require careful examination: size of population, nativity of population, educational attainments, and economic status.

Dinuba is roughly 20 percent larger in population than Arvin. Since the resource base is comparable, this divergence must be attributed in part to intensity of land use and in part to size of farm operations and degree of mechanization. Since approximately identical amounts of outside labor are brought into the community, migration of workers can hardly be held responsible. It would be difficult to explain differences in average level of living by the existence of fewer families, when these fewer families enjoy the same amount of natural resources. Since, however, the number of people are partially responsible for the existence of social agencies, such differences might be attributable to community size. While the population differences between the two communities may be contributing causes to the social differences, the towns are too nearly the same to account entirely for the difference of 2 to 1 or more in business establishments, clubs, churches, and community facilities.

The cultural background differs as follows: More Arvin residents are native American, but far fewer are native Californian; most Arvin residents come from the Dust Bowl states while the people of Dinuba represent a wide and even scatter of state origins; and finally the duration of residence of Arvin and Dinuba persons is greatly at variance.

The differences are most difficult to assess. It would be hazardous to suggest that the people from any one area have greater cultural or physical capability for creating a social environment more in keeping with American tradition than people from some other section of the nation. Local opinion is frequently derogatory of people from the Dust Bowl states, using the epithet "Okie" in referring to them and according them poor social standing. But upon closer questioning and examination, these references and social evaluations appear to be not actually directed at their place of origin but at their economic status and level of living. Cultural differences are recognized, of course. Religious behavior and beliefs stand out among such differences, but also manner of dress, colloquial expressions, and conceptions of morality show regional differentiation in America. But the differences between Arvin and Dinuba were not differences in culture but differences in the successful fulfillment of a common cultural tradition. Three fundamental reasons therefore appear which make it impossible to accord direct causative force to place of origin (keeping in mind always that we are not dealing with economic circumstances.) First, the difficulty of assessing cultural differences to separate states or regions in the United States. It would be impossible to assert that the people in the Texas-Arkansas-Oklahoma area either have social values which are universally poorer than those of the remainder of the United States or that they are socially or physically incapable of achieving such values. Second, the behavior patterns that are differentiable between people from that region—either differences in culture or in economic status—are rapidly sloughed and efforts are made to conform to dominant patterns. Older residents generally recognize that the faults found among "Okies" in their personal habits were changed "as soon as they learned better."

The religious beliefs brought by immigrants from the Dust Bowl is predominantly fundamentalist, and is a cultural characteristic which sets them off from older California residents. Yet a study made of this aspect of migrant workers' behavior shows that they readily take on the religious expressions of the older residents when resettling in California communities.[21] There is evidence

[21] Walter R. Goldschmidt, Class Denominationism in California Rural Churches, *op. cit.*

that the changes both in personal habits and religion follow from changes in economic conditions as much as or more than from cultural assimilation and education.

Third, while Arvin has a higher proportion of Dust Bowl migrants than Dinuba (66 percent as against 30), this is merely a reflection of the different occupation structures in the two towns. This can be shown, for laborers are predominantly from that area (80 percent in Arvin and 60 percent in Dinuba) whereas they make up relatively unimportant proportions of the independently employed category (40 and 24 percent from Arvin and Dinuba, respectively). Thus the preponderance of persons from the Dust Bowl states in Arvin results from the fact of large farms and the labor requirements. Furthermore, the group who are in a position of leadership in the community and who therefore can set the standards of its activities are not from this region.

Dinuba family heads have had nearly 1 year of schooling more than those of Arvin. This difference again is largely a result of the fact that farm labor has lower educational attainments than the remainder of the population. We find, for instance, that the average education of farm laborers in Arvin is 6.5 and of Dinuba 6.8 years, while that of farms and white-collar workers is 9.5 and 9.8 for Arvin and Dinuba, respectively. It can therefore be said that the difference in level of education of eight-tenths of a year is mostly the result of the difference in economic composition of the population. The difference in level attained among that group which offers leadership in community affairs is three-tenths of a year. Modal education for all groups is 8 years with a second and lower peak at 12 years. That educational attainment (as an index of personal capacity) could affect the quality of community life is an acceptable hypothesis, but the significance of this feature is diminished by the low observed differences not directly associated with economic status.

Arvin residents had but a short time in the community at the time of study, as compared with Dinuba residents. This in part is a function of the age of the two towns. However, a heavy turn-over in population is indicated by the fact that fewer than half of Arvin's residents had lived there in 1940 though by that time the community had achieved its present size.

That this turn-over is largely but not entirely a function of economic status can be shown by the device used for educational attainment and state of origin. If the farm labor group is singled out, 31 percent of the Arvin group and 27 percent of the Dinuba group came during the years 1943 and 1944 (prior to field work). The proportions are 61 percent and 47 percent for Arvin and Dinuba, respectively, when we consider all those who came in 1940 or later. Among farmers and white-collar workers, 37 percent and 15 percent, respectively, came in 1940 or later.

There is no doubt that community loyalty, positions of leadership, and the creation of social institutions are affected by length of residence, and that the recency of Arvin's development (which will be discussed below) and the turn-over in population have had an effect upon the social character of the communities. It is important to realize, however, that such turn-over is in part a function of economic and social conditions. Repeated statements by persons in all walks of life that they did not plan to remain in Arvin because of the inadequate facilities offer the best substantiation of this effect. Thus a vicious cycle is created which finds its origin in the fact that but a small portion of the community has a vested interest in it sufficient to create a sense of stability.

The foregoing has shown that each of the demographic differences is largely, but not wholly, a function of the occupational structure of the two communities. When residence, origin, and education are analyzed by occupation groups, half or more of the differential disappears. Furthermore, the influence of the economic conditions upon these factors goes beyond the simple change in percentage in some of these effects. These differences, whatever their origin, are certainly causes contributory to the relative social conditions in the two towns.

In Arvin 8 out of 10 families depend upon wages for their livelihood. In Dinuba 5 out of 10 are wage earners. These workers, especially those who are agricultural workers, have little economic or social investment in the community. Furthermore, they do not supply the leadership for social activities, which almost without exception comes from farmers and white-collar workers. The fact, therefore, that in one community there are approximately 1,000 families which make up the category from which such leadership normally arises, while in the other only about 250 families are in that position, is extremely important. It influences other demographic factors as well as the development of social institutions. This differential is, in turn, very largely a direct result of farm size—a simple arithmetical certainty. For the number of farmers that can be supported by a given resource base is a direct function of the amount of resources each one controls. The influence of size of farm on size of the merchant and other white-collar categories is less direct, but there is good reason to believe that such influence exists, as will be developed below.

HISTORIC FACTORS

There are two pertinent facts about the history of the two communities which have an influence upon the character of their social institutions. These are (a) The relative age of the two towns, and (b) the difference epochs or periods in which they came into being. Each deserves careful analysis.

It is difficult to say what point in time represents the beginning of a community. In Dinuba the year 1888 is generally accepted. It was in this year that the Alta Irrigation District was formed, that the post office was created, and the town officially inaugurated. Irrigation development had been coming in under a private corporation for 6 years. The following year a school was established at Dinuba, though schools had existed in the area nearly 10 years previously. A comparable date in Arvin is also hard to establish. Schools existed within the area in 1902, but none was created in Arvin proper till 1914. The earliest continuous settlement in this area based upon irrigation took place in 1910. The date should, therefore, be set between 1910 and 1914. Nineteen hundred thirteen, the year prior to the establishment of the Arvin school, is most comparable to that of 1888 for Dinuba and places the two towns just 25 years apart in point of origin.

The rate of growth in the two towns were nearly identical, though somewhat faster in Arvin than Dinuba, and the absolute figures are nearly the same. The Arvin figures are somewhat inflated, since one school was included which gets half or more of its pupils from outside the area of the community as delineated, while school lines and community lines in Dinuba are in close agreement. This accounts for the fact that the 1942 Arvin school attendance figure appears to be greater than Dinuba's on this graph (fig. 20), while schedule data showed Dinuba's population

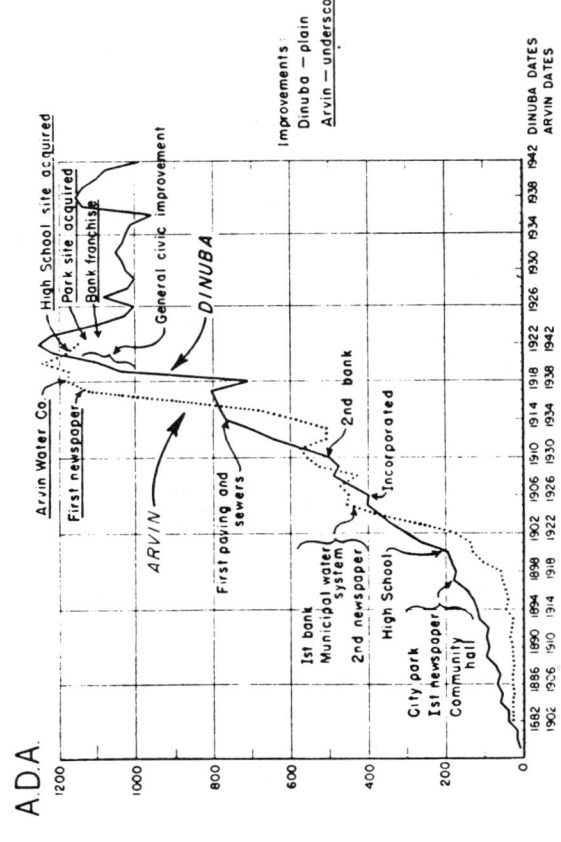

FIGURE No. 20

to be about 20 percent greater in 1944. This inflation is probably about 20 percent, but the effect of this on the rate and timing of the growth of these towns is not significant. Furthermore, the community in which these outside students fall offers fewer economic and social services than Arvin. Growth curves of the average daily attendance of the schools located in the towns of Arvin and Dinuba (leaving out schools in rural areas) show the same pattern as the curves presented here.

TABLE 43.—*Date of civic developments in Arvin and Dinuba*

Development	Approximate date of initiation		Age of community at initiation [1]		*Age difference [2]
	Arvin	Dinuba	Arvin	Dinuba	
Community hall	About 1938	Before 1900	25	12	13.
First newspaper	do	1896	25	10	15.
City park	1944 [3]	1898	31	10	21.
High school	1944 [3]	1899	31	11	20.
Second newspaper		1902		14	Over 17.
Water system as public utility	1938	1902	25	14	11.
First bank	1944 [3]	1902	31	14	17.
Incorporation		1906		18	Over 13.
Second bank		1910		22	Over 9.
First paving		1915		27	Over 4.
First sewer	1940	1915	27	27	0.

[1] Based upon origin of Arvin in 1913 and Dinuba in 1888.
[2] Number of years Arvin was older than Dinuba at time of development in each community.
[3] These were not accomplished facts in 1944 but had been initiated. County published notices for purchase of 10-acre park site in 1944; acquired school lands in 1941 but had not started building in 1944. Bank franchise issued in 1944 to Bank of America.

The effect of age of community per se—as distinct from the effect of the epoch of growth—can be eliminated if we examine the time at which facilities were developed with respect to the growth of the town. In table 43 are the approximate dates of these basic developments in Dinuba, the dates of comparable developments in Arvin, and the calculation of the age of the community at the time of each development. Five of the items cited for Dinuba have not been developed in Arvin at all, though all took place in Dinuba prior to 1920. Three others—park, bank, and high school—had not actually been brought to fruition at the time of field study though action had been initiated in each. Had these all been developed during 1944, they still would not have had a growth record comparable to that of Dinuba. In most of those items which Arvin has acquired, there were 10 or more years' difference in age, and only in a single instance did Arvin acquire improvements as soon as Dinuba, and in no instance sooner.

Figure 20 shows the time at which specific developments took place in relation to population growth, as shown by school attendance, and thereby gives graphic representation of the data discussed above. This tabulation and graph shows that according to the growth of Dinuba there has been ample time for the development of fundamental physical improvements and social services which have not come about and that virtually every feature which Arvin has was obtained at a later stage in growth than comparable ones in Dinuba.

The second aspect of this historical difference is the differing epochs or periods during which the community came into being as a community. This can be rephrased as follows: What difference in the character of the years preceding the First World War might create a community of a kind which could not come into being before the Second World War? On theoretical grounds it would be assumed that the years of the 1920's and 1930's would be years in which physical development would take place more rapidly than they had earlier, while the social institutions would develop less rapidly. Advanced technology would lead us to expect the former, while the universal use of the automobile and the resulting greater mobility of rural people would make us expect the latter. Arvin, however, is behind on both counts.

It would appear to be the case that communities developing in the 1920's and 1930's would be less likely to incorporate and would be less likely to have two competing banks and newspapers. They would be about equally likely to develop fine schools and good physical surroundings and a fairly rich social life. In order to determine the influence of this factor upon the condition of the community, it is necessary to examine briefly other towns in the area which are more nearly contemporaneous with Arvin.

The towns of Delano, Wasco, and Shafter lie about as far from Bakersfield as Arvin but in the opposite direction. Wasco was colonized in 1907 and Shafter a few years later, while Delano is somewhat older. These three towns have grown during the same period and at about the same rate that Arvin has; and yet, as social environments, they more nearly approach Dinuba than Arvin. In figure 21 the growth in average daily attendance in Wasco schools is plotted against that of Arvin but in this case without a time differential. It is seen that the two communities have grown at virtually the same speed and within 5 years of one another.

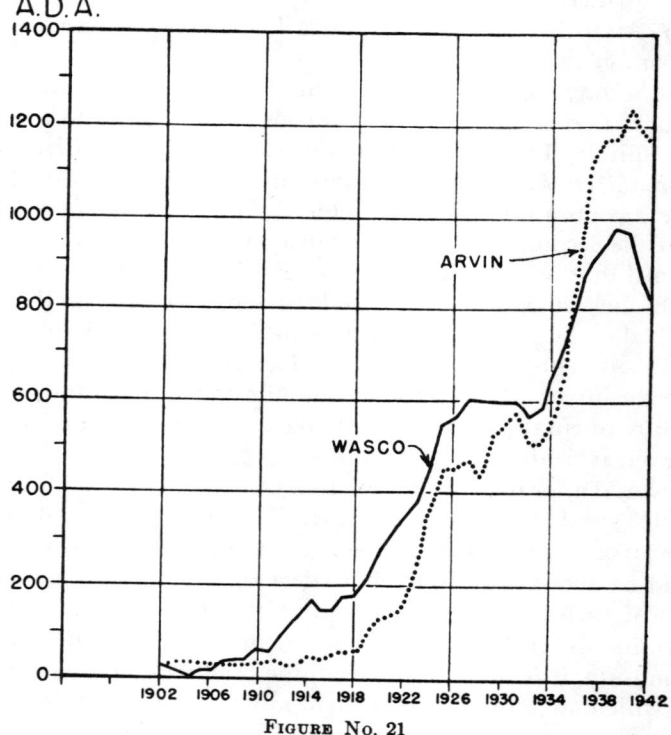

Figure No. 21

Comparable figures for Shafter are not at hand, but its beginnings are later than Wasco, so the coincidence with Arvin would be still sharper. Data for the early 1920's with respect to agricultural production show that these three towns had a similar agricultural base during the early years of their existence.

The following chart (fig. 22) shows the estimated carlot

shipments of fruit, grapes, and vegetables from each of the major small communities in Kern County, based upon the records of the Agricultural Commissioner. This chart shows a remarkably parallel growth in fruit and vegetable shipments in the four communities. The exceptionally high shipments in Arvin in the last 2 years recorded, and of Shafter in the late 1930's, are partly the result of heavy potato shipments, which bulk large relative to value as compared with fruits and other vegetables.

Since this tabulation does not include any data on either cotton or livestock feed or livestock products, the relative importance of these must be assayed. Table 44 presents information which gives us a clue. The acreage and proportion of land in intensive uses is given by four major classes for each of the four communities for the year 1940 based upon the Agricultural Adjustment Agency data. Community boundaries are less precise for Delano, Shafter, and Wasco than for Arvin, but are substantially correct. Records made contemporaneously by the agricultural commissioners for the Arvin-Weedpatch-Lamont area in 1931 and 1932 are also presented. The total area covered is about twice as large as the Arvin area used for the 1940 data.

The volume of shipment shown in figure 22 reflects the acreage in the first two categories presented in table 44. It is seen that these categories combined form very nearly the same proportion of total intensive acreage in each community, varying from 43.6 percent in Shafter to 58.4 percent in Delano, with Arvin in between. In Arvin, in 1931 and 1932, these classes represented still less of the ArvinWeedpatch-Lamont intensive acreage.

Therefore, the growth of the total Arvin production is not nearly so sharp as figure 22 indicates. Earlier figures are not available for the other communities, but general knowledge about them suggests that the shift of production from cotton and alfalfa to fruits and vegetables has not been any greater than indicated in Arvin. Therefore, the growth curve may be taken as showing the general relative position within broad limits of the several communities since 1921. On the whole, Arvin history from the standpoint of commodity production is reasonably like that of sister communities in Kern County, so that historical development can account for little of the difference found between them.

Delano, Shafter, and Wasco have had high schools for many

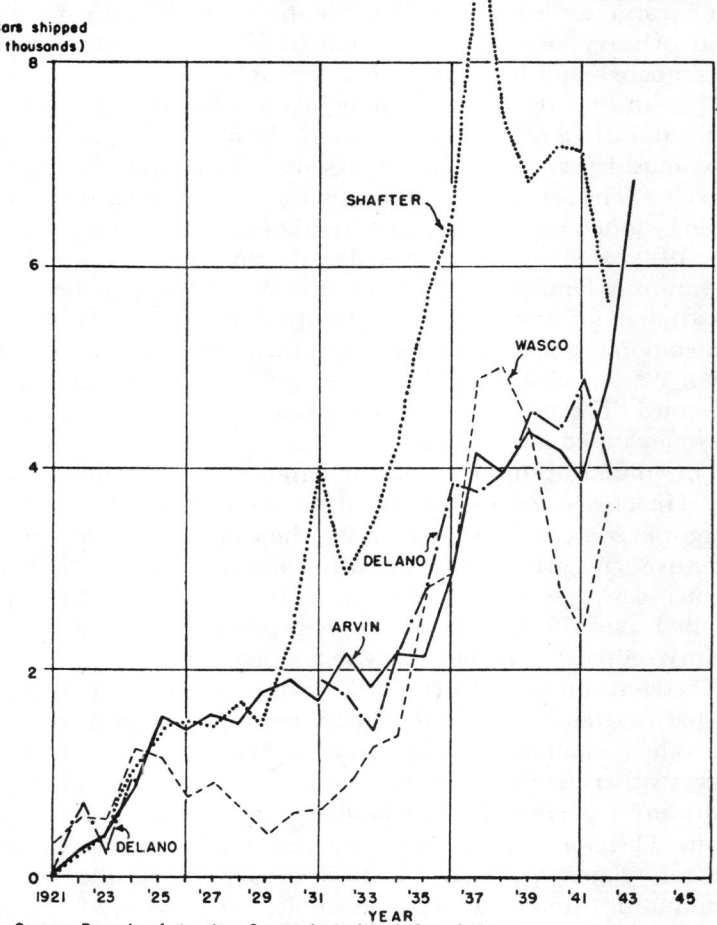

FIGURE No. 22

TABLE 44.—*Intensive land use in Arvin (1931, 1932, and 1940) compared with land use in neighboring communities*

Land use	Arvin-Weedpatch-Lamont [1]		Arvin [2]	Delano [2]	Shafter [2]	Wasco [2]
	1931	1932	1940	1940	1940	1940
Acreages:						
Orchards and vineyards	7,251	7,576	7,875	13,581	3,146	407
Vegetables, melons, and beets	1,094	1,139	2,707	1,033	9,464	5,569
Alfalfa	5,014	5,014	3,284	2,684	2,258	1,899
Cotton	7,756	9,306	6,274	7,741	8,672	4,836
Total	21,115	23,035	20,140	25,039	23,540	12,711
Percentages:						
Orchards and vineyards	34.3	32.9	39.1	54.3	13.4	3.2
Vegetables, melons, and beets	5.2	4.9	13.4	4.1	40.2	43.8
Alfalfa	23.7	21.8	16.3	10.7	9.6	14.9
Cotton	36.8	40.4	31.2	30.9	36.8	38.1
Total	100.0	100.0	100.0	100.0	100.0	100.0

[1] Data obtained from records in the Kern County office of the Extension Service, based upon a survey compiled by the Agricultural Commissioner in 1931 and 1932. The area includes a wider region than the Arvin community, but this region had no community as large as Arvin at that time, and the whole area has a comparable planting pattern. Absolute figures cannot be compared to present Arvin, but proportions are significant.
[2] Based upon Agricultural Adjustment Agency records.

years (Wasco since 1918), all have had a bank for many years, Shafter and Delano are incorporated, and these communities show physical improvements that go far beyond anything in Arvin, though in general not so far as Dinuba. Delano, Shafter, and Wasco are intermediate in social position to Arvin and Dinuba, and each has an average farm size that is also intermediate between the two communities studied here.

In view of this relative development of Arvin with her sister communities in Kern County, the similarity of growth on one hand and the difference in social conditions on the other, it is hardly possible to assign to the time of growth a major share of the differences between Arvin and Dinuba.

The most probable effects of the historic recency of Arvin as compared to Dinuba are these: The relative newness is contributory to the fact that a large portion of the population is relatively young, while the old-age brackets are underrepresented. Since Arvin grew during a period of migration of destitute persons from the Dust Bowl, the period of growth accounts in part for the preponderance of persons from that area. It seems likely that, despite the fact that other communities of like age have developed them, the influence of the automobile inhibited the growth of local social and economic services. At least it has made it possible for a community to function despite their absence.

AGRICULTURAL PRODUCTION FACTORS

The specific difference between Arvin and Dinuba with respect to farm production is that Dinuba is overwhelmingly a fruit—specifically grape—producing area, while Arvin is dominated by row crops, mostly cotton. Several measures of this difference have been presented. In terms of intensive land use Dinuba has nearly twice the proportion of orchard and vineyard (65 percent as against 36 percent) and only a fourth the proportion of row crops (11 percent as against 41 percent). In terms of value of production, Dinuba fruit is again twice as great as Arvin (69 percent compared to 36 percent), cotton is a third as great (7 percent compared to 20 percent), and all row crops a fifth (8 percent compared to 41 percent). Forage crops and livestock are, roughly, comparable in extent, while grain production is far more important in Arvin than in Dinuba. The financial importance of this class is minor, but the area of land use is greatest of any single class in Arvin.

Social poverty is frequently associated in American agriculture with cotton. The relation of the two in the South under the techniques and institutions which exist there is well established. It is, therefore, reasonable to assume a comparable relationship in California. Closer examination of the total production pattern shows great differences between cotton cultivation in the South and in the irrigated areas of the West. In the South it is associated with the sharecropper pattern of relationships, with the existence of a separate racial caste, with high degree both of farm specialization and area specialization, with long-term soil depletion, and with relatively low intensity of operations and comparably low yields. Institutionally, cotton production in the South is, therefore, quite different from cotton production in the West, so that it is improper to infer similar social conditions in the two areas from a single economic similarity. Since, however, impoverished social and economic conditions appear also to be associated with cotton in the West, it is necessary to examine the possibility further. The extent of such association is limited. Many of the communities offering the poorest facilities for social life are in cotton-producing areas. Tipton, Pixley, Buttonwillow, Firebaugh, and Mendota are all examples of cotton communities having relatively few business establishments and social facilities. They are also all associated with large-scale operations, and most of them, like Arvin, have had a relatively short existence. On the other hand, towns like Madera, Wasco, and Shafter offer far greater facilities than Arvin and are likewise associated with cotton culture to about the same extent.

The question therefore arises: Is the association between impoverished social milieu and cultivation of cotton a direct one, or does it result from the further association between cotton, on one hand, and, on the other, the existence of an economically destitute and socially impoverished labor class and/or the speculative cash production of the enterprise? Formulated this way, the question permits of but one answer—the latter. Yet this raises a real problem, if cotton per se is to be explanatory. The detailed analysis of farm production shows that both communities engage in production for the cash market and, furthermore, that the amount of labor required is higher in the grape-producing area of Dinuba than in the more diversified Arvin community. Requirements for labor are, therefore, not the differentiating factor and cannot explain the divergence between Arvin and Dinuba.

One other possibility presents itself, namely, that labor attracted to the cotton fields is measurably different from labor working in fruit-producing areas. We have seen that the laborers in Arvin are somewhat below those of Dinuba in educational attainments and that more of them come from the poorer states. It does not seem improbable that Arvin laborers are, on the average, persons with fewer cultural attainments and fewer advantages of background, though only within a very limited range. It is noteworthy that laboring groups in both communities receive median incomes in the same bracket but that the specific median (estimated) would be slightly lower in Arvin than in Dinuba. The effect of such differences would necessarily be slight. First, because the observable differences are very small. These differences could be accounted for by the fact that the social environment, as distinct from the character of economic opportunity, repels the workers whose capabilities are higher. Second, because labor in both categories is generally interchangeable; i.e., that farm laborers move from fruit to cotton to potatoes seasonally as a regular thing.

Third, because the social milieu of the California community quite clearly is created by the nonfarm labor population—the farmers and white-collar workers. It would, therefore, be impossible to claim that measurable differences in social and economic facilities are the result of fundamental differences in the characteristics of that element of the population which in neither community offers the leadership in creating such facilities.

Cultivation of cotton and other "row" crops, especially potatoes, may be partially responsible for the large operations in Arvin. Insofar as this is the case, the type of production is responsible for the proportions of farmers and farm laborers. However, the proportion of row-crop farms in the lower size categories is almost as great as the proportion of fruit operations, and some of the largest units are devoted chiefly to fruit production. Like the water situation, the kind of crops grown is therefore partially responsible for the size of farm pattern in Arvin.

FARM ORGANIZATION FACTORS

Three aspects of farm organization attract our attention as possible causative factors in determining the differences that exist between Arvin and Dinuba: tenure pattern, labor requirements, and size of farm operators.

Arvin has a high proportion of tenants whereas Dinuba has far fewer. Likewise, the proportion of absentee owners in Arvin—here defined as owners reported living outside the county—is over twice that in Dinuba. In general, it is expected that owner-operators and resident-owners are more concerned with community welfare and social services than are tenants and absentee owners. While nothing in the present study either corroborates or refutes this, it may generally be accepted as a working hypothesis.

It is therefore accepted that in some measure the relative social poverty rests upon tenure pattern. This difference in tenure pattern is partially the result of historic timing and outside social forces. It is also in considerable measure a function of scale of farm operations and social poverty. Table 12 (ch. III) shows that tenancy is more frequent on large farms, over 160 acres, than on small farms. It has also been shown that the general social conditions in Arvin have caused some owner-operators and other natural leaders to leave the community. How influential these forces are in creating the tenure pattern of Arvin cannot be assessed, but certainly they are not wholly negligible.

The second aspect of farm organization is the labor requirements of operation. This has been touched upon in the discussion of occupation structure. At that point, we saw that occupation structure is a very important aspect of the difference between the two communities. The question therefore arises as to whether differences in labor requirements on farms in the two communities create that differential in occupation structure. The answer is an unqualified no. For the production of commodities in Arvin requires just under 3 million man-hours of labor while the Dinuba production, reaching the same gross value, requires 3½ million man-hours of work. That the labor structure is a function of scale of operations becomes clear when we examine item (b) under this heading in the list appearing earlier in this chapter. Only a small fraction of Arvin labor is absorbed by farm operators while in Dinuba three-fifths of the work can be performed by farm operators.

It is generally accepted that seasonality of employment creates poor social conditions. Both Arvin and Dinuba have such an uneven demand for labor that severe hardships can be expected in normal times. Dinuba employment opportunities, because of the intensive devotion to grape production, fluctuate more than those of Arvin. An examination of figure 6 shows that Arvin regular workers can be fully employed locally for 6 months in the year, whereas Dinuba regular workers can be so employed only 4 months. The labor picture appears to be better in Arvin than in Dinuba.

It might be assumed however, that Dinuba labor tends to be performed by outsiders to a greater extent than Arvin labor does. Under such an assumption the poverty and poor social conditions which surround wage workers would not appear in Dinuba but would merely show up in other towns where these workers are resident. Such a factor would not affect the availability of social institutions and facilities, but merely the level of living, existence of slum conditions, etc. The sharp peak in the labor demand does, in fact, necessitate over a third more outside workers during a single month than are required in Arvin during its busiest month. This is a function of the sharply peaked demand, and therefore nullifies the effect of Dinuba's disadvantage in this respect. Though Dinuba requires more imported manpower during the single peak month of employment, the total amount of imported work required is very nearly the same. (See appendix C.) The proportion of imported labor requirements to the total is less.

Size of farm operations is the third characteristic of farm organization, and the one that the present study was designed to test. We find that the differences between average size of farm are great—in the neighborhood of 9 to 1 when taken on an acreage basis, 5 to 1 in value of products, and 3 to 1 if adjusted for intensity of operations. Nine-tenths of all farm land is operated in units of 160 acres or more in Arvin as against one-fourth in Dinuba.

Repeated allusions have been made to this factor. We have seen that water resources, historic timing, and type of farming were each to some measure responsible for the large farms in Arvin and the small ones in Dinuba. We have also seen that scale of farming operations had an effect upon the demography of the population, farm tenancy, and, above all, on the requirements for hired labor in each area and the occupation structure of the two communities. It is also true that throughout the intensively cultivated areas of the State, those communities with large-scale farming generally offer fewer economic and social services than those with moderate-sized farms. There remains no question that size of operations is therefore an important factor in establishing the kind of social environments found in Arvin and Dinuba. The place of this factor in the causal forces will be presented in detail in the succeeding section of this chapter.

AN EXPLANATORY HYPOTHESIS

It is now possible to formulate a hypothesis of the chain of causative forces which were responsible for the divergence of social conditions between the two communities whose fundamental cultural heritage and economic circumstances are similar. In formulating such an hypothesis all the pertinent known facts should be explained and their forces understood in terms of recognizable social process. Naturally such a formulation cannot be complete and final but can approach that only insofar as social processes are presently recognized and understood.

The physical landscape and the geographic position of Arvin

and Dinuba are sufficiently similar to produce an agricultural base to support communities equivalent in facilities offered, except that the water supply in Arvin created special circumstances. The necessary depth of the water level and the attendant need for larger capital investments delayed the intensive development of Arvin soils until adequate pumps were produced, and inhibited somewhat the growth of small farms. The delay in development made the land available to big operators at a time when industrialized fruit production in California was at its inception. Therefore, the water situation was doubly responsible for the fact that Arvin was a large farming community. It should be noted, however, that the water supply did not prevent small farms, and a few such units came into the community early and have been farmed continuously ever since. It is doubtful if the water supply had any other direct effects, though its cost may have created specific hardships in an earlier era. It is probable that other causes were contributory to the development of large-scale operations and the belated development of the area, but such causes are not readily apparent and were not the subject of specific analysis. High investment for farm development because of the water situation may also have been a contributory cause to the high tenancy in Arvin, since owners could rent to operators who irrigated several pieces of land from a single well.

The scale of operations that developed in Arvin inevitably had one clear and direct effect upon the community: It skewed the occupation structure so that the majority of the population could only subsist by working as wage labor for others. It probably had some effect upon the development of row crops. The relatively late development of Arvin placed it in a period of growing demand for vegetables and other row crops as contrasted with fruit. These two forces combined to give Arvin a large proportion of row crops, though fruits were also developed to a considerable extent. The large need for labor, and the period of major growth resulted in the aggregation of a large proportion of destitute white migrant labor with poor social and economic background. There is evidence that the quality of persons attracted by the kinds and conditions of work opportunities is somewhat poorer than was attracted to the situation in Dinuba.

The occupation structure of the community, with a great

majority of wage workers and very few persons independently employed and the latter generally persons of considerable means, has had a series of direct effects upon the social conditions in the community. These effects are applicable only given the total cultural situation that exists in America and particularly in California agriculture. The large labor population means inevitably large groups with poor economic circumstances, for the conditions of wage work in agriculture have permitted of nothing else. This in turn means poor housing, low level of living, existence of slum conditions and little money for community improvement. It means that a large portion of the population has little vested interest—economic or social—in the community itself. Such lack of ties, together with the seasonal nature of wage work in agriculture, results in a high turn-over of population (or instability of residence). The laboring population does not take leadership in general civic action and rarely supports organizations that exist, out of a usually well substantiated feeling of ostracism that results from the large differences in economic status. Thus general social facilities do not come into being for lack of leadership and support. This tendency is furthered by their own lack of funds and by their instability as residents in the community.

The occupation structure leaves few who are in an economic and psychological position of leadership. These few consist largely of people who can afford to engage in the social activities of urban centers and who regularly do so. This mobility tends to drain their social interests away from local activities and renders them a less valuable asset to local community welfare then are less well-to-do farmers, though their value to the broader area of activity may be equally great.

This social mobility engendered by their well-being was made possible by the fact that the automobile gave them physical mobility as well. That this mobility was available to them from the outset made it unnecessary to develop local satisfactions, whereas if they had once been developed they would likely have continued. Thus the period of development of Arvin was a contributory cause to its social poverty.

The fact that the large farming community is of necessity made up of large groups of laborers with low incomes on one hand, and a small group of well-to-do persons on the other tends to impoverish its social institutions of the leadership they require. It also impoverishes retail trade. For the farm laborer is generally unable to make a normal complement of purchases for family living because of his poverty, while the farm operator tends to make his purchases, as he does his social contacts, in the city. Thus the merchant group does not grow proportionate to the population, but lags behind it. This again reduces the proportion of independently employed.

The lack of economic and social facilities in the community has a continuative effect. The poor conditions tend to repel those very people who are most needed to enrich it. It was pointed out by farmers, merchants, and laborers alike that persons did not plan to make Arvin their home because of this very lack of facilities. It is very probably one cause for the high tenancy ratio in Arvin, since landowners will often prefer to live elsewhere and live off their rentals. It is possibly a cause for the fact that the average educational attainments of farm workers are below those in the same occupation in Dinuba.

The occupational structure has some influence upon political life in the community. The failure to develop real local interest in community affairs is a prime factor in this causal relationship. The mutual exclusiveness of the two major strata of society also inhibits the development of the community solidarity that would be expected in a more homogeneous group and thus prevents the development of a civic organization. The fact that the group from which natural leadership arises represents but a small minority, while those whose position is relatively insecure forms an overwhelming majority is a further reason for the failure of Arvin to incorporate. The existence of a strong and rich county government contributes to the fact that such political institutions were not developed.

The high rate of tenancy and absentee ownership may reduce further the proportion of persons who are willing to assume leadership. No information on participation by tenure, other than the operator-laborer dichotomy, was obtained. While such effect of tenure pattern upon the social organization is not supported by empirical evidence, the reverse effect, that the social environment increases tenancy, does receive some support.

The accompanying diagrammatic table presents a visual

TABLE 45.—*Diagrammatic presentation of causative forces responsible for the character of Arvin as contrasted with Dinuba* [1]

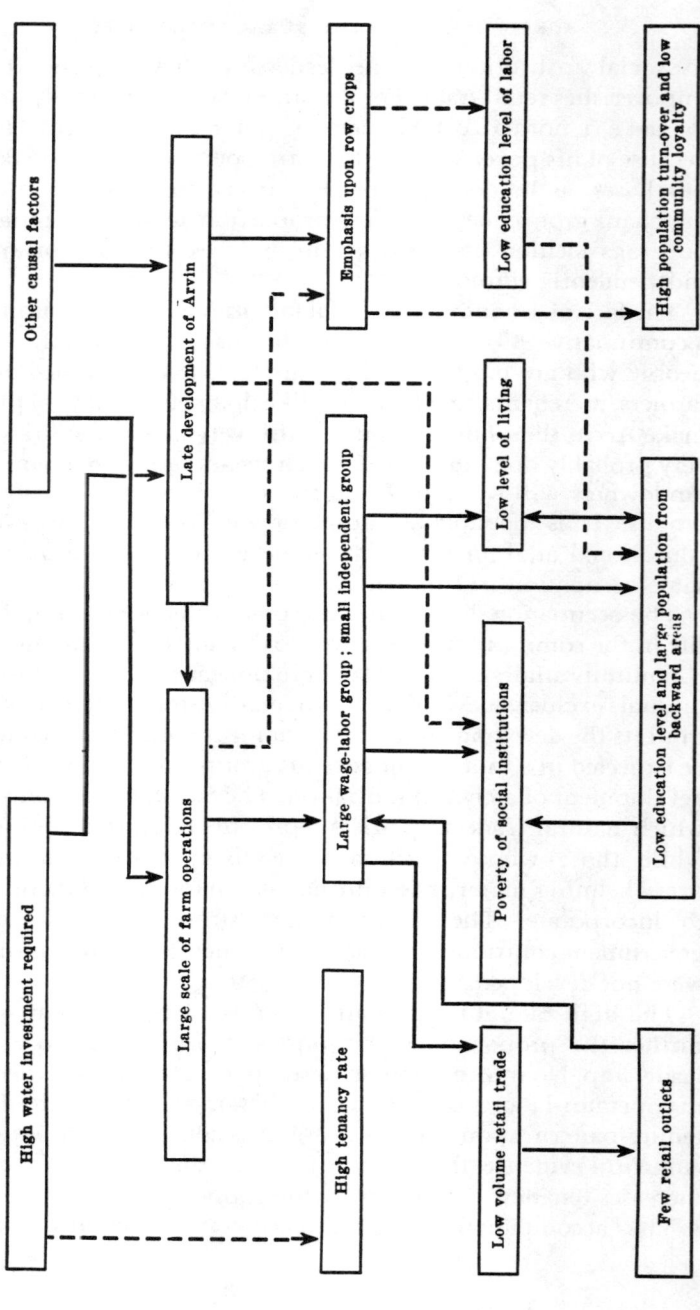

[1] For meaning of this table, and strictures on its usefulness, see text, pp. 110 and 112.

summary of the preceding discussion. The overconcreteness implied with lines and boxes is unavoidable and the chart should be read in terms of the text and other specific strictures. Foremost of these strictures is the fact that the whole chain of causation and intercausation is valid only within the frame of reference of the culture common to the two communities and the area of industrialized farming. Thus the scale of farm operations only creates the occupational structure found under the assumption that land is individually owned and requires hired labor. Cooperative farming would have a different effect. Again, the effect of occupation structure upon social institutions, retail trade, level of living, and demographic character of the population is applicable only in terms of accepted class patterns of behavior and wage scales general in the area. To be complete, therefore, these cultural forces would have to be recognized. Intermediate steps and causal mechanisms have frequently been left out. The second stricture is that all terms indicating qualitative or quantitative comparisons (low, few, poverty, etc.) have direct reference to the comparison of Arvin to Dinuba. Specifically, the causal forces relate to the explanation of the differences between those two communities.

Third, the importance of causal differences varies greatly. Two levels of importance are indicated on the chart. Those with significance which seems beyond question have been indicated with a solid line. Those which appear likely, but for which no specific evidence exists, and those where the presumed causative force or the observed phenomenon showed very small differences, have been indicated with a broken line. These differences are admittedly evaluative, and rest upon the content of preceding discussions. At the same time not all possible causal nexuses have been shown.

Finally, the causative analysis of why farms are large in Arvin and reasons for the belated development there were not subjected to specific analysis. Such analysis as was made shows that the character of the Arvin water supply was an important cause for both. It also indicated that other causative forces were partially responsible for each. Since the analysis of such forces was not made, they were simply lumped together as "other causative factors."

CONCLUSIONS

What, then, is the effect of scale of farm operations upon the character of the rural community? This is the question toward which this study of two California communities has been directed.

In the course of the analysis it has been shown that the two towns, selected for their divergence in scale of farm operations, were similar in most fundamental economic and geographic factors, particularly richness of potential resources, agricultural production, relationship to other communities, and the more general techniques and institutional patterns of production. At the same time they were found to differ in certain other, presumably fundamental characteristics, especially the kind of commodities to which the land was devoted, the age of communities, and the era of major growth. A number of less important differentials were also found to exist, of which origin of the population and tenancy rates were the most significant.

In the realm of social conditions, the two towns showed great divergence. In a series of measures of community character one community was found to meet the standards normally accepted for community life in America far better than the other. The differences were considerable in degree and consistent in direction, so that a causal explanation is immediately invoked.

The fact that the community surrounded by large-scale farm operations offered the poorer social environment according to every test made, could not suffice to show that scale of operations was, in fact, the crucial causative force. The relative importance of this fact and other known differences between the two towns had to be evaluated. As a result of such analysis a detailed hypothesis of the causative forces creating social differences was developed.

Large-scale farm operation is immediately seen to take an important part in the creation of the conditions found in Arvin. Its direct causative effect is to create a community made up a few persons of high economic position, and a mass of individuals whose economic status and whose security and stability are low, and who are economically dependent directly on the few. In the framework of American culture, more particularly that of industrialized farming, this creates immediately a situation where community participation and leadership, economic well-being, and business activities are relatively impoverished.

AGRIBUSINESS AND THE RURAL COMMUNITY 421

The central position of scale of operations and the resulting occupation structure of the community do not deny other contributory causes. The importance of such other forces is difficult to assess. That the period of community growth and the high tenancy rates have an impoverishing effect may be accepted. Other factors, such as the types of commodities produced and the state of origin of residents appear to have some significance.

Such force that these other causes may have in determining community conditions does not vitiate the central hypothesis that large-scale farming does create poorer social conditions in the rural community such farming supports. It is the position of the present writer, after detailed sifting of the evidence presented in this study, that large-scale farming does, in fact, bear the major responsibility for the social differences between Arvin and Dinuba. Several reasons may be summarized as to why such a position seems most tenable.

First of all, the causal mechanism by which large-scale farming creates social conditions is clear and understandable in terms of known social relationships and patterns of behavior. These were developed in earlier sections of this chapter and need no further discussion here.

Second, if we carry large-scale operations to their extreme, we reach the company town. Whatever physical assets may be developed in a company town, there inevitably remains something contrary to normal accepted standards of social life in such a community, with its social hierarchy and dependency ratio. Where company policy does not grant good physical conditions, then the company town is a miserable community indeed. The position of the large-scale farming community lies intermediate between the norm for America and such aberrations on community life. It must be remembered that, though Arvin is dominated by the large operation, a small nucleus of working farmers exists. In the light of the statement made about the function of the small farmer at the Farm Bureau Center, it seems highly probable that had this nucleus not existed, and the land all held in large farms, some of the existing Arvin institutions would not have developed.

Third, similar conclusions were reached by scholars and observers of the California scene a generation ago. A "before and after" picture of the city of Modesto, showing the effects upon community life of small-scale farming was presented in a pamphlet written in 1920 by Prof. R. L. Adams and W. W. Bedford for the Anglo and London Paris Bank of San Francisco.[22] These authors describe the difference between the pre- and post-irrigation as such, it is quite clear that size of holdings plays a prominent part in the differences they describe.

In the preirrigation period, the area around Modesto was described, in the Adams-Bedford book, as

an extensive strip of country devoted solely to grain growing and presents a rather monotonous succession of treeless and vineless fields.

Isolated groups of farm buildings [are found which] are not especially inviting or homelike. The holdings of necessity are large and social intercourse is somewhat restricted. The family keep rather much to themselves—extra help when it is needed, being recruited from a class of labor which is best satisfied if left to itself.

Its [Modesto's] general appearance reflected the declining prosperity of the country upon which a strictly agricultural town must rely for its existence—rough, unpaved streets—muddy in winter and dusty in summer, its stores a collection of mostly one-story unpainted, rickety frame buildings, its water supply from private wells, its sewerage nil, its lighting system coal oil lamps, its population but a few hundred people. (Pp. 15-17.)

In contrast is the postirrigation picture in which small units make for close association and the development of homes. The authors say:

Farming it is said, is a "mode of life." If this is so, then the real test of a section is to be found in the home building of its people. Applying this test, as a preliminary, to the Modesto district one soon finds full justification for all the time, thought, energy, and money spent in water development. For the outstanding feature which first strikes the investigator is that the district is essentially a home district. Pretty bungalows and tidy dwellings, lawns, vine covered porches, roses and old-fashioned flowers, shade trees and well-kept grounds are all strong testimonials that a home-loving people are settling in the community * * *. The small size of the holdings brings the houses rather close together, and a drive in any direction in the most fully settled sections

---

[22]R. L. Adams and W. W. Bedford, The Marvel of Irrigation: A Record of a Quarter Century in the Turlock and Modesto Irrigation Districts—California. Compiled by the Bond Department of the Anglo and London Paris Bank, Sutter and Sansome Streets, San Francisco. Second edition, 1921.

unfolds a succession of pretty homes and a general spirit of contentment.

Today it would be hard to find a more prosperous, bustling town than Modesto * * * [It] is essentially a "home" town. Civic pride is reflected in its flowers, its streets, its parks, its school system. (Pp. 17-20.)

Finally, cursory examination of other communities in California's intensively cultivated agricultural areas substantiates this point of view. In general, the following are associated: new communities, the cultivation of row crops, and large-scale operations. Where they are so found, communities in the Arvin pattern are found. But where the former two are found with small-scale operations, these communities acquire most of the characteristics of Dinuba. On the other hand, none of the towns whose agriculture is made up predominantly of large-scale operations has these amenities.

The study of Arvin and Dinuba shows, therefore, that quality of social conditions is associated with scale of operations; that farm size is in fact an important causal factor in the creation of such differences and that it is reasonable to believe that farm size is the most important cause of these differences.

APPENDIX A

SOURCES OF DATA, METHODOLOGY, AND SAMPLING TECHNIQUE

The nature of the study required the use of several methods and sources of data: community delineation, interviews, schedules, and statistical data on farming and business enterprises and data on membership in clubs and churches. The methods and sources are briefly described.

(1) *Community delineation.*[1]—The community, for purposes of this study, includes the farm area around the town, within which the people normally go to the town for their goods and services. The boundary of the community so defined was established by recognized techniques. First, the civic leaders were asked to indicate these boundaries on a map. Second, the margins were affirmed by interviewing persons living in doubtful areas as to their own community affiliations. In Arvin the boundaries were quite clear and there were no subcommunities or neighborhoods. In Dinuba there was considerable fluidity at the edges, especially toward the towns of Reedley and Kingsburg, and occasionally a "neighborhood" or a subcommunity based upon common religious tenets was found.

(2) *Interviews.*—About 30 persons in each community were interviewed. Such interviews were had with leaders in civic affairs in general, and leaders or representatives of different social, religious, and economic organizations. The interview was informal and designed to elicit information on the general character of the social and economic institutions of the community with particular reference to that phase of community life with which the person being interviewed had some direct connection. Data on the history of the communities were also obtained by

[1] The work of community delineation was done by Walter C. McKain, Jr., regional leader, Division of Farm Population and Rural Welfare, Bureau of Agricultural Economics.

means of interviews. Old records were sought, and provided valuable evidence on the development of the community. General statements concerning the effect of large farm enterprises on the community were obtained, as well as opinion of the present reclamation law. Especially important in this regard were the statements made by farm leaders. The interviews were not, however, in the nature of an opinion poll, but were designed to determine factually the social character of the community.

(3) *Schedules.*—Schedules were taken from a 10-percent sample of homes in each community by two trained investigators over a period of a month each in the two communities. The schedule falls into four sections: (A) Family composition, occupation, and history; (B) social participation in clubs, churches, and informal social events; (C) purchasing habits; and (D) level of living.

(4) *Sampling techniques.*—Each community was divided into two categories: town and rural. The town sample included the area of the town itself—in Dinuba bounded by the incorporated limits, in Arvin by the area of contiguous congestion. Every house in each sample was plotted on a map and the houses numbered consecutively, circling each block clockwise. (Figs. 12 and 13 in the text reproduce the maps of the town and show the houses sampled.) Every tenth number was selected as the sample, and the enumerators instructed to take only the house enumerated, making recalls where necessary. The number of actual houses covered by the survey was 1,304 in Arvin and 2,161 in Dinuba. Due to errors in numbering, two houses too many were included in Arvin, three too few in Dinuba, or a total sample of 132 in Arvin and 213 in Dinuba. No residents refused cooperation in Arvin, but seven refused to answer these questions in Dinuba. The occupation and number of persons in the household were obtained for each of these. Occasionally individual items were omitted because of reluctance on the part of the interviewee or for some other unavoidable reason. This technique was applied with all reasonable care, and can be assumed to represent an adequate random sample of the universe included.

This universe included all households within the area delineated as belonging to each of the respective communities. The only exception to this statement was the houses on the DiGiorgio property, where permission to enter was not granted the field workers. The approximate number of houses was obtained from the management, and these were included in the population estimates (assuming the average persons per family consistent with farm laborers in Arvin). They were not included for any other statistical analyses, not even the distribution of families by occupation of family heads. Most of the residents are farm laborers.

The universe, by definition, includes only residents at the time of field work. Field interviews were made in each community at a time (March-April in Arvin, April-May in Dinuba) when the local employment opportunities in agriculture were insufficient to employ fully the local labor supply (see fig. 6 of text, p. 35). Thus, itinerant workers with residence outside these communities were excluded from the analysis of schedule data.

(5) *Statistical information.*—Statistical data of various kinds, other than those developed from the schedule, form a crucial part of the evidence. Information on crop production was obtained from the agricultural commissioners of the respective counties and from other sources. School attendance and enrollment records were obtained from the superintendents of schools. Two special sources of statistical data were available. Data on farms, classified by size and type, and on acreage in the various major crops in each community have been obtained from Agricultural Adjustment Agency records. These data were collected on a three-county area for use in other studies, but special tabulations and analyses were made for Arvin and Dinuba.[2] Information on the volume and character of retail trade and the size of business establishments has been obtained through a careful analysis of the records of the California State Board of Equalization. A description of the nature of these data and the methods of analysis are given in appendixes B and G.

(6) *Church and club membership data.*—Because of the tendency for religious and social bodies to draw distinctions in membership which reflect the degree of social cleavage in the rural community, lists of membership showing occupation were obtained from several representative churches and clubs in each community.

---

[2] Edwin E. Wilson and Marion Clawson, Agricultural Land Ownership and Operation in the Southern San Joaquin Valley, Calif. Bureau of Agricultural Economics, Berkeley, Calif. (Mimeographed.) 1945.

APPENDIX B

AGRICULTURAL DATA, SOURCES, AND METHODS[1]

1. *Source.*—Data on the volume of agricultural production, number and types of farms, characteristics of ownership and tenure were obtained from records of the Agricultural Adjustment Agency. These records were obtained and analyzed for studies of the size of farm-operating and farm-ownership units and their use here was incidental to the major purpose for which they were obtained. Record data apply to the year 1940.

The base for these data was the "farm unit." The farm unit is a contiguous piece of land, all of which is operated by one single farmer and owned by one single owner who may or may not be the operator. One owner may have several such units, each with a different operator, and one operator may be farming several such units, each with a different owner. On the basis of these farm units, the operating units (a combination of farm units having the same operator) and ownership units (combinations of farm units owned by the same person or corporation) can be brought together. The former of these are called farms for purposes of this study, the latter are called ownership units.

The Agricultural Adjustment Agency data for each farm unit were recorded on cards and included the following: Location of unit, operator and owner, cross references to other farm units both owned and operated by the same man, total acres in the unit, and acreage by land-use classes, and yield of cotton, potatoes, and wheat. Land-use classes were: Range land, noncrop pasture, lanes and buildings, commercial orchard (including grapes), cotton, wheat for grain, rice, sugar beets, potatoes, commercial vegetables,

[1] The collection of the data from the Agricultural Adjustment Agency records was supervised by J. Karl Lee and the analyses by Edwin E. Wilson, both of the Bureau of Agricultural Economics, Berkeley. Credit for this material is due them, though responsibility for its use rests with the author.

barley for grain, wheat hay, other grain hay, grain sorghums, summer fallow, idle cropland, alfalfa, ladino, cropland pasture, and spaces for other soil-depleting and other nondepleting crops.

2. *Farm types.*—Farms were classifed into 10 types on the basis of these data by specialists in farm management. These types and brief definitions of them in terms of types of land use are as follows:

(1) *Stock ranches.*—Units engaged in the production of livestock by means of range. Included units over 320 acres with 90 percent or more of the land in range, pasture, or hay, but not over 30 percent in hay.

(2) *Forage-consuming livestock.*—Mostly dairies and a few other producers of animal products. Included units with 30 percent of more of the cropland in hay and pasture combined and at least 10 percent in each of these, but with less than 50 percent of their land in field crops. (Classification had to be made without direct knowledge of the number or even the presence of livestock on the unit.)

(3) *Specialized fruit ranches.*—Units with 80 percent or more of the cropland in commercial orchards, and at least 2 acres of fruit.

(4) *Major fruit farms.*—Fruit-producing units which are less highly specialized include those with from 25 to 80 percent of all cropland in fruit, provided that at least 2 acres are in fruit.

(5) *Winter field crops.*—Units were 80 percent or more of the cropland is devoted to winter field crops, which includes wheat, barley, oats, flax, small grain hay, or grain pasture.

(6) *Winter and summer field crops.*—Units with land in both winter and summer field crops, but with less than 80 percent of the cropland in either.

(7) *Summer field crops.*—Units with 80 percent of the cropland in summer field crops, which includes cotton, sugar beets, potatoes, commercial vegetables, truck crops, grain sorghums, grain hay, alfalfa, or hay.

(8) *Idle.*—Units where 90 percent of the cropland is not in production.

(9) *Part-time.*—All units except fruit farms having less than 5 acres of cropland.

(10) *Small ranches.*—Units of under 320 acres with 90 percent of the total in pasture.

3. *Farm size.*—The size of units in acres is given in the

Agricultural Adjustment Agency records. However, acreage is a poor measure of size as acres in various crops are not comparable in capital requirements, labor requirements, or income potential. For that reason, size in standard acres was calculated for the farms in Arvin and Dinuba. These standard acres were called acreequivalent acres, frequently abbreviated A-E acres.

A standard acre is a unit of land in any crop which under normal conditions for that crop in the Central Valley of California has the gross-income-producing potential of an acre of irrigated alfalfa in the same area. The size of each operating unit was calculated by multiplying the actual acreage in each crop by the conversion factor which expresses the ratio of income-producing potentiality of that crop to the income-producing potentiality of an acre of alfalfa. The factors used were developed by Arthur Shultis, of the Giannini Foundation of Agricultural Economics, University of California, and apply directly to Madera County. There is no reasonable question of the validity of extrapolation to the neighboring counties. The following is the table of factors used:

Alfalfa	1.00	Garden	1.00
Beans	.60	Grain	.15
Commercial orchard	2.00	Grain hay	.05
Commercial vegetables	1.80	Grain sorghums	.30
Corn	.50	Idle cropland and miscellaneous	.02
Cotton	1.40	Lanes, buildings, etc.	.02
Cropland pasture, dry	.05	Ladino	.60
Cropland pasture, irrigated	.40	Melons	1.00
Flax	.70	Noncrop pasture	.02
Nursery	3.00	Sugar beets	1.80
Oat and vetch hay	.20	Summer fallow	.01
Potatoes	1.80	Tomatoes	1.50
Rangeland	.01	Young and noncommercial orchard	1.00
Sudan grass	.20		

A slightly different method, involving the same assumptions but based upon the type of farm as classified above, was used for calculating A-E size in the communities listed in table 1. While this method is less direct, the comparability is great as shown by the fact that in Arvin the A-E size by the special method was 265 A-E acres as against 247 A-E acres by the method used for all communities. In Dinuba the respective figures were 89 and 84.

4. *Gross farm income.*—Gross farm income from all the farms in each community was calculated, using known 1940 acreages, 1937-41 yields, and 1935-39 prices for the San Joaquin Valley.

AGRIBUSINESS AND THE RURAL COMMUNITY

Estimation of income is fairly direct and highly reliable. Using yields and prices, returns per acre were calculated and these returns multiplied by acres in the various crops. Certain assumptions and manipulations were necessary, since crop data were not always broken down with sufficient exactitude. The following major assumptions were made:

(1) All commercial orchard was assumed to be vineyard. This is very nearly correct for Dinuba, less so for Arvin. Since returns per acre vary in both directions but not very greatly in either, the error of such an assumption is slight. Income was based upon Shultis' calculations.

(2) Commercial vegetables were given the average value of all commercial vegetables, developed by Shultis in his calculations of standard acres. Acreages in commercial vegetables were not broken down by type, so this average figure was necessary. Again, no great error can enter here.

(3) No income from crops was attributed directly to either milomaize or any of the pasture uses of land. It was assumed that income from these classes was realized through the sale of livestock and livestock products.

(4) Yields were based upon 1937-41 averages (irrigated land) for the San Joaquin Valley. Actual yields were used for cotton and potatoes. Wheat, barley, oats, and rye yields were based upon weighted average of irrigated and nonirrigated yields.

(5) Prices were based upon estimates of prices received by California farmers for the years 1935-39, made by the California Crop Reporting Service.

(6) All unspecified non-soil-depleting crops were assumed to be pasture and all unspecified soil-depleting crops were assumed to be oats.

A tabulation (table 46), based on these assumptions, shows gross income per acre and total gross income for crops.

These estimates can be considered reasonably exact. It is doubtful if there is any appreciable bias which would affect the relative gross returns between two communities, the most important aspect of this table.

Calculations of returns from livestock enterprises were more difficult to arrive at. Estimates of the number of livestock of each kind were made by assuming a proportionate distribution of the

TABLE 46.—*Gross income per acre and total gross income for crops: Arvin and Dinuba* [1]

Crop	Yield		Price	Income per acre	Arvin income		Dinuba income	
	Unit	Amount			Acres	Income	Acres	Income
			Dollars	Dollars		1,000 dollars		1,000 dollars
Grapes				107.50	7,875.0	847	16,294.9	1,752
Cotton				78.64	6,274.3	493	2,357.7	185
Lint	Pounds	629.0	.105	66.04				
Seed	Hundredweight	9.2	1.37	12.60				
Potatoes	Bushels	315.0	.71	223.65	2,047.3	458	10.4	2
Sugar beets	Tons	13.0	5.60	72.80	32.3	2		
Commercial vegetables				90.00	627.1	56	278.1	25
Milo	Bushels	39.0		112.8			951.6	
Wheat	do	16.2	.81	13.12	12,004.3	157	75.6	1
Barley	do	27.1	.50	13.55	3,990.2	54	944.3	13
Oats	do	27.4	.41	12.35	864.4	11	831.0	10
Alfalfa	Tons	4.9	10.16	49.78	3,283.7	163	3,060.1	152
Rangeland					170.0		7.7	
Noncrop pasture					1,078.3		4,234.6	
Summer fallow and idle	Pasture				3,472.4		2,307.7	
Ladino and crop pasture					377.3		737.2	
Other nondepleting					452.6		437.5	
Total						2,241		2,140

[1] For assumptions and explanations, see text.

TABLE 47.—*Estimated head of livestock and gross income from stock: Arvin and Dinuba*

Class of stock	Unit	Production [1]	Price [2]	Gross income per head	Arvin		Dinuba	
					Number [3]	Gross income	Number [4]	Gross income
			Dollars	Dollars		1,000 dollars		1,000 dollars
Horses and mules over 3 months.[5]					421		749	
Milk cows and heifers over 2 years.	Pounds butterfat	[6] 325	0.466	151.40	1,331	201	1,971	299
Beef cattle over 3 months	Pounds of meat	600	.0736	44.16	825	36	1,924	86
Sows and gelts to farrow	do	[7] 1,930	.0894	172.55	187	32	181	32
Sheep and lambs over 6 months.	do	[8] 58	.0790	4.58	262	1	70	1
	Pounds wool	[9] 10	.24	2.40				
Chickens over 4 months	Dozen eggs	14	.24	3.36	14,150	47	47,900	162
Chickens sold	Pounds meat	[9] 2	.25	.50	8,500	4	22,300	12
Turkeys raised	do	18	[9] .25	4.50	180	1	3,435	16
Total						322		608

[1] Fluharty, In Line Prices. Report to State Agricultural War Board.
[2] State Crop Reporting Service, Prices Received by California Farmers, 1935–39.
[3] Estimated on the basis of 1940 Census of Agriculture, using 31 percent of total for fifteenth township, Kern County, of which Arvin is a part.
[4] Estimated on the basis of 1940 Census of Agriculture, using 56 percent of total for Dinuba Township, Tulare County.
[5] No direct income, figure used to calculate feeding requirements.
[6] Assuming 4 percent butterfat.
[7] Based upon pork produced per sow.
[8] Assumed only ewes recorded in census, 80 percent lamb crop and selling lambs at 72 pounds gives an average of 58 pounds per sheep and lamb.
[9] Estimated production and prices.

total livestock within the minor civil division, as reported by the census of 1940, on an areal basis. That is, the area in farms in each community was calculated as a proportion of the total area in farms in the township, and stock apportioned according to this ratio.

Table 47 shows the number of stock by major classes, the annual income per head, and the annual returns to the community.

These two tabulations show the total gross income (except income from pasture lands and milo) to all farmers, first for crops, and second, for livestock and livestock products. However, it would not be appropriate merely to add these two figures. To do so would include considerable duplication, as no allowance has been made for crops grown which are fed to stock rather than sold.

For that reason calculations of the feed requirements of the livestock in the two communities have been made (table 48). On the basis of these feed requirements and estimated livestock numbers, it is possible to estimate the value of livestock feed. For purposes of bookkeeping, we can assume feeding of local products and purchase of similar feeds to make up the deficit, when such exists. In feeding grains; oats, barley, and wheat were fed in that order, and the remainder was sold after livestock requirements were met. Cottonseed was used as concentrates. The same purchase prices as sale price was used. Grain purchased was barley. Using these assumptions, we get the following value of grains, concentrates, and hay fed:

	Arvin	Dinuba
Grains	$36,000	$64,000
Concentrates	22,000	40,000
Hay	67,000	104,000
Total	125,000	208,000

For bookkeeping purposes it is appropriate to deduct the feed requirements either from gross value of livestock or from crop production. The latter procedure leaves certain crops deficit. Table 49 shows both allocations, while the text (see table 7, p. 26) shows the value of crops produced and the net value of livestock products.

5. *Cost of production and net profit.*—The calculations presented in the preceding section of this appendix indicate gross

TABLE 48.—*Feed requirements for livestock* [1]

Kind of livestock	Grains	Commercial by-product	Hay
	Pounds	*Pounds*	*Pounds*
Horses and mules, including colts	400.0		4,900
Milk cows over 2 years old	900.0	850.0	8,000
Dairy heifers under 2 years old	50.0	0	1,200
Beef cattle over 3 months old	50.0	15.0	,700
Sows and gelts to farrow	375.0	25.0	30
Sheep and lambs over 6 months old (hundredweight)	8.0	8.0	160
Chickens over 4 months old	66.0	18.0	
Chickens sold	6.7	3.9	
Turkeys raised	80.0	18.0	

[1] Pasture excluded.

Source: 1943 Maximum Wartime Production Capacity Study for California, p. 36, Appendix, Bureau of Agricultural Economics.

TABLE 49.—*Dollar value of commodities produced in Arvin and Dinuba*
[In thousands of dollars]

Commodity	Arvin			Dinuba		
	Produced	Amount fed	Net value	Produced	Amount fed	Net value
Fruit	847		847	1,752		1,752
Cotton:						
Lint	414		414	156		156
Seed	79	22	57	29	40	−11
Grain	222	36	186	24	64	−40
Vegetables	516		516	27		27
Forage crops	163	67	96	152	104	48
Total crop value	2,241	125	2,116	2,140	208	1,932
Value of livestock [1]	197	125	322	400	208	608
Total value of production	2,438		2,438	2,540		2,540

[1] For value of livestock the net value (above feed) appears first, and the gross value appears in the third column. This reversal is appropriate since the livestock consume the feed.

returns (deducting only cost of livestock feed). No calculations have been made either of the net returns to farm operator or of the unit cost of production. It has been assumed that net income and total cost of production per acre are the same for both communities. This assumption is reasonably accurate, though not exactly so. Cost of water (and perhaps other production factors) is somewhat higher in Arvin than in Dinuba, but labor costs in Dinuba appear to be greater. Since Arvin producers reach an extremely early market they probably receive higher prices. This is particularly true of fruits, potatoes, and commercial vegetables. Yields on the relatively new soils of Arvin are also advantageous.

The major cost of production disadvantage in the Arvin area is the cost of water. Because it seemed possible that the cost of water might be sufficient cause to account for the different economic conditions in the two communities, a careful analysis has been made of water costs in the two communities. It should be pointed out that, in the long run at least, water costs should be absorbed by land value, since the land values are very low without water and the two combined are an economic asset far exceeding the sum of each separately. Ignorance of irrigation requirements and costs may make this consideration inoperative on a short-run basis.

Water costs were calculated on units of average size for each community, and the cost of water in Arvin was also calculated on the basis of average size of units in Dinuba, in order to make more direct comparisons possible. These sizes are: Dinuba, 57 acres; Arvin, 497 acres and 57 acres.

The following assumptions were made:

(1) Duty of water: 2 feet 3 inches in Dinuba (average for San Joaquin Valley) and 2 feet 11 inches for Arvin (adjusted to allow for differences in precipitation). On this basis total annual water requirements per farm are: Dinuba, 143 acre-feet; Arvin 1,451 and 166 acre-feet.

(2) Irrigation season of 7 months with wells operated half the time during these months, and peak demands were assumed to be taken care of by full-time use of wells during those periods. Well requirements on this basis are: Dinuba, 309 gallons per minute; Arvin, 3,135 and 359 gallons per minute. Single wells would be sufficient for 57-acre farms, but three wells would be required for the 497-acre farm.

(3) Average water-level conditions in each community were used. A report of the Alta irrigation district, based upon 65 wells and made in 1931, indicated an average depth of 43.5 feet. A report to the Kern County Water Development Commission entitled "Cost per Acre-Foot of Pumped Irrigation Water in Kern County," by C. H. Monett, based upon eight Arvin wells and made in 1933 was used for Arvin. This report indicated a depth of 114 feet, but this was increased to 151 feet on the basis of information as to the recession of the ground water level since that date. These two reports indicated average draw-down of 8 feet in Dinuba and 26 feet in Arvin, and these figures were used. A pumping head of 54 feet and of 182 feet was used for Dinuba and Arvin, respectively,

allowing for discharge of water at a point a few feet above the ground, as indicated in these reports.

(4) Pumping efficiency was reported in these two sources and was calculated at 42 percent and 64 percent for Dinuba and Arvin. These figures are in keeping with observations made since that time, with considerably more efficiency on the larger pumps. The lower pump efficiency was used for the small farm in Arvin, in keeping with this observation.

(5) It was assumed that all pumping was done by electricity, since but few pumps are driven by gas or butane. On the basis of flow and pump efficiencies, the kilowatt-hours required per acre-foot of water were calculated on the basis of the following standard formula:

$$\text{Kw.-hr.} = \frac{43.560 \times 62.4 \times 746 \times \text{head}}{33,000 \times 60 \times 1,000 \times \text{efficiency}} = 1.024 \frac{\text{head}}{\text{efficiency}}$$

This resulted in a kilowatt-hour requirement of 132 for Dinuba and 291 for the large Arvin farm and 444 for the small Arvin farm (higher because of assumed lower efficiency). The total kilowatt-hours for each of these sizes, based upon water requirements are: Dinuba 18,860; Arvin, 422,241 on the larger unit, and 73,704 on the smaller.

(6) The size of motor was calculated on the basis of the above data according to the following standard formula:

$$\text{H. P.} = \frac{\text{G. P. M.} \times 62.4 \times \text{total head in feet}}{450 \times 550 \times \text{efficiency in percent}}$$

On the basis of this calculation, a 10-horsepower motor was required in Dinuba; three 75-horsepower motors on the large Arvin unit and one 45-horsepower motor on the smaller unit.

(7) The demand and energy charges for power were developed on the basis of rates used by the Pacific Gas & Electric Co., which serves these areas. It has three agricultural power rates, known respectively as schedule P-3-S, schedule P-12-S, and schedule P-13-S. The first two schedules embody demand charges which are based upon the connected horsepower load and energy charges which are based upon the number of kilowatt-hours consumed. The third schedule has only a charge for energy, but in using this schedule

the operator must guarantee a minimum charge per horsepower of connected load. Schedule P-12-S can only be used where the connected horsepower load amounts to 200 horsepower or more. Power bills were calculated on the basis of all applicable schedules and the lowest cost used, in keeping with actual procedure. It developed that schedule P-13-S resulted in the lowest total power bill for each unit.

The cost of pumps and motors was developed from information collected in the field observations made in the San Joaquin Valley in the winter of 1944, when records on size of motors and original cost were obtained. On the basis of these observations, costs were assigned. These costs are below present costs of such motors but in line with the cost of motors of these sizes over the past 20 years. The following costs resulted from these calculations: $800 for the pump and motors on the Dinuba farm, $2,500 each for the three pumps and motors on the large Arvin farm, and $1,700 for the pump and motor on the small Arvin farm.

(8) Records from the report for Kern County referred to in the foregoing indicate that the average depth of the well in the Arvin community is approximately 500 feet. This depth was used for all wells in that area. Comparable records were not immediately available for Dinuba. However, on the basis of the total pumping head and depth of wells required in other areas having a comparable head, 100 feet was assumed for Dinuba.

Current field reports indicate that it cost from $3 to $5 per foot to drill a well and put in the casing in these areas. An average of $4 per foot was assumed for wells in both communities regardless of required size of casing or depth of well. On the basis of this information the average investment in wells on farms of the size indicated was $1,200 for Dinuba, $3,700 for the small farm in Arvin, and $13,500 for the three wells on the large farm in Arvin. These costs would be higher under wartime prices.

(9) Because a large proportion of the water in the Dinuba area is surface water, brought by diversion from the Kings River, certain special adjustments must be made. It has been assumed that the facilities for a full water supply were maintained, but power, repair, and service costs were adjusted to actual requirements. During the past 12 years the amount of water delivered by the district varied from about 2 inches to nearly 2 feet per acre, so that

an assumed supply requires a well that will furnish virtually full water requirements.

Over 12 years, from 1930 to 1941, inclusive, the Alta irrigation district delivered an average of 1.18 acre-feet of gravity water to all land within the district. It was, therefore, assumed that 1.32 acre feet per acre of water would be pumped per year. This reduces the kilowatt-hour required from 18,876 to 9,931. Repair and service charges were arbitrarily reduced from $12 per year to $8 in light of this adjustment. These savings were partially offset by cost of surface water, as follows: The 1941 annual report of the Alta irrigation district indicates that the average assessment was 59 cents per acre. This resulted in a total bill for gravity water of $33.63 for the 57-acre farm.

(10) The tax rate used was based upon the Kern County report. Actually for tax purposes the pumping plants are valued considerably less than the figures used here while the tax rate is higher. The final result is very nearly accurate.

On the basis of these assumptions, the following table of water costs on three hypothetical units is presented:

TABLE 50.—*Itemized comparative costs of irrigation in Arvin and Dinuba by size of farm*

Item	Arvin		Dinuba—57-acre unit
	497-acre unit	57-acre unit	
Total investment in pumping plants	$13,500.00	$3,700.00	$1,200.00
Fixed costs:			
Interest at 5 percent	675.00	185.00	60.00
Depreciation at 5 percent	675.00	185.00	60.00
Taxes at 4 mills	54.00	15.00	5.00
Gravity water			34.00
Total	1,404.00	385.00	159.00
Variable costs:			
Repair and service	120.00	40.00	8.00
Energy	1,915.00	384.00	61.00
Total	2,035.00	424.00	69.00
Total costs	3,439.00	809.00	228.00
Cost:			
Per acre	6.92	14.19	4.00
Per acre-foot of water pumped	2.37	4.87	1.59

APPENDIX C
ANALYSIS OF MONTHLY LABOR REQUIREMENTS

The data on monthly labor requirements were based upon the acreage in various commodities and the requirements for all labor as established by detailed farm management records for most of those crops, supplemented by additional information for specific crops when not covered by these farm management records. Tables 51 and 52 (pp. 130 and 131) show the crops and acreages, the monthly per-acre labor requirement, and the total labor requirement in each community for Arvin and Dinuba, respectively.

Crop acreages were obtained from the Agricultural Adjustment Agency data. Alfalfa, cotton, grain, sorghums, pastures, and potatoes were given directly for the year 1940. Minor crop acreages were eliminated. Grapes were segregated from deciduous fruits in Arvin on the basis of average tonnage shipped during the 3 years 1941-43. Eleven percent of the total acreage was allocated to deciduous fruit and 89 percent to grapes. About 90 percent of all deciduous fruits were plums, and the seasonal labor requirements for plums was used for the total quantity. The error would amount to far less than 10 percent here, because all deciduous fruits compete heavily for labor. In Dinuba fruits were segregated into four classes, based upon proportions of each as indicated in the data obtained from the local farm labor office.

Monthly requirements for all labor were obtained from a series of records taken by the staff of the Bureau of Agricultural Economics from farm operators in the upper San Joaquin Valley. The following tabulation indicates the number of records used for each major crop, or the alternate source of data.

The data from farm records include all labor, while those from published sources refer to hired labor only. No correction was made for this difference, since the total amount of labor involved and the proportion of work performed by the operator is small.

Alfalfa	Old alfalfa, all sizes	9
Cotton	All sizes	27
Grain	Barley	4
Sorghum	Milo (medium size)	1
Pasture	Medium irrigated pasture	3
Potatoes	All sizes	7
Raisin grapes	Thompson seedless	8
Other grapes	Thompson seedless (leaving out turning and rolling of trays)	8
Deciduous fruit (Arvin)	Data on plums from R. L. Adams [1]	
Deciduous fruit (Dinuba)	Data on miscellaneous fruits from Farm Labor Advisory Committee.[2]	
Citrus fruit (Dinuba)	Data on citrus fruits from Farm Labor Advisory Committee.[2]	

[1] R. L. Adams, Agricultural Labor Requirements and Supply, Kern County. Mimeographed Report No. 70, Giannini Foundation of Agricultural Economics, June 1940, Berkeley. Table 9, p. 16.
[2] Tabulation entitled "1944 Estimate of Number of People Needed in Agriculture in Tulare County," summary of survey by Agricultural Extension Service in cooperation with Tulare County Farm Labor Advisory Office.

Probably the major source of error in these calculations derives from using selected crops. The total requirement is little affected by this, but for both communities it results in a slight tendency to accentuate the peaking for labor demand.

An estimate was made on the proportion of labor performed by the operator and by local labor. These are really estimates of potential labor rather than actual labor performed by these groups. Farm operators were assumed to work a maximum of 250 hours per month. The number of farm operators indicated in the Agricultural Adjustment Agency data is 133 for Arvin, 722 in Dinuba. Obviously all farm operators do not work at labor full time, so that the actual labor so furnished was less, and proportionately less, on the big operations in Arvin than on the small operations in Dinuba. However, availability of operator for management should compensate in increased efficiency at least to the extent of his own labor. On the basis of these calculations Arvin farmers have a potential supply of 33,000 man-hours of labor per month and Dinuba operators 180,000 per month.

The potential local labor supply was determined by the number of resident laborers (farm labor and farm foremen) recorded in the schedules. Assuming the recorded laborers represent 10 percent of the total, and adding the 140 laborers resident on the DiGiorgio farms, the available labor in Arvin was 940 and in Dinuba 550. It is assumed that this group normally worked 200 hours a month when work was available and can furnish a maximum supply of 188,000 man-hours of work in Arvin and 110,000 in Dinuba. Beside these, there are a number of workers available during the peak season. In Arvin 69 such part-time agricultural workers were recorded, while

AGRIBUSINESS AND THE RURAL COMMUNITY 441

in Dinuba there were 60. Assuming these represent 10 percent of the total (the sample proportion) and that they worked 100 hours per month when work was available, they could supply an additional sixty-nine and sixty thousand man-hours during peak months. Altogether, there are available, on the basis of these assumptions, 287,000 man-hours of labor per month in Arvin and 350,000 in Dinuba. Packing-shed labor was not included in any of these calculations. The following tables show the monthly breakdown of this labor supply against calculated demand:

TABLE 51.—*Calculations of labor requirements, by months and by crop classes: Arvin*

A. FACTOR USED IN CALCULATING LABOR REQUIREMENTS [1]

	Alfalfa	Cotton	Grain	Sorghum	Pasture	Potatoes	Grapes	Other deciduous fruit	Total
Month:									
January	0.1	5.0	0.4	0	0.9	8.2	9.6	29.9	
February	0	3.4	0	0	1.0	6.9	14.5	.3	
March	2.2	3.0	0	1.9	5.3	3.9	12.8	2.2	
April	12.0	2.9	0	0	12.4	11.6	9.9	62.8	
May	11.9	8.7	0	.7	12.2	47.6	6.1	1.3	
June	13.0	6.6	1.0	.4	12.1	36.8	8.0	104.2	
July	12.2	8.0	.2	4.5	14.0	.8	15.1	356.0	
August	11.7	6.0	.4	1.9	15.6	0	7.2	1.1	
September	12.1	13.5	1.4	0	14.9	0	29.9	0	
October	3.4	20.7	.7	0	19.7	.7	18.4	0	
November	0	16.6	.6	1.6	6.9	.4	2.1	0	
December	0	13.0	1.6	0	4.9	2.6	6.4	29.9	

B. ESTIMATED ACREAGE IN EACH CROP CLASS [2]

	Alfalfa	Cotton	Grain	Sorghum	Pasture	Potatoes	Grapes	Other deciduous fruit	Total
Acreage	3,284	6,274	15,996	113	1,078	2,047	7,009	386	

C. ESTIMATED LABOR REQUIREMENTS [3]

	Alfalfa	Cotton	Grain	Sorghum	Pasture	Potatoes	Grapes	Other deciduous fruit	Total
Month:									
January	328	31,370	6,398	0	970	16,785	67,286	25,893	149,030
February	0	21,332	0	0	1,078	14,124	101,631	280	138,425
March	7,225	18,822	0	215	5,713	7,983	89,715	1,905	131,578
April	39,408	18,195	0	0	13,367	23,715	69,389	51,385	218,489
May	39,080	54,584	0	79	13,152	97,437	42,755	1,126	248,213
June	42,692	41,408	15,995	45	13,044	73,283	86,072	90,237	332,776
July	40,065	50,192	3,199	509	15,092	1,638	105,836	308,296	524,827
August	38,423	37,644	6,398	215	16,709	0	50,465	933	150,807
September	39,736	84,699	22,393	0	16,062	0	209,569	0	372,459
October	11,166	129,872	11,197	0	11,535	1,433	128,966	0	294,169
November	0	104,148	9,597	181	7,438	819	14,719	0	136,902
December	0	81,562	25,592	0	5,282	5,322	44,858	25,893	188,509
Total	258,123	673,828	100,769	1,244	119,442	242,569	981,261	506,948	2,886,184

[1] Estimates of man-hours of labor required per acre during month. See text for fuller explanation.
[2] Acreage in crops for community area, as delineated.
[3] Calculation factor times acreage in crop.

TABLE 52.—*Calculations of labor requirements, by months and by crop classes: Dinuba*

A. FACTORS USED IN CALCULATING LABOR REQUIREMENTS [1]

	Alfalfa	Cotton	Grain	Sorghum	Pasture	Potatoes	Raisin grapes	Other grapes	Citrus fruit [2]	Other fruits	Total
Month:											
January	0.1	5.0	0.4	0	0.9	8.2	9.6	9.6		15.4	
February	0	3.4	0	0	1.0	6.9	14.5	14.5		14.5	
March	2.2	3.0	0	1.9	5.3	3.9	12.8	12.8		6.1	
April	12.0	2.9	0	0	12.4	11.6	9.9	9.9		14.1	
May	11.9	8.7	0	.7	12.2	47.6	6.1	6.1		14.5	
June	13.0	6.6	1.0	.4	12.1	35.8	8.0	8.0		11.1	
July	12.2	8.0	.2	4.5	14.0	.8	17.1	15.1		19.2	
August	11.7	6.0	.4	1.9	15.5	0	9.3	7.2		25.9	
September	12.1	13.5	1.4	0	14.9	0	37.0	29.9		21.7	
October	3.4	20.7	.7	0	10.7	.7	10.4	18.4		10.7	
November	0	16.6	.6	1.6	6.9	.4	2.1	2.1		5.4	
December	0	13.0	1.6	0	4.9	2.6	0.4	6.4		8.9	

B. ESTIMATED ACREAGE IN EACH CROP CLASS [3]

	Alfalfa	Cotton	Grain	Sorghum	Pasture	Potatoes	Raisin grapes	Other grapes	Citrus fruit	Other fruits	Total
Acreage	3,036	2,358	1,020	952	4,235	10	11,520	1,970	2,165	640	

C. ESTIMATED LABOR REQUIREMENTS [4]

	Alfalfa	Cotton	Grain	Sorghum	Pasture	Potatoes	Raisin grapes	Other grapes	Citrus fruit	Other fruits	Total
Month:											
January	304	11,790	408	0	3,812	82	110,592	18,912	9,488	33,341	188,729
February	0	8,017	0	0	4,235	69	167,040	28,565	3,020	31,393	243,239
March	6,679	7,074	0	1,809	22,446	39	147,456	25,216	3,424	13,207	227,350
April	36,432	6,838	0	0	52,514	116	114,040	19,503	5,256	30,527	265,234
May	36,126	20,515	0	666	51,667	476	70,272	12,017	11,240	31,393	234,372
June	39,468	15,563	1,020	381	51,244	358	92,160	15,760	10,040	94,032	250,026
July	37,039	18,864	204	4,284	59,290	8	196,932	29,747	4,760	41,668	392,756
August	35,521	14,148	408	1,809	65,643	0	107,130	14,184	4,290	56,074	229,123
September	36,736	31,833	1,428	0	63,102	0	426,240	58,903	3,744	46,981	663,967
October	10,322	48,811	714	0	45,315	7	223,488	36,248	3,444	23,166	391,515
November	0	39,143	612	1,523	29,222	4	224,192	4,137	13,392	11,691	120,916
December	0	30,654	1,632	0	20,732	26	73,728	12,608	16,072	19,269	174,741
Total	238,627	253,250	6,426	10,472	469,242	1,185	1,953,284	275,800	362,642	68,980	3,456,968

[1] Estimates of man-hours of labor required per acre during month. See text for fuller explanation.
[2] Data for citrus fruits based upon local estimates of requirements.
[3] Acreage in crops for community area, as delineated.
[4] Calculation factor times acreage in crop.

TABLE 53.—*Estimated monthly labor requirements and theoretical source of labor supply: Arvin*

[1,000 man-hours]

Month	Estimated man-hours required	Estimates of labor furnished by—			
		Farm operator [1]	Resident labor [2]	Resident seasonal labor [3]	Imported workers [4]
January	149	33	116		
February	138	33	105		
March	132	33	99		
April	218	33	185		
May	248	33	188	27	
June	335	33	188	69	43
July	525	33	188	69	235
August	151	33	118		
September	372	33	188	69	82
October	294	33	188	69	4
November	137	33	104		
December	189	33	156		
Total	2,886	396	1,823	303	364

[1] Work performed by 133 farm operators reported in Agricultural Adjustment Agency records, assuming each operator works 250 hours per month for a maximum of 33,000 hours in any 1 month.
[2] Work performed by 940 family heads who are laborers, assuming that each works 200 hours per month when work is available, for a maximum of 160,000 hours in any 1 month.
[3] Work performed by 690 family members other than head, assuming each works 100 hours per month during all months when work is available, for a maximum of 69,000 hours in any 1 month.
[4] Residual employment opportunity for itinerants, following from above assumptions.

TABLE 54.—*Estimated monthly labor requirements and theoretical source of labor supply: Dinuba*

[1,000 man-hours]

Month	Estimated man-hours required	Estimates of labor furnished by—			
		Farm operator [1]	Resident labor [2]	Resident seasonal labor [3]	Imported workers [4]
January	189	180	9		
February	243	180	63		
March	227	180	47		
April	265	180	85		
May	234	180	54		
June	250	180	70		
July	393	180	110	60	43
August	299	180	110	9	
September	669	180	110	60	319
October	392	180	110	60	42
November	121	121			
December	175	175			
Total	3,457	2,096	768	189	404

[1] Work performed by 722 farm operators, reported in Agricultural Adjustment Agency records, assuming each operator works 250 hours per month, for a maximum of 180,000 hours in any 1 month.
[2] Work performed by 560 family heads who are laborers, assuming each works 200 hours per month when work is available for a maximum of 110,000 hours in any 1 month.
[3] Work performed by 600 family members other than head, assuming that each works 100 hours per month during months when work is available, for a maximum of 60,000 hours in any 1 month.
[4] Residual employment opportunity for itinerants, following from above assumptions.

A comparison of these tabulations reveals a number of significant facts: The total labor requirement in Dinuba is greater than in Arvin, but because of the larger number of operators, over half the work can be done by the operators and the number of hired laborers required is greater in Arvin than Dinuba. While the number of workers resident in Arvin is greater, and they can have a longer season for working, both communities require imported labor for short seasons. The amount of such labor is approximately the same. If a thousand hours of work per month requires four laborers, then Arvin requires nearly 1,000 migrant workers in June, and Dinuba, 1,500 in September.

APPENDIX D
METHOD OF OBTAINING POPULATION FIGURES

Population data on the town proper and the rural area within the boundary of the community as delineated have been developed from the schedules. They are based upon the total number of houses and the average persons per family interviewed. In Arvin the number of housing units on the DiGiorgio farms were included and the population determined on the assumption that the number of persons per household was the same as the average number among Arvin farm labor families generally.

The number of houses was established by a map of the community in which each house was spotted. These maps were made for each rural area and each town proper, and may be considered as substantially accurate.

The size of family was taken from the schedule and included all persons living in the home at the time of interview. The following tabulation shows the basic data and calculations for the population of the two communities:

TABLE 55.—*Calculations in the computation of Arvin and Dinuba population from schedule data*

	Arvin	Dinuba
Number of houses in town	760	1,126
Average family size in town	4.13	3.33
Town population	3,139	3,750
Number of houses in open country	564	1,035
Average family size in open country	4.35	3.53
Country population	2,463	3,654
Reported number of DiGiorgio houses	155	
Average family size of Arvin laborers	4.67	
DiGiorgio population	634	
Total population	6,236	7,404

APPENDIX E

METHOD OF DETERMINING LEVEL—OF—LIVING INDEX

The level-of-living index is a figure which summarizes the quality of living conditions or material possessions of any group within the total sample from the two communities. It expresses differences within the sample, and should not be used to compare this sample with others in other parts of the country.

The index is based upon eight items, each weighted according to the square root of the inverse of the frequency of its occurrence, rounded to the nearest whole number. This may be expressed:

$$W = \sqrt{\frac{1}{r}}$$

where W is the weight of each item and r is the percent of the total population possessing that item. Table 56 shows the method of computing the value of each item.

The level-of-living index for any family is the sum of the values for each item, a range from 0 to 44. Because of the few items on the scale and the high degree of association between items, the resulting curve is not as smooth as would be desired.

The evaluation of the condition of the home was determined by assigning differential values to each of the categories within the three questions calling for such evaluation, and taking the sum of these values. The values were: 3 for best conditions, 2 for second best condition, 1 for third best condition, and 0 for poorest condition. In one question only three categories were supplied, and these were given the value of 3, 2, and 0, respectively. No special weighting was given since the data are not amenable to further refinements in quantitative evaluation.

TABLE 56.—*Frequency distributions of items on the material level-of-living scale and value of items*

Item	Frequency		Index calculation	
	Number	Percent	Inverse percent	Value [1]
1. House construction:				
A. Brick, stucco, or paint	256	77	23	5
B. Unpainted or other	75	23		0
2. Rooms per person:				
A. 2 and over	100	30	70	8
B. 1–1.9	126	37	33	6
C. Under 1	112	33		0
3. Water piped in house:				
A. Yes	283	84	16	4
B. No	54	16		0
4. Lighting:				
A. Electric	330	98	2	1
B. Other	7	2		0
5. Refrigeration:				
A. Mechanical	225	67	33	6
B. Ice, other, or none	112	33		0
6. Radio:				
A. Yes	302	89	11	3
B. No	35	11		0
7. Telephone:				
A. Yes	96	29	71	9
B. No	240	71		0
8. Automobile:				
A. 1938 or later	111	33	67	8
B. 1937 or earlier	165	49	18	4
C. No auto	57	18		0

[1] Square root of the inverse percent rounded to nearest whole digit.

APPENDIX F

ASSOCIATION BETWEEN SOCIAL PHENOMENA

The assumption that a whole series of social phenomena, from level of living to type of social activities, were associated with occupation and income was subjected to statistical tests. The Chi Square test of significance and the use of T as a measure of relative association were found most useful. The following tabulation shows the value of T for those associations subjected to the test, and the annotations indicate the level of significance by the Chi Square test. The value of T expresses the degree to which independent employment and higher income are respectively associated with (1) each other, (2) above median level of living as determined by the level-of-living index, (3) membership of individuals 12 years old and over in clubs, (4) reported social activities other than those sponsored by club or church, (5) above median in the index of condition of the home as established by subjective evaluation, (6) membership of persons 12 years old and over in any church, and (7) membership of persons 12 years old and over in churches of highest standing, in contrast with membership in the intermediate and lower status churches.

The procedure was to reduce all sets into dichotomous classifications, using for all seriated data the break nearest the median and for other data mutually exclusive attributes. The fundamental occupational dichotomy between laborers and independently employed persons was used. The remaining dichotomies are self-explanatory.

The formulas used were:

$$X^2 = \sum \frac{(f-f_o)^2}{f_o} \qquad (1)$$

when f=observed data
f_o=expected distribution if unrelated.

$$T=\sqrt{\frac{\overline{X^2}}{N}} \qquad (2)$$

when N=number of observations

Because Q is frequently used as a measure of degree of association, calculations of its value were made for a number of the associations here analyzed. Since Q is 1 when one cell is 0, since this is not actually a measure of perfect association, and since in some instances the number of cases in one cell is small, this measurement was rejected. Q values of items which meet the X^2 test of significance at the .001 level ran between .60 and .85.

TABLE 57.—*Association of social phenomena with occupation and income: Arvin and Dinuba*

Item associated	Value of T in the association of items			
	With occupation		With income	
	Arvin	Dinuba	Arvin	Dinuba
1. Income	0.25x	0.26		
2. Level of living	.40	.48	0.43	0.34
3. Club membership	.43	.45	.26	.27
4. Nonorganization social activity	.13xxx	.10xxx		
5. Condition of home	.28x	.23x	.33	.22x
6. Church membership	−.01xxxx	.06xxx	−.39	.12x
7. Class of church	.40	.28	.16xx	.27

The Chi Square test of the significance of associations was applied, and found to be greater than 0.001 in most cases. Those where the test was less significant have been marked as follows:
x, P=.01
xx, P=.1
xxx, P=.2
xxxx, P=.9

APPENDIX G

BUSINESS ENTERPRISE DATA: SOURCES AND METHODS

Information on type of enterprise and volume of retail trade was obtained from the records of the California State Board of Equalization assembled by staff members of the research and statistics section of the board in cooperation with the Bureau of Agricultural Economics.

California has a retail sales tax on all consumer commodities except foods purchased for off-premises consumption, and a few items covered by special taxes such as gasoline and cigarettes. In addition, it has a use tax which is paid by the consumer for items purchased from outside the State. The tax is always paid by the consumer to the merchant, who pays it over to the Board of Equalization, usually on a quarterly basis, occasionally on a monthly or annual basis. Each retail merchant selling taxable items, therefore, has an account with the board, and regularly reports the total sales tax, the total dollar volume of taxable merchandise sold, and the total dollar volume of business (including nontaxable sales). Services are not taxed, and certain types of enterprises, motion picture houses, banks, cleaning and pressing establishments, for example, are not covered unless they also sell taxable goods.

Since these taxes are an important source of revenue, the data on tax and taxable sales, and on enterprises selling such items, are closely watched and the data themselves are highly accurate. Since nontaxable items are not a factor in tax payments, records of sales of such merchandise are somewhat less reliable, and may be undernumerated. No estimates are available on such error, but it is assumed not to be large.

There is virtually universal coverage of all retail sales establishments, because no category of enterprise sells nontaxable goods exclusively. While groceries are not covered, soaps, paper towels, and so forth, are covered and therefore all grocers with a normal complement of goods must handle sales-tax moneys.

The most important stricture on the data is that the sales are recorded by class of business enterprise and not by type of merchandise sold. The board has worked out a classification of establishments which breaks them into 47 different groups, from general merchandise to industrial equipment. This classification, along with subcategories in each, has been published under the title "Business Classification Code of Permittees Licensed Under the California Retail Sales Tax Act" (California State Board of Equalization Sales and Use Tax Division, March 7, 1941, mimeographed). This publication indicates the general rules for classification, of which the following are significant to the present study: The classification should be made on the basis of the seller's principal line of business, whether taxable or not, but if he has two principal lines of equal importance, it should be made on the basis of the taxable one, or if the principal line of business is other than selling tangible property, it should be coded according to the principal retail trade sideline.

General knowledge of retail trade practices helps us to interpret data on the basis of the type of enterprise in which it was sold. While a vendor of packaged liquor in California frequently sells soft drinks and limes, it is known that his sales are usually so overwhelmingly in liquor that little doubt can be exercised. While grocers often sell wines and beers and nonedible merchandise, the great bulk of sales are of food, and the housewife usually classes under grocers all those things she gets at a grocery store. Some classes are less satisfactory—a general merchandise store may sell almost anything the local people require, from baby bottles to caskets. Within the broad categories used in the present study, this source of error is not very significant.

The fundamental procedure for extracting the data is simple. The account folders of all permittees with active accounts were withdrawn from the files, for each community, by class of enterprise. In this way the total number of enterprises subjected to analysis included all those with active accounts as of fourth quarter, 1943. The record of reported sales for the year (October 1942-September 1943) was recorded under the proper heading and the annual value indicated. At this point the name of the enterprise was dropped, and since this work was done by employees of the board, no information on individual accounts went outside the office.

Special assumptions and interpolation had to be made in some specific cases. Some enterprises had not been operating the full year. In these cases it was assumed that these businesses replaced others (every transfer of operator requires a new account) and that the missing months would have the average sale recorded for the months on record. Where heavy seasonal fluctuations were known to exist, appropriate adjustments were made. The second class of special cases was the chain stores. These stores are not required to report their sales by individual outlet, but report their total sales for the entire State and their taxable sales for the entire county. Total county sales were estimated by assuming that the ratio of taxable to total sales in any one county was the same as the ratio for the total enterprise. Allocation to individual outlets within the county had to be made by simply dividing evenly the county sales between the outlets in the county, the number of which is always reported. Such calculations are likely to overstate the total sales for the outlets in smaller communities (such as Arvin and Dinuba), but intimate knowledge of the region suggests that the error introduced in this way is not great. In Arvin, estimates were required for 10 outlets, 7 of which were only reported for only part of the year and 3 of which were chain stores. In Dinuba there were three partial accounts and four chain operations. Since the tendency of both types of estimate is to inflate total sales slightly, it is probable that the total difference between Arvin and Dinuba is slightly understated, though not to a very great extent. The large number of partial accounts in part reflects the growth in Arvin, in part the instability of its enterprises.

State law requires that no data be published which divulge the sales of any one enterprise. Therefore, combinations of different categories were made so that all published categories contain two or more enterprises.

PART III
Agribusiness and Political Power

AGRIBUSINESS AND POLITICAL POWER

The study of Arvin and Dinuba started a controversy across the breadth of the land when the study was being prosecuted and again after it appeared in print. This controversy is itself an expression of the effects of corporate farming on American life, and documenting its form and character will show how the machinery of propaganda is used to further corporate interests. This propaganda impeded the research, it prevented the prosecution of a crucial second phase, and it delayed and very nearly prevented the publication of the final product.

The controversy itself has engendered two studies, one hostile and one friendly.[1] It was said to have caused, and surely contributed to, the demise of the Bureau of Agricultural Economics. It demonstrates the vacillation of bureaucrats in the face of confrontation by corporate interests. The events surrounding this controversy therefore offer us a window through which we can see some of the broader social implications of corporate farming.

Before we enter into the controversy itself it is necessary to examine the situation and the aegis of the research. The Central Valley Project was established as a multipurpose water control system and built by the Bureau of Reclamation (BR). The BR was created in 1902 as a major element in Theodore Roosevelt's conservation program. Its major function was the construction of dams to make irrigation water available in the arid West. As the available homesteading lands were by then gone, it was also an extension of the principle of making farm lands available to those who wanted to establish family farms. Aware of the existing concentration of landholdings in the West, Congress included in the establishing legislation a provision designed to prevent the considerable subsidy incurred in the reclamation program from falling into the hands of a few rich individuals or large corporations. The instrumentality for accomplishing this is known variantly as the "acreage limitation provision" or the "excess lands law." This provision was a continuation of the homesteading principle in American agrarian history, written into the original law and periodically revised in form but always retained in essence. The law held that water developed by any Bureau of Reclamation project would be made available only to holdings of 160 acres or less, and that owners of larger tracts must sign "recordable contracts" making available to purchasers the acreage in excess of this amount, at a price not reflecting the incremental land value created by the availability of the irrigation water coming from the project itself. Inasmuch as the target area of the Central Valley Project was land held in large tracts, much in the hands of such landholding giants as the Kern County Land Company and the Southern Pacific Railroad, this provision was unpopular with the landed interests in California.

In order to anticipate the technical, economic, and social problems and consequences of this giant, multipurpose project, a coordinated interagency research program was launched, involving federal and state agencies and diverse private interest groups. Among the 24 problems to be addressed was the potential social consequences of the acreage limitation provision. The Bureau of Agricultural Economics of the U.S. Department of Agriculture took a leading role in the prosecution of research in the economic problems, under the general direction of Marion Clawson, an agricultural economist. I was at that time an employee in the Division of Farm Population and Rural Welfare of the BAE (the subdivision that dealt with sociological matters), and was appointed to the Central Valley Project studies. Clawson, Lloyd Fisher (a political economist), Mary Montgomery (a political scientist), Varden Fuller (an agricultural economist), and I, with the advice of Paul Taylor and others, formulated the research plans for the Arvin-Dinuba study. In essence, the problem we were addressing in the research was this: What difference does it make to the character of rural life if the farm units are large corporate holdings as against family-size units such as the acreage limitation provision was intended to create?

It is perhaps pertinent to mention the background I brought to this investigation. I was trained in anthropology: I had courses in economics but none in sociology, other than a special reading course offered me by Dorothy Swain Thomas (a demographic sociologist at the Giannini Foundation). The Wasco study, which later formed the basis for *As You Sow* and had then recently been accepted as my doctoral dissertation, had been sponsored by the BAE on funds provided by the Agricultural Extension Service. Following the classic study by Robert and Helen Lynd on "Middletown," several anthropological studies of American community life were made, mostly under the influence of W. Lloyd Warner. The BAE had also undertaken a series of such studies under the general title, "Culture of a Contemporary Community," of which my Wasco research was a kind of extension. John Provinse, an anthropologist who was an influential member of my division, had served as advisor to this research, as had Lloyd Fisher, a former student of the eminent anthropologist, Hallowell. I therefore brought to the Arvin-Dinuba study the holistic approach of anthropology, and a personal intellectual commitment to the examination of individual values in their social and cultural context. I also brought some limitations.

Some of the limitations were overcome with the help of scholars who provided the necessary expertise. Thus the delineation of the effective boundaries of the rural area centered on the towns was made by Walter C. McKain, a rural sociologist at the BAE, using techniques established by his discipline. The measures of farm size, the cost accounting analysis of water and similar economic information were provided by J. Karl Lee and Edwin E. Wilson, agricultural economists at the BAE.

The context within which the Arvin-Dinuba study was made may be summarized as follows:

1. The Central Valley Project, by developing irrigation water for a vast expanse of California land, created a great increment in wealth.

2. Much of the land for which this water was destined was held in large tracts.

3. The law under which the CVP was developed provided that these tracts must be broken into family farms under the acreage limitation provision.

4. Large landholders throughout the state and corporate interests generally opposed this provision, while diverse church and other agrarian-oriented interests wanted this law applied to California.

5. The comparative study of Arvin and Dinuba (and of other towns in the Central Valley) was designed to determine the social consequences that might be anticipated for the rural communities if the established law were applied or rescinded.

To these elements must be added the facts that the year was 1944; that it was becoming apparent that Roosevelt intended to run for his fourth term in office; and that the research was coordinated and supported by the Department of Interior, whose Secretary was Harold L. Ickes, the termagant and whipping boy of the New Deal.

It is therefore not surprising that the study was born in controversy.

PRESSURE IN THE FIELD

The issue reached public attention on the very day that research began. In a search for field assistants, the study was described in a letter sent to all recent graduates of the University of California, Berkeley, who had majored in sociology. One of these was the niece of a former president of the Associated Farmers, the dominant organization of agricultural corporations and business-oriented agriculturalists in the state at that time. The letter was forwarded (by her or some other recipient) to Congressman Alfred J. Elliott, representative from the district in which Arvin and Dinuba lie, who promptly put it in the *Congressional Record* along with an attack on the study.[2] Elliott had just managed to put a rider on the Rivers and Harbors Bill that would eliminate the acreage limitation provision. He was gearing up for the further fight that would lead to Senate concurrence. When my wife, Gale (who, along with Mrs. Beryl Strong, served as an interviewer for the project), and I arrived in Arvin to initiate the study, we picked up the *Arvin Tiller* and learned that a public social gathering was taking place that very afternoon. To our regret, we did not go to that event, for we later learned that the study had been the center of discussion there.

A few days later I called on the manager of the DiGiorgio Farms, the largest corporate landholding in Arvin, to request permission to interview the workers in the housing provided by the company. I had thought this a mere courtesy, but the manager told me that the matter would have to be taken up with his superiors. He asked for a copy of the questionnaire, which I readily provided him. (Permission to interview on the DiGiorgio premises was never obtained, though we were, despite efforts through official channels to get permission, never given a formal denial.) Perhaps coincidentally, according to the social notes in the next issue of the *Tiller,* Bob Franklin was also a visitor at DiGiorgio that day. (Franklin was the Associated Farmers' news broadcaster, operating out of Fresno. In a later interview he bragged that it was he who had organized the burning of *Grapes of Wrath* on September 1, 1939, and it was with a sense of tragedy, rather than irony, that he said that the impact of this action was severely blunted by Hitler's march on Poland.) With this, the second document came into the hands of those who wanted the study discredited.

In a few days the hostility became obvious in the field, and one early poignant scene stands out in my memory. Beryl Strong—the name is all too apt—was a woman of great force and capability, reminiscent of women from that rural world which itself inspires agrarianism. Her husband was in the Kern County agricultural advisory service (agricultural extension uses a different terminology in California), and when the pressure mounted, I feared for her and her husband's position. I remember looking directly into her cool grey eyes and saying that I realized her husband's position was delicate and that I would understand and sympathize if she wanted to withdraw from the study, carefully avoiding so charged a word as quitting. She looked directly back into mine—we were of the same height—thought just long enough so that I was sure she had reflected fully and said, "No, I will continue." The matter was closed.

The sampling procedure we followed involved a selection process in which households to be interviewed were preselected on a chance basis, *i.e.*, a "random sample." One household so selected was that of one of the largest growers in Arvin, a relative of the young woman who had received the letter inviting application to work. In view of the growing evidence of hostility to the research, we very naturally anticipated an unpleasant confrontation. It was not an interview that anybody looked forward to. However, when Gale finally called, she returned bearing a yellow rose from their garden, an invitation to bridge, and the following tale. She had been greeted by a woman through the screen door with "I know all about your study, and I won't answer your questions." "That," Gale responded, "is your privilege, but I would like to know your reasons for feeling that way." "Come in and I'll tell you!" Later, the woman suggested that her husband could give more accurate answers to some of the questions and might like to express his opinions, and she graciously drove Gale out to where he was supervising work in the field.

Everyone engaged in social studies expects personal objections and minor harassment. We, however, were subjected to a major attack, spearheaded by Congressman Elliott and then reflected in the press. The nature of this attack made it clear that it was a coordinated one, and that it was aimed at the central issue—the acreage limitation provision as applicable to the development of the Central Valley Project. The three central figures in this action were Elliott, news commentator Franklin, and John Pickett, editor of the *Pacific Rural Press*, published in San Francisco. Franklin had obtained the questionnaire from the DiGiorgio manager and undoubtedly supplied copies to Elliott and Pickett. Elliott made a second attack on the study on the floor of the House, reading some of the questions, especially those related to income, level of living, and social and religious participation.

He interjected such comments as: "These investigators are going out into the agricultural communities with a lot of silly asinine questions, when the farmers are trying to produce foodstuffs despite the [wartime] shortage of manpower . . ."[3]

His comments were converted into an AP release and reprinted in the local press (*e.g., Los Angeles Times,* April 30, 1944). On April 22, the *Pacific Rural Press* published an article under the heading: ARE YOUR RUGS DIRTY? HOW'S YOUR ETHNICS?, making fun of the questionnaire, suggesting that the purpose was secretive ("Why does the government want to know? Try to find out. It took a bit of doing to get a copy of the questionnaire away from the government social slummers. . . .") and avoiding the real issue. The item concluded with a suggestion that readers ask for a copy ("If you want light reading for these gas-less evenings, you might write the Bureau of Agricultural Economics . . ." giving the full address). A total of 451 persons requested copies of the questionnaire. Only about seven percent of them came from the Central Valley while most of the requests came from eastern cities.

On May 4, Fulton Lewis, Jr., devoted about two-thirds of his broadcast to the study. Lewis was then one of the most potent national radio news commentators, a strong proponent of big business interests and virulently anti-New Deal. His broadcast consisted chiefly of reading the questions in a derisive manner after an initial discussion, as follows:

> Now I have a little bedtime story for you tonight, ladies and gentlemen — a little romance to demonstrate that government does have its lighter moments, if you can hold on to your sense of humor.
> For several weeks past, I've been receiving a continuous string of protest letters from the Central Valley in California — from farmers, who complain that they've been annoyed by a federal government questionnaire, in which they were asked all sorts of weird and strange questions, and finally, yesterday, I actually received a copy of one of the questionnaires. I read it, and it was so utterly amazing that I could hardly believe my eyes, and I went to work to check it carefully to determine the genesis of it. It came from the United States Bureau of Agricultural Economics, and on inquiry there and elsewhere I found out the following:

Mr. Harold Ickes' Department of Interior has nearly completed a huge new reclamation project—an irrigation project to provide water for a large area in the rich Central Valley of California. But under an order, issued by Mr. Ickes under the terms of the Reclamation Law of 1904 [sic], no water from that project is to be sold to any farm larger than 160 acres. It so happens that more than half of the area to be served is in farms of more than 160 acres, but under Mr. Ickes' ruling those farmers either must sell off all land above 160 acres or not get any water. The congressman from that district, Rep. Alfred Elliott, a Democrat from California began receiving letters of protest from farmers, large and small, all through that valley. The small farmers were particularly loud in their protests, because they said that if the larger farms were ruled out, it would mean that the smaller ones would have to pay a larger share of the cost of the water. The larger farmers were not selling off land, to cut down size; they were keeping their farms intact because they were financially able to drill wells and get water.

Congressman Elliott introduced legislation to change the law of 1904, so as to terminate Mr. Ickes' 160-acre policy, and it passed the House of Representatives, and now is before the Senate. In the meantime, however, the Bureau of Agricultural Economics tells me that Mr. Ickes has called on them for statistical information, with which to fortify himself, in opposing the legislation in the Senate, and this questionnaire, circulated by special government representatives, among the farmers in the Central Valley, was in response to that request.

Remember, we have a manpower shortage, a paper shortage; we're supposed to be breaking our backs to try to win a war, and there has been bitter criticism that there still is part of the population that doesn't know there's a war going on.[4]

Note the following misrepresentations: implication that this questionnaire was difficult to receive, the association of the CVP with Ickes, failure to suggest that farmers' letters were responsive to Pickett's suggestion that people write, that small farmers would be hurt by the acreage limitation provision, and that Ickes had developed the research "to fortify himself." Such attacks clearly associated the study with the policy issue, for hearings had been initiated in Washington on the Elliott rider to kill the acreage limitation provision.

Franklin, in his daily "County Commentator" broadcast,

sponsored by the Associated Farmers, made regular attacks on the study starting about the time we moved from Arvin to Dinuba. The three of us would meet in the pleasant Dinuba park to listen to Beryl's car radio over lunch sandwiches. I am not certain how often the study was mentioned; it seemed to have been daily over a period of two or more weeks, but I have only three unofficial transcripts in my files. On May 1, 1944, he said in part:

> Congressman Elliott said that investigators for the Bureau are going out into the agricultural communities with a lot of these silly, asinine questions, and the farmers are trying to produce food stuffs despite the shortage in manpower. Then Congressman John Phillips interjected to say that he thought that the Congress should know that the snooper that did this is being paid $212.00 a month and $4.65 a day for his expenses for his car, and he is promised that the Bureau of Agriculture will see that he gets the necessary gasoline in spite of the fact that the farmers cannot get all of the gasoline they need.
> This came up during a debate upon the Department of Interior's appropriation bill because it was discovered that the Bureau of Reclamation, trying to keep acreage limitations on all the water here, so that the Secretary of Interior would say how big a farm would be, 10 acres to 160 acres, he could set the limit and say that a farm couldn't be over 10 acres for grapes if he wanted to, and if they used his water. Anyway, they found out and put into the record that the Bureau of Agricultural Economics is getting $70,000 of Central Valley Project money from Secretary Ickes' department to make these kind of surveys and then Congressman Johnson of Oklahoma came in to say that for months and months he had been fed up on what he called these insane, ridiculous and inexcusable questionnaires and so the Congressmen are out to do battle because of it.[5]

The following day, Franklin devoted virtually the entire session to the study,[6] having been contacted by Wendell Calhoun, the acting head of the Berkeley BAE office, who asked that Franklin meet with me. (Franklin broadcast that he had "challenged" me to come in.) I arranged the interview for Friday, May 5.

In this era of TV, it is hard to reconstruct what radio news was like. Commentators like Franklin and Lewis were masters at using intonation and innuendo. Franklin could make the word "doctor" sound like some indecent epithet, and he had obviously formed a mental picture of me that conformed to his own propaganda. When he came to his outer office where I was waiting, I could see he was visibly shocked to find I was an ordinary sort of person of his own age and I took advantage of this off-guard moment by asking why, as a reporter, he had not looked me up in Arvin when he picked up the questionnaire. This very cool man was visibly flustered. We had a long amicable conversation, some of which I have already reported, and on the following Monday (May 8) he made his last remarks, very altered in tone and character, which read in part:

> On Friday afternoon I talked at quite some length with Dr. Walter R. Goldschmidt, Social Science Analyst for the Bureau of Agricultural Economics of the United States Department of Agriculture. Dr. Goldschmidt is the man in charge of the social investigation to compare the social life and social factors in farming of different scales from small scales up to large scales, and out of that comparison to try to draw an analysis of what will happen in connection with the restrictions on acreage if imposed through the handling of Central Valley water through the Reclamation Bureau. I have been highly critical of this questionnaire business that's being circulated down there and have been very critical of this survey and the spending of government funds for that type of work during wartime.
> Now Dr. Goldschmidt is a very likable young man. He readily says that he is academic in his thinking, that he is a scientist who makes social studies based upon years of experimenting in studying social life as a science. He stoutly maintains that the survey is purely scientific and that he will make his analysis purely and simply to show what the comparison of the social life of the people involved is in the different scales of farming.[7]

On May 11, the "County Commentator" program was devoted to my response.[8] The station owner, for his own reasons, had insisted that I be given this opportunity. One fallout from this talk was that a Dinuba respondent to the questionnaire that afternoon refused to open the door for my wife, saying "I have just been listening to Dr. Goldschmidt on

the radio and he says nobody has to answer these questions."
This time, the resistance could not be overcome.[9]

While Franklin no longer attacked the study, either as a result of the interview which had exhausted its newsworthiness, or because the station operator objected, vituperations continued in the newspapers, particularly the *Los Angeles Times* and the *San Francisco Chronicle*. The *Chronicle* devoted two editorials to the subject, one of these as a response, on the same page, to a supporting letter by Marion Clawson (May 27, 1944). Articles and editorials appeared throughout the nation and ultimately the conservative columnist George E. Sokolsky devoted a column to it (dateline June 20), which duly found its way into the *Congressional Record*.[10]

Meanwhile, as Drew Pearson remarked in the "Washington Merry-Go-Round" (dateline May 4), hearings were scheduled "on a rider which Congressmen Elliott and Carter of California have skillfully smuggled into the Rivers and Harbors Bill—a rider permitting big landowners in California's Central Valley to benefit from Government low-cost irrigation." Marion Clawson was called to Washington to testify before hearings on this bill and asked me for a progress report, since the issue of the Arvin-Dinuba study would very likely arise.

The letter-writing campaign inspired by Pickett, Lewis and others resulted in considerable name-calling of the then familiar variety, *i.e.*, the imputation of communism.[11] Some of this has been documented by Kirkendall.[12]

There can be no doubt that the central purpose of this campaign was to sabotage the study itself. Nobody opposed to it had any doubt as to what the comparison meant or what the true differences between the two communities were, nor that these differences were a product of the scale of farm operations. Any number of personal comments to me during this period made this clear. When we did not scare off, when efforts to influence the local population did not prevent the prosecution of our research, pressure was put on the top—on the Director of the BAE in Washington. At some time in mid-May, when the work in Dinuba was near completion, I received a call from headquarters in Berkeley saying that they had protected my right to complete the Dinuba phase of the study (apparently with some difficulty), but that I must do so as quickly as possible and that the second phase of the research was to be cancelled. This was a major loss.

THE STUDY NEVER MADE

The research plan we devised had, from the outset, two phases. The first was the detailed examination of two representative communities. Out of this experience, I was to devise a series of measures of community organization that would reflect the quality of life in the towns, based upon data that was easily obtained, requiring no questionnaire and little interviewing. Among the items that we were considering were such things as the number of local business enterprises, social and civic clubs and organizations, churches, newspapers, and local schools; area in parks and other recreational facilities, prevalence of paved roads, sewers and other public facilities, rate of teacher turnover, and number of teachers resident in the community. It was my intention to formulate an index based upon such objective data, with which to rate the other 23 small towns of the upper San Joaquin Valley.

The economists of the BAE had measured the size of farms in all 25 communities, measured both by gross acreage and by "equivalent" acres (based upon the income potential) of diverse crops, as reported in Table 1 and Appendix B of the Arvin-Dinuba study. I had hoped to calculate a regression curve between these two variables but was prevented from making this sophisticated analysis. I have recently reexamined these data[13] and have found that they revealed a most important relationship. This I have already discussed in the Introduction (p. xl ff), where I showed that as the average size of farm increases, the number of persons supported in the rural area and local community declines.

With such a difference in basic support, it hardly seems doubtful that the other measures would have shown similar trends.[14] The refusal on the part of the officers of the BAE to support this second phase of the study was a most unfortunate retreat. It kept us from demonstrating, in incontrovertible terms, the relationship that the Arvin-Dinuba comparison established; it made it impossible to divest the analysis of the limitations that a case study imposes. This in turn had the effect of "personalizing" the results, so that just as Dinuba could take pride in the results, so too could Arvinites take umbrage.

A PROBLEM OF VALUES

Twenty years after the study was made, the controversy over the Arvin-Dinuba study was subjected to a detailed scrutiny by an historian, Richard S. Kirkendall, in *The California Historical Society Quarterly*.[15] I want here to interrupt the historic review of the study itself to examine my examiner, for he raises issues that are relevant to the purpose of this analysis.

Two quotes, respectively, at the beginning and the end of Kirkendall's paper, set the tone of his theme.

A social scientist employed by the government frequently finds himself in the midst of a political battle, the object of harsh criticism by some groups and warm praise by others. All of this results chiefly from the large role of values in his work. People with a point of view that conflicts with his own treat him in a rough fashion, while other groups who evaluate the situation as he does see him as an ally. And, try as he might to escape by assuming a neutral pose and insisting that as a scientist he is above the battle, the conflicting groups bar the door. His values determine his relations with other people, draw him into the fight and keep him there. [Page 195]

Perhaps if Goldschmidt and Clawson had been less militant in their approach and had accepted the theory of the proper role of the social scientist that Peter De Vries and Carl Taylor had pushed, the Bureau could have remained above the battle. But this seems unlikely. Surely any significant study that reached conclusions about acreage limitation was destined to be drawn into this very hot conflict. Furthermore, Goldschmidt's and Clawson's values pushed them into the battle. Having been influenced by the democratic side of the agricultural tradition, they thought first in terms of the democratic, rather than the business implications of a farm program. With such values, these social scientists found it difficult to stay out of the thick of the fight and impossible to avoid infuriating some people and pleasing others. [Pages 209-10]

Between these two statements lies a heavily documented account of the events that took place in 1944 and subsequently with respect to the Arvin-Dinuba research, chiefly referencing files relating to the project or the study—*i.e.*, correspondence, reports, etc. It is an interesting example of the historian's craft, demonstrating both its virtues and its faults. There are in the brief paper 76 footnotes and countless references. These notations are themselves strange, for it is not clear just what in the reference (often to archival matters and hence difficult to check) supports Kirkendall's contentions. I cannot, for instance, find support for the following: "As times passed, Goldschmidt developed some important reservations." As an anthropologist, I find most remarkable the kind of ritual purity that Kirkendall preserved. Though he carefully examined my subsequent writings and identified accurately my place of employment, he made no effort to contact me[16] for my version of what had happened—nor any of the other principals he criticizes. He had to treat this 20-year-old event as a matter of history, reconstructing it only from the available documents.

While I learned some facts about this "episode," as he calls it, from reading his article, he could have learned something from me as well. To take the most obvious and important example, Kirkendall makes no mention of the second phase of the study that I was prevented from undertaking. As I had myself been informed of the denial by phone, I have no way of knowing whether this action had been documented, though Kirkendall must have known of our intention to do so, inasmuch as he examined the planning phase of our investigation.[17]

The matter is important beyond the issue of methodology. For the issue that Kirkendall raises has to do with the degree to which my values (and of the others who initiated the study) were influencing our results. The important point is that we were subjecting a set of culturally based assumptions—

assumptions on which existing law had been based—to a severe empirical test; we wanted to go beyond the first-level, in-depth examination of two communities to make a general comparison of a large sample of communities. The fact that we believed that the test would support the agrarian assumption, and even that this was our social preference, is irrelevant. Scientists the world over want to find positive results, but proper scientists want to put their hypotheses to the most rigorous tests they can provide. This is precisely what the second phase was designed to do. That it was prevented from taking place strongly suggests that those who were sabotaging the study were also quite certain what this investigation would show, and knew that it was easier to refute the Arvin-Dinuba conclusions than it would be to dismiss the second level of investigation. Whether Kirkendall knew of this second phase and chose to ignore it for his own reasons, was too naive scientifically to understand its implications, or whether his methodology prevented him from discovering the very existence of the plan, the fact remains that the failure to comprehend the matter essentially deprived his analysis of the meaning he attributed to it.

This is also because he, like so many scholars, does not properly understand the relationship between research and values. On this subject, also in reference to this controversy, I wrote the following:

> There is a great confusion about the relationship between science and values. It is generally recognized that the reality of values is not amenable to scientific proof. This is clearly the case, for values are sentiments we hold and share. It is also said that science is value-free, by which it is properly meant that the scientist must set aside his own values in examining the reality of cause and effect. But these two points have led some to assert that science cannot deal with values at all. This is manifestly false, for values regularly enter into scientific study. For example, the President's current all-out effort to analyze the causes of cancer operates on the assumption that cancer is bad and that therefore a cure for cancer is good. These are values that all of us accept. Again, when an economist analyzes the profitability of an enterprise, he takes for granted that it is good to make a profit. Nothing the scientist does validates the assumption that cancer is bad

and profits are good; what the scientist does is to determine the causes and conditions under which [such perceived] good or evil will prevail.[18]

Now the Arvin-Dinuba study does not prove that social participation, democratic institutions, relatively equitable distribution of income, or high and relatively undifferentiated standards of living are good. There are many persons in the world who would argue the opposite, or that the individual's unfettered pursuit of gain is a value greater than those listed. My monograph does suggest that the values I enumerated are central to the American tradition (hence the initial quotations from Daniel Webster), and admittedly history could be quoted for alternative views. What the study does show is that these qualities are affected by the scale of farm operations and that large-scale farming creates a condition which undermines them. It is like a study that says, to use the examples in the passage quoted, if you smoke you will have a higher probability of cancer; if you operate your enterprise in a particular way, you will not make as much profit. Persons smoke or operate their businesses "inefficiently" because other values (perhaps habit or traditionalism) take precedence.

What is far more dangerous in research is the intrusion of values obliquely, either because the author is unaware of his own value presuppositions or because he wants to dissemble them. This is, in fact, illustrated by Kirkendall's article; there is a presumption of values in what he writes that are never made explicit.

Let us first see how he reshapes matters and falsifies my role. Kirkendall writes, "Hoping to preserve the principle [of acreage limitation], the Bureau of Reclamation called upon the BAE to see if it should be applied in California. The social scientists in the Department of Agriculture responded *eagerly* to this chance to *provide some guidance*. . . ."[19] Now aside from the falsification inherent in attributing *any* motivation to an institution, it is my opinion that personnel at the decision-making levels within the BR were far from eager to apply the acreage limitation law, a conclusion all too adequately documented by subsequent events.[20] But note that we were "eager" to provide guidance; not that we wanted to find out if in fact it did or did not make any difference. Surely this was, from the standpoint of a scientist, a unique opportunity to test a proposition, one that had both deep cultural and historical roots and immediate policy implications. But in Kirkendall's phrasing, we are already tarred with the brush of propagandizing.

Again, "Marion Clawson, an economist with years of experience in the BAE, was placed in charge of the investigation in the summer of 1942. Because of his special interest in farm management, he quickly designed a study to explore the relations between efficiency and size of farms. Efficiency, however, did not strike him as the only factor that should be considered, and so he was soon asking if there were 'any tangible evidences . . . of different social structures and social values that can be attributed to differences in size of farms or in size of land holdings.' "[21] But this was not a question Clawson asked; it was one of the issues inevitably raised, given the statutes on the books, when the whole set of impact studies was formulated; indeed, it was one of the 24 problems of the CVP studies. What Clawson and the rest of us did was to formulate a research program designed to answer a question already in front of us. There remains the problem of two different orders of consequences (profitability versus community virtues), each of which had to be assessed independently.

Finally, Kirkendall writes:

Even before the completion of the field work, Goldschmidt reported to Clawson in Berkeley that the differences between the towns were "overwhelming." They are apparent to the casual visitor and become greater and greater as more information is made available. At the root of the differences lay the contrast in size of farms. Believing that even these "preliminary results" would be of interest to those concerned with acreage limitation, he *hoped* that Clawson would present them to a Senatorial committee before which he was soon to appear.[22]

What this quotation fails to record is the fact that Clawson was in Washington to testify on the Elliott rider; that in view of the existing furor over the study, the issue might well be raised, and that Clawson therefore needed to be armed with up-to-date information on the study, which he therefore requested I supply. For this reason, and also because it is always useful to engage in stocktaking before leaving the field, I wrote up a detailed preliminary summary of what I had by then learned. Yet again, that little word "hoped" turned me from a scholar into a propagandist.

For an historian, Kirkendall treats temporal sequences rather cavalierly, for the imputations placed upon Clawson, myself, the BAE and the BR are developed before any mention is made of the Elliott rider and the attacks on the study. He returns to these with the following topic sentence: "Long before he [Goldschmidt] reached his Jeffersonian conclusions, however, other people with a somewhat different set of values began to attack his project."[23] It takes careful reading to sense what came first. He then presents the alternate set of values:

But the larger farmers and their friends had their own theories, ones that had long been important in American business thought, especially the idea that every man has the right to acquire property and to hold on to his acquisitions. Seldom criticizing the small farmer, they tended instead to argue that he should be allowed to expand his holding as far as his talents and energies would permit and with confidence that the government would protect the results. According to this view of farming, it should provide the same opportunities for ambitious men that other businesses did. In short, those who insisted that acreage limitation should not be applied to the project pictured themselves as traditionalists, defending old American principles against the "socialistic" and "communistic" tendencies of the proponents of limitation.[24]

By pushing me and my colleagues into the role of propagandists, by overlooking the desired second phase of the research, by obscuring the time sequence of events so as to confuse the contexts in which my actions were taken, by selective quotations too cumbersome to review here,[25] and by the failure to come to grips with the relation of science and values, Kirkendall transformed the episode into something it was not. Doing so, he could establish his main point, that scholars should remain remote from the fray. But there is a subtle point Kirkendall is making, wittingly or not, expressed in the final paragraph already quoted and repeated here: "Having been influenced by the democratic side of the agricultural tradition, they [Goldschmidt and Clawson] thought first of the democratic, *rather than the business implications of the farm program.*"[26]

The problem with values in social research, whether by an historian or an anthropologist, lies in not recognizing the values that enter into the equation and in letting them suffuse the analysis through word choice, implication, and other conscious or unconscious devices.

SUPPRESSION

Two and a half years were to lapse between our departure from Dinuba and the publication of *Small Business and the Community*. The delay was not fortuitous.

In the summer of 1944 I presented a paper based upon the Arvin-Dinuba study at a meeting of the Western Farm Economics Association. The report received enough publicity to make the papers. The *Pacific Rural Press* gave it a short paragraph under the heading "Goldschmidt Votes for Small Farms" (August 5, 1944). The *San Francisco Chronicle* gave the release developed from this paper almost a column of space, made only passing reference to the earlier controversy ("Part of Goldschmidt's findings were drawn from answers to a questionnaire circulated among farmers about which there was considerable controversy some months ago"), summarized the findings and indulged in no editorializing. Other papers were not so kind, but there was relatively little criticism or editorial comment. In August, the U.S. Department of Agriculture made a somewhat dramatized broadcast on the issue for release over Western Agriculture's "Blue Network," without noticeable repercussions. In November, Claude Wickard, then Secretary of Agriculture, cited the study in a speech before the National Farmers' Union in Denver. There was surprisingly little general criticism from those opposed to acreage limitation. I suspect that it was felt better to ignore than to refute this lightly documented summary.

The process of writing the detailed monograph continued. It was one thing to compare the towns on a series of measures, quite another to draw together the full documentation and analysis. It should perhaps be made clear that the qualitative differences between Arvin and Dinuba were apparent to the most casual visitor, and that the measures of the quality devised by me were essentially an adumbration and documentation of the obvious. What was by no means obvious, however, was that these differences were due to the size of the farm unit rather than to some other cause. The central problem in analysis was not so much to work out the detailed comparison of community facilities and character as it was to show that other differences between the two towns were not responsible for their divergent profiles.

The Arvin-Dinuba study was an example of what has since come to be known in anthropology as "controlled comparison." Unlike laboratory sciences, anthropology and sociology are naturalistic ones; that is, they examine ongoing events as these are taking place. A controlled comparison is one in which two sets of such events (in this instance, community life in Arvin and in Dinuba) are selected so that they are as alike as possible in all attributes except the "independent variable," the effect of which is to be tested (in this case, the scale of farm operation). This is an effort to operate as closely as possible in the manner of laboratory scientists. But naturalistic observations never simply control a single variable; there inevitably are other, potentially "contaminating" differences.

Thus our casual visitor would assume that Arvin was both a smaller and a poorer place than Dinuba. From our standpoint, it was of the greatest significance that the towns were approximately the same size and produced a closely comparable dollar-value product, *i.e.*, we had successfully controlled for these two most important variables.[27] Other variables could not be so successfully controlled, and much of the detail in the study endeavors to determine whether these other differences might be held accountable for the social variation that was recorded. I was engaged in this process for the remainder of 1944 and into the following spring. At that time, I received a long commentary on a completed draft from Clawson, mostly on minor editorial matters, concluding that "With these few specific and general statements the report should be ready for publication and I think it is excellent."[28] Clawson had dictated these words after sharing his views with Peter De Vries, then the BAE public relations officer in Washington. In his covering letter Clawson says "Pete was quite favorably impressed with the Arvin/Dinuba manuscript . . . I think these comments also reflect Pete's views."[29]

Neither my memory nor my files are adequate to detail the sequence of events that delayed publication, and I have neither time nor inclination to open the files that Kirkendall used. What I do recall is that the manuscript would be returned, either from Washington or by my own chief in Berkeley, Walter McKain, with objections of various kinds; I would meet the objections (thus strengthening the argument) only to go through the process again.[30] It eventually became clear to me that somebody was reluctant to publish the study.[31]

Meanwhile, I had gone on to other things, first within the BAE, then loaned to Interior for research among Alaskan Indians, and then to my teaching post in Los Angeles. It was during the fall of that always difficult first teaching year that I received an urgent call from Berkeley for a copy of the Arvin-Dinuba report. This avid propagandist could not even find his copy, to the disgust of the more orderly Clawson, who had to ferret out materials from the basement of my Berkeley house.

What had taken place is most revealing. Dewey Anderson, a sociologist who was then executive director of the Senate Small Business Committee learned about the report from Paul Taylor and brought it to the attention of Senator James E. Murray, its chairman. Murray, at Anderson's urging, decided it should be published. In October, 1946, Anderson tried to get the manuscript from the BAE. He wrote of his difficulties, first quoting from the BAE acting chief, Nichols:

". . . While the copy is pretty badly penciled, we believe that you could read it without too much difficulty. Please let us know whether or not you would like to borrow this copy and, if so, we would be very glad to send it over to you. You will realize of course that in its present form it has not been approved by our Bureau."

Second, [Anderson continued] I received on the 9th [of October, I presume] a letter from Wells himself which I quote as follows: "You asked about a copy of a manuscript on 'The Social Effects of Farm Operations' written by Dr. Walter R. Goldschmidt. The manuscript is not now in a form which is acceptable to the Bureau nor is it even in such shape as I feel it should or can be released (even on a confidential basis) for outside study or appraisal."

Finally after reference to a letter to the Secretary which I do not have, he writes:

I had a talk yesterday with Carl Taylor. I read him the letter to the Secretary and he was quite pleased with the steps taken. He assured me again that in his judgment the document was extremely important and that he wanted it published but thought I would have my difficulties.

I have just now talked with O. V. Wells, Head of the BAE, informing him of the steps taken to clear the matter through the Secretary. He assured me that he had had three people read the manuscript and while he had not done so completely himself, he had looked into it. He was convinced from the judgments received that considerable revision would have to be made in the document and that in its present form it presents a one-sided picture. He also said that the Secretary, who had been in Congress and knew the Congressional Delegation, insisted that he handle this matter himself so that it is out of Wells' hands. He expects that the Secretary might ask him for some data, but probably will not ask him to write the letter in reply to Senator Murray. He did expect, however, that the Secretary would talk to Murray directly.

What I am writing you about is not only to bring you up-to-date on this sequence of events, but to prevent something happening which may be the way the Secretary will seek to influence Senator Murray against publication of the manuscript. I told Wells to be on his guard against any move of the Secretary to obtain from him and his associates a judgment of the manuscript which would condemn it as a partial or unscientific work because I feel certain that will be the attempted characterization on the part of the Secretary when he tries to influence Murray. I told Wells that I was getting statements as to the reliability and validity of the manuscript, its impartial and scientific character, from qualified experts in the field who were willing to stake their reputations on it. I do so to forewarn him that he should not become a tool in this controversy.³²

This passage makes it clear that the Secretary of Agriculture³³ personally took charge of the matter and that Dewey Anderson felt that the Secretary would use personal influence to prevent its publication, and it implies that Wells, chief of the BAE, overrode his acting chief Elliott and refused to share the bureau copy with the Senate committee. It also indicates that Carl Taylor, who was throughout my whole involvement the national head of the Farm Population and Rural Welfare section of the BAE, favored releasing the study.

On October 25, Dewey Anderson wrote to me in part as follows:

> I have had clearance by telephone from the Secretary of Agriculture's Office to the effect that you are a free agent respecting the manuscript in your possession. You're furthermore not an employee of the Department of Agriculture. As a private citizen you are free to submit the document to the Senate Small Business Committee for publication. In writing your letter submitting it, will you be very sure to indicate that in the field hearings held by the Senate Small Business Committee in California, material of a preview nature was presented. The Committee Chairman evidenced considerable interest at the time and requested that the full report be submitted upon completion, which you are now doing.³⁴

It was, as I recall, the first evidence I had that I had been terminated; I thought I had taken a leave of absence for the then temporary appointment at UCLA.

I was told—for this there is no documentation—that when Murray called on Secretary Anderson in person, the manuscript was literally in the Secretary's desk. At any rate, the Secretary extracted from the Senator, as a *quid pro quo* in releasing the document, that no mention whatsoever be made of the Agriculture Department's involvement with the study.³⁵ Dewey Anderson communicated this to me as follows:

> You have a section on acknowledgements—my agreement with Secretary Anderson's office is that no mention is made of the

Department of Agriculture, I take it that applies also to acknowledgements. They are assuming no responsibility whatsoever for the printing of the document or the document in printed form, nor do they want any credit for having had part in its preparation.[36]

When the study was published, the situation was made public by Drew Pearson in the "Washington Merry-Go-Round" (dateline December 26) as follows:

> The study was recognized by economists as of great importance, but the pressure of large farmers and land holders was too great. It lay buried until it was brought to the attention of fair-minded Senator Jim Murray of Montana, Chairman of the Small Business Committee. He determined to publish it.
>
> His first difficulty was in getting it from the Department of Agriculture. Top officials there, fearful of offending the big farm operators, held out for weeks. Murray then had to beat down the opposition of Republicans on his own committee, who did not know much about the study, but had been warned it was something they should oppose.
>
> Murray persevered, however, until the study finally was made public this week.

All of this took place at a hectic pace. The November 1946 elections had returned, for the first time in 22 years, a Republican Congress and if the study was to be published at all it had to be before the 76th Congress died. It was published on December 26th. The effort to suppress the study had failed.

REACTIONS

Publication of the full study brought a second wave of reactions. The Senate committee not only made it the subject of a press release, but circulated it widely. "I think you would be interested in knowing that it has been one of our most popular prints. The individual requests seem to come mostly from colleges, college students, with many requests from religious groups and preachers."[37] The press release was widely published, usually without editorial comment. In the spring of 1947 several publications made large spreads based upon the study, notably the *Christian Science Monitor* (February 17, 1947, Second Section, page 9), complete with pictures. *Business Week* (April 12, 1947, pp. 17-18) identified the study as "one of the heaviest pieces of artillery that [proponents of acreage limitation] had added to their arsenal in years. . . ."

Negative reaction in the press came mostly from two centers of attack. The first of these was from the Arvin community and the surrounding Kern County area. It was of course reasonable for the citizenry to object to the unfavorable publicity,[38] though the nature of the response suggests other motives.

The Arvin Booster Club, according to a *Fresno Bee* article (January 9, 1947) had a meeting. "The two and a half hour long discussion varied between the potential effects of the 160 acre law on California agriculture and steps taken later to counteract the Goldschmidt report." The grower who was appointed head of the committee to take action was quoted as saying, "Goldschmidt has made many outright mistakes and ignored other factors." But the heart of the matter was expressed by an Arvin farmer quoted in the *Bakersfield Californian* (January 9, 1947) who said "Kill the 160 acreage limit law, and the Goldschmidt report would be meaningless." The Booster Club, together with the Kern County Chamber of Commerce ordered a study made of Arvin which, when eventually completed, presented inadequately documented indications of the entirely reasonable proposition that many in Arvin traded in Bakersfield.[39] This, at best, could merely controvert the data on trade, but in the absence of a comparative analysis with Dinuba, it could not even establish the significance of this point, for Dinubans also regularly traded in Fresno.

The accusations that the study was inaccurate, brought forth a response from Senator Murray. The *Bakersfield Californian* (January 10, 1947) reported:

> "I assure you that if any facts and conclusions in the report are brought to our attention as erroneous, we will use all means of publicity at our disposal to make them known", wrote Senator Murray in a personal communication to Emory Gay Hoffman, manager of the Kern County Chamber of Commerce.

No factual errors appear to have been submitted. Though the published attacks on the study were not extensive, one must not assume that the pressures from this quarter were insignificant. I had been contacted by *Life* magazine on the possibility of their making a picture essay on the two towns:

> Your study of Arvin and Dinuba as published for the Senate Small Business Committee interests me very much as a possible picture story for LIFE. Even taking into account your very proper reservations that the study deals only with two towns and that sweeping generalizations from your data would be unfair and misleading, it seems to me that your findings deserve wider circulation. Of course, a picture story might not be feasible; but it certainly is worth exploring.[40]

Further correspondence was followed by a phone call asking whether I still "believed in" my analysis. I heard that photographs were in fact taken by *Life* reporters—but no pictures ever appeared, so it is reasonable to assume, though impossible to prove, that their elimination was the result of pressure. I do remember that the *Life* editor said that it was difficult to take pictures in the two towns without making an editorial statement, for their appearance was so different. I asked him if he didn't "believe in" his own medium of communication. It was our last contact.

The major attack was spearheaded by Senator Sheridan Downey who, for reasons I never understood, staked his political future on fighting the acreage limitation law as applicable to California—and lost.[41] In 1947 he published a book attacking the Bureau of Reclamation under the title *They Would Rule the Valley*, in which one chapter was devoted to the Arvin-Dinuba study. The title itself was designed to evoke the notion of a communist plot, though that is not really the theme of the work. In March, Downey introduced a bill (S. 913, identical to HR. 2052) "Exempting certain projects from the land-limitation provision of the Federal reclamation laws and repealing all inconsistent provisions of prior acts."

The essence of Downey's attack on the study was the familiar one:

In reality, of course, Dr. Goldschmidt's determinism is a fake. He argues that small farm-units inevitably produce one kind of town, large farming units another—and worse—kind. Now, this may or may not be true, but nothing that Dr. Goldschmidt has brought forward will prove it. Why not? Because he has pinned the tail on the wrong donkey. He has ascribed to the size-factor what is rightly attributable to the age-factor. He has assumed that because Arvin and Dinuba differ both in social conditions and in farm sizes, therefore the former must be explained by the latter—a flagrant example of the danger of inferring causality from mere sequence. The factor which Dr. Goldschmidt has conveniently left out of the equation is the truly vital one; the difference in ages of the two towns. A very simple datum. But the key to the whole muddled debate.[42]

There is no mention of the fact that I devoted a dozen pages to this issue—nor, of course, the by now entirely lost fact that I was prevented from generalizing my findings by the elimination of the second phase.

In May, Dewey Anderson (now executive director of the Public Affairs Institute) wrote: "Senator Sheridan Downey has broken loose in hearings before the Harness Committee of the House, denouncing your study of Dinuba and Arvin. He is using pretty much the line he takes in his book. Senator Murray has asked me to provide him with a memo on the subject." He wanted my input on the memorandum.[43]

Downey entered the fray once again in 1949. Dewey Anderson wrote:

Dear Friend Goldschmidt: You are again a bone of contention. Senator Downey has attacked you (and us) in his appearance before the Sub-Committee of the Senate Committee on Appropriations on Tuesday, February 22. We are preparing an answer. He says in part:

"Instead of expressing my own opinion on this incredible brochure, let me say, well, that the liberal economists if not the left-wing economists in the Bureau of Agricultural Economics characterized this production as so biased and inaccurate that they not only would not print it as an agricultural document, but ordered its suppression, and I have talked to the economists who enunciated that. . . . I asked Senator Murray if he had been advised that the Bureau of Agricultural Economics had denounced this as a biased and unworthy publication, and he had no knowledge of that. . . . this pamphlet which the Bureau of Agricultural Economics condemns today, and did two years ago, in the very strongest kind of terms. . . . Mr. Wells (chief of the Bureau of Agricultural Economics) told me that the Bureau of Reclamation was very anxious to have it printed as a Bureau of Agricultural Economics document. Their economists found it to be biased and inaccurate, and declared it not only should not be printed, but that its name should not be used in connection with it ever having been produced, and they did not want to be identified with it. I may be wrong, but I do not think the pamphlet there is at all identified with the Bureau of Agricultural Economics that helped produce it."

Will you air mail me the facts as you know them?[44]

The repudiation of which Downey wrote was of course the action forced upon the BAE by the external pressure. It was not the character of the response from the sociological sector of that organization. The acting director of the Division of Farm Population and Rural Welfare wrote, "We [in the Division] do not wonder that you have received generally favorable comment on this job for that has been the nature of the reaction to it among our staff."[45]

Academic acceptance outside the BAE was most favorable. My files show evidence that it was used in advanced classes at Harvard (by Carl C. Zimmerman) and at Columbia (by Edmond DeS. Brunner) and I was told it was used to exemplify scientific method for students at Chicago. F. Stuart Chapin, a prominent sociologist at Minnesota, J. Lossing Buck of FAO, and other educators and scholars wrote personal notes of appreciation regarding this work. But the most important evidence of its acceptability in scholarly circles was the fact that it was used extensively in several textbooks in sociology written over the next few years (including one by the Chief of the Division of Farm Population and Rural Welfare, Carl C. Taylor).

IMPLICATIONS

The history of the study of Arvin and Dinuba is a document on the social effects of corporate farming as telling and as important as the study itself. Let us review what it reveals.

An investigation, as scientifically sound and carefully conceived as is possible in the field of social behavior, is initiated in response to a matter of public policy. This issue, as old as the nation itself, has to do with the character not only of our rural life, but of democratic institutions as a whole.

From the first indication that the study was under way, the Associated Farmers, an organization dominated by agribusiness, and a representative of DiGiorgio Farms, one of the giants in the field, initiated a propaganda campaign, by releasing material from me (the letter and the questionnaire) to Elliott and the sympathetic—or captive—media. The first efforts of this campaign were directed at the study itself, endeavoring to prevent the completion and succeeded in aborting the important second phase of the study. The similarities in statements and the general pattern of this activity indicate it was a coordinated and centrally orchestrated campaign.

The second effort was to suppress the full study. Relatively little attention was given to the preliminary report, which did not contain the full documentation and could therefore easily be condemned and overlooked; better not to give it too much attention. Suppression was successful for nearly two years, and was overcome only by the forceful and courageous action of a liberal senator, who quite evidently received a continuous barrage of flack from the opposition as a result.

Once published, efforts were made to discredit the study itself. This was done in part by condemning the authors, by stating that the study was factually in error and by arguing that it had failed to consider the alternate explanations to account for the differences. No factual errors were ever brought to public attention and no recognition was given to my careful examination of those very alternate explanations, especially the crucial matter of difference in the age of the two towns, which were repeatedly mentioned. No personal accusations against me could be sustained for I was never confronted with them, even though I was heavily investigated when I sought a commission and again, I was told, when I came up for a regular appointment at UCLA.

That the Arvin-Dinuba study was eventually published,

received wide circulation, and became (as *Business Week* indicated) artillery for the proponents of the acreage limitation law, these facts might suggest that the influence of agribusiness is minimal. Such a conclusion might lead one to believe that these large growers do not have much power. This, unfortunately, is not the case. They succeeded in preventing the second phase of the study which I believe would have deprived them of *any* case for discrediting the study. They succeeded in delaying the report and in forcing its publication in a relatively obscure form that is (despite its widespread use) difficult of access.

Above all, they deprived the study of the opportunity for rational examination; they changed the arena of discourse from one of judicious review of the facts, from the importance of the underlying acreage limitation law and the agrarian principle, to one of propaganda involving diverse irrelevancies. This was achieved to such a degree that Kirkendall, in his examination 20 years later, saw only the propagandistic aspects of the situation.[46]

But there were more important repercussions. I left the BAE[47] because I preferred an academic appointment to a transfer to the Washington office, when the regional offices of that organization were abandoned by legislative fiat. In an article in *The Nation,* Alden Stevens concluded a report on Dinuba after reviewing the Arvin-Dinuba materials as follows:

> This proof that small irrigated farms are better than large brought about a resolution by the directors of the California Farm Bureau Federation, a friend of the big farmers, disapproving ". . . the personnel of the BAE spending a considerable portion of their time in preparing reports on various Central Valley study problems." In the next Department of Agriculture appropriation bill the following provision mysteriously appeared:
>
> "No part of the funds herein appropriated or made available to the Bureau of Agricultural Economics shall be used for state and county land-use planning, for conducting cultural surveys, or for the maintenance of more than one worker in the respective regional offices."

Howard R. Tolley, realizing that the bureau he had built and directed was now stripped of its fact-finding ability and of its freedom, resigned as chief, and the usefulness of the bureau came virtually to an end. The Dinuba study, which showed that its small family farms make a better way of life than the large factory farms of Arvin, and that less than 160 acres of irrigated land is enough to support a family, was used to destroy one of the most honest and courageous organizations in Washington, the Bureau of Agricultural Economics.[48]

I wrote a letter to *The Nation* saying that the study was not manifestly responsible for this action.

Many of my former colleagues in the Bureau of Agricultural Economics would be dismayed to learn that their agency was destroyed. It was, to be sure, heavily curtailed in its activities by the Seventy-ninth Congress, but it continues to function as an important research agency of the government. Mr. Stevens states that the fall from grace which the bureau suffered was the result of my investigations into the effect of large farms on community life. There is no evidence in the hearings on the Agricultural Department appropriation bill for 1947 that the study of Dinuba and Arvin had anything to do with the curtailed budget. Failure to mention this study cannot be attributed to Congressional reticence, since there was none evidenced when the study was being prosecuted in the field and attacked on the radio and in Congress.[49]

I am not so sure as I was when I wrote that letter to *The Nation* that the Arvin-Dinuba investigation was not a major factor in the curtailment of the BAE and its subsequent demise. An investigation of this matter was made at the request of the Senate Small Business Committee in 1972. Hugh P. Prince, legislative attorney at the Library of Congress wrote:

We have located the statement referred to in "The Nation" for September 28, 1946, page 352, and enclose xerox copy thereof. We have not located a provision in the appropriation acts for the Department of Agriculture which is in the exact language of that quoted. We have located similar language in the regular appropriation acts for the Department of Agriculture beginning with the Department of Agriculture Appropriation Act of July 12, 1943 and extending through all subsequent acts to and including the Act of July 28, 1953.⁵⁰

The Department of Agriculture Appropriation Act for Fiscal Year 1947 includes the following codicil: "That no part of the funds herein appropriated or made available to the Bureau of Agricultural Economics under the heading 'Economic Investigation' shall be used for state or county land and planning, *for conducting cultural surveys, or for the maintenance of regional offices.*"⁵¹

Kirkendall has written a book detailing the growth and demise of the BAE.⁵² In this work he places the role of the Arvin-Dinuba study in broader context. He makes it clear that criticism of this study, and even stronger objections to an examination of race relations in Mississippi, are specific issues used in the pressure to demote the role of the BAE. But more importantly, agricultural leaders, and especially corporations with close ties to agricultural production had from the outset objected to the New Deal agricultural policies that were promulgated by agricultural economists. In this way, the propaganda against the study was but a small but significant element in a larger fight over control of American agriculture. Kirkendall writes as if this was an issue between farm leaders and social scientists, though he is not unaware of big business interests in the agricultural enterprise. The business involvement in these issues has been documented by others, notably Wesley McCune, who shows the degree to which industrial leaders had organized anti-New Deal propaganda.⁵³ We must thus see the pressure as a small battle in a major campaign favoring industrial interests in the organization of our farming. At any rate, whether or not the attacks on the Arvin-Dinuba research were responsible, it is clear that the Department of Agriculture ceased to have an effective research unit engaged in studying the social aspects of agriculture, as Jim Hightower has documented extensively in *Hard Tomatoes, Hard Times*. Thus agribusiness interests have successfully curtailed those research activities not devoted to economic profitability and the techniques of production and marketing. The research arm of the Department of

Agriculture is a notably weak one, and it can only be seen as the handmaiden of that very agribusiness group who fought the Arvin-Dinuba study.

Wasco, Arvin and Dinuba tell us what industrialized agriculture does to the *local community* and how corporate agricultural operations exacerbate the disadvantages in this industrial system. The examination of the treatment of the Arvin-Dinuba study, however, tells us what this industrialized agriculture does to our *national life*. It shows how knowledge gets suppressed and truth distorted, how bureaucracies are entered and destroyed, how national policies are subverted, and the character of our nation reshaped. As I testified before Senator Harris:

. . . there are few who doubt that the nature of rural land tenure is intimately related to the character of the social order. Since the dawn of civilization, when intensive agriculture became the means by which man supplied his basic wants, the control of land has been a basic element in forming the character of society. By and large, where democratic conditions prevail, the man who tilled the soil was a free holder and in control of his enterprise. Where, on the other hand, the farming lands are owned and controlled in the urban centers, and the men engaged in production are merely peasants, serfs, or hired laborers, democratic institutions do not prevail. Those who framed our constitution and set the course of American history believed that this relation was paramount. It lay behind Jeffersonian democracy, it lay behind the Homestead Act, and it lay behind the extension of the homestead principles in the development of irrigation under the Reclamation Act as formulated at the beginning of this century.[54]

NOTES

1. Richard S. Kirkendall, "Social Sciences in the Central Valley of California: An Episode," *The California Historical Society Quarterly* (September 1964), pp. 185-218. Paul S. Taylor, "Walter Goldschmidt's Baptism in Fire. Central Valley Water Politics," *Paths to the Symbolic Self: Essays in honor of Walter Goldschmidt*, in *Anthropology UCLA*, Vol. 8, Nos. 1 and 2 (Los Angeles: Department of Anthropology, University of California, 1976), pp. 129-40.

2. *Congressional Record*, House, March 23, 1944. p. 3039-40.

3. *Congressional Record*, House, April 27, 1944. p. 3755.

4. Reprint of Broadcast by Fulton Lewis, Jr., Mutual Network, May 4, 1944. Personal files. This item and other relevant materials have been reproduced in the Hearings before the Subcommittee on Monopoly of the Select Committee on Small Business, United States Senate, 92nd Congress, First and Second Sessions; *The Role of Giant Corporations in the American and World Economies* (November 23 and December 1, 1971; March 1 and 2, 1972); hereinafter, *Giant Corporations*.

5. "County Commentator" broadcast, May 1, 1944. Personal files; also *Giant Corporations*, Part 3B, p. 4657.

6. "County Commentator" broadcast, May 2, 1949. Personal files; also *Giant Corporations*, Part 3B, pp. 4657-59.

7. "County Commentator" broadcast, May 8, 1944. Personal files; also *Giant Corporations*, Part 3B, pp. 4663-64.

8. *Giant Corporations*, Part 3B, pp. 4664-66.

9. Aside from the DiGiorgio refusal, however, there were no failures to respond in Arvin and only seven in Dinuba, or less than two percent overall. This record is in itself an accolade to the quality of the interviewers.

10. *Congressional Record*, House (June 21, 1944), Appendix A, p. 3489.

11. A few months later, when I sought a commission in the U.S. Navy, the investigation was unusually thorough. I was found "not to possess the qualifications for an officer in the United States Naval Reserve." I am certain, though cannot prove, that the rejection was based upon the public attacks.

12. Kirkendall, p. 200.

13. I wonder now why it did not occur to me, or anybody else involved with the study, at the time. Perhaps the pressure we were under had prevented us from reflection.

14. It would certainly have influenced the level of local business activity, a difference between Arvin and Dinuba that seems to have caused more consternation among those who opposed the study than did the differences in social conditions. The ratio of total family income (based on questionnaires) to total farm income in Arvin was 1.3:1; in Dinuba it was 2:1.

15. Kirkendall, *op. cit.*, p. 195.

16. Nor did he see fit to favor me with a copy after publication. I learned of the study wholly by accident from a fellow guest at a party who was a reader of the relatively obscure journal. "Goldschmidt?" he queried at the introduction; "Why I have just read an article about you." "*By* me, you mean?" "No, *about* you."

17. Kirkendall, *vide op. cit.*, footnote 8, p. 211.

18. Walter Goldschmidt, "Research into the Effects of Corporate Farming on the Quality of Rural Community Life," statement prepared for the Subcommittee of the Select Committee on Small Business, Hearings before the Subcommittee on Migratory Labor of the Committee on Labor in Public Welfare, United States Senate, 92nd Congress, 1st and 2nd Sessions, *Frameworks in Rural America* (1971-1972), Appendix Part 5A, p. 33323.

19. Kirkendall, p. 196 (emphasis supplied).

20. The repeated failure of the BR to enforce the acreage limitation provision has been documented in detail by Angus McDonald, *Reclamation Law Violation of the Department of Interior*, MS. (1977). Personal files, courtesy McDonald.

21. Kirkendall, p. 196.

22. *Ibid.*, p. 198 (emphasis supplied). This subtle imputation of propagandist zeal appears again when Kirkendall writes, "His biggest opportunity came on May 11, when Bob Franklin granted him radio time." First, Franklin did not grant the time; he was forced to do so by the manager of the station; second, I did not request it, but the request was made by BAE officials. It was my maiden radio speech, and I was far from eager, as Kirkendall's sentence implies. Again, in the closing paragraph, Kirkendall has me being "pushed" into the controversy by my values, rather than drawn into it by events.

23. *Ibid.*, p. 199.

24. *Ibid.*, p. 201. Presenting this argument without recognition that the Central Valley Project constituted a massive subsidy, makes this statement highly suspect.

25. Some of these contradictions will appear in the following section. Kirkendall indicates that the study was rejected by the Washington staff of the BAE (pp. 206-207). He does not take cognizance of the pressure exerted by congressmen on the BAE personnel to make such rejection. Furthermore, the study was sociological and the sociologists in my division did not reject the study (see below). Kirkendall takes no notice of this distinction and the normal disagreements between members of different disciplines. As a matter of fact, there was no little expression of anxiety among the career social scientists that the study might create such pressures as would endanger their jobs—a sentiment not without foundation, as we shall see.

26. Kirkendall, p. 210 (emphasis supplied).

27. There is a correlation between average farm size and population per acre in the rural communities of the lower San Joaquin Valley (Walter Goldschmidt, *The Relation Between Farm Size and Population*, MS., 1977). Arvin is unusual in this respect, for the population per acre is greater than any of the other communities with farms above median size; indeed, it is identical with that of Dinuba. Thus our effort to control for size led us to select a community that in this respect is unique. The effect of this has undoubtedly been to *understate* the full effects of large-scale farming in the rural communities of the area. No doubt it was this fact that made those who opposed the study recognize that the communities selected constituted a "fair" choice, according to comments I received at the time.

28. Comments by Marion Clawson on manuscript, *The Social Effects of the Scale of Farm Operations* by Walter Goldschmidt, p. 8. Personal files.

29. Clawson to Goldschmidt, April 7, 1945. Personal files. This stands in direct contrast to Kirkendall's report of De Vries' opinion.

30. Objections to the manuscript indicated that I had treated the discussion "like a lawyer's brief" (*vide* Kirdendall, p. 206). This ticking off and refutation of alternate explanations developed from the manner in which objections were raised seriatim.

31. Kirkendall gives us a glimpse of this, though he is more interested in displaying the criticism of the research than in demonstrating that it was being buried. It is another example of his selective reporting; he nowhere indicates that the new Secretary of Agriculture personally held up publication (see below).

32. Dewey Anderson to Paul Taylor, October 10, 1946. Personal files.

33. Claude Wickard had by now been replaced by Clinton Anderson, a former and subsequent member of Congress.

34. Dewey Anderson to Goldschmidt, October 25, 1946. Personal files.

35. It was a personal embarrassment to me that I could not make appropriate acknowledgements to the many persons whose contribution to the study were vital to its accomplishment. Among those who should receive their due at this late date are the following: Paul S. Taylor, Walter Packard, Marion Clawson, Lloyd Fisher, Mary Montgomery, Eshrev Shevky, and Varden Fuller, who helped in formulating the research design; Walter McKain who used techniques of the rural sociologists in delineating the two communities; J. Karl Lee and Edwin E. Wilson who analyzed much of the data on farm size and production; Gale Goldschmidt and Beryl Strong who took the schedules in Arvin and Dinuba under somewhat less than ideal circumstances and came up with an astonishing record; and numerous secretaries, cartographers, others at the BAE who helped in the preparation of the manuscript and undoubtedly many others whose memory has been dimmed by the passage of time, as well as the citizens of Arvin and Dinuba and various local officials who, whether friendly or hostile, contributed to my understanding of California rural life.

36. Dewey Anderson to Goldschmidt, November 20, 1946. Personal files.

37. Dorothy Holshouser (committee staff person) to Goldschmidt, May 13, 1947. Personal files.

38. It would of course have been better if the community names could have been obscured. It has been common practice in community studies, dating from Robert and Helen Lynds' study of Muncie, Indiana ("Middletown"), to give fictitious names to the communities investigated, in order to protect them and their citizenry from adverse publicity. Naturally, I gave considerable thought to following the same procedure, though inasmuch as anybody who cares, particularly the inhabitants, can easily unmask such pseudonyms, the procedure is of doubtful value. The decision not to do so was made, however, because long before the study reached print there had already been vast public exposure, so that to do so would have been both vain and ludicrous. It is a source of personal unhappiness that I was therefore in the position of "condemning" a community. Had the second phase of the study been permitted, there would have been some amelioration of this effect. The study does not, of course, "blame" the community or its citizenry, but assesses the consequences of farm tenure.

39. Cecil L. Dunn and Philip Neff, *The Arvin Area of Kern County: An Economic Survey of the Southeastern San Joaquin Valley in Relation to Land Use on the Size and Distribution of Income*, prepared for the Board of Supervisors of Kern County and the Water Resources Committee of the Kern County Chamber of Commerce. Mimeographed (1947).

40. Robert H. Garrison to Goldschmidt, December 24, 1946. Personal files.

41. Downey did not run for election again; Helen Gahagan Douglas won the primary and was defeated by Richard Nixon. Downey had begun his career as a New Deal liberal.

42. *Giant Corporations*, Part 3B, p. 4679.

43. Dewey Anderson to Goldschmidt, May 12, 1948. Personal files. See also *Giant Corporations*, Part 3B, p. 4678. The memorandum appears also in *Giant Corporations*, Part 3B, pp. 4678-82.

44. Dewey Anderson to Goldschmidt, Feb. 26, 1949. Personal files. See also *Giant Corporations*, Part 3B, p. 4682.

45. Nichols to Goldschmidt, Jan. 28, 1947. Personal files. Also *Giant Corporations*, Part 3B, p. 4684.

46. And by succumbing to this orientation, becomes a part of the propaganda.

47. Had I not happened to have opted for this choice, it is very likely that the suppression of the study would have been totally successful, since the Secretary of Agriculture could have denied me permission, as an employee, to publish the work.

48. "Small Town America VII: Dinuba, California," Alden Stevens, *The Nation*, Sept. 28, 1946. See *Giant Corporations*, Part 3B, pp. 4686-87.

49. Walter R. Goldschmidt, "Alive and Kicking," *The Nation* (January 18, 1947).

50. *Giant Corporations*, Part 3B, p. 4685. A footnote lists the relevant entries.

51. *Giant Corporations*, Part 3B, p. 4699. The italicized material in this codicil indicates what was new in 1946, and it was continued, according to Prince's documentation, until 1953.

52. Richard S. Kirkendall, *Social Scientists and Farm Politics in the Age of Roosevelt* (Columbia: University of Missouri Press, 1966). See especially pages 224-25.

53. Wesley McCune, *Who's Behind our Farm Policy?* (New York: Praeger, 1956).

54. See reference 18.

INDEX

AAA (see Agricultural Adjustment Administration)
Abourezk, Sen. James, xxv
Absentee owners, 412, 417
Acreage limitation provision, 456, 458-60, 462, 470, 480
Acre-equivalent units, defined, 310, 430
Adams, Frank, 297, 298
Adams, R. L., xxxviii, 39, 82, 422-23
Adohr Milk Farms, 10
Adult education, 239, 263-69
Age-grading, 77, 115
Agribusiness (corporate agriculture), xxv-xxx, 245; and American culture, xxxix-l; contract farming, xxvi-xxviii; in controversy on Arvin-Dinuba study, 455, 482-87; corporate advantage in, xxxii-xxxix; in farm policy, xlviii-l; growth of, xxv-xxvi; and research agencies, xxxviii-xxxix; subsidiaries, xxxiii; tax advantages, xxxiv-xxxviii; vertical integration, xxvi-xxviii
Agribusiness and the Rural Community (W. R. Goldschmidt), xxiv, xli, xlii
Agricultural Adjustment Act, 247-48
Agricultural Adjustment Administration, 184, 187-89, 204, 239-40, 255; and disadvantaged farmers, 247-48; hostility toward, 46-47; local committee, 174; and Wasco, 46-47
Agricultural Adjustment Agency, data from, 294, 304-5, 315, 428, 430, 439, 440
Agricultural Extension Service, 239, 251, 260, 268-70
Agricultural labor (see Labor, agricultural)
Agricultural Packers, 172
Agricultural production (see Farm production)
Agricultural Workers' Union, 102
Alabama, poultry farmers' strike, xxvii-xxviii
Alcorn, G. B., 31
Alfalfa, 38, 295
Alta Irrigation District, 298, 402, 435
Altmeyer, A. J., 250-51

American Cyanamid, xxix
American Exodus (Lange and Taylor), 53
American Legion: in Dinuba, 197, 356-57; in Wasco, 102, 166
Amusement (see Entertainment; Recreational activities)
Anderson, A. C., 30
Anderson, Clinton, 476-77
Anderson, Dewey, 475-78, 481-82
Arizona, recruiting of labor from East, 162
Arkansas, migrants from, 19-21, 50, 207, 232
Arkies, 51
Armenian church, 198, 367, 369
Armenians in Dinuba, 192, 193, 322
Arvin, 9, 186, 187, 190, 191, 227 *et seq.*, 252, 257, 269; age distribution of residents, 324-25, 327; agriculture and crops in, 203-5, 289, 294-95, 304-20, 410-12; appearance, 342, 344; Booster Club, 346, 353-54, 373, 374, 377, 479; business in, 282-83, 381-91; changing conditions in, xli-xlii; churches, 212-14, 367-72; civic action, 213-17, 344-46; civic developments, 404; clubs, 210-12, 353-59; community solidarity in, 375-76, 401, 416-17; compared with Dinuba, 217-20, 282-85, 289-91, 301-3, 342-43, 376-80, 392-423 (*see also* Arvin-Dinuba study); compared with Wasco, 217-20; educational level, 328; ethnic groups in, 291, 321-22; family heads, birthplace and year of arrival, 325, 326; family size, 322-24; Farm Center, 212, 353, 354; farm labor requirements, 315-20, 439-43; farm laborers, social position and rights, 323, 328-29, 354-56; farm size, 203-20, 306-14; flower festival, 353; fruit and vegetable shipments, 407-8; glider meet, 353; government, 344-49; gross farm income by principal sources, 306-8; history, 293-96, 303, 402-10; income, 211, 330, 332; intensive land use, 306, 407, 409; irrigation, xli, 204, 293-96, 301-3; land tenure, operators and tenants, 314-15; land use and com-

modity value, 204; large farms, 203–20, 282–85, 287; level-of-living index, 333–37; Lions Club, 353, 354, 373, 374, 377; living conditions, 332–39, 342; occupations, 328–29, 331; Parent-Teachers Association, 212, 353–56; population, 205–7, 321–22, 398; reaction to publication of Arvin-Dinuba study, 479; recreation, 119–20, 210; schools, 216–17, 303, 349–53, 402–4, 406; setting, 292–93; social background and structure of, 207–10, 325–28, 376–80, 398–402; social evaluations of, 373–76; social participation, 210–12, 353–64, 376–78; soil compared with Dinuba, 302; speculative developments in farming, 295–96; water supply, 397–98, 415, 434–38; youth problems and services, 364–67

Arvin-Dinuba study, 392–423; causative differentials, 395–96; controversy on, 455, 458–87; cultural and demographic factors, 398–402; cultural similarities, 392–94; data sources and methodology, 425–50; environmental factors, 396–98; explanatory hypothesis, 414–19; farm labor, 398–401, 411–17, 439–43; farm organization factors, 412–14; farm production factors, 410–12; historic factors, 402–10; interviews, 425–26, 459–60; large- and small-scale farming, conclusions on, 412, 414–23, 474, 482–87; origin of, 456–58; purpose and methods of, 286–91; sampling techniques, 426–27; social conditions, 415–21; social differences, 394–95; summary of, 281–85; unfinished, 466–67

Asiatics (see also Chinese labor; Japanese labor): in California, 15–19, 49, 176; in Dinuba, 192, 193; restriction on immigration, 20

Assembly of God church, 136, 198, 213–14, 367, 369

Associated Farmers, 102, 166, 483; and union activities, 182–83

Associations (see also Clubs): in Arvin, 210–12, 360–64; in Dinuba, 196–97, 360–64; in Wasco, 101–12

"Backwardness" of farm population, 239

Bailey, Warren R., xxxi

Bakersfield, 209, 216, 356, 378, 479

Bakersfield Californian, 170, 479

Balfour-Guthrie Investment Company, 10

Bancroft, Philip, 182

Banking: in Dinuba, 299–300; in Wasco, 42

Bank of America, xxvi

Baptist church, 367, 369

Bedford, W. W., 422–23

Beef production and agribusiness, xxxv–xxxvii

"Bindle stiff," 49

Black churches, 124, 141

Blacks: in Arvin and Dinuba, 291, 322; in California, 16–18; housing for, 74–75; in labor force, 4, 49, 120, 123; petition of, 173–74; religious segregation of, 134–35; in Wasco, 55, 59, 66–68, 70–71, 93–94

Boeing, xxvi

Boom periods, 155–56, 299

Boswell, J. G., Co., xxxii

Boy Scouts, 365–67

Brunner, Edmond deS., 482

Buck, J. Lossing, 482

Bureau of Agricultural Economics, xxxix, 304, 439, 449; and Arvin-Dinuba study, 455–58, 461–63, 465–67, 470, 472, 475–77, 481–82, 484–86

Bureau of Reclamation, 186, 455–56, 470, 472

Business: in Arvin, 282–83, 381–91; data sources and methods of study, 449–51; in Dinuba, 282–83, 381–91; farming as, 22, 28–29, 40–41; number of enterprises and gross volume of sales, 381–89; in Wasco, 42–45

Business Week, 479, 484

Buttonwillow, 410

Calhoun, Wendell T., 14, 463

California: agribusiness and changing conditions in, xli–xlvi; agriculture in American life, 3–21; communities, failure to incorporate, 215–16; ethnic groups (see Ethnic groups); farm production, 13–14; home-produced foods, 31; immigration, 49–54; industrialized farming, growth of, 280–81; land acquisition in, 7–8; land tenure in, 6–13; population growth, 19–20; water districts, study of, xliii–xlv

California Farm Bureau Federation, 102, 170, 181, 231, 269, 484

California Fruit Growers, 182

INDEX 495

California Packing Corporation, 10
California State Board of Equalization, 381, 391
California State Relief Administration, 46, 177
Campbell Soups, xxix
Camps, workers' (*see* Laborers' camps)
Canadians in Dinuba, 192
Cannery and Agricultural Workers' Union, 171
Capital and industrialization, 33-41
Capitals, political, 221
Cash cropping, 27-30
Caste barriers, 4 (*see also* Segregation)
Catholic church: in Arvin, 214, 367, 369; in Dinuba, 198; in Wasco, 55, 56, 67, 125, 136, 138
Cattle (*see* Beef production; Livestock)
Cemetery district, 111
Central Soya, xxviii, xxix
Central Valley Project of California, xxiv-xxv, xli, 186, 286, 287, 455-58, 460, 462-65
Chamber of Commerce, 170, 181
Chapin, F. Stuart, 482
Chapman, William S., 7
Chicken farming (*see* Poultry industry)
Child labor laws, 249-50
Children: advancement of, 161; in school (*see* Schools)
Children's Bureau, U.S., 249
Chinese labor, 15-18, 23, 49
Chi square, 332n, 335, 368, 477-48
Christian church, 198, 367, 369
Christian Science church, 136
Christian Science Monitor, 479
Churches, 71, 228, 230; in Arvin, 212-14, 367-72; attendance of recent arrivals, 144; civic influence of, 146-47; class character of, 124-47, 198-99, 213, 368-71; and cliques, 117; in Dinuba, 197-99, 299, 367-72; in large-farm and small-farm communities, 284; membership in, by occupations, 103, 368, 370-72; segregation in, 133-38; social mobility of, 138-43; social status in, 133-38, 368-71, 378-80, 399-400; underprivileged in, 141; in Wasco, 65, 67, 71, 124-33
Church of Christ, 136, 198, 367, 370
Church of God, 198, 367, 370
Church of the Nazarene, 136, 146, 198, 213-14, 367, 369
Cities, heterogeneity of, 222-23
Citizenship, full, 262

City, defined, 222
Civic action, 237-38; in Arvin, 213-17, 344-46; in Dinuba, 199-202, 344-49; in Wasco, 110-12
Civil War, 4
Class-consciousness, 172
Classes, 55-79 (*see also* Social participation; Social structure); in rural America, xlv-xlvi; in Wasco, 58-63
Clawson, Marion, 13, 456, 465, 467, 471-73, 475
Clerical workers, 57
Cliques, 75-76; and social recreation, 115-17
Clubs: activities and individual status, 107-10; age-grading and sex division in, 115; in Arvin, 210-12, 353-59; civic action and, 110-12; in Dinuba, 195-97, 356-60; occupational membership in, 103-5, 358-59; public opinion and, 110-12; special interest, 102, 106; in Wasco, 101-15; women's, 102-4, 106, 108, 109, 114-15, 165, 357
Cohesive factors: nuclear group, 161-62; outsider group, 149-53
Cole, Ralph C., 30
Collective bargaining, 266
Colonization: in California, 6-9; in Wasco, 24-27
Committee on Interstate Migration of Destitute Citizens, 19
Committee on Violation of Free Speech and Rights of Labor, 19; *Supplementary Hearings*, 243, 249
Commodities, value of: in Arvin, 204; in Dinuba, 188-89
Commodity loans of AAA, 247
Communism, 166-67
Communists, 171; and strikes, 182
Community action, 237-38; in Arvin, 214-17; in Dinuba, 199-202; in Wasco, 110-12
Community of interest and geographical community, 112-13
Conflict: economic, 163-66; political, 167-68; situations, external leadership in, 169-72; social, 163-72; on unionization, 166-67
Congregational church, 136, 367, 369
Congress, attitudes on labor relations, 252
Consolidated holdings, 10, 12-13
Consumers Purchases Study, 30, 119
Consumer subsidies, 264
Contract farming, xxvi-xxviii

Controls, social (see Social control)
Cooley, Charles H., 92
Cooperative colonies, 9
Cooperatives in Wasco, 44–45
Corn Belt, mechanization in, 244
Corporate agriculture (see Agribusiness)
Corporate interests, 231; in Wasco, 42–45, 63–64
Costs of land (see Land costs and values)
Costs of production (see Farm production costs)
Cotton, 27, 28, 409; in Arvin, 289, 294–95, 410–12; costs of production, 34, 36–38; harvesting, 88; poverty associated with production, 410–11; seasonal rhythm, 80–81
County government, 221; in Arvin, 344–46
County Land Use Planning Committee, 181
Creel, George, 183
Crops produced (see Farm production, crops)
Cultural backgrounds, 17, 18, 55, 59, 66–68, 233, 236; in Arvin and Dinuba, 398–400; in Wasco, 55
Cutler, 296

Dairying in Wasco, 44–45
Dancing as recreation, 195
Delano, 405, 407–9
Democracy, 4, 5; in schools, 106, 161
Department of Agriculture, xxxviii, xxxix, 251, 473, 478, 486–87
Department of Agriculture Appropriation Act (1947), 486
Depression, 259; of 1920s, 299–300
Desert, 26
De Vries, Peter, 467, 475
DiGiorgio Fruit Corp., 292, 294, 483
DiGiorgio housing units, 10, 203, 205, 229, 329, 444, 459
Dinuba, 9, 12, 13, 227 et seq., 252, 267; age distribution of residents, 324–25, 327; agriculture and crops, 187–90, 289, 296–97, 304–20, 410–12; appearance, 342, 344; boom and depression of 1920s, 299–300; business in, 282–83, 381–91; changing conditions in, xli–xlii; churches, 197–99, 299, 367–72; civic action, 199–202, 344–49; civic developments, 404; clubs, 195–97, 356–60; community solidarity, 375–76, 401; compared with Arvin, 217–20, 282–85, 289–91, 301–3, 342–43, 376–80, 292–423, (see also Arvin-Dinuba study); compared with Wasco, 217–20; educational level, 328; ethnic groups, 192–93, 291, 321–22; family heads, birthplace and year of arrival, 325, 326; family size, 322–24; Farm Center, 357; farm labor requirements, 188, 315–20, 439–43; farm laborers, social position and rights, farm laborers, social position and rights, 357–60; farm size, 187, 306–14; government, 344–49; gross farm income by principal sources, 306–8; history, 297–301, 303, 402–10; income, 190, 330, 332; incorporation of, 199, 215, 299, 346; intensive land use, 306; irrigation, 298, 300–303; land tenure, operators and tenants, 314–15; land use and commodity value, 189; large-scale farming operations, 187, 300–301; level-of-living index, 333–37; living conditions, 332–37, 340–41, 342; newspapers, 284, 299; occupations, 191, 328–29, 331; population, 190–92, 321–22, 398; recreation, 119–20, 195, 299; schools, 298, 299, 303, 349–53, 402–404; setting, 296–97; as small-farm community, 282–84, 287; social background and structure, 192–94, 325–28, 376–80, 398–402; social evaluations of, 374–76; social participation, 195–97, 299, 356–64, 376–78; soil compared with Arvin, 302; study of, 186–202 (see also Arvin-Dinuba study); water supply, 397–98, 415, 434–38; youth problems and services, 364–67
Dow Chemical, xxix
Downey, Sen. Sheridan, 480–82; *They Would Rule the Valley*, 480
Drinking, 76–77
Drought, 26, 150
Ducoff, Louis J., 258
Dust Bowl, 20, 50, 73
Dust Bowl migrants (dust-bowlers), 93, 207, 398–400, 409; differentiated from Okies, 73

Earl Fruit Company, 10
Economic basis of social distinctions, 55–79
Economic conflict, 163–66
Economic neighborhoods, 92–94
Economic sanctions, 255–56

INDEX

Economics of scarcity, 254-55
Economy of scale, xxx-xxxii
Education: adult, 239, 268-69; educational level of family heads, 328, 400; levels in Arvin and Dinuba compared, 400; schools (*see* Schools)
Edwards, Alba M., 57
Elite, 224-25; social control by, 179
Elliott, Rep. Alfred J., 458-63, 465, 471, 472, 477, 483
El Solyo Ranch, 10
El Tejon Ranch, 292, 293
Employment security, 89
Employment service, 268, 270-71
Entertainment, commercial, 101, 117-23; motion pictures, 117-20, 195, 362-64, 366-67; radio, 120, 121; reading, 120-22; various types of, 122-23
Entertainment, social, organized, 101-17
Equity: for commercial farmers, 257; and inequities, 255-56; in policy, principle of, 256-62; in rural society, 262-72
Ethnic groups, 17, 18, 49, 55, 59, 66-68, 233, 236; in Arvin, 291, 321-22; in Dinuba, 192-93, 291, 321-22
Evangelical sects, 143
Evans, Rudolph M., 255
Excess lands law, 456
Extension Service, 239, 251, 260, 268-70
External control, 179-85; AAA, 46-47; in conflict situations, 169-72

Factories in the Fields (Carey McWilliams), 19, 22
Factory farm production, 10 (*see also* Industrialized farming)
Fair Labor Standards Act, 250
Family, 75-77; size of, in Arvin and Dinuba, 322-24
Family farm, 253, 279-80
Family labor, unpaid, 15, 40, 257
Farm Bureau, 102, 170, 181, 231, 269; in Arvin, 353
Farmers: "backwardness" of, 239; commercial, equity for, 257; independent (self-employed), decline of, xxv; mobile, 10-12; noncommercial, 257, 258; part-time, 257; "submissiveness" of, 240; subsistence, 257; and workers, interdependence of, 62-63
Farm income (*see* Income)

Farming: in American life, 3-21; as business, 22, 28-29, 40-41; contract, xxvi-xxviii; corporate (*see* Agribusiness); decline of independent farms, xxv; factory farms, 10; family farms, 253, 279-80; farmer-intensive and labor-intensive areas, xlii-xliii; general farms, defined, 28; industrialized (*see* Industrialized farming); intensive, 31-34, 306, 407, 409; large-scale (*see* Large scale farming); mechanized, xxxi-xxxii, 32-33, 150, 242-43; productivity and waste of resources, xxxii; self-sufficient farm, 30; small-farm pattern, 3, 186-202, 265 (*see also* Small-scale farming); specialized (*see* Specialized farming)
Farm labor (*see* Labor, agricultural)
Farm Labor Act of 1943, 252
Farm Labor Service, 162
Farm operators, 57, 58; in Arvin and Dinuba, 305; in Wasco, 84-85
Farm policy: agribusiness in, xlviii-l; on labor, 249-53; need for, 254; on price support, 245-49; principles for, 253-56
Farm production, costs, 34-41; in Arvin, 204; cotton, Kern County, 34, 36-38; in Dinuba, 188; potatoes, 34, 35; sugar beets, 34, 35
Farm production, crops: in Arvin, 203-4; in Arvin-Dinuba study, 410-12; in California, 13-14; in Dinuba, 187-88; efficiency and farm size, 24; in Kern County, 38; marketing, 34-36; on small farms, 3, 186-202, 265; in Wasco, 27-32
Farm relief, xxxii, 240
Farm Security Administration, 169, 183
Farm size, 242-45; in Arvin, 203-20, 306-14; in Dinuba, 187, 306-14; and efficiency, 24; in Wasco, 22-27
Farm values (*see* Land costs and values)
Farm wages (*see* Wages, farm)
Farm workers' camps (*see* Laborers' camps)
FHA loans, 65
Filipino labor, 16-19, 49, 291, 322; as "stoop" labor, 86
Firebaugh, 410-11
Fisher, Lloyd, 456, 457
Folk culture, 226
Folsom, J. C., 164
Four-Square church, 198, 367, 370

Fowler, Henry R., 164
Franklin, Bob, 459, 460, 462-65
Fraternal orders: in Arvin, 210-11; in Dinuba, 196-97, 357; in Wasco, 102-4, 107
Fresno County, 296
Friedlander, Isaac, 8
Fruits: in Arvin, 294-95; in California, 13-14; in Dinuba, 289, 410, 411; shipments for Arvin and other communities, 407-8
Fujimoto, Isao, xlii
Fuller, Varden, xxxvii, 22, 50, 53, 69, 152, 161, 456

Gardens, farm, 28
Garrison, Walter, 182
Gates, Paul Wallace, 7-8
Gemeinschaft, 222
General farms, defined, 28
Geographical community and community of interest, 112-13
Germans: in Dinuba, 192, 193, 198, 291; Mennonites, 55, 192, 193, 198, 291
Gesellschaft, 222
Giffen, Inc., xxxiii
Gillette, J. M., 248
Girls, organizations for, 365, 366
Goldschmidt, Gale, 459, 460
Goldschmidt, Walter R., 187, 257; *Agribusiness and the Rural Community*, xxiv, xli, xlii; in Arvin-Dinuba study, 456-58; in controversy on the study, 464-87; delayed publication of report by, 473-78; *Small Business and the Community*, xxiv, 473, 478
Goodall, Merrill, xlii
Goodyear, xxvi
Government agencies and social controls, 184-85, 245-75
Government Camp, 174, 181, 329
Grange, the, 102, 231, 353, 356, 357
Grapes, 27, 38; agribusiness in production, xlvii; in Arvin, 294, 295; in Dinuba, 289, 296, 297, 301, 306, 410, 411
Grapes of Wrath, The (John Steinbeck), 19, 51, 112, 118, 181, 459

Hacienda, Spanish, 5, 6
Haggin and Carr, 24
Hamilton, C. Horace, 43
Handbills, 162

Harvesting: cotton, 88; potatoes, 86-88
Haskell, Sen. Floyd K., xxv
Health department, 175
Heffernan, William D., xlvii
High schools, 98-100; in Dinuba, 349, 352-53; lack of, in Arvin, 351-53
Hightower, Jim, xxxvii, xxxix, 486
Hindu labor, 16, 19, 49
"Hired hands," xxxvii, 252, 257, 258
Hired man, 48-49
Holy Roller church, 139
Home-produced foods, 31
Homestead Law, 3-4, 8, 253
Housing, 224, 235; for blacks in Wasco, 74-75; cheap, 162; level of living and, 333, 335, 337; programs, 268, 271-72; shortage, 174-75

Ickes, Harold L., 458, 462, 463
Immigration, 15-16, 49-54, 227
Imperial Valley, 11, 296
Improvement Club, 113
Income: in Arvin, 211, 330, 332; in Dinuba, 190, 330, 332; farm, calculation of, 430-32; in Kern County, and cotton, 37; and level of living, 335, 336; and social worth, 55-56
Incorporation: Arvin's failure to incorporate, 344-45; of communities in California, 215-16, 344, 345; of Dinuba, 199, 215, 237, 299, 346; of Wasco, 174, 178, 237
Indians: in California, 17, 18; impression of, 6, 15, 19; Kwakiutl, 224; Pueblo, 223; Zuñi, 224
Individual status: and athletic prowess, 100, 161; and club activities, 107-10; and religious participation, 143-46
Industrialized farming, 13, 280-81; in Arvin, 203-206; in Arvin-Dinuba study, 393-94; and capital, 33-41; in Dinuba, 187; and laborers, 15, 48-54; national trend toward, 242-45; nature of, 22-24; power equipment, 32-33; and rural community, 22-54; and urbanized farm people, 221-38; in various states, 243; in Wasco, 24-48
Inequities, 255-56
Intensive farming, 31-34, 306, 407, 409
Irrigation, 24, 26-27 (*see also* Water supply); in Arvin, xli, 204, 293-96, 301-3, 397-98, 434-33; Arvin and

INDEX 499

Dinuba compared, 302, 438; in Dinuba, 192, 193, 298, 300-3, 397-98, 434-38; pivot, in Nebraska, xxix-xxx, xxv, xlv; in Wasco, 32

Jackson, Joseph Henry, xxiv
Janow, Seymour, 49
Japanese Buddhist group, 198, 367
Japanese labor: in California, 16-18, 49, 176; in Dinuba, 192, 193, 291, 322
Jehovah's Witnesses, 367, 370
John Hancock Mutual Life Insurance Company, xxix
Johnstone, Paul H., 40-41, 182
Juvenile delinquency, 364-65

Kern County, 287, 296, 314, 381; Agricultural Planning Committee, 34; Chamber of Commerce, 479; cotton production costs, 34, 36-38; county government of communities, 345; farm equipment growth, 33; fruit and vegetable shipments, 407-8; incorporation in, 215; labor requirements in, 38-41, 288; migrant labor in, 50-52; Northern, crop acreages, 30; population and farming, 290; potatoes, 31; recreation of migrants, 119; seasonal workers in, 39-40; strikes in, 164-66
Kern County Land Company, 9, 24, 25, 456
Kerr, Clark, 163, 165, 166, 170
Key, Leon, 6
Kingsbury, 296
Kirkendall, Richard S., 465, 467-73, 475, 484, 486
Koehler, Leighton F., 30
Kolb, J. H., 92
Korean Presbyterian church, 367, 369
Koreans in Dinuba, 192, 193, 291, 322
Kwakiutl Indians, 224
Kyle, xlix

Labor (see Workers)
Labor, agricultural, 15-21, 247; in agribusiness, xxix, xxxii, xxxvii-xxxviii; in Arvin, 315-20, 323, 328-29, 354; in Arvin-Dinuba study, 398-401, 411-17, 439-43; barred from community action and social life, 111, 201, 214, 237, 323, 328-29, 354-60, 364; definition, broadening of, 250-51; in Dinuba, 315-20, 323, 328-29, 349, 357-60, 439-43; educational level, 400; and Fair Labor Standards Act, 250; family, unpaid, 15, 40, 257; family size, 323; gainfully employed in U.S., 257; government policy on, 249-53; "hired hands," xxxvii, 252, 257, 258; importance of, 176-77; and industrialized farming, 15, 48-54; in Kern County, 38-41, 50-52; in labor-intensive and farmer-intensive areas, xlii-xliii; not protected by National Labor Relations Act, xxxvii; organization of, 266-67 (see also Unionization); pools, 268; recruiting of 162; seasonal (see Seasonal workers); social participation, 361-64, 378-80; strikes (see Strikes); tenure, 267-68; types of, 48-49; wages (see Wages); in Wasco, 85-89
Laborers' camps, 169, 174, 181
La Follette, Sen. Robert, 243, 245, 264
La Follette Committee, 19; *Supplementary Hearings*, 243, 249
La Follette Hearings, 180; on wage settlement, 170, 171
Lamont, 292-93, 351, 407
Land acquisition in California, 7-8
Land costs and values, 33-41; in Arvin, 204, 293; in Dinuba, 188-89; in Kern County, 33; in Wasco, 33-41
Land grabs, 6
Land Grant colleges, 221
Land leasing, 10-12
Landrum-Griffin amendment to National Labor Relations Act, xxxvii
Land tenure: in Arvin and Dinuba, 314-15; in California, 6-13; Spanish, 6; in U.S., 3-6
Land Use Planning Committee, 174
Lange, Dorothea, 51, 53
Large-scale farming, 10, 242-45, 280-81; in Arvin, 203-20, 282-83, 287, 412, 414 (see also Arvin-Dinuba study); in Dinuba, 187, 300-301; and industrialized farming, 24, 393; in Wasco, 22-27
La Rose, Bruce, xli
Lasley, xlvii
Lee, J. Karl, xxxi, 24, 457
Leisure-time activities, 101
LeVeen, Phillip, xlii, xliii
Level-of-living index: in Arvin and Dinuba, 333-37; determination of, 445, 446; housing in, 333, 335, 337;

income in, 335, 336; occupation in, 333-35
Lewis, Fulton, Jr., 461-63, 465
Liberal thinking, fear of, 177
Life, 480
Lindsay, M. A., 31
Liquor, sales of, 387, 391
Little Oklahoma City, 65, 74, 152, 233
Livelihood, means of, 80-92, 283
Livestock (*see also* Beef production); and agribusiness, xxxv-xxxvii; calculation of income from, 431-34
Loans: commodity, of AAA, 247; FHA, 65
Longfellow, H. W., 31
Loomis, Charles P., 222
Los Angeles, 216
Los Angeles Times, 461, 465
Lutheran church, 367, 379
Lynd, Helen, 457
Lynd, Robert, 457

McConnell, Beatrice, 249
McCune, Wesley, 486
McEntire, Davis, 49, 50
McKain, Walter C., 457, 475
McWilliams, Carey (*Factories in the Fields*), 19, 22
Madden, J. Patrick, xxx-xxxi
Madera, 411
Madera County, 287, 381; population and farming, *table*, 290
Managers, 57; farms operated by, 248
Marginal social group, 65-66
Material possessions and social worth, 55-56
Matthews, S. F., xxxvi-xxxvii
Meat production (*see* Beef production; Livestock)
Mechanized farming, 32-33, 242-43 (*see also* Industrialized farming); power consumption in, xxxi-xxxii; as reason for migration, 150
Meisner, Joseph C., xxxv-xxxvi
Melons, 27
Mendota, 411
Mennonites: in Dinuba, 192, 193, 198, 291, 322, 367, 369, 379; in Wasco, 55
Merchants, status of: in Arvin, 206-207; in Dinuba, 191, 201; in Wasco, 58, 63-64
Metcalf, Sen. Lee, xxv
Methodist church, 136, 367, 369
Metzler, William H., 259
Mexican labor, 16-19, 49, 120, 123, 176; in Arvin, 207; in Dinuba, 192; housing for, 75; as "stoop" labor, 86; in Wasco, 55, 59, 66-68, 70, 75, 93-94, 125, 126
Mexican Pentecostal church, 124, 367
Mexican period, 7
Mexicans: in Arvin and Dinuba, 291, 322, 325; churches, 367; religious segregation, 135
Middle social group, 64-65; in Dinuba, 194
Middle West, 226, 227
Migrant workers, 48-53; camps for, 169, 174, 181; cultural characteristics, 399-400; defined, 49; recreation of, 119; in various states, 243; in Wasco, 69-71
Migration: of 1920s, 19; of 1930s, 19-21, 49-53; reasons for, 150-53
Miles, Sara, 49
Miller, E. H., 8, 9
Miller, Henry, 7
Miller and Lux, 7-9
Minimum wages, 264-66
Minnesota, land sales to investors, xxxv
Minority ethnic groups (*see* Ethnic groups)
Missionary Baptist church, 367, 370
Missouri, grape production area, xlvii
Mitchell, John W., 8
Mobility, social (*see* Social mobility)
Modesto, study of, 421-23
Monett, C. H., 435
Money, 225
Montgomery, Mary, 456
Morality, 97-98, 178
Mormon church, 124, 198, 367
Morse, Sen. Wayne, xlix-l
Motion pictures, 17-20, 195, 362-64, 366-67
Mountaineers, 226
Murray, Sen. James, 476-79, 481

Nation, The, 484-85
National Council of Agricultural Employers, xxix
National Labor Relations Act, xxxvii
National Planning Association, xxxvii
Natural resources: conservation of, 255; power consumption and misuse of, xxxi-xxxii
Nazarene church (*see* Church of the Nazarene)
Nebraska, pivot irrigation in, xxix-xxx, xxxv, xlvi
Negroes (*see* Blacks)

INDEX

Neighborhoods, economic 92-94
Nelson, Sen. Gaylord, xxv
New Deal, xxxiii, 240, 249, 486
New England farming tradition, 3
Newspapers, 238, 284, 299; advertisements in, 162
Nichols, 475-76
Nikolitch, Radoje, xlvi
Noncommercial farmers, 257, 258
North, social system in, 5
North Atlantic farming tradition, 3
North Dakota, Bottineau County, 248
North Dinuba, 296
Nuclear group: in Arvin, 209; attitudes toward strikes, 172; cohesive factors, 161-62; defined, 59; in Dinuba, 194; as employer group, 163; social controls in, 177-79; in Wasco, 63-66
Nuts produced in California, 13, 14

Occupational ambitions of high school students, 99
Occupational characteristics: of churches, 136, 137; of library subscribers, 121; of organizations in Wasco, 103-5
Occupations, 77; in Arvin, 328-29, 331; in Arvin-Dinuba study, 415-17; church membership and, 103, 368, 370-72; in Dinuba, 191, 328-29, 331; groupings, 57, 58; level of living and, 333-35; shifts in Wasco, 153-61; and social worth, 55-56; of voters in Wasco, 93, 103
Oil production near Arvin, 290-91, 301
Okies, 20, 51, 53, 172, 399; differentiated from dust-bowlers, 73; popular picture of, 61-62; in Wasco, 66, 111
Oklahoma, 50, 71, 73, 192, 207, 232; migration from, 19-21; recruiting of labor from, 162
Old-age insurance, 250
Onions, 38
Orange Cove, 296
Organizations (*see* Clubs; Social participation)
Organized entertainment (*see also* Recreational activities): cliques in, 115-17; social, 101-17, 360-67
Orosi, 296
Outsider group: in Arvin, 209; attitudes toward strikes, 172; cohesive factors, 149-53; defined, 59; in Dinuba, 194; domination of, by nuclear group, 173-77; in Wasco, 66-75
Owen, Bruce C., 30

Paarlberg, Don, xxvii
Pacific Rural Press, 460, 461, 473
Packing industries, 250
Palomares, Frank, 162
Parent-Teachers Association: in Arvin, 212, 353-56; in Wasco, 102, 165
Parity (parity price): calculations, 246; nature of, 245; program, 245-49
Parlier, 296
Pearson, Drew, 465, 478
Penn Central, xxvi
Pentecostal church, 124, 131-33, 136, 140, 143-45, 367, 370
Peterson, George M., 17, 18
Phillips, Rep. John, 462
Pickett, John, 460, 462, 465
Piece work, 86
Pike, Ray, 181
Pillsbury, xxviii, xxix
Pixley, 410
Plains area, 227
Plainville, U.S.A., 242
Plantation system, 3, 4, 241
Political capitals, 221
Political conflict, 167-68
Population: of Arvin, 205-7, 321-22, 398; data sources, 444; of Dinuba, 190-92, 321-22, 398; farm labor, of California, 15-21; growth, in California, 19-20; of Wasco, 51, 52, 56-77
Potatoes, 27-29; cost of producing, 34, 35; harvesting, 86-88; seasonal rhythm, 80-83
Poultry industry: agribusiness in, xxvii-xxix, xlvii; Alabama farmers' strike, xxvii-xxviii
Power farming (*see* Industrialized farming)
Pre-emption laws, 253
Presbyterian church, 367, 369
Price support, 245-49
Primary groups, 92, 94
Primitive societies, 223-24
Prince, Hugh P., 485-86
Production, farm (*see* Farm production)
Professionals, 57, 58
Promoters, 9
Proprietors, 57

Prospectors, land, 9
Protestant churches, 124, 136, 158, 369
Protestant ethic, xl, 142
Protestant Ethic (Max Weber), 142
Provinse, John, 457
Prudential Insurance, xxvi
Public forums, 179
Public lands, 3-4, 6
Pueblo Indians, 223
Purex, xxvi, xxix

Rabbits, 26
Race relations: in Dinuba, 193; in Wasco, 66-75
Racial groups (*see* Ethnic groups)
Radical thought, fear of, 177
Radio, 120, 121
Railroads, land grants to, 6
Ralston Purina, xxviii, xxix
Raup, Philip, xxxiv, xxxv
Reading as entertainment, 120-22
Realtors and laboring class, 162
Reclamation Act of 1902, xxiv, 186
Reclamation Lands Family Farm Act, xxv
Recreational activities: in Arvin, 210; in Dinuba, 195, 299; in large-farm and small-farm communities, 283-84; of migrants in Kern County, 119; in Wasco, 101-17
Redfield, Robert, 222
Reedley, 296, 298
Relief, 174; farm, xxxiii, 240; parity program as, 246; state, case load, 82-83
Relief workers, attitude toward, 177-78
Religion, 77 (*see also* Churches)
Religious life and participation: individual status and, 143-46, 399-400; social status and, 124-47
Reseach agencies, agricultural, xxxviii-xxxix
Resettlement, attractions of, 150
Retail trade (*see* Business)
Retzer, J. L., 30
Revivalist churches, 126-30, 141
Reynolds, Charles N., 17, 49
Rhodes, James, xxxv-xxxvii, xlix
Rivers and Harbors Bill, 458-59, 465
Roosevelt, Franklin D., 458; administration, xxxiii, 240, 249
Roosevelt, Theodore, 455
Roy, Ewell Paul, xxvii
Rural society: equity in, 262-72; in future world, 272-75; industrialized farming and, 22-54; urban life and, 221-26
Russians in Dinuba, 192

Sacramento-San Joaquin Delta, 296
Sacramento Valley, 7
Salinas Valley, 11, 296
Sanctions, economic, 255-56
San Francisco Chronicle, 465, 473
Sanger, 296
San Joaquin Valley, xxv, xli, xlii, 7, 11, 191, 281, 297, 315, 325; churches in, 124; strikes in, 165; study of, 13
San Joaquin Valley Agricultural Labor Bureau, 170-71
Scarcity economics, 254-55
Schenley Corporation, 13
Schismatic Pentecostal church, 124, 131-33, 136, 140, 143-45
Schneider, John B., 31
School lunches, free, 174
Schools: in Arvin, 216-17, 303, 349-53, 402-4; consideration in resettlement, 151-52; democracy in, 100, 161; in Dinuba, 298, 299, 303, 349-53, 402-4; high schools, 98-100, 349, 351-53; in large-farm and small-farm communities, 283; in Wasco, 45-46, 94-100, 406
Schultz, Theodore W., 246, 247
Schwartz, Harry, 252
Seasonal rhythm, 80-84
Seasonal workers, 257; in Arvin-Dinuba study, 413-14; farmers' dependence on, 161-62; in Kern County, 39; in Wasco, 86
Secret orders, 102-4, 107
Segregation: in churches, 133-38; in Dinuba, 192-93; in motion picture theaters, 120; in Wasco, 94
Self-sufficient farm, 30
Selma, 296
Semi-skilled labor, 57, 58
Senate Small Business Committee, 477-78, 480, 485
Service clubs: in Arvin, 353-54; in Dinuba, 196-97, 356-57; in Wasco, 102, 110-13
Seventh-Day Adventist church, 136, 198, 367, 369, 379
76 Ranch & Water Co., 297-98
Sewage system, petition for, 173-74
Sex: division in club life, 115; social status and activities, 91
Shafter, 405-9, 411
Sharecroppers, 4, 55, 247, 257, 258, 266

INDEX

Shultis, Arthur, 430
Size of farms (see Farm size)
Skilled labor, 57, 58
Slavery, 4
Slums, 224, 233
Small-scale farming, 3, 186-202, 265; in Dinuba, 282-84, 287, 414
Smith, T. Lynn, xlv-xlvi
Social conflict, 163-72
Social control, 172-85; by elite, 179; external, 179-85; government agencies and, 184-85, 245-75; in nuclear group, 177-79
Social Darwinism, xxx
Social directions, 239-75
Social distinctions, economic basis of, 55-79
Social experience and social status, 80-123
Social mobility, 153-61; in Arvin-Dinuba study, 416; case stories, 155-60; of churches, 138-43
Social participation: in Arvin, 210-12, 353-64, 376-78; in Dinuba, 195-97, 299, 356-64, 376-78, laborers in, 361-64, 378-80; in Wasco, 101-17
Social reality, stereotype and, 239-41
Social recreation (see Organized entertainment; Recreational activities)
Social Security Act, 250-51
Social status: church membership and, 133-38, 368-71, 378-80, 399-400; clique and, 115-17; commercial entertainment and, 117-23; economic neighborhoods and, 92-94; educational system and, 94-100; individual (see Individual status); occupations and, 55-56; organized recreation and, 101-15; sex and activities, 91; social experience and, 80-123; social participation and, 101, 376-80; system, 5-6
Social structure: in Arvin, 207-10, 325-28, 376-80, 398-402; in Dinuba, 192-94, 325-28, 376-80, 398-402; in Wasco, 55-79
Social worth, determination of, 55-56
Sokolsky, George E., 465
South, 253; blacks from, 68; cotton culture, 410; plantation system, 3, 4; social system, 5
Southern Pacific Railroad, 456
Southern Plains, laborers from, 49, 50
Southwest: agriculture, 4-5; migration from 19-21
Spain, California's heritage from, 6

Spanish grants, 23
Spanish *hacienda*, 5, 6
Spanish surname population in labor force, xliii
Specialized farming: in Arvin, 204-5, 293-94; in Dinuba, 188, 289; Wasco, 27-29
Speculators, 6-9
Spreckels Sugar Company, 10
Squatting, 175
Standard of living, 258-59
Standard Oil of California, xxvi
Status (see Individual status; Social status)
Steffens, Lincoln, 224
Steinbeck, John (*The Grapes of Wrath*), 19, 51, 112, 118, 181, 459
Stereotype and social reality, 239-41
Stevens, Alden, 484-85
Stiebeling, Hazel K., 31
"Stoop" labor, 86
Strikes: Alabama poultry farmers, xxvii-xxviii; "communist" dominated, 182; cotton pickers, 163; in depression, 164-66; of 1933, 180; in San Joaquin Valley, 165
Strong, Beryl, 459-60
Students: choice of subjects, 98; occupational ambitions, 99-100
"Submissiveness" of farmers, 240
Subsidies: consumer, 264; in corporate operations, xxxiii
Subsistence farmers, 257
Sugar beets, 27; cost of production, 34, 35
Sultana, 296
Swift & Co., xxviii, xxix

T, value of, 447-48
Taft-Hartley amendment to National Labor Relations Act, xxxvii
Tagus Ranch, 10
Tawny, R. H., xl
Taxes, agribusiness advantages, xxxiv-xxxviii
Taylor, Carl, 467, 476, 477, 482
Taylor, Paul S., 22, 23, 50, 53, 150, 165, 166, 170, 244, 456
Teachers: in Arvin and Dinuba, 350-51; tenure, 97, 351; in Wasco, 95-98
Tenants (tenancy), 247, 266; in Arvin and Dinuba, 314-15, 412-13, 417; in California, 18
Tenneco, xxvi, xxix
Tenure, land (see Land tenure)

Texas, migrants from, 19–21, 50, 192, 207, 232
Textron, xxix
Thomas, Dorothy Swain, 457
Tipton, 410
Tocqueville, Alexis de, xl
Tolan Committee, 19, 255
Tolley, Howard R., 484–85
Tönnies, Ferdinand, 222
Town-country relationships, 221–75; in Arvin, 211–12; in Dinuba, 193–94; in Wasco, 41–48
Townspeople: in Arvin, 205–7; in Dinuba, 190–92; in Wasco, 41–48
Tractors, 32–33
Trade Union Unity League, 171
Traver, 297, 298
Tulare *Advance-Register*, 163, 165
Tulare County, 287, 314; *map*, 288; population and farming, 290

UCAPAWA, 172
Under-employment, 88, 259
Unemployment, 46, 82–83
Unemployment insurance, 250
Union Congregational Church, 367, 369
Unionization, 70, 71, 266–67; conflict over, 166–67; of farm labor, 182; resentment toward, 185
United Cannery, 172
United States vs. *California Fruit Growers Exchange*, 203
Unskilled labor, 57–63
Urbanism: differentials in, 235–38; diffusion of, 226–27
Urbanized culture: and industrialized agriculture, 221–38; in rural areas, 227–35, 393–94
Urban life: definitions, 222; and rural life, 221–26

Value of farms (*see* Land costs and values)
Vasey, Tom, 22, 23
Veblen, Thorstein, 5
Vegetables: in Arvin, 289, 294–95; in California, 14; shipments from Arvin and other communities, 407–8
Vertical integration in agribusiness, xxvi-xxviii
Vineyards (*see* Grapes)

Wages, farm, xxxviii, 258–59; minimum, 264–66; on monthly basis, 89; in potato harvest, 87

Wagner Act, xxxvii, 251, 266
Ward, James E., 259
Warner, W. Lloyd, 457
Wasco, 8–13, 228 *et seq.*, 239, 242, 247, 252, 257, 258, 260, 265, 267, 269, 405–9, 411; agricultural industry, 24–48; Arvin and Dinuba compared with, 190, 217–20; associations, 101–12; blacks and whites in, 67–68; building restrictions, 175–76; chain operation, 42–45; churches, 65; cliques, 115–17; commercial entertainment, 117–23; cooperatives, 44–45; corporate interests in, 42–45; creamery, 12–13, 44–45; crops in, 27–28; cultural backgrounds, 55; ethnic groups, 66–68; farm size and value, 32; housing, cheap, 162; incorporation, 174, 178, 237; land costs, 33–41; leisure-time activities, 101; means of livelihood, 80–92; migrant labor, 50–52; nuclear group, 63–66; outsider group, 66–75; population growth, estimates, 51, 52; post office, 162; schools, 45–46, 94–100, 406; seasonal rhythm, 80–84; settler's organization, 25–26; social classes, 58–63; social groups, 55–79; social status and social experience, 80–123; specialization in, 27, 28; state relief case load, 82–83; study of, 457, 487; voting precincts, occupational characteristics, 93; water corporation, 26–27; women's work, 89–92
Water districts, California, government of, xliii–xlv
Water supply: in Arvin and Dinuba, 397–98, 415, 434–38; in Bureau of Reclamation projects, 456; control of, 173; costs in Arvin-Dinuba study, 434–38
Weber, Max (*Protestant Ethic*), xl, 142
Webster, Daniel, 279, 470
Weedpatch, 292–93, 351, 353, 356, 407
Wells, O. V., 476, 477, 482
Wesley, John, 142
West, James, 242
Western Worker (San Francisco), 170
Wheat Belt, 248
White collar workers, 57, 58, 91, 93
Wickard, Claude, 473
Williams Management Company, xxix–xxx
Wilford, Harrison, xxvii–xxix
Wilson, Edwin E., 13, 457

Wirth, Louis, 222
Women's auxiliaries, 115
Women's clubs, 102-104, 106, 108, 109, 114-15, 165, 357
Women's work in Wasco, 89-92
Workers: black, 4, 49, 120, 123; equity for, 257; farm (*see* Labor, agricultural); farmers and, interdependence, 62-63; occupational shifting, 153-61; semi-skilled, 57, 58; skilled, 57, 58; unskilled, 57-63; white, 18-19, 49, 59-63; white collar, 57, 58, 91, 93

Workers' Alliance, 168
WPA, 303, 367
Wright Act, 298, 300, 398

Yettem, 296
Youth problems and activities, 355, 364-67

Zimmerman, Carl C., 482
Zion Mennonite church, 198, 367
Zuñi Indians, 224